THE MAPS OF THE WILDERNESS

*An Atlas of the Wilderness Campaign, Including all
Cavalry Operations, May 2-6, 1864*

Bradley M. Gottfried

SB

Savas Beatie

California

First edition, first printing

ISBN-13: 978-1611212587
eISBN: 978-1-61121-259-4

Library of Congress Control Number: 2015945527

SB

Published by
Savas Beatie LLC
989 Governor Drive, Suite 102
El Dorado Hills, CA 95762
Phone: 916-941-6896
(E-mail) sales@savasbeatie.com

Savas Beatie titles are available at special discounts for bulk purchases in the United States by corporations, institutions, and other organizations. For more details, please contact Special Sales, P.O. Box 4527, El Dorado Hills, CA 95762. You may also e-mail us at sales@savasbeatie.com, or click over for a visit to our website at www.savasbeatie.com for additional information.

The sixth volume of
The Savas Beatie Military Atlas™ Series

To Senator Thomas (Mike) V. Miller, Jr.
An avid historian, who has done so much for the State of Maryland

Contents

Contents (continued)

Contents (continued)

Contents (continued)

Contents (continued)

Map Set 12: May 5 Fighting Ends,
and the Armies Prepare for May 6

Map Set 13: Fighting Begins on the Union Right (May 6)

Map Set 14: Hancock Strikes A. P. Hill's Third Corps (May 6)

Map Set 15: Longstreet Reaches the Battlefield (May 6)

Contents (continued)

Contents (continued)

Contents (continued)

Contents (continued)

Introduction

The idea for this series came about when I was seeking several years ago a better way to visualize, understand, and appreciate the battle of Gettysburg and other major campaigns in the Eastern Theater. What began as a simple idea in my home library has since developed into the book you are holding—the sixth volume in the Savas Beatie Military Atlas Series™. My goal is to research and illustrate every major campaign of the Eastern Theater; the intent of the series is to cover the entire Civil War.

The first effort in 2007 resulted in *The Maps of Gettysburg*, which served as a springboard for a second book two years later, *The Maps of First Bull Run*. Soon after the Gettysburg volume appeared, my publisher expressed an interest in expanding the series to the Western campaigns. I was flattered and agreed it was a good idea, but because my primary interest rests in the East, other historians would have to be found to assist elsewhere. The first two who came aboard were David Powell (text) and David Friedrichs (cartography), whose outstanding collaboration produced *The Maps of Chickamauga* in 2009—the same year my First Bull Run study appeared. Other Western Theater campaign studies are in various stages of completion (Chattanooga, Franklin and Nashville, the Atlanta Campaign), as are atlas books dealing with Napoleon's 1812 invasion of Russia and WWI campaigns. This is personally gratifying. The only way to really understand a military campaign (besides walking the ground) is through good maps, and the unique presentation of these Savas Beatie atlas titles *unlocks* other books on the same subjects and makes them more usable and accessible. My third title, *The Maps of Antietam: An Atlas of the Antietam (Sharpsburg) Campaign, Including the Battle of South Mountain, September 2 - 20, 1862*, appeared in 2011, with the fourth, *The Maps of the Bristoe Station and Mine Run Campaigns*, appearing two years later. You now hold what is my fifth book (the sixth in the series)—*The Maps of the Wilderness*. I have also largely completed *The Maps of Fredericksburg*, and when that is finished intend to turn to Spotsylvania and beyond.

Like all my books, *The Maps of the Wilderness* includes the all related cavalry operations and is intended to be neutral in coverage. The text and maps cover the movement of the armies from where *The Maps of the Bristoe Station and Mine Run Campaigns* ends—the late winter of 1864 as the armies prepare for the coming spring operations. Despite its size, bloodshed, importance, and high-profile commanders, surprisingly little has been written about the Wilderness. Part of this sparse coverage is a lack of battle reports (especially on the Confederate side), and the astounding complexity of the fighting. The best full-length in-depth effort did not appear until nearly a century after the battle (1960) with the appearance of Edward Steere's *The Wilderness Campaign*. As anyone who is familiar with this series will attest, the purpose of these atlas books is to offer a broad and richer understanding of topic at hand, rather than a micro-history of a particular event or day based upon exhaustive new research. Delving deep enough into any subject to map it, however, always turns up interesting questions that challenge earlier conclusions. As a result, some of my maps and text coverage in this volume differ from previous authors. For example, I believe the Confederate right flank line of battle straddling the Orange Plank Road on May 5 (Harry Heth's magnificent defensive effort, punctuated with sharp local counterattacks) was much closer to the Brock Road than others have described or mapped it.

No other single source has endeavored to pull together the movements and events of this campaign and offer it in a cartographic form side-by-side with reasonably detailed text complete with endnotes. Like the books before it, *The Maps of the Wilderness* dissects the actions within each sector of a battlefield for a deeper and hopefully more meaningful understanding and reading experience. Each section of this book includes a number of text and map combinations. Every left-hand page includes descriptive text corresponding with a facing original map on the right-hand page. One of the key advantages of this presentation is that it eliminates the need to flip through the book to try to find a map to match the text. Some sections required only a few map and text pages, while others required as many as eleven map and text pages. Wherever possible, I utilized firsthand accounts to personalize the otherwise straightforward text. I hope readers find this method of presentation useful.

As I have written in previous introductions, the plentiful maps and sectioned coverage make it much easier to follow and understand what was happening each day (and in some cases, each hour). The various sections may also trigger a special interest and so pry open avenues ripe for additional study. I am hopeful that readers who approach the subject with a higher level of expertise will find the maps and text not only interesting to study and read, but also truly helpful. Hopefully someone will place this book within easy reach and refer to it now and again as a reference guide while reading other studies on these campaigns. If so, the long hours invested in this project will have been worthwhile.

A few caveats are in order. *The Maps of the Wilderness* is not the last word or definitive treatment of this campaign or any part thereof—nor did I intend it to be. Given space and time considerations, that is simply not possible. The endnotes offer additional avenues of study and discussion, and should be read carefully. My primary reliance was upon firsthand accounts (diaries, journals, books, newspaper accounts, etc.) and battle reports, followed by quality secondary scholarship. Therefore, other than a handful of new theories or conclusions (such as the location of Heth's line of battle on May 5, for example), evaluations of why the battle unfolded as it did are fairly traditional. I am also familiar with the battlefield and have visited it several times, often in the company of other students of the war. Whenever a book uses short chapters or sections, as this one does, there will inevitably be some narrative redundancy. I have endeavored to minimize this as much as possible.

Sources can and often do conflict on many points, including numbers engaged, who moved when and where and why, what time a specific event unfolded, and of course, casualties. No one knows the exact location of every unit at all times (this is especially true when it comes to the Wilderness), and in many cases I have pieced the evidence together to come to a educated conclusion. I am sure some of my conclusions or maps will spark some level of debate, but they represent my best effort to get them as right as the sources will allow at this time. It is also important to realize that the time a particular action occurred is always approximate. Not only did various participants disagree, but watches were not synchronized and memories are notoriously unreliable.

A study like this makes it likely mistakes of one variety or another end up in the final text or map, despite endless hours of proofreading. I apologize for any errors and assume full responsibility for them. Any mistakes discovered will be fixed in subsequent printings.

*   *   *

This book could not have been written and produced without the assistance of a host of people. As always, Theodore P. Savas of Savas Beatie heads the list. A good friend and effective editor, he has always supported my efforts. Because Ted is also a distinguished historian and author in his own right, he understands the researching and writing process and is always helpful. His fine eye, honed from his own cartography, helped to refine and improve the maps.

A number of individuals provided invaluable assistance by reading all or portions of the manuscript. Phillip Greenwalt and Kristopher White performed yeoman service by reviewing the entire manuscript. Their comments were invaluable. NPS Ranger Greg Mertz reviewed the Orange Turnpike section and made a number of vital observations that vastly improved the text. Chris Mackowski and Robert Krick weighed in on a important Orange Turnpike issues that helped clarify a few significant matters.

Any study of the Fredericksburg-area battlefields would be incomplete without spending time with the 500-plus bound volumes maintained at the Chatham House. Donald Pfanz, Staff Historian (recently retired) at the Fredericksburg & Spotsylvania National Military Park, allowed me access to this tremendous resource. Don is always accommodating of his time. Othere individuals who helped with access and other pertinent matters include John Hennessey, Chief Historian at Fredericksburg and Spotsylvania National Military Park, and Eric Mink, Cultural Resources Manager at the same location.

Finally, I would like to thank Linda, my friend, my partner, and my wife. She travels with me on my many of trips to the fields, listens with amazing patience to my steady stream of stories, and graciously allows me the time and space to complete my work.

Bradley M. Gottfried
Cobb Island, Maryland

"For two days nearly 200,000 veteran troops . . . groping their way through a tangled forest, the impenetrable gloom of which could be likened only to the shadow of death. . . . Officers could rarely see their troops for any considerable distance, for smoke clouded the vision, and a heavy sky obscured the sun. Directions were ascertained and lines established by means of the pocket-compass, and a change of position often presented an operation more like a problem of ocean navigation than a question of military maneuvers. It was the sense of sound and of touch rather than the sense of sight which guided the movements. It was a battle with the ear, and not with the eye. All circumstances seemed to combine to make the scene one of unutterable horror . . . the wind howled through the treetops, mingling its groans with the groans of the dying, and heavy branches were cut off by the fire of the artillery, and fell crashing upon the heads of the men, adding a new terror to battle. Forest fires raged; ammunition trains exploded; the dead were roasted in the conflagration; the wounded roused by its hot breath, dragged themselves along, with their torn and mangled limbs, in the mad energy of despair, to escape the ravages of the flames; and every bush seemed hung with shreds of blood-stained clothing. It was as though Christian men had turned to fiends, and hell itself had usurped the place of earth."

— Horace Porter

THE MAPS OF THE
WILDERNESS

An Atlas of the Wilderness Campaign,
Including all Cavalry Operations, May 2-6, 1864

Map Set 1: Preparing for a New Kind of War

Map 1.1: The Confederate Army in Winter Quarters

General Robert E. Lee experienced a miserable string of winter months. The war's third year started off well with the victory at Chancellorsville. Southern fortunes spiraled downward thereafter when Thomas Jackson succumbed to his wounds, the Army of Northern Virginia suffered a bloody repulse at Gettysburg, and Vicksburg fell in Mississippi. Against Lee's wishes, Richmond stripped much of Lt. Gen. James Longstreet's First Corps from Lee's grasp and shipped it to the Western Theater that September. The troops played a pivotal role in a major victory at Chickamauga, but Longstreet and his veterans were still detached and would not return any time soon. The Bristoe and Mine Run campaigns that Fall made it readily obvious that neither the chronically ill A. P. Hill nor his fellow lieutenant general and corps commander Richard Ewell could execute his designs in the field.

There was also the matter of food and forage. Securing enough of both for his men and animals was an endless and largely unsatisfying endeavor; cajoling, pleading, and begging for Richmond's support did not suit the general. The last month of 1863 and early weeks of 1864 frustrated the aggressive Lee, who admitted to Gen. Braxton Bragg, "My hands are tied" while his men and horses starved. To President Jefferson Davis, Lee wrote, "Unless there is a change, I fear the army cannot be kept effective, and probably cannot be kept together," and to Secretary of War James A. Seddon, "I fear that the discipline of the army is suffering from our present scarcity of supplies." The food issued to each man shrunk to barely subsistence level. "[I]f supplies are not accumulated here," warned Lee, "a demoralized Army pillaging its countrymen may be looked for, with the loss of Richmond."[1]

The effects of an unhealthy diet were compounded by inadequate clothing during a frigid winter and a lack of shoes. A Georgia soldier wrote home, it was "enough to make tears come from the eyes of the most hardened soul to see our brave men marching through the mud & snow almost naked & barefooted." Only five or six men in his company had shoes. Lee tried to alleviate this dire condition by buying hides and putting men to work fashioning shoes. Twenty-two men in Charles Field's Division produced 1,500 shoes for their comrades that winter.[2]

A slow and inadequate transportation system aggravated the situation. It took 60 hours to travel by train from Raleigh, North Carolina, to Orange Court House, Virginia, for example. At one point, North Carolina had 30,000 tons of forage, but no way of getting it where it was needed.[3]

Lee also worried about the number of men who would remain in the ranks come spring, for the terms of enlistment of many of them were about to expire. Patriotic rallies, coupled with religious fervor and a sense of duty led to "a flurry of re-enlistments for the war." According to one historian, "Although the act was more symbolic than real—the Confederacy would never have let them leave the service by expiration of their terms—it represented a passion to see the war through to victory in this, the decisive year."[4]

Like the army he led, the hard field service had taken its toll on Lee's health. The heart problems that would eventually kill him were present that summer in Pennsylvania, and incidences of incapacitation would plague him through the end of the war. "I am becoming more and more incapable of exertion," wrote the 57-year-old Lee to President Davis, "and am thus prevented from making the personal examinations and giving the personal supervision to the operations in the field which I feel to be necessary." Davis would hear nothing of it. Lee would remain at the head of his army.[5]

While the abilities of his corps commanders remained suspect (see Map 1.6), the loss of so many mid-level and field-grade officers to battle, illness, and resignation continued to plague Lee and reduce the efficiency of his army.

With most of Longstreet's First Corps in Tennessee, the remaining two-thirds of Lee's army held strong positions just south of the Rapidan River from Barnett's Ford in the west to Morton's Ford—a distance of almost 20 miles. General Hill's Third Corps occupied the left of the line, while General Ewell's Second Corps held the right. Several brigades defended each ford. A sudden Union thrust across Morton's on February 6, 1864 was thwarted, and it would not be repeated.[6]

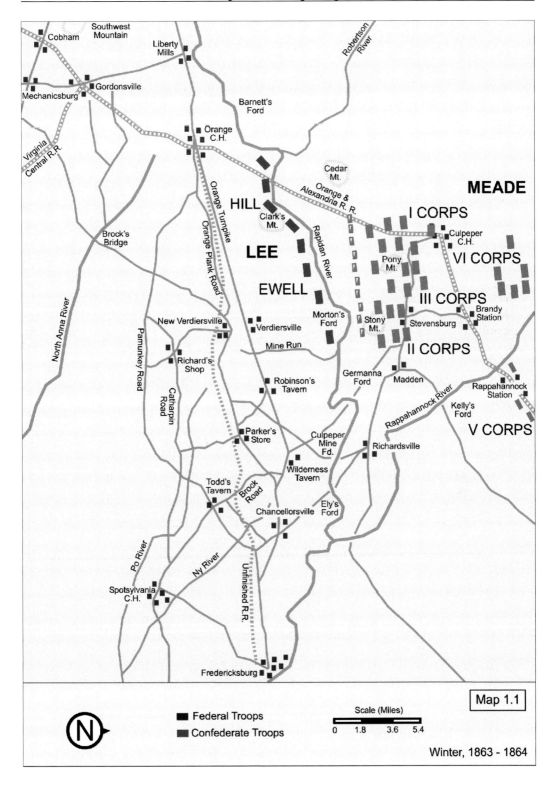

Map 1.1

Federal Troops
Confederate Troops

Scale (Miles)
0   1.8   3.6   5.4

Winter, 1863 - 1864

Map 1.2: The Union Army in Winter Quarters

The campaigns that Fall in Virginia ended on an ambivalent note for the veterans in the Army of the Potomac. On November 30, 1863, more than 30,000 men were poised to march a mile over open terrain to attack the heavily entrenched enemy behind Mine Run. The attack was called off at the last possible moment, and the men would never forget the courage Maj. Gen. George G. Meade exhibited in doing so.[7]

While Lee's army suffered through a winter with short rations and supplies, the opposite was true for Meade's army. With a good transportation system and better access to all manner of supplies, Meade's men spent the winter in relative comfort. Goods poured into Brandy Station, and sutlers made it easy for the men to supplement their rations with oysters, beer, fish, and milk. Their insulated huts contained fireplaces, and activities like cards, reading, games, religious services, plays, and even snowball fights helped pass the time. One New Jersey veteran recalled that winter as "the most pleasant experience in our army experience." Still, the men had to deal with the cold and dampness, illness, and the Virginia mud. "[A]man's shoes must be well tied," noted a Vermont soldier, "or he will leave them buried in this red clay." Cold and mud notwithstanding, observed a modern historian, "The four months prior to the Overland campaign would leave their morale and physical condition excellent in every respect."[8]

Of more concern was the approaching end of the three-year enlistments for thousands of troops. The Lincoln administration went to extremes to convince the men to reenlist. The incentives were almost irresistible to the men of the First New Jersey Brigade: a $402 bounty and a 30-day leave. Some counties, anxious to reach their quotas, tossed in an additional $300. While many men took advantage of these incentives, others had seen too much and no amount of money could induce them to remain in the army.[9]

The Army of the Potomac's winter camps were scattered across 100 square miles in and around Culpeper Court House, covering the roads leading to and from Lee's army. The I and III Corps were about two miles south of Culpeper Court House, and therefore the closest to the enemy. The II Corps was near Stevensburg and the VI Corps near Welford's Ford on the Hazel River. The V Corps protected the vital Orange and Alexandria Railroad, which stretched from the Rappahannock River to Bristoe Station. The powerful IX Corps (acting as an independent command) was brought up from North Carolina to strengthen the army for the upcoming spring offensive.[10]

The army's leadership was a mixed bag of personalities and abilities. George Meade continued to lead the army, despite his post-Gettysburg actions and inactions that often frustrated and angered Lincoln and Halleck. The I Corps was led by Maj. Gen. John Newton, who was known more for his indolent nature and general inattention to detail than battlefield abilities. Major General Winfield Hancock, who was still recovering from a wound suffered while throwing back Pickett's Charge on July 3, 1863, left the reins of his II Corps in the hands of Maj. Gen. Gouverneur Warren, one of many heroes of Gettysburg. Warren's performance during the Fall campaigns was mixed, expertly extracting his corps from near-extinction at Auburn and Bristoe Station, but sacrificing some of his reputation at Mine Run when he misjudged his ability to attack the enemy's right flank. The III Corps was led by Maj. Gen. William French. Known for heavy drinking, French turned in an abysmal performance in the Mine Run Campaign. Major General George Sykes headed up the V Corps. "Tardy George" was known as a reliable but plodding leader, a trait that did nothing to endear him to his superiors in Washington. The final corps—the VI—was led by Maj. Gen. John Sedgwick, next to Meade, the army's most experienced commander. He had a reputation as a cautious but sturdy leader. The newly arrived IX Corps was under Maj. Gen. Ambrose Burnside. The former head of the Army of the Potomac operated as an independent commander reporting directly to General U. S. Grant—a problematic command structure at best.[11]

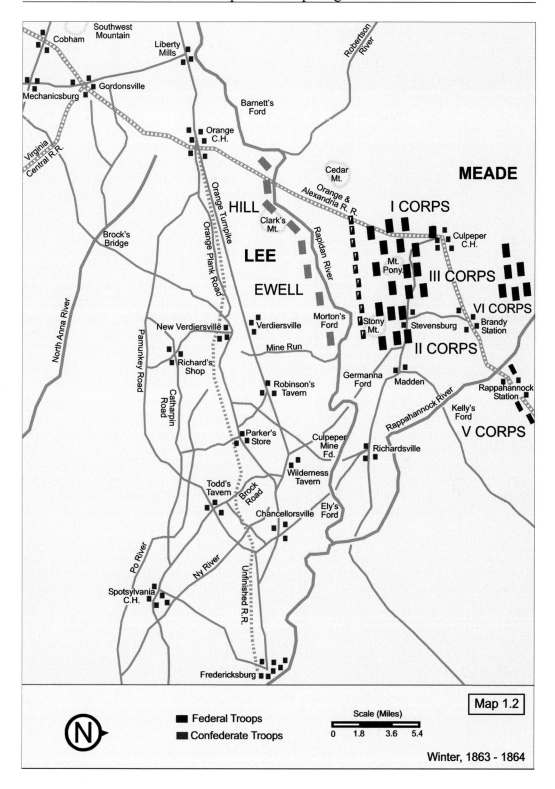

MEADE

HILL

LEE

EWELL

I CORPS

III CORPS

VI CORPS

II CORPS

V CORPS

Southwest Mountain
Cobham
Liberty Mills
Robertson River
Gordonsville
Mechanicsburg
Barnett's Ford
Virginia Central R.R.
Orange C.H.
Cedar Mt.
Orange & Alexandria R. R.
Culpeper C.H.
Clark's Mt.
Brock's Bridge
Orange Turnpike
Rapidan River
Mt. Pony
North Anna River
Orange Plank Road
New Verdiersville
Verdiersville
Morton's Ford
Stony Mt.
Stevensburg
Brandy Station
Pamunkey Road
Richard's Shop
Mine Run
Germanna Ford
Madden
Rappahannock River
Rappahannock Station
Catharpin Road
Robinson's Tavern
Kelly's Ford
Parker's Store
Culpeper Mine Fd.
Richardsville
Todd's Tavern
Brock Road
Wilderness Tavern
Chancellorsville
Ely's Ford
Po River
Ny River
Unfinished R.R.
Spotsylvania C.H.
Fredericksburg

N

■ Federal Troops
▦ Confederate Troops

Scale (Miles)
0   1.8   3.6   5.4

Map 1.2

Winter, 1863 - 1864

Map 1.3: The Union Army Experiences Major Changes (March 1864)

Major changes visited the Army of the Potomac during the fall and winter of 1863-64. Through the Gettysburg Campaign, the army had been composed of seven corps: I, II, III, V, VI, XI, and XII. That number shrank to five in late September 1863, when the XI and XII—the army's two smallest—were shipped to Tennessee after the Union disaster at Chickamauga and to help counter the movement of nearly one-third of Lee's army to the same theater of the war. None of these units would ever fight with the Army of the Potomac again.

A less dramatic, though more traumatic event occurred on March 23, 1864, when Meade consolidated the remainder of the army into three corps by merging the venerable I and III into the II, V, and VI. The II Corps' three divisions were consolidated into two, and two more divisions arrived from the III Corps, with its remaining division merged into the VI Corps. The I Corps' depleted divisions were added to the V Corps. The men of the deactivated corps retained their old badges, but this did little to salve their wounded pride. "The history and associations of these organizations were different," noted Maj. Gen. Andrew A. Humphreys, who had led a division in the III Corps but was now the army's chief of staff. "When they were merged in[to] other organizations their identity was lost and their pride and espirit de corps wounded."[12]

Meade blamed the reorganization on the "reduced strength of nearly all the regiments . . . [which had] imperatively demanded . . . [the] temporary reduction of the number of army corps to three." Despite his claim, he knew this action was permanent. The fact that the reorganization would also rid the army of two problematic leaders, the I Corps' John Newton and the III Corps' William French may have also played a role in the decision. Meade hoped the consolidation would facilitate the movement of large units. He knew Lee's army was composed at various times of two or three corps, each containing as many as 30,000 men, a fact that may have contributed to the Virginia army's success. Yet another series of command changes occurred when Winfield Hancock returned to the army after recovering from his Gettysburg wound. Gouverneur Warren was now shifted to lead the V Corps, leaving Maj. Gen. George Sykes without a command.[13]

President Lincoln also made a major decision that would dramatically influence the Army of the Potomac and the course of the war. His frustration with Meade was common knowledge. Despite Meade's inability to effectively confront Lee and bring him to battle, Lincoln knew he could not remove the victor of Gettysburg without an uproar of public protest. He was also increasingly discontented with the performance of Maj. Gen. Henry Halleck, his general in chief. Lincoln only needed to look to the West to find the answer to his dilemma. Ulysses S. Grant had won most of his battles, including Shiloh, Vicksburg, and Chattanooga, and Lincoln promoted him in March 1864 to command all the Union armies. "Grant," Lincoln was overheard to say, "is the first general I've had." Continuing, he added, "He hasn't told me what his plans are. I don't know, and I don't want to know. I'm glad to find a man who can go ahead without me." With his ascension to the rank of lieutenant general, Grant outranked every American in U.S. history with the exception of George Washington.[14]

While most Confederates believed Grant would fail just as all of his predecessors had, those who knew him disagreed. General Longstreet, who knew Grant well from West Point and early service, noted "we can not afford to underrate him and the army he now commands...that man will fight us every day and every hour till the end of this war. In order to whip him we must out maneuver him, and husband our strength as best we can."[15]

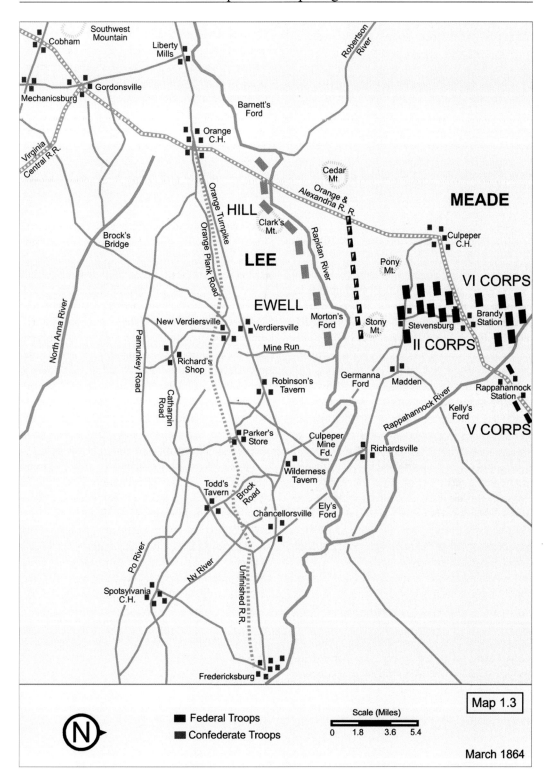

Southwest Mountain
Cobham
Liberty Mills
Robertson River
Gordonsville
Mechanicsburg
Barnett's Ford
Virginia Central R.R.
Orange C.H.
Cedar Mt.
Orange & Alexandria R.R.
MEADE
HILL
Clark's Mt.
Culpeper C.H.
Brock's Bridge
Orange Turnpike
Rapidan River
Pony Mt.
VI CORPS
LEE
EWELL
North Anna River
Orange Plank Road
New Verdiersville
Verdiersville
Morton's Ford
Stony Mt.
Stevensburg
Brandy Station
II CORPS
Pamunkey Road
Richard's Shop
Mine Run
Germanna Ford
Madden
Rappahannock Station
Catharpin Road
Robinson's Tavern
Rappahannock River
Kelly's Ford
V CORPS
Parker's Store
Culpeper Mine Fd.
Richardsville
Todd's Tavern
Wilderness Tavern
Brock Road
Chancellorsville
Ely's Ford
Po River
Nv River
Unfinished R.R.
Spotsylvania C.H.
Fredericksburg

N

■ Federal Troops
■ Confederate Troops

Scale (Miles)
0   1.8   3.6   5.4

Map 1.3

March 1864

Map 1.4: The Union Army Prepares for the Spring Campaign (March 1864)

Grant wasted little time in making the trek from Washington to Brandy Station to visit Meade and the Army of the Potomac. Grant originally believed he could oversee the armies from the Western Theater, but he soon realized he needed to remain closer to the Northern capital. Eschewing Washington, however, he decided to make his headquarters with the Army of the Potomac, where he arrived to a decidedly cool reception on March 10, 1864.

Worried about his job security, Meade was extremely anxious when Grant assumed command. Meade had already endured two long days of grilling (March 4-5) at the hands of the Joint Congressional Committee on the Conduct of the War, and he told his wife the politicians were "conspiring to have me relieved." When Grant arrived, Meade went right to the heart of the matter that caused him so much anguish. As Grant later recalled, Meade said "that I might want an officer who had served with me in the west, mentioning Sherman especially, to take his place; if so, he begged me not to hesitate about making the change." Grant reassured Meade he had "no thought of substituting anyone for him." The relieved general wrote his wife that he was "very much pleased with General Grant," who showed "much more capacity and character than I had expected." Meade, however, was also a realist and prescient. In the future, he added, "the ignorant public [would place] laurels on the brow of another rather than your husband" when the army won great victories.[16]

Grant spent the next seven weeks shuttling back and forth between Brandy Station and Washington. The troops were anxious to see Grant, and they got their wish once the rains abated. Artilleryman Charles Wainwright's conclusions seemed to capture the general consensus of the army when he recorded in his diary that Grant was "stumpy, unmilitary, slouchy, Western-looking; very ordinary in fact."[17]

In the end, the consolidation of the corps, good rations, and new leadership sat well with the Army of the Potomac. The report for April 30, 1864, showed 99,489 soldiers "present for duty equipped," which included 73,390 infantry, 12,444 cavalry, and 10,230 artillerymen, or just over 96,000 men. Burnside's IX Corps arrived from Annapolis on May 1, adding 19,331 more men, swelling the army to almost 120,000. All told, once Longstreet returned from Tennessee, Lee would be able to field about 64,000 men.[18]

The IX Corps relieved the V Corps along the Orange and Alexandria Railroad, which moved to Culpeper. The VI Corps camps were between Brandy Station and the Rappahannock River, and the II Corps was camped between Stevensburg and Brandy Station.[19]

Grant understood that in order to win, the North needed to move on all fronts simultaneously. "[T]he armies in the East and West acted independently and without concert, like a bulky team, no two ever pulling together," he explained, "enabling the enemy to use the great advantage of interior lines of communication for transporting troops from east to west." Only a "simultaneous movement all along the line" would bring about victory. To that end, Grant decided that Meade's army would cross the Rapidan River and strike hard at Lee, while Benjamin Butler's Army of the James advanced up the river of the same name toward Richmond to sever Lee's supply lines and perhaps combine with Meade to take on Lee. At the same time, a third column under Franz Sigel would march up (south) the Shenandoah Valley and threaten Lee's left flank while destroying his much-needed supplies there. In the Western Theater, Sherman would drive south for Atlanta against the Army of Tennessee under Gen. Joseph Johnston. Grant also hoped to launch an amphibious campaign against Mobile, Alabama, with troops now in Louisiana.[20]

The only change Grant made to the Army of the Potomac's command structure was to its mounted arm. Few were happy with the uninspired leadership of Maj. Gen. Alfred Pleasanton, and the same day Grant met with General Halleck (March 23), a telegram was sent west to fetch Maj. Gen. Philip H. Sheridan. Brigadier General Judson Kilpatrick, a cavalry division commander, was also removed from command and replaced with Brig. Gen. James Wilson. Both Sheridan and Wilson had served with Grant in the Western Theater.[21]

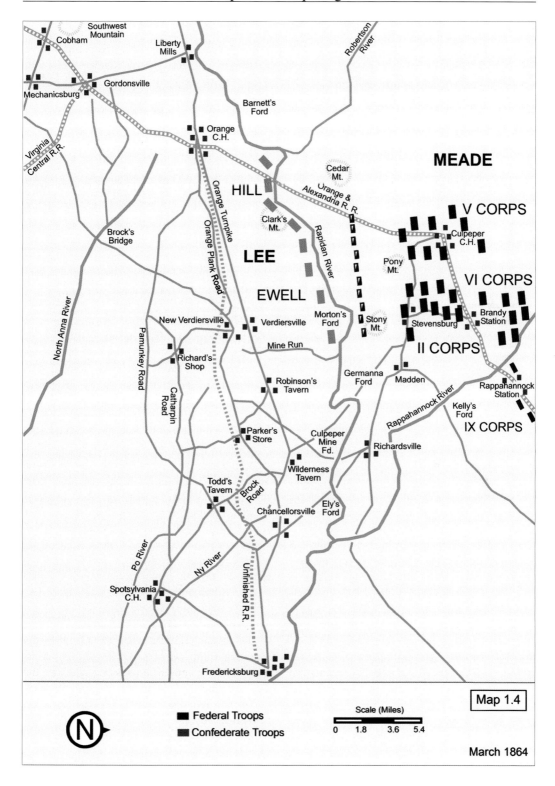

Map 1.4

Federal Troops
Confederate Troops

Scale (Miles)
0   1.8   3.6   5.4

March 1864

Map 1.5: The Confederates Prepare for the Spring Campaign (March 1864)

To General Lee's immense relief, Longstreet and his two First Corps divisions received orders to return to Virginia from Tennessee on April 7, 1864. They had made the trek west seven months earlier to reinforce Braxton Bragg's Army of Tennessee. Within hours of their arrival they were engaged at Chickamauga, where they played a significant role in defeating William Rosecrans's Army of the Cumberland. The high of victory went downhill quickly when Longstreet and Bragg clashed and the latter was defeated at Chattanooga. By that time Longstreet was in East Tennessee, where his attack on Knoxville was repulsed with heavy losses. Old Pete and his men were more than happy to return to their familiar haunts in Virginia. Several other detached brigades were also returned to Lee.[22]

Despite the change in his chief lieutenants the previous year with the death of Jackson and elevation of Hill and Ewell, Lee's leadership style remained the same. "I do everything in my power to make my plans as perfect as possible and to bring the troops upon the field of battle," he explained to a foreign visitor in mid-1863, "[and] the rest must be done by my generals and their troops, trusting to Providence for the victory." This hands-off approach worked well for Jackson and Longstreet, who both knew how to handle large numbers of men in combat and take advantage of opportunities. However, attrition and illness had culled some of the army's most effective leaders from its ranks. The reorganization into three corps after Jackson's death left the reliable Longstreet in charge of the First Corps. The two new corps commanders, Richard Ewell (who replaced Jackson) and A. P. Hill (who took over a new corps), had both been tested during the Gettysburg Campaign and found wanting. Their record thereafter during the Bristoe Station and Mine Run campaigns did not engender any cause for optimism that they would grow into their positions.[23]

One of the army's finest early-war division commanders under Jackson, Ewell returned a changed man after being severely wounded during the Second Manassas Campaign in August 1862. As staff officer Randolph McKim put it, the new commander of the Second Corps "arrived in camp with his wife, a new acquisition, and with one leg less than when I saw him last. From a military point of view the addition of the wife did not compensate for the loss of the leg. We were of the opinion that Ewell was not the same soldier he had been when he was a whole and a single one."[24]

Lee gave the Third Corps to A. P. Hill, an aggressive and capable division leader. Recurring bouts of illness, sensitivity to criticism, and prickly temperament reduced his effectiveness, and his aggressive tactics often crossed the line into bloody impulsiveness. His management of his corps on the first day at Gettysburg was a mix of rashness and sloppy preparation, two traits that raised their heads once more during the Bristoe Station Campaign when he launched a bold, but poorly thought-out attack that was repulsed with heavy losses. Hill was not learning from his experiences.[25]

Even though the Army of Northern Virginia lacked the men and resources to mount a viable offensive once the weather moderated, Lee wrote to Longstreet on March 28 that unless he could devise some offensive plan, he would be forced to "conform his plans and concentrate wherever they are going to attack us." Leaving the initiative to the enemy never sat well with Lee, and the hard winter and questions about Hill and Ewell made him less confident about controlling future events against an aggressive successful general like Grant.[26]

Lee's options were therefore limited: remain where he was behind the Rapidan and fight the enemy there once he crossed, or retreat south behind the North Anna River. Lee decided to stay put. He could always give up the ground and fall back behind the North Anna if forced to do so.[27]

Longstreet's men arrived on April 20 and went into camp between Gordonsville and the small hamlet of Mechanicsville six miles to the south. From this position Longstreet could reinforce either Hill or Ewell, or move to Richmond or the Shenandoah Valley as circumstances warranted. Lee arrived nine days later to meet with Longstreet and review his troops. The men were overjoyed to see their venerable commander. As artillery officer E. Porter Alexander observed, "all felt the bond which held them together. There was no speaking, but the effect was of a military sacrament."[28]

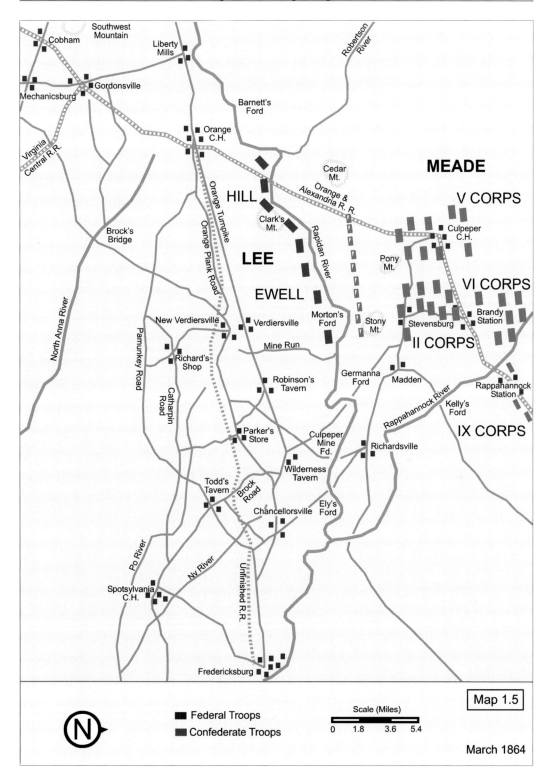

Map 1.5

Federal Troops
Confederate Troops

Scale (Miles)
0   1.8   3.6   5.4

March 1864

Map Set 2: The Armies Approach the Wilderness

Map 2.1 Grant Plans His Route

As general in chief, Gen. Ulysses S. Grant understood he oversaw the activities of every army in the field, but he ensured that their commanders were "independent in their commands." Major General George G. Meade was a different situation, since Grant elected to accompany the Army of the Potomac. "I tried to make General Meade's position . . . what it would have been if I had been in Washington or any other place away from his command," Grant insisted. While he sent orders directly to Meade instead of to his subordinates, Grant's presence alone fundamentally altered the equation within the army.[1]

How best to win the war was uppermost in Grant's mind, and as far as he was concerned Lee's army was the objective. Because Lee's defenses behind the Rapidan River were too strong to attack, he decided to maneuver him out of this stronghold and fight him in the open, where superior numbers would crush or seriously damage the Confederate army. "The only point upon which I am now in doubt is whether it will be better to cross the Rapidan above or below him," Grant mused to Meade.[2]

Both routes presented opportunities and threats to the Union movement. A move by the right flank around the Confederate left would require the army to march upriver from Barnett's Ford, passing Orange Court House and Gordonsville on the enemy's left flank toward Southwest Mountain, about 40 miles away. Because the country was largely open, Lee's men would easily see the movement and take counter-measures, including the building entrenchments near or on Southwest Mountain. In addition, the Army of the Potomac would be forced to rely upon the Orange and Alexandria Railroad to supply its needs (No. 1), and a relatively large force would have to be detached to protect it.

Moving around the Confederate right flank also posed advantages and disadvantages (No. 2). Once across the Rapidan the Federal army would march through an area known as the Wilderness. This thick second-growth forested region was choked with undergrowth, creeks, swampy low patches, and few roads for easy passage. Much of Chancellorsville had been fought on that ground in May 1863, so both commanders knew of its appeal and its dangers. Tramping nearly blind for up to 15 miles through the thickets would expose the army to potentially grave peril should Lee decide to attack it there. Meade's superior cavalry and artillery would be of little or no use in the tangled thickets. "[S]uperiority in numbers on such a field would be of less value than on any other," observed Maj. Gen. A. A. Humphreys, who added that "an encounter in the Wilderness [would] neutralize the disparity in numbers." However, the route also had an advantage for the Unionists. A move around Lee's right would make it possible to supply the army by the rivers emanating from the Chesapeake Bay. In addition, a quick thrust through the Wilderness would put the army beyond Lee's right in more open terrain, closer to Richmond than the Confederates.[3]

After weighing all of his options, Grant chose to move around Lee's right flank. The supply line was apparently the deciding factor. Although he knew Lee would be tipped off to the movement almost from the start because of the Confederate observation post on Clark's Mountain, Grant knew that during the prior fall, it had taken Lee almost 30 hours to mobilize his men when Meade moved to open the Mine Run Campaign. If the army could move quickly, it could get through the Wilderness unscathed and offer battle to Lee on ground of Grant's choosing.[4]

"Lee's army is your objective point," Grant informed Meade in no uncertain terms. "Wherever Lee goes, there you will go also." Wagons would be kept to a minimum: "two wagons to a regiment of five hundred men is the greatest number that should be allowed," cautioned Grant.[5]

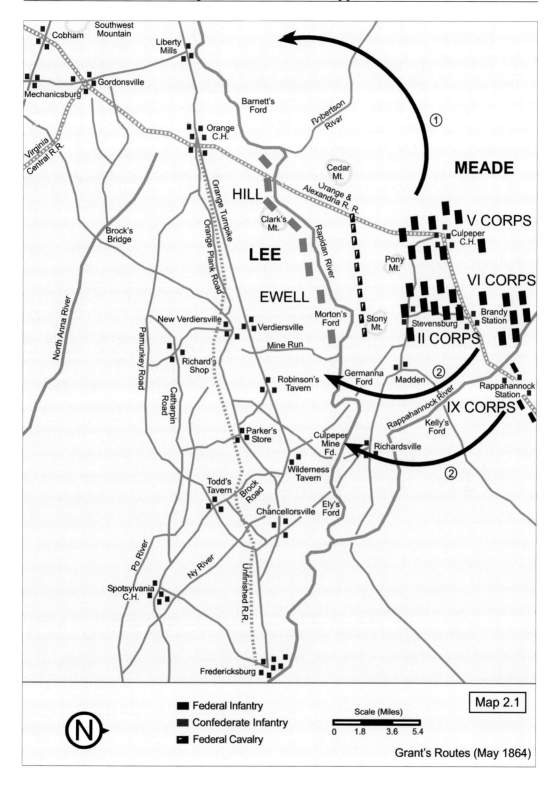

Map 2.1

Federal Infantry
Confederate Infantry
Federal Cavalry

Scale (Miles)
0   1.8   3.6   5.4

Grant's Routes (May 1864)

Map 2.2: Grant Prepares to Put the Army in Motion (May 2)

With the general plan decided upon, Maj. Gen. Andrew A. Humphreys, the army's chief of staff, went to work charting specific routes of march. Speed was of the essence, and the army needed to cross the Rapidan and penetrate through the Wilderness around Lee's flank before the Confederate general could intercept the effort. The Army of the Potomac would utilize two fords, Germanna and Ely's, about five miles apart, in order to expedite the crossing. Both fords offered fairly level banks and could be easily spanned with pontoon bridges.

Brigadier General David McM. Gregg's cavalry division was tasked with leading the Federal left wing to Ely's Ford at about 2:00 a.m. on May 4. Major General Winfield Hancock's II Corps would cover the road behind the ford (No. 1). Engineers accompanying the cavalry would transport a dozen canvas boats and 14 wooden French pontoons to provide a pair of ribbons to span the narrow river. Once across, the left wing (screened by cavalry) would march to Chancellorsville along Catharpin Road, and then head southwest toward Todd's Tavern. Several miles farther right (west), Brig. Gen. James Wilson's cavalry division and engineers, with the V and VI Corps tramping behind, would lead the way to Germanna Ford at midnight (No. 2). Once across, the column had orders to head for Wilderness Tavern on Germanna Plank Road while the cavalry scouted along the Orange Plank and Catharpin roads. Both columns would march to the Orange Turnpike, a major thoroughfare through the Wilderness.

Each man was issued 50 rounds of ammunition, three days of full rations packed in his haversack, and a three-day supply of bread and small rations in his knapsack. Each corps was allowed to bring half of its ambulances and a few other wagons loaded with ammunition and entrenching tools. The remainder would roll with the wagon train across the Rapidan on a fifth pontoon bridge at Culpeper Mine Ford.[6]

Orders circulated cautioning the men against setting their camps on fire, which would alert the Southerners that something major was afoot, and General Meade ordered his officers to adopt the "most vigorous measures to prevent any bonfires being made . . . [because of] the importance of concealing our movement from the enemy." The same orders (Special Orders Number 134) guarded against "marauding and pillaging" along the route of march.[7]

While these organizations moved south of the Rapidan, Brig. Gen. Alfred Torbert's cavalry division and Maj. Gen. Ambrose Burnside's IX Corps would remain on the north side. The recently arrived IX Corps' initial task was to protect the army's line of communications and not cross the river until at least May 5. When "the crossing of Meade's army is perfectly assured," Grant wrote Burnside, "I will notify you . . . which will be the signal for you to start" toward the river. The decision to have Burnside and his 20,000 men move separately and last would have important consequences in the upcoming battle.[8]

As General Humphreys saw it, General Lee had three alternatives: do nothing and the Union army would fall on his right flank and rear; turn and face the threat, or; retreat farther south, where he would be forced to fight out in the open. Planning his marches with an eye toward avoiding a fight in the Wilderness, Humphreys calculated that if the army began crossing the Rapidan about midnight on May 3-4, it could reach Mine Run by the evening of May 4. He was well aware of all the intangibles, particularly when trying to move large numbers of troops on just two roads. And of course, there was the question of what Lee would do. If he learned of the crossing by the morning of May 4, he could quickly put his troops on the road and have them facing the threat by mid-afternoon that day. Surprisingly, it appears as though little thought was given to dispatching Burnside's powerful corps to the fords closer to Lee's left flank to freeze him or a large position of his army in place.[9]

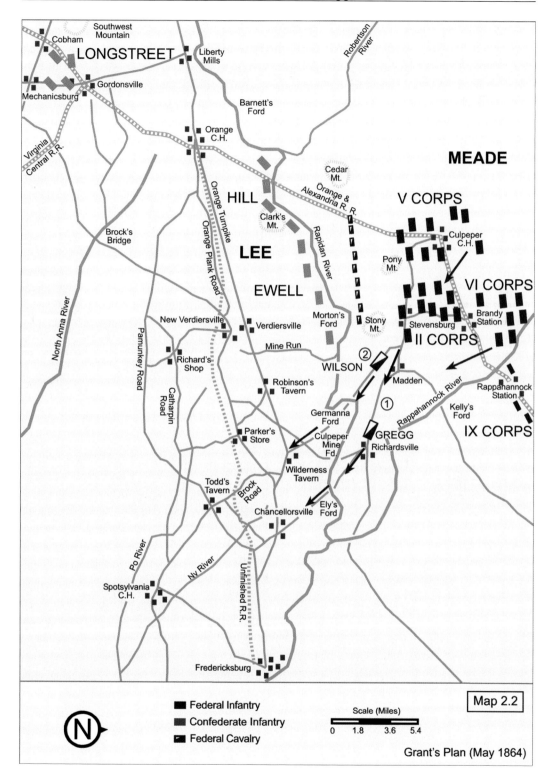

Southwest Mountain
Cobham
LONGSTREET
Liberty Mills
Gordonsville
Mechanicsburg
Barnett's Ford
Virginia Central R.R.
Orange C.H.
Cedar Mt.
MEADE
V CORPS
Orange & Alexandria R. R.
HILL
Clark's Mt.
Culpeper C.H.
Orange Turnpike
Brock's Bridge
LEE
Orange Plank Road
Rapidan River
Pony Mt.
VI CORPS
EWELL
North Anna River
New Verdiersville
Verdiersville
Morton's Ford
Stony Mt.
Stevensburg
Brandy Station
Pamunkey Road
Mine Run
II CORPS
Richard's Shop
Catharpin Road
Robinson's Tavern
WILSON
②
Madden
Rappahannock River
Rappahannock Station
Kelly's Ford
Germanna Ford
①
IX CORPS
Parker's Store
Culpeper Mine Fd.
GREGG
Richardsville
Wilderness Tavern
Todd's Tavern
Brock Road
Chancellorsville
Ely's Ford
Po River
Nv River
Unfinished R.R.
Spotsylvania C.H.
Fredericksburg

N

■ Federal Infantry
■ Confederate Infantry
▰ Federal Cavalry

Scale (Miles)
0   1.8   3.6   5.4

Map 2.2

Grant's Plan (May 1864)

Map 2.3 The Offensive Begins
(May 3-4)

The grand offensive began without a hitch on the night of May 3-4. The Union left wing, composed of Hancock's II Corps, broke camp between Stevensburg and Brandy Station before midnight on May 3 and moved toward Ely's Ford (No. 1). Two divisions under Brig. Gens. Francis Barlow and John Gibbon marched along the Culpeper Fredericksburg Road past Madden's Tavern while the divisions under Maj. Gen. David Birney and Brig. Gen. Gershom Mott took a more northerly route. The two portions of the left wing came together at Richardsville by sunrise.

The right wing was also on the move. When buglers with the V Corps broke the silence about midnight, the men boiled coffee and prepared for their march to Germanna Ford (No. 2). As one soldier recalled, we "rolled our blankets and stumbled at a snail's pace through the almost pitch darkness of the night for some two hours and a half before we had light enough to . . . distinguish our surroundings." Lines of men were deployed at various places along the road to prevent the column from taking the wrong path in the darkness. A division under Brig. Gen. Charles Griffin led the V Corps, followed by Brig. Gen. Samuel Crawford's, Robinson's, and Wadsworth's. General Warren split and marched his divisions on parallel roads before pulling them together again. The head of the column reached Germanna Plank Road about sunrise. Behind them Stevensburg burned—fired despite Meade's orders to the contrary.[10]

Sedgwick's VI Corps, slated to follow Warren's V Corps to Germanna Ford, was not roused until 3:30 a.m. and fell into line at about 4:00 a.m. (No. 3). Brigadier General George Getty's division was in the van, followed by divisions under Brig. Gen. Horatio Wright's and Brig. Gen. James Ricketts. Getting the troops up and on the road was no easy task. Sedgwick halted his column at 7:00 a.m. for a quick breakfast.[11]

The first crossing was affected by Maj. William Patton's 3rd Indiana Cavalry, which splashed across the Rapidan at Germanna Ford at 3:00 a.m. Pickets from the 1st North Carolina Cavalry fired a few scattered shots before dispersing into the darkness. With the south bank secured, the Federal engineers went to work on the pontoon bridges about 4:00 a.m. and by 5:30 they were ready to be used. The van of Warren's V Corps appeared about 30 minutes later—the first infantry to tramp across the river about 7:00 a.m. The second growth and heavy brush enveloped the men as they marched south into the Wilderness. A few short miles to the east, troopers from the 1st New Jersey Cavalry crossed the river and also easily scattered the Rebel pickets. Within minutes engineers there were also busy completing two pontoon bridges at Ely's Ford.[12]

Meade and his staff were in the saddle heading south from Brandy Station before dawn on May 4. One of Meade's aides noted the roads were hard, good for marching, and "full of wagons and black with troops." The sights and sounds of an army on the move was magnificent: "Corps, divisions . . . were moving on in a waving sea of blue; headquarters and regimental flags were fluttering, the morning sun kissed them all, and shimmering gaily from gun-barrels." Another veteran noted that the lines entered "the dark woods and dreadful fields where death should hold high carnival."[13]

Grant and his staff watched the movement but did not mount until 8:00 a.m. The men cheered Grant, whose reputation as a winner was new to them and their army. A war correspondent noted he had "never seen the army move with more exact order, with a less number of stragglers, and with so little apparent fatigue to the men." Grant crossed the river at Germanna Ford at noon and established his headquarters near Meade's.[14]

This was a long, hard march for the Army of the Potomac's veterans and green troops alike. The former were out of marching trim because of their months of inactivity; the latter were similarly unused to the physical strain and did not understand the value of traveling light. Most experienced soldiers had given up carrying knapsacks and packed their belongings in what was affectionately called a "horse collar."[15] The veterans watched and laughed at the extra belongings being carried by the new troops. As artilleryman Frank Wilkenson observed, veterans confidently predicted "they will throw away those loads before camp tonight." By the time the troops crossed Ely's Ford and had to scale its steep southern bank, continued the gunner, "Spare knapsacks, bursting with richness, were cast aside near its base."[16]

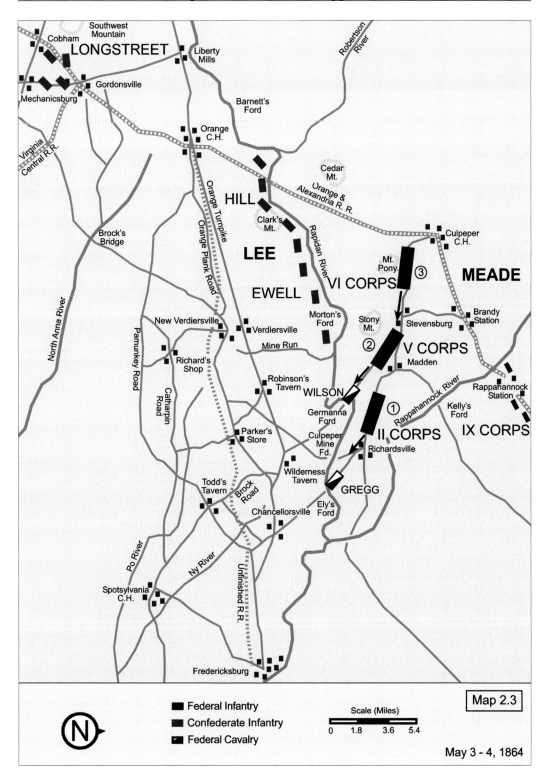

Federal Infantry
Confederate Infantry
Federal Cavalry

Scale (Miles)
0   1.8   3.6   5.4

Map 2.3

May 3 - 4, 1864

Map 2.4: The March Into
the Wilderness (May 4)

In addition to all their other responsibilities, Generals Meade and Grant spent most of May 4 pondering how and when General Lee would react to the crossing. The hours slipped past without incident, however, and the men drew near their evening bivouac sites without meeting enemy activity. "[W]e have succeeded in seizing the fords and crossing the river without loss or delay," Grant told his aides. "Lee must by this time know upon what roads we are advancing, but he may not yet realize the full extent of the movement. We shall probably soon get some indications as to what he intends to do."

Two sources provided Grant and Meade with a stream of information about the enemy army. One was the cavalry patrols riding upon the roads winding through the thickets. Except for a stray Rebel, all was quiet. The signal station atop Stony Mountain was also watching for enemy movements and intercepting enemy messages being sent via signal station flags atop Clark's Mountain. An ominous message was deciphered at 11:00 a.m.: "We [Lee's army] are moving . . . toward New Verdiersville," a small hamlet within the Wilderness.

This initial indication Lee was moving in his direction did not disturb Grant. He expected Lee would move toward the marching Union columns. Moving in his direction also meant Lee was not heading for Washington. Orders went out for Burnside to move his IX Corps toward the Rapidan and join Meade's army: make "forced marches until you reach this place. . . . Start your troops now in the rear . . . and require them to make a night march." Because it did not appear Lee's infantry had made much progress into the Wilderness, Grant believed he could keep his timetable and pass through the thickets before having to deal with the Rebels.[17]

By late afternoon, Meade's men were settling into their camps after a long uneventful march. Shortly after 3:00 p.m., Warren notified Meade that "the men are almost all in camp washing their feet and with a good night's rest will feel fine." Warren's V Corps camped near the intersection of Germanna Plank Road and the Orange Turnpike. Griffin's division, which led the march that day, camped at the crossroads. Behind it, Wadsworth's division camped east of Wilderness Run, and Crawford's division on the opposite side of it. Robinson's division brought up the rear of the V Corps, camping along Germanna Plank Road about halfway back to the river. Getty's division of the VI Corps bivouacked behind Robinson's division along Germanna Plank Road. Stretching toward the river were Sedgwick's remaining divisions under Wright and Ricketts.

The exhausted men of General Hancock's II Corps, some having marched 25 miles, dropped to the ground around Chancellorsville.[18] Their bivouac added to the men's discomfort: scattered in every direction were human skulls and bones comprising the hastily buried remains of men who had fallen a year earlier at Chancellorsville.[19] Some of the men were now camped on the same spot where they had fought during the gruesome battle.[20]

However well they slept that night, Meade's men would have slept much worse had they known that Lee had rapidly mobilized his army and large numbers of enemy troops were approaching their positions. Lee's observation post atop Clark's Mountain picked up that something was afoot almost as soon as Meade's men broke camp after dark on May 3; telltale flickers indicated that troops were marching in front of the campfires. What the observers could not determine was the destination of the troops and how many were involved. About 1:00 a.m., Lee sent a message to General Ewell holding the right of his line, "Have your command ready to move by daylight." Lee did not yet know whether Grant would attempt to cross the Rapidan River above or below his position. The enemy's intent became clearer when, at 9:30 a.m. on May 4, the signal station messaged, "Everything seems to be moving to the right on Germanna Ford and Ely's Ford roads, leaving cavalry in our front."[21]

Lee left behind Maj. Gen. R. H. Anderson's Division of Hill's Third Corps and Brig. Gen. Stephen Ramseur's Brigade and six regiments from others of Ewell's Second Corps and rushed the remaining men to the right. He also ordered Longstreet to bring up his First Corps from near Gordonsville, which would approach via Richard's Shop and Todd's Tavern. The men were ordered to quickly prepare three days' rations, but they were on the march before the task was completed. Hill's men marched east along the Orange Plank Road, while Ewell's marched along the Orange Turnpike.[22]

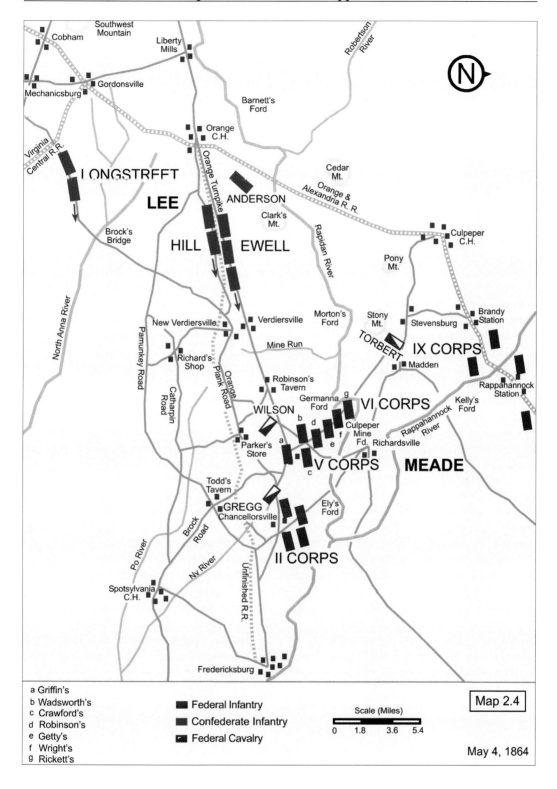

a Griffin's
b Wadsworth's
c Crawford's
d Robinson's
e Getty's
f Wright's
g Rickett's

Federal Infantry
Confederate Infantry
Federal Cavalry

Scale (Miles)
0   1.8   3.6   5.4

Map 2.4

May 4, 1864

Map 2.5 Lee Puts his Army in Motion (May 4)

Lee and his generals knew if they could catch the Army of the Potomac strung out marching in the Wilderness, its superiority in muskets, cavalry, and artillery would be neutralized. Still, the odds of battlefield victory were stacked against them. Even with Longstreet's command, the Army of Northern Virginia fielded roughly one-half of what Meade and Grant thrust across the Rapidan. Long odds were nothing new to the Confederates, and though they had suffered through a long and difficult winter, the army emerged with renewed confidence that spring. William Dame of the Richmond Howitzers recalled that despite the disparity in numbers, "these lunatics [Lee's men] were sweeping along to the appallingly unequal fight, cracking jokes, laughing, and with not the least idea in the world of anything else but victory. I did not hear a despondent word, nor see a dejected face among the thousands I saw and heard that day."[23]

Lee's men were on the road by noon of May 4 and maintained a blistering pace toward Mine Run. When night fell, Ewell's Second Corps was along the Orange Turnpike near Robinson's Tavern (also Robertson's Tavern or Locust Grove), with Maj. Gen. Jubal Early's Division camped near the buildings. His two other divisions under Maj. Gens. Edward Johnson and Robert Rodes camped behind Early. A. P. Hill's Third Corps had farther to march and so ended the day a few miles short of where Ewell had reached farther north. Major General Henry Heth's Division was in the van and camped beyond New Verdiersville on the Orange Plank Road, while Maj. Gen. Cadmus Wilcox's Division bivouacked near New Verdiersville. Hill's last division under Maj. Gen. Richard Anderson had been left behind to keep an eye on the fords and what had been Lee's left flank. Lee's cavalry corps under Maj. Gen. James Ewell Brown (Jeb) Stuart, minus Maj. Gen. Fitzhugh Lee's Division, camped just east of the town. The latter division was near Hamilton's Crossing just south of Fredericksburg. Several miles to the southwest, two infantry divisions comprising James Longstreet's First Corps had crossed the North Anna River and camped nearby. Lee knew that he may well have to fight in the open without his most experienced corps commander and some of his best troops, which had another 32 miles to march before reuniting with the rest of the army. In order to ensure he took the most direct route, Longstreet acquired an experienced local guide.[24]

While his army rested, Lee had his tent pitched at New Verdiersville, near the location of his prior camp during the Mine Run Campaign, and planned for the coming day. A flurry of intelligence reports, many of them contradictory, reached him. Even though Longstreet was not up and Anderson's Division was still well behind the tail of Ewell's Corps, Lee decided to seize the initiative and attack Meade with the roughly 30,000 men he had on hand. Orders were issued to both Ewell and Hill to advance along their respective roads on the morning of May 5 and strike the Union troops wherever they were found. "If the enemy moved down the river, he [Lee] wishes to push after him. If he comes this way, we will take our old line. The general's desire is to bring [the enemy] to battle as soon now as possible."[25]

While Lee issued his orders that would trigger one of the war's large-scale battles (and fighting that, with few exceptions, would rage in one form or another until Appomattox in April 1865), every Union regiment was assembled and read a patriotic message prepared by General Meade before falling out for rest. After the war, with the benefit of hindsight, some of the veterans questioned the wisdom of halting for the night of May 4-5 within the Wilderness where Lee had the advantage. As the historian for Hancock's II Corps put it, "the troops had made a stiff, but, except in the case of the Second Corps, not an exhausting march, and were in the best of condition and spirits." Other historians writing more recently questioned this analysis, believing the other two corps had marched for 15 hours and were in no shape to continue on into the night.[26]

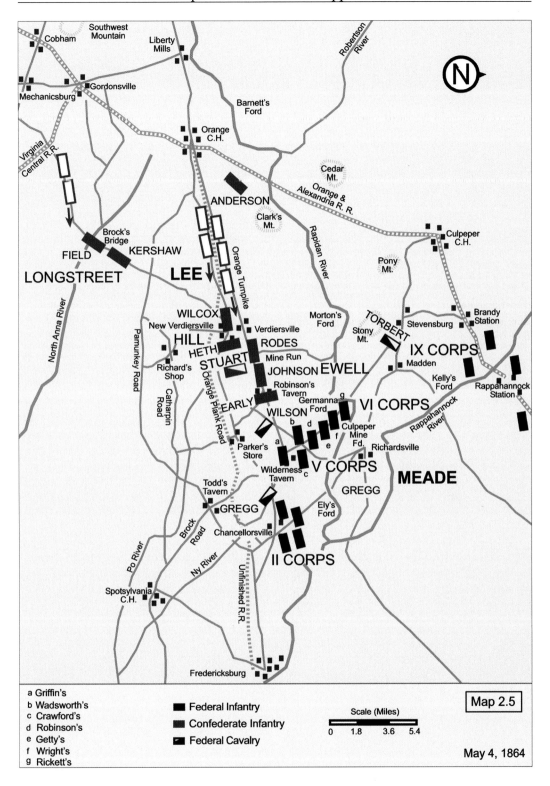

a Griffin's
b Wadsworth's
c Crawford's
d Robinson's
e Getty's
f Wright's
g Rickett's

■ Federal Infantry
■ Confederate Infantry
◩ Federal Cavalry

Scale (Miles)
0   1.8   3.6   5.4

Map 2.5

May 4, 1864

Map Set 3: The Armies Come into Contact (May 5)

Map 3.1: The Wilderness Battlefield

The large sprawling area referred to as the "Wilderness" extended from the Rapidan River on the north to Spotsylvania Court House in the south, and from Chancellorsville to the east to Locust Grove (Robinson's Tavern) to the west. The area was once the home of rich virgin timber, most of which had been cut down years earlier to feed nearby iron smelting furnaces. In its place sprouted a dense secondary thicket of scrub pine and black oak with a heavy mixture of dogwood, hazel, and chestnut. Without large numbers of animals to graze among the trees, thick undergrowth had taken root.

The undulating ground within the Wilderness was creased with ravines, creeks, and swampy terrain in its low areas, with sweeps of incline and prominent knolls marking its highest elevations. Though few in number, sizeable clearings would play a significant role in shaping the upcoming combat. Saunders' Field, several hundred yards long and wide, extended along both sides of the Orange Turnpike. Higgerson's Field and Jones' Field, which connected with the high and open ground surrounding the Chewning farm, lay farther south. The few structures within this forbidding landscape included commercial establishments like the Wilderness Tavern (built in 1810), Robinson's Tavern, and Parker's Store. Places of worship included Shady Grove Church, Craig's Meeting House, and New Hope Church. The most prominent of the few farms included Lacy's, Higgerson's, Chewning's, and the Widow Tapp's.[1]

A spider's web of roads and waterways traversed the Wilderness. Several major arteries cut east to west, including the Orange Turnpike, Orange Plank Road, Catharpin Road, and Pamunkey Road. Some of the north-south roads included Spotswood Road, Germanna Ford Road, and Brock Road. One of the most important creeks winding through the region was a tributary of the Rapidan named Wilderness Run. The meandering waterway flowed northeast, crossing both Germanna Ford Road and the Orange Turnpike. Several streams branched off Wilderness Run. The Po River ran south of Orange Plank Road and Robertson's Run flowed into it.

Moving a large army through the Wilderness was a slow and fitful affair on the roads, and nearly impossible off them. Visibility was usually measured in a handful of yards. It was easy within this living quagmire to lose one's bearings. The region, remembered Col. Horace Porter of Grant's staff, "is well described by its name. It was a wilderness in the most forbidding sense of the word."

During the evening of May 4-5, pickets from Griffin's division were thrown forward on Germanna Plank Road in the direction Lee's army would approach. One officer unimpressed with the effort later wrote that the picket line was not established "with such care as should be exercised in the presence of the enemy." The men were exhausted and most of the officers allowed them to rest rather than perform rigorous duty. The Union soldiers mistakenly believed that Brig. Gen. James Wilson's cavalry division was deployed ahead as a protective screen. What they did not know was that the relatively inexperienced Wilson, who was tasked with probing the army's front for signs of Lee's army, had neglected to post a picket line on either the Orange Turnpike or Orange Plank Road. If he had done so, the Union high command would have learned that Lee's infantry was camped but a short march away.[2]

General Wilson's probes, however, were communicated to General Lee by his cavalry commander, Jeb Stuart, at about 11:15 p.m. The commander of Ewell's artillery and General Lee's former staff officer, Brig. Gen. Armistead Long, spent the night at Lee's headquarters. The army commander, wrote Long, "expressed himself surprised that his new adversary had placed himself in the same predicament as 'Fighting Joe' had done the previous Spring. He hoped the result would be even more disastrous to Grant than that which Hooker had experienced. He was, indeed, in the best of spirit," continued Long, "and expressed much confidence in the result."[3]

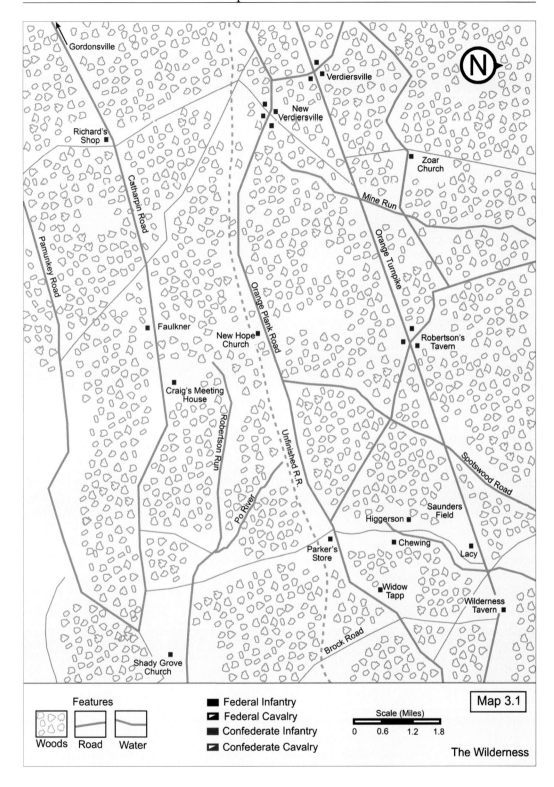

Gordonsville

Verdiersville

New Verdiersville

Richard's Shop

Zoar Church

Mine Run

Catharpin Road

Orange Turnpike

Pamunkey Road

Orange Plank Road

Faulkner

New Hope Church

Robertson's Tavern

Craig's Meeting House

Robertson Run

Unfinished R.R.

Spotswood Road

Po River

Saunders Field

Higgerson

Parker's Store

Chewing

Lacy

Widow Tapp

Wilderness Tavern

Brock Road

Shady Grove Church

Features

Woods   Road   Water

■ Federal Infantry
◪ Federal Cavalry
■ Confederate Infantry
◪ Confederate Cavalry

Scale (Miles)

0   0.6   1.2   1.8

Map 3.1

The Wilderness

Map 3.2: The Confederate Army Moves East (4:00 - 5:00 a.m.)

General Meade's original orders tasked Wilson's division with screening the army's right column (V Corps and VI Corps) while Gregg's division screened the left column (II Corps). After accompanying the vital wagon train, the remaining cavalry division under Brig. Gen. Alfred Torbert was to join Wilson's troopers in front of the V Corps and VI Corps. The army's cavalry commander, Phil Sheridan, was firmly against dividing his cavalry, and when he learned enemy horsemen were at Hamilton's Crossing below Fredericksburg, lobbied Meade to pull Gregg's division from in front of the II Corps and, together with Torbert's troopers, ride eastward to take on the enemy cavalry. Meade's assent left only Wilson's division to attend to the vital task of screening all the infantry columns. If he encountered Lee's army, Wilson was to engage the enemy while Union infantry converged upon his position. Wilson was inexperienced in handling a division, and his was the smallest of Meade's cavalry divisions. Even a more experienced leader would have struggled with his mission because he did not have enough troopers to handle the task assigned to him.[4]

Farther west, the troops under Generals Ewell and Hill were stirring before daylight. Ed Johnson's Division of the former corps was bivouacked about one mile east of Locust Grove with Robert Rodes' Division just behind it and Jubal Early's Division camped in and around the small hamlet. Two divisions of A. P. Hill Corps under Generals Wilcox and Heth were in and around New Verdiersville. His third, under Richard Anderson, was shaking off sleep on Rapidan Heights guarding Lee's rear but was now heading toward Plank Road to rejoin the rest of Hill's command.[5] Almost all of these men were on the march at first light, with Ewell's troops filling the Orange Turnpike streaming east and A. P. Hill's tramping upon the Orange Plank Road a couple miles to the south.

A curious junior officer approached Ewell as he rode west with Johnson's Division and asked if he had any objections about revealing his orders. "No sir, none at all; just the orders I like—to go down the plank road [turnpike] and strike the enemy wherever I find him."[6]

The head of Ewell's Corps had only been on the road a short time when a small picket line was discovered about two miles beyond Locust Grove. The one-legged commander sent his new son-in-law, Campbell Brown, to find and tell General Lee the news, and that he would keep pushing east. Brown found Lee on the Plank Road opposite Locust Grove. The army leader may have had the disasters of Gettysburg and Bristoe Station on his mind when he counseled caution. As Brown recorded the instructions, "General Ewell was not to advance too fast, for fear of getting entangled with the enemy while still in advance & out of reach of Hill. If the enemy were found in large force," Lee added to Brown, "he did not want a general engagement brought on till Longstreet cd come up (which wd hardly be much before night). If the enemy advanced & showed a willingness to fight he preferred falling back to our old position at Mine Run. Above all, Gen. E was not to get his troops entangled, so as to be unable to disengage them, in case the enemy were in force. If he found them, he cd feel them with skirmishers, well supported & ascertain their strength—then act as above shown."[7]

Marching near the head of Ewell's Corps that morning, John Worsham of the 21st Virginia (John M. Jones' Brigade, Johnson's Division), recalled how that fateful May day began: "As the streaks of day were just beginning to show themselves, we were ordered to fall in, and resumed our march. We had gone only a short distance when the stillness in our front was broken by the sound of a drum, and the sweet notes of music from a band. Every man clutched his gun more tightly, as the direction of the music told him that the enemy were in front. There was no need of urging us to hurry, no need to inquire what it meant. All knew now that Grant had crossed the Rapidan, and soon the tumult of battle would begin. The march continued, the command was 'Close up,' soon the order, 'Halt! Load your guns!' then 'Shoulder arms! March!'[8]

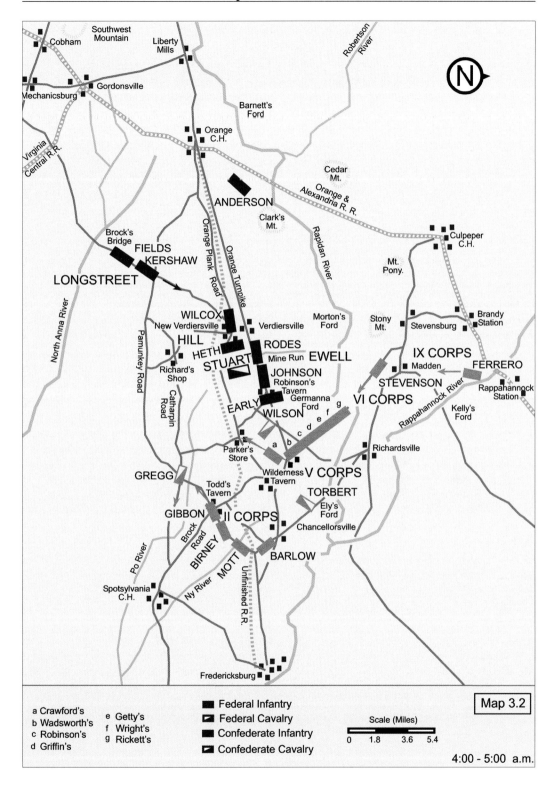

a Crawford's   e Getty's
b Wadsworth's   f Wright's
c Robinson's   g Rickett's
d Griffin's

■ Federal Infantry
◤ Federal Cavalry
■ Confederate Infantry
◤ Confederate Cavalry

Scale (Miles)

0   1.8   3.6   5.4

Map 3.2

4:00 – 5:00 a.m.

Map 3.3: The Federal March Begins
(5:00 - 6:00 a.m.)

On the morning of May 5, Meade's army formed something of a convex line stretching from the Rapidan River to Shady Grove Church. Hancock's II Corps had orders to march to Catharpin Road while Warren's V Corps headed to Parker's Store to connect with Hancock's right flank. Sedgwick's VI Corps would follow Warren and assume the V Corps' former position. Sedgwick was to maintain a division at Germanna Ford until Burnside's IX Corps appeared. The cumbersome miles-long wagon train would head to Todd's Tavern at the intersection of Catharpin and Brock's roads. Once those positions were reached, "the army will be held ready to move forward," but not until Burnside's men crossed the Rapidan. This strategy may have stemmed from Grant's and Meade's belief that Lee would again assume a defensive posture in his strong works west of Mine Run—the same entrenchments he had occupied the prior December.[9]

The Union men were also up and about early, grabbing breakfast and forming in the roads about 5:00 a.m. Happy to be once again in the field leading his men after his debilitating wound at Gettysburg, General Hancock marched his II Corps toward Shady Grove Church 12 miles away. Gibbon's division was in the lead, followed by Birney's, Mott's, and Barlow's. The corps filtered southward along a variety of roads, including Furnace Road, Brock Road, and Catharpin Road. General Warren's V Corps headed south on Parker's Store Road toward its namesake about four miles distant. The "road" was really little more than a narrow trail. Crawford's Pennsylvania Reserve division led the column, followed by Wadsworth, Robinson, and Griffin. Marching behind Warren, General Sedgwick's VI Corps had the shortest march (less than four miles to the Wilderness Tavern). Getty's division took the lead, with Wright and Ricketts trailing. General Burnside's IX Corps was also on the move, with Stevenson's division marching well in front as it approached Germanna Ford.[10]

Wilson's cavalry division, which had spent the night near Parker's Store, was also on the move by 5:00 a.m. when its men rode to Craig's Meeting House on Catharpin Road. Wilson was also ordered to send patrols west along the Orange Turnpike and Orange Plank Road. He ordered Lt. Col. John Hammond's 5th New York Cavalry to reconnoiter on the latter road toward Parker's Store, but did not send any troopers to ride the Orange Turnpike. Meade would not learn until much later that Sheridan had sent most of his cavalry on a fruitless expedition, for Fitzhugh Lee's Confederate cavalry division had already vacated Hamilton's Crossing.[11]

The lack of a Federal cavalry screen allowed Ewell's men to march east on the Orange Turnpike toward wholly unsuspecting enemy infantry. Screened by the 1st North Carolina Cavalry, the vanguard of Johnson's Division reached the western edge of Saunders Field about 6:00 a.m. When he spotted enemy soldiers on the opposite side several hundred yards distant, Johnson sent a message to Ewell that he had found the enemy, ordered his artillery to the rear, and deployed his division on both sides of the road. Brigadier General John M. Jones' Virginia brigade at the head of the column moved south of the Plank Road. It was a fine defensive position with an unobstructed view of Saunders Field. Brigadier General George Steuart's mixed brigade of Virginians and North Carolinians deployed across the road from Jones' men. Brigadier General Leroy Stafford and his Louisiana troops assumed a line on Steuart's left, while James Walker's Stonewall Brigade of Virginians formed perpendicular to the rest of the division to guard against a flank attack. Jones' and Steuart's men had a fairly easy time getting into their assigned positions, but the same was not true for Stafford and Walker, whose men had to make their way through a "jungle of switch, twenty or thirty feet high, more impenetrable, if possible, than pine," noted one of the Rebs. Another observed that "a more difficult and disagreeable field of battle could not well be imagined." Walker's men reached their destination by marching along a narrow trek generously called the Spotswood or Culpeper Mine Ford Road. Once in position, Johnson's men clawed out a crude series of trenches and felled some of the smaller trees for additional protection.[12]

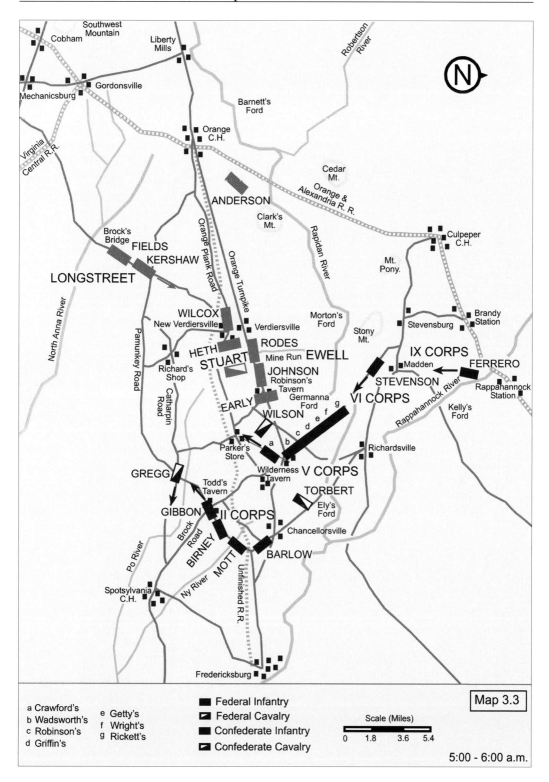

a Crawford's
b Wadsworth's
c Robinson's
d Griffin's

e Getty's
f Wright's
g Rickett's

Federal Infantry
Federal Cavalry
Confederate Infantry
Confederate Cavalry

Scale (Miles)

0   1.8   3.6   5.4

Map 3.3

5:00 - 6:00 a.m.

Map 3.4: Griffin's Men
See the Enemy (6:00 a.m.)

Dressed in a fine uniform and mounted on his large horse, General Warren headed toward the front of his V Corps column at 6:00 a.m. on May 5. Not known for his sunny disposition, he was especially irritable that morning. He had plenty to be worried about, for it was his responsibility to maneuver his 24,000 soldiers through the dense Wilderness along narrow winding roads, and do so without any knowledge of the location of the enemy. Because his corps was the farthest west and thus the closest to the Confederates, the odds were high that Lee's veterans would pitch into his men first. While his troops headed toward Parker's Store, Warren's engineers threw three bridges across Wilderness Run to permit ready passage for the artillery and wagons following the infantry. Without a visible cavalry screen, the naturally cautious Warren eased his column forward slowly, "well closed and held well in hand, ready to meet an attack at any moment." He also wisely threw out scores of pickets to the front and to the right. The last thing Warren wanted was a surprise in any form.[13]

Griffin's division remained behind at the intersection of the Orange Turnpike and Germanna Ford Road to protect Warren's rear and await the arrival of Sedgwick's VI Corps marching up from Germanna Ford. The night before, Griffin had thrown out pickets from each brigade in the general direction of any anticipated Confederate approach. Griffin's men were packing up that morning to join the march when members of the 1st Michigan (Bartlett's brigade) spotted figures off to the west along the Orange Turnpike. The Michiganders had already been called to move out, but Lt. Col. William A. Throop instead extended his line to the right across the turnpike and called up his reserve company, and notified his brigade commander of what was transpiring. Meanwhile, Col. David T. Jenkins of the 146th New York, commanding the picket line, sent a message to Warren that "rebel infantry have appeared on the Orange Court House turnpike and are forming a line of battle, three quarters of a mile in front of General Griffin's line of battle. I have my skirmishers out, and preparations are being made to meet them."

Griffin jotted off a similar message to the V Corps commander. What none of the Federals knew yet was that the grayclad figures in the distance represented the vanguard of Ewell's Second Corps.[14]

Warren, in turn, was penning a note to Meade's chief of staff, Maj. Gen. Andrew Humphries at about 6:00 a.m. that "a force of the enemy has been reported to him [Griffin] coming down the turnpike . . . until it is more definitely ascertained no change will take place in the movements ordered" when another arrived from Griffin. Warren scribbled a second note, this one with the time of 6:20 a.m. that "General Bartlett sends in word that the enemy has a line of infantry with skirmishers out advancing," and sent a courier to Griffin with orders to "push a force out at once against the enemy and see what force he has."[15]

General Lee was up and dressed long before daylight on May 5 at his camp near Verdiersville. Cheerful and full of energy, Lee could not contain his pleasure at the news that the Army of the Potomac had camped for the night within the gloomy Wilderness. As one aide recalled, Lee believed his "antagonist would be at his mercy while entangled in these pathless and entangled thickets, whose thickets disparity in numbers lost much of its importance."[16]

Lee mounted his horse and rode with A. P. Hill's Third Corps along the Orange Plank Road, screened by Jeb Stuart's cavalry. The men prepared to halt when they reached their former Mine Run fortifications, but their officers kept them moving along. Lee had no intention of fighting a defensive battle, a realization that coursed through the ranks. "Marse Bob is going for them this time," was passed along the line in a mixture of excitement and dread.[17]

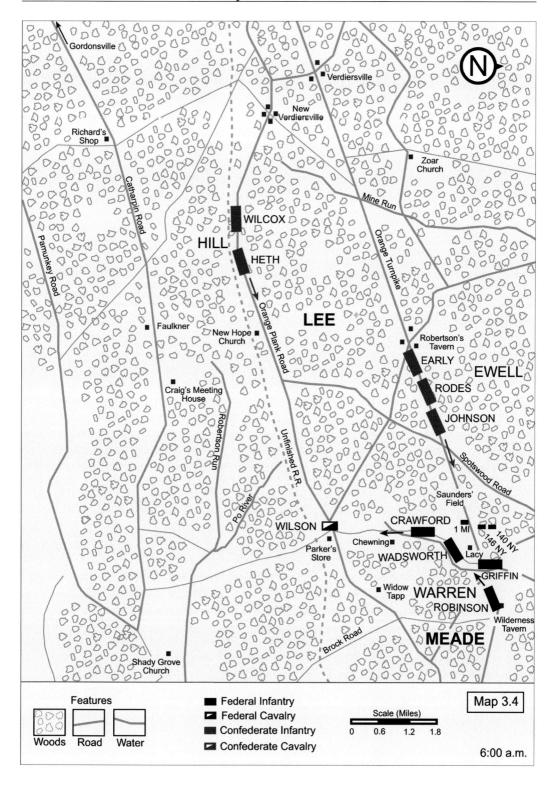

Map 3.4

6:00 a.m.

Map 3.5: Initial Encounter
(7:15 - 7:30 a.m.)

The naturally aggressive Lee was inclined to send Ewell straight into the ill-prepared Federals, but caution prevailed. Ewell would advance methodically to avoid getting too entangled with the enemy without ready support from either Hill or Longstreet. Even when Hill's corps pulled up roughly even with Ewell's right, Lee counseled caution. The two corps were still separated by a couple miles of heavy terrain, and Longstreet's First Corps was still many hours away. As far as Lee was concerned, the army could issue a devastating blow once it was collected and organized accordingly. And so while skirmishers from Johnson's Division's slowly picked their way east a few yards at a time, the balance of the command busily dug trenches and threw up crude breastworks in the woods lining the western portion of Saunders Field.[18]

On the opposite side of the field, General Griffin pondered his options. He had no idea of who he was facing, if infantry or cavalry, or how many Rebels were waiting in the woods. To find out, so he ordered Brig. Gen. Joseph Bartlett to probe westward. Bartlett tapped the 18th Massachusetts and 83rd Pennsylvania (No. 1) and placed the regiments under the command of Col. Joseph Hayes of the 18th. Hayes advanced slowly west toward the V Corps' skirmish line. "With the aide [sic] of my glasses," he wrote, "I could plainly see the enemy filing off to the right and left of the road and apparently massing his forces." Too far away to be able to get a real understanding of the situation, Hayes threw out two companies of the 18th Massachusetts south of the pike and a pair Keystone companies to the north, and sent them toward Saunders Field. The open patch of ground, which had grown corn the previous year, was about 400 yards east to west and 800 yards north to south, with the Orange Turnpike running roughly through its center. Although the field was open, it did not offer a smooth easy crossing. The ground was bumpy, and a deep swale oriented along a roughly north-south axis sliced across much of it.[19]

The approaching Federals soon realized the enemy was hard at work fortifying the top of the slope. Johnson's advance line opened with a patchwork of musketry that convinced the four companies to fall back. During the retreat, a bullet found an 18-year-old Massachusetts farmer named Charley Wilson. He was the first fatality of the Wilderness fighting.

Meanwhile, General Wilson with a single mounted division was doing his best to screen and scout the broad front of Meade's army while his other two divisions rode toward Fredericksburg for what would be a completely useless waste of good horseflesh. Without new orders, Wilson decided to follow his old ones. His men were in the saddle at 5:00 a.m., riding southwest from Parker's Store toward Craig's Meeting House on Catharpin Road. He left behind Lt. Col. John Hammond's 5th New York Cavalry to watch the Orange Plank Road until Warren's infantry appeared (No. 2). Because he did not push scouts westward along the road, Wilson had no idea an entire Confederate infantry corps (A. P. Hill's) was marching east toward the critical Parker's Store intersection.

Hammond, meanwhile, ordered a company under Capt. William Cary to ride west on the Orange Plank Road to find—but not engage—the enemy while the rest of the regiment ate breakfast at Parker's Store. Within minutes Cary's Spencer-armed troopers were driving back Confederates. Most of the prisoners were from Brig. Gen. William W. Kirkland's Brigade—the van of Hill's Third Corps. When the news filtered back to Colonel Hammond at Parker's Store, he sent reinforcements to Cary and ordered the erection of barricades. One of Warren's staff officers arrived with the welcome news that Crawford's infantry division was nearby.[20]

The rest of Wilson's division headed southwest toward Craig's Meeting House four miles away. Wilson detached Col. John B. McIntosh's brigade at Robertson's Run to prevent an ambush by Longstreet's men, rumored to be marching toward the battlefield. Wilson rode on to the intersection of the Catharpin Road, where with Col. George H. Chapman's brigade (No. 3) he turned west. Led by the 1st Vermont Cavalry, the column trotted a short distance before finding Rebels belonging to Brig. Gen. Thomas L. Rosser's brigade riding toward them. "The heat of the night had been oppressive and the men poorly refreshed by broken slumbers, were called early into the saddle," recalled the historian for Rosser's command. The first cavalry fight of the battle was about to erupt.[21]

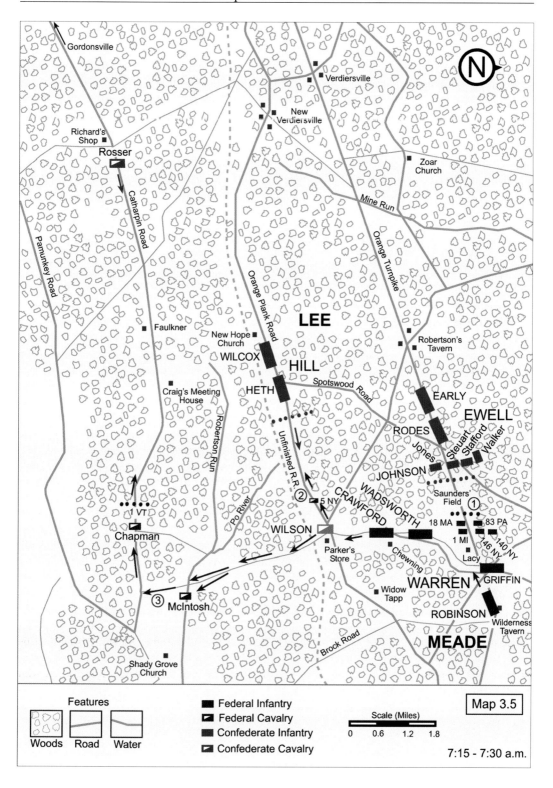

Gordonsville

Verdiersville

New Verdiersville

Richard's Shop

Rosser

Zoar Church

Mine Run

Catharpin Road

Pamunkey Road

Orange Turnpike

Faulkner

New Hope Church

Robertson's Tavern

WILCOX

LEE

HILL

HETH

Spotswood Road

EARLY

Craig's Meeting House

Orange Plank Road

Robertson Run

RODES

EWELL

Jones

Steuart

Stafford

Walker

Unfinished R.R.

JOHNSON

Po River

WADSWORTH

CRAWFORD

Saunders' Field ①

② 5 NY

1 VT

Chapman

WILSON

18 MA

83 PA

1 MI

146 NY

140 NY

Parker's Store

Chewning

Lacy

③ McIntosh

Widow Tapp

WARREN

GRIFFIN

Brock Road

ROBINSON

Wilderness Tavern

Shady Grove Church

MEADE

Features

Woods   Road   Water

■ Federal Infantry
◣ Federal Cavalry
■ Confederate Infantry
◣ Confederate Cavalry

Scale (Miles)

0   0.6   1.2   1.8

Map 3.5

7:15 - 7:30 a.m.

Map 3.6: Meade Halts
His Army (7:30 - 8:30 a.m.)

General Meade caught up with General Warren at Wilderness Tavern between 7:30-7:45 a.m. After a quick update, Meade was heard to exclaim, "If there is to be any fighting this side of Mine Run, let us do it right off!" He canceled all marching orders and notified his corps leaders to form a line roughly perpendicular to the Orange Turnpike. General Hancock, marching east of Warren's V Corps, was ordered to halt his II Corps at Todd's Tavern and wait "until the matter develops." The dispatch did not reach Hancock until about 9:00 a.m., and by that time the head of his column was two miles beyond Todd's Tavern. Hancock began retracing his steps. Meade could not count on that corps to arrive any time soon. The VI Corps and IX Corps were also hastened forward. The former (under General Sedgwick) was ordered to form on Warren's right, while the latter continued crossing the Rapidan River.[22]

Forming his corps into a defensive line would not be easy for Warren because his four divisions were strung out over some four miles in the dense thickets of the Wilderness. Holding Robinson's division in reserve near the Wilderness Tavern, Warren sent Griffin's division "forward [to] attack the enemy, and await further instructions, while the other troops are forming." The "other troops" consisted of Wadsworth's and Crawford's divisions, which were on the trail leading to Parker's Store.[23]

Back in front of Griffin's position, the men of the 20th Maine moved forward to fell trees, strip the branches and leaves, and stack the trunks to form a defensive barrier about 50 yards in front of the rest of the division, which went to work digging a trench behind the breastworks, topping it off with a few feet of soil. By this stage of the war, "the opposing sides . . . entrenched even before the first shot was fired." This precaution would become the norm for the balance of the war.[24]

The anxious and frustrated Warren now knew some part of Lee's army was massing in his front, but the size and composition remained to be determined. Almost as worrisome was the fact that Warren had little idea of the whereabouts of the rest of the Army of the Potomac. Amidst this uncertainty, the head of the V Corps oversaw the alignment of his troops in the heavy and foreboding thickets. Woe to the subordinate, whether a general or a lowly foot soldier, who did not follow orders promptly or proved tardy in his movements.[25]

Meade, meanwhile, informed General Grant about 7:30 a.m. that part of Lee's army had been found. "The enemy have appeared in force . . . and are now reported forming line of battle in front of Griffin's division," wrote Meade. "I have directed General Griffin to attack them at once with his whole force. Until this movement of the enemy is developed, the march of the corps must be suspended." Meade received a response about one hour later: "If any opportunity presents itself for pitching into a part of Lee's army, do so without giving time for disposition."[26]

Meade's decision, now confirmed by Grant, was just what Lee desired: a confrontation within the Wilderness where the heavy terrain favored the understrength Confederate army. Rather than continue moving south to get beyond Lee's right flank, Meade was preparing his troops to fight the enemy in what could only be a series of frontal assaults. Severely hampered by a lack of information from the cavalry, the infantry thrust along the Orange Turnpike would acquire both vital information about the enemy and buy time for the rest of the army to assemble.[27]

Meanwhile, farther south along the Plank Road, the 5th New York Cavalry continued battling the forward elements comprising A. P. Hill's Third Corps. By this time Captain Cary's men were falling back to Parker's Store, and Colonel Hammond knew the enemy would soon appear behind them. Within minutes Confederate troops made there appearance "in almost a solid battle line." One of Hammond's troopers wrote that "it was almost impossible not to hit our mark" with their seven-shot carbines. About this time cavalry brigade commander Col. John McIntosh appeared to help defend the vital crossroads. The direct approach to the barricade sheltering the New Yorkers proved more than the Tar Heels of Kirkland's Brigade wanted to bite off, so they slipped around the flank of the embattled troopers and eased them back from Parker's Store. The withdrawal proved short-lived, for Hammond reestablished his line and continued felling North Carolinians as fast as his Spencers could fire.[28]

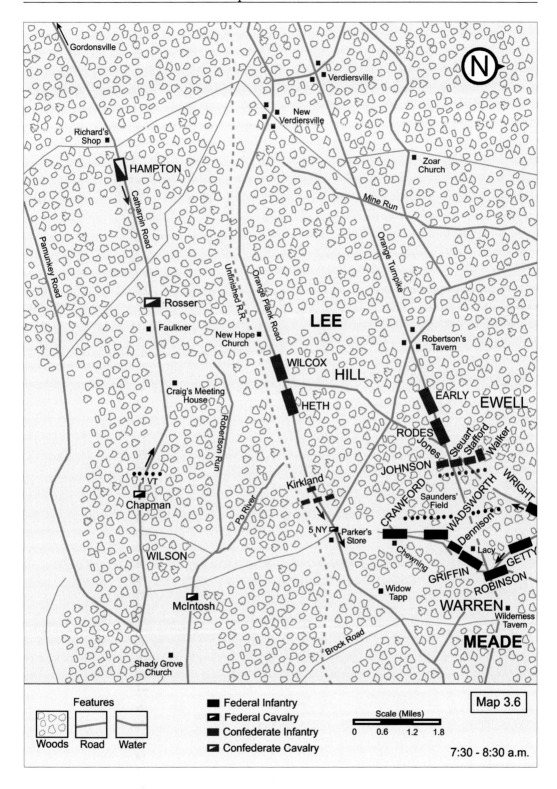

Gordonsville

Verdiersville

New
Verdiersville

Richard's
Shop

Zoar
Church

HAMPTON

Mine Run

Pamunkey Road

Catharpin Road

Rosser

Faulkner

New Hope
Church

LEE

Robertson's
Tavern

Orange Turnpike

Unfinished R.R.

Orange Plank Road

WILCOX

HILL

EARLY

EWELL

Craig's Meeting
House

HETH

RODES

Jones

Steuart

Stafford

Walker

Robertson Run

JOHNSON

1 VT

Kirkland

CRAWFORD

Saunders'
Field

WRIGHT

Chapman

Po River

WADSWORTH

Dennison

5 NY

Parker's
Store

Lacy

GETTY

Chewning

WILSON

GRIFFIN

ROBINSON

McIntosh

Widow
Tapp

WARREN

Wilderness
Tavern

MEADE

Brock Road

Shady Grove
Church

Features

Woods   Road   Water

■ Federal Infantry
◥ Federal Cavalry
■ Confederate Infantry
◤ Confederate Cavalry

Scale (Miles)

0   0.6   1.2   1.8

Map 3.6

7:30 - 8:30 a.m.

Map 3.7: Wilson's Cavalry Clashes with the Enemy (8:00 - 8:30 a.m.)

Colonel McIntosh quickly sized up the situation and sent a dispatch directly to Meade: "We are now formed at the junction of the Parker's Store Road and [Orange Plank Road] without ammunition. . . . I understand that General Crawford is on my right. He should extend his line at once across the Parker's Store Road." Brigadier General Samuel Crawford, who had won accolades for his performance at Gettysburg, had already thrown out the 13th Pennsylvania Reserves on the skirmish line toward Parker's Store to ascertain what was on his left flank (No. 1). The Bucktails had not moved far before Kirkland's North Carolinians developed both of McIntosh's flanks (No. 2). The Rebels, wrote one Union trooper, "made things buzz from all sides, and we were obliged to skip out for our horses." Pulling back about a quarter of a mile, McIntosh halted the New Yorkers and deployed them as a heavy skirmish line across the road. He yelled to one of the officers, "For God's sake, captain, hold this line!" Holding the intersection was vital for the Union effort, and the situation looked grim.

The Pennsylvania Bucktails, who could see the left flank of Kirkland's line following Hammond's cavalry east, opened fire. The rounds surprised and temporarily halted the Tar Heels. When an officer ordered his North Carolinians to turn and attack what he thought was Federal cavalry, one of his veterans replied, "Cavalry, hell! Cavalry don't carry knapsacks and wear bucktails!"[29]

The implications of losing Parker's Store to the Confederates were immense. Its loss would cut off Wilson's cavalry division from the rest of the Army of the Potomac and leave Hill's Third Corps squarely on Crawford's left flank. It would also allow Hill ready access east to the Brock Road, another vital intersection that, if taken by the Rebels would cut off Hancock's II Corps.[30]

While the 5th New York Cavalry gamely tried to blunt Hill's advance east on the Orange Plank Road, Col. George Chapman's cavalry brigade continued reconnoitering west along the Catharpin Road (No. 3). When he reaching Craig's Meeting House, Chapman wisely halted his command and threw a battalion of the 1st Vermont Cavalry westward toward Richard's Shop. The Vermont boys rode cautiously ahead, looking closely into the thickets lining either side of the road. After about one mile they passed the Faulkner farm and encountered videttes from the 12th Virginia Cavalry at about 8:00 a.m. This was enough for the Vermonters, who turned and set their spurs to rejoin their command with the gray troopers in close pursuit.[31]

The pursuing Virginians were brought up short when they reached the edge of the open field surrounding Craig's Meeting House and spied Chapman's brigade deployed and ready for battle. Dismounting, the Rebels opened fire from the woods lining the field, but there were too many Yankees with too much firepower, and the Southern troopers slowly gave ground. Chapman's men pursued and drove the Virginians back more than a mile to the Faulkner farm, where the flow of battle slowed when the rest of Brig. Gen. Thomas Rosser's Brigade reached the scene. According to General Wilson, the fighting began immediately because "both sides were anxious to gain the first advantage, it [the fight] soon became furious." Both sides fought dismounted, and as one Rebel noted, "for some time the battle was of an infantry character." The Virginians, "after a very sharp fight and several handsome charges" were driven back a couple of miles. The enemy troopers, reported Chapman, "contest[ed] hard every inch of ground."[32]

The Union tactical success gave Wilson pause. From his new headquarters at the Faulkner house, the cavalry leader ordered Chapman to halt and hold his position because he was too far in advance of McIntosh's brigade back near Robertson's Run. The colonel dismounted his 3rd Indiana Cavalry in a deep ravine bisecting the Catharpin Road and formed the men there in a line of battle. The rest of his brigade, meanwhile, stood in readiness in a field about half a mile farther east. Wilson had additional firepower in the form of two six-gun horse batteries under Lt. Charles Fitzhugh and Lt. A. C. Pennington marking time at his headquarters. During the lull, General Rosser reorganized his brigade for a counterattack.[33]

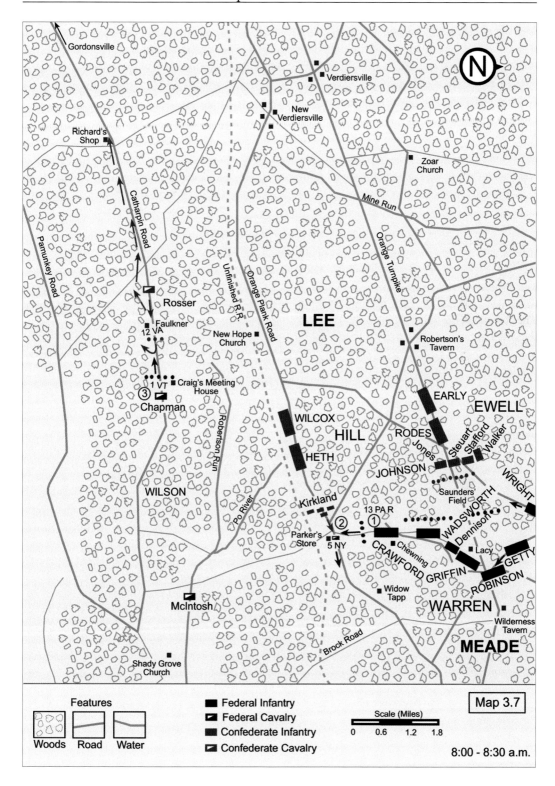

Features

Woods   Road   Water

■ Federal Infantry
◤ Federal Cavalry
▨ Confederate Infantry
◤ Confederate Cavalry

Scale (Miles)
0   0.6   1.2   1.8

Map 3.7

8:00 - 8:30 a.m.

Map 3.8: General Grant Arrives
(8:30 - 11:00 a.m.)

As noted earlier, about 7:30 a.m., Meade ordered Warren to attack Ewell. Warren knew he was expected to press ahead immediately, but he was not about to attack without his four divisions properly aligned, and the terrain made shifting troops from column into line of battle difficult. General Griffin's division formed on Warren's right opposite Saunders Field perpendicular to the Orange Turnpike with that road cutting through his front. General Wadsworth moved his three brigades into position below Saunders Field on Griffin's left, with his right flank on Mill Branch and his left facing Higgerson's Field. Finding a gap between the two divisions, Warren moved Col. Andrew W. Denison's reserve brigade (General Robinson's division) up to plug it. In a textbook example of how hard it was to maneuver in the Wilderness, Denison lost his way and never accomplished his mission. It was the larger gap farther south, however, that most worried Warren. His last division under General Crawford was in line fronting south by southwest below the Chewning farm toward the intersection around Parker's Store. Crawford, however, was about half a mile from Wadsworth's left flank, which meant the flanks of both divisions were exposed. Warren ordered Crawford to slide his men right and connect with Wadsworth.

Samuel Crawford, a doctor by training who had performed well at Gettysburg, questioned the wisdom of his order. The brigadier general controlled an ideal defensive position around the Chewning farm. He also noted, with growing concern, the intensity of Union carbine fire coming from the vicinity of Parker's Store. Because Warren was unaware of the terrain and situation, Crawford kept his men in place and sent a message, received at headquarters about 9:00 a.m., that he was holding his position.

Crawford deployed his small two-brigade Pennsylvania division into two lines. The first line formed, from left to right: 1st-10th-12th-6th Pennsylvania Reserves. The second support line formed, from left to right: 2nd-5th-7th-8th-11th Pennsylvania Reserves. On the skirmish line, the 13th Pennsylvania Reserves formed across most of the front while a couple companies of the 1st Pennsylvania Reserves stretched out on their left facing south. The skirmishers eased slowly toward the Orange Plank Road. Despite repeated orders from Warren, Crawford refused to budge.[34]

Warren's frustration increased with each passing minute. Crawford's recalcitrance was bad enough, but now General Griffin astride the turnpike was refusing to attack across Saunders Field. There was still a gap between his left and Wadsworth's division, and his right above the road petered off into nothing. Until most or all of the corps was in position and could support his attack, and troops from General Sedgwick's VI Corps arrived to protect his northern (right) flank, Griffin was not going anywhere. Wadsworth, whose division was also in position, remained in place.[35]

The situation changed with the arrival of General Grant. The general in chief of the Union armies was still adjusting to his new role and his uneasy relationship with Meade. He had openly pledged to allow Meade to fight his Army of the Potomac as he saw fit, and had spent the early morning hours near Germanna Ford waiting for Burnside's IX Corps to cross. Meade's messages urging aggressive action buoyed the offensive-minded Grant, but he grew antsy when the expected swell of battle failed to materialize. A courier from Meade arrived at 8:30 a.m. with news the advance had halted and Warren's V Corps would attack "at once." After waiting another 20 minutes for Burnside, Grant left written instructions for the IX Corps, hopped into his saddle, and rode to the front.[36]

When he spotted Brig. Gen. James Ricketts's division (VI Corps) parked by the Rapidan River, Grant broke his pledge and ordered it to the front. What he did not know was that Meade had ordered Ricketts to guard the Federal right flank. Within a short time Grant was on a small knoll near the Lacy house behind Warren's position conferring with Meade. He did not like what he heard: a large enemy force was in front of the V Corps, and intelligence suggested Rebels were moving around both flanks. The brief conference resulted in a flurry of orders rearranging the army (See Map 3.9). Grant took a seat near the Lacy house, lit a cigar, pulled out a pocket knife, and began to whittle. He was so distracted that bits of fabric from one glove fell to the ground at his feet, alongside the wood shavings.[37]

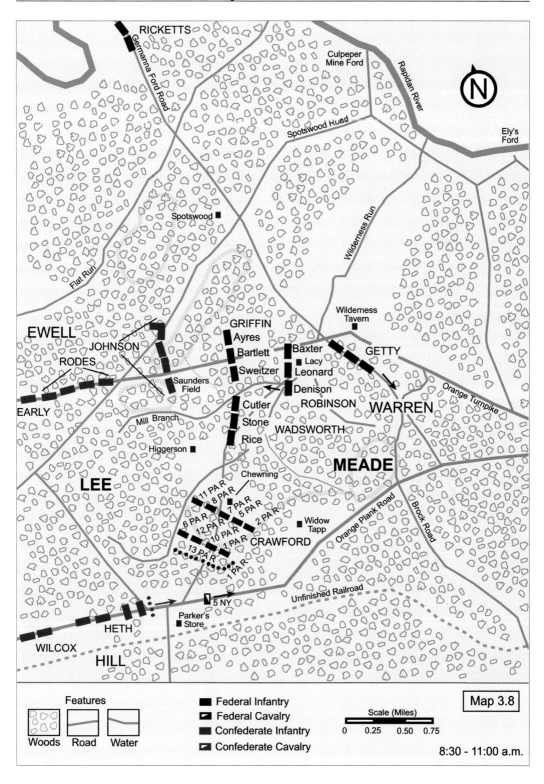

RICKETTS

Germanna Ford Road

Culpeper
Mine Ford

Rapidan River

Ely's
Ford

Spotswood Road

N

Spotswood ■

Flat Run

Wilderness Run

GRIFFIN
Ayres
Bartlett
Sweitzer

Baxter
■ Lacy
Leonard

Wilderness
Tavern ■

GETTY

EWELL
JOHNSON
RODES

Saunders
Field

Denison

Orange Turnpike

EARLY

Mill Branch

Cutler
Stone
Rice

ROBINSON

WARREN

WADSWORTH

Higgerson ■

MEADE

Chewning

LEE

11 PA R
8 PA R
7 PA R
6 PA R
12 PA R
10 PA R
5 PA R
2 PA R
1 PA R
13 PA R
1 PA R

Widow
Tapp ■

Orange Plank Road

Brock Road

CRAWFORD

5 NY

Unfinished Railroad

Parker's
■ Store

HETH

WILCOX

HILL

Features

| Woods | Road | Water |

■ Federal Infantry
◪ Federal Cavalry
■ Confederate Infantry
◪ Confederate Cavalry

Scale (Miles)

0   0.25   0.50   0.75

Map 3.8

8:30 - 11:00 a.m.

Map 3.9: Getty's Division Saves the Day (11:00 - 11:30 a.m.)

Grant rarely avoided a fight when he had a chance to engage the enemy—even if his flanks were threatened. He wanted Warren to shove his V Corps into the attack without delay and without excuses. To bolster Warren's right flank, he ordered Brig. Gen. Horatio Wright's division of the VI Corps, reinforced by Brig. Gen. Thomas Neill's brigade of Brig. Gen. George Getty's division, west and south down the Spotswood Road (No. 1).

With matters seemingly in hand on the right, Grant turned his attention farther south, where a strong enemy infantry column (A. P. Hill) was driving east down the Orange Plank Road threatening the vital intersection with the Brock Road. Hancock's II Corps was the obvious choice to reinforce the crossroads and block Hill, but the head of the II Corps was still four miles away, and the rest of it stretched six miles behind that. Even if it arrived before the enemy, it would take hours for enough men to arrive and deploy to provide a secure defensive line. Meade and Grant settled instead on Getty's division (VI Corps), which had reached Wilderness Tavern by 7:30 a.m. and spent the next three hours waiting for orders. When they arrived Getty put his men in motion for the two-mile trek south. "[H]e is a cool man, is Getty, quite a wonder," wrote Meade's aide Lt. Col. Theodore Lyman. Still, Getty would need help, and the II Corps was ordered to expedite its march to assist him.[38]

By 11:30 a.m., Hammond's 5th New York Cavalry had been pushed all the way back to the intersection of the Orange Plank and Brock roads. The troopers breathed a sigh of relief when they spied Getty's VI Corps division approaching (No. 2). Foot soldiers were rarely fans of cavalrymen, and this day would be no different. Despite the hard fighting thus far by the New Yorkers, the only comment one of Getty's officers could muster was the troopers were strung out "like a flock of wild geese."[39]

Knowing the seriousness of the situation, Getty trotted ahead of his foot soldiers to get a better grasp of what he was facing. "On approaching the cross-roads our cavalry was found hastily retiring. Hastening forward with my staff, I reached the cross-roads just as the enemy skirmishers appeared rapidly advancing to gain possession of this point," recalled Getty in his report. "The presence of my small retinue . . . standing firmly at the point in dispute, although under fire, served to delay their advance for a few minutes." Bullets zipped past endangering man and beast alike, but Getty stood firm. "We must hold this point at any risk," he announced to his staff. "Our men will be up soon."[40]

While their commanders squabbled near Saunders Field, the men of Warren's V Corps settled down to consume their midday meal. All knew a fight was in the offing and it was a whole lot easier to engage the enemy on a full stomach. "Had it not been for the bullets that tore through the branches of the trees at frequent intervals, sending showers of leaves or pine needles upon those below, one might have supposed we were awaiting the start of some pleasure excursion rather than the beginning of a furious battle," noted a New Yorker. Somewhat disconcerting were the sounds of falling trees and digging in the distance as the enemy continued constructing breastworks.[41]

While the Union army struggled to get into position to attack the gathering Confederates, additional enemy units slid into position on the opposite side of Saunders Field (No. 3). Ed Johnson's Division occupied the front line, supported by Robert Rodes' Division, which deployed with Brig. Gen. Cullen Battle's Brigade of Alabamians dug in astride the Orange Turnpike, with Brig. Gen. George Doles' Georgians and Brig. Gen. Junius Daniel's North Carolinians continuing the line south below Mill Branch. Jubal Early's Division was behind Rodes, ready to provide support. By noon, some 10,000 Southerners were in line on or near the edge of Saunders Field, and another 4,500 of Early's command prepared to advance, as needed.

Some two miles to the southeast on the Orange Plank Road, meanwhile, Maj. Gen. Harry Heth's 6,500-man division of A. P. Hill's Third Corps continued advancing east toward the Brock Road intersection. About noon, Brig. Gen. John Cooke's Brigade replaced General Kirkland's exhausted men and pressed ahead. The other division Hill had on hand under Maj. Gen. Cadmus Wilcox was on the road about a mile west near Parker's Store.[42]

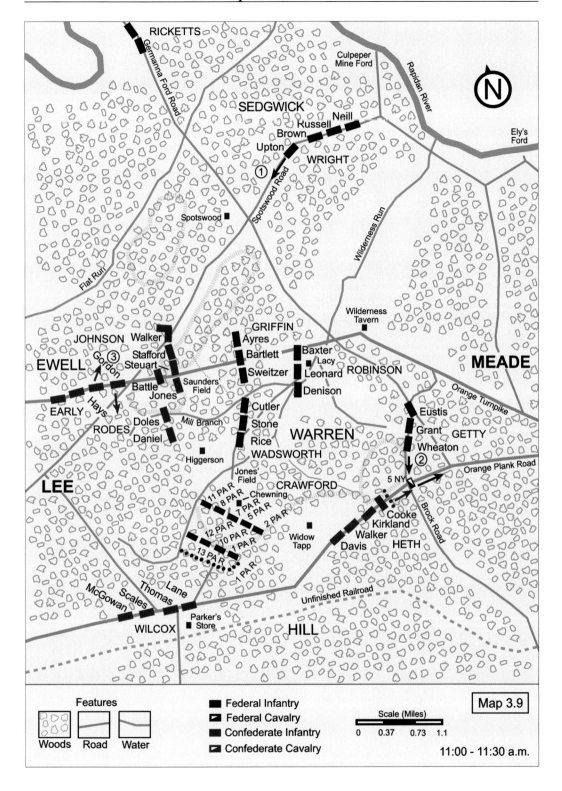

RICKETTS

Germanna Ford Road

Culpeper
Mine Ford

Rapidan River

SEDGWICK

Neill

Russell

Brown

Upton

WRIGHT

Spotswood Road

①

Ely's
Ford

Spotswood

Wilderness Run

Flat Run

JOHNSON   Walker

Wilderness
Tavern

GRIFFIN

Ayres

EWELL

Stafford
Steuart

Gordon

③

Bartlett

Baxter
Lacy

ROBINSON

MEADE

Battle
Jones

Hays

Saunders'
Field

Sweitzer

Leonard

Denison

Orange Turnpike

EARLY

Doles

Mill Branch

Cutler

Eustis

RODES

Daniel

Stone

Grant

GETTY

Higgerson

Rice

WADSWORTH

WARREN

Wheaton

②

Jones'
Field

5 NY

Orange Plank Road

LEE

CRAWFORD

Chewning

11 PA R

8 PA R

7 PA R

5 PA R

2 PA R

Cooke
Kirkland
Walker

Davis

HETH

Brock Road

12 PA R

10 PA R

1 PA R

Widow
Tapp

13 PA R

1 PA R

McGowan   Scales

Thomas   Lane

Unfinished Railroad

WILCOX

Parker's
Store

HILL

Features				Federal Infantry		Scale (Miles)				Map 3.9

Features
Woods   Road   Water

Federal Infantry
Federal Cavalry
Confederate Infantry
Confederate Cavalry

Scale (Miles)
0   0.37   0.73   1.1

Map 3.9

11:00 - 11:30 a.m.

Map Set 4: The Fight for Saunders Field (May 5)

Map 4.1: Grant, Meade, and Warren Lose Their Patience (11:30 - noon)

While Brig. Gen. George Getty and members of his staff sat on their horses and braved Rebel bullets, one of his aides rode back to hasten the infantry to the vital Orange Plank and Brock Road intersection. When the leading brigade under Brig. Gen. Frank Wheaton arrived, several men were struck by enemy fire. Getty yelled "Halt! Front! Fire!", and a ragged volley knocked Rebel skirmishers off their feet. Wheaton's regiments straddled the Orange Plank Road while Brig. Gen. Henry Eustis moved his brigade into position on Wheaton's right and Col. Lewis Grant did the same on the left (No. 1). Some of the Union men may have learned or were experienced enough to realize their task was to hold the crossroads, but none knew the II Corps was rapidly moving to assist them. Union skirmishers fanned out and encountered dead and wounded Confederates within 30 yards of the intersection. "Sure enough, Robert E. hasn't many men," declared one defiant prisoner, "but what he's got are the right good ones, and I reckon you'll find it out before you leave here."[1]

Farther north on the Orange Turnpike, Warren's efforts to coordinate an attack failed. Orders were orders, but all three division leaders exhibited uncharacteristic lethargy and a strain of recalcitrance. On the right, General Griffin's brigadiers argued against an advance because the right flank was unprotected. In the center, General Wadsworth's flanks were supported, and farther south on Warren's left, General Crawford still stubbornly refused to slide north and establish a link with Wadsworth. Crawford wasn't the only one who disagreed with Warren about vacating the Chewning heights. Warren's aide, Maj. Washington Roebling, told him "It is of vital importance to hold the field where Crawford is. Our whole line of battle is turned if the enemy get possession of it."[2]

This resistance, coupled with increasingly strident orders to advance from Generals Meade and Grant, weighed heavily upon the meticulous and cautious Warren. His officers did not want to attack, and neither did Warren, who thought an assault across an open field into thickets against an enemy of unknown strength was unwise.[3]

His inordinate delay resulted in a summons to headquarters, where "unpleasant things [were] said to him by General Meade, and that General Meade had just heard the bravery of his army questioned [by Grant]." Chastised, Warren was riding back when he encountered Lt. Col. William Swan, an aide to Brig. Gen. Romeyn Ayres. Swan had the unenviable task of reiterating Griffin's position that the attack was ill-advised. The frustrated corps leader let fly a stream of insults against Griffin, his officers, and his men. "I remember that he answered me as if fear were at the bottom of my errand," wrote the angry staff officer, who added, "I remember my indignation" (No. 2).[4]

Meade's tongue-lashing, added to Warren's interactions with Griffin and Wadsworth, put the final pieces for an attack in motion, but Crawford would not budge (No. 3). He held good ground, but news his pickets had spotted Rebels (Cooke's Brigade, Heth's Division) on the Plank Road on his left put the doctor-turned- general in a state of some anxiety. After the series of exchanges failed to convince Warren, however, he had little choice but to ultimately obey his commander. Crawford adopted a midway measure by ordering Col. William McCandless's brigade to slide left toward Wadsworth while Col. Joseph Fisher's brigade maintained its position on the heights.

On the Rebel side of the line, Henry Heth deployed his remaining three brigades into line of battle well east of the Orange Plank and Brock Road intersection (No. 4). To the shock and dismay of Lt. Col. William Poague, Heth ordered up a battery of guns from his artillery battalion. When the baffled gunner explained to Heth that only one gun could be safely deployed along the road, Heth insisted on keeping all four there in column "right up at the front until I prevailed on him to let me send three of them back." Heth acquiesced and Poague shifted the exposed tubes (and the rest of his battalion) to the Widow Tapp farm. "This is but one of the many examples of infantry officers' manner of handling artillery," griped Poague. Two miles north along the Orange Turnpike, Ewell had better fields of fire and deployed 13 guns "on a commanding ridge" overlooking Saunders Field. The balance of his artillery was kept back near Robertson's Tavern.[5]

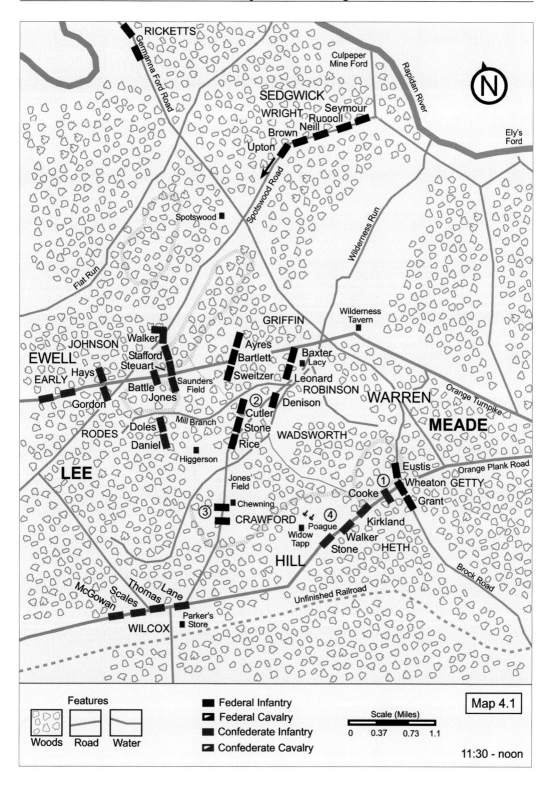

RICKETTS

Germanna Ford Road

Culpeper
Mine Ford

Rapidan River

SEDGWICK

Seymour

WRIGHT   Russell
Neill
Brown
Upton

Ely's
Ford

Spotswood Road

Spotswood

Wilderness Run

Flat Run

GRIFFIN

Wilderness
Tavern

JOHNSON   Walker

Ayres

EWELL   Stafford
Steuart

Bartlett

Baxter
Lacy

Hays

Sweitzer

Leonard

EARLY

Battle   Saunders'
Field

ROBINSON

WARREN

Orange Turnpike

Gordon   Jones

② Denison

MEADE

Cutler

RODES   Doles   Mill Branch

Stone

WADSWORTH

Daniel

Rice

Higgerson

LEE

Jones'
Field

Eustis

Orange Plank Road

① Wheaton GETTY

Cooke

Chewning

③   CRAWFORD   Poague
Widow
Tapp

④

Grant

Kirkland

Walker   HETH
Stone

HILL

Brock Road

McGowan   Scales   Thomas   Lane

Unfinished Railroad

WILCOX   Parker's
Store

Features			Federal Infantry		Map 4.1

Features

Woods   Road   Water

◼ Federal Infantry
◪ Federal Cavalry
◼ Confederate Infantry
◪ Confederate Cavalry

Scale (Miles)

0   0.37   0.73   1.1

Map 4.1

11:30 - noon

N

Map 4.2: Warren Maneuvers Into Position (noon - 1:00)

Out of excuses, General Griffin finally pried his men from behind their hastily constructed earthworks. It was only a half mile to their jump-off point along the edge of Saunders Field, but the thickets created immediate havoc. The woods were so thick, observed a New Yorker, that "not even a hare can get through." In an effort to keep formations together, some of the regiments moved in column, but even this was not entirely successful. Navigating through briers, stumbling through underbrush, dodging vines, and splashing through swamps made it nearly impossible to pay attention to fellow soldiers or follow orders. According to one staff officer, the "density of the woods prevented orders from being given by brigades, [and] staff officers had difficulty in carrying the orders to regimental commanders, and I feel certain that some of the regiments went forward merely because they saw others leave the woods."[6]

Colonel Andrew Denison's earlier experience was proof that the Wilderness could swallow entire brigades. A few hours earlier, Denison had been ordered to advance his brigade to fill the gap between Wadsworth's right and Griffin's left. It moved out, but never arrived. In an effort to reach Saunders Field for the planned attack, Col. Jacob Sweitzer's brigade began on the left of Brig. Gen. Joseph Bartlett's brigade but ended up directly behind it. Farther right, General Ayres' brigade stumbled through undergrowth and was more than tardy in assuming its position north of the turnpike. The result was a winded and frustrated horde of Union foot soldiers gathered along the edge of Saunders Field. It was not a pretty sight. "All semblance of line of battle was gone," confessed one of Warren's aides, "and there were gaps everywhere between regiments and brigades."[7]

The men of Wadsworth's division experienced similar difficulties reaching their jump-off positions on the edge of Jones' and Higgerson's fields. Farther left, Crawford finally had some of his men in motion to connect with Wadsworth and the rest of the V Corps. Warren's final communication of 11:50 a.m.— "You must connect with General Wadsworth and cover and protect his left as he advances"—finally sparked Crawford into action and by about noon McCandless's brigade was inching northward. Crawford could not resist telling Warren that he was complying with his orders, but added "the enemy hold the Plank Road and are passing up." Potential threat to his left or not, Warren was intent on driving the enemy in his front and getting Meade off his back.[8]

By 1:00 p.m., two Federal divisions—Griffin's and Wadsworth's—were finally ready to attack, with Robinson's division ready in support. Warren's attack front stretched for about two miles, with each flank unsupported. According to historian Gordon Rhea, "Meade, in his hurry to bring on a fight, had thrown his numerical advantage to the winds and forced Warren to attack on terms that offered little chance of success."[9]

Bartlett's brigade straddled the Orange Turnpike in two lines: the 18th Massachusetts, 83rd Pennsylvania, and 44th New York in the first line, and the 118th Pennsylvania and 20th Maine in a supporting second line. The alignment of Sweitzer's brigade remains unclear. It probably began in two lines, with the 9th Massachusetts, 4th Michigan, and 62nd Pennsylvania in the first and the 22nd and 32nd Massachusetts in the second. A short time later, however, the second line was pulled to the right of the road. General Ayres also deployed his brigade in two lines, with the 140th New York, 2nd U.S., 11th U.S., 12th U.S., 14th U.S., and 17th U.S. manning the first, and the 146th New York, 91st Pennsylvania, and 155th Pennsylvania forming the second.[10]

Across the field to the west a pair of veteran divisions comprising Edward Johnson's and Robert Rodes' divisions waited for the assault, with Jubal Early's command in support. The men in front had spent the last four hours digging and erecting a line of breastworks that General Ewell would later characterize as "slight," but the men would have ample time during the remainder of the battle to improve upon them. The Rebels, observed a member of the 140th New York, "were posted on the crest of the hill opposite us, just in the edge of the woods that skirted the hollow."[11]

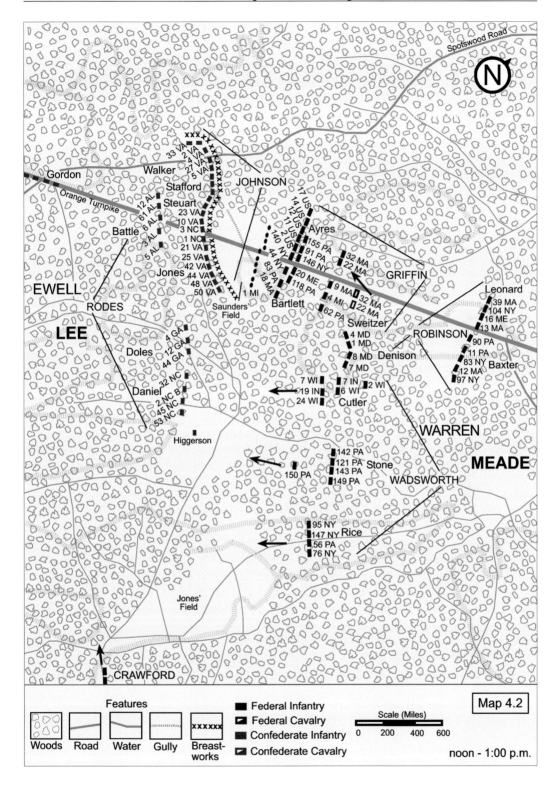

Spotswood Road

N

xxxx
33 VA
2 VA
4 VA
27 VA
5 VA

Gordon   Walker
Stafford   JOHNSON
12 AL   Steuart
61 AL   23 VA
6 AL   10 VA
Battle   3 AL   3 NC
5 AL   1 NC
21 VA
25 VA
42 VA
Jones   44 VA
48 VA
50 VA   1 MI

EWELL
RODES   Saunders'   Bartlett
Field
LEE

Orange Turnpike

17 US
14 US
12 US
11 US
2 US   Ayres
140   155 PA
PA   91 PA
44   146 NY   32 MA
NY   22 MA
83   20 ME   GRIFFIN
PA   118 PA   9 MA
18   4 MI   32 MA
MA   62 PA   22 MA

Leonard
39 MA
104 NY
16 ME
13 MA
Sweitzer
4 MD   90 PA
Doles   4 GA   1 MD   ROBINSON   11 PA
12 GA   8 MD   Denison   83 NY   Baxter
44 GA   7 MD   12 MA
32 NC   97 NY
Daniel   2 NC B   7 WI   7 IN   2 WI
45 NC   19 IN   6 WI
53 NC   24 WI   Cutler

Higgerson

WARREN

142 PA
121 PA   Stone
150 PA   143 PA
149 PA   WADSWORTH

MEADE

95 NY
147 NY   Rice
56 PA
76 NY

Jones'
Field

CRAWFORD

Features

Woods   Road   Water   Gully   xxxxxx
Breast-
works

■ Federal Infantry
◪ Federal Cavalry
▦ Confederate Infantry
◪ Confederate Cavalry

Scale (Miles)
0   200   400   600

Map 4.2

noon - 1:00 p.m.

Map 4.3: Griffin's Attack
Begins (1:00 - 1:15 p.m.)

And so Warren's two divisions waited for the order to advance. The composition of the assault was quite different than the two corps Meade had originally intended to use to strike Ewell's Confederates straddling the Orange Turnpike. Warren knew both flanks were hanging in air, inviting targets for the opportunistic Lee. Fortunately for the Federals, the same heavy terrain that made organizing and moving a simple line of battle such a difficult task also concealed its weaknesses from the Confederates.

Ewell's men, meanwhile, issued forth a heavy sheet of fire against the Federals gathered along the skirt of Saunders Field. According to one on the receiving end, the bullets reminded him of "big drops of a coming shower you have so often seen along a dusty road." A volley ripped into the 140th New York (Ayres' brigade) as it approached the clearing. "Its effect was serious," admitted one of the officers. To avoid senseless losses, orders sent the men to the ground, where they waited, watched, and worried. A member of the 118th Pennsylvania, also known as the Corn Exchange Regiment, part of Barlett's brigade, recalled the "wild, wicked roar of musketry, reverberating through the forests with a deep and hollow sound." Unable to see more than a few yards in any direction the men resorted to yelling back and forth, as if to reassure one another that everyone was still in place and they would not be alone in their trek across the open field. According to Porter Farley of the 140th New York, "the suspense and dread and hope which possess men during such minutes cannot be adequately told in words."[12]

When the order came to advance, Bartlett's skirmish line, composed of the 1st Michigan, sprinted toward its Confederate counterpart made up of the 25th Virginia (Jones' Brigade). The Michiganders overwhelmed the Virginians, killing, wounding, and capturing a sizable portion of the regiment. Bartlett's first battle line (the 18th Massachusetts, 83rd Pennsylvania, and 44th New York) quickly closed the distance with the victorious Wolverines. Once out of the woods, reported one of the New Yorkers, "they were

splendidly in line, moved rapidly, their colors all unfurled, and formed as they advanced one of the finest battle pictures I can remember." Directly ahead of them waited Brig. Gen. John M. Jones' Virginia brigade in its hastily constructed breastworks. Jones' alignment remains unclear.[13]

Once Bartlett's first line was well into the field, "bugles sounded the charge" for the second line, composed of the 20th Maine and 118th Pennsylvania. One of the men in the former regiment recalled looking across Saunders Field and seeing "the first line of battle about half way across it, receiving a terribly fatal fire from an enemy in the woods on the farther side."[14]

Across the Turnpike to the north on Bartlett's right, Romeyn Ayres' brigade also broke from its cover and headed across the field. The commander of the 140th New York, Col. George Ryan, expected a tough fight that would require every man he could muster. Prior to the charge, he called up his non-combatants and ordered them into the fight, telling them to pick up a rifle when one became available. Despite the desperate nature of their mission, "when the order to charge was given, every man in line moved forward with a rush; not a single man hesitated." The first line, composed of the 140th New York on the left and the U.S. Regulars battalions on the right, almost immediately absorbed a heavy fire that killed many and sent "wounded men plunging to the ground." This murderous small arms fire, coupled with the dry stream bed, broke the first line into two parts: the New Yorkers drifted south until their left flank guided upon the road, and the Regulars drifted right. The result was a gap that left all four flanks of the advancing line vulnerable.[15]

Confidently awaiting the approaching Unionists from behind their hastily built breastworks on Jones' left were the veterans of Brig. Gen. George "Maryland" Steuart's Brigade. The 1st North Carolina was on the right (south side) of the road next to Jones' Virginians, with the 3rd North Carolina extending the line left (northward) across the road. Steuart's three Virginia regiments (2nd, 4th, and 33rd) extended the line north. These veteran infantrymen were anything but the dismounted cavalrymen Ayres' men had been told they faced.[16]

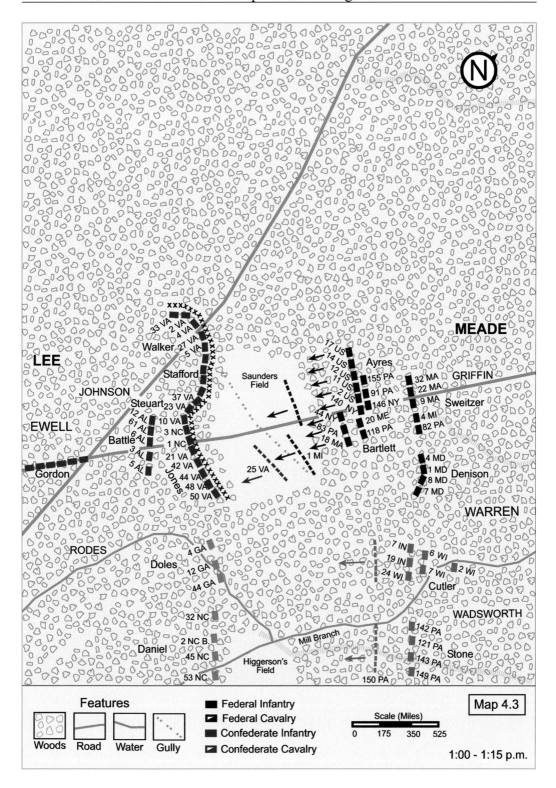

Features

Woods | Road | Water | Gully

■ Federal Infantry
◪ Federal Cavalry
■ Confederate Infantry
◪ Confederate Cavalry

Scale (Miles)

0   175   350   525

Map 4.3

1:00 - 1:15 p.m.

Map 4.4: The Two Sides Engage
(1:15 - 1:30 p.m.)

South of the Orange Turnpike, General Griffin's division suffered horrifying losses rushing across Saunders Field. Once its troops in the front ranks were well out into the open, it did not take them long to realize that retreating was just as dangerous as advancing, and that perhaps their salvation rested in the tree line on the opposite side of the field. Unfortunately, the trees teemed with enemy infantry. "The bullets fly like hail," recalled an officer in the 140th New York. "Men fall by the dozen; and thus we reach the other border of the woods where the rebels lie entrenched not more than thirty feet away."[17]

Just north of the turnpike, Rebel division commander General Johnson watched the Federal advance and reminded Capt. McHenry Howard, one of General Steuart's aides, "It was not meant to have a general engagement." The staffer responded, "But, general, it is evident that the two lines will come together in a few moments, and whether it is intended to have a general engagement or not, will it not be better for our men to have the impetus of a forward movement in the collision?" Johnson agreed. "Very well, let them go ahead a little." Without communicating the order to Steuart, the captain raised his sword and ordered the men forward. The Confederate advance a short distance into Saunders Field afforded them a better field of fire than did their earthworks, most of which were on the reverse slope of the wooded ridge.[18]

Griffin, an artillerist by training, added firepower to his attack by calling up a section of Lt. William Shelton's Battery D, 1st New York Light Artillery. Shelton called the order "wholly unpracticable," for long-range rifle fire started dropping his men almost as soon as they wheeled into position along the turnpike (No. 1). The distant trees were full of Rebels who had scaled them to better acquire targets of opportunity.[19]

North of the pike, once he realized his first line (140th New York and the Regular battalions) was separating and flagging, General Ayres ordered his second line into the assault (No. 2). The 146th New York and 91st and 155th Pennsylvania regiments in a tight line stepped out of the trees and marched smartly toward their comrades. Within seconds they met dead and wounded men from the first battle line, and their numbers increased with each passing yard. The Zouave-clad New Yorkers drove on to the "rattle of the musketry [that] was interspersed [by] the booming of the cannon stationed on the road." One man wrote the Federal guns were so close "we could feel the strong wind of the discharges."[20]

As his second line picked its way over the dead and wounded, Ayres' first line approached the woods on the far side of Saunders Field. The 140th New York on the left could see the Rebels fall back into the woods. Emboldened by this withdrawal, the New Yorkers rushed forward into the trees (No. 3). The U.S. Regular battalions to their right, however, were hit by hundreds of Virginian rounds in the front and Louisiana musketballs from Leroy Stafford's men on the right flank. It was at this point that the decision to go in with General Warren's right flank unsupported looked worse than rash. General Sedgwick's VI Corps had not yet arrived, and there was no one to the north to protect the attackers. Unbeknownst to the Union high command, General Ewell had extended his front well to the north, snaking it along a spine of ground to cover the northern reaches of the field and deep into the woods beyond. One of Stafford's Louisiana men recalled that the brigade occupied a ridge that provided a perfect platform to take on the enemy and "The way we poured lead into them was a sin." Unable to take the pounding, the Regulars broke for the rear (No. 4).[21]

South of the turnpike, Griffin's left-front brigade under General Bartlett rushed toward General Jones' Rebel line with Brig. Gen. Lysander Cutler's Iron Brigade of General Wadsworth's division attempting to keep pace on its left (No. 5). Although they suffered heavily, Bartlett's first line reached the trees, halted, fired a volley, and charged with bayonets fixed. While Bartlett was pinning and pressing Jones' Virginians from the front, some of Cutler's men (7th Indiana) found their exposed right flank and rear. Hit on two sides, the 50th Virginia on the right of the Rebel line fought, wavered, and finally stampeded to the rear. Their rout exposed the 48th Virginia's right flank, and the process repeated itself. A supporting brigade under Brig. Gen. Cullen Battle was stationed behind Jones, but the heavy vegetation blocked their view of what was taking place, so the men stayed put as the front began to crumble.[22]

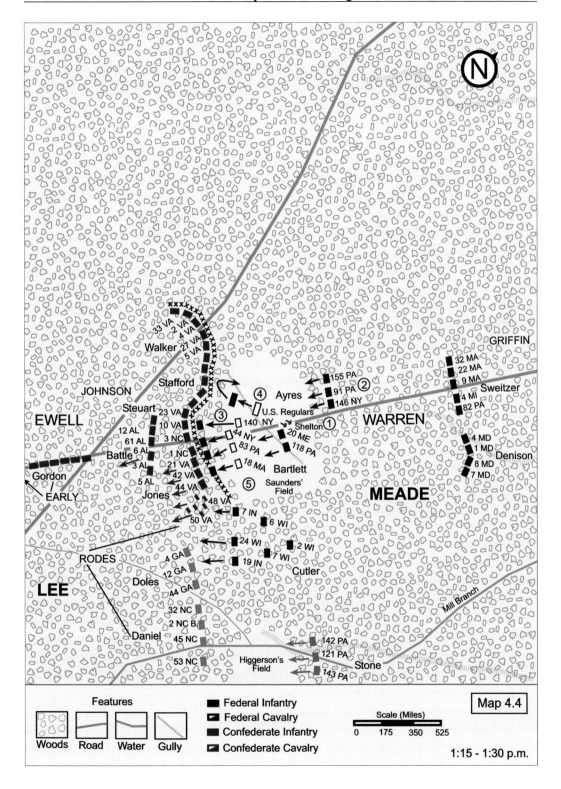

N

GRIFFIN

xxx
33 VA
2 VA
4 VA
Walker 27 VA
5 VA

32 MA
22 MA
9 MA
Sweitzer
4 MI
82 PA

155 PA
91 PA ②
146 NY

JOHNSON   Stafford

Ayres ④

Steuart 23 VA
10 VA
EWELL   3 NC

U.S. Regulars ③
140 NY

WARREN

12 AL
61 AL
6 AL
Battle 3 AL
1 NC
21 VA
42 VA
5 AL
44 VA
Gordon /
EARLY   Jones
48 VA
50 VA

44 NY
83 PA
18 MA Bartlett

Saunders'
Field ⑤

Shelton ①
20 ME
118 PA

4 MD
1 MD
8 MD
7 MD
Denison

MEADE

7 IN
6 WI

24 WI
19 IN
7 WI
2 WI

RODES
Doles
4 GA
12 GA
44 GA

Cutler

LEE

32 NC
2 NC B.
Daniel 45 NC

53 NC   Higgerson's
Field

142 PA
121 PA

143 PA

Mill Branch

Stone

Features

Woods Road Water Gully

■ Federal Infantry
◪ Federal Cavalry
■ Confederate Infantry
◪ Confederate Cavalry

Scale (Miles)

0   175   350   525

Map 4.4

1:15 - 1:30 p.m.

Map 4.5: The Tale of Two Union Brigades (1:15 - 1:30 p.m.)

John M. Jones was meeting with Generals Ewell, Rodes, and Early when Bartlett's men moved against his brigade. "Suddenly a heavy skirmish fire open on the front, swiftly followed by volleys along the line," wrote an aide. Without a word, Jones spurred his horse to rejoin his men. Federal lead flew into the Rebel ranks, killing and wounding scores of men. One was General Jones, and another his aide, Capt. Robert Early (Jubal Early's nephew). Both tumbled dead from their horses.[23]

The fleeing Virginians scattered through the woods and brush into Cullen Battle's shocked Alabama troops behind them (No. 1). Thick vegetation had prevented Battle's men from seeing the fight. The first inkling of a problem was the swarm of "panic stricken" men running through their ranks. Already unnerved by the heavy firing and the gloomy thickets surrounding them, some of Battle's men joined in the retreat. General Battle had been cautioned by both Generals Rodes and Ewell to not "become involved, but to fall back slowly if pressed." This admonition had unforeseen consequences. In the hasty retreat, one of Jones' officers yelled to Col. Charles Forsyth of the 3rd Alabama, "Fall back to Mine Run!" When Forsyth asked, "Is that a general order?" the Virginian replied, "Yes, the army falls back to Mine Run." A similar exchange occurred with the leader of the 5th Alabama, with the result that both regiments headed for the rear. A large segment of the right side of Ewell's front was in a chaotic retreat that threatened to escalate into a wholesale rout.[24]

Like Battle's troops, Bartlett's also had a limited field of vision, but the nature of the fighting and lack of heavy resistance meant the enemy was on the run, and they followed into the woods for hundreds of yards. An advance under any circumstances will disorder an attacking line, but it was impossible to maintain cohesion in the Wilderness. Bartlett's men advanced in small groups without knowing the whereabouts of the rest of their comrades or of other regiments. One officer in the 83rd Pennsylvania recalled the push into the foliage this way: "we kept on yelling and firing into the woods at every jump; for now we had the Johnnies on the run . . . o'er briar, o'er brake, o'er logs and o'er bogs, through the underbrush and overhanging limbs, for about three quarters of a mile, yelling all the while like so many demons, until we came to a small opening and there we halted."[25]

North of the Orange Turnpike, a weakened 140th New York (Ayres' brigade) slugged it out with Steuart's Rebels in the fringe of woods along the western edge of the field (No. 2). Many New Yorkers lay dead or wounded behind them, and those still on the firing line were in some disorder because of casualties and the resulting confusion. "The regiment melted away like snow," recalled a member of the 140th. "Men disappeared as if the earth had swallowed them." Hand-to-hand combat broke out along this part of the line, but most of the time the combatants fired blindly into the vegetation or thrust their bayonets in the morass as they advanced, hoping to find flesh.[26]

Ayres' second line was well across the field when the two Pennsylvania regiments were struck front and flank much like the Regulars who had just fallen back through their ranks. And like the Regulars, the Keystone soldiers were unable to continue in the face of the lead storm and fell back to their stepping-off position (No. 3). The retreat left only the 146th New York, which had been behind the 140th New York on the left side of Ayres' second line (No. 4). "Just as we reached the gully," wrote the regiment's historian, "a withering volley of musketry was poured into our line, followed a moment later by another. Many threw their arms wildly into the air as they fell backward, the death-rattle in their throats. . . . Paying but slight heed to our stricken comrades, the rest kept on, with clenched teeth." Despite heavy losses, the New York regiment reached the western edge of the field. The officers maneuvered the regiment into the woods on the right of the 140th New York—the position that was to have been held by the Regulars. Losses continued to mount.[27]

Lieutenant William Shelton, meanwhile, advanced his section of Battery D, 1st New York Light Artillery to the swale and opened fire (No. 5). The gunners were anxious to strike the Rebels, most of whom they could not see, that they simply loaded and fired blindly in their general direction, forcing the men of the 140th New York to throw themselves to the ground to avoid flying friendly iron. Many were unable to do so.[28]

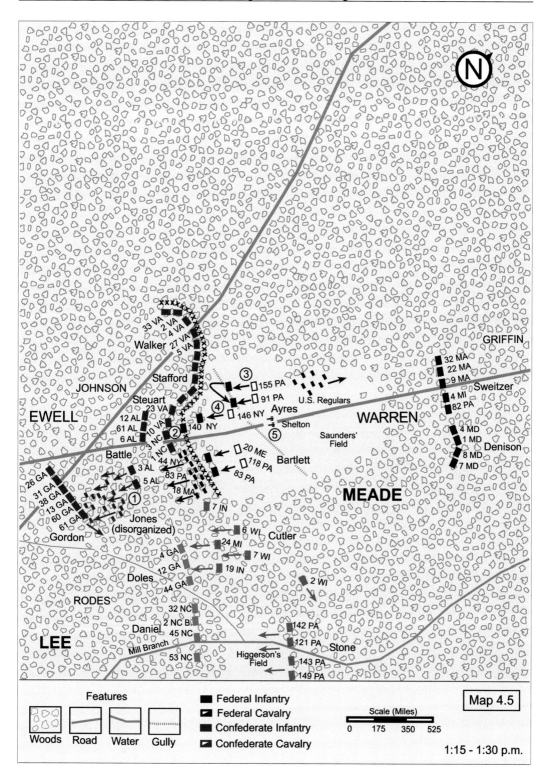

N

GRIFFIN

33 VA
2 VA
4 VA
Walker 27 VA
5 VA

JOHNSON   Stafford   ③   155 PA
                 Steuart   91 PA   U.S. Regulars
EWELL   23 VA   ④   146 NY   Ayres
            12 AL   140 NY   Shelton
            61 AL   10 VA   ⑤
            6 AL   3 NC ②
Battle   1 NC   20 ME   Bartlett
            44 NY   118 PA
      3 AL 83 PA   83 PA
26 GA 5 AL 18 MA
31 GA   ①   7 IN
38 GA
13 GA   6 WI   Cutler
60 GA   Jones   24 MI
61 GA (disorganized)
Gordon   7 WI
            4 GA   19 IN
      12 GA
Doles   44 GA   2 WI

RODES   32 NC
      2 NC B.
Daniel 45 NC   142 PA
LEE   121 PA   Stone
     Mill Branch   53 NC   Higgerson's
                             Field   143 PA
                                      149 PA

32 MA
22 MA
9 MA   Sweitzer
4 MI
82 PA

4 MD
1 MD
8 MD   Denison
7 MD

WARREN

MEADE

Features

Woods   Road   Water   Gully

■ Federal Infantry
▨ Federal Cavalry
■ Confederate Infantry
▨ Confederate Cavalry

Scale (Miles)
0   175   350   525

Map 4.5

1:15 - 1:30 p.m.

Map 4.6: Griffin Withdraws
(1:30 - 2:00 p.m.)

Although successful, Bartlett's brigade "by this time got into such a snarl that no man could find his own company or regiment," admitted a member of the 83rd Pennsylvania. "In fact," he added, "the whole brigade had to be unraveled before we could again form line and continue the pursuit." About this time, a heavy oblique fire from Battle's Alabamians slammed into the 20th Maine on the right of the second line and into other regiments manning the front ranks. A private in the 6th Alabama recalled, "we were soon within forty paces of the Yankees who we found standing erect and firing . . . but the woods were . . . very thick and they had not discovered our true position. . . . They appeared at once amazed, as soon as we commenced pouring into their ranks our well-directed storm of lead."

Initially, Bartlett's men thought the rounds were "friendly fire" because Ayres' troops advanced with them and were off to their right-front. When the firing continued, the men realized they were wrong; it was about to get much worse. Alone and confused in the heavy woods and far from support, the men of the 18th Massachusetts on Bartlett's left watched as the first line of Cutler's Iron Brigade "gave way and retired in confusion." A Massachusetts officer later wrote that "we then found ourselves isolated, the enemy upon both flanks and reported to be in [the] rear also." Bartlett had little choice but to order an "about face" and move back toward the western fringe of Saunders Field (No. 1). What began as an organized movement degenerated into flight. As one Pennsylvanian wrote, "every man saw the danger, and without waiting for orders . . . broke for the rear on the double quick." The Rebels responded by "yelling and sending minnies after us, killing and wounding many of our men."[29]

Not everyone heard the retreat order, and some who did could not comply. For example, when a 20th Maine company turned to retreat, an enemy line of battle was behind them. It was either surrender or cut through the Rebels in an effort to reach safety. The Maine men chose the latter, yelling, "Surrender!" The ruse worked and most of the Rebels melted into the foliage. The balance threw down their arms. The hearty men from Maine reached the other side of the bloody field with about 30 prisoners.

While the Unionists were taking a beating, General Rodes was reforming the right side of Battle's Brigade, which he led into place to plug the hole in his line (No. 2). Reinforcements from Early's Division (Brig. Gens. George Doles and John B. Gordon) were also put into line and marched east below the turnpike to bolster Steuart's right flank and cover Jones' collapse.

For Bartlett's men, reaching Saunders Field was only the beginning of their exhausting bloody withdrawal. Separated from his staff, Bartlett began the hazardous journey back across the open terrain. His usually impeccable uniform was torn and his face bloodied from sharp briers. When a line of Rebels appeared in his rear and ordered his surrender, Bartlett galloped toward the deep and wide stream bed that would surely trap him. Hundreds of Rebels lined the edge of the woods and fired, but Bartlett somehow jumped his mount across the gully. At least one bullet found his airborne horse, which somersaulted and fell dead atop him. The Union soldiers who witnessed the event thought their general was as dead as his mount. When several rushed to secure his body, they found their beloved leader dazed but very much alive, and hustled him off to safety—much to the chagrin of the pursuing Rebels.[30]

Back in the woods, meanwhile, many exhausted Union infantry simply surrendered rather than risk the return journey to their side of the field. As one Confederate put it, "behind every tree and stump were several who seemed to remain there in preference to running the gauntlet of our fire." When Bartlett's survivors reached the safety of the woods on the eastern side of Saunders Field, wrote a Pennsylvanian, "we laid down on our backs and panted like so many hounds which had just come back from a . . . chase after a gang of foxes."[31]

Ayres' 140th and 146th New York on the north side of the turnpike also relinquished the strip of woods they had captured and retreated (No. 3). Captain Howard, Steuart's redoubtable staff officer, watched as the Confederates emptied their rifled muskets into the backs of the fleeing New Yorkers and wrote, "It appeared to be the ground was more thickly strewn with their dead and wounded than I had ever seen."[32]

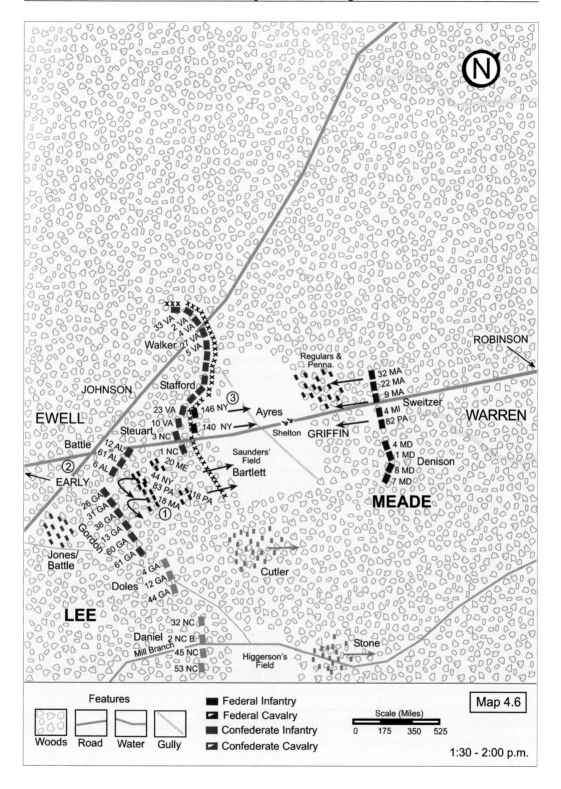

ROBINSON

N

xxx xxxx
33 VA 2 VA 4 VA
Walker 27 VA
5 VA

Regulars &
Penna.

32 MA
22 MA
9 MA
Sweitzer

JOHNSON   Stafford

EWELL

23 VA   146 NY   Ayres
10 VA
Steuart 3 NC   140 NY
Shelton   GRIFFIN

4 MI
82 PA

WARREN

Battle
12 AL
61 AL
6 AL

1 NC
20 ME
Saunders'
Field
Bartlett

Shelton

4 MD
1 MD
Denison
8 MD
7 MD

EARLY

44 NY
83 PA   118 PA
18 MA   ①

MEADE

26 GA
31 GA
38 GA
13 GA
60 GA
61 GA

Gordon

Jones/
Battle

Cutler

Doles

4 GA
12 GA
44 GA

LEE

32 NC

Daniel 2 NC B.
Mill Branch 45 NC
53 NC

Stone

Higgerson's
Field

Features				Federal Infantry	
Woods	Road	Water	Gully	Federal Cavalry	

Federal Infantry
Federal Cavalry
Confederate Infantry
Confederate Cavalry

Scale (Miles)
0   175   350   525

Map 4.6

1:30 - 2:00 p.m.

Map 4.7: The Fight for Shelton's Guns (2:00 - 2:30 p.m.)

The Union retreat did not end the fighting in Saunders Field. Seeing Shelton's pair of New York artillery pieces alone on the turnpike and unsupported, members of the 1st and 3rd North Carolina of Steuart's Brigade gathered in the woods directly to the west, and, together with knots of other men from other commands, surged forward on their own to capture the guns. The artillerists, however, were not about to relinquish their prized guns without a fight. Since most of their horses were dead or wounded, as were their officers, the gunners grabbed rammers, revolvers, and any other weapon that could be used to save their pieces. According to one North Carolinian, "the fighting was desperate, clubbed-guns and bayonets being used. . . . Twas claw for claw, and the devil for all of us." Another recalled the disorder: "there was such an intermingling of troops that confusion decidedly predominated; every man was going it on his own hook, for it was a hand-to-hand contest." An officer with Battle's Brigade who had rushed into the melee, Lt. Col. James Lightfoot of the 6th Alabama, climbed atop one of the guns and waved his regiment's flag claiming victory. This act of bravado angered the Tar Heels. For a short time it appeared as though a mini-Civil War would break out in a fight for who had the honor of capturing the guns.[33]

The Yankees had other ideas and had no intention of sitting by while the guns were lost. About 200 men from the 140th and 146th New York who had sought temporary shelter in the gully charged the Rebels gathered around the pieces. Fresh Union troops appeared on the eastern edge of the field, the result of General Warren's decision to pull the brigades of Brig. Gen. Henry Baxter and Col. Samuel Leonard (Brig. Gen. John Robinson's division) from around Wilderness Tavern and trot them to the embattled field. Major Abner Small of the 16th Maine of Leonard's brigade recalled the events:

> A scattering of men was running in, some of them crying disaster; and ahead of us there was an uproar of yelling and firing. We came to a clearing and filed off to the right of the turnpike and went into line along the edge of an old field. . . . The fight had swept across it and back again, and now the hollow was filled with wounded, and out where the pike went over it were two field pieces, abandoned, the dead horses lying near by. The rebels wanted those guns and tried to get them, but our brigade, and the reserve of the troops that were in action before we came up, were now in line, and sent so hot a fire from our side . . . that the rebels drew back to their side and stayed there. . . . The guns on the pike stood lonely in the sun.[34]

Before abandoning the guns, some of the Rebels adorned them with small flags. According to a soldier in the 9th Massachusetts (Sweitzer's brigade), this was done to "tantalize us on." If that was the plan it worked, for the Irish regiment charged into the field. The men were hit by devastating volleys that knocked men, weapons, and accouterments into the air. The regiment lost 12 officers and 138 soldiers in a few minutes. The survivors had barely reached their original line when brigade commander Col. Jacob Sweitzer, who had not witnessed the slaughter, ordered his men forward. "We have been in, and just come out!" shot back the 9th's commander. This did not sit well with Sweitzer, who retorted, "Well, take 'em in again!" Just before the regiment was to advance a second time, a divisional aide told Sweitzer, "General Griffin's orders are not to take the 9th in again." Sweitzer, who would not learn the full extent of the deadly charge across Saunders Field until the next day, apologized to the colonel. "If Colonel Sweitzer's irrational orders had not been countermanded," claimed the regiment's historian, "few, if any, of the Ninth would have come out of 'that hole' fit for duty."[35]

Saunders Field was now a bloody no man's land. Despite the heartrending pleas of the wounded for water and medical care, any attempt to provide succor would do nothing but generate more losses. Both sides reorganized their fronts and awaited further developments.

Union losses had been especially heavy, with the regiments on the front line suffering the most. For example, the 140th New York (Ayres' brigade) crossed the field with 529 men but only 261 returned (a loss of 51%), while the 20th Maine in the second line of Bartlett's brigade lost about 20% of its men.[36]

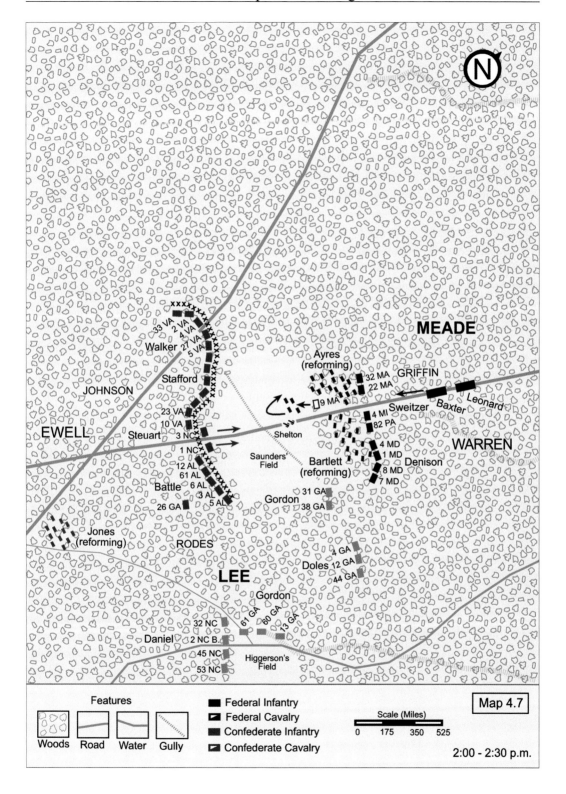

Map 4.7

2:00 – 2:30 p.m.

Map Set 5: Wadsworth's Division Enters the Fight (May 5)

Map 5.1: Wadsworth's Division Prepares for Action (1:00 - 1:15 p.m.)

Neither General Warren nor General Meade intended for General Griffin's division to attack Ewell's Confederates alone. On Griffin's left was another of Warren's V Corps divisions under Brig. Gen. James Wadsworth, three tough brigades who were supposed to attack with Griffin.

Holding Wadworth's right was Brig. Gen. Lysander Cutler's Iron Brigade, which except for a battalion of New Yorkers, was composed entirely of Western men from Indiana, Michigan, and Wisconsin. Cutler's men would go in and support the otherwise exposed left flank of General Bartlett's brigade of Griffin's division. The Iron Brigade adopted an unusual three-line deployment. The first was comprised of the 24th Michigan on the left, followed by the 19th Indiana and 7th Indiana. The 6th Wisconsin was about 100 yards behind the 7th Indiana with the 7th Wisconsin on its left. The 2nd Wisconsin was alone in a third line.[1]

Colonel Roy Stone's Pennsylvania regiments were aligned on the left of the Iron Brigade on the east side of Higgerson's Field. The brigade's deployment is unclear, but likely formed in two lines behind a skirmish line composed of the 150th Pennsylvania. The 149th and 143rd Pennsylvania were in the first line, followed by the 121st and 142nd Pennsylvania.[2]

The brigade General Cutler had commanded at Gettysburg was now under Brig. Gen. James Rice, who had earned accolades for his heroism on Little Round Top on July 2, 1863. Rice's units were deployed in one line, with the 76th New York on the left, and the 56th Pennsylvania, 147th New York, and 95th New York extending the line to the right.[3]

Just getting the men into position for the jump-off was difficult. The terrain was so thick and disruptive that a Pennsylvanian was convinced the jungle-like vegetation had not been disturbed for centuries. "The troops were compelled to cut alley-ways through the thickets with axes and hatchets, in order to proceed," he

added. Some of Wadsworth's men did not know they were about to make a desperate assault, being told instead their effort was merely a "reconnaissance."[4]

The Iron Brigade's advance was aimed just south of Saunders Field and, as luck would have it, into a yawning gap between two Confederate brigades that formed the hinge of two Southern divisions. The northernmost brigade was under Brig. Gen. John Jones (Johnson's division) facing east toward Saunders Field. Jones' right flank was in the air and about to be struck and turned by the Union Western men. The Confederate line picked up again well beyond Jones' right in the form of two brigades from Robert Rodes' Division. The first under Brig. Gen. George Doles was comprised of three Georgia regiments. The second was a four-regiment brigade of North Carolinians under Brig. Gen. Junius Daniel, whose line extended south to front Higgerson's Field.

When the order to advance arrived, Wadsworth's brigades set out more or less in unison, fighting the brambles and thickets every step of the way as they struggled toward the enemy lines. The thick vegetation immediately exerted its influence, separating regiments and disorienting the men and their officers. As a young soldier in the 143rd Pennsylvania recalled, "soon the 149th Pennsylvania, that was on our left when we advanced, was compelled to unlock from our left and instead of moving a little by the left flank, until they uncovered our left, then came in on our rear." The situation further deteriorated when "some of their men fired upon us, but lucky for us they fired low and their bullets tore the ground under our feet."[5]

The Iron Brigade was able to align its march with Bartlett's brigade on its right, but Stone's and Rice's brigades drifted left and quickly lost their connection to the Westerners. When they reached a boggy area around Mill Branch, their movement slowed to a crawl.[6]

Following normal practices, the officers originally formed their men into lines of battle, but the thickness of the vegetation forced them to modify their approach. When it became obvious that maintaining ordered lines was impossible, they resorted to "flank marches, bringing platoons and companies into line whenever possible," noted a historian. The result was hopelessly intermingled regiments and mass confusion.[7]

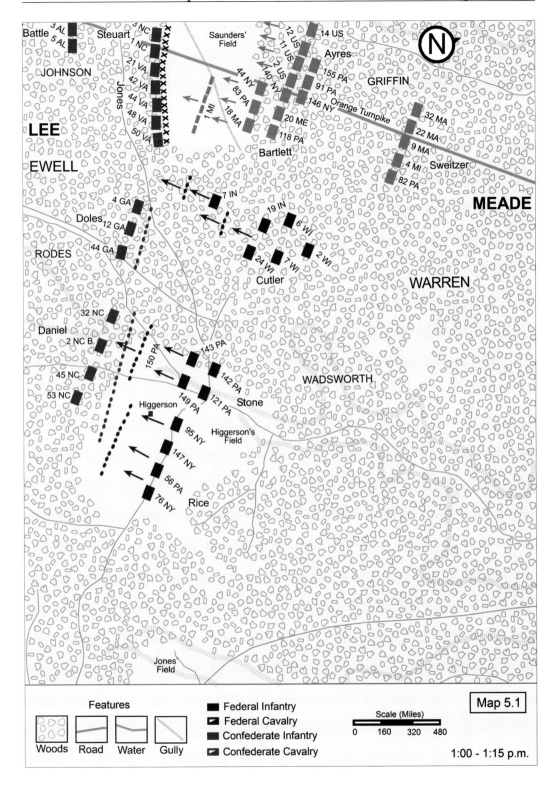

Battle 3 AL
5 AL
Steuart 3 NC
1 NC
Saunders'
Field
14 US
12 US
11 US
Ayres
JOHNSON
21 VA
42 VA
44 VA
48 VA
50 VA
Jones
44 NY
140 NY
83 PA
18 MA
1 MI
2 US
155 PA
91 PA
146 NY
Orange Turnpike
20 ME
118 PA
GRIFFIN
32 MA
22 MA
9 MA
LEE
EWELL
Bartlett
4 MI
82 PA
Sweitzer
MEADE
Doles 4 GA
12 GA
7 IN
19 IN
6 WI
RODES
44 GA
24 WI
7 WI
2 WI
Cutler
WARREN
32 NC
Daniel
2 NC B.
143 PA
150 PA
142 PA
121 PA
Stone
WADSWORTH
45 NC
53 NC
149 PA
Higgerson
95 NY
Higgerson's
Field
147 NY
56 PA
76 NY
Rice

Jones'
Field

Features

Woods   Road   Water   Gully

■ Federal Infantry
◢ Federal Cavalry
■ Confederate Infantry
◢ Confederate Cavalry

Scale (Miles)
0   160   320   480

Map 5.1

1:00 - 1:15 p.m.

Map 5.2: Wadsworth Engages Rodes' Division (1:15 - 1:30 p.m.)

The vaunted Iron Brigade was the first of Wadworth's commands to make contact with the Rebels. Together with the left regiments of General Bartlett's brigade (Griffin's division) in Saunders Field, the 7th Indiana and part of the 19th Indiana struck the 48th and 50th Virginia—the front and right of Jones' Brigade (No. 1). The Virginians, who were already contending with Bartlett's men in their front, panicked when they saw the Federal soldiers crashing through the vegetation against their unsupported flank. This part of the fighting involved only the first line of the Iron Brigade because the 6th Wisconsin in the second was working hard to catch up with the Hoosiers who had "disappeared into the woods," wrote the 6th's Lt. Col. Rufus Dawes.

There is some evidence that Abram Buckles, the flagbearer of the 19th Indiana in the middle of the Iron Brigade's first line, believed a charge was the best way to deal with whatever enemy was in front of his regiment. Unable to spot any officers, he unfurled his tattered flag, and waving it, took off toward the enemy with the serrated regimental line trying to keep up. Buckles almost immediately took a bullet, but rather than falling, he planted the flag in the ground and supported himself with it. Another soldier took the flag and advanced a few steps before a bullet tore through his skull. Two more men would eventually carry the banner during the assault against and pursuit of Jones' men. The Westerners captured over 300 prisoners and carried off the flag of the 50th Virginia. Whether their officers tried to stop them to reorganize is unknown, but what is certain is that the victors continued advancing southward into the thick foliage behind where Jones' men had first stood. The panic within the Rebel ranks was palpable and, in their haste for the rear and safety, barreled into the right side of Cullen Battle's Brigade, taking with it the 3rd and 5th Alabama (see Map 4.4).[8]

The left front of the Iron Brigade (24th Michigan and perhaps part of the 19th Indiana) probably struck the left front of George Doles' small Georgia brigade (No. 2). As the historian of the 24th Michigan recalled, "after a short but very sharp engagement, the Iron Brigade with its old-time yell, charged the enemy, completely destroying the first line of battle." The enemy line, however, may have been Doles' skirmish line and not his primary line of battle.[9]

As the combat intensified, Wadsworth rode up to the 2nd Wisconsin deep in the rear of the advancing Iron Brigade and ordered it to move left and form behind Stone's brigade (No. 3). Its controversial orders, confirmed by two of its veterans, were to "fire on some Penn. Regiments in its immediate front if they broke." The Badgers noted with no little relief that "no necessity arose for executing these instructions."[10]

There was "no necessity" because Stone's men could barely move in any direction. They and Rice's men had drifted left during the advance and most of Stone's men were caught up in a swampy waist-deep morass fed by Mill Run. They were mired in place when their horrible situation took an even worse turn. The historian of the 121st Pennsylvania (Stone's brigade) described what happened next: "the regiment had not progressed far through the swamp when, without seeing a single foe, a sheet of fire opened on the line—if line it could be called. . . . Here the men were almost entirely at the mercy of the foe, who, no doubt, had been lying in wait for them for some time." The fight between Stone's men and Daniel's Tar Heels was "of short duration," he added, "but quite lively while it lasted, and not at all satisfactory to our men, who could not do much execution while floundering about in the mud and water up to their middle." Neither side could see the other in the thick undergrowth, but the Tar Heels got the better end of that deadly bargain (No. 4).[11]

Rice's brigade was also having a tough time of it on the far left of Wadsworth's now-scattered and chaotic line. After thrashing through the dense vegetation, the brigade was "met by a heavy fire of musketry from an unseen enemy," wrote Col. J. William Hofmann of the 56th Pennsylvania. The Keystone men had met the right flank of the 53rd North Carolina of Daniel's Brigade (No. 5).[12]

Doles' Georgians, meanwhile, could tell from the nature of the fighting off to their left that Jones' Brigade was falling back. They knew Daniel's North Carolinians were on their right, but there were no supporting troops behind them. That meant their left flank was completely exposed. What they did not know was that Jubal Early's Division was nearby and available for support, if needed.[13]

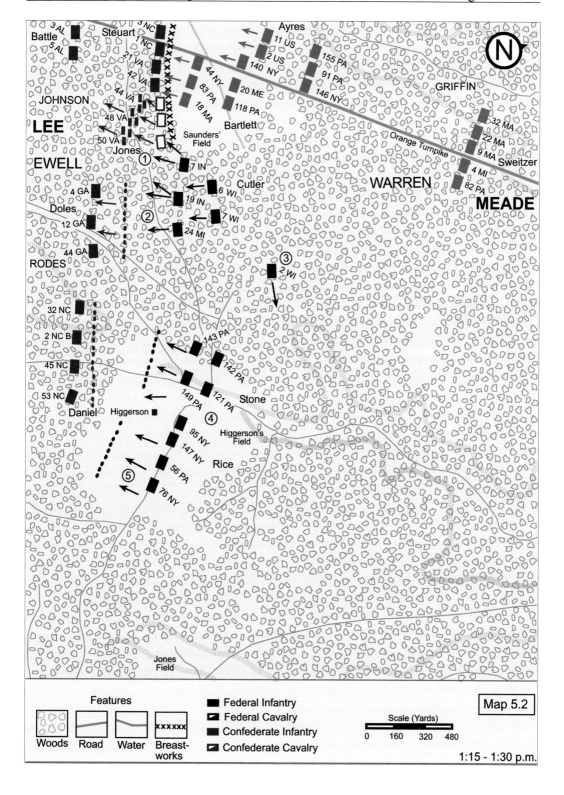

Features

Woods	Road	Water	Breast-works

xxxxxx

■ Federal Infantry
◨ Federal Cavalry
■ Confederate Infantry
◨ Confederate Cavalry

Scale (Yards)

0   160   320   480

Map 5.2

1:15 - 1:30 p.m.

Map 5.3: Wadsworth's Men Begin to Break (1:30 - 1:45 p.m.)

A member of the 4th Georgia on the left of Doles' line recalled that "a sudden attack by the enemy stampeded the [Jones'] command," and this had the effect of "leaving our flank unprotected and we were attacked from front, flank and rear." The attacking troops were probably from the 6th Wisconsin and 7th Indiana (No. 1). Doles' center and right, composed of the 12th and 44th Georgia, were also having their share of trouble (No. 2). According to the historian of the 24th Michigan fighting on the left of the Iron Brigade, the Western troops pushed ahead "without waiting to reform its own ranks," and was soon engaged "in another sharp fight with this second line."[14]

Doles' Georgia veterans, who had been in tough places on many fields, lowered their musket barrels and fired. The volley crashed into the oncoming Union soldiers. The losses could have been much heavier, but the Westerners were experienced enough to know what was coming and had thrown themselves to the ground. Once the volley ended, the men were up again and advancing. Small in number, and with the enemy advancing steadily, Doles' Brigade's historian noted with pride, "the regiment [4th Georgia] never showed to better advantage than in this emergency, for, notwithstanding [that] the loss in killed and wounded was appalling, when the order to change front was given the movement was effected without the least evidence of panic or nervousness." The change in position probably involved a swivel to the northwest to face the threat to its left flank. Meanwhile, as the 44th Georgia was on the verge of breaking, the 12th Georgia charged, halting the left side of Cutler's advance.[15]

While Doles and part of Cutler's brigade slugged it out, Stone's brigade on the left of the Iron Brigade was stymied by its hellish situation (No. 3). Stone's ranks were completely disordered by the dense vegetation, most of the men stuck deep in mud and unable to return an effective fire, and the air filled with whizzing lead balls that told them large numbers of Rebels were arrayed across their front. A soldier in the 121st Pennsylvania recalled that "neither combatant could see the other, and the only guide as to the locality of the opponent was the noise of the scrambling through the network of briers and floundering through the mud and water, as well as the irregular musketry fire on either side."[16]

Many of Stone's officers realized their situation was helpless. The historian of the 121st Pennsylvania recalled it was "evident before long that this locality was altogether too unhealthy; and when the order to retire was given, the scrambling to get out of that mud hole was amusing as well as ridiculous." Many of the units withdrew without orders. Some reported a "sheet of flame" hitting them as they moved through the morass, which triggered a stampede to the rear. Colonel Stone "rode behind [the 149th Pennsylvania] . . . cursing them as though that were a part of his education. Swinging his sword, he drove them back into the line again." Given what they faced in front and beneath their feet, the swinging sword of a swearing officer offered little incentive to stay in line, and the men "went to the rear, pell mell, like a flock of scared sheep."[17]

Rice's men on the extreme left of Wadsworth's line experienced their own challenges during their approach toward Daniel's battle line (No. 4). "We had not, up to this moment, seen an enemy," recalled a member of the 45th North Carolina. When a Union volley crashed through the brush and timber, he went on to note that "The aim [of Rice's men] was too high and hardly a man in the regiment was touched. Without waiting for a command, every gun was leveled, and into the line of smoke we poured a terrible volley, and with a shout, went at them." The two sides exchanged volleys. The officer commanding the left side of Rice's skirmish line rushed back with an erroneous report that Rebels were "advancing in a line extending far beyond our left. Almost simultaneously with this report the line on our right [Stone's brigade] fell back in considerable disorder and was followed by this brigade." Most of Rice's skirmish line was captured by the onrushing Tar Heels.[18]

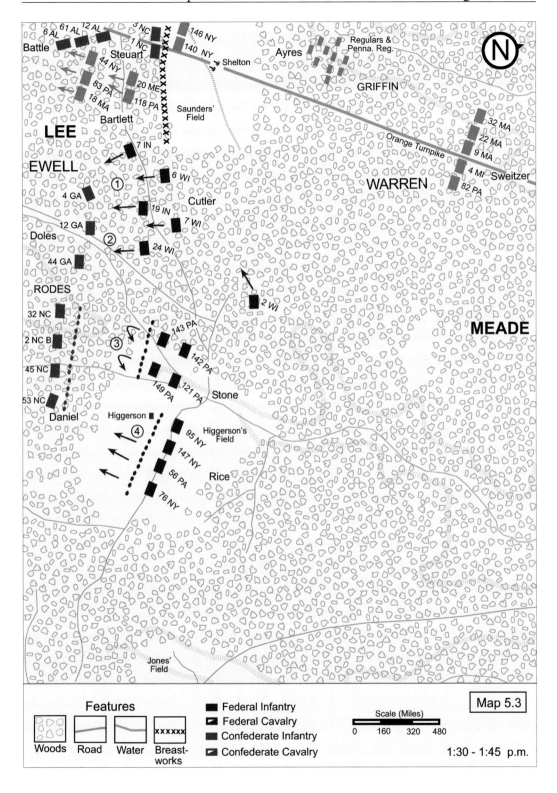

N

6 AL
61 AL
12 AL
3 NC
146 NY
140 NY
Battle
1 NC
Steuart
44 NY
Shelton
83 PA
20 ME
18 MA
118 PA
Bartlett
Saunders' Field
Regulars & Penna. Reg.
Ayres
GRIFFIN

LEE

EWELL
7 IN
6 WI
①
4 GA
Cutler
19 IN
7 WI
12 GA
②
24 WI
44 GA
Doles
RODES
2 WI
32 NC
143 PA
2 NC B
③
142 PA
45 NC
149 PA
121 PA
53 NC
Stone
Daniel
Higgerson
95 NY
④
Higgerson's Field
147 NY
56 PA
Rice
76 NY

Orange Turnpike

WARREN
32 MA
22 MA
9 MA
4 MI Sweitzer
82 PA

MEADE

Jones' Field

Features

Woods Road Water xxxxxx Breast-works

■ Federal Infantry
🏴 Federal Cavalry
■ Confederate Infantry
🏴 Confederate Cavalry

Scale (Miles)
0   160   320   480

Map 5.3

1:30 - 1:45 p.m.

Map 5.4: Gordon Smashes into the Iron Brigade (2:00 - 2:30 p.m.)

General Ewell was in trouble and he knew it. Two Federal divisions had attacked his line, Jones' Brigade had collapsed and taken part of Battle's Brigade with it, and Doles' Brigade was barely holding on. Grabbing a flag, Ewell plunged it into the Orange Turnpike and tried to rally the retreating infantry and send them back to the front. Before doing so, he turned to his aide, Maj. John Daniel, and yelled in an excited shrill voice, "Major, you will find Gordon a short distance up the pike. Ride to him as fast as you can and tell him to bring up his brigade as quick as possible." When Daniel found Gordon and conveyed the orders, the brigadier replied, "Do me a favor. Give the instructions yourself to each of my regimental commanders while I ride to the front and see the situation and prepare for the charge." As the Georgia foot soldiers "alternately trotted and quick-stepped forward," Gordon conferred with Early and Ewell and reunited with his arriving troops. Majestic in his immaculately tailored uniform and ramrod-straight posture, Gordon surveyed his troops as they formed into line of battle a short distance south of and roughly perpendicular to the Turnpike. Gordon, recalled Major Daniel, sat "erect, his countenance intense, and his sword drawn."

The Georgians could hear the noisy advance of the Iron Brigade in front and Bartlett's brigade off to their left by their shouts, screams, and increasing number of bullets coming their way. The Federals were probably no more than 200 yards away and quickly closing. Calmly riding to the center of his brigade, Gordon stood up in his stirrups and with a clear voice yelled, "Forward!" Screaming at the tops of their lungs the Georgians pushed through the foliage.[19]

The orientation of Gordon's attack has been debated since the battle. Some place his Georgians much farther south on the right of Daniel's Brigade going in against Rice's Union brigade. Other historians have Gordon going in between Doles and Daniel. Ewell and Early knew Jones' Virginians had collapsed and the resulting hole in the line destabilized Doles' left while his Georgians were attempting to hold against attacks on their front, left flank, and rear.

Almost certainly Gordon went in just below the turnpike on Doles' embattled left flank, with Battle's remaining Alabama regiments fighting somewhere on Gordon's left.[20]

Gordon's left, composed of the 26th and 31st Georgia, assisted Battle's men in driving portions of Bartlett's brigade to the rear (No. 1). "We swept forward through the thick undergrowth," recalled Pvt. Gordon Bradwell of the 31st Georgia, "slowly at first, until we struck the enemy, only a hundred yards or so away, when pandemonium broke loose. Their line crumbled immediately under our first volley as our men rushed over them, I could see them to the right, left, and in front throwing up their hands and surrendering by scores."[21]

The 6th Wisconsin's (Iron Brigade) Lt. Col. Rufus Dawes was probably one of the first to see Gordon's advance. When an officer screamed "Look to the right!" Dawes spotted "the enemy stretching as far as I could see through the woods, and rapidly advancing and firing upon us." Attacked on two sides, Dawes ordered his regiment to change direction to face the oncoming Rebels. The officer in charge of the left flank was wounded before the order could be given, so it remained in position, leaving only half of the regiment to face the new threat to its flank and rear (No. 2). "We here lost forty or fifty men in a very few moments," Dawes recalled after the war.[22]

The rest of the long line of Georgians (38th, 13th, 60th, and 61st regiments) hit the left flank, left front, and center of the crumbling Iron Brigade (No. 3). Despite its distinguished past, the Westerners could not stand under these conditions. The brigade, wrote a recent historian of the 19th Indiana, "was rolled up like a wet blanket and put to flight. The Hoosiers . . . were routed for the very first time in the war as they fell back before the screaming Rebels." The confusion, losses, and dense terrain made escape a real challenge. A member of the 7th Indiana succinctly described the Iron Brigade's fight on May 5: "Drove the enemy 1 ½ miles and were repulsed."[23]

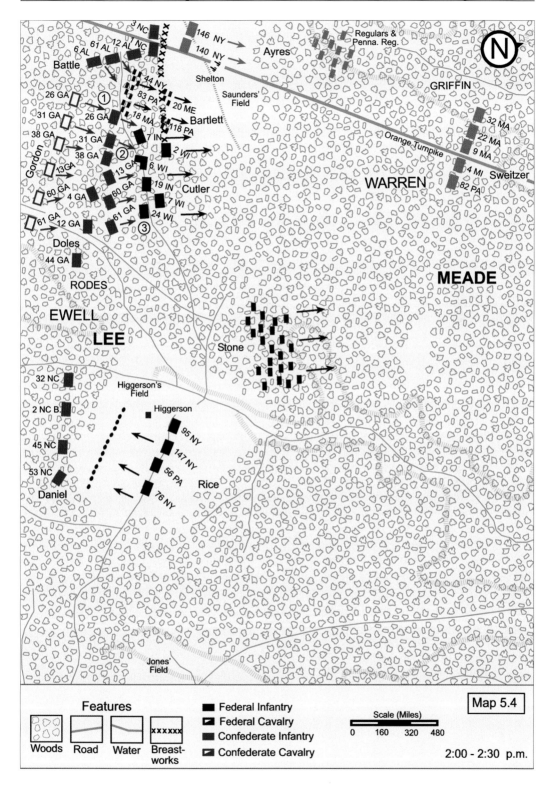

Features

Woods   Road   Water   Breast-
                        works

■ Federal Infantry
▨ Federal Cavalry
■ Confederate Infantry
▨ Confederate Cavalry

Scale (Miles)

0   160   320   480

Map 5.4

2:00 - 2:30 p.m.

Map 5.5: Wadsworth's Division in Full Retreat (2:00 - 2:30 p.m.)

Gordon's success in driving back Cutler's Iron Brigade put his command in a precarious position. The Georgians had punched a hole in the Union line, but enemy troops were on both of their flanks. Driving farther eastward would imperil the brigade, so Gordon improvised a unique plan. While the 31st and 38th Georgia remained in place as the pivot point, the regiments on their right (13th, 60th, and 61st Georgia) and left (26th Georgia) swung outward like a hinged door (No. 1). The 26th Georgia on the left swung to the left and smashed into the flank of Bartlett's brigade, which had broken Jones' line. Hit in front by Battle's men and in the flank and rear by the Georgians, Bartlett's men broke and headed back out of the woods and into Saunders Field (No. 2). The 13th, 60th, and 61st Georgia on the right of the brigade swung right and headed southward to strike Rice's flank. With Daniel's Brigade in its front and the Georgians in its flank and rear, Rice's men also called it quits (No. 3). Most of its skirmish line did not enjoy this choice and surrendered.[24]

With the enemy on the run, Gordon ordered his two regiments that had remained in place (31st and 38th Georgia) to drive eastward after the fleeing Union soldiers. The move scooped up scores of prisoners. "The brush now served us well. Our smaller body of men could move faster than the heavy lines of the enemy could follow," noted Rufus Dawes of the 6th Wisconsin. "The rebels came on yelling and firing."[25]

Into this mayhem rode General Wadsworth, who had never seen the Iron Brigade in flight. The sight unnerved him. "Where is my second line?" he screamed to his aides, referencing Col. Andrew Denison's Maryland brigade. "Bring up my second line!" Denison's brigade was to have advanced in support of Wadsworth's three-brigade attack (No. 4). The strong brigade composed of the 1st, 4th, 7th, and 8th Maryland was new to the Army of the Potomac, having served mainly garrison and picket duty until it was incorporated into Meade's command after the Gettysburg Campaign.[26]

Denison's men knew all was not well when they saw "suspicious numbers of supernumerary

attendants [among] the wounded, soon followed by stragglers with the usual discouraging reports." When a frantic aide appeared and asked the identity of the commander of the Maryland troops and someone referred him to Colonel Denison, the aide shook his head and yelled back that he had no time to find him. "Tell him [Denison] the rebels are driving our right, and there is no support on that flank." When he heard the news, Denison replied "with great composure" that he had just received a similar communication from his left flank. Just then, growing hordes of men from the Iron Brigade barreled out of the woods and into the brigade, throwing Denison's ranks into disarray. The retreating troops created "some confusion for a moment, which, however was promptly allayed."

The Iron Brigade's retreat was more disorganized than its chaotic advance. Many of its new members refused to turn and face the enemy once they began their retreat. The same was not true for most of the veterans, who periodically halted to fire into the enemy, but there were too few of them to stop the swarming enemy. According to Lt. Col. William Swan, an aide to General Ayres, the "fearful confusion [and the] calamity spread to all the troops in that region." Still, he added, it was "not altogether a disgraceful retreat." In some places the retreat and resistance was fairly organized. For example, the 6th Wisconsin "clung around its colors," noted Lieutenant Colonel Dawes. "We rallied and formed twice or three times and gave the enemy a hot reception as they came on," but before being overpowered, the retreat continued. According to Colonel Hofmann, the end of half a mile the officers succeeded in rallying about 350 men on the crest of a slight elevation and intended to hold the ground. At this moment an aide of General Wadsworth arrived with instructions to move some distance to the rear where the division was reforming.[27]

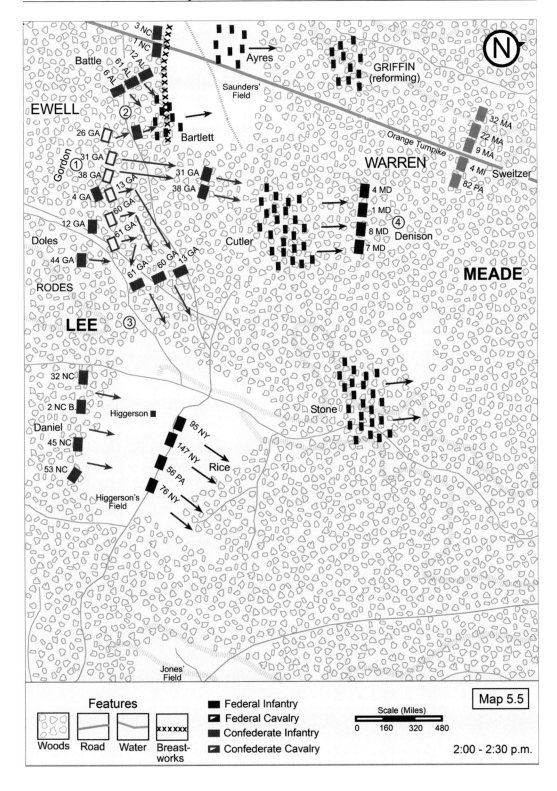

3 NC
1 NC
12 AL
Battle
61 AL
6 AL

Ayres

GRIFFIN
(reforming)

Saunders'
Field

EWELL

32 MA
22 MA
9 MA

26 GA
Bartlett

WARREN

4 MI Sweitzer

Gordon ①
31 GA
38 GA
31 GA
38 GA

82 PA

4 GA
13 GA

4 MD

60 GA
1 MD

12 GA
61 GA
8 MD Denison

Doles
Cutler
7 MD

44 GA
61 GA 60 GA 13 GA

RODES

MEADE

LEE ③

32 NC

2 NC B.
Higgerson

Stone

Daniel
45 NC

95 NY

53 NC
147 NY

Higgerson's
Field
56 PA Rice

76 NY

Jones'
Field

Orange Turnpike

②

Features

- Federal Infantry
- Federal Cavalry
- Confederate Infantry
- Confederate Cavalry

Scale (Miles)

0   160   320   480

xxxxxx

Woods Road Water Breastworks

Map 5.5

2:00 – 2:30 p.m.

Map 5.6: Retreat Back to the Lacy House (2:00 - 2:30 p.m.)

By this time Denison's Maryland brigade was the only organized command facing the Confederate onslaught. Once the last of the fugitives cleared their front, the Marylanders leveled their muskets and fired volleys into the approaching but still largely unseen "furious and desperate" enemy assault. According to an eyewitness, the Marylanders "defeated and severely punished" the Rebels, who rallied and fired back as they advanced anew. The brigade, admitted Col. Samuel Graham who later commanded the unit, "suffered severely." Hit in front and flank, the 1st and 4th Maryland on the right of the line were forced to the rear. The remaining 7th and 8th Maryland spotted enemy approaching their front and both flanks and were ordered back to the Lacy house with the command to "fall back steadily." (No. 1).[28]

The whooping and hollering victorious Confederates, composed of portions of Gordon's, Daniel's and Doles' brigades, pursued the fleeing Union troops all the way to the Lacy property. There, a number of V Corps guns were deployed with "fixed prolonges,"—ropes to allow the guns to be withdrawn by hand while firing. This may have disheartened some of the infantry, who knew it meant the officers were unsure there would be enough time to limber up in the traditional manner. The canister belched from the guns tossed Confederate bodies in every direction. When several attempts to take the guns failed, the Rebels fell back to the opposite side of Lacy's Field.[29]

It was about this time that men from General Warren's absent division under Samuel Crawford, which had been farther south near the Chewning farm, made its appearance at Higgerson's Field (No. 2). After several protestations about his orders to slide right to connect with Wadsworth's division, Crawford relented, but only sent the 2nd, 7th, and 11th Pennsylvania Reserves under brigade commander Col. Joseph McCandless. The men moved quickly up the small country road and the 2nd Pennsylvania Reserves spread out on the skirmish line and cautiously entered Higgerson's Field with the other two reserve regiments

behind it. Thin groups of Rebels (probably from Daniel's command) fell back before their advance, but resistance stiffened when they came up against the three regiments of Gordon's Brigade that had just driven off Rice's brigade.[30]

As the fighting intensified, McCandless grew more uneasy with each passing minute. Worried about his flanks, he finally ordered his command to fall back. The 61st Georgia, however, had already worked its way around McCandless' left flank and had now formed in his rear (No. 3). Initially, the Pennsylvania troops thought these men hailed from their own division, which they believed was approaching in support. A deadly volley dispelled the notion. According to the historian of the 7th Pennsylvania Reserves, "an effort was made to break through to the left, but was met by an unyielding resistance. The right was then tried . . . with like ill success." The 7th's commander, Col. H. C. Bollinger, had a decision to make: fight on or surrender. Unwilling to sacrifice his command, Bollinger surrendered 272 officers and men. "As it was," wrote a veteran, "many of his brave men were left in the Wilderness, never to be heard from again." The survivors ended up at Andersonville prison, which prompted a survivor to write after the war, "had they known the fate to which their inhuman captors were to subject them, they would, doubtless, have preferred slaughter upon the field." According to several Confederate veterans, a Maj. Van Valkenberg with a company of the 61st Georgia on detached duty watching the regiment's flank encountered the 7th Pennsylvania Reserves. Feigning more men than he actually had, he convinced the Pennsylvanians' commander to surrender, which he reluctantly did.[31]

The 11th Pennsylvania almost shared the same fate. According to the regiment's historian, the unit "succeeded, after several fruitless attempts, in cutting its way out and reaching the union lines; but not without serious loss." The 2nd and 11th Pennsylvania Reserves, together with about 40 men from the 7th Pennsylvania Reserves, made their way back to the safety of the division. The handful of survivors from the latter regiment was attached to the 11th Pennsylvania Reserves. McCandless's command was in shambles and narrowly escaped destruction.[32]

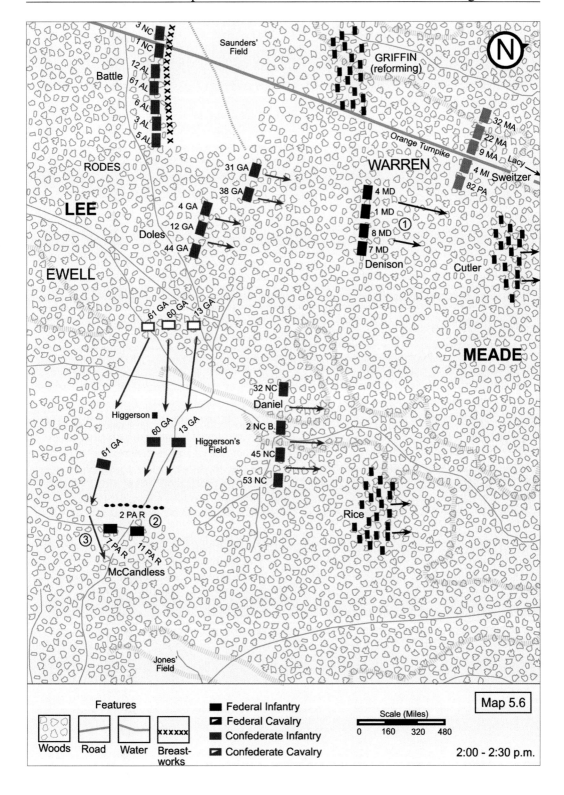

Map 5.6

2:00 – 2:30 p.m.

Map 5.7: The Fighting Ends on Warren's Front (2:30 - 3:00 p.m.)

The early afternoon combat on May 5, explained one historian, "more closely resembled a riot than a battle." Almost all of the Union problems of coordination were the result of dense vegetation and inadequate roads. Communication between army headquarters and corps commanders made it difficult to get the various corps into their proper places, and once an attack began this same brush and timber disorganized the alignment, marching order, and direction of every regiment, brigade, and division. With visibility often limited to a handful of yards, Union men fought alone or in small groups. A thick layer of smoke from both discharging weapons and smoldering fires hung like a pall across the battlefield and further obscured visibility. The fighting and smoke left the men hot, exhausted, unable to see far, and nauseated—a debilitating combination of factors that caused one of General Wadsworth's aides, Capt. Robert Monteith, to conclude that a "strange lethargy" had overtaken the men. Many of the men, both friend and foe, likened the retreat to a flock of frightened sheep.[33]

Many of the Union soldiers believed that if they could only get back to their jump-off point near the Lacy house, all would be well. One of General Ayres' aides, Lt. Col. William Swan, observed that the "fearful confusion [and the calamity] spread to all the troops in that region," yet "every soldier . . . seemed to know the way to the Lacy house." Avery Harris of the 143rd Pennsylvania recalled "when we went out of the woods . . . I saw what was to me the most satisfactory sight in my life. That was our own colors. Down below in the field near some buildings [our commander] was rallying the men around the colors." The reactions by the regimental, brigade, and division leaders were decidedly mixed. Most were content to reassemble their broken commands, but Colonel Hofmann of the 56th Pennsylvania was still full of fight. He prepared his men for a counterattack, but as he later wrote, "General Wadsworth, who had a remarkable capacity for keeping a clear head in the most trying situations" dissuaded him from undertaking such a futile act. Wadsworth, he wrote, was

"deeply mortified and in high temper," and was only able to rally his division "with great exertion." Ordnance officer Morris Schaff claimed "it only took a moment" to reform these veteran troops. The men immediately began throwing up breastworks.[34]

One of the most dramatic incidents at this stage of the combat involved General Griffin, who was both devastated and "in miserable humor" by his division's defeat. According to Meade's aide, Lt. Col. Theodore Lyman, the ill-tempered brigadier was searching for Warren when he spotted a tent under which Meade was conferring with Grant, Brig. Gen. John Rawlins (Grant's adjutant general), and other staff officers. Griffin dismounted and demanded to know why his attack was unsupported and his division needlessly sacrificed. When no one replied Griffin continued, explaining how he had pushed Ewell's men back for more than half a mile, but Wadsworth's men broke on his left and General Wright's VI Corps division failed to go in on his right as promised. Griffin's censure of his own corps commander (Warren) and two fellow division commanders stunned Grant and appalled Rawlins, who denounced Griffin's behavior and demanded his arrest. Grant seemed to agree when he said to Meade, "Who is this General Gregg? You ought to arrest him!" Once again Meade was in a difficult situation. Griffin had indeed crossed a line, but Meade respected his former comrade's fighting abilities as much as he disliked Grant's growing influence on his army's actions. "It's not Gregg but Griffin," Meade replied. "And its only his way of talking." Rawlins, added Lyman, "asked me what he had done; [I] told him his reputation as an officer was good." When Grant sat back in his chair and fired up a cigar, Griffin stomped away and the unusual episode came to a close.[35]

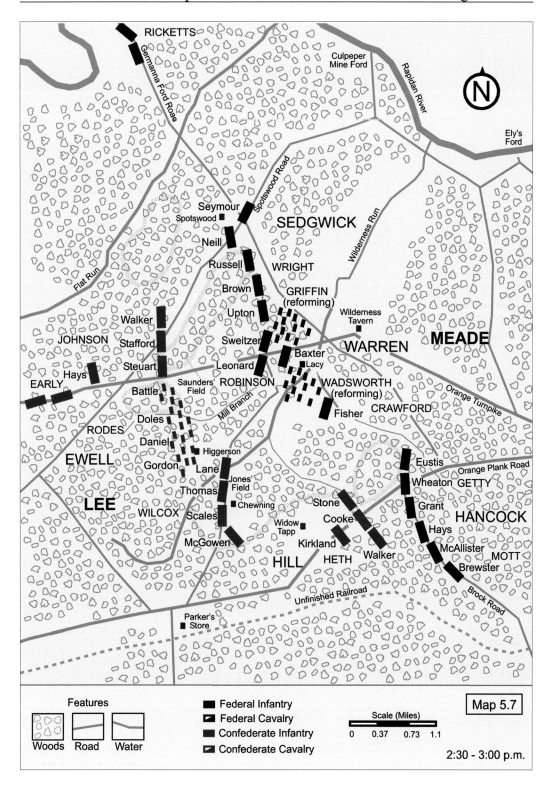

RICKETTS

Culpeper
Mine Ford

Germanna Ford Road

Rapidan River

Ely's
Ford

Spotswood Road

Seymour
Spotswood

SEDGWICK

Wilderness Run

Neill

Russell

WRIGHT

Brown

GRIFFIN
(reforming)

Wilderness
Tavern

Upton

Flat Run

Walker

JOHNSON   Stafford   Sweitzer

WARREN

MEADE

Baxter

Steuart   Leonard   Lacy

Hays
EARLY   Battle   Saunders'
Field   ROBINSON

WADSWORTH
(reforming)

Orange Turnpike

Mill Branch

Doles

Fisher   CRAWFORD

RODES   Daniel

Higgerson

EWELL   Gordon   Lane   Jones'
Field

Eustis

Orange Plank Road

Wheaton GETTY

Thomas   Chewning

Stone   Grant

LEE   WILCOX   Scales   Widow
Tapp   Cooke   HANCOCK
Hays

McGowen   Kirkland   Walker   McAllister   MOTT

HILL   HETH   Brewster

Unfinished Railroad

Brock Road

Parker's
Store

Features

Woods Road Water

■ Federal Infantry
▰ Federal Cavalry
■ Confederate Infantry
▰ Confederate Cavalry

Scale (Miles)

0   0.37   0.73   1.1

Map 5.7

2:30 - 3:00 p.m.

Map 5.8: Warren Reforms His V Corps (3:00 p.m.)

General Warren had been against launching a hasty attack in the first instance, and now he and his officers were faced with a corps in disarray and the enemy approaching. They quickly rounded up the men, did their best to reform shattered ranks, and formed a coherent defensive front. Although thinned by casualties, within a relatively short time the companies, regiments, and brigades reassembled in a line stretching from north of the turnpike south past the Lacy house and south across Wilderness Run into the woods beyond. Some of the units had lost as many as one-half their number. Heavy losses were an especially bitter pill to swallow because the terms of enlistments for some units, such as the Iron Brigade, were up within a few weeks.

While those who had made it back were relatively safe, the same could not be said for most of the wounded who were lying where they fell in or near Saunders Field. The bullets and shells that had injured them also triggered small fires in the undergrowth, and parts of Ewell's breastworks erupted into flames that quickly spread. The ambulatory wounded hobbled or crawled out of harm's way. "The bare prospect of fire running through the woods, where they lay helpless," Frank Wilkeson recalled, "unnerved the most courageous of men, and made them call aloud for help." For some, safety represented the turnpike itself, which acted as a firebreak. Unfortunately, the flames inexorably found those unable to move or move fast enough, and also ignited their cartridge boxes, which exploded and inflicted additional wounds. Some of the injured preferred to take their own lives rather than burn alive.[36]

One veteran provided a vivid description of these horrible moments: "The almost cheerful "Pop! Pop!" of the cartridges gave no hint of the dreadful horror their noise bespoke. Swept by the flames, the trees, bushes, and logs which Confederates had thrown up as breastworks now took fire and dense clouds of smoke rolled across the clearing, choking unfortunates who were exposed to it and greatly hindered the work of the rescuers. The clearing now became a raging inferno in which many of the wounded perished.

The bodies of the dead were blackened and burned beyond all possibility of recognition. It was a tragic conclusion to this day of horror."[37]

General Warren never forgot the events of May 5 or forgave those who forced his men into premature battle. Warren knew his attack had failed because of inadequate support by Sedgwick's VI Corps, and he was not afraid to say so. Soon after the battle Warren noted as much in his battle report: "The attack failed because Wright's division, of the Sixth Corps, was unable on account of the woods to get up on our right flank and meet the division (Johnson's) that flanked us." Ten years later Warren was of like mind, writing, "If we had waited until the 6th Corps or two divisions of it got up with the enemy on the road the 6th Corps was taking, we should have begun the attack on Ewell's corps." The premature attack, he concluded, was the "most fatal blunder of the campaign." Historian Gordon Rhea agreed, noting that "the ultimate fault, of course, lay with Meade. There was no excuse for his forcing Warren forward until he was ready and until Wright's full weight could be brought to bear."[38]

While Wright's absence played a significant role, so too did the fact that too few men participated in the attack. Bartlett's and Cutler's brigades met with initial success and broke through Ewell's front, but no reinforcements were available to press the advantage. Warren had two other divisions (Crawford's and Robinson's), but was unable to organize his front sufficiently to get them into the fighting. In addition, the terrain negated the significant Federal advantage in artillery, which played virtually no role in the fighting. And of course, the Confederates had something to do with it. Overall, Ewell and his men turned in a strong performance. After the initial collapse of Jones' Brigade, Ewell quickly regrouped his men, rushed in reinforcements, and sealed the breach.[39]

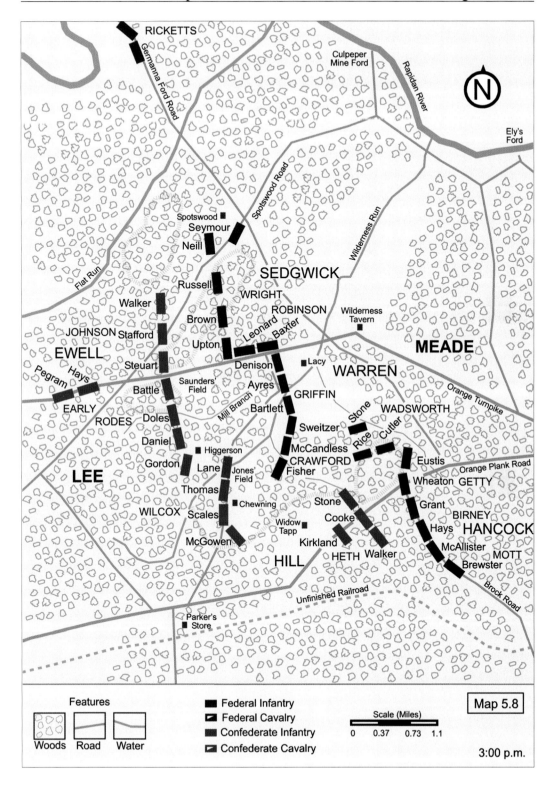

RICKETTS

Germanna Ford Road

Culpeper
Mine Ford

Rapidan River

Ely's
Ford

Spotswood Road

Spotswood

Seymour

Neill

SEDGWICK

Russell

WRIGHT

Walker

Brown

ROBINSON

Wilderness
Tavern

Flat Run

JOHNSON Stafford

Upton

Leonard

Baxter

MEADE

EWELL

Pegram

Hays

Steuart

Denison

Lacy

WARREN

Orange Turnpike

Battle

Saunders'
Field

Ayres

GRIFFIN

EARLY

Doles

Bartlett

Stone

WADSWORTH

RODES

Mill Branch

Sweitzer

Rice

Cutler

Daniel

Higgerson

McCandless

Gordon

Lane

Jones'
Field

CRAWFORD
Fisher

Eustis

Orange Plank Road

LEE

Thomas

Chewning

Stone

Wheaton GETTY

WILCOX

Scales

Widow
Tapp

Cooke

Grant

BIRNEY

McGowen

Kirkland

Hays

HANCOCK

HILL

HETH

Walker

McAllister

MOTT

Brewster

Brock Road

Unfinished Railroad

Parker's
Store

Wilderness Run

Features

Woods Road Water

Federal Infantry
Federal Cavalry
Confederate Infantry
Confederate Cavalry

Scale (Miles)

0   0.37   0.73   1.1

Map 5.8

3:00 p.m.

Map Set 6: Wright's Division Engages the Confederate Left

Map 6.1: Wright Approaches its Jumping-Off Point (3:00 p.m.)

The division Maj. Gen. Gouverneur Warren and Brig. Gen. Charles Griffin had so fervently looked to for support on the right of the V Corps was Brig. Gen. Horatio Wright's command of Maj. Gen. John Sedgwick's VI Corps.

Wright had his four brigades ready to march about 6:30 that morning, but orders to move out were not in hand because George Meade was sifting through intelligence reports in an effort to better understand the confusing tactical situation unfolding across his front. About 9:00 a.m., he decided to move General Wright southwest to support the Warren's V Corps' right flank. Wright, however, was instructed to wait for reinforcements. When Brig. Gen. Truman Seymour's brigade (Brig. Gen. James Ricketts' division) arrived at 11:00 a.m., Wright set off. This delay, however, helped seal the fate of Griffin's ill-timed charge across Saunders Field.[1]

Colonel Emory Upton's brigade led Wright's division along Spotswood Road, followed by Col. Henry Brown's brigade, and Gen. David Russell's. Wright's last brigade, Brig. Gen. Alexander Shaler's, remained back to protect the wagons. Wright received two other brigades: Brig. Gen. Thomas Neill (Brig. Gen. George Getty's division) followed Brown, and General Seymour's. Wright put Neill's brigade behind Brown's and ordered Seymour to bring up the rear (see Map 3.9). The head of the column took fire quickly from Maj. W. H. Cowles' 1st North Carolina Cavalry, which had screened Edward Johnson's division during its march to Saunders Field. By 11:00 a.m. that morning it was scouting toward Germanna Ford. The troopers did their best to delay the infantry column, like a giant arrow was pointed directly at Ewell's exposed left flank. It was but a short march of one and one-half miles to Wright's objective, but what should have taken an hour consumed closer to four hours because of Rebel resistance and the impenetrable vegetation masking what might be lurking within.[2]

With Confederates in their front, Wright left the lane and headed southwest. It was a difficult slog. In addition to the heavy vegetation, snake-like tributaries spilled into Wilderness Run and Flat Run, cutting "steep-banked gullies that knifed off to all points of the compass," explained one modern historian of the battle. "Hills popped up expectedly, separated by dark little swamps and streams. Obscure depressions and ridges, clogged with choking second growth, offered irresistible opportunities for ambush." Upton noted in his report that "the advance was made by the right of wings, it being impossible to march in line of battle on account of the dense pine and nearly impenetrable thickets which met us on every hand." A foot soldier thought it was the "awfullest brush, briars, grapevine, etc., I was ever in."[3]

Edward Johnson spent the hours of Wright's fitful approach regrouping his division after repulsing Griffin's Unionists. John M. Jones was busy reforming his disrupted Virginians in the rear after their stampede from the front line. George "Maryland" Steuart's mixed brigade remained in its forward position straddling the turnpike. Johnson rearranged his remaining two brigades, positioning Leroy Stafford's Louisianans on Steuart's left and James Walker's Stonewall Brigade on the far left flank well north of the turnpike.[4]

Cowles' dismounted cavalry was joined by skirmishers from Walker's Stonewall Brigade, and continued tormenting Wright's marching column on its slow approach to Saunders Field. A Union doctor recalled the difficulties: "as our line advanced, it would suddenly come upon a line of graycoated rebels, lying upon the ground, covered with dried leaves, and concealed by the chaparral, when the rebels would rise, deliver a murderous fire, and retire." The strength of the Union column made it impossible to stop the approach, so the Rebels resorted to firing the woods. According to Upton, "the ground had previously been fought over and was strewn with wounded of both sides, many of whom must have perished in the flames, as corpses were found partly consumed."[5]

Despite these difficulties Wright pressed ahead until he connected with the right of Warren's V Corps. There, the VI Corps division formed a line of battle perpendicular to the pike. Wright's staff officer, Maj. Henry Dalton, reported that, "having made connection with the Fifth Corps, the troops remained in position till the next morning, having been engaged only in brisk firing."[6]

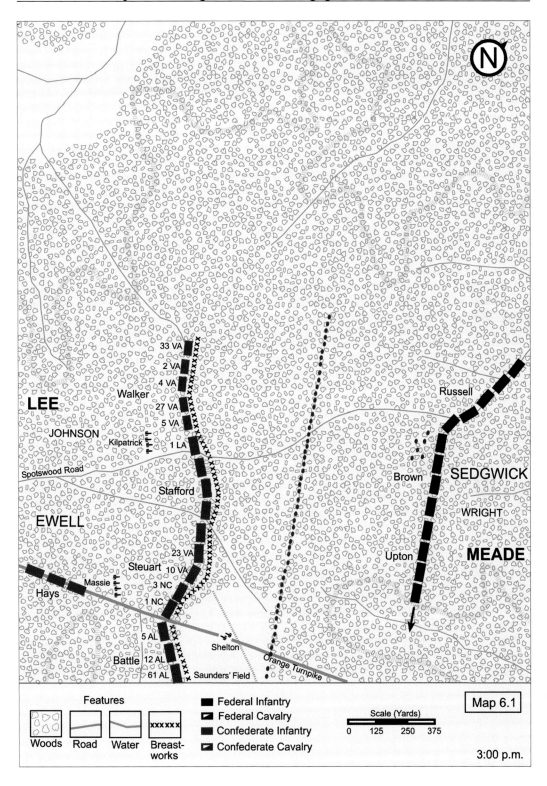

Features

Woods Road Water Breastworks

xxxxx

■ Federal Infantry
▰ Federal Cavalry
■ Confederate Infantry
▰ Confederate Cavalry

Scale (Yards)
0   125   250   375

Map 6.1

3:00 p.m.

Map 6.2: Wright Advances Against the Enemy (3:00 - 3:30 p.m.)

Colonel Emory Upton's brigade formed the left of Wright's divisional front with the 95th Pennsylvania on the far left next to the turnpike, and the 96th Pennsylvania, 121st New York, and 5th Maine extending the line to the right. The historian of the 5th Maine recalled that "skirmishers were sent forward to feel the enemy's position, or rather to discover if there were any rebels in that vicinity" (No. 1). He described the advance as slow and measured because "the underbrush was so dense it was highly dangerous to advance rapidly." It was not long before Upton's men encountered some of Cowles' dismounted cavalrymen on the skirmish line. This broke the silence and gunfire erupted all along the line. "Almost simultaneously with the advance, came a deafening roar of artillery, and shots and shells flew lively above our boys," recalled George Bicknell of the 5th Maine.[7]

On Upton's right was Brown's First New Jersey Brigade (No. 2), whose members discovered that forming into line of battle was almost impossible. The briars were so thick along the Jerseymen's front they had to stamp them down before they could move a yard. Brown formed his men in two lines with the 10th and 15th New Jersey in the front and the original regiments (1st, 2nd, and 4th New Jersey) tucked behind them. The remaining regiment—the 3rd New Jersey—appears to have gotten lost. John Judd of the latter regiment noted in his diary that his unit "maneuvered around through the woods and bushes all day under a heavy fire but was not actually engaged." Confusion also reigned when the 15th New Jersey on Brown's left front was ordered to guide left while the 5th Maine of Upton's was ordered to "guide right." The result was a confused mess that had to be sorted out before the troops could continue their advance.[8]

The next brigade in line under Russell also experienced difficulties (No. 3). Russell's men were also formed in two lines, with the 5th Wisconsin on the left, and the 49th Pennsylvania and 6th Maine extending the front northward, with the 119th Pennsylvania alone in the rear. A member of the 49th Pennsylvania noted that the regiment "formed in line of battle parallel with the road, and had advanced a quarter of a mile through shrub-oaks, stunted pines, and towering green briars, alias the Wilderness." The regiment ran into difficulty when, "on account of the woods and underbrush the four old companies and colors of our regiment [49th] was cut loose from our new companies."[9]

Thomas Neill's brigade, part of Getty's division, formed on the right end of Wright's three brigades. When the order to advance arrived, they drove the enemy skirmish line before them (No. 4). At some point during the advance the Rebel skirmishers stood their ground along a ridge, forcing Neill's men to charge. The attacking Unionists reached and took the designated position, where they halted, dressed ranks, and awaited further orders.[10]

General Sedgwick and his staff arrived on the scene about 3:30 p.m. to help supervise Wright's advance, which met not only difficult terrain and enemy lead, but a host of grisly sights—especially on Upton's front. The sights and smells of charred flesh from wounded men caught up in the spreading flames discouraged the men, who were forced by Rebel bullets in many cases to drop down next to a blackened corpse.[11]

Ewell and his staff, meanwhile, remained near the Orange Turnpike actively receiving couriers and dictating orders for the front line commanders.[12] Three brigades of Johnson's Division (Steuart, Stafford, and Walker) were deployed behind breastworks, while Jones' men continued forming and resting in the rear. A series of comical events occurred within Stafford's line to break up the tension of waiting for the real combat to begin. The hilarity began when a fox suddenly appeared being chased by Col. Zebulon York of the 14th Louisiana. "Suddenly a wild turkey starts out from the undergrowth and our boys letting out a wild yell pour a volley after the affrighted bird," recalled the chaplain of the 14th Louisiana. "Soon a rabbit jumps out in front and makes in the direction of the enemy. Some of the boys pursue and bring back the animal amidst the cheers of their companions."[13]

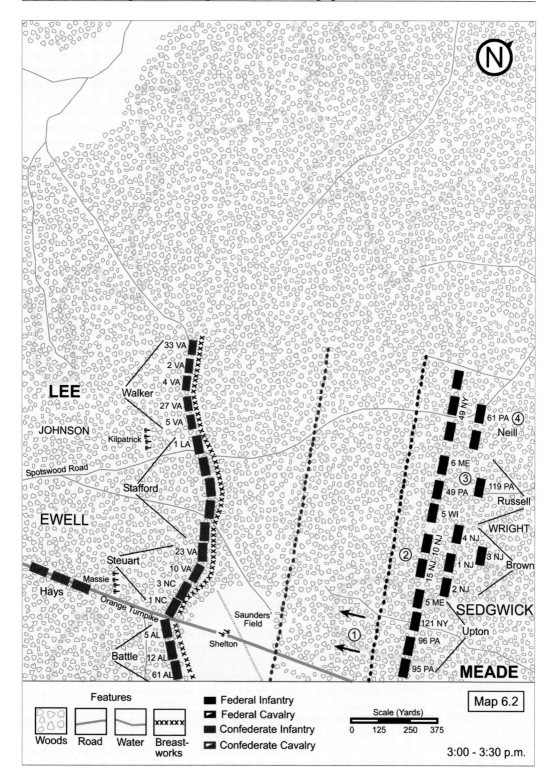

LEE

JOHNSON

Walker

33 VA
2 VA
4 VA
27 VA
5 VA
Kilpatrick
1 LA

Spotswood Road

Stafford

EWELL

23 VA
10 VA

Steuart

Massie

Hays

3 NC
1 NC

Orange Turnpike

5 AL

Battle

12 AL

61 AL

Saunders'
Field

Shelton

49 NY

61 PA ④
Neill

6 ME
③
49 PA

119 PA
Russell

5 WI

WRIGHT

4 NJ

15 NJ 10 NJ

②

1 NJ

3 NJ
Brown

2 NJ

5 ME

121 NY

SEDGWICK

Upton

96 PA

①

95 PA

MEADE

Features

Woods   Road   Water   Breast-works

xxxxx

Federal Infantry
Federal Cavalry
Confederate Infantry
Confederate Cavalry

Scale (Yards)

0   125   250   375

Map 6.2

3:00 - 3:30 p.m.

Map 6.3: Initial Contact
(3:30 - 3:45 p.m.)

George Bicknell of the 5th Maine recalled how the relatively peaceful advance ended. "And soon it came," he wrote. "A few hundred yards of advance, and the quick sharp crack of a rifle, followed by a full volley of musketry, announced the presence of the rebel infantry." Upton's brigade was up against Steuart's Brigade, which had effectively repulsed the earlier charge of Ayres' brigade (Griffin's division).

Upton's 121st New York was led into position by one of Wright's staff officers. The regiment's historian noted that "he led it so rapidly that it became scattered in the thicket and a portion of it ran squarely into the ranks of the enemy. In the resulting confusion, some prisoners were taken by both sides as the Confederates fell back to a safer position. The unit settled down, but could not be called a cohesive group as clumps of men were scattered in the sector.[14]

The most severe fighting occurred on Upton's left flank. Riding ahead of his men, Lt. Col. Samuel Carroll of the 95th Pennsylvania, on the left of Upton's line, "came suddenly upon a group of the enemy, who fired upon him, killing him instantly." Seeing the enemy up ahead posted on a small hill, a couple of Carroll's companies charged, driving the Rebels back toward the main Confederate line. The Pennsylvanians sent 30 enemy soldiers to the rear.[15]

Worried about the vulnerable left flank of his line, General Sedgwick rode up to the 15th New Jersey of Brown's brigade and quickly sent it to the left to help bolster the 95th Pennsylvania's line. The regiment would remain here for the rest of the battle, attached to Upton's brigade. Colonel Upton reported that the regiment "behaved under all circumstances with a steadiness indicative of the highest state of discipline."[16]

The advance continued. Upton's men finally reached the edge of Saunders Field. The men of Steuart's Brigade fingered their muskets on the opposite side of the field. As the officers and men pondered their options, all were in agreement that to attempt to cross the open, already bloody field would be folly. The men's enthusiasm on both sides was dampened by the number of dead and dying men in Saunders Field. One Confederate foot soldier noted that the "ground was strewn thick with bluecoats, so close that they could not be moved." Colonel Upton, conferring with Generals Wright and Sedgwick was emphatic—"It was madness" to attempt to attack the well-defended Confederate line. The decision made, the men hunkered down and showed their aggressiveness in ways other than a charge. The historian of the 5th Maine recalled that, "there was considerable sharp rifle practice during the remainder of the day, which made it a little more safe to be behind shelter than to be exposed to rebel bullets."[17]

A soldier in Upton's sector recalled the tense situation:

> It was impossible to see the enemy; and though we peered into the thick woods, we were fighting invisible foemen. We soon began intrenching. Our men scraped the stones and earth before them as best they could, until spades were brought. All the time the enemy were sending a shower of bullets over and past us. It would at times lessen, then start again afresh. We lay, on the crest of the hill, stooping low as every fusillade swept over. It was wonderful that our casualties were not greater in that leaden storm. We replied by occasional volleys, but could not see what damage we inflicted. We were screened by bushes on our front. The enemy before was screened in the same manner. Between the two lay an open, cleared flat, of small extent, through which passed the Orange pike.[18]

The Confederate artillery continued pounding the Federal lines. Lying prone on the ground, a soldier in the 15th New Jersey (Brown's brigade) recalled that the "shells flew over our heads at a lively rate. The trees rattled and the branches fell; but though we bowed our heads low to the ground and knew not what was to follow, no man left his place."[19]

The other Federal brigades also reached their positions and hunkered down.

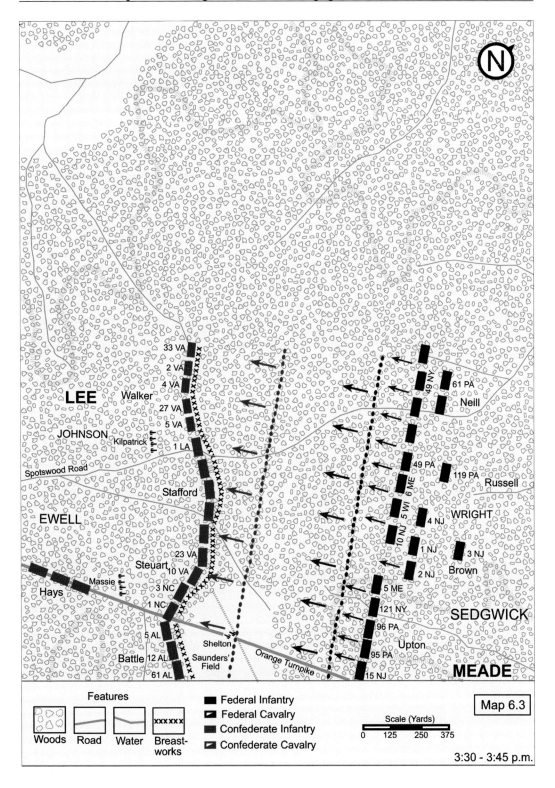

LEE

Walker

JOHNSON

Kilpatrick

Spotswood Road

Stafford

EWELL

Steuart

Massie

Hays

Battle

33 VA
2 VA
4 VA
27 VA
5 VA
1 LA

23 VA
10 VA
3 NC
1 NC
5 AL
12 AL
61 AL

Shelton
Saunders'
Field

Orange Turnpike

49 NY
61 PA
Neill

49 PA
6 ME
5 WI
10 NJ
5 ME
121 NY
96 PA
95 PA
15 NJ

119 PA
Russell

4 NJ
1 NJ
2 NJ
3 NJ
Brown
WRIGHT

Upton

SEDGWICK

MEADE

Features

| Woods | Road | Water | Breast-works |

Federal Infantry
Federal Cavalry
Confederate Infantry
Confederate Cavalry

Scale (Yards)
0   125   250   375

Map 6.3

3:30 - 3:45 p.m.

Map 6.4: The Stonewall Brigade Makes a Stand (3:00 - 4:00 p.m.)

Wright's commanders struggled to align their scattered ranks and reposition their troops. For example, the 121st New York (Upton's brigade) moved to the left to bolster the 15th New Jersey on the left (No. 1). Brown's brigade by this time was badly divided: the 3rd and 10th New Jersey moved to the right to form behind Russell's brigade (No. 2). Brown's remaining regiments, the 1st, 2nd, and 4th New Jersey, had been in the second line but were now moved forward to replace the two regiments that had originally been in the first line.[20]

A member of the 49th Pennsylvania (Russell's brigade) recalled that his regiment "suddenly came upon the enemy, receiving his fire at less than thirty yards distance. The line wavered for an instant, but soon closed up, and poured in a well directed fire with good effect, breaking his line and occupying his ground (No. 3)." They had probably encountered the 5th Virginia of Walker's Brigade manning the left side of Johnson's divisional line.[21]

On the Confederate side, Walker's Virginians and Stafford's Louisianans hopped over their protective breastworks and headed through the heavy undergrowth toward the enemy. The tangles of vegetation hindered their movement as bullets fired by a largely unseen enemy whizzed through the foliage. Walker's regiments apparently encountered the enemy first. The men in the brigade's right regiments, the 5th, 27th, and 4th Virginia, were waiting when their skirmishers scampered back yelling that the enemy was right behind them. Before they had a chance to react, the 49th Pennsylvania fired a devastating volley into the front and flank of the 5th Virginia manning the brigade's right side. This volley, fired from a distance of only 40 yards, staggered the Virginians who quickly gave way "in some confusion." The panicked soldiers barreled into the 27th Virginia on their left (No. 4), which was taking heavy frontal fire. The confusion of men from the 5th entering their ranks and the volleys from the front was too much to stand and this also gave way. The disorder, admitted one men, "was so great & unexpected that there was fear lest the brigade could not sustain its position." As the right side of Walker's Brigade melted away, the balance of the men together with Stafford's Brigade on their right stood their ground and opened fire.[22]

Cognizant that his men were breaking on the right or barely maintaining their position on the left, General Walker stood in his stirrups and yelled, "Remember your name!" When the 5th and 27th regiments fell back in confusion, the next regiment to the left, the 4th Virginia, found itself exposed to being turned on the right. Its commander, Col. William Terry, ordered his regiment to pull back its exposed flank and form at right angles to its former position (No. 5). As a result, Neill's approaching Federals ran into an effective wall of Rebel small arms fire rather than an exposed flank to turn and crush.[23]

The left side of Walker's embattled brigade was faring only slightly better. The 33rd and 2nd Virginia were desperately attempting to halt the onslaught of the right of Neill's brigade (No. 6). According to Thomas Doyle of the 33rd Virginia, the battle "raged with inconceivable violence along the whole front." Colonel William Randolph of the 2nd Virginia called the regiment's flag-bearer to his side and ordered him to vigorously wave the flag to help maintain the men's confidence to hold strong against the Federal onslaught. A bullet hit Randolph in the head and instantly killed the 27-year-old regimental commander.[24]

Realizing his brigade was on the verge of complete collapse, Walker pulled back about 75 yards to reform and reorder his ranks. According to Doyle, the movement was executed "in great order under a most galling fire from the enemy who were pressing the line heavily at all points." He also recalled the Union enemy seemed to be "indisposed to press their (seeming) advantage but contented themselves by keeping up a heavy skirmish fire which did the Confederates but little damage."[25]

The attacking Federals experienced a variety of frustration of their own. In the midst of the wild confusion that was disordering their own ranks, the 119th Pennsylvania leveled their rifled muskets and fired into the backs of the 49th Pennsylvania. "We drop to the ground, and are very angry," wrote the regiment's historian. "We say some bad words and fire a few shots at them and [holler] that they are firing into the Forty-ninth Pennsylvania Volunteers."[26]

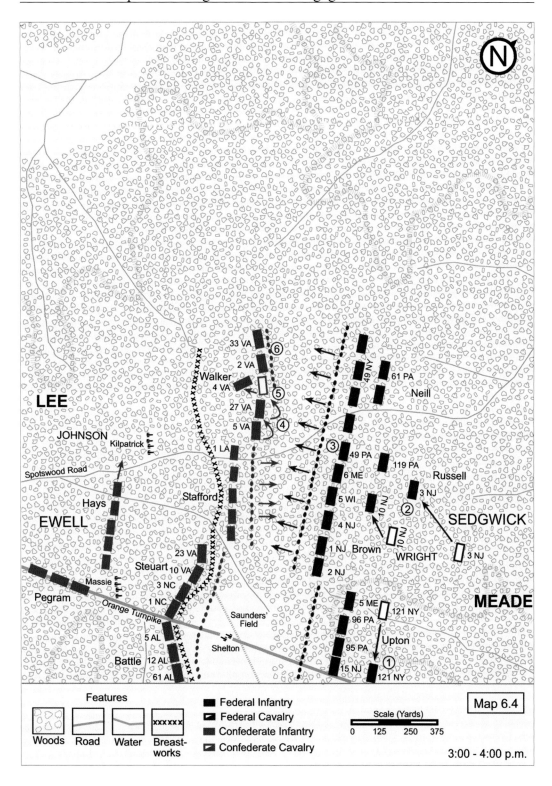

Features

Woods   Road   Water   Breast-
                        works

■ Federal Infantry
◪ Federal Cavalry
■ Confederate Infantry
◪ Confederate Cavalry

Scale (Yards)
0   125   250   375

Map 6.4

3:00 - 4:00 p.m.

Map 6.5: Stafford's Tigers vs. Russell's and Neill's Brigades (3:00 - 3:30 p.m.)

Stafford's Brigade in the center of Johnson's divisional line left its works and crashed through the dense vegetation toward the enemy. The men felt reassured knowing the sturdy Stonewall Brigade was advancing with them on their left. Within a short time the Louisianans encountered a line of blue soldiers about a quarter mile from their breastworks. Hat in hand, Stafford leaped his horse over a gully and urged his men to follow his lead. None of his men could ascertain the enemy's strength; all they could see was some blue on a low ridge ahead. It was about this time that a giant crash of muskets broke out on Stafford's left in the direction of Walker's Virginians. The firing, recalled a staff officer, was "the most tremendous roll of musketry it was ever my fortune to hear." Someone else called the sounds "almost deafening."[27]

Stafford's Brigade's impulsive charge out of its protective works took Brown's and Russell's men by surprise. The Unionists halted and inched backward a short distance before regrouping and holding their ground. A courier galloped up to Stafford and screamed, "They are coming!" pointing to the left. No enemy troops were visible in that direction, however, and Walker's Stonewall Brigade was fighting in that direction; Stafford discounted the information. He changed his mind, however, when a short time later a large mass of enemy troops tramped into Stafford's view and moved past his left flank into his rear. It was only then that Stafford realized the Virginians were no longer covering his left. The experienced brigadier reacted by ordering the small 1st Louisiana to bend back to face the new threat (No. 1).[28]

The orders were clear, but the response was not. Whether the 1st Louisiana commander misunderstood his orders or the men panicked is unclear, but the small group of fifty or so soldiers merely mobbed around Stafford. He responded by waving his sword in the air. Stafford realized these men were in no position to hold off a determined flank attack, so he ordered his brigade to begin filing right in an attempt to link with Steuart's Brigade (No. 2). Southerners would later describe the retreat as orderly, but a member of the 49th Pennsylvania (Russell's brigade) wrote that "we drove the rebels in our front like a lot of sheep." Sitting calmly astride his horse, Stafford patiently encouraged his troops and waited until the last man in the 1st Louisiana had flew past him before turning his horse to follow.

Just then a bullet slammed into Stafford and knocked him off his horse. The round entered just beneath his left armpit and severed his spine. In terrible pain, the general was carried back to the original line of works and laid under a tree, where the men realized Stafford was paralyzed. Reinforcements arrived and marched past Stafford's prone body (No. 3). They were the other brigade of Louisianans under Harry Hays. Although in agony, Stafford became animated when his former regiment, the 9th Louisiana, trotted past. According to Capt. William Seymour, a staff officer, "we passed poor Stafford, lying under a tree on the side of the road [Spotswood Road] suffering terribly from his wound. To those who stopped to express their sympathy, he spoke encouragingly, urging them to fight to the last and expressing a perfect willingness to yield up his life for the glorious cause in which he had so long borne arms."[29] Stafford lingered for three days before dying in Richmond. His death was said to have "cast a gloom over the city." President Jefferson Davis and his wife attended the funeral. Robert E. Lee reported that Stafford, was "mortally wounded while leading his command with conspicuous valor."[30]

Few firsthand accounts exist documenting the Federal side of this part of the fighting, and the few regimental histories available are also largely silent. For example, the historian of the 119th Pennsylvania wrote only that "The attack was repulsed, and the Federals withdrew to their own ridge, firing from tree to tree as they went." With this action over, Wright's men began entrenching. One Jerseyman wrote, "it was impossible to see the enemy; and though we peered into the thick woods, we were fighting invisible foemen. We soon began entrenching. Our men scraped the stones and earth before them as best they could, until spades were brought. All the time the enemy were sending a shower of bullets over and past us."[31]

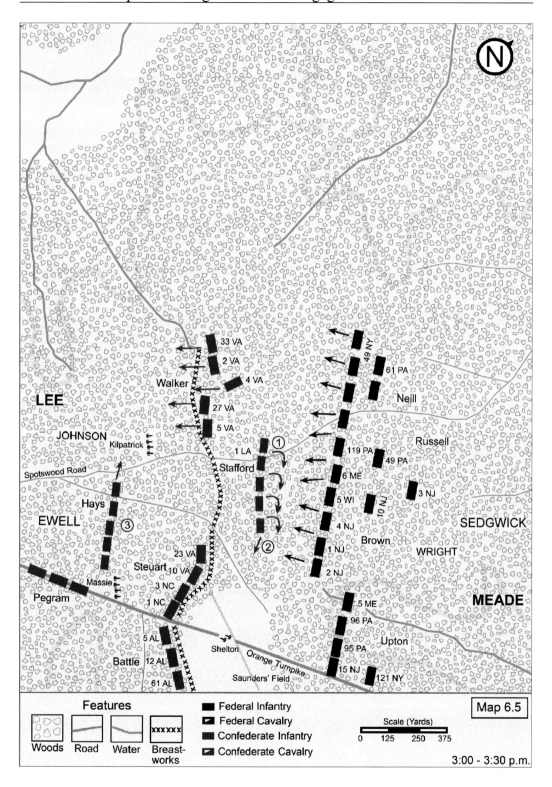

Features

Woods Road Water Breastworks

■ Federal Infantry
◪ Federal Cavalry
■ Confederate Infantry
◪ Confederate Cavalry

Scale (Yards)

0   125   250   375

Map 6.5

3:00 - 3:30 p.m.

Map 6.6: Hays' Louisianans Enter the Fight (3:30 - 4:30 p.m.)

While Walker and Stafford were waging their chaotic slugfest with Federal brigades under Neill, Russell, and Brown, help was on the way for the beleaguered Confederate left flank.

General Early had retained two of his three brigades in reserve along the Orange Turnpike under Harry Hays and Brig. Gen. John Pegram. His third under John Gordon had rushed south of the pike to plug the gap created when Jones' Virginians had spilled out of the line. With that threat ended, the two reserve brigades were sent north of the pike. Hays arrived first and formed on Walker's left. Pegram's men arrived later and extended the line northward (No. 1).

Both brigades had colorful histories. Hays' command was composed of tough Louisiana men who had earned distinction on many battlefields including Gettysburg, where they successfully stormed Cemetery Hill on the evening of July 2, 1863. Later that year, in November, the brigade was decimated during a night attack at Rappahannock Station and now numbered but 1,000 muskets. Pegram's Virginians had been under the command of eccentric William "Extra Billy" Smith, but when he left to become governor of Virginia, Pegram was assigned to command the brigade.

While Hays and Pegram were threading through the foliage behind the earthworks, some of Neill's Federals were running out of ammunition. This was especially true of the regiments on the right of his line. When the Rebels in their front retreated, these Federal did likewise, though in a more orderly manner. The historian of the 49th New York noted that his regiment "had to conform to the movement by swinging the men to the rear." It is possible Neill's entire line pulled back during this time.[32]

Hays, who had arranged his men in line on the far left of the line, received orders to advance in conjunction with Walker's Virginians, who were also in line on his right. Hays did as ordered, but when the Virginians didn't budge Hays sent an aide to find General Walker "to acquaint him with these orders." According to Captain Seymour, Walker "promised to accompany us; but for some unexplained reason, he failed to do so."[33]

Alone with both flanks in the air, Hays pushed his Louisiana troops eastward through the thickets, firing as they advanced (No. 2). Whatever Federals were in their front were easily driven, and after advancing about half a mile the Louisiana Tigers spotted a long line of enemy troops partially hidden in the pines. Russell's and Neill's brigades heavily outnumbered Hays. As they drew closer to the enemy, the foliage allowed for a fuller view of the Federal line. "We could see that the Federals outflanked us by the breadth of an entire brigade," wrote a staff officer. "Notwithstanding the danger of attacking such an extended line, our men were too eager and impetuous to be halted." The Federal foot soldiers patiently waited with leveled rifled muskets and when the Louisiana troops stepped within killing range fired a devastating volley that cut down scores of them.[34] A Rebel corporal recalled after the war that "the enemy opened a [devastating] broad-side into our ranks."

Frederick Bidwell of the 49th New York remembered Hays' Confederate attack. "The Confederates now charged, making a desperate effort to turn the Union flank, but without avail," explained Bidwell. "Again and again their columns rushed with great fury upon the Union lines, without being able to move them." According to the historian of the 61st Pennsylvania, the men "fired about 100 rounds apiece, their Springfield rifles getting too hot to hold where the hand came in contact with the barrel."[35]

The Federals could also see what they faced, including that both of Hays' flanks dangled in the air. Someone ordered an advance and the Federal troops moved forward (No. 3). "It soon became apparent that the enemy were rapidly closing in upon both of our flanks, with the intention of enveloping our Brigade," wrote Captain Seymour. General Hays decided the only way to save his command was to extricate his men, so he ordered his veterans to fall back. The already small brigade lost about 250 men. Many were killed and wounded, but large numbers were captured when they either refused to retreat or were unable to do so once they got the order. Seymour rationalized the losses by writing that "though we were driven back, this charge had the desired effect of staying the progress of Sedgwick's flanking movement." In reality, the Union attack had already ended.[36]

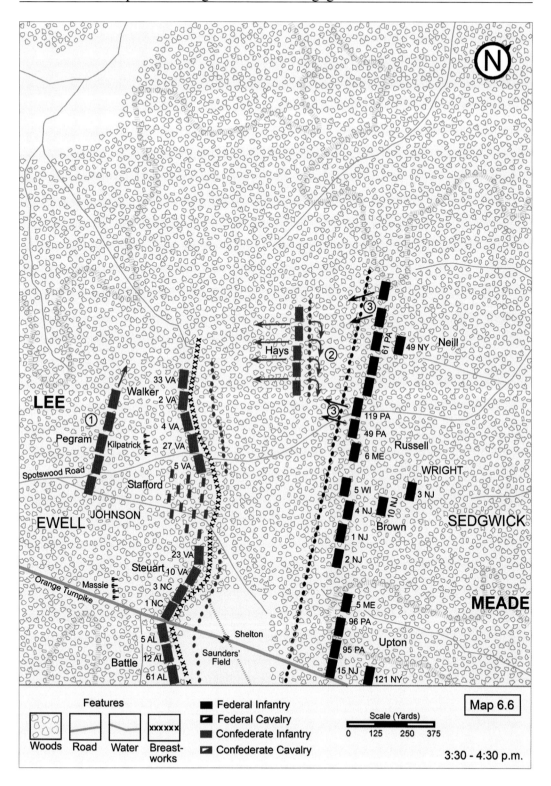

Features

Woods Road Water Breast-
                    works

Federal Infantry
Federal Cavalry
Confederate Infantry
Confederate Cavalry

Scale (Yards)

0   125   250   375

Map 6.6

3:30 - 4:30 p.m.

Map 6.7: Stalemate (5:00 - 5:30 p.m.)

Tumbling back to Ewell's reforming defensive line, Hays' men reorganized their ranks and counted their losses. The men immediately began throwing up crude breastworks with whatever tools they could find including axes, bayonets, cups, and bare hands. A VI Corps surgeon recalled that the "woods resounded with the strokes of their axes, as the busy workmen plied their labor within three hundred yards, and in some places less than one hundred yards of our line, yet so dense was the thicket that they were entirely concealed from our view." Although Hays' order of deployment is not clear, it appears that the 6th Louisiana was on the left flank.[37]

John Pegram's Brigade arrived about this time and slid into position on the left of the Louisiana men and also began entrenching. During the trek north Pegram's men passed hundreds of wounded and dying men and listened to the sound of the one-sided fight between Hays and Neill. The lonely feeling holding the flank of the army was alleviated to a small degree when company arrived in the form of the 37th Virginia from Steuart's Brigade. The regiment had remained behind to picket the Rapidan River. When it finally arrived on the battlefield that afternoon, Steuart was holding his front without issue and, with no space to accommodate the regiment, sent it north to augment Pegram's defensive line.[38]

The Union commanders were also reorganizing their front in preparation for additional combat. Upton's brigade remained on Wright's left, with its own left near the Orange Turnpike. Russell's brigade, followed by Neill's, extended the line northward (to the right). Brown's New Jersey brigade was by this time broken up, its units scattered all along Wright's defensive line. The lull in the action gave the Northern officers time to regroup and throw up breastworks of their own.[39]

The bloody fighting north of the Orange Turnpike that afternoon stripped many hundreds of men from their respective brigades but achieved absolutely nothing. A Union medical officer summed up the afternoon by writing:

the battle had raged furiously along the entire line. The rattle of musketry would swell into a full continuous roar as the simultaneous discharge of ten thousand guns mingled in one grand concert, and then after a few minutes, become more interrupted. . . . Then would be heard the wild yells which always told of a rebel charge, and again the volleys would become more terrible and the broken, crashing tones would swell into one continuous roll of sound, which presently would be interrupted by the vigorously manly cheers of the northern soldiers, so different from the shrill yell of the rebels, and which indicated a repulse of their enemies. Now and then the monotony of the muskets was broken by a few discharges of artillery, which seemed to come in as a double bass in this concert of death, but so impenetrable was the forest that little use was made of artillery, and the work of destruction was carried on with the rifle.[40]

Another VI Corps Federal officer boiled down the late afternoon actions of the men thusly: "the afternoon passed in a succession of charges and counter-charges. The shrill rebel yell alternated with the deep hurrah of our people, and neither side gained much, though we got a few hundred prisoners."[41]

As the day wound down, it became obvious that the effort to crush Ewell's Corps had failed. Part of the Confederate success can be attributed to Ewell's skillful handling of his units and their outstanding fighting abilities. Generals Meade and Grant contributed by ordering attacks before their subordinates were in position. Given the heavy Federal numbers, the odds that a coordinated Federal attack would have succeeded were high. Historian Gordon Rhea probably summed it up best when he wrote, "Warren had faltered because he had been forced to attack before Wright arrived. Wright had got nowhere because he, too, had been compelled to fight alone." Meade's style of not fighting until all was ready and Grant's approach of headlong assault with whatever force was available, were as incompatible as a pair of horses pulling in opposite directions.[42]

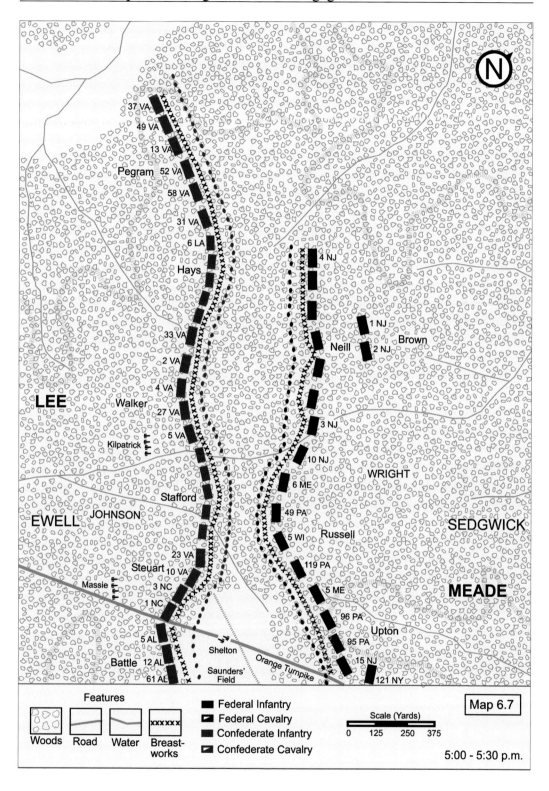

Features

Woods | Road | Water | Breast-works

Federal Infantry
Federal Cavalry
Confederate Infantry
Confederate Cavalry

Scale (Yards)
0   125   250   375

Map 6.7

5:00 - 5:30 p.m.

Map Set 7: The Attack is Renewed Against the Confederate Left

Map 7.1: Seymour's Brigade Reinforces the Federal Right (4:00 - 6:00 p.m.)

Though only hours into their first campaign, a schism between Generals Grant and Meade was present and growing. The contradictory orders issued by them and their respective staffs was a prominent example, as was Grant's desire to pitch into Lee whenever and wherever possible, and Meade's desire to organize the pieces of his army first before attacking. The handling of Brig. Gen. James Ricketts' division brought their differences into stark relief.

Meade's orders to General Ricketts (part of Sedgwick's VI Corps) were to "hold the roads leading from the enemy's line to our right flank." Grant, however, had other ideas. When it was obvious the attacks against Ewell's Corps had failed, Grant unilaterally ordered Ricketts' division—without Meade's knowledge—to march to the battlefield when Maj. Gen. Ambrose Burnside's IX Corps' leading elements crossed the Rapidan River at Germanna Ford.[1]

Caught between two contrary directives, Ricketts decided to sit tight and not act on either (No. 1). It would be three long hours before Ricketts finally began moving toward the battlefield. The stalemate ended about 4:15 p.m. when Meade sent General Warren the following message: "General Ricketts has been ordered to report to you and will be up immediately."[2]

Ricketts' two-brigade division finally approached Warren's sector after 4:00 p.m. Splitting his brigade, he sent Brig. Gen. William Morris' south to join Warren's V Corps east of Saunders Field, halting about a mile from the Wilderness Tavern (No. 2). His second brigade under Brig. Gen. Truman Seymour broke off and marched to the right to reinforce Sedgwick's VI Corps, well north of the Orange Turnpike. Guided by one of Meade's aides, Seymour's men slogged their way toward the right side of Neill's brigade to extend the army's right flank (No. 3). Once Ricketts' men were up, Meade looked for a way to launch yet another attack against Ewell. With two corps finally in place, he reasoned, a coordinated attack could break through and collapse the Confederate front. This seems even more likely because Warren's signal stations reported Rebels moving away from Ewell toward the Confederates right where A. P. Hill's Third Corps was fighting Brig. Gen. George Getty's division (VI Corps). What Meade did not know was that the moving body was Maj. Gen. Cadmus Wilcox's fresh division of Hill's own corps moving back south to the Orange Turnpike, and not a weakening of Ewell's front (No. 4).[3]

Perhaps Meade's most immediate problem was how to deal with two of his corps commanders. Neither Warren nor Sedgwick showed any inclination to resume the offensive. The irascible Andrew Humphreys, Meade's chief of staff, was in no mood to brook defiance from Warren. The aide was still frustrated by Warren's unwillingness to attack across Saunders Field earlier in the afternoon. Now, Humphreys demanded a concerted attack with Sedgwick. Warren received a message from Humphreys about 4:00 p.m. stating, "the major-general commanding [Meade] directs that you make dispositions to renew the attack if practicable." This same communication, which noted that Maj. Gen. Winfield Hancock's II Corps and Getty's division were attacking farther south along the Orange Plank Road, ended with a statement intended to preempt Warren from arguing that he needed reinforcements: "you will have one brigade of Ricketts,' besides Robinson and Crawford, who have not been engaged."[4]

Planning for the intended attack went went awry when the intense fighting along the Orange Plank Road forced Brig. Gen. James Wadsworth's men to shift their front and attention to their left and move out in that direction (No. 5; see Map 10.1). Wadsworth's withdrawal (which also removed some of the V Corps' most seasoned and effective officers and men) left Warren with only three divisions with which to make the attack.[5]

Sedgwick was also weighing the best way to strike during this time. He learned that the Rebels had entrenched opposite his entire line, which suggested Ewell's front was probably spread thin. Rather than throw his men through bad terrain against earthworks, Sedgwick decided to find Ewell's left flank and turn it, while striking the front. The coordinated action would roll up Ewell's entire line. The arrival of Seymour's brigade provided the troops needed to strike the Confederate flank, but the regiments had seen but limited action and their commander had a checkered past.[6]

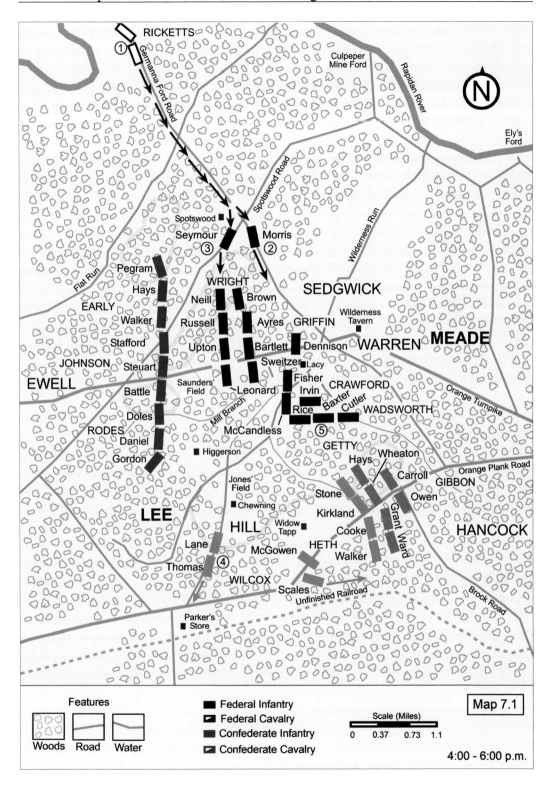

Map 7.1

4:00 - 6:00 p.m.

Map 7.2: Seymour's Brigade Advances to the Attack (6:00 - 7:00 p.m.)

Once on the right flank, General Seymour threw out a skirmish line to ascertain the enemy's position. A West Point veteran, Seymour had fought well from the Seven Days' Battles through the 1862 Maryland Campaign, but his luck turned when his attack against Battery Wagner in South Carolina was repulsed in 1863, and as the head of the Department of Florida he was soundly defeated at the battle of Olustee in February 1864. The new arrivals fanned out and replaced the 4th New Jersey's skirmish line. Seymour deployed his brigade in two lines: the first line consisted of the 6th Maryland on the left and the 110th Ohio on the right, with the 122nd Ohio on the left, the 138th Pennsylvania in the center, and 126th Ohio holding the right of the second line. As Seymour recalled the situation, "an attack was [to be] made along the line, and under the impression that we overlapped the enemy's left, and that he was weak in our front, from the detaching of troops to his right, I was to swing around so as to take him in flank." One of the veterans described the maneuver as a "left half-wheel."[7]

Seymour put the experienced Col. J. Warren Keifer of the 110th Ohio in charge of the first line, and likely remained himself with the second. After an hour passed without word from his skirmishers, who were to have developed the Confederate position, Seymour lost his patience and ordered his entire brigade forward. He ordered Keifer to "press the enemy, and, if possible, outflank him upon his left." About 6:00 p.m., the order "Forward, men!" rang out and the "slight swinging motion" immediately began as the brigade stepped off in search of the Rebel left flank.[8]

The first line, Keifer noted in his report "charged forward in gallant style." The Unionists tramped through perhaps half a mile of vegetation with enemy bullets zipping through their ranks with increasing frequency. They stopped in their tracks, explained Seymour in his report, because "the enemy was soon found, but sheltered by log breast-works and extending so far beyond me that his fire came upon the prolongation of our line with the greatest severity."[9]

Rather than coming in on Ewell's exposed left flank, Seymour's regiments faced the left end of Hays' Brigade and the right and center of Pegram's Virginia command. The latter brigade had arrived earlier in the afternoon to shore up and extend Ewell's left flank and they began throwing up breastworks as soon as they reached their destination. Captain James Bumgardner of the 52nd Virginia recalled that "the men worked very reluctantly, they were tired and grumbled a good deal." They had built breastworks before, but the Yankees were never foolhardy enough to attack them. Captain Samuel Buck of the 13th Virginia recalled that "dead trees were rolled together and soon every man and officer was busy throwing up dirt on the logs with tin plates, hands." By the time the sunlight was fading the men had thrown up a respectable line of works three to four feet high, and whatever grumbling was still being offered ended when a long line of blue soldiers stepped into view. The vegetation was so dense the Rebels were surprised by the sudden appearance of Seymour's line of battle. Pegram ordered his men to hold their fire until the enemy had stepped to within 20 paces.[10]

Colonel Keifer was just as shocked by the unpleasant discovery stretching across his front as anyone under his command. Once his leading line stopped, he conferred with Col. John Horn of the 6th Maryland about what to do. Both had expected Neill's brigade to advance with them to protect their left, but Neill was nowhere to be found. Keifer sent word back to Seymour that "the advance line of the brigade was unsupported upon either flank, and that the enemy overlapped the right and left of the line, and was apparently in heavy force, rendering it impossible for the troops to attain success." The reply surprised Keifer: attack as ordered. Hoping his superior had not yet received his message and was prompting him out of ignorance, Keifer waited. When a second messenger arrived with the same order, Keifer had no choice but to wave his men forward.[11]

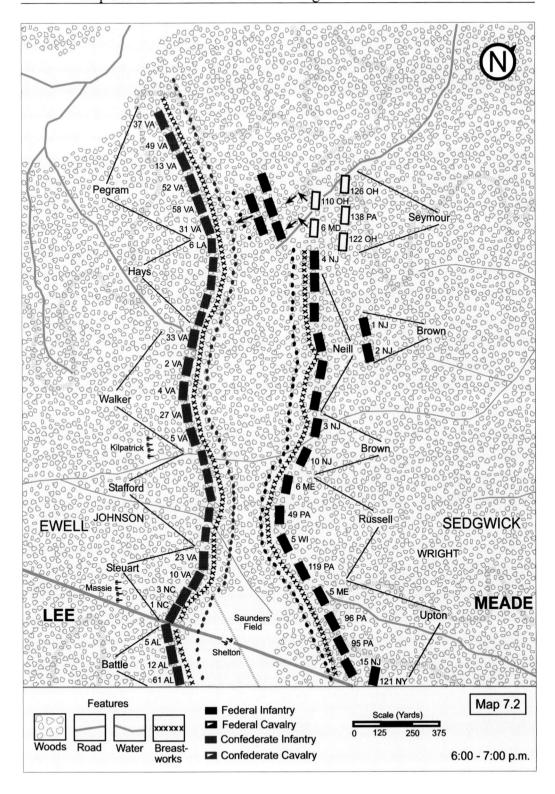

N

37 VA
49 VA
13 VA
Pegram
52 VA
58 VA
31 VA
6 LA
Hays

126 OH
110 OH
138 PA
6 MD
122 OH
Seymour
4 NJ

33 VA
2 VA
4 VA
Walker
27 VA
5 VA
Kilpatrick
Stafford
JOHNSON
EWELL
23 VA
Steuart
10 VA
Massie
3 NC
1 NC
LEE
5 AL
Battle   12 AL
61 AL

Neill
1 NJ
Brown
2 NJ

3 NJ
Brown
10 NJ
6 ME
49 PA
Russell
5 WI
119 PA
5 ME
96 PA
95 PA
15 NJ
121 NY

Saunders'
Field
Shelton

SEDGWICK
WRIGHT
MEADE
Upton

Features

Woods	Road	Water	Breast-works

Federal Infantry
Federal Cavalry
Confederate Infantry
Confederate Cavalry

Scale (Yards)
0   125   250   375

Map 7.2

6:00 - 7:00 p.m.

Map 7.3: The Renewed Union Offensive North of the Turnpike Fails (7:00 - 8:00 p.m.)

When Seymour's men closed on Pegram's breastworks, the Virginians opened fire with devastating effect. One Confederate officer noted that he "never heard anything like it except at Gain's [sic] Mill. The enemy did not advance a step after we gave them the first volley." Keifer essentially agreed with that assessment when he noted the advance suffered under "the most terrible fire from the front and flanks. It was impossible to succeed." Keifer never forgot the horror of that May 5 assault. "The presence of a general officer in authority, or an intelligent staff officer representing him, would have averted the useless slaughter," he noted in his memoirs in a not-so-subtle stab at Seymour.[12]

The Rebel small arms fire shredded Keifer's two regiments. A member of the 13th Virginia recorded that "nothing could stand that fire and in a few moments the blue line swayed and fell back but only to be replaced by another and another . . . each one melted as did the first; death was in every shot and we held fast to our works." The 6th Louisiana on Hays' left joined in the killing, and "poured [volleys] into the thick Yankee columns as they advanced." The losses were horrendous. In just minutes the 6th Maryland lost 180 men and the 110th Ohio lost 113. Amongst the losses were Colonel Keifer, who fell with a shattered arm, and General Pegram, who took a bullet to his leg while sitting on his horse. Colonel John Hoffman of the 31st Virginia assumed command of the brigade.[13]

A Confederate ventured out after dark to check on Seymour's position and was "astonished at the number of dead and wounded lying on the ground. I never saw dead and wounded lying more thickly anywhere. Evidently the rear lines stood, after the front lines fell back out of sight and our fire was into a packed mass which retired slowly under it."[14]

The grand assault was supposed to include all of Sedgwick's command, and not just Seymour's isolated brigade. Exactly what happened depends upon who you believe. The reason behind Neill's misfire is unclear. There is no doubt the brigade assisted in repulsing Hays' earlier assault, but whether it participated in Seymour's charge is in dispute. Historian Edward Steere argued that at least some of his regiments charged ahead on Seymour's left. A close reading of the primary references, however, suggests Neill's men may never have left their defensive positions, from which they laid down a steady fire in the direction of the distant Confederate line. For example, the historian of the 61st Pennsylvania, one of Neill's regiments, wrote, "one feature of this fight was disagreeable in the extreme, and that was in many places the rebels could not be seen, and it was impossible to tell what effect the 61st's fire had on their antagonists."[15]

On Neill's left, the brigades of Russell, Brown, and Upton appeared content to hunker down behind their crude breastworks and periodically fire in the direction of the Rebel line. Farther south, the men of Warren's V Corps also remained in their defensive works; their commander convinced that a renewed attack would simply kill and wound more men to no advantage. The lone exceptions seem to have involved the 90th Pennsylvania (Baxter's brigade) and 39th Massachusetts (Leonard's brigade). Led by Col. Peter Lyle of the former regiment, these men slipped over their breastworks on the edge of Saunders Field and headed for the two abandoned artillery pieces sitting alone on the turnpike. One of the soldiers recalled that "quite a number of the brigade were killed and wounded crossing the road; the missiles would come with a swi-s-s-s-h, killing the air full." Fully exposed in the open field, the veterans knew a hopeless mission when they saw one. Lyle also realized the folly of the venture and called his men back to the safety of their works.[16]

Night and Rebel lead put an end to the fighting along Sedgwick's front. Both sides, however, worked to improve their breastworks. Captain Buck of the 13th Virginia waxed poetically about the horrors of the day: "Shall that terrible night ever be erased from my memory, the terrible groans of the wounded, the mournful sound of the owl and awful shrill shrieks of the whippoorwill; the most hideous of all noises I ever heard on a battle field after firing had ceased. The loneliness is of itself sufficient, and these birds seemed to mock at our grief and laugh at the groans of the dying. Pen and words fail to describe the scene."[17]

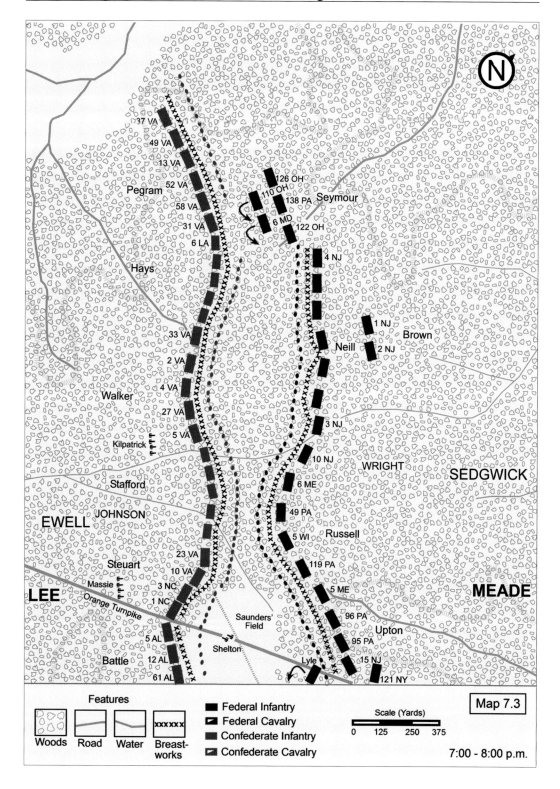

Features

Woods Road Water Breastworks

■ Federal Infantry
◢ Federal Cavalry
■ Confederate Infantry
◢ Confederate Cavalry

Scale (Yards)

0   125   250   375

Map 7.3

7:00 - 8:00 p.m.

Map Set 8: The Orange Plank Road: Getty and Heth Battle for the Crossroads (May 5)

Map 8.1: Getty Prepares for Action (3:30 - 4:00 p.m.)

Brigadier General George Getty quick-stepped his Federal division from the Wilderness Tavern to the critical intersection of Orange Plank Road and Brock Road (see Map 3.9). His infantry arrived just in time to see Brig. Gen. James Wilson's cavalry division flying past, followed by a persistent skirmish line that signified the advance of Maj. Gen. Henry Heth's Division. While Heth deployed his brigades, Gen. Robert E. Lee, together with Maj. Gens. Jeb Stuart and A. P. Hill, conversed at the Widow Tapp farm. Without warning, a group of Federal skirmishers walked warily out of a line of trees. Lee and his generals slowly turned their mounts and moved away, and the enemy foot soldiers followed suit in the opposite direction.[1]

With Ewell fully engaged to the north and A. P. Hill's Third Corps heading east along the Orange Plank Road toward the Brock Road, Lee knew he desperately needed Lt. Gen. James Longstreet's First Corps (which was on its way from Gordonsville) to reach the field. Hill mustered but two divisions; his third under Maj. Gen. Richard Anderson had been left behind to guard the Rapidan River crossings. As Heth's Division approached the intersection with Brock Road, Lee pulled Maj. Gen. Cadmus Wilcox's Division from its rear position and dispatched it north in an effort to connect with Ewell's exposed right flank. None of the Confederate generals in this sector realized Heth's men were on a collision course with Getty's VI Corps division, and that the entire II Corps was marching hard to support him.[2]

Lee's orders to Heth were reminiscent of those he had issued on July 1, 1863 that had triggered the battle of Gettysburg: move forward to the Brock Road intersection "without bringing on a general engagement." Ten months earlier Heth did not heed Lee's orders, and his infantry became heavily engaged. This time Heth was more cautious, halting his men to send an aide to Lee with information that "the enemy are holding the Brock Road with a strong force.

Whether I can drive them from the Brock Road or not can only be determined by my attacking with my entire division, but I cannot tell if my attack will bring on a general engagement or not." Heth explained that he was "ready to try" if Lee agreed. To the north, Wilcox left two brigades at the Chewning farm and continued north with his other two brigades in an effort to find Ewell's flank.[3]

Heth, meanwhile, deployed Brig. Gen. John R. Cooke's Brigade with its right just below the road and the balance stretching above it, with Col. John Stone's brigade extending Cooke's line farther left. Heth's remaining brigades under Brig. Gens. Henry Walker and William Kirkland remained in reserve. Lt. Col. William Poague's artillery battalion supported Heth. Though he wrote "the men had no protection other than that afforded by the growth of timber in their front," other reports discuss the erection of breastworks.[4]

Almost a mile to the north, General Getty prepared for the combat he knew was about to break out. Orders had arrived about 3:15 p.m. that his "attack up the Plank Road must be made at once." According to Lt. Col. Theodore Lyman, who carried these orders, Getty was "very cool—evidently did not think it good strategy to attack till more of the 2d Corps was up." Orders were orders, however, so he sent his own aides to have Brig. Gens. Henry Eustis and Frank Wheaton prepare for the battle that would begin here in earnest about 4:15 p.m. Getty seemed to believe that a short delay of half an hour would allow the II Corps to join in the attack or at least come up. Wheaton's and Eustis's brigades formed Getty's right by deploying along the Brock Road above the Plank Road, and to their left below the Plank Road, Col. Lewis Grant arranged his Vermont brigade. Getty was shy one brigade; Brig. Gen. Thomas Neill's command had been sent to reinforce the far right of the Federal line well above the Orange Turnpike.

Once deployed, Heth's left flank overlapped Getty's right, but the opposite was true on the other end of the line, where the Federal's overlapped the Rebels. The two divisions were about the same size (Getty's mustered 6,700 and Heth's 7,200), but Maj. Gen. Winfield Hancock's II Corps was rapidly approaching. Its arrival would heavily tip the balance in favor of the Federals. A section of Capt. R. Bruce Ricketts's Battery F, 1st Pennsylvania Light Artillery, under Lt. Charles Brockway, dropped trail at the intersection.[5]

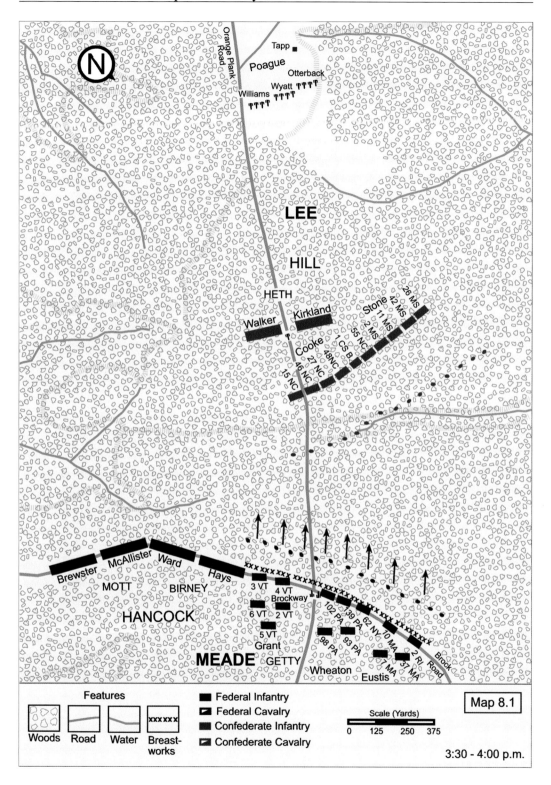

Orange Plank Road

Tapp

Poague

Otterback

Wyatt

Williams

LEE

HILL

HETH

Walker   Kirkland

Cooke

Stone   42 MS   26 MS
11 MS
2 MS
55 NC
1 CS B
48 NC
27 NC
46 NC
15 NC

Brewster   McAllister   Ward
MOTT   BIRNEY   Hays

HANCOCK

3 VT
4 VT
Brockway
6 VT   2 VT
5 VT
Grant
102 PA   39 PA   62 NY   10 MA   2 RI Road
98 PA   93 PA
7 MA   37 MA
Brock

MEADE   GETTY
Wheaton
Eustis

Features

Woods	Road	Water	Breast-works

◼ Federal Infantry
◪ Federal Cavalry
◼ Confederate Infantry
◪ Confederate Cavalry

Scale (Yards)
0   125   250   375

Map 8.1

3:30 - 4:00 p.m.

Map 8.2: Getty Attacks Heth
(4:00 - 4:15 p.m.)

Getty's men unhappily received the order to scale their makeshift defenses and head for the enemy line. The three-brigade line moved forward in tandem but soon became disordered in the thick tangled brush. Regiments veered this way and that, often running into one another. Confusion in the ranks is often accompanied by potentially dangerous consequences, and that was certainly the case for the 3rd Vermont holding the division's extreme left. These Vermonters drifted so far to the left that both of their flanks were exposed to attack (No. 1). The ranks became "more and more crooked and disordered" as the division advanced, admitted a staff officer.[6]

The division's skirmish line, meanwhile, engaged its counterparts after an advance of perhaps one-eighth of a mile. Colonel Grant, on Getty's far left, reported the Rebels did not field much of a skirmish line in front of his brigade, but this was not true in front of Eustis's brigade, where Colonel Stone had established an abundant and active skirmish line across the front of his Mississippians and North Carolinians. The disparity was the result of an initial dearth of Rebel foot soldiers south of the Orange Plank Road. When he realized his right flank was imperiled, Heth quickly responded by sending Walker's Brigade from its reserve position to form on Cooke's right (No. 2).[7]

"Now came the holocaust," recalled Lt. Col. John Lewis of the 5th Vermont. Without the impediment of a skirmish line and realizing the enemy had closed to within 100 yards, Walker's Virginians, Alabamians, and Tennesseans unleashed a staggering volley. "Hundreds of our men fell at that first volley, but it was immediately returned," reported Grant with some exaggeration. "By some misapprehension of orders," wrote Heth in his report, "Walker's Brigade, instead of prolonging Cooke's line, and holding the line, so prolonged, charged the enemy, driving him back." Once they had blunted Grant's assault, Walker's men returned to their intended position and threw up light breastworks during the short lull that followed.[8]

General Wheaton, commanding the brigade in the center of Getty's division, recalled that his men advanced to within 50 yards of the enemy line when both sides blazed away at each other for nearly an hour (No. 3). The combatants could not see each other, but bullets zipped through the vegetation and knocked men to the ground. According to Grant, "the men aimed at the wall of fire and smoke in our front." These were extraordinary conditions, even for veterans. "The distance between the two lines was so short," Grant continued, "that under ordinary conditions we could have charged upon the enemy with the bayonet before giving time to reload. But a bayonet charge under these conditions was nearly impossible. A line could advance only slowly and with great difficulty even when unopposed. Anything like a dash upon the enemy was simply out of the question."[9]

The terrain on this part of the field confounded the attackers and reduced their effectiveness. Heth's line, explained Grant, "was partially protected by a slight swell of ground, while ours was on nearly level ground." There was nothing the boys in blue could do except fall to the ground to protect themselves from the storm of bullets. A staff officer recalled that after a short time on the ground, a bugle would sound "Advance" and the men would instinctively rise to comply—only to be mowed down by Rebel bullets. Grant's men were hopelessly pinned down.[10]

Wheaton's and Eustis's brigades were experiencing much the same thing on the right of the Orange Plank Road. Wheaton's men were up against Cooke's North Carolinians, while Eustis faced off against Stone's (Davis's) Brigade. Wheaton noted that "the fighting was incessant, and the loss proportionately great, but the enemy was too strongly posted and could not be dislodged." Berea Willsey, a new recruit in the 10th Massachusetts, part of Eustis's command, recalled the reaction of the veterans: "they say they never saw anything like it. It seemed to come from two or three lines of battle, one above the other, a perfect hail of balls. . . . Men dropped like the leaves of autumn."[11]

Federal rounds were also causing havoc within Rebel ranks. A young soldier in the 11th Mississippi recalled that "the musketry was fearful, men fell on every side and our newly issued ANV battle flag received it share of bullets."[12]

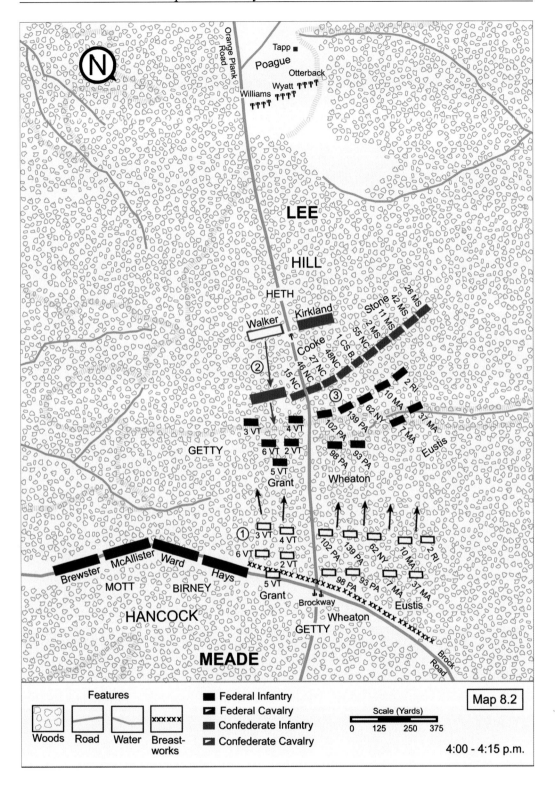

Tapp

Poague

Otterback

Wyatt

Williams

LEE

HILL

HETH

Walker   Kirkland

Cooke   Stone 11 MS 42 MS 26 MS

2 MS

55 NC

1 CS B.

48 NC

27 NC

46 NC

15 NC   2 RI

10 MA

62 NY   37 MA

139 PA   7 MA

3 VT   4 VT   102 PA   Eustis

GETTY   6 VT 2 VT   98 PA 93 PA

5 VT   Wheaton

Grant

3 VT   4 VT   102 PA   139 PA   62 NY   10 MA   2 RI

6 VT   2 VT   98 PA   93 PA   7 MA   37 MA

Brewster McAllister Ward Hays   5 VT   Eustis

MOTT   BIRNEY   Grant

Brockway   Wheaton

HANCOCK   GETTY

MEADE   Brock Road

Features

Woods Road Water Breast-works

■ Federal Infantry
▱ Federal Cavalry
■ Confederate Infantry
▱ Confederate Cavalry

Scale (Yards)

0   125   250   375

Map 8.2

4:00 - 4:15 p.m.

Map 8.3: Getty and Heth Fight to a Stalemate (4:15 - 5:00 p.m.)

Worried about his isolated 3rd Vermont, which had veered well to the left, and the growing casualties being collected by his front line troops, General Grant ordered up his second line, composed of the 2nd and 6th Vermont. Chewed up by Rebel lead, the 4th Vermont pulled back (No. 1). The 2nd Vermont, which included soldier Wilbur Fisk, moved ahead to replace the 4th Vermont. Fisk recalled the enemy "poured their bullets into us so fast that we had to lie down to load and fire." Moving into their new positions was not easy, and some of the men had to literally crawl forward to reach it. Grant had one last reserve regiment—the 5th Vermont—but did not want to commit the regiment until it was absolutely necessary. Everyone in Getty's division was convinced they were being thrown in to fight all three of A. P. Hill's divisions. The heavy gunfire and sheets of bullets seemed to support their contention. To help compensate, Getty ordered up Charles Brockway's section of Ricketts's battery about 4:30 p.m. (No. 2). The men had a duty to attack and fight hard until Hancock's reinforcements arrived. Heth's Confederates knew that holding their position was critical to the army's safety. A soldier in Stone's Brigade claimed their line "never wavered. The officers and men of the regiment realized that the safety of the army depended upon our holding the enemy in check until the forces left behind would come up, and there was a fixed determination to do it, or to die."[13]

On Getty's right, just above the road, Wheaton's first line (composed of the 102nd Pennsylvania, 139th Pennsylvania, and 62nd New York) was maintaining its position but ammunition was becoming scarce. Like Grant to the left, Wheaton called up his second line, the 93rd and 98th Pennsylvania to replace his first (No. 3). Fresh troops, however, did not change the fact that there was no viable way to close with Cooke's North Carolinians. The fresh Keystone troops fell to the ground and fired from that position as best as possible.[14]

The situation was even grimmer on Wheaton's right, where Eustis's brigade battled Stone's Mississippians and North Carolinians (No. 4). Stone's line significantly overlapped Eustis's right flank. Elisha Hunt Rhodes recorded in his diary that his 2nd Rhode Island was "on the extreme right of the line and were harassed by a flank fire from the enemy." Unable to sustain this pounding, the veteran regiment, which was one of the first to see action at First Bull Run, fell back. The historian of the 10th Massachusetts observed that the 2nd Rhode Island "could not stand the terrible ordeal to which it was subjected, and gave way in some confusion, and then a most destructive fire was poured into the right flank of the Tenth [Massachusetts]. Men dropped like leaves of autumn." The veteran also noted that "all this time not an enemy could be seen. Perfectly covered by the woods and abattis, we could only fire at the direction of the flashes of light, and puffs of smoke from their rifles, while our men could undoubtedly be very distinctly seen by them." The 10th Massachusetts, which was now the only regiment remaining on Eustis's first line, was running out of ammunition.[15]

General Eustis compensated for these problems by moving the 37th Massachusetts forward to occupy the position of the recently departed 2nd Rhode Island, which was reforming in the rear. He also replaced the 10th Massachusetts with the 7th Massachusetts. All these fresh troops could do was to hug the ground and pray the deadly havoc would quickly end (No. 5).[16]

Once the second line troops were engaged without changing the fortunes of the attack, Getty's front was in serious jeopardy. The general summed up the situation by stating in his report that the enemy's lines "outflanked the division, and though forced back some distance in the center, they held in the main their ground and repulsed every attack." Fortunately for him and his embattled division, two II Corps infantry divisions were up and ready for action.[17]

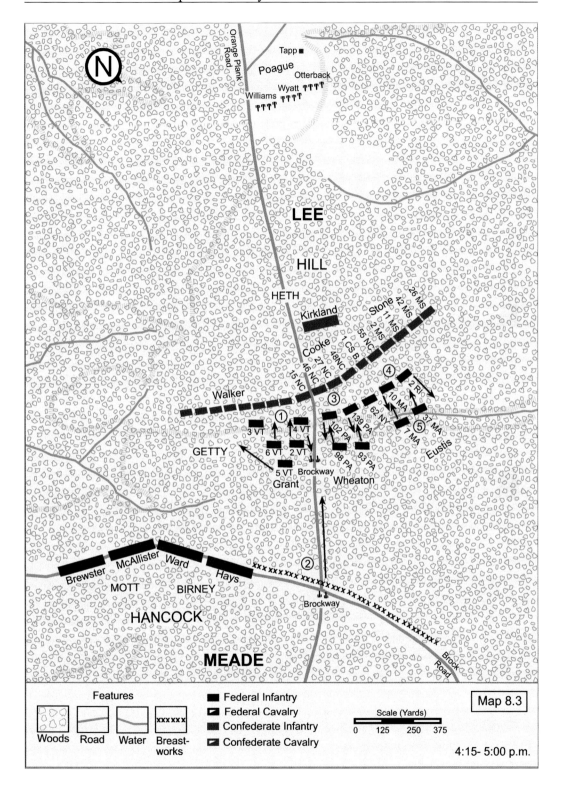

Map 8.3

4:15- 5:00 p.m.

Map 8.4: Heth Counterattacks
(5:00 - 5:45 p.m.)

Getty's men were supported during their attack by a section of Ricketts's battery under Lt. Charles Brockway, which had been ordered to advance his two guns several hundred yards along the Orange Plank Road about 4:30 p.m. (No. 1). While Getty's men were protected by the tangles of the Wilderness, Brockway's men were fully exposed. The guns opened on the Rebels with percussion shells but the initial impact was primarily felt by the men of the 4th Vermont. "The first shot killed eight men on the left of my company," wrote one disgusted Vermonter. "A few more shots were fired when some soldiers got back to the guns and told the gunners what was being done." Set straight, the gunners found their range and targets. One soldier observed that the guns were "used constantly all afternoon throwing grape and canister, and were double and treble shotted with this deadly material. This no doubt killed hundreds of our enemies and added a base to the treble of musketry in the terrible music of the afternoon."

In an effort to answer Ricketts's guns, a 12-lb. Napoleon from Poague's Battalion galloped up, unlimbered, and opened fire with canister, tearing splinters from the wheels and knocking down a horse and man from time to time (No. 2). "Here was a tangible enemy," Brockway wrote, "and we all breathed freer in seeing something definite to fire at." One of Brockway's shots exploded a caisson and killed or wounded several Rebel gunners and their horses. The duel, such that it was, lasted but a few moments before the Federal guns overwhelmed their lone Southern counterpart. "Our percussion shell was superior and their artillery was soon withdrawn," was Brockway's matter-of-fact analysis.[18]

While Brockway's guns held their ground, Getty's assaults were thrown back time and again. About an hour after the infantry attack began, Cooke's Tar Heels climbed out of their lines and charged Getty's front. Little is known about this action from the Confederate point of view (No. 3). Getty noted that the attack occurred about 5:30 p.m.: "The enemy charged and forced back our lines some 50 yards, when they were checked and repulsed." When they spotted the Confederate infantry surge, Brockway's gunners opened with solid shot and shifted to canister when the enemy closed on their position. The giant shotgun rounds cleared Brockway's front. Enemy soldiers who survived on either side of the blast radius in the dense vegetation made for the guns. With their horses down, the cannoneers could not remove the guns and hand-to-hand combat broke out around them. According to Getty, the enemy "planted a color at one of the guns of Ricketts' section." Federal infantry on either side of the road from Wheaton's and Grant's brigades surged inward, overwhelmed the Confederates, and forced them from their prize.[19]

While this localized drama was unfolding, the fighting up and down the line continued unabated. "An army of drummers beating the long roll could not have made a more continuous sound," recalled a Confederate sharpshooter. Getty grimly noted that "it was with the utmost difficulty and only by the most stubborn fighting and tenacity that the division could hold its ground, outnumbered and outflanked as they were by the whole corps of A. P. Hill." (Getty's reaction when he later learned that his men had only faced Heth's Division is unknown.)[20]

By this time most of the officers in Grant's brigade were down and his losses exceeded 1,000 men. Wheaton's and Eustis's brigades suffered comparable casualties. The returns they eventually filed were for the entire battle, but the commander of the 102nd Pennsylvania on the second line of Wheaton's brigade reported losing 119 men on May 5. Confederate losses from this portion of the Wilderness struggle are not known, but were almost certainly much lower because they had fought primarily behind their breastworks or other improvised defensive barriers.[21]

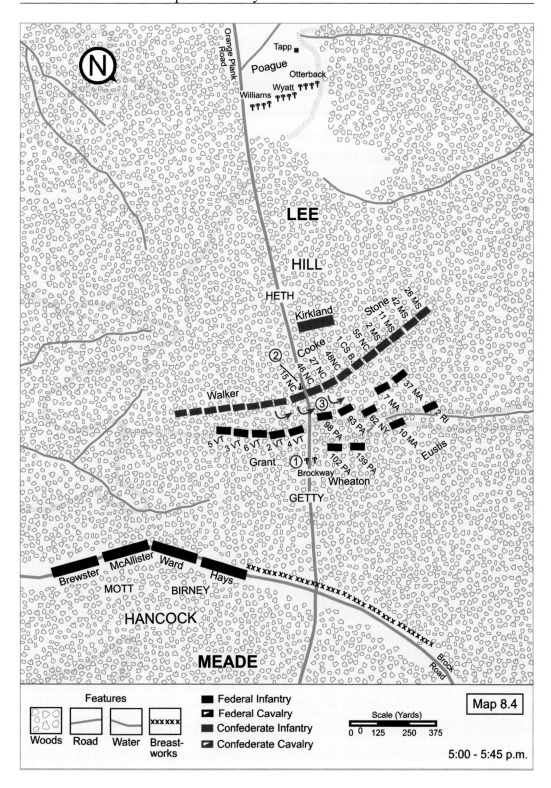

Features

Woods   Road   Water   Breast-
                        works

■ Federal Infantry
▱ Federal Cavalry
■ Confederate Infantry
▱ Confederate Cavalry

Scale (Yards)

0 0   125   250   375

Map 8.4

5:00 - 5:45 p.m.

Map Set 9: Getty is Reinforced on the Orange Plank Road (May 5)

Map 9.1: The II Corps Approaches (9:00 a.m. - 2:30 p.m.)

Major General Winfield Hancock, arguably the best combat general in the Army of the Potomac, led what was probably the army's finest fighting unit. His II Corps, comprised of four veteran divisions totaling 27,000 officers and men, was also the Federal army's largest. Three of its four division commanders were first class field officers, while the fourth, new to division leadership, had yet to prove his abilities at that distinguished level. Rumor had it that if President Lincoln deemed a change in army command necessary, Hancock would be the man to replace George Meade.

The II Corps began the day at Chancellorsville with its destination Shady Grove Church on Catharpin Road (No. 1). When the Army of Northern Virginia was discovered moving eastward, however, the combative Hancock was ordered at about 9:00 a.m. to halt at Todd's Tavern, at the juncture of the Brock and Pamunkey roads, "until the matter develops." The head of his corps was already two miles beyond the tavern when the order arrived. At 11:40 a.m., another dispatch arrived from Meade to "move up the Brock road to the Orange Court-House plank road." Meade issued the order about 10:30 a.m., and it took more than an hour to reach Hancock (No. 2). The historian of the II Corps, using a healthy dose of "what if thinking," believed a better solution would have been for the Corps to continue its march, which would have carried it beyond A. P. Hill's right flank and rear. Instead, Hancock guided his men into a position for a head-to-head clash with Hill's Corps.[1]

Stretched out for miles along the Pamunkey Road, countermarching the head back to the Brock Road intersection proved a time-consuming and frustrating task. The van had already reached the Catharpin Road and its rear was still near Chancellorsville, meaning the Brock Road bisected the long column clogged with wagons and artillery on a road lined with heavy brush and trees along both sides. Hancock, as able a manager as any who wore blue, immediately began sorting out the marching mess. Another message penned at noon at Army headquarters was also on the way to Hancock, but he would not receive it until early afternoon: "The enemy's infantry . . . are moving down it [Orange Plank Road] in force. . . . General Getty's division has been sent to drive them back, but he may not be able to do so." Hancock was to "move out the plank road toward Parker's Store, and supporting Getty, drive the enemy beyond Parker's Store, and occupy that place and unite with Warren on the right of it." Meade's order was based on the mistaken assumption that Hancock was within supporting distance of Getty.

Once he had his men moving north along the Brock Road, Hancock rode ahead to confer with Getty. He had not yet received the noon dispatch. In an effort to clarify his role, Hancock sent his chief of staff, Lt. Col. Charles Morgan, to find Meade and obtain additional orders. Stamped at 1:30 p.m., the order reiterated the noon directive: "Attack them; Getty will aid you." Morgan did not return with these orders until 2:40 p.m., about the same time the original noon order arrived. Hancock immediately responded by indicating that his lead elements were moving into position on Getty's left, but that "the ground over which I must pass is very bad—a perfect thicket."[2]

The day's march proved frustratingly difficult for the men. The roads were narrow, not in the best condition, and filled with troops and wheeled vehicles, all of which required frequent detours. One Massachusetts soldier recorded in his diary, "Marched round more everywhere in all sorts of directions, frequent halts." The fact that they were marching toward combat without the accustomed cavalry screen did not help matters.[3]

Major General David Birney's division led the II Corps, followed by divisions under Brig. Gens. Gersham Mott and John Gibbon. Hancock's last division under Brig. Gen. Francis Barlow brought up the rear, shy Col. Paul Frank's brigade, which had been left behind to hold the intersection of Brock and Pamunkey roads. The intersection was a mess. "Numerical superiority was seen here at its worst," quipped one of the Federals. "There were more troops than could be utilized, almost a huddle."[4]

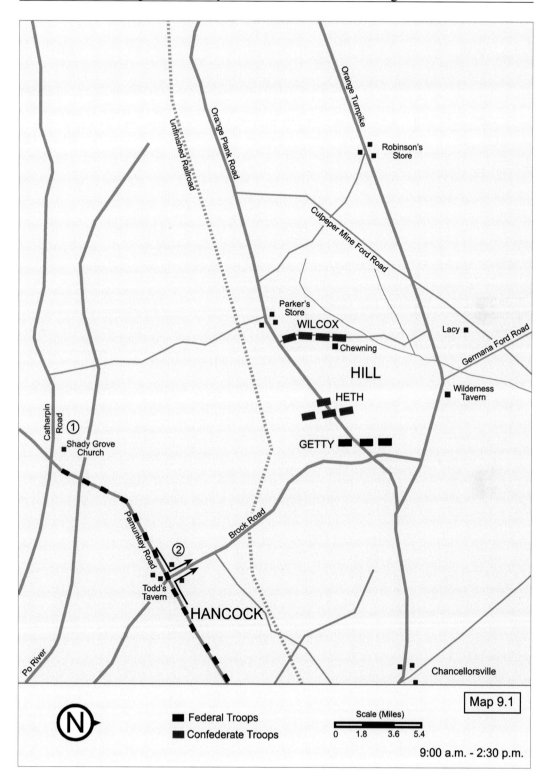

Map 9.1

Federal Troops
Confederate Troops

Scale (Miles)

0   1.8   3.6   5.4

9:00 a.m. - 2:30 p.m.

Map 9.2: The II Corps Begins Reinforcing Getty (2:30 - 4:30 p.m.)

David Birney's two-brigade division was the first division of the II Corps to approach the Orange Plank Road and Brock Road intersection (No. 1). Once there, Birney formed his men in two lines along the Brock Road and had them construct breastworks. Gershom Mott's division followed and its two brigades formed on Birney's left. Hancock knew that Meade wanted an attack and he prepared his men accordingly. He wrote to Meade at 3:00 p.m. that he would make the attack with "two of my divisions . . . as soon as troops can get into position. I shall keep one division on their left and keep one division in reserve." Another message arrived from Meade at this time telling Hancock to support Getty with "one division on his right and one division on his left, the others in reserve." Dictated from afar, the order threw a wrinkle into Hancock's deployment and necessitated a more complex and time-consuming movement. Hancock complied and Birney and Mott marched to the right to comply with the new orders.

According to the II Corps' historian, "General Hancock found General Getty anxious to make an early attack, in consequence of repeated instructions from General Meade, who addressed similar urgent representation to Hancock himself upon his arrival on the ground; but the latter was strongly desirous of getting his whole corps up and in hand before beginning the fight. It is no small matter to bring up twenty-five to thirty thousand men by a single road and form them for battle." Getty launched his men toward Heth's Division at about 4:15 p.m. All three of Getty's brigades soon found themselves in trouble, and requested support from Hancock, who was pleased to oblige.[5]

Perhaps because of Mott's relative inexperience, Hancock put Birney in charge of both divisions. When Col. Lewis Grant, just south of the Orange Plank Road, requested support, Birney complied by sending three veteran regiments (141st Pennsylvania, 40th New York, and 20th Indiana, right to left) from Brig. Gen. J. Hobart Ward's brigade (No. 2). The 141st Pennsylvania headed toward the right of Grant's line held by the 4th Vermont while the latter two regiments (40th New York and 20th Indiana) struggled to reach the left side of Grant's line, where the 5th Vermont was having difficulty maintaining its position.[6]

Lewis Grant was one of the army's finest brigade commanders and was always looking for an advantage against his opponent. As the battle was raging, he approached Maj. Charles Dudley, now commanding the 5th Vermont on his left flank. Grant "called his attention to the fact that the position of the enemy in his front was less protected than it was in front of the rest of the brigade and asked him if he could, with the support of the regiments in his rear, break the enemy line." Dudley briefly pondered the question and replied, "I think we can." When Grant asked the same of the two new supporting regiments, "The men rose with a cheer and answered, 'We will!'"

The three regiments (the 40th New York and 20th Indiana, with the 5th Vermont between them) rushed forward and immediately began taking casualties but closed with the Rebel works with surprising speed. The 55th Virginia of Walker's Brigade apparently occupied a weak position along an otherwise strong line. Hand-to-hand combat broke out near the breastworks and the Hoosiers captured the 55th's flag. All of the men, reported Grant, "advanced in good style, and the enemy partially gave way." The Virginia regiments on either side of the beleaguered 55th regiment, however, turned their guns on the exposed flanks of the attacking column, driving it back outside the line. When chaos and confusion coursed through the ranks of the 20th Indiana and 40th New York, their officers wisely counseled calm and ordered the men to halt and lie down, which they did. Major Dudley did the same with his Vermonters (No. 3). One of the New Yorkers wrote after the war that "the action continued [for] three hours with the most intense fury and with repeated and desperate assaults, but the enemy met us at every point of our line and delivered volleys which were bravely encountered."[7]

While Ward's three regiments were moving to reinforce Grant's Vermont brigade, the rest of his brigade and all of Mott's division prepared for combat. To better reinforce and support the right side of Getty's embattled division, Birney directed his second brigade under Brig. Gen. Alexander Hays to move via the right flank to get into position (No. 4).[8]

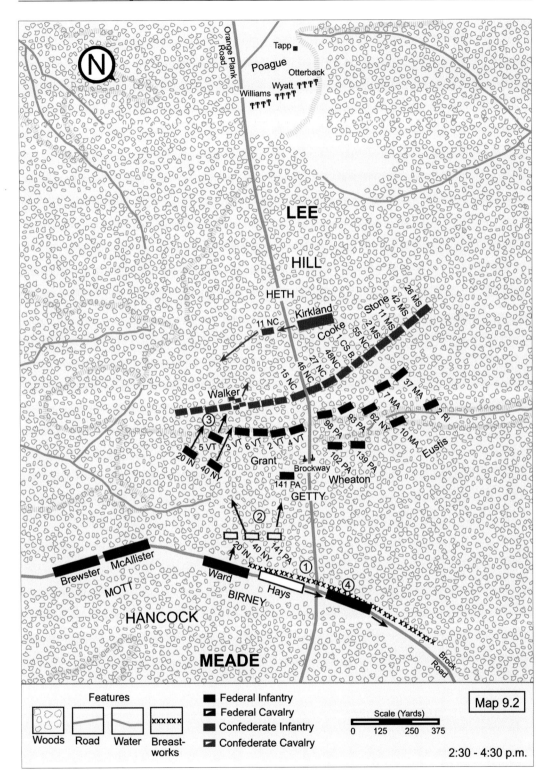

Map 9.2

2:30 - 4:30 p.m.

Map 9.3: Three II Corps Brigades Enter the Fray (4:30 - 5:30 p.m.)

Harry Heth's bloodied men were still holding, but the might of the II Corps was about to fall upon them. To help bolster the right of his line, Heth detached the 11th North Carolina from Kirkland's Brigade and sent it through the thickets (see Map 9.2).

More reinforcements were on their way to bolster Getty's beleaguered division as three more II Corps brigades readied themselves to advance off the Brock Road into the dense thickets. Mott's two-brigade division approached the Brock/Orange Plank intersection about 4:00 p.m. Colonel Robert McAllister's brigade, holding the division's right, was composed of nine regiments hailing from Massachusetts, New Jersey, and Pennsylvania. Mott's second brigade, under Col. William Brewster, formed on McAllister's left and was composed of eight regiments from Massachusetts, New York, and Pennsylvania. The Federals began throwing up breastworks along the former road.

"We had no entrenching tools," wrote a man in McAllister's brigade. "Hastily throwing together what rails and fallen timber we could find, we covered them as best we could with dirt, using our bayonets to loosen the earth, and cups, tin-plates and hands to throw it up. Quite a respectable line of defense against infantry was soon constructed, but it would have been useless had it been possible for the enemy to have brought artillery against it." A Massachusetts soldier recalled that "old trees were rolled up and cleared of their branches . . . new ones cut down as fast as the few axes procurable could be made to do service; dirt, stones, and rocks thrown up in rear; and in an hour's time a passable line of earthworks was completed."[9]

Before they had a chance to rest, orders arrived to form into line of battle. McAllister wrote in his report, "over breastworks we went, but the dense thicket of underbrush made it impossible for the troops to keep their proper distance." His brigade's front line was deployed from right to the left as follows: 8th New Jersey-5th New Jersey-11th New Jersey-7th New Jersey-16th Massachusetts-1st Massachusetts. The 115th Pennsylvania and 6th New Jersey held the second line. The 26th Pennsylvania and part

of the 5th New Jersey were thrown out on the skirmish line. Little is known about Brewster's deployment except that it was probably in two lines, as were most of the rest of the brigades. Both of Mott's brigades advanced toward the left flank of Grant's Vermont brigade.[10]

As it had elsewhere, the dense vegetation and undulating terrain created havoc in the advancing ranks. "The men went forward, however, in very irregular lines, going round the trees, creeping under the branches, and keeping as closely together as they were able," recalled a soldier in the 1st Massachusetts. Captain Thomas Thompson of the 7th New Jersey in the middle of McAllister's first line reported that after tramping about 300 yards "through a dense jungle of scrub oak," the line had to halt to reform. This simple exercise was almost impossible because the regiments on its right and left overlapped nearly the entire New Jersey command. Thompson ordered his men back "a few paces" to reform his line, and then continued his advance. Brewster's Excelsior Brigade added to the confusion by drifting rightward, crowding into McAllister's brigade. According to Lt. Col. John Schoonover of the 11th New Jersey in the middle of McAllister's first line, "it was impossible to form a line of battle in the space I occupied." By detaching three companies, Schoonover was able to form something that resembled a line of battle. As the brigade approached the front, its right apparently overlapped Grant's Vermont brigade, probably because Grant had redeployed his brigade into one line, which had stretched it to the left.[11]

While Mott's division headed for Getty's left flank, Brig. Gen. Alexander Hays' brigade left the works on the right of the intersection and headed for Getty's right flank. The brigade was aligned in two lines with the first composed from right to left as follows: 17th Maine-63rd Pennsylvania-57th Pennsylvania-4th Maine. The second line was composed of the 3rd Michigan, 105th Pennsylvania, 93rd New York, and 5th Michigan. Hays, one of the most capable brigadiers in the Union army, had led a division that helped repulse the Gettysburg attack on July 3 known as the Pickett-Pettigrew-Trimble Charge.[12]

Whether Hays' brigade stepped off at the same time as Mott's division is unknown, but we do know it had a longer distance to traverse to reach Getty's right flank.

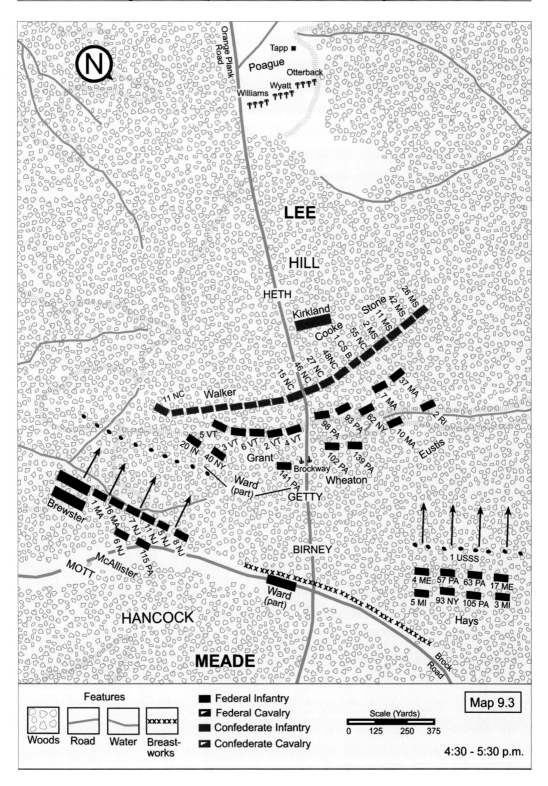

Map 9.3

4:30 - 5:30 p.m.

Map 9.4: Mott's Division is Defeated
(4:30 - 5:30 p.m.)

Mott's division continued advancing toward Heth's extended Confederate front with Brewster's brigade on the left and McAllister's on the right. Colonel McAllister ordered his skirmishers to accelerate their movement, to no avail. Exasperated, McAllister ordered the main brigade line to push past his skirmishers, an act that immediately invited deadly volleys from Walker's Confederates. The Rebels, recalled a Massachusetts soldier, "opened a double volley, which sent thousands of bullets crashing through the woods into their faces. This fire, so sudden, so unexpected, and so deadly, was returned in but a feeble and scattering manner." Regimental control was already evaporating.[13]

"To my astonishment," wrote the capable and experienced McAllister in his after-action report, "the line began to give way on the left [Brewster's]." Why Brewster's brigade unceremoniously broke and headed to the rear has never been adequately explained (No. 1). McAllister surmised its unsteady service was related to "the fact that a large number of troops were about to leave the service," and no one wanted to die within a month of their discharge. The 11th New Jersey's Lt. Col. John Schoonover (McAllister's brigade) suggested another reason: "We had been in position but a short time, when a few volleys of musketry were heard to the extreme left and rear, and immediately the left of the line . . . commenced falling back in confusion." If correct, this suggests that some of Walker's men (and perhaps the 11th North Carolina) may have left their earthworks to strike Brewster's exposed left flank, which like a domino effect triggered a stampede of one regiment after another.[14]

Whatever the reason, Brewster's rout spread like a contagion. "My left regiment—First Massachusetts Volunteers—and then regiment after regiment, like a rolling way, fell back and all efforts to rally them short of the breastworks [on Brock Road] were in vain," McAllister explained (No. 2). According to Schoonover, "the troops seemed panic-stricken, and for what reason I was never able to imagine. They acted as if their only safety was in the works which they had so hastily erected." McAllister's second line, composed of

the 115th Pennsylvania and part of the 6th New Jersey, may have held a bit longer. The commander of the 7th New Jersey, in McAllister's front line, recalled that his routing command "passed over the second line of battle" to regain the breastworks. It is doubtful the two regiments remained long on their own once all their comrades had fled the scene.[15]

General Hancock never mentioned the stampede of Mott's division in any of his reports, but Colonel McAllister admitted in a letter to his wife that "our division did not do well." The effort to bolster Getty's left and crush Heth had failed.[16]

While Mott's attack was falling apart, Hays' brigade was tramping westward to take up a position next to Eustis's brigade on the right side of Getty's Union line (No. 3). Hays also had orders to, if possible, stretch farther right to find the V Corps to the north. In addition to the typical difficulties traversing thick underbrush, the men had to deal with their commander's explosive temper. John Halsey of the 17th Maine described Hays as "tearing and swearing. His English was exceedingly vigorous and confusingly copious…General Hayes, who always had a select litany of imprecations to dispense, was cursing one and damning the other."[17]

The 1st U.S. Sharpshooters, Hiram Berdan's crack unit, led Hays' advance. At first the front was eerily quiet. "[We] could see no one but the one on our right & left [and] hear no noise except what we made ourselves wading through the brush," recalled a sharpshooter. The 17th Maine on the far right of the first line drifted to the right.[18] It was about now, when the attack below the Orange Plank Road had failed, that the remaining regiments in Ward's brigade left the Brock Road works and marched west to reinforce and support Mott's beleaguered division (No. 4).[19]

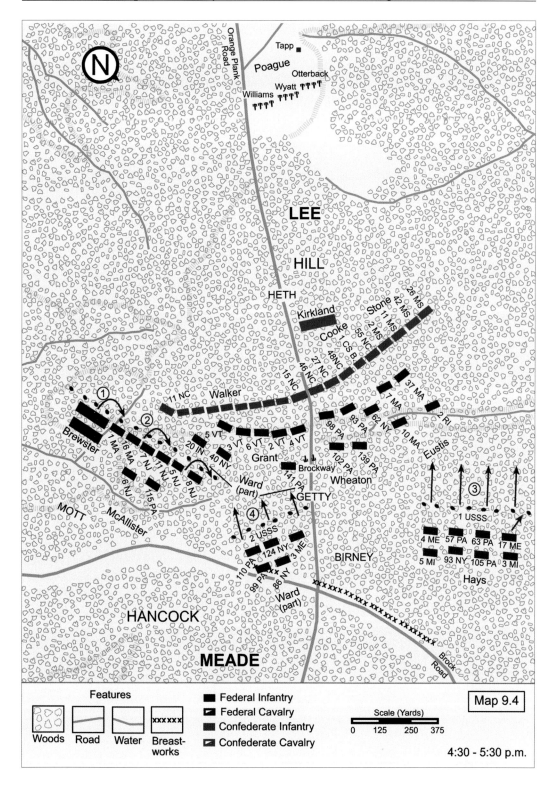

Map 9.4

4:30 - 5:30 p.m.

Map 9.5: Hays' and Ward's Brigades
Attack Heth's Division
(4:30 - 5:30 p.m.)

The eerie silence in front of the 1st U.S. Sharpshooters on Hays' skirmish line ended when distant gray figures were spotted through the foliage. A smattering of gunfire broke the silence as the skirmishers continued advancing. Suddenly, "a reb line of battle rose out of the fringe and let us have it full in the face. Talk about astonishment, or surprise, or dismay," recalled one of the sharpshooters years later. Hays' losses mounted as he drove his brigade lines of battle up to relieve his battered skirmish line. Major Charles Mattocks of the 17th Maine, who was in temporary command of the regiment's sharpshooters, pulled his new command back some distance. When he learned some of the men on his right were still engaged, the major rode in that direction, only to be captured with some of his men.[20]

Hays' men couldn't see any enemy soldiers in front of them. "Only by the flash of the volleys of the forming lines can we know where is posted the enemy with which we are engaged," wrote a New Yorker in the 93rd regiment. "The woods light up with the flashes of musketry, as if with lightning, while the incessant roar of the volleys sound like the crashing of thunderbolts."[21] When he finally found Eustis's exhausted regiments, Hays halted his men so Eustis's troops could fall back to allow the rein-forcements to take their positions. The incessant small arms fire prompted Hays to order his men to lie down. Samuel Dunham of the 63rd Pennsylvania recalled that "the faster we fired the hotter they poured it into us." Despite the deadly situation, General Hays rode up to the front and stopped a few yards from the 63rd's regimental flag. This was his old regiment, and he likely realized the men were in need of some encouragement. Hays was in the process of drawing his sword when a bullet struck him in the temple. The mortally wounded general pulled on the reins, causing the horse to rear and throw him to the ground. Several Pennsylvanians placed their general in a blanket and carried him to the rear, where he died a few hours later. Colonel John Crocker of the 93rd New York assumed command of the brigade.[22]

The historian of the 3rd Michigan described the tenacity displayed by both sides that late May afternoon: "The slaughter is fearful, men fall on every side, and my flag is receiving its share of bullets. Charge after charge is made by each side. Sometimes we drive the enemy, and then they rally and drive us, until both sides are almost exhausted, and night puts an end to our first day's struggle." Another eyewitness noted that "brave men are falling like autumn leaves, and death holds high carnival in our ranks." The opposing lines often fought only 40 yards apart. "One by one Hays' disjointed elements went into the merciless ambuscade of Stone's Mississippi riflemen," wrote modern historian Edward Steere. "Here, in a few frightful minutes, was the bloodiest shambles of the Wilderness." The stationary Confederates enjoyed the initial benefit of surprise and stability, but the superb discipline of Hays' veterans kept them in line and their return knocked an impressive number of Southerners off their feet.[23]

As was usually the case, the number of losses suffered by a specific unit depended in large part on their location in the line of battle. For example, the 57th Pennsylvania in the first line sustained losses of 22 killed, 128 wounded, and three missing for a total of 153 men. The 93rd New York behind it lost just two killed and 30 wounded.[24]

While Hays' men were slugging it out with Stone's Brigade, the remainder of Hobart Ward's brigade continued its approach to help stabilize the left of the line now that Mott's division was heading for the rear.[25]

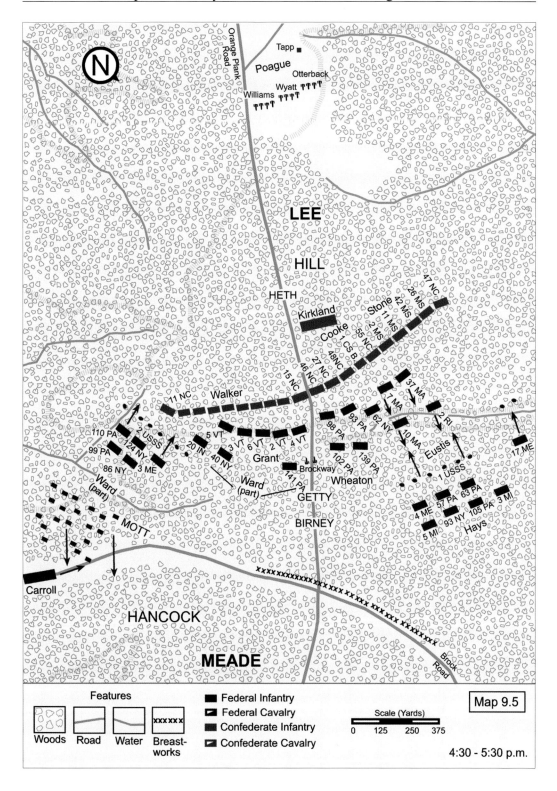

Map 9.5

4:30 - 5:30 p.m.

Map 9.6: Hancock Feeds More Troops into the Fight (4:30 - 5:30 p.m.)

With the 2nd U.S. Sharpshooters on the skirmish line, the remaining five regiments of Ward's brigade had advanced to reinforce its three sister regiments that had been already been sent to the front (No. 1). The brigade went into action to the left of Grant's brigade about where Mott's division had entered the combat.[26]

Scores of men from Mott's division, most of them from McAllister's brigade, were still full of fight and joined Ward's regiments on the firing line. According to the historian of the 124th New York (the Orange Blossoms), the enemy fired a "wild storm of bullets, which rattled through the brush, pattered against the trees, and hissed and whistled through the air." As with the other units fighting in the gloomy Wilderness, "we could seldom see the enemy's battle-line because of the denseness of the foliage; but powder flashes from the opposing lines often told that they were but a few yards apart."[27] Amos Bean of the 3rd Maine recalled that the Rebels saw his regiment being relieved and charged his line "with such a yell or screech as no pack of wolves ever made." The Maine troops fixed bayonets and charged, driving Walker's Virginians back into their defenses.[28]

II Corps commander Winfield Hancock had planted himself throughout the fight at the intersection of the Orange Plank and Brock roads, where a stream of reports—none of them good—reached him (No. 2). "Sir! Gen. Getty is hard pressed and his ammunition nearly out," was one, and a bit later, "Sir! Gen. Mott's division is broken, and is coming back." Hancock ordered an aide to return to Getty and "tell him to hold on, & Gen. Gibbon will be up to help him!" To another aide he yelled, "Tell him [Mott] to stop them!" To the mob of men returning from the front, Hancock roared, "Halt here! Halt here! Form behind this rifle pit." Within a short time, the two divisions under Birney and Mott (or half of his corps) had arrived and been fed into the battle with little to show for it.

The most immediate problem facing Hancock was just to the right of the Orange Plank Road, where Wheaton's exhausted brigade of Getty's division was being pushed steadily back by Heth's Confederates. The attackers, likely all North Carolinians, were steadily pushing closer to the critical intersection screaming at the tops of their lungs. John Gibbon's three brigades would soon be up, but rather than wait, Hancock ordered his aide to "go to Gibbon and tell him to come up on the double-quick!" Just as the aide galloped off, a cloud of dust appeared to the south and the head of Col. Samuel Carroll's brigade representing the tip of Gibbon's column appeared (No. 3).[29]

Brigadier General Alexander Webb's brigade arrived next. It was about this time that Gibbon reported "the enemy was close to the Brock Road, firing rapidly upon our disordered troops." Webb's men halted, faced left, and threw volleys into the approaching Confederates, halting them in their tracks and sending them to the rear (No. 4). Brigadier General Joshua Owen's brigade was also now up and Gibbon ordered it to the right of Webb's brigade (No. 5).[30]

On the Confederate side of the line, no one yet realized the full extent of the Federal juggernaut being assembled against them. Getty's attack brought with it about 6,000 men, or roughly the same strength as Heth's Division. Hancock's II Corps added another 27,000 fresh troops, but their attacking power had thus far been muted because of piecemeal attacks through heavy terrain. Somehow Heth's four brigades had managed to not only hold their own, but launch periodic spoiling counterattacks against various parts of the Federal line. Their ammunition, however, along with their energy, was rapidly dwindling. Heth had already committed his reserve brigade under Brig. Gen. William Kirkland's, splitting it up and sending its regiments to wherever they were most needed (No. 6). Two regiments ended up in the middle of the divisional line (26th and 44th North Carolina) where they replaced some of Cooke's regiments, and one on each flank of the division (11th and 47th North Carolina).[31]

Help, however, was not far away and would arrive in the form of Maj. Gen. Cadmus Wilcox's Division. Wilcox's men, it will be recalled, had followed Heth east down the Orange Plank Road, before being sent north (to their left) in an attempt to link up with Ewell's Corps. Within minutes it would be their turn at the front (No. 7).[32]

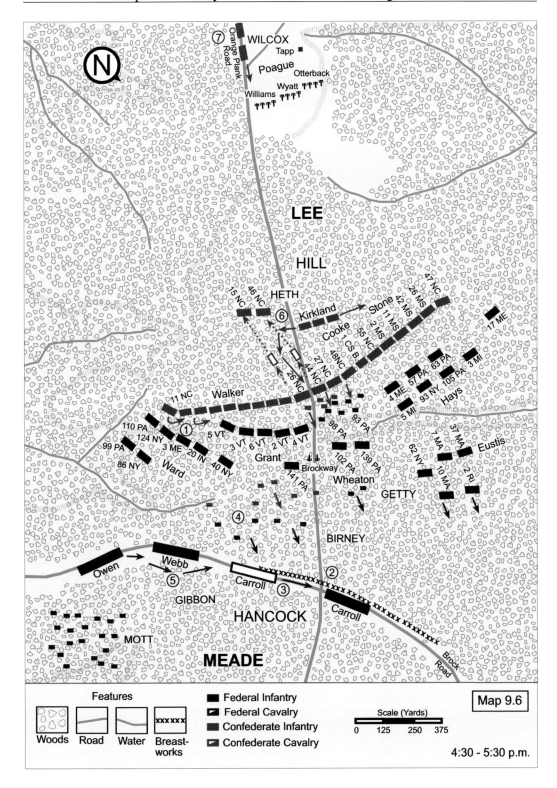

Map 9.6

4:30 - 5:30 p.m.

Map Set 10: Wilcox's Division and the Rest of Hancock's II Corps Enter the Fight (May 5)

Map 10.1: Wilcox's Division Approaches Heth's Line (2:30 - 5:30 p.m.)

The yawning two and one-half mile gap between A. P. Hill's Corps and Richard Ewell's Second Corps gravely concerned General Lee, so much so that he halted Maj. Gen. Cadmus Wilcox's Division near the Widow Tapp field about 2:30 p.m. to send it northward along a narrow road toward the Chewning farm in an effort to link up with Ewell's right flank (No. 1). Lee did this almost certainly without knowing that Maj. Gen. Winfield Hancock's II Corps was approaching the Orange Plank Road to reinforce Brig. Gen. George Getty's division, which was now attacking Maj. Gen. Henry Heth's Division.

Brigadier General James Lane's Brigade led Wilcox's column, followed by brigades under Brig. Gens. Edward Thomas, Alfred Scales, and Samuel McGowan. When they reached the Chewning farm about 4:00 p.m., Wilcox deployed McGowan and Scales there and rode with Thomas and Lane toward Ewell's right (No. 2). McGowan and Scales at the Chewning farm rested and were led in prayer by chaplains. J. F. J. Caldwell, an officer with the 1st South Carolina (McGowan), recalled, "on the left thundered the dull battle; on the right the sharp crack of rifles gradually swelled to equal importance; above was the blue, placid heavens; around us a varied landscape of forest and fields, green with the earliest foliage of spring; and here knelt hirsute and browned veterans shriving for another struggle with death."[1]

Wilcox met Maj. Gen. John B. Gordon near Higgerson's Field, and they discussed the fluid combat situation (No. 3). Gunfire from the Orange Plank Road ended the conversation. Within a short time an aide from General Lee arrived with orders for Wilcox to retrace his steps and return to the Orange Plank Road to reinforce Heth. Short of troops, Lee had to choose between connecting his wings by filling in the gap, or supporting Heth's embattled division. Wilcox left orders for Thomas and Lane to reform and head back, and rode back to the Chewning farm. The farm was devoid of troops

because McGowan and Scales were already marching back to the Plank Road to reinforce Heth (No. 4). "In the midst of the prayer," South Carolinian Caldwell recalled, "a harsh, rapid fire broke out right on the plank-road . . . the order was issued to face about and forward; and then we went, sometimes in quick-time, sometimes at the double-quick, towards the constantly increasing battle. The roar of musket became continuous, augmented occasionally by the report of cannon, and always by the ringing rebel cheer."[2]

V Corps signalmen operating near Maj. Gen. Gouverneur Warren's headquarters at the Lacy home observed Wilcox's movement about 5:30 p.m. and sent a message to General Meade: "a heavy column of enemy's infantry moving in a field this side of the Plank Road and going toward General Hancock." Grant and Meade assumed these troops belonged to Ewell's Corps, sent by Lee to reinforce A. P. Hill in the struggle along the Orange Plank Road. Two major orders flew out of Army headquarters. First, Generals Warren and Sedgwick were instructed to renew their attacks against Ewell's weakened Rebel line straddling the Orange Turnpike. Second, Brig. Gen. James Wadsworth's division, reinforced by Brig. Gen. Henry Baxter's brigade of Brig. Gen. John Robinson's division, was ordered south to strike what was believed to be Heth's left flank (No. 5). Wadsworth's men had been roughly handled earlier in the afternoon, but several hours of rest and reforming around the Lacy house had them again ready for action. Wadsworth's strike force set out through the thick vegetation about 6:00 p.m.[3]

Back at Lee's headquarters at the Widow Tapp farm, the army leader closely monitored the action and plotted his next move. Stretched thin, darkness could not come soon enough. He knew Lt. Gen. James Longstreet's two divisions, along with Maj. Gen. Richard Anderson's Division (Hill's Corps) would likely arrive during the night to stabilize the front and perhaps tip the balance of power. Wilcox sent word of enemy troops massing near the Lacy house, possibly for a move against Hill's left flank. While this may have disturbed Lee, he knew Wilcox's Division was on hand to reinforce Heth. Like his Union counterparts Meade and Grant, Lee believed that if Federal troops were heading south, the Union right was being denuded of manpower. As a result, both army commanders sought to exploit a nonexistent opportunity along the Orange Turnpike.[4]

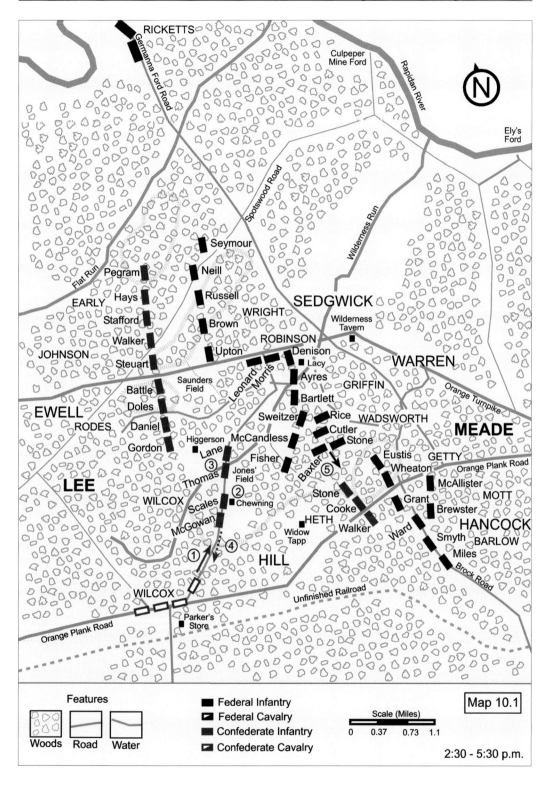

Features

Woods   Road   Water

■ Federal Infantry
◤ Federal Cavalry
■ Confederate Infantry
◤ Confederate Cavalry

Scale (Miles)
0   0.37   0.73   1.1

Map 10.1

2:30 - 5:30 p.m.

Map 10.2: Reinforcements Move into the Plank Road Sector (5:30 - 6:30 p.m.)

Both sides viewed the fighting in the Orange Plank Road sector as increasingly important. Harry Heth's lone extended Confederate division had sustained attack after attack by three Union divisions. Although exhausted and almost out of ammunition, it remained firmly in place. Lee and A. P. Hill, however, knew there were precious few troops on the army's right flank, Longstreet would not be up any time soon, and only a single additional division (Wilcox) was available to maintain the front.

The Federal troops on the front lines threw up breastworks whenever they could, and several of Heth's regiments launched preemptive attacks against when local tactical opportunities beckoned. In one example, a soldier in the 11th North Carolina (Kirkland's Brigade) recalled the prophetic words of Col. William MacRae of the 15th North Carolina (Cooke's Brigade). When MacRae learned that the 11th was preparing to attack part of Ward's brigade (No. 1), the colonel "sneered sardonically: 'Go ahead; you'll soon be back.' And sure enough we did. We struck as he had done the Federal line behind intenchments, from which in vain we tried to dislodge it, and recoiled lying down in turn. . . . I fancy he smiled sardonically then."[5]

On the Union side, Hays' and Ward's relatively fresh brigades of Birney's division were widely separated on the opposite flanks of the line, but Grant's and Wheaton's brigades of Getty's division in the middle of the line had shot their bolt and were at their breaking point.

Help was also on the way for these four embattled brigades. Colonel Samuel Carroll's brigade (Gibbon's division) was ordered out of the breastworks lining Brock Road and ordered to head west to relieve Wheaton with the Orange Plank Road guiding its left flank (No. 2). According to the 1st Delaware's historian, the brigade was aligned in three lines: the first composed (left to right) of the 10th New York and 12th New Jersey, the second of the 14th Connecticut, 1st Delaware, and 108th New York, and the third line of the 7th West Virginia, 14th Indiana, and 8th Ohio. A few minutes later Brig. Gen. Joshua Owen's brigade (Gibbon's division) repeated the process south of the road

(No. 3) bound for Grant's position. The men of the 152nd New York, who had never heard shots fired in anger, stepped out of the woods and soon trod over and around "the bodies of those who had fallen before." The men "forced a passage through the thick undergrowth, becoming separated and considerably mixed up."[6]

Grant, who knew reinforcements were coming, began pulling his men away from Heth's blazing defensive position (No. 4). The regiments on his right (2nd and 4th Vermont) were the first to fall back. Before Grant could order his remaining regiments back, however, the Confederates launched a bayonet charge. "So sudden was the enemy's advance," recalled the brigadier, "that the staff officer who was sent to order back the Fifth [on the left of the line] fell into the hands of the enemy." Without much prompting the 5th Vermont speedily vacated its position.[7]

While Carroll and Owen were advancing their brigades to relieve what was left of Getty's division, Cadmus Wilcox was marching his Confederate division along the Orange Plank Road toward Heth's embattled front (No 5). The South Carolinians of Sam McGowan's Brigade held the van, alternately quick-stepping and trotting down the road, with Alfred Scales's North Carolinians right behind them. Wilcox's remaining brigades under Edward Thomas and James Lane were still some distance in the rear and would take a bit longer to come up. As they passed the limbered guns of Poague's Battalion, the cannoneers whooped and hollered, threw their caps in the air, and waved their gun rammers in salute. A short distance beyond, when McGowan's men encountered General Lee and his staff, it was their turn to loose a throaty cheer.[8] The Carolinians remembered the twin moments of martial pride for the rest of their lives.

McGowan's Brigade continued forward and replaced Cooke's Brigade, whose front ran perpendicular to the Orange Plank Road. McGowan deployed his regiments (from left to right) as follows: 1st South Carolina-Orr's Rifles-12th South Carolina-13th South Carolina-14th South Carolina. Scales, meanwhile, slid off the road to the right, where the fighting was increasing in intensity. It was there that Walker's Brigade, with support from some of Kirkland's regiments, were battling Ward's Federal brigade.[9]

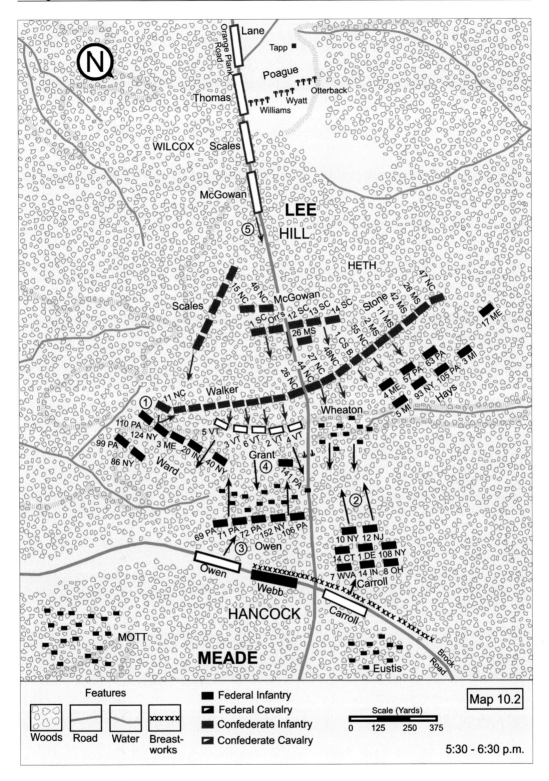

Features

Woods Road Water Breastworks

■ Federal Infantry
▰ Federal Cavalry
■ Confederate Infantry
▰ Confederate Cavalry

Scale (Yards)

0   125   250   375

Map 10.2

5:30 - 6:30 p.m.

Map 10.3: The Reinforcements Prepare for Action (5:30 - 6:30 p.m.)

The chaotic fighting up and down the line resulted in stacked and overlapped Federal regiments and large gaps in the front through which aggressive Confederate commanders charged toward the Brock Road. One North Carolinian called the fighting there a "storm center," and doubted "any more violent or sanguinary contest occurred during the entire Civil War than here." The road, continued the North Carolinian, "was swept by an incessant hurricane of fire, and to attempt to cross it meant almost certain death."[10]

Carroll's and Owen's brigades (Gibbon's division) were pushing forward in the growing darkness to relieve Getty's men (No. 1) as Wilcox's Division was deploying to replace Heth's men and meet them. The result promised a new outbreak of heavy fighting between fresh combatants. Getty's brigades, meanwhile, under Grant and Wheaton fell back toward the Brock Road (No. 2).

North of the Orange Plank Road, wrote historian Edward Steere, "Carroll passed over Wheaton's lines and struck with the vigor that fresh troops usually bring to an exhausted battle front." The same could not be said for Owen, who, "coming up on the left . . . was unable to hit with the power exhibited by Carroll." According to division commander John Gibbon, the Rebels were nearly to the Brock Road. His "leading regiments [of Carroll's brigade] came up they were faced to the left, and by their fire soon drove the enemy back, took possession of the road and held it . . . the day closed with heavy skirmishing." While Gibbon's two brigades cleared their fronts of Heth's exhausted troops, he was not as inclined as previous commanders to vigorously attack the enemy's light breastworks, which were now being reinforced by Wilcox's fresh brigades. William Landon of the 14th Indiana in the third line of Carroll's brigade recalled that the unit, "blazed away [at the enemy] until dark [when] we were relieved by a strong, double line of skirmishers."[11]

It was General Lee himself who urged McGowan's and Scales's brigades to continue moving northeast along the Orange Plank Road. General Wilcox, who had galloped ahead of his remaining two brigades, conferred with General Heth just behind the front. "I gave him [Wilcox] my views," recollected Heth, "which were briefly that, having successfully resisted all of the enemy's attacks up to the present time, we should now, in our turn, attack."[12]

Wilcox readily agreed and ordered McGowan's and Scales's brigades into the fight. Rather than hitting Getty's worn-out brigades, however, his men met Carroll's and Owen's fresh units (No. 3). McGowan was so anxious to charge that when the order was given he drew his sword and, leaping over Heth's prone men, headed for the enemy followed by his screaming infantry. "We should have charged without uttering a word . . . as it was, we drew upon ourselves a terrific volley of musketry," admitted a soldier in the 1st South Carolina. Besides Carroll's fresh troops ahead of them, McGowan's men had to struggle against the thick undergrowth and friendly fire. In their attempt to support the charge, some of Cooke's and Kirkland's troops accidentally fired into what they thought was the enemy, but were in reality the backs of the South Carolinians.[13]

McGowan's South Carolinians were also contending with Federal artillery fire. To help reduce the effectiveness of the latter's fire, McGowan's men began zigzagging along the road, which helped reduce casualties. Watching this tactic, a Federal staff officer thought that "the object of the performance was seen; namely, to draw the fire of our guns, when the enemy charge in force on both sides of the road."[14]

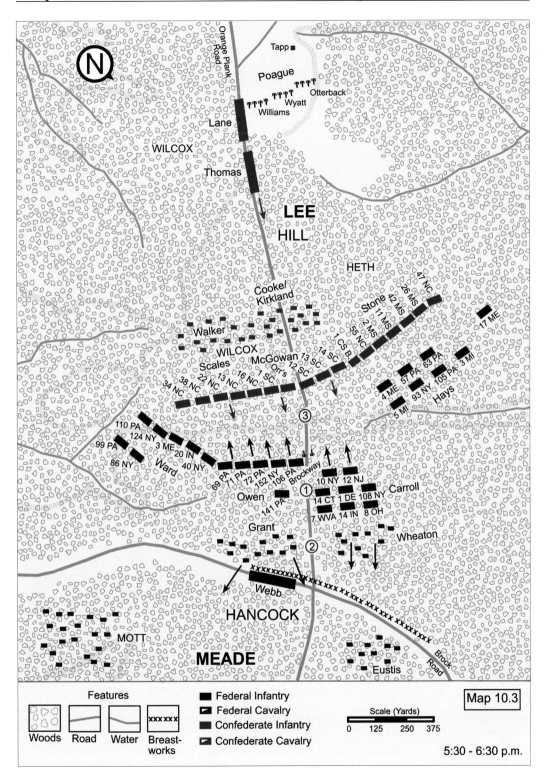

Map 10.3

5:30 - 6:30 p.m.

Map 10.4: McGowan's Brigade Takes on Gibbon's Division (5:30 - 6:30 p.m.)

Because of the terrain, the 1st South Carolina and Orr's Rifles on the right side of the Orange Plank Road had the toughest going (No. 1). Mostly because of the rough terrain, "all idea of a charge had to be abandoned," recalled the brigade's historian. Orr's Rifles halted on some high ground, but when its losses quickly mounted, the South Carolinians withdrew behind the incline for protection. This left the 1st South Carolina alone with the enemy to its front and on both flanks. Enemy gunfire pattered through the heavy vegetation, which deflected many of the lead balls.[15]

Unfortunately, the accounts of this action by Owen's men are not particularly helpful in following the course of the fighting. The historian of the rookie 152nd New York recalled a "sharp crackling of musketry and the whizzing of many bullets caused the men to stagger and fall. The attack was so sudden that it caused the line to waiver. . . . Instantly recovering, we began to fire at will, and poured volley after volley in the darkness of the night. We fell back a few paces and formed the picket line."[16]

McGowan's three regiments fighting on the left side of the Orange Plank Road had an easier time of it against Carroll's men. The 12th South Carolina, closest to the road, advanced faster than the other two regiments, a move the brigade's historian called "too impetuous." Up ahead of the South Carolinians was Francis Snider's section of Ricketts's battery, which had been sent galloping forward to support Brockway's section of guns. Brockway was only too happy to order his men to pull his guns back to safety, using prolongs because the enemy was so close and time was of the essence. Snider's gunners had hardly manhandled their guns into position before the 12th South Carolina surged over the cannons, driving the gunners to the rear (No. 2). The 12th was so far in advance of the rest of the brigade that Federals began enveloping its flanks and slipping into its rear. Its officers realized a lost cause when they saw one and ordered a retreat to reconnect with the other regiments. As they fell back, portions of the 8th Ohio and 14th Indiana in Carroll's second and third lines surged forward and retook the guns.[17]

Once the 12th South Carolina reformed with the other two regiments, McGowan's advance continued. George Bowen of the 12th New Jersey, fighting in the first line of Carroll's brigade, recorded in his diary that the enemy made a tenacious attack that was beaten off, but not without some heavy losses to the Jerseymen. Carroll's men redoubled their efforts to drive the South Carolinians from their front. "They pressed on us, filling the air with shouts and the roll of arms, and sweeping the woods with balls," reported McGowan.[18]

The terrain, confusion, limited visibility, and deadly enemy lead squeezed the three South Carolina regiments into what one soldier described as "the shortest, most huddled, most ineffective line-of-battle I ever saw." Fire was zipping through their ranks from the front and both flanks. "The balls of the enemy at one point crossed the road from each side," recounted one of the survivors. There was nothing left to do but pull back, and McGowan reluctantly gave the order to reform on Heth's original defensive line (No. 3).[19]

Scales was apparently ordered to advance his brigade simultaneously on McGowan's right, but it lagged behind and never connected with the South Carolinians (No. 4). A soldier from the 13th North Carolina declared his regiment made "charge after charge," which if true, had little if any effect on the tactical situation south of the road. Another Tar Heel, this one in the 34th North Carolina, summed up the fighting rather simply when he wrote, "the regiment, with the brigade, fought on the right side of the Plank Road, holding the position till night against a strong opposing force."[20]

At some point during the fighting, four Confederate guns were brought forward to support the offensive. It was not a good move, for within minutes most of the gunners and many of the horses were cut down (No. 5). A detachment of 40 men from the 44th North Carolina ran over to pull the guns to safety. They were successful, but only three men returned unhurt.[21]

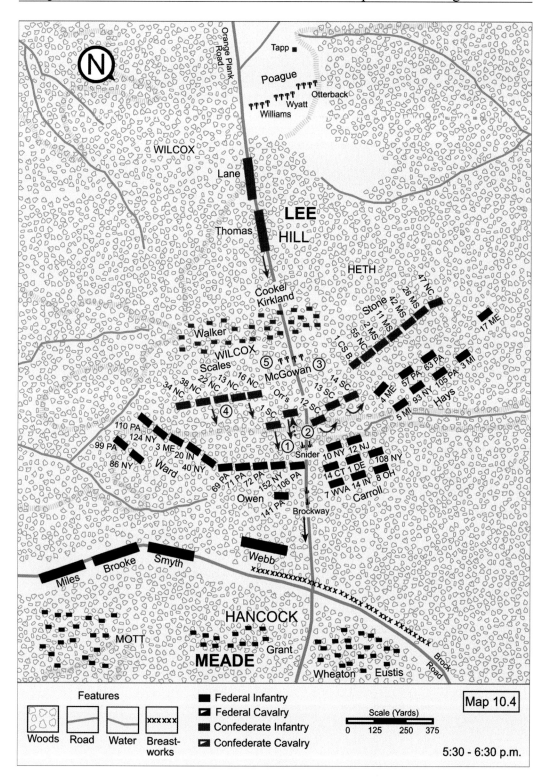

Tapp

Poague

Otterback

Williams   Wyatt

WILCOX

Lane

LEE

Thomas   HILL

HETH

Cooke/
Kirkland

Stone 42 MS 26 MS 47 NC

11 MS

2 MS

55 NC

1 CS B.   17 ME

Walker

WILCOX

Scales   McGowan ③

22 NC 13 NC 16 NC   14 SC   4 ME 57 PA 63 PA 3 MI

38 NC   Orr's 13 SC   93 NY 105 PA

34 NC   7 SC 12 SC   5 MI   Hays

④   ①

②

Snider 10 NY 12 NJ   108 NY

110 PA

124 NY

99 PA 3 ME 20 IN   14 CT 1 DE 8 OH

86 NY   40 NY   7 WVA 14 IN   Carroll

Ward   69 PA 71 PA 72 PA 152 NY 106 PA

Owen   141 PA   Brockway

Miles   Brooke Smyth   Webb
xxxxxxxxxxxxxxxxxxxxxxxx
xxxxxxxxxxxxxxxxxxxx

HANCOCK

MOTT   Grant

MEADE   Wheaton Eustis   Brock Road

Features

Woods	Road	Water	Breast-works
			xxxxx

■ Federal Infantry
▰ Federal Cavalry
■ Confederate Infantry
▰ Confederate Cavalry

Scale (Yards)

0   125   250   375

Map 10.4

5:30 - 6:30 p.m.

Map 10.5: The Remainder of Wilcox's Division Arrives (6:00 - 7:30 p.m.)

Heth's Division fought Getty's men more than two hours, staving off a large segment of Hancock's II Corps. His Rebels managed to launch their own attacks, some penetrating as far east as the Brock Road. By early evening Heth's men were played out and their ranks depleted. Except for a few regiments, the arrival of Wilcox's Division allowed three of Heth's brigades—Walker's, Cooke's, and Kirkland's—to pull back a few hundred yards to reorganize. They were replaced by McGowan's Scales's brigades.

Stone's Brigade on the left of Heth's line, however, was still engaged (No. 1). Stone's men had withstood attacks from Eustis's brigade (Getty's division) and Hays' brigade (Birney's division). Adjutant Charles Cooke of the 55th North Carolina counted seven charges against his regiment, but "our line never wavered. The officers and men . . . realized that the safety of the army depended upon our holding the enemy in check." One man fired his musket 61 times that afternoon. "I was nevor in as clost a place as I was the first day—not more than 2 hundred yards from them," he later recalled.[22]

By 6:00 p.m., the situation was so desperate Stone's officers met to discuss what to do. No support was in sight, ammunition was low, and "the enemy were pressing us so heavily with their successive lines of fresh troops it was thought that they would annihilate us before nightfall." Colonel Stone was particularly upset because "he had sent for cartridges repeatedly, but the men who were sent were killed or wounded." His 42nd Mississippi had all but stopped firing. The officers decided their best hope was to launch an unexpected bayonet charge. As Adjutant Cooke put it, the men "expressed hope that it might not be necessary . . . but there was no disposition to shirk the duty if it had been imposed." One of the sharpshooters recalled that the order was given "in cold blood . . . as calmly as if it was meaningless." Several lines of enemy troops were visible through the trampled vegetation. Stone's men had been "thinned almost to a skirmish line, with empty guns and bayonets fixed."

Luckily, Thomas's Brigade (Wilcox's Division) arrived. General Wilcox had already shoved McGowan and Scales to the right and center to replace Walker, Cooke, and Kirkland, so he sent the Georgians left to relieve Stone, whose regiments fell back below the Orange Plank Road to rest and regroup. Although Stone's losses on May 5 are not known, they were surely heavy. It is known that of the 340 men carried into battle by the 55th North Carolina, for example, 34 had been killed and another 167 wounded. A soldier in the ambulance corps ventured forward the following day and counted 157 dead Union troops in front of their position.[23]

Thomas's transition to the front did not go as smoothly as hoped. In his battle report, Wilcox observed the brigade "did not succeed in getting into line on the left of the latter [Stone's Brigade] but encountered the enemy in [the] rear of that flank and fought in a line parallel with the plank road while the remainder of the line was at right angles to it." Thomas was deploying his line when James Lane's Brigade arrived. Wilcox used his ears to place it—the firing was heaviest to his right—so he sent it to form on Scales's right. Every man General Lee had available from A. P. Hill's Third Corps was either fighting or fought out.[24]

What none of the Rebel commanders knew was that powerful Union reinforcements were also on the move in heavy numbers toward both Confederate flanks. Hancock's last division under Brig. Gen. Francis Barlow was approaching the intersection of the Orange Plank and Brock roads. Webb's brigade (Gibbon's division) was already behind light works. Colonel Thomas Smyth's brigade, in the van of Barlow's division, formed on Webb's left and began throwing up dirt and logs. (No. 3). The brigades of Cols. Nelson Miles and Paul Frank followed suit, formed on Smyth's left, and took to crafting anything that could stop a bullet. Barlow's last brigade under Col. John R. Brooke was about a mile to the rear and closing fast. Every brigade but Frank's would soon advance to find and crush the Confederate right flank below the Orange Plank Road.[25]

Perhaps the greatest threat to Lee's line, however, was approaching from the north, where three brigades of Wadsworth's division and one of Robinson's were aiming straight for his left flank and rear (No. 4). If these four brigades hit Thomas's Brigade's flank, the entire Rebel line would be rolled up and defeated.[26]

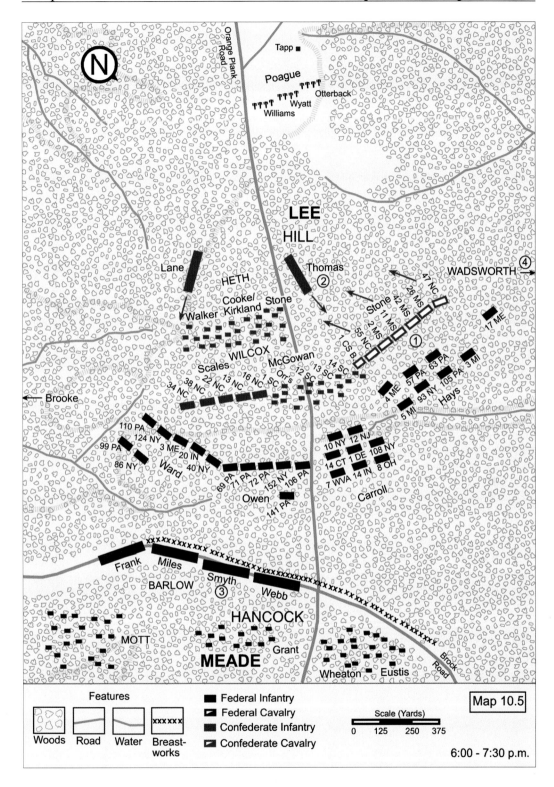

Map 10.5

Features

Woods   Road   Water   Breast-
                        works

■ Federal Infantry
◪ Federal Cavalry
■ Confederate Infantry
◪ Confederate Cavalry

Scale (Yards)
0   125   250   375

6:00 - 7:30 p.m.

Map 10.6: Lane Brigade Slugs it Out with Barlow's Division (6:30 - 7:30 p.m.)

Despite their overwhelming superiority in numbers, the Union troops and their leaders in the Brock Road-Orange Plank Road sector were growing increasingly pessimistic of victory. One of Meade's aides sent a message to headquarters at 5:50 p.m.: "we barely hold our own; on the right the pressure is heavy. General Hancock thinks he can hold the plank and Brock roads, in front of which he is, but he can't advance." It was an odd communication given that Hancock outnumbered A. P. Hill by some 20,000 men. All that faced Hancock's right was Stone's worn-out brigade, which was in the act of being relieved by Thomas's Georgians, and some of McGowan's men. The fact that Hancock believed he could not advance was a testament to Southern tenacity and the tricks played on human senses by the Wilderness. Southern prisoners being herded to the rear continued to spread fear by swearing that Longstreet's powerful First Corps was already up. Few Union men wanted to advance to test the veracity of the information.[27]

The arrival of Barlow's division provided Hancock with a strong fighting force to both attack the enemy's right flank and at the same time guard against the possibility of a flank attack by Longstreet's men rumored to be lurking beyond the Rebel left. Colonel Smyth, in command of the venerable Irish Brigade, was the first to move out from its defenses and, using the road as a guide for its right, head toward the Confederate line where Owen's brigade was battling for its life (No. 1).[28]

A soldier in the 116th Pennsylvania on Smyth's left recalled "the crash of musketry filled the woods, the smoke lingered and clung to the trees and underbrush and obscured everything. Men fell on every side, but still the Regiment passed steadily on. One by one the boys fell—some to rise no more, others badly wounded."[29]

Next to move was Colonel Miles, who advanced his brigade on Smyth's left. When orders reached Colonel Brooke to send two regiments from his brigade in support, he selected the 64th and 66th New York and shoved them west out of sight into the forbidding brush and timber (No. 2).[30]

Barlow's officers used the tremendous roar of battle in their front to guide their movements. The Federals were approaching the vulnerable Rebel right just as A. P. Hill's last fresh brigade under Lane got into position on the right of Scales. Within seconds Union skirmishers appeared and opened fire. Lane dispatched the 37th North Carolina, bringing up the rear of the brigade, to deal with the threat by forming parallel to the Orange Plank Road. About this time, Hill informed Lane that Scales's line was shaken and needed to fall back and reestablish its front. This required Lane to form in front of Scales, rather than on his right. The 7th North Carolina on the left of Lane's line was about 100 yards from the road, where it was to make contact with the right elements of McGowan's Brigade. Lane cautioned the men to not fire into the South Carolinians. It was helpful advice, for as one of the men related, "at the time, owing to the darkness, smoke, and density of the swamp, it was impossible to distinguish friend from foe."[31]

Once aligned, Lane ordered his men to advance, which they did "handsomely," although swampy ground about 250 yards wide hindered their passage (No. 3). As the brigade slogged through the swamp, enemy troops opened fire on them, forcing the line to halt. The front was somewhat elongated with the addition of the 38th North Carolina (Scales's Brigade), which remained in the forefront. When the firing ceased, the line continued forward. The Tar Heels pushed through thick growth and over fallen trees to confront Smyth's newly arrived men.[32]

Once they reached firmer ground, Lane's men spied a strong line of enemy soldiers on higher ground to the front: Smyth's and Miles's brigades were up. When he realized the enemy line stretched far beyond his own right, Lane refused his right-most regiment (the 18th North Carolina) to keep from being turned. Unbeknownst to Lane, the situation was much worse than he knew, for Wilcox had just pulled McGowan's Brigade off the line to reform in the rear. As a result, enemy soldiers were on Lane's front and threatening both flanks. "We soon discovered that no one was in our front but the enemy, and we commenced firing on them," recalled Lt. Col. Robert Cowan of the 33rd North Carolina.[33]

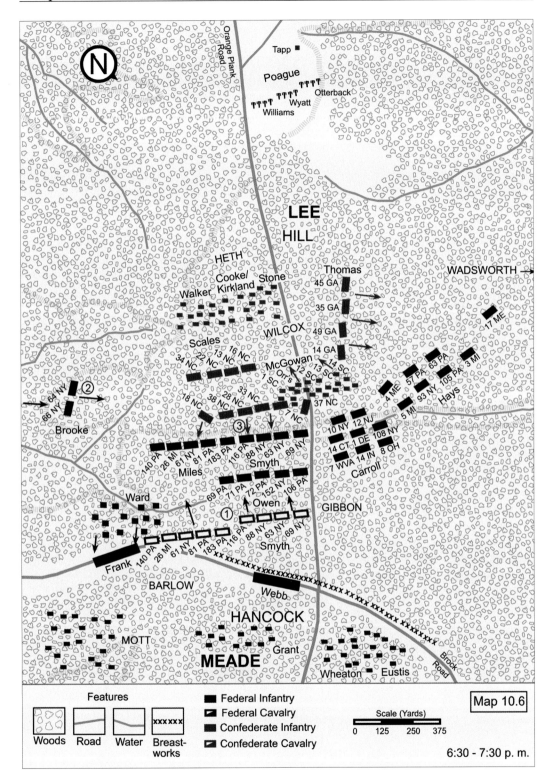

Map 10.6

Features

Woods   Road   Water   Breast-
                         works

■ Federal Infantry
◤ Federal Cavalry
■ Confederate Infantry
◤ Confederate Cavalry

Scale (Yards)

0   125   250   375

6:30 - 7:30 p. m.

Map 10.7: More Union Troops Threaten A. P. Hill's Flanks (7:30 - 9:00 p.m.)

Emerging from the swamp and approaching to within 75 yards of Federal troops straight ahead of them, the North Carolinians were hit by what Lane called "a terrible fire." A sharpshooter fighting with Lane's men recalled "neither side making a charge, as it ought to have done. Either side by a charge could have driven the enemy." Smyth's troops yelled for the 7th North Carolina on the left of Lane's line to surrender and, when they did not, continued firing into it (No. 1). "The right of the regiment fell back a short distance, and the left, owing to the proximity to the enemy, and the heavy fire poured into it, fell back in considerable disorder," admitted Capt. James Harris.

Prior to being ordered to withdraw, the 18th North Carolina on the right of the line was also in trouble (No. 2). These Tar Heels were up against the left wing of Miles's brigade. "We went in on the double-quick . . . yelling like mad . . . then fired front, then right, then left, then front until no enemy returned our fire," boasted a Pennsylvanian. The 64th and 68th New York of Brooke's brigade compounded the Tar Heels's misery when they appeared directly on its right flank (No. 3). The regiment apparently put up quite a fight, for Colonel Brooke reported that the New Yorkers's losses were "considerable." More bad news was on its way as Brooke had been ordered to reinforce the 64th and 68th New York with the rest of his brigade. However, Brooke reported, "it was by this time quite dark, and very difficult to pass through the dense thicket of the Wilderness." [34]

"This exposed condition of my flanks," concluded Lane, "induced me to order the balance of my brigade back to the high ground in the rear of the swamp." By his timepiece it was about 9:00 p.m. Slogging to the rear, Lane encountered Scales's men behind protective breastworks, and so ordered his men behind their fellow North Carolinians (No. 4).[35]

The 28th North Carolina fighting in the middle of Lane's line did not get the order to withdraw. After driving the enemy before them, the North Carolinians realized they were well in advance of their fellow Tar Heels, which prompted their commander, Lt. Col. William

Speer, to halt his men. It was dark now, a factor that favored the otherwise exposed Confederates, who were almost out of ammunition. Speer ordered his men to rifle through the cartridge boxes of dead and dying soldiers before pulling back to rejoin the rest of the brigade.[36]

With most of Barlow's attack against the right of A. P. Hill's defensive line stalled by opposition and darkness, the more powerful threat approaching Hill's left flank finally made its appearance. There, General Wadsworth's three brigades, with another from Robinson's division, approached from near the Lacy house as part of Grant's orders to continue the offensive. They had been in motion since about 6:00 p.m., trying to keep their lines arranged as they slowly, step by step, tramped through the tangled thickets. There were far fewer of them than earlier in the day when Ewell had so roughly handled them, and their enthusiasm was dampened by their earlier experience. The Confederates probably learned about this threat about 7:00 p.m. or shortly thereafter.

A. P. Hill had nothing left to combat the mass of enemy troops approaching his vulnerable left flank except the 150-man 5th Alabama Battalion, which had been guarding an ever-growing number of enemy prisoners in the rear. The Alabamians were rushed to the left and deployed as a strong skirmish line. The Southern arrivals advanced screaming at the top of their lungs and firing as they did so. The thousands of Federals advancing hesitated, peering into the smoky darkness unsure of what lie ahead—and halted (No. 5). The generals consulted, unsure how or whether to proceed. Wadworth's adjutant wrote after the battle that Col. Roy Stone's men in the second line broke "in a disgraceful manner on seeing the fire of Baxter's skirmishers in front of them." Colonel John Irvin assumed command of the brigade when Colonel Stone's horse reared in panic, throwing its rider to the ground and falling on top of him. The fall knocked the colonel out of action for the rest of the campaign.

The advance stalled as the men had no stomach to go further.[37]

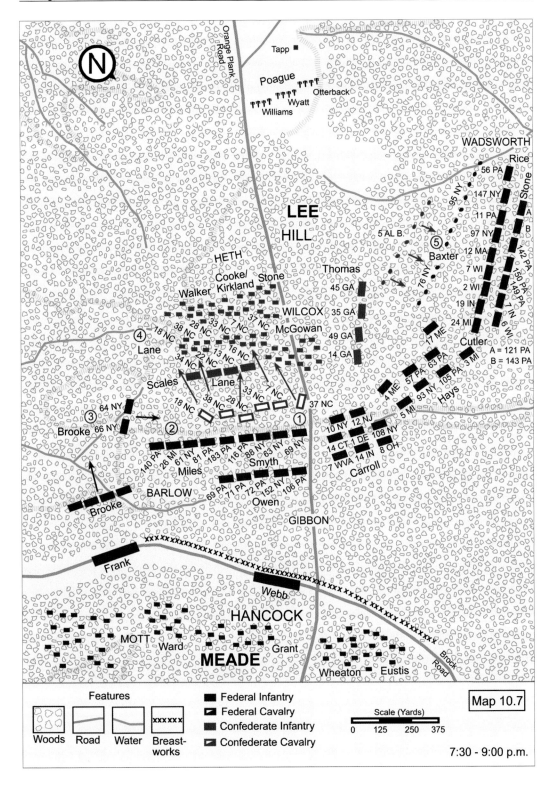

Features

Woods   Road   Water   Breastworks

■ Federal Infantry
◪ Federal Cavalry
■ Confederate Infantry
◪ Confederate Cavalry

Scale (Yards)
0   125   250   375

Map 10.7

7:30 - 9:00 p.m.

Map Set 11: Afternoon Cavalry Actions (May 5)

Map 11.1: Wilson's Division Escapes (12:00 - 2:30 p.m.)

May 5 was not a good day for the Union cavalry. When newly minted cavalry commander Maj. Gen. Phil Sheridan heard that Maj. Gen. Jeb Stuart's main body of Rebel cavalry was camped at Hamilton's Crossing near Fredericksburg, he petitioned army commander George Meade for permission to ride after it. The aggressive Sheridan viewed the mission as an opportunity to catch and destroy enemy cavalry, but Meade thought of the effort as a preemptive strike to protect the Army of the Potomac's vulnerable supply wagons. Whatever the rationale, two of Sheridan's three divisions (one each under Brig. Gens. Alfred Torbert and David McM. Gregg) left the army with only a small division left behind under Brig. Gen. James Wilson, who had never led men in battle (see Map 3.2).[1]

The effort to catch Stuart began inauspiciously when Torbert's mounted division became intertwined with wagons on a clogged road. The situation for Torbert was even worse, for he was suffering from a painful abscess at the base of his spine, which finally forced him to turn his command over to Brig. Gen. Wesley Merritt.[2]

Not having heard from General Wilson for some time, Meade sought help from Sheridan, just back from Fredericksburg without having found any Rebel cavalry. Sheridan sent General Gregg's division to find the missing division. Wilson was not that hard to locate. A brigade under Brig. Gen. Henry Davies, Jr. leading Gregg's column found his men at Todd's Tavern at the intersection of the Brock and Catharpin roads about 2:30 p.m. "General Wilson is falling back to this point, followed by the enemy," Gregg dispatched to Sheridan. "I have my command here and will receive the enemy."[3]

Wilson was having a tough time of it. His men had been fighting against Brig. Gen. Thomas Rosser's cavalry brigade throughout the early afternoon (see Map 3.7). At one point in the action Wilson found himself and but 50 soldiers of the 8th Illinois Cavalry facing hundreds of Rosser's men near the Faulkner house on the Catharpin Road (No. 1). In an effort to buy time,

Wilson ordered a bold charge that initially scattered the enemy troopers. With A. P. Hill's Third Corps on the Orange Plank Road to the north and Rosser's cavalry in front of him, Wilson directed his troopers to fall back toward the Brock Road (No. 2). With Rebel horsemen clogging the main roads, Wilson was in real trouble until he found a wagon track above Robertson's Run that met the Catharpin Road just before Todd's Tavern, and ordered his men onto it (No. 3).

Colonel George Chapman's brigade led the way, followed by Col. Timothy Bryan's brigade, with Bryan's former regiment, the 18th Pennsylvania Cavalry, acting as a rear guard. With Rosser's men trotting east along Catharpin Road, it became a race to the intersection (No. 4). Wilson's head start gave his men the jump they needed and they galloped into the main road before Rosser's men could block them. As Wilson was leading his men eastward to safety, the 18th Pennsylvania Cavalry (with orders to "hold the ground at all hazards") valiantly attempted to hold back Rosser's men. As a Pennsylvanian later explained, "In our front, the Confederates were literally swarming. The right-hand road was crowded with them, while their batteries were belching hot shot into us on our left." Surrounded on three sides, the Keystone men attempted to cut their way out with a charge, but it failed, as did a second attempt. The unit finally melted into the dense forest to the east. "Imagine, if you can," wrote one eyewitness, "a cavalry regiment tearing through woods and underbrush, over logs, floundering through swamps, caps and cuss words flying in all directions, and you have a faint idea of our escape." The disheveled troopers eventually emerged on the Brock Road later that evening.

The 1st Connecticut Cavalry with a section of artillery deployed across Catharpin Road to provide support for the rattled Pennsylvanians. Portions of the 7th and 11th Virginia Cavalry recklessly charged into the reinforcements "like a solid shot in the ranks of the Federals, who now broke and ran," recalled one of Rosser's men. Wilson's men were a long way from being out of danger. "We were outflanked on both sides," noted a Connecticut trooper, "and being under orders to hold the position at all hazards, were in immediate danger of being surrounded."[4]

This was the situation Gregg's division discovered when they reached the vicinity of Todd's Tavern (No. 5).

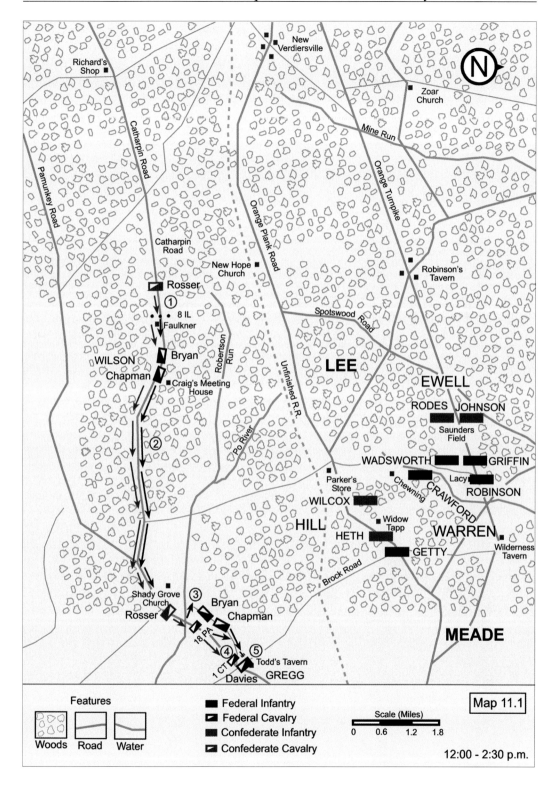

Features

Woods Road Water

Federal Infantry
Federal Cavalry
Confederate Infantry
Confederate Cavalry

Scale (Miles)

0   0.6   1.2   1.8

Map 11.1

12:00 - 2:30 p.m.

Map 11.2: Gregg's Division Stems the Confederate Advance (2:30 - 7:00 p.m.)

While Maj. Erastus Blakeslee's 1st Connecticut Cavalry (Bryan's brigade) tried to hold back Rosser's attempt at cutting off Wilson's division, General Gregg deployed for action. Preparing for battle was never a simple task, but Wilson's troopers made it harder by galloping past the new arrivals for the rear in what one of Gregg's officers labeled a "very disordered state." Gregg dispatched Col. John Kester's 1st New Jersey Cavalry to engage Rosser. Kester peeled off a company and sent it flying toward Rosser's men, who broke in confusion when the line of fresh Union cavalrymen charged toward them with sabers raised. According to Kester, his Jerseymen were "in turn met by the charge of a rebel regiment, which again turned the tide of battle." The colonel brought up reinforcements. "Hastily forming these squadrons in line of battle, the whole line moved forward and gave the enemy such a sharp volley, followed by a rapid fire at will, that they desisted from their charge and endeavored to keep back the advancing line of my regiment, but without success." The Jersey brigade's historian boasted that, "with this skirmish line of two hundred and fifty men we actually bore back the effective force of the entire opposing brigade."[5]

Flushed with victory, the Jerseymen pressed their advantage, joined now by elements of the 1st Massachusetts Cavalry on their left. However, the Rebels rallied and charged, hitting the Federals squarely in the front. Gregg's men held them off, but knew it was time to withdraw when more Rebel troopers began moving around their left flank toward their rear. Many of the troopers had dismounted in a wet field, and the sudden enemy counterattack forced them to leave more than one pair of boots mired in the mud. Chew's Confederate horse battery added to the Union confusion when its shells rained into Gregg's unsuspecting men. The troopers redeployed across Catharpin Road with the 1st Massachusetts Cavalry on the left, the 1st New Jersey Cavalry in the center, and the 10th New York Cavalry on the right.[6]

With his troops deployed and ready for action, Davies gave the order to attack.

According to a Jerseyman, "Our skirmishers wheeled with one accord, and with a wild cheer the whole body made a simultaneous and resistless charge." "Forward we moved, as steady as on parade," Colonel Kester reported, "the rebels endeavoring to check us by showers of canister, but with no avail; and they hastily limbered their guns and fell back, just in time to prevent their capture." Kester's chaplain recalled how Davies's men swept on "without a halt or a check, over the dead and wounded rebels, crushing before them every attempt to rally." The troopers drove Rosser's cavalrymen about two miles until someone wisely gave the order to halt. Rosser's men acknowledged the events, but considered the climax a tactical withdrawal rather than a repulse.[7]

While Davies's brigade fought with Rosser's determined troopers, a new threat developed along the Brock Road, where the forward elements of Maj. Gen. Fitzhugh Lee's cavalry division were arriving from Hamilton's Crossing (not shown on map). Gregg blunted their arrival by sending the 1st Pennsylvania Cavalry galloping in their direction which, together with the 1st Massachusetts Cavalry, battled Brig. Gen. Lunsford Lomax's 6th and 15th Virginia Cavalry regiments until nightfall.[8]

During the long day of fighting, Rosser reported his losses as 114 from all causes, while Federal casualties came in at about 700 (with some 91 of the killed and wounded from Gregg's division). More important than the losses, Sheridan's handling of the cavalry cost the Army of the Potomac dearly. Wilson's division alone could not provide an effective screen for the Federal infantry, and was unable to identify the location of General Lee's advancing troops. According to historian Gordon Rhea, Sheridan's "dereliction enabled Lee to surprise Grant and to exploit the awkward Union deployments." Concluded Rhea, "blame for the Union army's misguided use of cavalry lay at all levels of command," including Meade.[9]

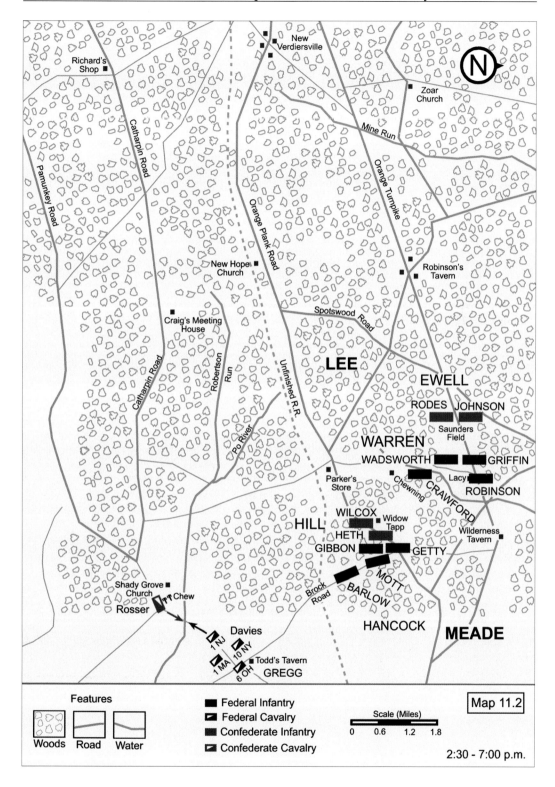

Features

Woods   Road   Water

Federal Infantry
Federal Cavalry
Confederate Infantry
Confederate Cavalry

Scale (Miles)
0   0.6   1.2   1.8

Map 11.2

2:30 - 7:00 p.m.

Map Set 12: May 5 Fighting Ends, and the Armies Prepare for May 6

Map 12.1: The Fighting Finally Ends (9:00 - 10:00 p.m.)

Many who wrote about the long and bloody day noted their overwhelming fatigue by the time darkness fell. W. M. Waddell of the 46th North Carolina (Brig. Gen. John R. Cooke's Brigade, Hill's Corps) summed up the action along Orange Plank Road as "a butchery pure and simple it was, unrelieved by any of the arts of war in which the exercise of military skill and tact robs the hour of some of its horrors. It was a mere slugging match in a dense thicket of small growth, where men but a few yards apart fired through the brushwood for hours, ceasing only when exhaustion and night commanded a rest."[1]

One of Union Brig. Gen. George Getty's officers wrote that the "musketry was terrific and continuous. Usually when infantry meets infantry, the clash of arms is brief. One side or the other speedily gives way. Here neither side would give way, and the steady firing rolled and crackled from end to end of the contending lines, as if it would never cease. But little could be seen of the enemy," he added. "Whenever any troops rose to their feet and attempted to press forward, they became a target for the half-hidden foe, and lost severely." A Rebel wrote how hard it was to attack, for it was impossible to "keep even a regiment well dressed. Then the enemy open fire . . . Some men will . . . return the fire. Gradually all join in it; and once the whole roar of battle opens, there is an end to unison of action."[2]

The May 5 fighting was different than earlier combats. Whenever possible, soldiers threw up dirt and piled rocks or logs for protection. It was also the first major battle fought almost entirely with infantry (few artillery pieces managed to fire a round). "The men who noted this fact were men accustomed to warfare," explained a Vermont historian, "and who knew that the fire of infantry was much more deadly than that of artillery, and never before had they heard such continuous thunder or confronted such a storm of lead as on this occasion."[3] The result was a slaughter on a horrific scale at close quarters.

A member of Lewis Grant's Vermont brigade exclaimed, "Oh, you have no idea of the scenes we are passing through. Tongue can never tell the suffering, the hardships, the alternate rising of hope and falling of hope. The successes of the battles are various, though we have made steady gain from the first. Which (if our men last) will give us the victory in the end." Another man in the same brigade wrote, "Oh how I felt after the battle could I have cried. Our boys fought like men."[4]

The moonless dark night brought little relief. Ambulances rumbled along the dark paths and roads packed with wailing wounded. Fires flared up in the dense vegetation—"pulsing beacons over the dark woods" was how one soldier described them—and burned to death those who could not escape. Concern for the wounded was expressed at the highest levels. Once the fighting died down, one of General Grant's first thoughts was for the stricken. Most could not be found let alone moved, and attempts to do either triggered new fighting. Grant "manifested intense anxiety in regard to relieving the wounded, and the medical officers and the commanders of troops were urged to make every possible effort to find the sufferers and convey them to the rear," wrote Horace Porter.[5]

The day was filled with inept Union assaults against stout Rebel defensive efforts. Richard Ewell handled his Second Corps well on the northern end of the field, extending his line as needed and launching limited counterattacks, both aimed at maintaining a cohesive front. A. P. Hill's battle farther south, however, was one of the war's most brilliant defensive efforts. There, the 7,000 men of Heth's Division fought to a standstill a similarly sized VI Corps division (Getty) followed by one assault after another from General Hancock's II Corps—altogether some 30,000 men. A historian writing for the 11th Mississippi (Davis's/Stone's Brigade) estimated that they fired more than 100,000 bullets. The men did not "waste time to aim and fired point blank into the masses 'floundering toward them.'" The leaden rain devastated the vegetation between the two lines. A member of the 11th Mississippi recalled that the "undergrowth was very thick, and during the fight all the bushes as large as a man's wrist were cut down about two and one-half feet above the ground by musket balls." Heth's report observed that the "enemy's dead marked his line of battle so well, and even in such numbers, that, if living, they would have formed a most formidable line."[6]

The tireless efforts of Ewell and Hill erased at least some of the stain of Gettysburg.[7]

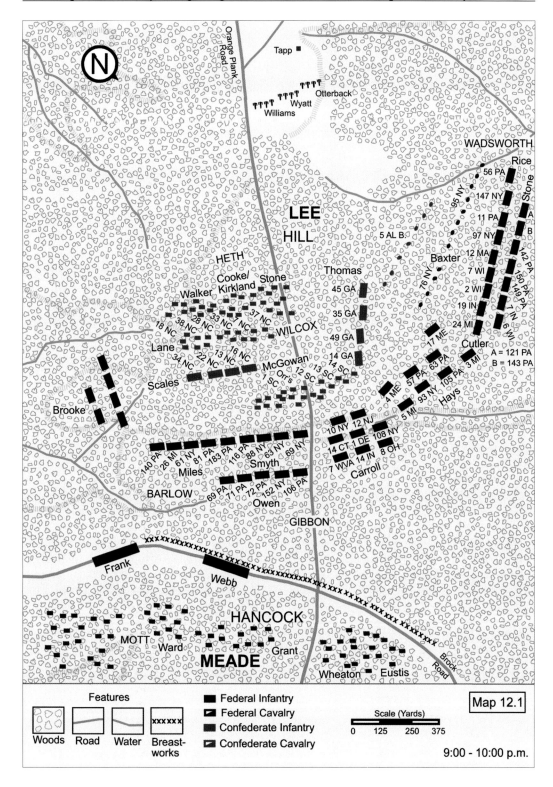

Map 12.1

9:00 – 10:00 p.m.

Features

Woods   Road   Water   Breast-works

Federal Infantry
Federal Cavalry
Confederate Infantry
Confederate Cavalry

Scale (Yards)
0   125   250   375

Map 12.2: Meade and Grant Prepare for May 6 (9:00 p.m.)

The day that began with so much promise for the Army of the Potomac melted into one bloody frustration and failure after another. This was the first time the army went into battle with two commanders. Grant's general theory was to pitch into the enemy whenever and wherever he was found, while the meticulous Meade wanted to make sure his attacking pieces were in place before doing do. Sometimes Grant gave orders to Meade directly, and sometimes he bypassed Meade and went directly to his corps leaders. As the army's direct commander, Meade also issued his own orders. These men, together with their separate staffs, made for a "curious form of dual command," noted one historian. The resulting confusion was evident everywhere.[8]

Sitting before a fire at his headquarters that night, Grant said, "I feel pretty well satisfied with the result of the engagement; for it is evident that Lee attempted by a bold movement to strike this army in flank before it could be put into line of battle and be prepared to fight to advantage; but in this he has failed." The general's staff officer who recorded the conversation also indicated that Grant noted that neither Maj. Gen. Ambrose Burnside's Union IX Corps nor Lt. Gen. James Longstreet's Confederate First Corps had reached the field, which meant the two armies "have been occupied principally in struggling through thickets and fighting for position." Now, with that position determined, he added, "to-day's work has not been much of a test of strength." The arriving reinforcements for both sides would test all of them come sunup.[9]

Despite his comments, May 5 frustrated Grant. Throwing units piecemeal into a raging battle seldom had the desired effect. He intended for May 6 to be very different. With all of his men up and in position, Grant intended to employ his favorite tactic—large-scale attacks to overwhelm the enemy's line. Meade's three corps (Hancock's II, Sedgwick's VI, and Warren's V, together with Burnside's independent IX Corps, would assault in unison. As one historian put it, "the secessionists would be flattened like dough under a rolling pin."[10]

Grant modified his thinking as the evening wore on. The main action would be on the left, where at 4:30 a.m. Hancock would launch his corps, together with Getty's VI Corps division, against A. P. Hill's Third Corps straddling Orange Plank Road. Farther north on the Union right, Sedgwick's VI Corps and Warren's V Corps would continue their attacks, primarily intended to hold Ewell's Corps in place to keep reinforcements from propping up Hill's front. The key to Federal success would be to strike hard early and crush Hill before Longstreet's veteran infantry reached the field. Francis Barlow's division would remain in reserve to keep an eye out for Old Pete's expected arrival. To better ensure victory, General Wadsworth's (Warren's V Corps division) would strike for Hill's left flank in an effort to catch the Confederate Third Corps in a vise.

Grant and Meade would also have four more divisions comprising General Burnside's IX Corps. Brigadier General Thomas Stevenson's division would tramp south to reinforce Hancock and serve as a reserve, while Brig. Gens. Robert Potter and Orlando Willcox used their divisions to plug the gaping hole between Warren's left and Hancock's right. These troops could be used to reinforce either flank as needed. Burnside's last division under Brig. Gen. Edward Ferrero, composed of African-American troops, would remain in the rear guarding the army's extensive wagon trains.[11] Grant and Meade knew the army had lost heavily on May 5 and would need as many men in the ranks as possible. Between 8:00 and 9:00 p.m., orders went out to each corps: "all train guards as well as every man in your command capable of bearing arms, to join your troops at the front before daylight tomorrow morning . . . every man who can shoulder a musket must be in the ranks."[12]

Meade met with his corps commanders to outline the coming day's plans. Everyone realized Burnside's participation would be critical to success. Burnside, however, was generally viewed as a slow marcher. Why begin the main attack at 4:30 a.m. when Burnside would probably not be up in time to join in (even though he was set to begin marching at 2:00 a.m.)? When the corps commanders argued for a delay of 90 minutes Meade agreed and composed a tactfully worded message to Grant at 10:30 p.m. Grant agreed to delay the attack until 5:00 a.m.[13]

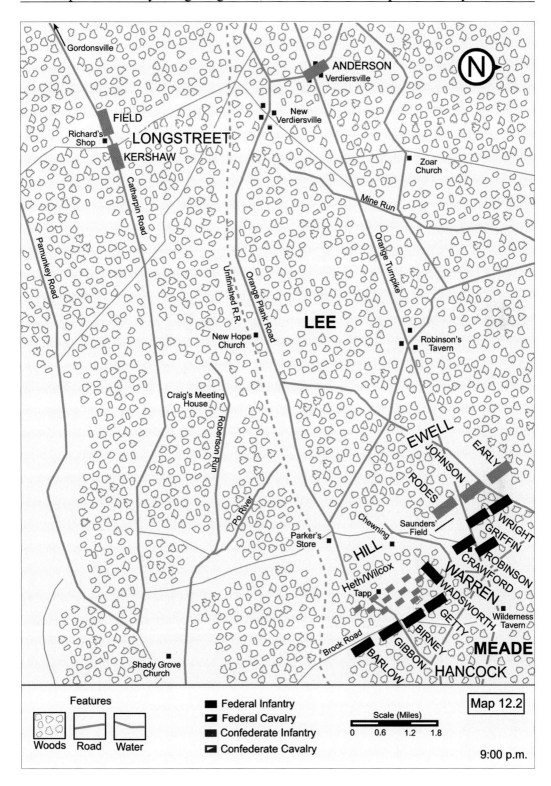

Gordonsville

ANDERSON
Verdiersville

FIELD

Richard's
Shop

LONGSTREET

KERSHAW

New
Verdiersville

Zoar
Church

Mine Run

Catharpin Road

Pamunkey Road

Unfinished R.R.

Orange Plank Road

Orange Turnpike

LEE

New Hope
Church

Robinson's
Tavern

Craig's Meeting
House

Robertson Run

Po River

EWELL

JOHNSON

EARLY

RODES

Chewning

Saunders'
Field

WRIGHT

GRIFFIN

Parker's
Store

HILL

ROBINSON

CRAWFORD

WARREN

Heth/Wilcox

Tapp

WADSWORTH

Wilderness
Tavern

GETTY

Brock Road

BIRNEY

MEADE

GIBBON

HANCOCK

Shady Grove
Church

BARLOW

Features

Woods   Road   Water

■ Federal Infantry

◪ Federal Cavalry

■ Confederate Infantry

◪ Confederate Cavalry

Scale (Miles)

0   0.6   1.2   1.8

Map 12.2

9:00 p.m.

Map 12.3: Lee Prepares for May 6
(9:00 p.m. - 1:00 a.m.)

General Lee also spent the night of May 5-6 reorganizing his command, assessing the day's action, and planning for the combat sure to resume at first light. The day had severely strained the understrength Army of Northern Virginia. It had beaten off the determined but piecemeal Federal attacks, though just barely, and now Lee looked anxiously for the pre-dawn arrival of Longstreet's two divisions and Maj. Gen. Richard Anderson's division of A. P. Hill's Corps. Always seeking a way to maintain the initiative, Lee's initial plan for May 6 was to attack with fresh troops east down Catharpin Road in an effort to turn Meade's left flank and roll it up toward the Rapidan River.

Ewell and Hill, Lee's two corps commanders on the field that night, prepared their troops for the coming dawn in very different fashion. On the Rebel left, Ewell double-checked his front, and rearranged his Second Corps for an attack against Sedgwick. John Gordon's Brigade was shifted to the far left of the line, and Brig. Gen. John Jones' reformed brigade headed back in line on the turnpike. Artillery was repositioned. His three divisions would be ready for the dawn. The same could not be said about A. P. Hill's Third Corps. Despite a thoroughly disordered right flank, Lee ordered Hill to allow his men (Heth and Wilcox) to sleep. Longstreet and Anderson, he reasoned, would be up before sunrise to relieve Hill's jumbled pair of divisions.[14]

The generals closer to the front were more than uneasy with the current arrangement. General Wilcox described his line as "very irregular and much broken and required to be rearranged." Heth agreed, noting that "Wilcox's troops and my own were terribly mixed up." The two divisions, admitted one soldier, "lay in the shape of a semicircle, exhausted and bleeding, with but little order or distinctive organization." This was a dangerous situation, and neither Heth nor Wilcox was content to let matters be. According to postwar accounts, they made several trips to see Hill, alone and together, and were rebuffed each time. At one point Heth suggested, "let me take one side of the road [Orange Plank] and Wilcox the other side and do

the same; we are so mixed and lying at every conceivable angle, that we cannot fire a shot without firing into each other. A skirmish line could drive both my division and Wilcox's, situated as they are now." Hill was in no mood to listen, however, for just as he had been at Gettysburg and elsewhere he was sick. "Longstreet," he assured Heth, "will be up in a few hours. He will form in your front. I don't propose that your division shall do any fighting tomorrow . . . I do not wish them disturbed."[15]

General Wilcox would claim after the war that he was so frustrated he personally sought out General Lee. When he arrived at his tent about 9:00 p.m. to plead his case, Lee merely held up Anderson's note that his division was bivouacking at Verdiersville and could be in position before daylight. Wilcox left without the orders he desired. Hill, perhaps with second thoughts, painfully mounted his horse and rode to see Lee around midnight. The army commander reassured him Longstreet would soon be up and that he should not worry. One recent historian put it best when he wrote, "only pulling back from its advanced position could have saved the Third Corps from disaster, and only Lee could have issued that order."[16]

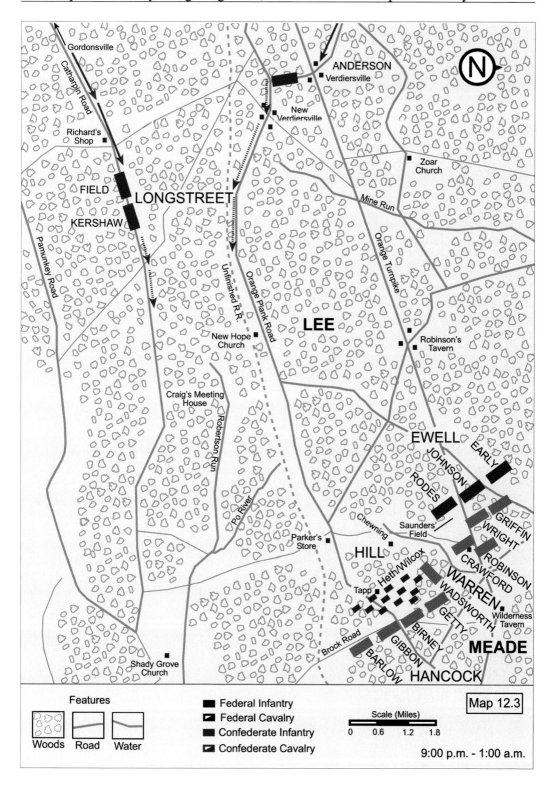

Features

Woods   Road   Water

◼ Federal Infantry
◪ Federal Cavalry
◼ Confederate Infantry
◪ Confederate Cavalry

Scale (Miles)
0   0.6   1.2   1.8

Map 12.3

9:00 p.m. - 1:00 a.m.

Map 12.4: Lee's Gamble
(1:00 - 5:00 a.m.)

Often forced to gamble against long odds, Lee was betting the integrity of his right flank on the arrival of his anticipated reinforcements. He would need them to not only stabilize the weak Orange Plank Road sector, but to deliver a crushing attack to turn back the Union army and end the latest campaign on his terms. Grant's aggressiveness, which may have surprised Lee, combined with the wretched condition of Hill's Corps, convinced him to modify his plan from a sweep around the Union left flank to a direct reinforcement of Hill's front. Lee redirected Longstreet to march east down the Orange Plank Road to replace Hill's Corps, whose two divisions under Heth and Wilcox, augmented by Anderson's, would shift north to finally plug the gap between Hill and Ewell. Once in position, Longstreet's fresh troops would go over to the offensive and collapse the Union left flank.[17]

Had Lee fully understood the unfolding situation he would have been far less optimistic about his chances on May 6. Longstreet and his troops had only recently returned to Virginia after their largely unhappy six-month sojourn in Georgia and Tennessee. Lee had positioned Longstreet's corps at Gordonsville, almost 50 miles from scene of the May 5 combat. Once he was called forward, Longstreet marched his men hard under grueling circumstance—some 32 miles in 24 hours. He finally halted for the night at Richard's Shop, about 15 miles from the battlefield, where his veterans dropped to the ground and fell asleep. Longstreet's orders were to have his men marching again by 1:00 a.m. on May 6. They would move east down the Catharpin Road and north to Parker's Store to the Plank Road, which would put them at the Tapp farm at least by daylight.[18]

Longstreet had his men on the road at the prescribed hour. Major General Joseph Kershaw's Division was in the van, followed by a division under Maj. Gen. Charles Field and the artillery. The column almost immediately ran into trouble. We marched, explained one soldier, "along blind roads, overgrown by underbrush, through fields that had lain fallow for years, now studded with bushes and briars." The roads were narrow and the night dark as pitch. On several occasions the front of the corps took the wrong route, which forced the entire miles-long column to halt and, at least part of it, retrace its steps. Another soldier recalled some of the roads were "overgrown by rough bushes, except the side-tracks made by the draft animals and the ruts of wheels which marked occasional lines in its course." Longstreet was smart enough to use local guides to lead the column, but even they on occasion became disoriented.[19]

As the night hours slipped past, Lee openly worried about their timely arrival and ordered his aide, Catlett Taliaferro, to find Longstreet and urge him to "strain every nerve to reach our lines before day." The tired Longstreet, who had already received a number of Lee's messengers, appeared irritated by the appearance of yet another. "Return to General Lee and tell him to rest easy," he told the aide. He explained he "would be with him before day and prepared to execute any order he desired." Taliaferro turned his horse and made the long dangerous ride back to Lee.[20]

Meanwhile, Richard Anderson's Division, which had been guarding the Rapidan fords, went into camp at Verdiersville on the evening of May 5. He received orders from Lee to resume the march as soon as possible to arrive on the Plank Road. Anderson had his men on the road by 2:00 a.m.[21]

Four o'clock in the morning arrived and passed with no sign of reinforcements. The tension along Hill's front was increasing by the minute. One Mississippi soldier wrote that "all were praying for the arrival of Longstreet." In the east, the very first hint of dawn was beginning to emerge. Wilcox longed to put shovels into the hands of his men, but the enemy was too close. Many Confederates had spent the night listening to Union officers speaking to their men. Heth wrote that he could not sit still and turned his horse around and rode west down the Orange Plank Road in search of Longstreet. He claims to have ridden several miles without catching sight of the approaching First Corps. During a ride along the Plank Road about this time artilleryman William Poague "was surprised to see the unusual condition of things. Nearly all the men were still asleep. One long row of muskets was stacked on the road. Another row made an acute angle with the road and still another was almost at right angles, and here and there could be seen bunches of stacked arms."[22]

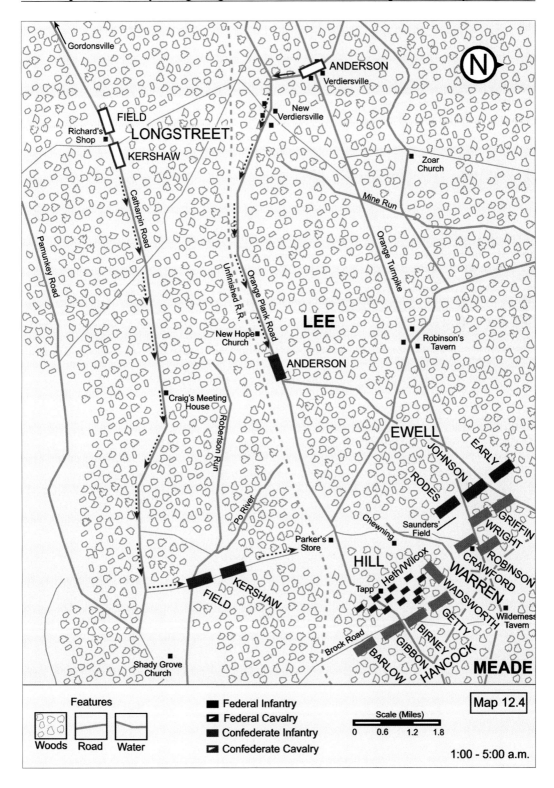

Gordonsville

ANDERSON
Verdiersville

New
Verdiersville

FIELD
Richard's
Shop
LONGSTREET

KERSHAW

Zoar
Church

Catharpin Road

Mine Run

Pamunkey Road

Orange Turnpike

Unfinished R.R.

Orange Plank Road

LEE

New Hope
Church

ANDERSON

Robinson's
Tavern

Robertson Run

Craig's Meeting
House

EWELL

JOHNSON

EARLY

RODES

GRIFFIN

Po River

Chewning

Saunders'
Field

WRIGHT

ROBINSON

Parker's
Store

HILL

CRAWFORD

WARREN

Heth/Wilcox

Tapp

WADSWORTH

FIELD

KERSHAW

GETTY

BIRNEY

Wilderness
Tavern

Shady Grove
Church

Brock Road

GIBBON

HANCOCK

BARLOW

MEADE

Features

Woods   Road   Water

■ Federal Infantry
◨ Federal Cavalry
■ Confederate Infantry
◨ Confederate Cavalry

Scale (Miles)

0   0.6   1.2   1.8

Map 12.4

1:00 - 5:00 a.m.

Map Set 13: Fighting Begins on the Union Right Flank (May 6)

Map 13.1: Fighting on the Union Right Flank (4:30 - 7:00 a.m.)

Generals U. S. Grant and George Meade rose before dawn on May 6. The massive attack by troops under Gens. Winfield Hancock and James Wadsworth against A. P. Hill's battered Third Corps was scheduled to being at 5:00 a.m. A ground fog shrouded the fields. Grant munched a cucumber bathed in vinegar, and washed it down with a cup of strong coffee. He was sitting down to smoke one of the many cigars he would consume that day when artillery fire from the army's right flank broke the silence.[1]

General Richard Ewell had spent considerable time realigning his troops during the night, including his artillery. There were few places to put it to good use, but openings to Saunders Field along the Orange Turnpike and on each flank offered opportunities and he massed guns accordingly. He was especially concerned about the gap between his right and Hill's left, so he posted Lt. Col. Carter Braxton's artillery battalion there as well, supported by Brig. Gen. Stephen Ramseur's Brigade, which had not been involved in the first day's fighting. Ewell also ordered his men to construct abatis (sharpened sticks facing the enemy) in front of their lines. If the Federals attacked, the additional barrier would delay them long enough for musket and artillery fire to break it up. "The enemy could be heard all night falling trees, making abatis, constructing fortifications and cutting roads for the movement of artillery," recalled A. T. Brewer of the 61st Pennsylvania (Brig. Gen. Thomas Neill's brigade). Ewell also stationed sharpshooters in front of the abatis to pick off the enemy as they advanced.[2]

Across the way, Union soldiers in Maj. Gen. Gouverneur Warren's and John Sedgwick's corps were also busy. According to a Pennsylvanian, the "lines were also strengthened and better positions secured. The cartridge boxes and pockets were refilled, guns were examined to see that they were in good order for the next day, when a battle was expected so colossal that the first day's engagement would hardly constitute a respectable prelude."[3]

It was about 4:45 a.m., just when Grant was finishing breakfast and about to enjoy a cigar, when Ewell opened the fighting. Several authors, veterans and modern historians alike considered this effort to be a "full-scale" attack. For example, the historian of the 49th New York (Neill's brigade) observed that "the battle was opened at daylight by a fierce charge by the Confederates on the Sixth Corps, and soon it raged along the whole line." He also recalled that "at five A. M. a battery opened on the 49th Regiment, doing terrible execution with shell and solid shot. The loss was so great that Colonel Bidwell ordered the regiment to double quick to the front about one hundred feet, to get out of their line of fire, and then to lie down upon the ground." The historian of the 61st Pennsylvania described the situation as, "In front of the 6th Corps the rebels charged fearlessly and maintained their assault with great determination. They were supported by artillery which had been skillfully placed during the night."[4]

As impressive as the assault looked to the men in blue, no Confederate reports, memoirs, or unit histories confirm the Union claim of a determined full-scale attack against Neill's men or anyone else's. They do, however, confirm that a heavy skirmish line advanced against Brig. Gen. Truman Seymour's and Neill's brigades, but was beaten off. This probing attack against the Union right flank confirmed the enemy remained in position, and in strength. The Confederates were falling back when at least some of the Union regiments in Neill's brigade, including the 61st Pennsylvania, launched a counterattack about 5:00 a.m. that had the effect of "driving them back into their rifle pits."[5]

The Federal counterthrust was much more organized in Seymour's brigade on the army's extreme right flank. According to Joseph Keifer of the 110th Ohio, "the brigade formed in two lines of battle and assaulted the enemy works in front. . . . The assault was most vigorously made, but the enemy was found to be in too great numbers and too strongly fortified to be driven from his position. After suffering very heavy loss, the troops were withdrawn to their original position, where slight fortifications were thrown up."[6]

Far to the south, meanwhile, the roar of gunfire erupted. Hancock was attacking.

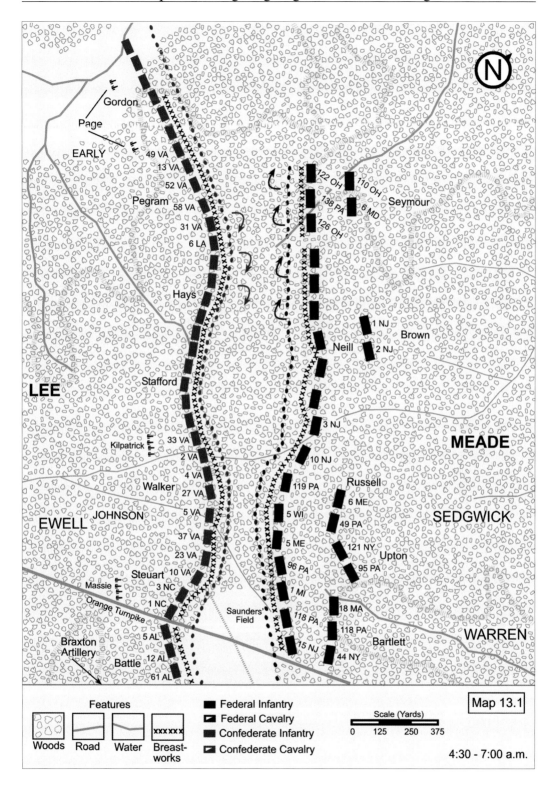

Features

Woods   Road   Water   Breast-
                         works

Federal Infantry
Federal Cavalry
Confederate Infantry
Confederate Cavalry

Scale (Yards)
0   125   250   375

Map 13.1

4:30 - 7:00 a.m.

Map 13.2: Burnside's Difficult Journey (2:00 - 5:00 a.m.)

The vicious fighting on May 5 ended without discernable gain to either side. Even before night fell, General Warren likely suspected his men would be ordered into action again on May 6. Soon enough orders arrived for him to launch a large-scale diversionary attack at 5:00 a.m. with that part of his command still with him, joined by a portion of Sedgwick's Sixth Corps. Much of whatever success Warren's attack would enjoy rested with Maj. Gen. Ambrose Burnside's IX Corps, one-half of which was to take position on Warren's left.[7]

Burnside's corps had camped for the night on the Germanna Plank Road near the Spotswood Plantation. None of his men were more than five miles from Wilderness Tavern, the jump-off point for their attack. Burnside put his men on the road between 1:00 and 2:00 a.m. so he could arrive at the tavern by 4:00 a.m. Problems began almost immediately, for according to Burnside's biographer, "every step of the way they were bucking artillery, ammunition, and ambulance trains [of V Corps] that choked the few existing roads." Marching around the obstacles was all but impossible because the heavy brush and second growth timber hugged each side of the narrow roads. Other factors, such as thick smoke from burning vegetation and fatigue contributed to the slow march.[8]

Warren sent an aide galloping down the Germanna Plank Road at 4:00 a.m. to help lead the van of Burnside's corps into position, but the object of his search was nowhere to be found, to the corps commander's dismay. Meade followed up the news by dispatching another rider who returned to announce that the road was choked with artillery that blocked Burnside's progress. The aide volunteered to return and order the artillery off the road, but Meade snapped, "No, sir! I have no command of General Burnside." Everyone working in proximity to the army commander could see the impact Grant's presence had on Meade's nerves and behavior.[9]

The head of Burnside's column finally tramped into view about 5:00 a.m. and began settling in around the Wilderness Tavern. They arrived with the sound of battle welling up from the south, where Hancock was pitching into A. P. Hill. "Off down the Brock Road to the south, in front of the Second Corps, came the crash of musketry," observed an officer, "with the occasional declaration of artillery. The sound came nearer. It rolled up the line toward us like the closing of a gigantic pair of shears." The approaching roar of combat signaled that part of the V Corps had entered the engagement.[10]

One of Warren's aides, Lt. Morris Schaff, was tasked with escorting Burnside's column to the road leading to Parker's Store. According to the young officer, Burnside was "accompanied by a large staff . . . he was mounted on a bobtailed horse and wore a drooping army hat with a large gold cord around it. Like the Sphinx, he made no reply, halted, and began to look with a most leaden countenance in the direction he was to go."[11]

Burnside's slow approach to the battlefield dismayed (but did not surprise) his fellow corps commanders, just as it did Meade and Grant. Hancock, whose II Corps had attacked on time and was already driving the Confederates (see Map Set 14), was the most vocal about the delayed reinforcements when he felt that he needed them most. Told that Burnside's two divisions would be delayed, Hancock exploded.[12]

Meanwhile, along what was now the Union center held by part of the V Corps and Maj. Gen. Horatio Wright's division of the VI Corps, the faint traces of dawn brightening Saunders Field revealed Ewell's formidable line of works. The fortifications were "plainly to be seen across the open field, a quarter of a mile ahead," wrote one Pennsylvanian lying on the edge of the field. Everyone was within killing range noted another Federal, who observed, "any one who assumed a perpendicular position was sure to make himself a target for the enemy."[13]

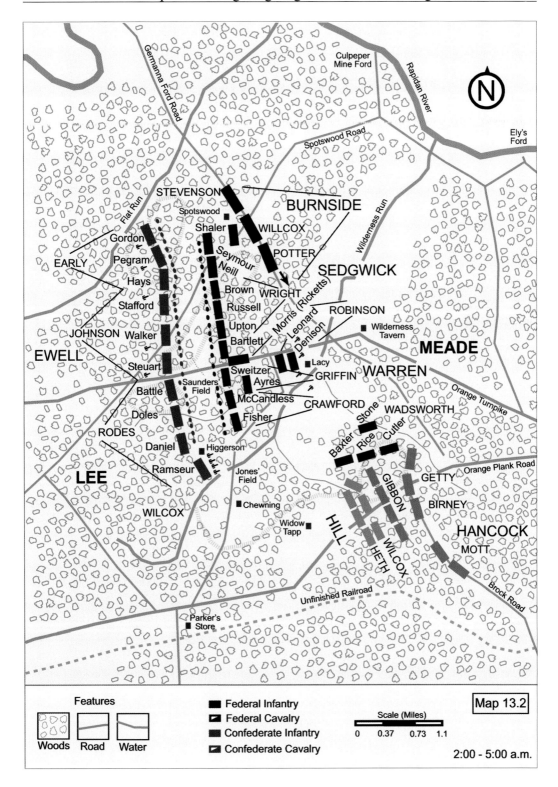

Features

Woods Road Water

■ Federal Infantry
▰ Federal Cavalry
■ Confederate Infantry
▰ Confederate Cavalry

Scale (Miles)

0   0.37   0.73   1.1

Map 13.2

2:00 - 5:00 a.m.

Map 13.3: Warren Hesitates
(5:30 - 7:30 a.m.)

At 5:30 a.m., Warren sent a message to Meade notifying him that all of his troops "are disposed for the assault." All that is, except for two brigades of Brig. Gen. John Robinson's division held in reserve to be used as needed. A newly formed infantry brigade of heavy artillery under Col. Howard Kitching (about 2,900 men) was also available, sent by Warren to bolster Wadsworth's line. Warren did so because "the head of Burnside's column is just going on the field." In other words, Burnside was yet not in position to assist Hancock, and Warren felt compelled to send his own reinforcements.[14]

A frustrated Warren examined Ewell's works that morning through his field glasses, still smarting over his repulse the previous day for what he believed was an ill-advised and poorly planned attack. The Rebels had obviously used the nighttime hours to their advantage, and their front was even stronger than before. Any attack was bound to fail. Meade viewed the situation differently. The primary attack was Hancock's (assisted by Wadsworth and Burnside from the north) against A. P. Hill. Meade needed Warren to attack convincingly in order to prevent Ewell from sending reinforcements to the Rebel right. The attack had been delayed because of Burnside's tardiness. Nearing the end of his patience, Meade sent a message at 6:00 a.m. telling Warren to "throw your pickets and skirmishers well out to the front."[15]

Warren knew it was his job to comply with orders, so he directed Griffin and Crawford to move their divisions forward. Griffin's two battle lines emerged from woods north of the Orange Turnpike to once again cross Saunders Field. Brigadier General William Morris's brigade (Ricketts's division) formed on the left of Bartlett in column of regiments. South of the turnpike, Col. Jacob Sweitzer's brigade, with Brig. Gen. Romeyn Ayres's brigade in support, also headed toward the enemy lines. To its left, Crawford's two brigades under Cols. Joseph Fisher and William McCandless also advanced.[16]

The Confederates opened with small arms fire while their artillery remained silent, probably because the gunners were hoarding their dwindling supply of fixed ammunition if the musketry did not do its job. To counter the expected artillery fire, Warren had several of his own artillery batteries wheeled into position.

It appears only the skirmish line moved toward the Rebel line. The historian of the 44th New York (Bartlett's brigade) noted, "The 6th Corps on our right was to commence the assault and when it became actively engaged our corps was to advance to the attack at once. We waited . . . in anxious expectancy but did not attack. Our position in the mean time was one of extreme discomfort. That our position might be concealed as much as possible from the enemy our troops were ordered to lie upon the ground and remain inactive."[17]

At 6:25 a.m., or about half an hour after the V Corps was ordered to attack, Warren indicated to Meade that his skirmishers had driven their counterparts back to their main line, but "I think it best not to make the final assault until the preparations are made." Warren's foot-dragging infuriated Meade. By this time the Union high command knew Hill's front had collapsed, but that James Longstreet's First Corps was up and counterattacking Hancock on the Federal left. The army leader shot off another, more pointed order to Warren at 7:15 a.m.: "your attack should be pressed with the utmost vigor. Spare ammunition and use the bayonet." Warren's subordinates strongly counseled caution because like him, they considered the enemy works impregnable. He had not wanted to attack the previous day, and he was even more dead set against throwing lives away in what he saw as a senseless charge. Despite Meade's directive, Warren was not going to be budged.[18]

Where was Burnside? With reports of the arrival of Longstreet along the Orange Plank Road, Grant's headquarters shot off a series of orders to Warren and Burnside. The latter was instructed to leave Brig. Gen. Thomas Stevenson's division at Wilderness Tavern and continue marching with his remaining two divisions under Brig. Gens. Robert Potter and Orlando Willcox to the Chewning farm as previously planned.[19]

Their journey began about 6:30 a.m., with Potter's division in the lead. Two regiments, the 48th Pennsylvania and the 6th New Hampshire, were thrown out to protect the front and right flank of the column. The column had barely gotten underway when Burnside called a halt—it was time for the men to have their breakfast.[20]

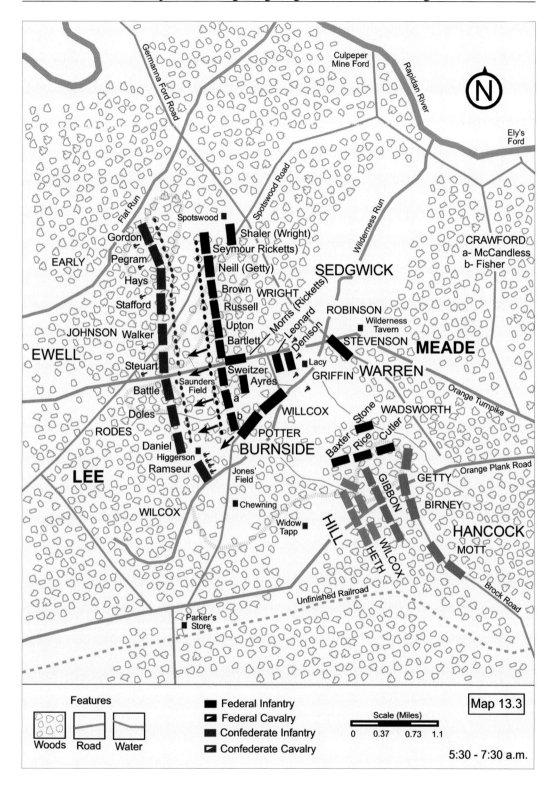

Culpeper
Mine Ford

Rapidan River

Ely's
Ford

Germanna Ford Road

Flat Run

Spotswood Road

Wilderness Run

N

Spotswood

Gordon

Shaler (Wright)

Seymour Ricketts)

CRAWFORD
a- McCandless
b- Fisher

EARLY   Pegram

Neill (Getty)

SEDGWICK

Hays

Brown   WRIGHT

Stafford

Russell

Morris (Ricketts)

ROBINSON

JOHNSON   Walker

Upton

Bartlett

Leonard
Denison

Wilderness
Tavern

STEVENSON   MEADE

EWELL

Steuart

Sweitzer

Lacy

WARREN

Battle

Saunders'
Field

Ayres

GRIFFIN

Doles

a

b

WILLCOX

Orange Turnpike

RODES

POTTER

Stone

WADSWORTH

Daniel

BURNSIDE

Baxter

Rice   Cutler

Higgerson

Ramseur

Jones'
Field

Orange Plank Road

LEE

GIBBON

GETTY

WILCOX

Chewning

BIRNEY

Widow
Tapp

HILL

HANCOCK

HETH

MOTT

WILCOX

Unfinished Railroad

Brock Road

Parker's
Store

Features

Woods   Road   Water

■ Federal Infantry
▱ Federal Cavalry
■ Confederate Infantry
▱ Confederate Cavalry

Scale (Miles)

0   0.37   0.73   1.1

Map 13.3

5:30 - 7:30 a.m.

Map Set 14: Hancock Strikes A. P. Hill's Third Corps (May 6)

Map 14.1: Hill Rests While Hancock Prepares (Midnight - 4:30 a.m.)

Lieutenant General A. P. Hill was a troubled man on the night of May 5-6. In addition to being ill yet again, he was under severe stress: would daylight arrive before James Longstreet? The Third Corps commander painfully mounted his horse about midnight and rode toward Parker's Store in the hope of receiving more news about the two First Corps divisions marching to reinforce his battered front. Frustrated in his effort, Hill rode to army headquarters for the latest information, but none was forthcoming. His exhausted men, he was assured once more, would be relieved before dawn and should be left to sleep. According to Col. William Palmer, one of Hill's aides, "we expected an attack in overwhelming numbers at first blush of dawn."[1]

Although Hill had adamantly rebuffed efforts by Maj. Gens. Harry Heth and Cadmus Wilcox to reorganize their haphazard lines, a certain amount of reorganization of the front took place that night. In Wilcox's Division, Brig. Gen. Samuel McGowan consolidated his scattered brigade on the left of the Orange Plank Road and refused his left, while Brig. Gen. Edward Thomas, whose brigade had been on the left of the line, shifted to McGowan's right with the Plank Road dividing their commands and their lines coming together at an acute angle to form a small salient. Two brigades of North Carolinians held the tenuous right, with Alfred Scales's Brigade in front (on Thomas's right) with James Lane's command in a support position behind Scales and Thomas.[2]

Heth's Division is more difficult to firmly place and was in a more confused state. Brigadier General William Kirkland's Brigade may have been on McGowan's left in the front line, and if so was surely refused to align itself with McGowan's angled line. Colonel Stone, commanding Joe Davis's Brigade, was ordered to return his men to the front and slid his troops near Kirkland, though likely behind his left flank. Heth's final brigades under Brig. Gens. John Cooke and Henry Walker are very difficult to place. The former, which had been hammered

the day before holding the center of Heth's line, was resting in a stubble field somewhere north of the Plank Road, probably behind Stone's position as a general reserve. Walker's Brigade may have been behind Cooke, or may have shifted south, straddling the road as a reserve for both flanks.[3]

Most of the reordering and preparations took place just prior to dawn. Whether the troops constructed breastworks depended upon the brigade commander. For example, General Cooke (Heth's Division), whose men were in reserve, ordered his troops to throw up light works during the night. General Scales's Tar Heels (Wilcox's Division) south of the road in the front line, however, did not erect any works. General Wilcox later reported that he ordered the pioneers forward to begin building breastworks about 3:30 a.m. once he realized Longstreet was unlikely to appear before dawn. Hancock, however, attacked before the pioneers could begin their work.[4]

A Tar Heel in Lane's Brigade recalled many regiments were lying, "just as they had fought." Another noted that many of his fellow soldiers were "out of ammunition and the arms so badly fouled from the firing in the engagement of the 5th that but few of them would fire." Unfortunately for the Confederates, Hill's front was neither well ordered nor cohesive. That night, a single leader was desperately required to reorganize the battered Third Corps front, and only A. P. Hill or General Lee had such authority. Neither man exercised it.[5]

While Hill's Corps largely rested on its arms, a short distance east Hancock developed his attack formation. He divided his command into two wings: Brig. Gen. John Gibbon led the left wing (his own and Brig. Gen. Barlow's divisions), while Brig. Gen. David Birney headed up the right wing (his own division along with those of Brig. Gen. Gershom Mott and George Getty of VI Corps). Birney's division straddled the intersection, with Mott's division stacked on his left. Getty was positioned in a second line behind these two divisions. Gibbon's division was behind Getty.

The responsibility for protecting the left against a surprise attack by Longstreet fell to Gibbon, who deployed Barlow's division, along with most of his artillery, well to the south—which removed Barlow from the subsequent attack column. Gibbon stretched Col. Nelson Miles' brigade across Brock Road and placed his remaining three brigades behind barricades running north along the road.[6]

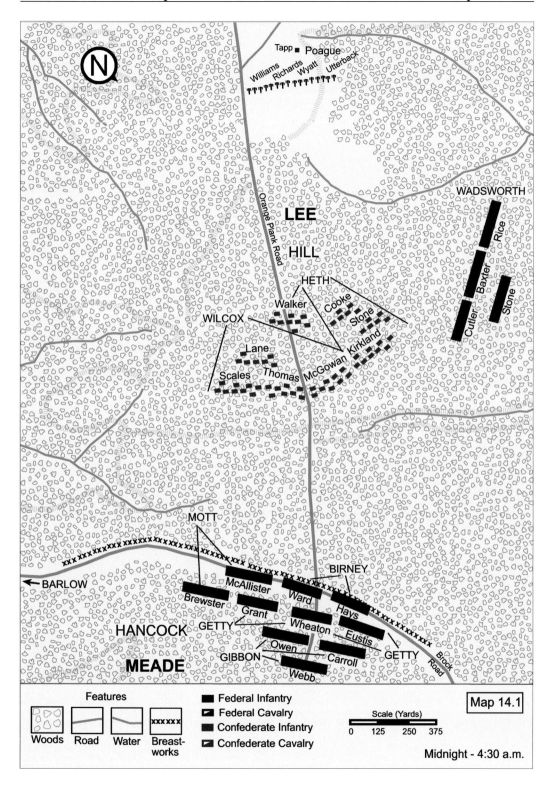

Tapp ■ Poague

Williams Richards Wyatt Utterback

WADSWORTH

LEE

HILL

HETH

Walker   Cooke

Stone

Rice

Baxter

Cutler

Stone

WILCOX

Lane

Scales   Thomas   McGowan   Kirkland

MOTT

BIRNEY

BARLOW

McAllister   Ward   Hays

Brewster   Grant

GETTY   Wheaton   Eustis

HANCOCK

Owen   Carroll   GETTY

GIBBON

MEADE   Webb

Brock Road

Features

Woods Road Water Breast-works

■ Federal Infantry
▰ Federal Cavalry
■ Confederate Infantry
▰ Confederate Cavalry

Scale (Yards)
0   125   250   375

Map 14.1

Midnight - 4:30 a.m.

Map 14.2: Hancock Attacks
(5:00 a.m.)

Robert Robertson of the 93rd New York (Hays' brigade) recalled how he and his comrades were "asleep upon our arms in a field near the crossroads, dreaming of home and the fireside, forgetting the frightful scene through which we had just passed. Not long were we left to our dreams, for at half past three on May 6 we were waked and moved rapidly to the position we first occupied yesterday on the open ridge, the line extending a little further to the left." "At daybreak," wrote the historian of the 152nd New York (Owen's brigade), "we arose and prepared for action. Hastily eating a few mouthfuls from the haversack, we fell in line." These and dozens of other regiments were part of four divisions in attack formation, the whole fronted by a strong skirmish line west of the Brock Road as Hancock prepared to strike A. P. Hill's Third Corps. A fourth division under Barlow was off to the south in reserve to guard the left flank.[7]

Hancock organized a deep attack instead of a broad one. The first line was organized by brigade, McAllister-Ward-Hays, from left to right. The last two brigades comprised Birney's division, while the first brigade was from Mott's. A second line, composed of brigades under Grant and Brewster formed left of the road behind the first line. Grant's men had performed well the day before, but Brewster's brigade had fallen apart almost as soon as it came in contact with the enemy. On their right across the Plank Road were the remaining brigades of Getty's division under Eustis and Wheaton. Gibbon's division comprised Hancock's third line, with Owen's and Carroll's brigades on either side of the road. Webb's brigade formed in the rear, ready to move where needed. This concentrated formation was designed to hit fast and hard and break Hill's front, with enough depth to drive deep into the Rebel rear. They did not receive orders, but the men knew from their officers' frenzied actions that it was but a short time before they would be called into action.[8]

Well to the right (north) and somewhere ahead of Hancock's men in the thickets was James Wadsworth's V Corps division, also prepared for an attack against what the Union command believed was Hill's vulnerable left flank. The division was arranged with Brig. Gen. James Rice's brigade on the right, Brig. Gen. Lysander Cutler's on the left, and Brig. Gen. Henry Baxter's (Robinson's division) in the center. Wadsworth maintained Col. Roy Stone's brigade, under Col. Edmund Dana, as a reserve. The troops had been resupplied with ammunition during the night.[9]

Most of the Confederates were unaware of the storm that was about to hit, and were content to sleep and recuperate from the previous day's ordeal. Some of the Confederate officers worried that there would be an attack. For example, Gen. Kirkland paced back and forth in front of his lines, "casting his eyes toward his men and toward . . . the enemy."[10]

The signal gun triggering the attack shook the predawn darkness just before 5:00 a.m. and within a short time Wadsworth's and Hancock's troops were on the move. "Owing to the nature of the ground, level and covered with a dense forest growth," explained the historian of the 63rd Pennsylvania, "artillery was used very little. The woods were almost impassable even for individuals, and it was impossible to see the entire length of a regimental line." Cornelius Van Santvoord of the 120th New York (Brewster's brigade) remembered "the Union dead lay thick on the ground over which we advanced. Shortly after we crossed the small stream, suddenly there was a loud crash in our front, and the woods were again filled with the messengers of death."[11]

A member of Wadsworth's division wrote with pride: "As its first rays came streaming through the woods, we moved forward on the enemy's position. To a looker-on, I think the advance . . . was the grandest display of military strength that was ever seen on this continent. We press on in six parallel lines of battle . . . it seemed as if nothing could check its progress."[12]

Nine Federal brigades constituting four divisions numbering some 20,000 men were tramping parallel to the Orange Plank Road toward A. P. Hill's mixed up front lines while another 5,000 men in four brigades angled southwest for Hill's left flank. If all went according to plan, another two IX Corps divisions would also drive in to crush Hill's flank. Opposing these various Union juggernauts were eight battered Rebel brigades in two divisions, fewer than 9,000 men in various states of readiness and disarray.[13]

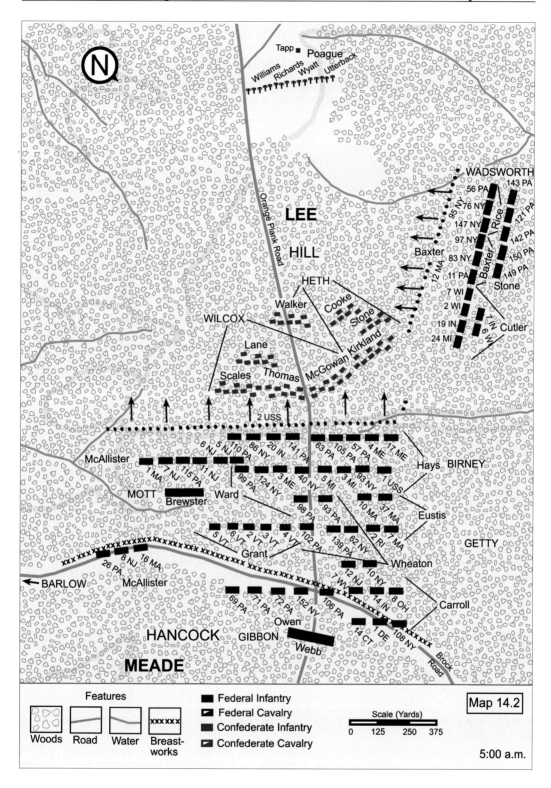

Map 14.2

5:00 a.m.

Map 14.3: Hancock Drives A. P. Hill: Fighting South of the Plank Road (5:00 - 5:45 a.m.)

General Wilcox would vividly recall the morning of May 6 for the rest of his life. Writing in the third person, he noted that "Wilcox, in front, was in an irregular and broken line; Heth's men had slept close in rear, without regard to order." A scattered fitful skirmish fire along his front did not alarm him, but he knew immediately what the volleys "of the heaviest kind" off to his distant left indicated: large bodies of troops fighting. Although most of his men were on the right side of the Plank Road, the sounds of the engagement suggested the enemy was approaching both Hill's front and his left simultaneously.[14]

What part of Hill's front was struck first will never be known with certainty. The Federal troops south of the road under McAllister and Ward struck hard against Thomas's and Scales's brigades, hitting them in front, flank, and rear. A portion of McAllister's brigade was behind part of Hays' line at the beginning of the attack and obliqued left to clear its front. Once free, these men extended beyond the Confederate right and turned and broke the enemy line.[15]

Captain R. S. Williams of the 13th North Carolina (Scales's Brigade) was not quite fully awake when a sergeant yelled, "Look in front!" To Williams's horror, the "woods were blue with the enemy." General Scales took note of the irresistible tide about to engulf his men and called out for them to follow his lead. "He dashed off at right angles . . . and took his brigade out by the right flank," wrote the captain. Most of the men retreated and, in some cases, "stampeded [troops] circled back to the road." Some of Scales's Tar Heels decided to stay and fight, including several from the 38th North Carolina. Their stand, however, was wholly ineffective and onrushing Federals were soon among and through them. "The boys in blue passed right along beside us and yelled at us, 'get back to the rear, Johnnies, to the rear,'" recalled one of the unfortunate Rebels.[16]

George Verrill recalled that his 17th Maine (Ward's brigade) began moving against the enemy in "quick time," and when the Rebel pickets fired on them the pace changed to "double quick time." "The enemy had thrown up a low line of shelter," he wrote, "a single volley from this line was all we received and to the rear they went."[17]

Hill's front was melting away without more than a few minutes of hard fighting anywhere it was challenged. The precipitous withdrawal of Scales's Brigade left Thomas's command on its left and Lane's Brigade behind it in untenable positions. Captain James McElvany of the 14th Georgia (Thomas's Brigade) described what happened that early May morning: "A column of the enemys force attacked our right flank and another our front, [we] fell back again in confusion (No. 2)." Woodson Moon of the 35th Georgia wrote home, "they pored a heavy fire in to us from boath ways and Thomas Brigade had to turn tale and get up or the last one of us would of bin taken prisoner." A member of the 45th Georgia added, "a good many [of our men] were taken prisoner." A veteran in the 16th North Carolinia whose own comrades did not perform much better, complained that the Georgians "gave way at once, almost without firing a gun."[18]

Within minutes James Lane found his brigade in the second line under tremendous pressure. Following A. P. Hill's orders, Lane had not reorganized his men during the night. "In this disorganized fix we received the heavy attack of Hancock," wrote Octavius Wiggins of the 37th North Carolina, part of Lane's command. "The men were willing to fight," he continued, "but had no chance, 'twas confusion worse confounded." Much of the confusion resulted from Scales's foot soldiers barreling into their front in their frenzied retreat to safety. His regiment, complained Wiggins, was "borne gradually back by other disorganized troops without firing a gun." Those not carried back, reported Lane, "fought like heroes, but could not long stand the terrible fire on our front and rear."[19]

Within minutes of contact, most of Hill's front south of the Orange Plank Road had collapsed, Hancock's men had barely broken stride, and the vast majority of the Federals had yet to pull a trigger.

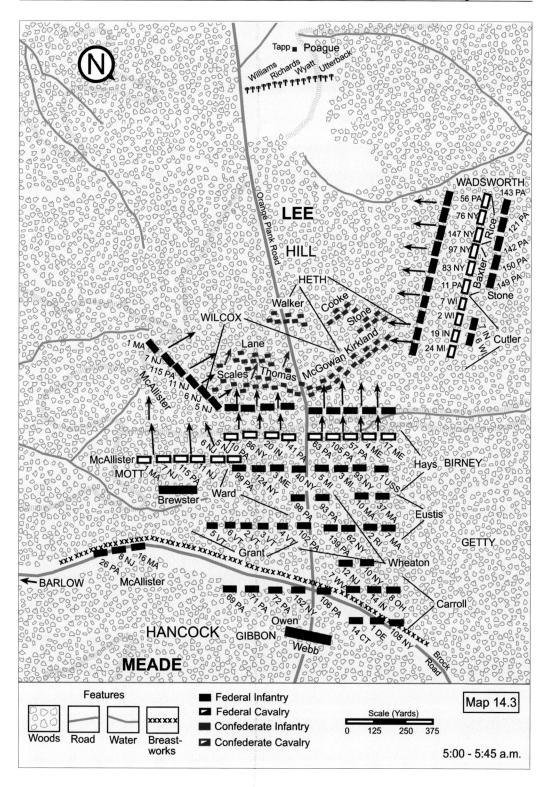

Map 14.3

5:00 - 5:45 a.m.

Map 14.4: Hancock and Wadsworth Drive A. P. Hill: The Fighting North of the Orange Plank Road (5:00 - 5:45 a.m.)

Hancock's front line of brigades north of the Orange Plank Road (Hays, Eustis, and Wheaton) had farther to march to hit the enemy line, which in their front was held by McGowan's and Kirkland's brigades. The attack was supposed to be coordinated with Wadsworth's division coming down from beyond their right.

McGowan's South Carolinians, who had valiantly helped restore the Rebel line the evening before, faced generally north with their right flank touching the Plank Road—directly in the path of the oncoming blue wave. According to McGowan, his men spent the night with their weapons nearby "in the same broken order in which they were at the close of the fight; the line [A. P. Hill's], if any, was something like an irregular horse-shoe—no two brigades touching each other. . . . Hungry, thirsty and fatigued, they had to pass a sleepless night, during the long hours of which the enemy could be distinctly heard making arrangements to envelop them."[20] When the first rays of light broke the darkness, "the enemy could be seen moving on our front, rear, and right, completely enveloping us." The brigade's history claims McGowan's right was unprotected because Thomas's Brigade had fled. "The enemy may have struck their flank, or overlapped them, or they may have not been well in line. . . . The first intimation we had of the state of affairs was the mass of disorganized men who rushed up the road."

The Federal onslaught caught the 12th South Carolina, on the brigade's right flank, in the front, flank, and rear. The regiment tried to refuse its flank, but was too disorganized to make this complicated maneuver under fire. With the bullets killing and wounding up and down the line, the regiment withdrew. Like a line of dominos, the rest of the regiments unraveled in turn (No. 1). J. F. J. Caldwell, who would one day write a history of the brigade, claimed there was "no panic and no great haste; the men seemed to fall back from a deliberate conviction that it was impossible to hold the ground, and, of course, foolish to attempt it. It was mortifying."[21]

Kirkland's North Carolina brigade on McGowan's left was holding the most dangerous part of the entire line that morning, and as a result, was hit on its left by Cutler's Iron Brigade (Wadsworth's division) and in front by Hays' men (No. 2). According to a member of the 11th North Carolina, "a furious attack was made on our left flank and the unformed line was rolled up as a sheet of paper would be rolled without the power of effective resistance." Few Union attackers mentioned this part of the fight, probably because the Confederates fled without putting up much of a struggle and the heavier fighting was yet to come. Breastworks of varying strength delayed parts of the Federal onslaught, and the dense vegetation made it hard for both attackers and defenders to tell whether they were fighting alone or as part of a larger force. General Kirkland sent an aide to the left-rear to see if Stone's Brigade was still in position, but all the staffer found was Yankees. Hit from three directions, Kirkland ordered his men to find their way to the rear as best they could. Fortunately for the Tar Heels, Cutler's left became entangled with Hays' right, which triggered enough confusion to delay that part of the advance for a time. A few regiments tried to maintain their front. The 44th North Carolina, for example, stood fast for a few minutes, but when nine men were shot down attempting to hold the flag high, the soldiers broke for the rear.[22]

Stone's men, on Kirkland's left and rear, had more time to prepare for the onslaught and put up a stronger fight (No. 3). They had to battle both the right side of the Iron Brigade and Kirkland's chaotic tide of retreating North Carolinians, which carried some of the Mississippians "backward amidst the struggling mass, some of whom were firing toward the enemy through their own ranks." A member of the 26th North Carolina who crashed through the line of Magnolia soldiers called the retreat "perfectly disgraceful. I am ashamed to say it, but I don't think I ever saw troops behave so badly."[23]

Colonel Stone did everything he could to keep his brigade from joining the disheveled mass fleeing toward the Plank Road. Riding his buckled line, he rallied his men shouting, "Steady men! Steady! Form on your colors." Stone reformed parts of his line and threw forward a line of sharpshooters to keep the enemy as far away as possible. Somehow the line held—despite the victorious Union troops on their right and rear.[24]

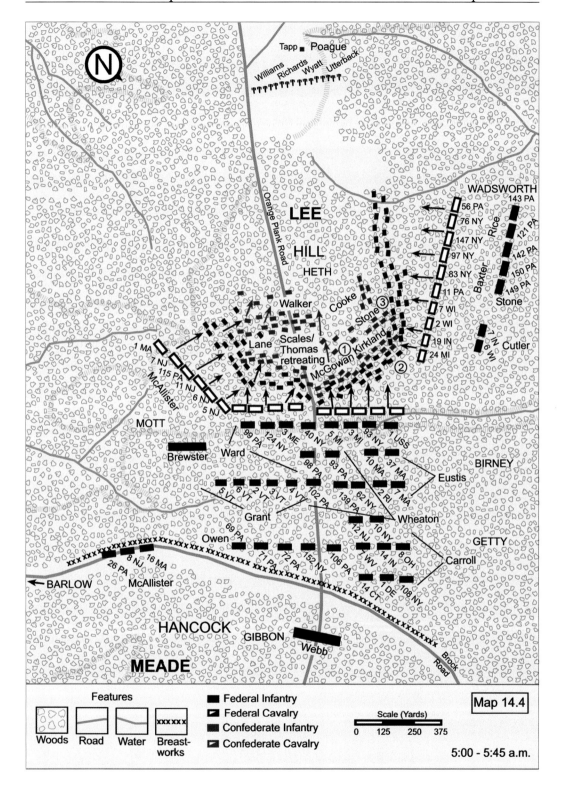

Map 14.4

5:00 - 5:45 a.m.

Features

Woods Road Water Breast-works

■ Federal Infantry
▨ Federal Cavalry
▨ Confederate Infantry
▨ Confederate Cavalry

Scale (Yards)
0   125   250   375

Map 14.5: A. P. Hill's Front Collapses (5:00 - 5:45 a.m.)

A. P. Hill's Confederates were falling back everywhere except on Colonel Stone's narrow front and on his left rear where Cooke's Brigade was maintaining its position. The retreats continued when Walker's Brigade, Heth's deep-left flank unit, joined in the collapse, which cleared the front of Poague's guns. Stone and Cooke fought side-by-side the day before, and they valiantly attempted to repeat their May 5 performance by holding their positions against long odds. Both had been pulled out of the front when Wilcox's Division arrived the day before, but what had been the reserve area was now the front once more, with Wadsworth's attacking Federals approaching from the northwest.

Contrary to orders, the men had spent considerable time that night fortifying their front. After the war, Lt. H. C. Kearney of the 15th North Carolina explained how the men "worked all night throwing up breastworks, which gave us protection and enabled us to hold our position."[25] A member of the 48th North Carolina (Cooke's Brigade) recalled how the fire from Maj. William Poague's Battalion deployed in Tapp field helped the men maintain their front. The rounds tore gaps in Rice's brigade, which was already disordered by its difficult approach.[26]

The pressure, however, was unrelenting and Cooke's North Carolinians and Stone's Mississippians and Tar Heels had no choice but to fall back or be engulfed and destroyed. All of General Hill's infantry in the Orange Plank Road sector were now in full retreat. Only one organized force stood between Hancock's and Wadsworth's men and complete victory: the 16 guns of William Poague's Battalion deployed in the center of Widow Tapp's field. The gunners knew the situation in the woods beyond their vision was grave. According to Poague, "closer and closer the uproar came, [and I] directed our men to pile up rails, logs, etc., at each gun for protection from bullets that now came constantly our way."[27]

Thus far Hancock's massive hammer stroke had struck nothing but victory. Hill's front had dissolved, and hundreds of enemy soldiers were in Federal hands. Some had to run a gauntlet of fire just to reach the Federal lines to be captured. "They were evidently badly frightened, as well they might be, but we shouted encouragingly to them, 'Come on in, Johnny'…and carefully held our fire until they were within our lines," wrote a soldier in the 14th Connecticut.[28]

General Hancock, who had remained at the intersection of Brock and Plank roads, could barely contain his excitement. When Meade's staff officer, Lt. Col. Theodore Lyman, encountered him there, the II Corps commander yelled, "Tell Gen. Meade we are driving them most beautifully. Birney has gone in and he is just cleaning them out beautifully." Lyman, however, was there to share some bad news with Hancock: "I was ordered to report only one division of Burnside up; but he would attack as soon as he could." "I knew it! Just what I expected!" Hancock replied. "If he could attack, now, we could smash A. P. Hill all to pieces."[29]

By this time Hancock's men were also disordered by their rapid advance and the defeat of Hill's Corps. "In some cases they [the Union troops] were heaped up in unnecessary strength," wrote the historian of the II Corps. "Elsewhere great gaps appeared; men, and even officers, had lost their regiments in the jungles." Birney halted the advance to realign his lines. A brief pause ensued.[30]

The Federal onslaught had now reached the edge of Tapp field. Seeing an enemy skirmish line appear at the edge of the clearing, Poague knew that a line of battle was usually behind it, so he ordered his men to open a slow fire with "short-range shells." To his surprise, he continued, "no force showed itself, for I surely expected our guns would be charged." W. H. Lawhorn of the 48th North Carolina (Cooke's Brigade) recalled that "the smoke from cannon was so dense" it partially obscured their view of the approaching foe. The historian of Lee's artillery described Poague's stand as, "The gunners worked with almost superhuman energy, the muzzles belched their withering blasts, the twelve pieces blended their discharges in one continuous roar." Realizing the threat had to be neutralized, General Rice sent the 56th Pennsylvania and 76th New York from his right flank to drive back the guns.[31]

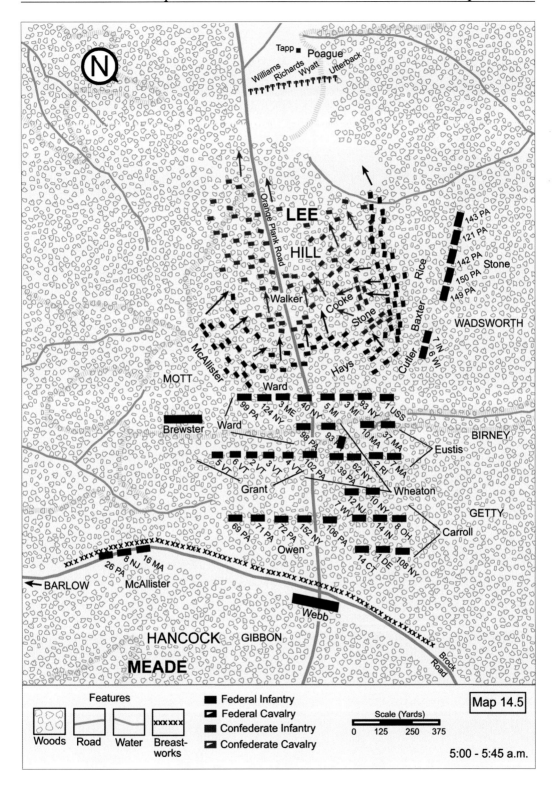

Map 14.5

5:00 - 5:45 a.m.

Map Set 15: Longstreet Reaches the Battlefield

Map 15.1: Robert E. Lee in Crisis (5:45 - 6:00 a.m.)

The only time Robert E. Lee had ever faced a crisis as serious as the one confronting his army that dawn of May 6 was during the battle of Sharpsburg on September 17, 1862, when Burnside's IX Corps turned his right flank and threatened to get behind the Confederates and block Lee's route of retreat. Now, along the Orange Plank Road, Lee's right flank was once again collapsing. At Sharpsburg, A. P. Hill executed a forced march to rescue Longstreet's beleaguered wing. In the Wilderness on May 6, 1864, A. P. Hill's front was collapsing and Longstreet's First Corps reinforcements were marching hard to save it.

Ironically, Burnside played a role in both battles. In the former he was slow to cross Antietam Creek and attack Lee's right. In the latter, he was slow to get his IX Corps up and in position to support Maj. Gen. Winfield Hancock's attack, which became less effective with each tick of the clock as the lines jumbled up, officers went down, and confusion and chaos permeated the ranks. One of Hancock's aides, Francis Walker, wrote many years later how "great gaps appeared [in the line]; men, and even officers, had lost their regiments in the jungle; the advance had not been, could not have been made uniformly right to left, and the line of battle ran here forward, and there backward, through the forest; thousands had fallen in the furious struggle; the men in front were largely out of ammunition." The nearly impassible vegetation compelled the troops to "break up into squads and march by the flank; regiments would thus become separated from brigades, and brigades from divisions, and when the attempt was made to reestablish a line, numerous gaps existed," recalled a New Yorker.[1]

Facing these problems, Hancock and Maj. Gen. James Wadsworth halted their men to reorganize the shattered ranks. By this time the left side of Wadsworth's division (Cutler's brigade) was intermingled with the right side of Brig. Gen. David Birney's division (Hays' brigade). An officer in Cutler's 6th Wisconsin observed that "when the two came together, the men became jammed and crowded, and there was much confusion." Untangling the lines would take time, which was something Hancock simply did not have. He knew Longstreet's men had to be approaching somewhere against the army's left, and if Hill was going to be crushed and dispersed, it would have to be soon.[2]

Although Hancock's line was disordered, it still had considerable depth. By this time only the 16 guns of Poague's Battalion deployed in the Widow Tapp field and pockets of Confederate infantry resistance were standing in the way of a potentially decisive Union victory. Hill's front had collapsed. His soldiers, recalled Porter Alexander in his memoirs, "fell back from both flanks into the Plank Road, and came pouring down the road past the open field near the Tabb [Tapp] house, where Lee stood among the small and scattered pines." When he spied Brig. Gen. Samuel McGowan approaching, Lee rode up to him and exclaimed, "My God! General McGowan, is this splendid brigade of yours running like a flock of geese?" "General, the men are not whipped," he replied. "They only want a place to form, and they will fight as well as ever they did."[3] One of McGowan's foot soldiers later claimed that "General Lee and Hill were here, evidently excited and chagrined. The former expressed himself rather roughly to us, especially us file-closers; but I am not sure but his anger implied a sort of compliment to our past performances." Poague's blazing line of guns provided some measure for recovery, and behind them some of the men ceased their retreat and began to reform.[4]

Poague's veteran artillery was making one of the most gallant gunnery stands of the entire war. One piece was deployed in the middle of the Plank Road, its rounds forcing exposed Federal troops to dash into the underbrush. Poague's remaining guns covered a wide swath of ground that included terrain below the Plank Road. A single battalion of 16 guns, however, regardless of how well they were handled, could not stop a large and determined infantry column converging on three sides.[5]

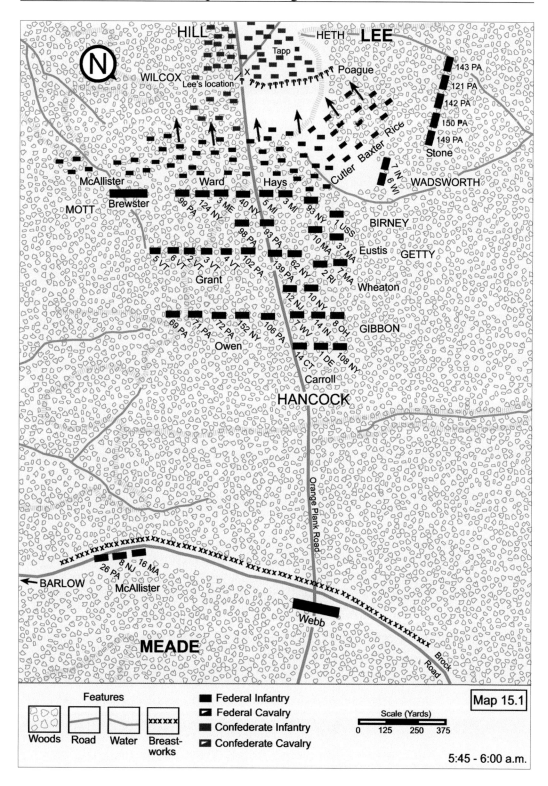

HILL HETH LEE

Tapp

WILCOX Poague 143 PA
Lee's location X 121 PA
142 PA
150 PA
149 PA
Cutler Baxter Rice Stone
7 IN
6 WI

McAllister Ward Hays WADSWORTH

MOTT Brewster BIRNEY
99 PA 124 NY 3 ME 40 NY 5 MI 3 MI 93 NY 1 USS
98 PA 93 PA 10 MA 37 MA Eustis GETTY
5 VT 6 VT 2 VT 3 VT 4 VT 102 PA 139 PA 62 NY 2 RI 7 MA
Grant Wheaton
12 NJ 10 NY
69 PA 71 PA 72 PA 152 NY 106 NY 7 WV 14 IN 8 OH GIBBON
Owen 14 CT 1 DE 108 NY
Carroll

HANCOCK

Orange Plank Road

8 NJ 16 MA
26 PA
←BARLOW McAllister
Brock Road

Webb

MEADE

Features

Woods Road Water Breast-works

■ Federal Infantry
◪ Federal Cavalry
■ Confederate Infantry
◪ Confederate Cavalry

Scale (Yards)
0 125 250 375

Map 15.1

5:45 - 6:00 a.m.

Map 15.2: Longstreet Finally Arrives
(6:00 - 6:30 a.m.)

By the time he encountered Maj. Gen. Cadmus Wilcox along the Orange Plank Road, General Lee's typical poise and control had left him. "Longstreet must be here. Go bring him up!" he shouted to Hill's division commander before turning to ride back to Poague's gun line. The confusion surrounding Lee and his men was as nearly absolute as the stress was overwhelming: choking smoke, screaming gunners, officers shouting at their men while waving swords and pistols, and soldiers overcome with exhaustion or fear or both, "scarcely conscious of the orders given them."[6]

For Major Poague, these long minutes in the Wilderness crowned a career of Confederate service studded with examples of stellar performances. His guns had opened fire even before those pulling the lanyards could see any blue-clad soldiers. The increasing intensity of fighting south of the Plank Road convinced Poague to turn his right pieces south to fire across the road and into the woods beyond. When the enemy appeared in large numbers there, he ordered additional guns to pivot and pour iron into their ranks. "It was our belief that this flank fire checked their advance," Poague proudly penned after the war. He did much of his fighting under Lee's watchful eye. An aide near Lee heard him ask, "Why does not Longstreet come?" For Samuel Harper of Hill's staff, "the minutes seemed like hours, and the musketry was getting uncomfortably near and everything looked like disaster." A. P. Hill dismounted and assisted the gunners in their strenuous labors.[7]

When all seemed hopelessly lost, and large numbers of Hancock's men could be seen moving and firing through the vegetation to the east, Lee took note of a body of men, muskets at the ready, running east toward Poague's guns. "Who are you, my boys?" Lee yelled out. The newcomers replied, "Texas boys!" Behind them, additional reinforcements crowded forward. Longstreet was on the field, with John Bell Hood's former Texas Brigade, now under Brig. Gen. John Gregg, leading the way north of the Plank Road to halt the enemy onslaught. Unable to contain himself, Lee waved his hat in the air and shouted, "Hurrah for Texas! Hurrah for Texas!"[8]

Regaining his composure, Lee ordered the men into line of battle. Riding to the left, he could not help but admire the line of veterans who had fought so magnificently on so many fields. As the line advanced, so did Lee closely behind it. When the men realized what was happening, those in proximity yelled out, "Go back, General Lee, go back!" When the army commander continued with them, several men admonished Lee with the equivalent of, "We won't go on unless you go back." About this time General Gregg appeared to plead his case for Lee to remain behind, as did a tall sergeant who tried to grab his bridle. It was only when Lee's trusted aide, Charles Venerable, arrived to announce that all of Longstreet's men were arriving and his corps commander needed orders that Lee heeded the realities of the situation, turned Traveller about, and trotted to the rear to find Longstreet.[9]

Colonel Venable had encountered Longstreet about a half mile west of the Widow Tapp's field. The event was so critical to the safety of the army that the aide admitted, "my heart beats quicker to think about it even at this distance of time." He found Longstreet's "imperturbable coolness, which always characterized him in times of perilous action," reassuring.[10]

What was transpiring on the Confederate side of the field is generally known, but the positions of the various Union brigades that had driven in Hill's left flank remain murky at best. The front lines of the attacking columns were in deep disarray, but how Wadsworth's division (with Baxter's brigade in tow), aligned with Hancock's II Corps is unclear. According to General Cutler, "the division was then formed in four lines, the left resting on the plank road. These lines were, by order of General Wadsworth, closed in mass to avoid the artillery fire of the enemy." However, Col. Richard Coulter wrote 11 days after the battle that his brigade (Baxter's) straddled the Plank Road. These two reports suggest that during the advance, Baxter's brigade shifted to the left of Cutler to form on the Plank Road and that the rest of Wadsworth's men were on Baxter's right.[11]

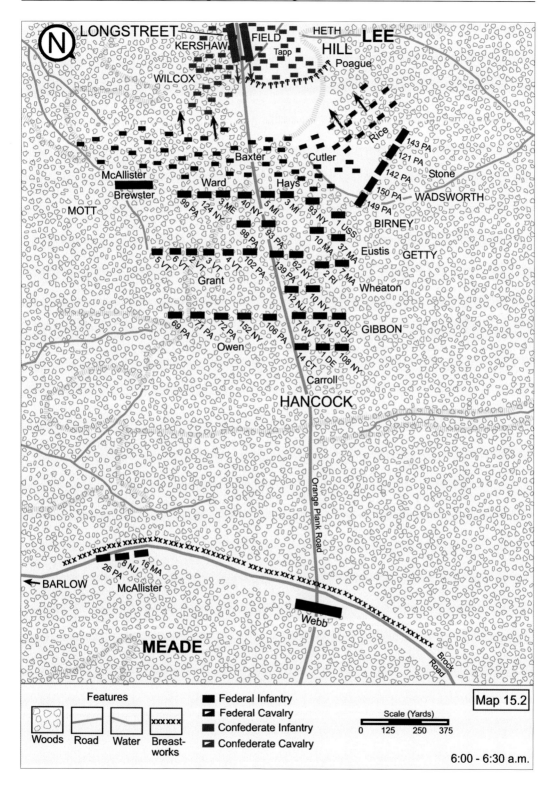

N

LONGSTREET

KERSHAW   FIELD   HETH   LEE
Tapp   HILL
WILCOX   Poague
Poague

Baxter   Cutler   Rice
143 PA
121 PA
McAllister   142 PA   Stone
Ward   Hays   150 PA   WADSWORTH
Brewster   149 PA
MOTT   99 PA   124 NY   3 ME   40 NY   5 MI   3 MI   93 NY   1 USS   BIRNEY
98 PA   93 PA   10 MA   37 MA   Eustis   GETTY
5 VT   6 VT   2 VT   3 VT   4 VT   102 PA   139 PA   62 NY   2 RI   7 MA
Grant   12 NJ   10 NY   Wheaton
69 PA   71 PA   72 PA   152 NY   106 PA   7 WV   14 IN   8 OH   GIBBON
Owen   14 CT   1 DE   108 NY
Carroll

HANCOCK

Orange Plank Road

XXX XXX XXXXXXX XXXXXXXXXXXXXXXXXXX XXXXXXXX
6 NJ   16 MA   XXXXXXXXXXXXXXXXXXXXX
26 PA
BARLOW   McAllister   XXXXXXXXXXXXXX

Webb   Brock Road

MEADE

Features

Woods   Road   Water   Breast-works

■ Federal Infantry
◿ Federal Cavalry
■ Confederate Infantry
◹ Confederate Cavalry

Scale (Yards)
0   125   250   375

Map 15.2

6:00 - 6:30 a.m.

Map 15.3: Longstreet Deploys for Action (6:00 - 6:30 a.m.)

Longstreet's two divisions under Maj. Gen. Charles Field and Brig. Gen. Joseph Kershaw jogged their way to the scene of the action abreast of one another to ensure as many trigger-pullers as possible arrived where they were most needed in the shortest span of time. The detritus of A. P. Hill's broken Third Corps stood in their path like rocks around which washed an unstoppable gray flood tide. "Before reaching the Plank Road we knew from the continued roll of musketry that the battle was on in earnest," recalled R. T. Coles of the 4th Alabama, part of Brig. Gen. Evander Law's Brigade (on this day under Col. William Perry) in one of the finest descriptions of the moment. "Directly in our front as we were hastening forward, the sun, blood red, from the effect of the smoke of battle, was just appearing above the Wilderness. . . . Litter bearers were continually passing with the severely maimed and a stream of wounded able to leave the battle line filled both sides of the Plank Road. I never before or after witnessed such excitement and confusion. It was perfectly appalling. Staff officers were urging their mounts at topmost speed back and forth; orders were repeatedly received for us to quicken our steps. The number of wounded and stragglers increased as we drew nearer the firing line, all stating that we were holding our own, unwilling to acknowledge that disaster had befallen them."[12]

Gregg's Texas Brigade (Field's Division) was not the first of Longstreet's troops to reach the field. That honor belonged to Kershaw's Division, the head of which arrived first and flowed to the right (south) of the Plank Road. Kershaw knew his men would immediately plunge into a bitter fight because General Wilcox had ridden back to advise him of the state of the front and give him Lee's orders to deploy south of the road. Kershaw's own brigade, commanded by Col. John Henagan, spearheaded the column. Getting into position was not easy for the South Carolinians. Before they could deploy, "retreating masses of Heth's and Wilcox's division broke through my ranks and delayed Colonel Henagan until they had passed to the rear," explained Kershaw in his report.

Regimental leadership, always critical, was especially needed at this time, and Longstreet's officers were up to the task. The men opened ranks to allow the fugitives to pass through without extensive disruption, reorganized their ranks, and stepped forward into the maelstrom.[13]

North of the Plank Road, Colonel Venable encountered Longstreet encouraging his men as they deployed. Worried about General Lee's reckless state of mind, the staff officer asked Longstreet to convince the army commander to stay out of harm's way. Longstreet agreed, rode to Lee's side, and with his "affectionate bluntness" told him he needed a free hand to command his corps. "If my services [are] not needed," he told Lee, "I would like to ride to some place of safety, as it [is] not quite comfortable where we [are]."[14]

Most of Longstreet's men were still on the back side of a rise on Widow Tapp's field, so the Federal commanders did not yet know the First Corps had arrived. Longstreet's seasoned eye quickly sized up the situation. One of Lee's aides watched Longstreet and reported after the war that Old Pete "rode down the line, his horse at a walk, and addressing each company said, 'Keep cool, men, we will straighten this out in a short time—keep cool.' In the midst of the confusion his coolness and manner was inspiring." Longstreet also personally halted scores of men from McGowan's and Stone's brigades and helped reform them behind Poague's gun line. They were in no condition to participate in the counterattack, but they could support the artillery.[15]

And the victorious but disorganized Federal troops were in no condition to meet a concentrated fresh Confederate thrust. As noted earlier, after his successful attack General Hancock stopped the advance to "adjust its formation before advancing farther." Some of the troops would later criticize his decision. According to John Haley of the 17th Maine (Hays' brigade, Birney's division), "our troops had moved with wonderful celerity and had turned the Rebs right out of their blankets, pursuing them for two miles. No one knows where our division would have driven them if Hancock hadn't felt it imperative to halt and make some kind of alignment."[16]

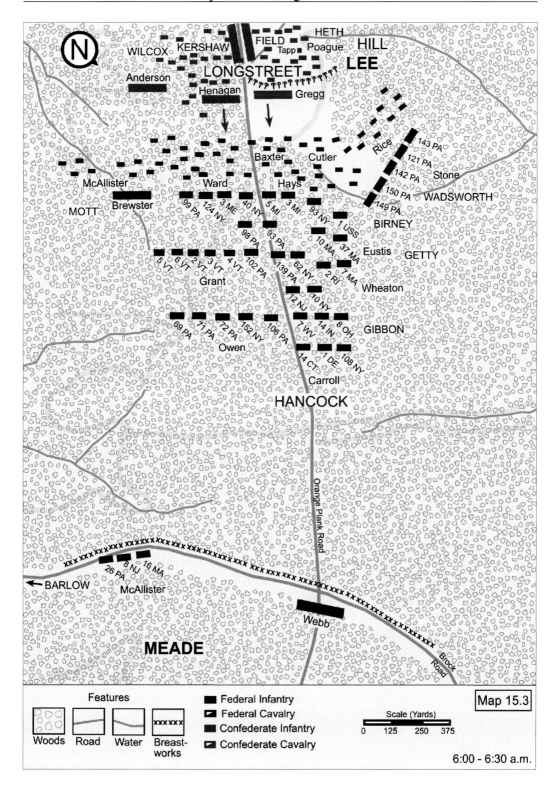

Map 15.3

6:00 - 6:30 a.m.

Map Set 16: Longstreet Counterattacks North of the Orange Plank Road

Map 16.1: Gregg's Texans Crash into the Federal Line (5:45 - 7:00 a.m.)

The collapse of A. P. Hill's Third Corps demanded immediate address, and the veteran Longstreet knew exactly what to do to stabilize the front. Waiting for his entire command to arrive was impractical given the emergency at hand, so he thrust each brigade into the fighting as it reached the front. Major General Charles Field's Division, Hood's former command, formed on the left (north) of the Orange Plank Road (No. 1), with Brig. Gen. John Gregg's Texans in front. This was Gregg's first experience with Lee's army, having been placed in command of the famous Texas Brigade in January while still in Tennessee.[1]

With Lee now behind them, the Texans advanced east with Gregg shouting, "The eyes of General Lee are upon you!" The brigade was composed of three Texas regiments and the 3rd Arkansas. The alignment of the 800-man unit is unclear, although it appears the 5th Texas was on the right with the rest—4th Texas, 1st Texas, and 3rd Arkansas—extending the line left. The brigade's right flank was at least 100 yards from the Plank Road, a front filled with the 2nd South Carolina of Colonel Henegan's Brigade (No. 2).[2]

As the line moved out, recalled one veteran, "the jingle of hundreds of iron ramrods up and down the line denoted that something horrible was soon to take place." The quick-stepping Rebels scattered the Federal skirmish line and entered the tangles of the Wilderness. According to the historian of the 3rd Arkansas, "the Rebels fired in their faces and went in with the bayonet. The Federals didn't drive. They stubbornly stood their ground and slugged it out." A Confederate officer remembered the opening of the fight this way: "there was a terrible crash, mingled with wild yells, which settled down into a tremendous roar of musketry." A member of Brig. Gen. Henry Baxter's brigade found he and his comrades in a rather chaotic state at the front and roughly center of the attack along the road when Longstreet's men came up to greet them. The enemy poured "a fearfully murderous volley.

The effect was electrical," added Phil Faulk of the 11th Pennsylvania, "our entire line . . . rising at once to repel the attack. It was a moment of deadly peril and wild excitement." Baxter's rounds cut through Gregg's right and struck his front and left.[3]

The murderous fire brought the Texans and Arkansans to a halt just 20 or so yards from the Yankees, where the two sides exchanged a deadly fire (No. 3). "Death seemed to be our portion," recalled one of Gregg's men. Realizing he could not maintain his exposed position, Gregg pulled his men back, reorganized his ranks, and launched a new attack. This one was more successful and drove the front Union units into retreat. According to the historian of the 17th Maine (Hays' brigade, Birney's division, Hancock's II Corps), "the enemy, having gained a position on the Plank Road, opened upon our lines a most deadly fire, both with musketry and artillery, so that the advance was checked. . . . [The regiment] was unable to hold the position, as it was flanked by the enemy, and the command was forced to retire." Major Merit of the 7th Indiana, part of Cutler's Iron Brigade fighting somewhere on the right of the 17th Maine, reported that the "rebels charging in front and on right flank caused us to slowly retire, losing the ground gained this day."[4]

Gregg's assault stunned and then threw back the advanced enemy front. The depth of the Union attack, however, made itself known when the first line of Federal troops was replaced by a second line. The cost of sealing the breach in Hill's front was high. "For 25 minutes we held them steady," recalled one of the survivors, "and at the expiration of that time more than half of our brave fellows lay around us dead, dying, and wounded, and the few survivors could stand it no longer." During the last minutes of their fight, it looked as though the right regiments (4th and 5th Texas) would be cut off. By the time the fighting ended only about 250 of the 800 men Gregg carried into battle were present.[5]

After losing two-thirds of his men, Gregg fell back near Poague's guns. According to one story, a lieutenant was his company's sole survivor and for months after paraded alone with the rest of his regiment's companies. "As we were forming [in the rear]," wrote J. B. Polley of the 5th Texas, "another brigade passed over us on its way to hold the enemy in the position to which we had driven him." The Georgians of Brig. Gen. Henry "Rock" Benning's Brigade were about to enter the fight.[6]

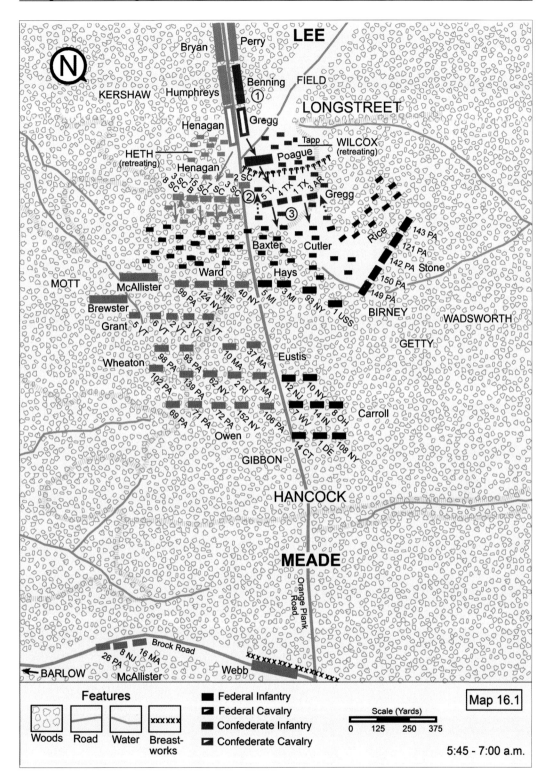

Map 16.1

5:45 - 7:00 a.m.

Map 16.2: "Rock" Benning's Georgians Enter the Fray (5:45 - 7:00 a.m.)

The brigade of Georgians under Henry Benning numbered about 1,000 trigger-pullers when it arrived at the Widow Tapp farm. With the route ahead of them open, Benning thrust his command ahead with a step and a shout. "Benning's Brigade," observed Col. William Perry, the commander of Law's Brigade, "passed over the ground stained by the blood of the heroic Texans."[7]

"We . . . had many 'close calls' during the war," recalled George McRae of the 20th Georgia, part of Benning's Brigade, "but I think as a command the closest grapple we had with death was on the morning of May 6, 1864, at the Wilderness." There was little time for the men from the Deep South to halt in Widow Tapp's field, for Gregg's men were falling back in some disorder. An anonymous foot soldier in the 15th Georgia acknowledged as much when he wrote home soon after the battle, "after reaching the scene of the strife, we only halted sufficiently long to load our guns and then hastened in the fight, without ever taking time to form line of battle." General Lee was still sitting on Traveller in the Tapp field when Benning's men came up. Many saw the army commander wave his hand toward the south side of the road and say, "We are driving them on the right." From the sounds of battle, J. H. Gresham of the 15th Georgia knew the news to be true, though he did not know that Joe Kershaw's Division was doing the fighting there.[8]

Benning's alignment is unclear, but a recent map study indicates it was, from left to right as follows: 15th Georgia - 17th Georgia - 2nd Georgia - 20th Georgia (No. 1). Once the fresh troops entered the woods on the edge of the field, they encountered a swampy area and, after slogging nearly 200 yards through soggy ground, discovered a strong line of enemy troops. According to McRae, "the opposing lines of battle commenced firing on each other as soon as they came in sight of each other." Firing as they advanced, the two sides halted within a murderously close distance and killed one another in a stand-up fight. Colonel Perry recalled that Benning's Brigade, "being a larger brigade [than Gregg's], it produced more impression."[9]

The Union troops directly in front of the Georgians melted away into the vegetation. "Heavy masses were pressing by and beyond its left," recalled Perry, and within a short time a deadly volley ripped through the exposed flank of the 15th Georgia on the far left of the brigade line (No. 2). The regiment's commander, Col. Dudley DuBose, refused the left four companies to face this new threat, which hailed from the ranks of James Wadsworth's division. "For fifteen minutes or more our boys stood the enfilading fire," wrote McRae. "It was, however, impossible for any troops to withstand such a galling fire [for] any length of time." Another Georgian recalled that no orders were issued during this fight, and even if they were, the sounds of battle were so loud, no one would have heard them.[10]

The problems increased for the embattled Georgians when Benning, mounted on an impressive steel-gray steed and with "spurs rattling like as many trace irons," was struck in the left shoulder by a bullet that fractured several bones. A surgeon later decided he was "severely, but not dangerously wounded." Colonel DuBose of the 15th Georgia assumed command of the brigade.[11]

Realizing that the brigade could not hold its position much longer, DuBose was faced with the difficult task of safely extracting the men. He attempted to do so by boldly "endeavoring to force the [enemy] line in our front, hoping to cause those on the flank [Wadsworth's Division] to fall back also." The tactic failed, however, when the Rebels "found a wet, muddy marsh, over which it was impossible to pass in any order." By the time the Georgians fell back in some disorder to the Widow Tapp field, another brigade was advancing to replace it (No. 3).[12]

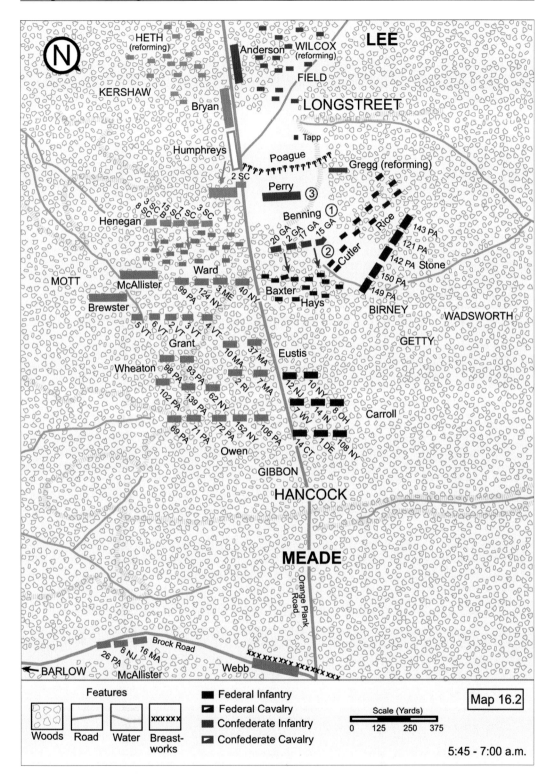

Map 16.2

Features

Woods Road Water Breastworks

xxx xxx

Federal Infantry
Federal Cavalry
Confederate Infantry
Confederate Cavalry

Scale (Yards)

0   125   250   375

5:45 - 7:00 a.m.

Map 16.3: Perry's Brigade Attacks
(7:00 - 8:00 a.m.)

The initial brigade-size attacks north of the Orange Plank Road by Gregg and then Benning blunted and in some cases drove back parts of two Federal divisions (Wadsworth's and Birney's).[13] Given the dire circumstances and difficult terrain, the piecemeal manner in which they were fed into battle was not strong or cohesive enough to do much more than that. Portions of Hays', Baxter's, Cutler's, and Rice's brigades still manned the front lines north of the road. Organized regiments, if there were any, were few and far between, with most of the front consisting of masses of men desperately trying to hold their positions. Wadsworth's right flank was reinforced by two large regiments of green heavy artillerymen armed with muskets and expected to behave like infantry. The 6th and 15th New York Heavy Artillery under Col. J. Howard Kitching entered the sector with about 2,400 men (No. 1). Colonel Roy Stone's brigade was also here, and fairly intact. Into this inferno stepped Col. William Perry at the head of Law's Brigade.[14]

Perry began shifting the brigade into line of battle while quick-stepping toward the edge of Widow Tapp's field. Unlike Benning and Gregg, Perry halted to form his final line. As he had been all morning, General Lee was present to witness Perry's arrival and was still anxious about the safety of his army. When he inquired as to the identity of the passing infantry, one of the foot soldiers replied, "Law's Alabama Brigade, Sir." A delighted Lee exclaimed, "God bless the Alabamians!" The army leader guided Traveller back and forth along the assembling line until he spied a rotund officer, at which point Lee rode along him and called out, "Go on my brave Alabama captain and drive them back."[15]

The five regiments deployed from left to right as follows: 15th Alabama - 48th Alabama - 44th Alabama - 47th Alabama - 4th Alabama. Colonel P. D. Bowles of the 4th Alabama recalled General Field telling him to "place his right on the Plank Road, and keep it there." Several uncomfortable minutes passed before the men were finally unleashed at a "double-quick" pace. The 1,255-man brigade, large in comparison to Gregg's and Benning's swept across the Widow Tapp field with its right along the Plank Road and its left substantially farther northwest than either of the aforementioned brigades had reached. It is possible that Colonel Perry oversaw the regiments on the left of the extended line and that General Field, at least early in the fighting, guided those on the right.[16]

The Alabamians on the right of the line fired a volley into the Federals, who were barely visible through the thickets, before advancing into the tangles (No. 2). The clots of enemy soldiers fell back in confusion. An advance of about 100 yards brought the Alabama men face-to-face with a fresh line of breastworks. According to the 4th Alabama's commander, Colonel Bowles, the works "consisted of logs piled up here and there sufficiently arranged to satisfy me that the enemy had just reached it and were hastily erecting it from logs lying indiscriminately in the woods." Bowles, who was also in command of the 47th Alabama on his immediate left, ordered his men to take shelter behind this rough barricade when it became obvious its recent occupants were fleeing.[17]

The situation facing the rest of Perry's long line was much different (No. 3). According to Perry, his center and left regiments "found themselves confronted by dense masses of the enemy." With a large measure of audacity, Perry's men "fired a volley without halting, and the whole line bounded forward with their characteristic yell." The surprised Federals—probably the remains of Rice's and Cutler's brigades—gave ground. It was about this time, however, that Perry "became aware, from the direction of the balls . . . [that] a force of the enemy has crossed the morass, ascended the heights and occupied a body of woods at the farthest limit of open ground." Heavy lines of enemy infantry were only about 200 yards from his vulnerable left flank. What he did not know what that these men represented Colonel Kitching's two large regiments of heavy artillerymen. Showing solid tactical ability, Perry sent his sizable 15th Alabama on his left flank looping back to the left-rear in an effort to confront the new threat (No. 4). It was a bold move that split his attenuated front into three separate parts.[18]

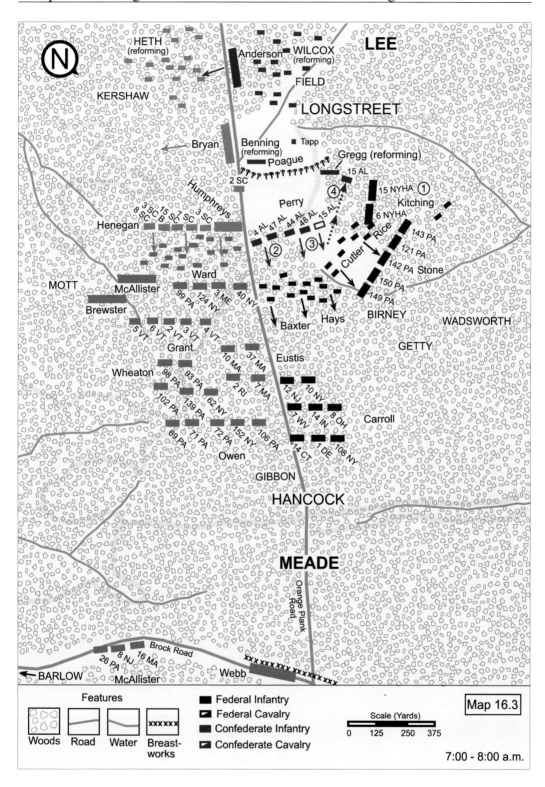

HETH
(reforming)

Anderson   WILCOX
              (reforming)

LEE

FIELD

KERSHAW

LONGSTREET

Bryan

Benning
(reforming)
Poague

Tapp

Gregg (reforming)

15 AL

2 SC

Humphreys

Perry

④

15 NYHA ①

Kitching

3 SC
8 SC 15 SC 1 SC 3 SC
       B

4 AL 47 AL 44 AL 48 AL 15 AL

6 NYHA

Henegan

②   ③

Rice

143 PA

121 PA

Cutler

142 PA Stone

Ward

150 PA

149 PA

BIRNEY

WADSWORTH

MOTT

McAllister

99 PA 124 NY 3 ME 40 NY

Baxter   Hays

Brewster

5 VT 6 VT 2 VT 3 VT 4 VT

GETTY

Grant

10 MA 37 MA

Eustis

Wheaton

98 PA 93 PA 2 RI 1 MA

62 NY

102 PA 139 PA 152 NY 106 PA

12 NJ 10 NY 8 OH

Carroll

69 PA 71 PA 72 PA

7 WV 14 IN

14 CT 1 DE 108 NY

Owen

GIBBON

HANCOCK

MEADE

Orange Plank Road

Brock Road

26 PA 8 NJ 16 MA

BARLOW   McAllister

Webb

xxxxxx xxxxxxxxxxxxx

Features

Woods   Road   Water   Breast-
                        works

xxxxxx

Federal Infantry
Federal Cavalry
Confederate Infantry
Confederate Cavalry

Scale (Yards)

0   125   250   375

Map 16.3

7:00 - 8:00 a.m.

Map 16.4: Perry's Brigade Continues Its Advance (7:00 - 8:00 a.m.)

After detaching the 15th Alabama, Perry threw the 44th and 48th Alabama against the Federal troops in their front (No. 1). The going was tough for the two regiments, for they faced perhaps three brigades, though all three were in various states of exhaustion and confusion. By that time Federal casualties were taking their toll and two brigade commanders were down. General Baxter fell with a gunshot wound to his leg, leaving Col. Richard Coulter of the 11th Pennsylvania in command, and Colonel Stone fell from his horse and re-injured his leg, which elevated Lt. Col. John Irvin of the 149th Pennsylvania.[19]

The disappearance of enemy troops from in front of his center and left allowed Perry to focus his attention on Kitching's heavy artillerymen off his vulnerable left flank (No. 2). "The safety of the brigade," concluded Perry, "might be compromised by an advance far to the front, while a force of the enemy—I knew not how large—was upon my flank and rear." He had already dispatched the 15th Alabama to address this threat, a large veteran regiment led by the competent and experienced Col. William C. Oates. After swinging tightly to its left, Oates found his regiment of 450 men on the flank of the 1,200-man 15th New York Heavy Artillery. Beyond was the 6th New York Heavy Artillery of roughly similar size. The bold Oates, a veteran of many battles including the fighting on Little Round Top, attacked. According to Alabama soldier William Jordan, "we charged them resolutely with a Rebel yell that terrified the Blue Jackets so that they limbered to the rear, shedding their haversacks and baggage as they moved in a hurry, half bent. This certainly was the richest battle field that I ever beheld." The New Yorkers put up a short fight before scampering for the rear. The assault cost the 15th Alabama but one man killed and another 11 wounded. Colonel Oates later attributed his scant losses to the enemy's inexperience and the suddenness of his flank attack. Colonel Perry later described the 15th Alabama's action as "one of the most brilliant movements I have ever seen on a battlefield."[20]

With the threat to his left and rear neutralized, Perry knew he had to reestablish his brigade front and rode back to his two center regiments—but not before ordering the 15th Alabama to rejoin them. As the colonel soon discovered, however, the 44th and 48th Alabama had veered to the left during their advance to confront a large number of enemy troops (perhaps Stone's brigade, now under Colonel Irvin). "These two regiments," he reported, "had crossed the morass, and were pressing steadily up the hill, firing as they advanced." Their drive left a large gap between them and his right wing (47th and 4th Alabama) fighting closer to the Orange Plank Road.[21]

Perry's two right regiments were nowhere to be seen, for they had obeyed orders and maintained a connection with the Plank Road, halting to take cover behind the hastily constructed breastworks as noted earlier (No. 3). It appears that remnants of Hays' and Baxter's brigades still occupied their front. A soldier fighting with the 11th Pennsylvania of Baxter's brigade wrote that the earlier Rebel advance had caused "the whole front [to be] lighted up with deadly volleys. . . . Longstreet's attack on the left-first lines with the force of an avalanche."[22]

The shredding of the front line brigades under Baxter, Hays, and Cutler, which had formed along the Orange Plank Road, prompted General Birney to order up Eustis's and Wheaton's brigades from Getty's division (No. 4). According to General Getty, these troops had shifted from their original positions north of the road to the south as they were squeezed to the left when they collided with Wadsworth's division approaching form the west. Now they were needed back above the road to stop Field's Division. General Wadsworth was also there, ordering Eustis into battle even though the brigade did not belong to his command.[23]

Wadsworth was probably feeling more confident now that reinforcements from Getty's division were up. Eustis's brigade crossed the road in column of regiments, with the 37th Massachusetts in the lead, and Wheaton's brigade following. Wadsworth met the regiment as it filed across the road and made a sweep with his arm from right to left to indicate a half wheel as it advanced toward the enemy line.[24]

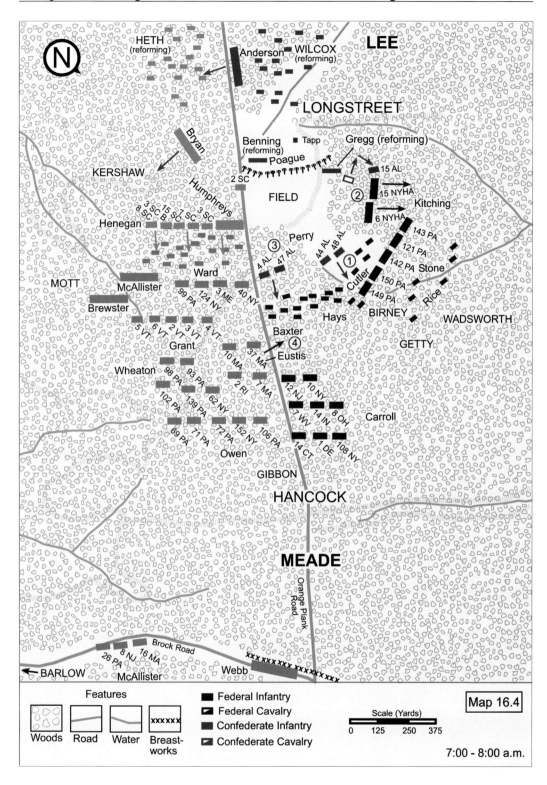

Features

Woods Road Water Breast-works

Federal Infantry
Federal Cavalry
Confederate Infantry
Confederate Cavalry

Scale (Yards)
0   125   250   375

Map 16.4

7:00 - 8:00 a.m.

Map 16.5: Perry's Right Fights the 37th Massachusetts and Part of Carroll's Brigade (8:00 - 9:00 a.m.)

Leading Brig. Gen. Henry Eustis's column was Col. Oliver Edwards's 37th Massachusetts, which complied with Wadsworth's orders as it made its half-wheel toward the 4th and 47th Alabama of Perry's Brigade (No. 1). Eustis, however, found the situation unsettling and ordered his brigade to halt. The Massachusetts men in front, however, did not receive the order and continued their steady advance, noted the regiment's historian, "with a cheer and a dash as one man the gallant battalion threw itself against the advancing line." Wadsworth accompanied the regiment during the initial stages of its advance.[25]

According to Colonel Bowles of the 4th Alabama, the 37th Massachusetts "fired very low, so that their shots were having a very perceptible effect on my line." Realizing he could not maintain his position, Bowles ordered his regiment to charge with the 47th Alabama on its left. When Colonel Edwards learned his regiment was facing a strong enemy alone, with the Rebels lapping his vulnerable right flank (No. 2), he had little choice but to order a withdrawal. An ordered retreat under those bloody chaotic conditions was easier said than done. Somehow Edwards managed to withdraw by pulling back half of his command a short distance, where it would halt and open fire while the other half repeated the process. This brilliant tactical move was repeated several times until the 37th Massachusetts was able to rejoin the rest of the brigade, where it formed on the right of the line.[26]

The pair of Alabama regiments under Colonel Bowles continued advancing until they reached some light breastworks thrown up the previous day by A. P. Hill's Third Corps. Their reprieve behind the works proved short, for within a few minutes a large Federal force was spotted advancing against them. The identity of these troops is unclear, but they were probably the 14th Indiana, 8th Ohio, and 7th West Virginia of Col. Samuel Carroll's brigade, which had moved forward into the vacuum created by the withdrawal of the Bay Staters and failure of Eustis to fully advance. Carroll had been ordered

south of the Orange Plank Road (No. 3) when Longstreet's attack began to help absorb and beat back the hammer blow delivered by Kershaw's Division. The arrival of Field's Division above the road, however, coupled with its stunning success there, triggered new orders for Carroll to send back three of his regiments. These regiments probably slid into position when the 37th Massachusetts was pulling back from its ill-advised attack. Carroll remained with the balance of his brigade below the road, leaving the three regiments above it under the command of Col. John Coons of the 14th Indiana. According to Col. Franklin Sawyer of the 8th Ohio, his regiment moved by the right flank behind the 14th Indiana, while the 7th West Virginia followed the Buckeyes.[27]

Bowles, meanwhile, knowing the 47th Alabama on his left had already pulled back, watched with growing alarm as the new threat materialized along his front and to his right. Like so many commanders before him, he was now isolated and his only realistic option was to fall back (No. 4). He halted his 4th Alabama at the first line of breastworks they had recaptured, linking up there with the 47th Alabama which was already in the works. Together, the two regiments opened a blistering fire against Carroll's advancing troops. The 20th Georgia of Benning's Brigade appeared on their right flank and faced the Plank Road, forming a rough inverted "L" (No. 5). When he heard a series of Union commands suggesting the enemy was readying a full-scale attack, and believing he was severely outnumbered, the audacious Colonel Bowles ordered his men to charge. Screaming the Rebel Yell, the Alabama men leaped the works and advanced. According to Colonel Sawyer of the 8th Ohio, the 14th Indiana suffered the most just as it crossed the road, "when it was furiously attacked." Colonel Coons, at the head of Carroll's trio of regiments, calmly ordered his men to "face to the front and open fire." The 8th Ohio and 7th West Virginia ran into position, formed on the right of the embattled Hoosiers, and prepared to throw back the Rebels (No. 6).[28]

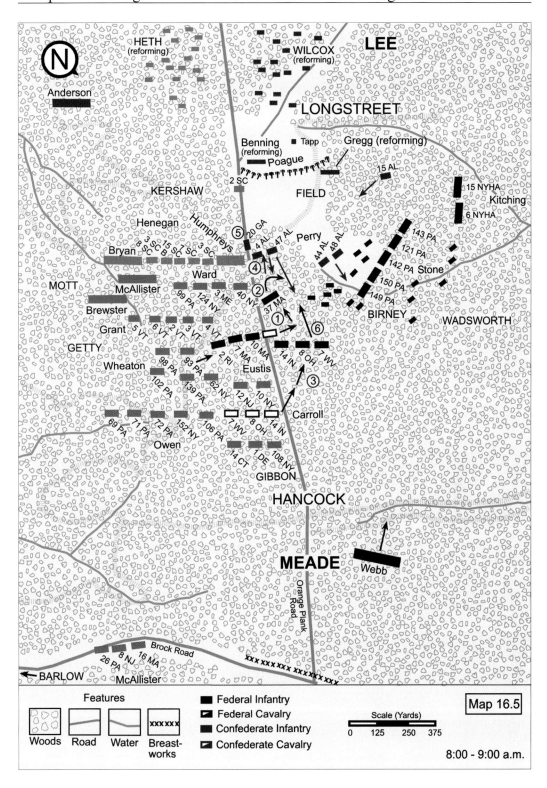

HETH (reforming)

WILCOX (reforming)

LEE

Anderson

LONGSTREET

Benning (reforming)   Tapp   Gregg (reforming)

Poague

15 AL

2 SC

KERSHAW

FIELD

15 NYHA
Kitching
6 NYHA

Henegan

Humphreys

Bryan   3 SC 15 SC 7 SC 3 SC
B

20 GA
4 AL   47 AL   Perry

143 PA
44 AL 48 AL   121 PA
142 PA Stone
150 PA
149 PA

MOTT

McAllister

Ward

99 PA 124 NY 3 ME 40 NY

37 MA

BIRNEY

WADSWORTH

Brewster

Grant   5 VT 6 VT 2 VT 3 VT 4 VT

GETTY

Wheaton   98 PA 93 PA 2 RI

7 MA 10 MA 14 IN 8 OH 7 WV

Eustis

102 PA 139 PA   62 NY

12 NJ 10 NY
14 IN

Carroll

69 PA 71 PA 72 PA 152 NY 106 PA   7 WV 8 OH

Owen

14 CT 1 DE 108 NY

GIBBON

HANCOCK

MEADE   Webb

Orange Plank Road

Brock Road
8 NJ 16 MA
26 PA
BARLOW   McAllister

Features

| Woods | Road | Water | Breast-works |

Federal Infantry
Federal Cavalry
Confederate Infantry
Confederate Cavalry

Scale (Yards)
0   125   250   375

Map 16.5

8:00 - 9:00 a.m.

Map 16.6: The Federal Line North of the Plank Road Holds (8:00 - 9:00 a.m.)

The 14th Indiana was deploying to repel the Alabamians's advance when the Buckeyes of Colonel Sawyer's 8th Ohio trotted into view. Colonel Coons ordered Sawyer to march his command "past his regiment, and 'file into line,' and commence firing as soon as possible." Colonel Sawyer recalled that "the fire now became severe as we moved forward" into position on Coons' right. "[W]e almost fell into the embrace of the whole of Longstreet's Corps," thought Sawyer. "The woods were literally black with ranks of men as far as we could see."[29]

The Buckeyes and Hoosiers were forming to repulse the Rebels when the 7th West Virginia arrived on the right of the line. With all three regiments in hand, Coons ordered an advance against the 4th and 47th Alabama, who may have fallen back because they were no longer visible. The advance was not well executed, and the 14th Indiana moved well ahead of its sister regiments. "[A] terrific volley of musketry struck us," recalled Sawyer, "and our officers and men went down all along the line." Colonel Bowles of the 4th Alabama ordered an attack, which was supported by some of Kershaw's men advancing from south of the road.[30]

Thomas Galway of the 8th Ohio recalled that the line advanced but a few yards when word filtered through the ranks that they were being flanked (No. 1). "To our left and rear across some openings some distance to the left of the Plank Road, we could see the Confederates advancing almost at a run to our rear." Colonel Sawyer attempted to "change front to the left" to face this new threat, but as Galway explained, "the stiff and crooked hazel brush that surrounded us prevented any sort of a regular formation at all." Much of the regiment was composed of new recruits, "who had not learned the cool courage with which veterans maneuver under fire. They began to give way one by one, then in twos and threes," continued Galway, "until at last they went in such numbers as to give the appearance of a general skedaddle."[31]

Colonels Sawyer and Coons realized the futility of attempting to maintain their advanced position. "We sent our colors back and carried the men back carefully, but with as much expedition as possible," reported Sawyer. Charles Myerhoff of the 14th Indiana credited the enemy with helping them along, recalling how "the Johnnies gave us a blast that hurried us to the rear of the line; our brave two hundred did not feel sufficiently strong to cope with the enemy alone in that isolated position." Despite Galway's observation of "a general skedaddle," Colonel Sawyer insisted the retreat was made "in good order." The victorious 4th and 47th Alabama followed as closely as possible. Within a few minutes they were sheltered behind the second line of breastworks they had occupied earlier.[32]

While Colonel Perry's two right Alabama regiments (the 4th and 47th) waged their seesaw battle against a variety of Yankee units, the brigade's three left regiments (the 15th, 48th, and 44th) continued advancing north of the road. "The fire was severe," Perry later related, "but the enemy, being a little back of the crest of the hill, sent most of their balls over our heads." The 15th Alabama returned at this time after driving away the inexperienced heavy artillery regiments of Kitching's brigade. Colonel Oates, the 15th Alabama's commander, found the 48th Alabama "giving way slowly under the well-directed volleys which came from Wadsworth's regulars in its front, who were firing by rank." Perry's recollection notwithstanding, the "regularity and effectiveness" of the Yankee's method of fire impressed Oates (No. 2).

With no enemy troops in his immediate front, Colonel Oates undertook another flanking move by swinging his regiment around to the left (No. 3). This put his veterans on the right flank of Stone's brigade, where Oates ordered his men to open fire. "One volley in the enemy's flank 'stopped their racket,' and caused them to retreat," boasted Oates. The single volley impressed Perry, who reported that after it was fired, "the work was done. The enemy instantly disappeared, and the heights were carried."[33]

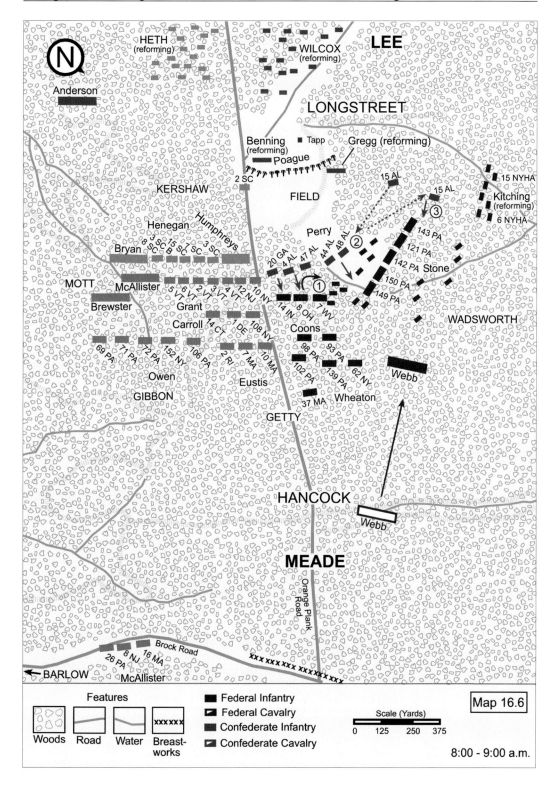

Map 16.6

Features

- Woods
- Road
- Water
- Breast-works xxxxxx

- Federal Infantry
- Federal Cavalry
- Confederate Infantry
- Confederate Cavalry

Scale (Yards)
0   125   250   375

8:00 - 9:00 a.m.

Map 16.7: The Collapse of the Federals North of the Plank Road (9:00 - 10:00 a.m.)

General Wadsworth desperately attempted to reorganize his broken units under Rice and Cutler and ordered them back into line. The Union right flank was now more stable, albeit temporarily, but with the 15th Alabama wreaking havoc on the right flank and the 44th and 48th Alabama chipping away at his front, Wadsworth's men soon had enough and began bolting for the rear (No. 1).[34]

According to Maj. Rufus Dawes of the 6th Wisconsin (Cutler's Iron Brigade), "the line on my left retreated in confusion before the pressure around our right." Realizing he could no longer hold his position, continued Dawes, "I endeavored to preserve the integrity of my command by retiring slowly through the woods, but outflanked both ways and pressed by the enemy from all sides, the line broke in disorder"—a rare occurrence for the venerable Iron Brigade. While large numbers of Federals began making their way back through the thickets in the general direction of the Lacy house and the Brock Road, Col. Richard Coulter, now in command of Baxter's brigade, claimed he rounded up about 600 men of various commands and was ordered by Hancock to report to Brig. Gen. John Gibbon's division on the left of the line south of the Orange Plank Road (No. 2).[35]

In charge of all of the troops in this sector, including Wadsworth's division, Hancock realized that he needed to act fast to stabilize the line to the right of the Plank Road. Unfortunately, he was running out of troops, so he decided to send Brig. Gen. Alexander Webb's brigade through the thickets. General Webb and his brigade spent the morning in reserve along the Brock Road, despite the fierce fighting in front of them. The unit was now thrown forward north of the Orange Plank Road (see Map 16.6) with orders to report to General Birney (No. 3). Despite the fact that none of Birney's men were still in the fight, he still commanded the sector between the Plank Road and Wadsworth's troops. Agitated by the turn of events, Birney welcomed the fresh brigade and ordered Webb to move forward and join George Getty's division. The intent was to form on the right of Wheaton's line. "I deployed and advanced as ordered," Webb reported. "I of course failed to find the line of General Getty, since I do not know that any of our troops ever had been where I was ordered."[36]

A physician, Dr. John Perry, accompanied Webb's advance. "We pushed forward," wrote the doctor, "and very quickly were walking over rows of dead bodies piled at times two and three deep, as they lay in lines, exactly as if mowed down." Informed that Getty's men were in his front, Webb pushed his men through the thickets without a skirmish line because he did not expect to find any enemy. Unfortunately for Webb and his men, Getty's men would prove impossible to locate, but they had little trouble finding Perry's Alabama brigade, which was advancing after driving off the rest of Wadsworth's men. "I had been distinctly ordered to relieve Brigadier-General Getty with my brigade by Major-General Birney in person," a frustrated Webb would later write. "From this moment to the time when my line was destroyed by the forcing in of the troops on my left [Perry's Alabamians], I was left totally unaware of any special object in disposing of my command, and I am still at a loss to determine whether or not it was my duty to attack and attempt to drive the enemy on the plank road or to hold my position in connection with a line taken up by the rest of the army."[37]

Webb's men moved up and into a deadly vise, where the 47th Alabama fired into their left flank and Perry's 15th, 44th, and 48th Alabama into its front and right flank (No. 4). Webb explained that he "tried to drive the enemy and failed to do so, and I believe because I struck him at a time when I had no reason to suppose that I would meet any but General Getty's command. The enemy, finding that my line was but a few hundred yards in length and entirely without support, forced me to change front to rear at a double-quick" (No. 5).[38]

With his unsupported men falling fast, and unable to stabilize his line, Webb ordered a general withdrawal. No Union or Confederate attack followed on the heels of Webb's retreat, and the heavy fighting in this sector fell away into fitful small arms fire.

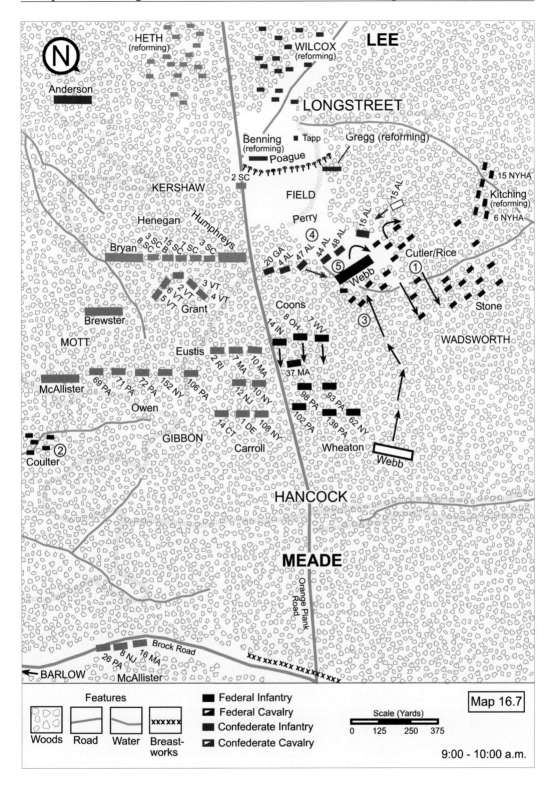

Map 16.7

Features

Woods   Road   Water   Breast-works (xxxxxx)

■ Federal Infantry
◤ Federal Cavalry
■ Confederate Infantry
◤ Confederate Cavalry

Scale (Yards)
0   125   250   375

9:00 - 10:00 a.m.

Map Set 17: Longstreet Counterattacks South of the Orange Plank Road

Map 17.1: Henagan Drives into the Enemy Line (5:45 - 7:00 a.m.)

While Maj. Gen. Charles Field's Division was pounding the Federals north of the Orange Plank Road, another Rebel division under Maj. Gen. Joseph Kershaw was doing much the same south of the road. Joe Kershaw's former South Carolina brigade under Col. John Henegan arrived at the front of the division that morning. During the approach to the Tapp farm, Kershaw ordered Henagan to "file to the right and form line of battle." Henegan formed his left flank on the road. The Gamecocks faced a challenge even before taking on the Yankees when A. P. Hill's routed infantry stormed out of the woods and barreled into their ranks with the enemy in close pursuit as Henagan was deploying his men. This "created some confusion and some uneasiness on my part; fearing that the stampede might communicate itself to my command," Henagan admitted. This was a potentially pivotal moment, and as historian Edward Steere observed, "only the superb troop leadership of Kershaw's regimental officers, and the steady confidence of their men, averted a complete catastrophe." Augustus Dickert, the brigade's historian, would recall years later, "in my long experience, in war and peace, I never saw such a picture as Kershaw and his war-horse made in riding down in front of his troops at the Wilderness. It seemed an inspiration to every man in line." The veterans calmly opened their ranks to let their comrades fly past to the rear before closing them to confront the approaching enemy.[1]

Although Henagan's task was to blunt the Union advance south of the road, he sent the 2nd South Carolina to the left to help protect Poague's vulnerable artillery line fighting in the Widow Tapp field (No. 1). Henagan deployed his remaining regiments from left to right as follows: 3rd South Carolina - 7th South Carolina - 15th South Carolina - 3rd South Carolina Battalion - 8th South Carolina. There was no time to dress the lines, for a sea of blue from Ward's brigade, together with parts of Hays' and Baxter's, was washing toward them. The South

Carolinians knew the enemy was rapidly approaching but could not yet see them. "Down the gentle slope the brigade marched," wrote Dickert, "over and under the tangled shrubbery and dwarf saplings, while a withering fire was being poured into them by as yet an unseen enemy." "The shock came," he continued, when the line reached the bottom of the hill. It was there, "just in front of us, and not forty yards away, lay the enemy. The long line of rifles; the red flashes of their guns seemed to blaze in our very faces." Henagan's veterans leveled their own rifled muskets, took aim, and returned fire.[2]

The Union troops barely knew what hit them. Not long before, elements of four Federal divisions had advanced west below the Plank Road against but little resistance while seeing the backs of fleeing Rebels. Now, without warning, a well-formed line of Confederates lined the front. One of the Federal soldiers recalled that the first sign of a problem was the "rattle of musketry like the boiling cauldrons of hell, as is represented to us by our good Chaplains."[3]

David Craft of the 141st Pennsylvania, which had been in the first line of Hobart Ward's brigade during the initial attack, recalled that "without supports, without ammunition, with lines badly broken by the long distance through the rough thickets, the Regiment was forced to retire, and with fixed bayonets slowly and sullenly fell back to near the position of the morning on the line of the Brock road, when there followed a short lull in the contest." Ward's second line moved forward to confront the Southern reinforcements (No. 2).[4]

Fighting at such close quarters tested the men's mettle. "Men rolled and writhed in their last death struggle; wounded men groped their way to the rear, blinded by the stifling smoke," noted a South Carolinian. Most of the men fought the battle on their own hook, for the ear-splitting noise precluded them from hearing the commands of their officers. Casualties on both sides mounted quickly. Henagan's officers were especially hard-hit, and within a short time the commanders of the 2nd, 3rd, and 7th regiments were on their way to the rear.[5]

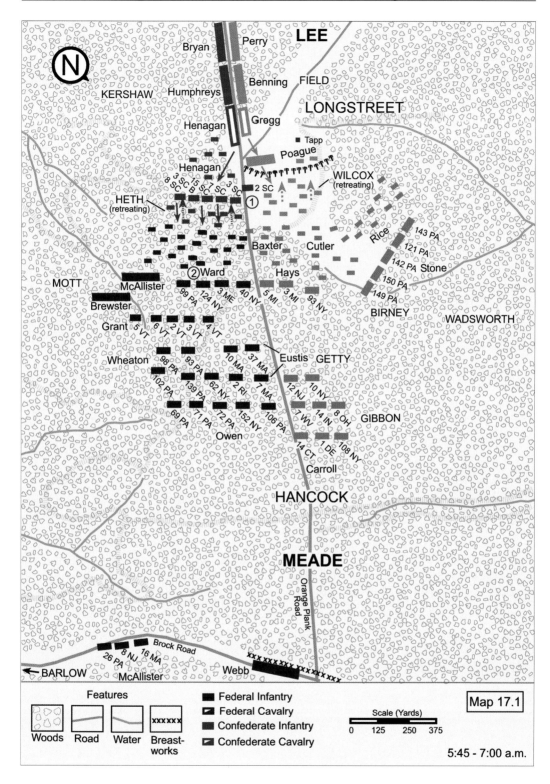

Features

Woods   Road   Water   Breastworks

Federal Infantry
Federal Cavalry
Confederate Infantry
Confederate Cavalry

Scale (Yards)
0   125   250   375

Map 17.1

5:45 - 7:00 a.m.

Map 17.2: More Confederate Troops Enter the Fighting (5:45 - 7:00 a.m.)

The 2nd South Carolina left of the Plank Road had the unenviable task of defending Poague's guns in the face of a strong enemy attack (No. 1). According to the regiment's leader, Col. William Wallace, it was touch and go until the rest of Henagan's regiments deployed below the road on its right. The 2nd regiment, wrote Wallace, "although completely flanked at one time by the giving way of the troops to the right [Wilcox's Division], gallantly stood their ground, although suffering terribly, they and the battery keeping up a well-directed fire to the right oblique until the enemy gave up."[6]

Henagan's initial advance angled away from the road and left a gap between the right flank of the 2nd South Carolina and the left flank of the rest of the advancing brigade. General Longstreet spotted the breach and rode back to the next brigade in line under Brig. Gen. Benjamin Humphreys, and yelled, "Form your line, General," pointing to the gap (No. 2). The brigade was William Barksdale's prior veteran Mississippi command. The men "had just halted and were panting like lizards," recalled W. Garth Johnson of the 18th Mississippi, when Longstreet's directive sent the men moving east. "Wounded men and minnie balls were coming through our ranks before we got loaded."[7]

Within a short time Longstreet had two crack brigades in place below the Orange Plank Road and a third under Brig. Gen. Goode Bryan about to leave the road to take up a position on the division's right (No. 3). The Mississippians moved promptly into the action, triggering a bitter and intense firefight. "The enemy got within a few steps of us in the dense cedar thicket," recorded one Mississippian, "but we stood it until they began to back, then it was our time to press." The fighting would soon claim almost one-half of his company "in a very few minutes."[8] The brigade's historian wrote of the intensity of the fight: "It seemed for a time as if the whole Federal Army was upon us—so thick and fast came the death-dealing missiles. Our ranks were being decimated." The enemy, he added, "held their position with a tenacity, born of desperation, while the Confederates pressed them with that old-time Southern vigor and valor that no amount of courage could withstand."[9]

"All commands were drowned in this terrible din of battle—the earth and elements shook and trembled with the deadly shock of combat," wrote a Rebel. Only veterans could have withstood these hellish conditions, whose only reprieves were a wound or death. "Our brigade had done good fighting before," wrote a Mississippian, "but I thought it reached a climax on that occasion."[10]

The double assault of first Henagan and then Humphreys was more than the Federals of Ward's and a portion of Hays' brigade could stand, and within perhaps 15 minutes they began heading for the rear (No. 4). Despite the wide array of Federal troops that had been deployed and advanced south of the road, only a few intact commands remained. The brigades of Brig. Gens. Henry Eustis and Frank Wheaton, both of Getty's VI Corps division, had been shifted to fight against Kershaw's men (No. 5), but given the progress of Field's Division, they were shifted to the right side (see Map 16.4). Hearing gunfire to the left of the road, Colonel Carroll led his brigade there, but was ordered to send three regiments back (No. 6). Lewis Grant's crack Vermont brigade was already in position. It had tenaciously slugged it out on May 5 with Maj. Gen. Henry Heth's Division, only pulling back when ordered to do so. Grant's brigade and about two-thirds of Carroll's were available to contest Kershaw's fresh two-brigade assault.

Other Federal units in the sector could provide support, if necessary. On the far left, Brig. Gen. Gershom Mott's II Corps division had halted after helping drive Hill's Corps that morning. One of his brigades under Col. Robert McAllister was still in the front line, but its ranks were disordered after the initial attack. Mott's second brigade under Col. William Brewster was behind McAllister and comparatively fresh, but was not considered a wholly reliable command. A third brigade, Brig. Gen. Joshua Owen's Philadelphia Brigade of Gibbon's division was farther to the rear.[11]

During the early stages of the assault that morning, General Getty was wounded with a bullet in the arm and relinquished command of his VI Corps division to Brig. Gen. Frank Wheaton. General Meade's aide, Theodore Lyman, returned to headquarters after delivering a message and was surprised to find Getty there "looking pale." When Lyman inquired as to his condition, Getty yelled, "I am shot through the shoulder; I don't know how badly."[12]

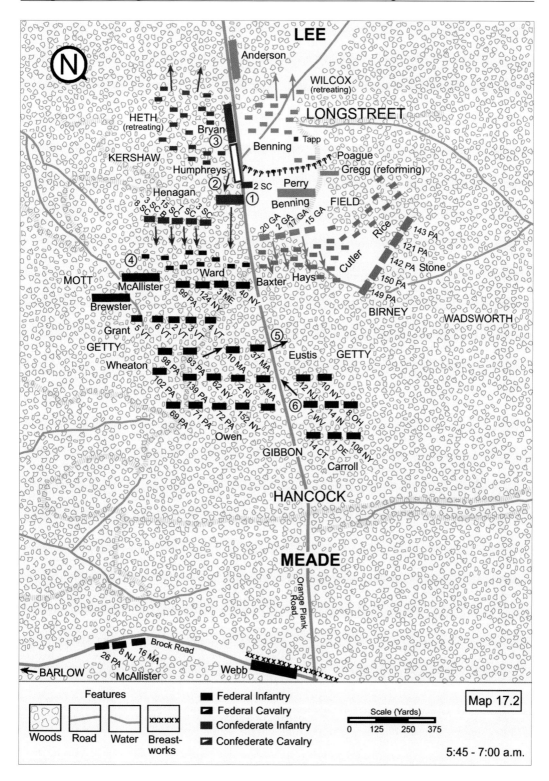

Map 17.2

5:45 - 7:00 a.m.

Map 17.3: Hancock Attempts to Stabilize the Front (7:00 - 8:00 a.m.)

Colonel Grant advanced his Vermont brigade to occupy the front line during this period. According to Grant and his men, there were Union troops to his immediate right and left (No. 1). It appears that a portion of Colonel Carroll's brigade was on Grant's right, and General Mott's division on his left. Carroll had earlier spun off three regiments to the right (north) of the road to confront part of Perry's Alabama brigade. The regiments fared poorly there and were forced to withdraw. The remainder of the brigade moved up to assume the first line against the brigades under Colonel Henagan and General Humphreys. According to Carroll, the brigade remained there until it ran low on ammunition and was replaced with Grant's Vermonters. Historian Gordon Rhea contested this recollection by concluding that units of Carroll's brigade fought beside the Vermont boys (No. 2). Colonel McAllister's brigade of Mott's division was in position to the left of Grant (No. 3). It is likely by this time that General Owen's Philadelphia Brigade had advanced and formed a supporting line behind these troops (No. 4).[13]

Grant's Green Mountain boys woke early on May 6 and received bad news by 4:30 a.m.: they would advance into the area they had vacated the day before, the same place where so many of their comrades had fallen. "There were pale and anxious faces in our regiment when that order was given," admitted Pvt. Wilbur Fisk of the 2nd Vermont. "We had had very insufficient rest for the two nights previous, and the terrible nervous exhaustion of fighting had left us in hardly a fit condition to endure another such an ordeal so soon." Orders were just that, however, and as Fisk added, "I do not know that a single man failed to take his place." During the advance, he continued, we found "our dead comrades . . . on the ground, just as they had fallen, many of whom we recognized. We would gladly have fallen out to give them a decent burial, but we had no time to think of that."[14]

The news of another advance depressed Grant: "To me, personally, the order came like a death-warrant. If the struggle of the day before

was to be repeated, it evidently meant death to many of us." Grant was just one of many who believed he would fall in the coming fight, so he took off his watch and handed it and his wallet to an aide with instructions for disposing of them upon his demise.[15]

As the Vermont boys advanced, they were fortunate to find shelter behind the crudely constructed enemy breastworks composed of "two irregular lines of old logs and decayed timber." Even better, the works were atop a small knoll. The works were oriented the wrong way, but the men quickly adjusted them to their best advantage.[16]

As the Union line south of the Orange Plank Road stabilized, Joe Kershaw's third brigade under General Bryan moved off the road and slid into position on the right of Henagan's South Carolinians. With a trio of veteran brigades across his front, Kershaw ordered the line forward against the Union defenders. According to General Bryan, his troops encountered the same problem other Confederate reinforcements faced: "Here again the discipline of the command was severely tried, for while forming line of battle in a dense thicket under a severe fire of the enemy the line was constantly broken through by men hurrying to the rear." Once their ranks were realigned, the Georgians scattered the Union troops (probably part of McAllister's brigade) in their front. According to Charles von Santvoord of the 120th New York of Brewster's brigade, which was behind McAllister's, "shortly after we crossed the small stream, suddenly there was a loud crash in our front, and the woods were again filled with the messengers of death. . . . Our line was soon broken by the terrible fire, and we again fell back in the same manner as the day before, and formed behind the breastworks, and again checked the enemy's advance."[17]

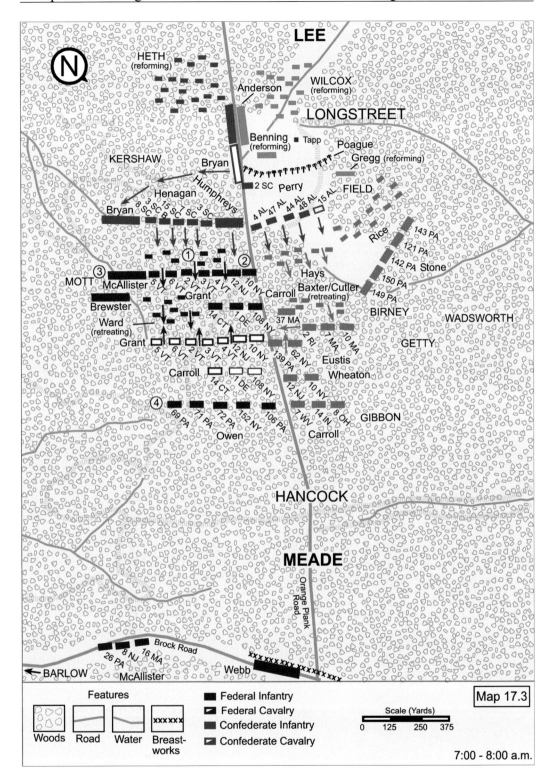

LEE

HETH (reforming)

Anderson

WILCOX (reforming)

LONGSTREET

Benning (reforming)   Tapp

Poague

Gregg (reforming)

KERSHAW   Bryan

Humphreys

Henagan

2 SC   Perry   **FIELD**

Bryan

3 SC   15 SC   3 SC   3 SC B

4 AL   47 AL   44 AL   48 AL   15 AL

Rice   143 PA

121 PA

142 PA   Stone

①   ②

③   Hays   150 PA

MOTT   McAllister   5 VT   6 VT   2 VT   3 VT   4 VT   12 NY   10 NY   Carroll   Baxter/Cutler (retreating)   149 PA

Grant

Brewster   **BIRNEY**

Ward (retreating)   14 CT   1 DE   108 NY   37 MA   **WADSWORTH**

Grant   5 VT   6 VT   2 VT   3 VT   4 VT   12 NJ   10 NY   139 PA   62 NY   2 RI   7 MA   10 MA   **GETTY**

Eustis

Carroll   14 CT   1 DE   108 NY   12 NY   10 NY   Wheaton

④   69 PA   71 PA   72 PA   152 NY   106 PA   12 NJ   7 WV   14 IN   8 OH   GIBBON

Owen   Carroll

HANCOCK

MEADE

Orange Plank Road

Brock Road

26 PA   8 NJ   16 MA

BARLOW   McAllister   Webb

Features

Woods   Road   Water   Breast-works

■ Federal Infantry
▰ Federal Cavalry
■ Confederate Infantry
▰ Confederate Cavalry

Map 17.3

Scale (Yards)
0   125   250   375

7:00 - 8:00 a.m.

Map 17.4: Kershaw Pressures Hancock's Line (7:00 - 8:00 a.m.)

On the right of the line, Carroll's regiments beat off several attacks from behind breastworks thrown up the day before by the enemy. At one point, the 10th New York Battalion on the right of this line was hit by fire along its front from Humphreys's Mississippians, and in the right-front by Perry's Alabamians north of the Plank Road.[18] The 10th's commander responded by refusing his two right companies (No. 1). The battalion was composed of a number of new recruits, and when the right companies were hit by the oblique fire, they fell back to reload. Unfortunately, this caused a chain reaction and "the battalion, company by company, similar to the fall of a row of bricks," wrote an eyewitness, headed for the rear. The battalion's color-bearer waved the flag and ran to the front in an effort to stop the retreat. "The effect was electrical," noted the unit's historian, and just as quickly the entire battalion was moving back to its original position. The Rebel fire, however, was simply too heavy to sustain for an extended period, and the New Yorkers vacated their position on the front line and fell back some distance.[19]

The rest of Carroll's brigade maintained its position. According to Charles Page of the 14th Connecticut, the bullets from the enemy flew thick and fast. Only the effective work delivered by scores of Sharp's breech-loading rifles held the enemy in check for about 20 minutes, with some of the men firing 80 rounds during that period.[20]

Despite their enervated state, Grant's Green Mountain boys demonstrated their mettle anew this morning (No. 2). According to Grant, "the enemy's advancing lines came upon us in great force. They were met by a terrible fire of musketry, broken and sent back in confusion. They reformed, and with fresh troops returned to the attack to be again slaughtered and sent back. This was repeated, and each time the attack in our front was met and repulsed."[21] Grant also kept an eye on the troops on either side of his brigade. After the war he recalled that "at each advance the Confederates gained substantial advantage on our right and left . . . [and] the

repulse, however, was complete only in front of this brigade."[22]

Brewster's brigade manning the Federal left in the front line was having its share of problems holding back Bryan's Georgians. According to Bryan, "after a few well-directed volleys the enemy broke from behind their intrenchments" (No. 3). The Pennsylvanians of the Philadelphia Brigade were behind Brewster's men, but they did not advance to link up with Grant's left—the small arms fire from Bryan's Georgians was too severe to do so (No. 4).[23]

The steady pressure against Carroll's men burned off their dwindling supply of ammunition and they were finally forced to give ground. This left Grant's Vermonters in a precarious situation. After the war, Grant recalled that "our line on either flank was pressed back, so the Vermont Brigade stood well out in front, like a bulge or a great knot in the line." Wilbur Fisk thought the line resembled the letter "V" (No. 5). Matters worsened with "the rebels rapidly closing up the sides. On they came, double quick, elated with the prospect of capturing a fine lot of Yankees."[24]

Although the brigade suffered about a quarter of the casualties it had sustained the day before, most of the men believed the fire was heavier and more destructive on May 6. "Bullets came from the right and left," Grant recalled, "and my flanking regiments changed and directed their fire to meet that coming from the flanks." The breastworks behind which the Vermonters fought helped reduce the losses.[25]

Frank Wheaton's Federal brigade appears to have advanced along the north side of the Plank Road about this time. The mixed brigade of Pennsylvania and New York troops formed to the right of Grant's embattled line and opened an oblique fire upon Humphrey's advancing Mississippians that dampened some of their ardor (No. 6). Grant's line held. The iron nature of this defensive effort allowed General Hancock to stop Kershaw's heavy push through the Federal left toward Brock Road. The victory came at a heavy price, as Maj. Richard Crandall of the 6th Vermont, part of Grant's command, recorded in his diary: "the battle raged hotly . . . the 6th held its ground and . . . drove back the rebel hordes, but our dead lie in windrows."[26]

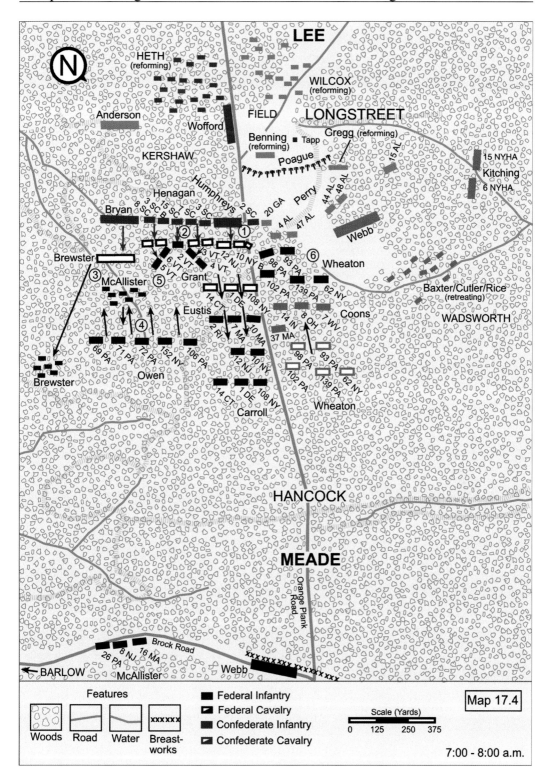

LEE

HETH
(reforming)

WILCOX
(reforming)

Anderson

FIELD

LONGSTREET

Wofford

Benning
(reforming)

Tapp

Gregg (reforming)

15 AL

15 NYHA

KERSHAW

Poague

Kitching

6 NYHA

Humphreys

Henagan

44 AL

48 AL

Perry

8 SC

3 SC

15 SC

1 SC

3 SC

2 SC

20 GA

Bryan

4 AL

47 AL

Webb

Brewster

③

McAllister

②

①

3 VT

2 VT

12 NJ

10 NY

98 PA

93 PA

⑥

Wheaton

6 VT

4 VT

Baxter/Cutler/Rice
(retreating)

5 VT

Grant

⑤

102 PA

139 PA

62 NY

Eustis

14 CT

1 DE

108 NY

14 IN

8 OH

7 WV

Coons

WADSWORTH

④

2 RI

7 MA

10 MA

37 MA

98 PA

93 PA

62 NY

69 PA

71 PA

72 PA

152 NY

106 PA

12 NJ

10 NY

102 PA

139 PA

Brewster

Owen

14 CT

1 DE

108 NY

Wheaton

Carroll

HANCOCK

MEADE

Orange Plank Road

Brock Road

8 NJ

16 MA

26 PA

←BARLOW

McAllister

Webb

Features

Woods Road Water Breastworks

▆ Federal Infantry
◪ Federal Cavalry
▆ Confederate Infantry
◪ Confederate Cavalry

Scale (Yards)
0   125   250   375

Map 17.4

7:00 - 8:00 a.m.

Map Set 18: Cavalry Action Along the Brock Road

Map 18.1: Custer Encounters Rosser's Brigade (7:00 - 8:30 a.m.)

Part of the preparation for the major attack along the Orange Plank Road included Maj. Gen. Winfield Hancock's decision to leave Brig. Gen. Francis Barlow's II Corps division and a sizable array of artillery deployed along the Brock Road to protect his otherwise exposed left flank. "Longstreet's corps was passing up the Catharpin road to attack my left flank," was how Hancock explained the decision after the battle. The II Corps commander was also concerned about the aggressive Rebel cavalry operating in that sector and knew he needed a buffer between those horsemen and his infantry columns.[1]

Hancock was not the only corps commander who worried about Longstreet's whereabouts. With the various corps of the Army of the Potomac caught up in the midst of a major battle within the tangles of the Wilderness, it was critically important for Maj. Gen. Phil Sheridan's Cavalry Corps to protect the army's vulnerable, exhausted and bloodied components during the night of May 5-6. Brigadier General David McM. Gregg's division remained at Todd's Tavern on the Brock Road protecting the left wing of the army, while Brig. Gen. Alfred Torbert's division, under Brig. Gen. Wesley Merritt, camped about two miles southwest of Chancellorsville at Catharine Furnace to protect the army's rear. Sheridan's third division under Brig. Gen. James Wilson had been roughly handled on the first day of the battle. According to a trooper in Brig. Gen. George Custer's brigade (part of Torbert's division), Wilson's exhausted horsemen "seemed much chagrined over their defeat." Sheridan ordered Wilson to ride back to Chancellorsville to rest and refit.[2]

Sheridan decided to bolster Gregg's division with two brigades from Torbert's command. Orders reached Custer at 2:00 a.m. on May 6 to leave Catherine Furnace with his brigade and Col. Thomas Devin's and ride west to the intersection of Furnace Road and Brock Road (No. 1). Doing so would put this command just north of Gregg's division, a cluster of five veteran Federal cavalry brigades with which Sheridan could defend the left or release on a variety of operations. Custer deployed his Michigan cavalry regiment in the woods on the left side of the Brock Road, from left to right as follows: 7th-5th-1st-6th (No. 2). Once in position the troopers munched on hardtack and awaited further orders.[3]

Dawn was just about to break when the crash of small arms fire broke out to the north. A desperate infantry fight was underway. The cacophony of death was unnerving. What the troopers did not yet know was that Hancock's men were in the act of crushing A. P. Hill's Third Corps along the Orange Plank Road and following the fleeing fugitives toward the Widow Tapp farm. Meade and Hancock knew that Longstreet's two powerful divisions were approaching the battlefield, but could only guess where they would appear. A thrust against the Federal left was a good bet, so Hancock retained Barlow's division here and the Federal cavalry was tasked with determining Longstreet's actual location. Custer received orders about 8:30 a.m. to "harass Longstreet's corps, which was reported to be moving on Hancock's left flank." The aggressive Custer never needed prodding to get his men into their saddles for action. Within minutes his men were heading north on the Brock Road in the direction of the Federal army's left and, more importantly, the probable route of Longstreet's infantry (No. 3).[4]

Unbeknownst to Custer, troopers in gray were also on the move and heading in his direction. Brigadier General Thomas Rosser's Rebel cavalry brigade, which had gotten the better of Wilson's division the previous day, had been resting in the rear. However, when the all-too-familiar bugles sounded at sunrise on May 6, the men were soon atop their mounts and heading for Todd's Tavern (No. 4). The diminished brigade crossed the Poe River on Corbin's Bridge and turned left at the Chancellor plantation to head north. Rosser sent Col. Elijah White's 35th Virginia Battalion ("Comanches") ahead of the column to reconnoiter and, wrote the unit's historian, "run over anything he came to." The vague directive puzzled White, who asked the aide delivering the orders, "How far must I go?" The aide galloped back to ask Rosser and soon returned with his reply: White was to "drive [the enemy] as far as he can." This was all White needed, and he headed north up the road.[5]

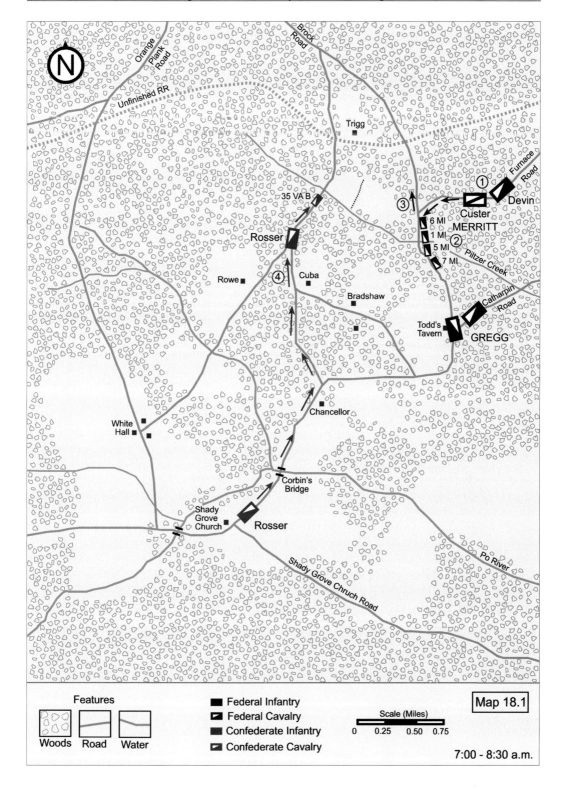

Orange Plank Road

Brock Road

Unfinished RR

Trigg

N

Furnace Road

① Devin
Custer
MERRITT
③ 6 MI
1 MI ②
5 MI
7 MI
Piltzer Creek

35 VA B

Rosser

Rowe ④ Cuba

Bradshaw

Catharpin Road

Todd's Tavern
GREGG

Chancellor

White Hall

Corbin's Bridge

Shady Grove Church
Rosser

Po River

Shady Grove Chruch Road

Features		
Woods	Road	Water

■ Federal Infantry
◪ Federal Cavalry
■ Confederate Infantry
◪ Confederate Cavalry

Scale (Miles)
0   0.25   0.50   0.75

Map 18.1

7:00 - 8:30 a.m.

Map 18.2: The Custer–Rosser Fight Escalates (8:30 - 10:00 a.m.)

Before reaching the Trigg house, Col. White's "Comanches" encountered some of Custer's pickets in an open field to the right of the road (No. 1). One Virginian recalled how they were greeted "with a rattling, whizzing blaze of carbines" delivered "by a squadron of the enemy not twenty steps distant." White's men returned the fire and charged, screaming the war whoop their namesakes had made famous. The blue-coated troopers beat a hasty retreat to the woods lining the Brock Road.[6]

The sudden appearance of White's 35th Virginia Battalion necessarily voided Custer's orders to ride north on the Brock Road to find Longstreet's infantry. Most of Custer's men were deeper in the woods and although they could not see White's charge, they certainly heard it. Colonel James Kidd of the 6th Michigan painted the picture: "thicker and faster the spattering tones were borne to our ears from the woods in front. It was the 'rebel yell;' at first faint, but swelling in volume as it approached."[7]

Custer was out on the picket line when White's men made their sudden appearance, and dashed to safety with his scrambling troopers. When he reached his main line, Custer pulled up and ordered his band to play a ditty. In his after-action report, the brigade commander explained that "most of my command was concealed by the woods, only the pickets and reserves being visible to the enemy. This fact induced the enemy to charge." Orders to the 1st Michigan Cavalry soon followed and a solid mass of Federal horsemen emerged from the woods and headed for White's charging Virginians, who numbered barely more than 100. A deep gully running diagonally across the field prevented the two sides from closing upon each other, but Federal carbine fire convinced White to withdraw across the field while Custer's band played "Yankee Doodle" (No. 2).[8]

General Rosser witnessed the mass of Federal troopers in the clearing and deployed the rest of his men for battle (No. 3). Unsure of what he was facing, Rosser ordered the 11th Virginia Cavalry forward. According to its commander, Col. William McDonald, his regiment "now charged in fine style, and again the pines

resounded with the 'shout of the captains' and the roar of battle." The Virginians were overwhelmed by enemy firepower when Custer ordered his brigade forward. When he realized the 11th Virginia Cavalry was being forced back, Rosser ordered the 12th Virginia Cavalry in to support the embattled regiment and, when that outfit encountered problems, followed up with the 7th Virginia Cavalry. Rosser's decision to drip his veteran brigade into battle one piece at a time proved unwise.

The two sides, wrote one Federal officer, galloped toward each other "in full career" as Custer threw in the rest of his legions (No. 4). The right side of his line was quickly thrown into disarray when the 6th Michigan Cavalry became inextricably mixed with the 1st Michigan Cavalry, reducing the fighting effectiveness of both units.[9]

Within a short time the engagement became a fight across the gully where pistols and carbines ruled the day. Some riders on both sides, by accident or exuberance, rode into the gully where they engaged in hand-to-hand combat. According to Custer, "the enemy made repeated and desperate attempts to drive me from this position, but was defeated each time with heavy loss."[10]

Frustrated by his lack of progress, Rosser tried to outflank the Michiganders by slipping around Custer's right. Thinking that the Rebels were trying to reach the Furnace Road and his rear to cut him off, Custer quickly responded by facing the 6th Michigan Cavalry to the right, and, with the added firepower of the 5th Michigan Cavalry, effectively confronted the new threat (No. 5). Custer knew Tom Devin's brigade was in the rear with some artillery pieces, but he had no idea if and when they would appear.[11]

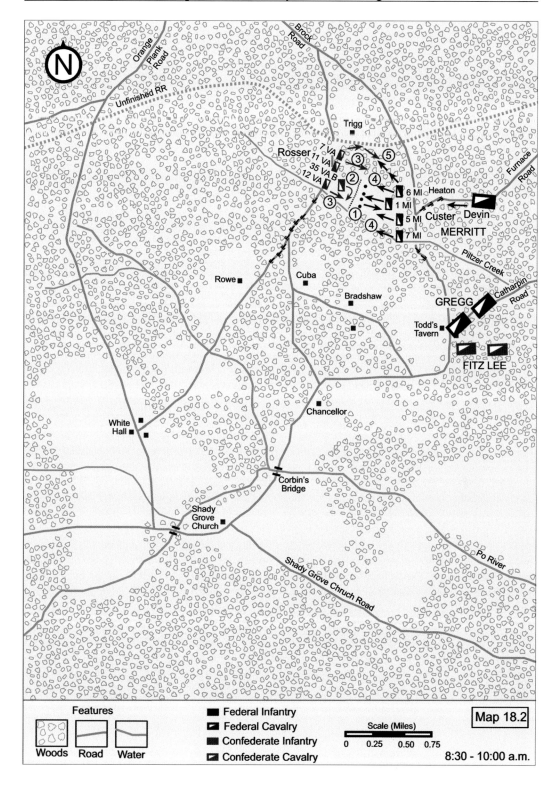

Map 18.2

8:30 - 10:00 a.m.

Features

Woods   Road   Water

■ Federal Infantry
◪ Federal Cavalry
■ Confederate Infantry
◪ Confederate Cavalry

Scale (Miles)

0   0.25   0.50   0.75

Map 18.3: Custer Victorious
(10:00 - 11:30 a.m.)

Reinforcements for the embattled Custer and his troopers arrived in the form of a six-gun horse artillery battery under Lt. Edward Heaton. The guns dropped trail along the Brock Road and opened fire on Rosser's Virginians. The battery was soon joined by a section of Lt. Rufus King's Battery A, 4th U.S. attached to Gregg's division (No. 1). Gregg had no need for the guns, so he sent them galloping up the Brock Road to support Custer, who ordered the eight pieces to "fire as rapidly as they could be loaded and aimed." The gunners wreaked havoc upon the Virginians. Custer was also pleased to see Tom Devin's four regiments swing into view to bolster his deteriorating position (No. 2). As Devin recalled, his initial orders were to "take up a position on the right of General Custer, and to endeavor to communicate with and watch the left of our infantry line."[12]

The nearly overwhelming Federal firepower sent Rosser's men tumbling back to the edge of the woods on the western side of the field. Rosser was still full of fight, but he needed to buy time to reform. Unlike Custer, all he could count on in the way of artillery was a single gun from Lt. James W. Thomson's Battery. The gun crew, which had recently reached the scene of the fighting, valiantly opened fire on Custer's eight guns. Fortunately for the Confederate artillerists, seven more guns rumbled up—the remaining pieces from Thomson's command and the four comprising Capt. John J. Shoemaker's Battery (No. 3). Within minutes a large-scale counter-battery affair was underway. When some of the Federal gunners shifted to enfilade the Rebel position, Yankee flying iron began to produce the desired results. As one Confederate reported, he and his comrades endured Federal shells "crossing in mid-air, and spreading considerable alarm in our ranks." Thomson's Battery moved to the left to counteract the firing. The gray cannoneers were surprised they did not sustain more casualties during the action, noting that many of enemy's rounds flew over their guns and slammed into the woods behind them. They could, however, hear the screams of horses and men from the rear area, which was loaded with caissons and reforming cavalry.[13]

Custer dismounted his men and once again sent them forward, driving Rosser's troopers before them (No. 4). The Federal brigadier noted in his report that the enemy troopers were "driven from the field in great disorder, leaving his dead and many of his wounded upon the ground." Custer also claimed to have captured "a considerable number of prisoners." With more breathing room, his men headed for the Confederate artillery. When the gunners saw them edging in their direction, they knew it was time to depart (No. 5). "[W]e came out hastily," admitted one of the crew.[14] The cavalry action along the Brock Road was over.

While Custer's men were beating off Rosser's rash attack, General Gregg's division was farther south deployed near Todd's Tavern against Fitzhugh Lee's Division of Virginians (No. 6). Unlike Rosser, Lee was content to confront Gregg without triggering any serious fighting. The two sides, reported Gregg, skirmished throughout the day. "The whole force of the enemy appeared to be dismounted, and studiously kept under the cover of the dense woods surrounding the tavern. Their long extended lines were everywhere protected by hastily built defenses."[15]

The always aggressive Custer was cautioned to "not pursue the enemy beyond this point," so he did not budge from his position. Devin claimed in his report that with the fighting over, his right, composed of the 17th Pennsylvania, connected with the left of Hancock's II Corps (No. 7) and that his left flank, composed of the 6th New York Cavalry, connected with the right of Gregg's division (No. 8).[16]

The losses suffered by the battling cavalry were not well recorded, but may have been sizable. Major Kidd of the 6th Michigan Cavalry admitted that "the casualties among enlisted men were numerous." The historian of Rosser's Brigade wrote that "the ground was strewn with the dead and dying" of his unit. A sergeant in the 11th Virginia Cavalry admitted his regiment was "badly cut to pieces." Many of these losses were a direct result of Rosser's tactics. "He is no general at all," complained an officer after the battle. "As brave a man as ever drew a breath, but knows no more about putting a command into a fight than a school boy. We have lost confidence in him so fast that he can't get a good fight out of us any more unless we know positively what we are fighting."[17]

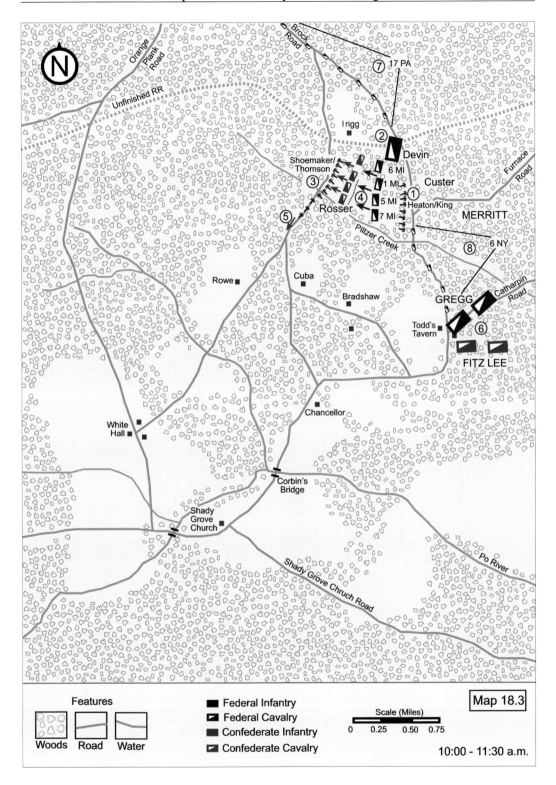

Map 18.3

10:00 - 11:30 a.m.

Features

Woods Road Water

Federal Infantry
Federal Cavalry
Confederate Infantry
Confederate Cavalry

Scale (Miles)
0   0.25   0.50   0.75

Map Set 19: Federal Command Confusion

Map 19.1: Burnside's Trials and Travails (2:00 - 8:00 a.m.)

From generals to bayonet-wielding privates, the bloody Wilderness fighting had thus far had been an exasperating experience. The mix of tough veterans leavened with thousands of new recruits that was the Army of the Potomac in May 1864 had fought about as well as could be expected given the exceedingly difficult terrain, objectives, and their well-led opposition. By the morning of May 6, however, with the sun well up and Confederate reinforcements striking back, the Union army had nearly shot its bolt. The II, V, and VI corps had been thrown into the spreading conflagration without any decisive result. All three were exhausted, bloodied, and in various states of confusion. The only fresh corps at Maj. Gen. George Meade's disposal belonged to Maj. Gen. Ambrose Burnside—four divisions totaling some 19,000 men. Some of its units were battle-tested and led by reliable officers, while others, like Brig. Gen. Edward Ferrero's division of African-American troops, were untested.

Burnside's march to the battlefield had been anything but smooth. Left behind to guard the army's communications and wagons, the IX Corps did not cross the Rapidan until May 5, when the battle was already raging. The original plan called for Brig. Gen. Thomas Stevenson's division to march south to reinforce Hancock's II Corps while two other IX Corps divisions under Brig. Gens. Robert Potter and Orlando Willcox slid southwest to plug the wide gap between General Warren's V Corps and Hancock's II Corps near the Chewning farm and turn the left flank of A. P. Hill's embattled Rebel corps. From that point, Potter and Willcox would also be in a position to reinforce either flank of the army. Burnside's final division under Ferrero was left behind to guard the wagon trains. The march on May 6 began at 2:00 a.m., but clogged roads ground the march to a crawl. The head of the column finally reached Wilderness Tavern about 5:00 a.m., a full 90 minutes behind schedule (No. 1). Hancock's massive attack against Hill was already underway and audible to every man in the column.[1]

Burnside's column set out for Parker's Store at 6:30 a.m. with Potter's division leading. Stevenson's division stayed at Wilderness Tavern. The 48th Pennsylvania and 6th New Hampshire were thrown out as flankers. The route led directly between the Rebel flanks and into Hill's left-rear. The column had barely gotten underway, however, before Burnside called a halt for breakfast. The men resumed their march an hour later. According to Burnside, Potter's division in the front was deployed with Col. Simon Griffin's brigade in the lead, supported by a brigade under Col. Zenas Bliss protecting Griffin's left.[2] The head of the column quickly ran into enemy pickets, whose firing slowed the march considerably. Within minutes enemy shells began flying overhead, probably from Lt. Col. William Pegram's Battalion.[3]

Lt. Col. Henry H. Pearson's 6th New Hampshire (Griffin's brigade) crossed Wilderness Run and found Brig. Gen. Stephen Ramseur's Brigade (Early's Division) deployed behind a rail fence on the far edge of Jones' Field (No. 2). The Tar Heels had spent May 3-4 guarding the Rapidan crossings before rejoining the army on May 5 on the Orange Turnpike. Ramseur was ordered south to extend General Ewell's right flank earlier that morning (No. 3). "Moving at a double-quick," he wrote, "I arrived just in time to check a large flanking party of the enemy."[4] Unsure what was in his front, Burnside called a halt to see what might develop. Ramseur, meanwhile, extended his skirmish line about half a mile farther right. Some of Burnside's troops, including the 17th Vermont (Griffin's brigade), crawled on their hands and knees and drove back the Rebel videttes, but a sharp counter-thrust sent them packing in turn.[5]

With his march along the back road to Parker's Store halted, Burnside focused his attention on the Chewning farm. Large numbers of enemy troops were occupying this high ground beyond Jones' Field (No. 4). What he did not know was that these enemy units belonged to A. P. Hill's wrecked Third Corps, reforming after their defeat that morning. When Lt. Col. Cyrus Comstock from General Grant's staff arrived, he and Burnside and his aides engaged in a lively discussion about what to do next. During this delay, General Potter was preparing to charge Ramseur's blocking Confederates. As Potter recalled, "I received an order to withdraw my command, move to the left, and attack on the right of General Hancock, near the plank road."[6]

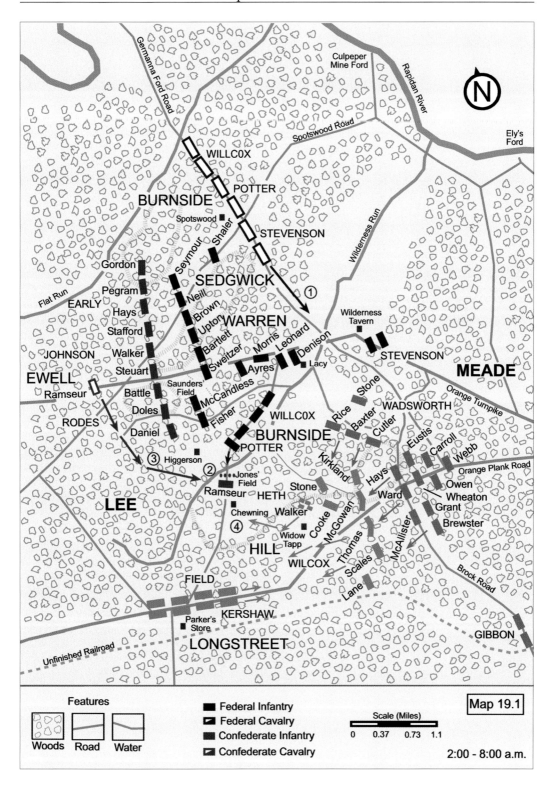

Map 19.1

Features

Woods   Road   Water

■ Federal Infantry
▨ Federal Cavalry
■ Confederate Infantry
▨ Confederate Cavalry

Scale (Miles)

0   0.37   0.73   1.1

2:00 - 8:00 a.m.

Map 19.2: Hancock's Dilemma
(7:00 - 9:00 a.m.)

May 6 began with great promise for Winfield Hancock even before the sun rose. It was still dark when his assault column, together with troops from Brig. Gen. James Wadsworth's division on his right, smashed into A. P. Hill's unprepared corps. Within minutes, two veteran Rebel divisions were in chaotic retreat to and through the Widow Tapp field. Routing any part of Lee's Army of Northern Virginia was a rare occurrence, and Hancock knew he had a narrow window to complete his victory before Longstreet's First Corps arrived, likely somewhere off his own left flank. He hoped to disperse Hill's troops and gain the high ground around the Chewning farm before Old Pete made his appearance. It was not to be.

By the time the sun was barely visible, elements of two of Longstreet's divisions under Maj. Gens. Charles Field and Joseph Kershaw had stopped Hancock's and Wadsworth's victorious, if brief, assault in its tracks. With Longstreet up and the entire assault on the verge of bogging down in failure, Hancock now had to directly concern himself with his left flank. The II Corps commander believed Longstreet had all three of his divisions on the field (or soon would), so had placed five brigades under John Gibbon with an array of artillery near the Trigg house to prevent his left from being turned. Hancock was also concerned about the whereabouts of Hill's third division under Maj. Gen. Richard Anderson.[7]

Hancock later spent eight months re-fighting the action on May 6 in an effort to discern what went wrong. "It appears that the expected movement of Longstreet on the left flank . . . had a very material effect upon the result of the battle," he concluded. "I was not only cautioned officially that the movement was being made, but many incidents . . . such as the skirmishing and artillery firing on Barlow's flank, the heavy firing from the direction of Todd's Tavern, where Sheridan was to attack Longstreet, and the report of infantry moving on the Brock Road from the direction of Todd's Tavern, confirmed me in the belief that I would receive a formidable attack on my left. This paralyzed a large number of my best troops,"

added Hancock, "who otherwise would have gone into action at a decisive point on the morning of the 6th."[8] The failure of at least two divisions of Burnside's IX Corps, probably 10,000 strong, to arrive as promised was at least as responsible for the failure to crush Hill as was the siphoning off of II Corps troops mentioned by Hancock.

When he realized that his attack was in danger of turning into a defeat, Hancock had no choice but to release some of the reserve troops he had stationed on his left flank. He could no longer wait for Burnside's troops to pierce into Hill's deep left-rear when his remaining front-line units were in desperate need of assistance. The II Corps leader instructed a staff officer at 7:00 a.m. to gallop to General Gibbon on the far left with the information about "our success on my right," and order him to "attack the enemy's right with Barlow's division, and to press to the right toward the Orange plank road." As it turned out, no large-scale assault developed. The order, reported a disappointed Hancock, "was only partially carried out."[9]

At the same time, also about 7:00 a.m., General Meade notified Hancock that Stevenson's division of Burnside's IX Corps was available to support him. This gave Hancock a seventh division to focus against the embattled Confederate right flank—or more than one-half of the Army of the Potomac. When Stevenson finally had his division up about 9:00 a.m., he personally led his First Brigade under Col. Sumner Carruth forward to reinforce Wadsworth's decimated command (No. 1). The Second Brigade under Col. Daniel Leasure remained in reserve (No. 2).[10]

Hancock now had three fresh brigades moving forward or in reserve to stabilize the front: Stevenson's pair under Carruth and Leasure, and Frank's brigade of Barlow's division. Additionally, Alexander Webb's brigade had reformed after its earlier ordeal. As related earlier in Map 16.7, Webb's brigade had advanced with vague orders and little if any support, was routed on the right, and forced to retreat. Fortunately, Carruth's brigade came up and formed on Webb's right. Later, Webb candidly admitted that the bloody confused encounter with the Rebels had left his men demoralized (they "had lost their dash").[11]

Gibbon's brigade under Col. Paul Frank, meanwhile, was thrown forward to provide support for General Mott's left flank (No. 3).

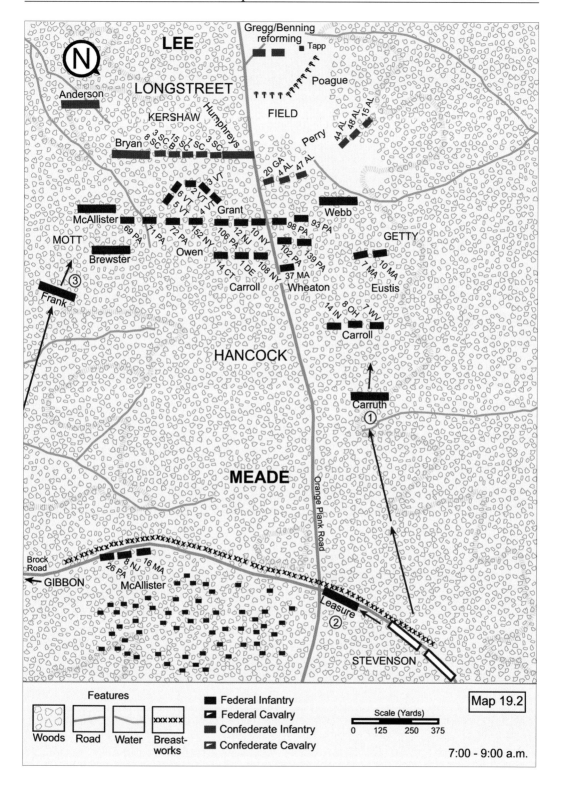

LEE

Gregg/Benning
reforming

◾ Tapp

Ṉ

LONGSTREET

Anderson

Poague

FIELD

KERSHAW

Humphreys

44 AL
48 AL
15 AL

Bryan   8 SC 3 SC B 15 SC 1 SC 3 SC
Perry

20 GA 4 AL 47 AL

3 VT
2 VT
6 VT   4 VT
5 VT

McAllister   Grant   Webb

69 PA 71 PA 72 PA 152 NY 106 PA 12 NJ 10 NY 98 PA 93 PA

GETTY

MOTT   Owen

Brewster   14 CT 1 DE 108 NY 102 PA 139 PA

7 MA 10 MA

Eustis
③   102 PA 37 MA

Frank   Carroll   Wheaton

14 IN 8 OH 7 WV

Carroll

HANCOCK

Carruth

①

MEADE

Orange Plank Road

Brock
Road   ×××××××××××××××××××××××××××××××××

8 NJ 16 MA
26 PA

← **GIBBON**   McAllister

×××××××××××

Leasure
②

STEVENSON

| Features | | | | | Scale (Yards) | Map 19.2 |

Features

Woods   Road   Water   Breast-works

■ Federal Infantry
◪ Federal Cavalry
■ Confederate Infantry
◪ Confederate Cavalry

Scale (Yards)
0   125   250   375

Map 19.2

7:00 - 9:00 a.m.

Map 19.3: Stalemate on the Federal Left (9:00 - 9:15 a.m.)

The troops moving to support Hancock's left flank consisted of a lone brigade of New Yorkers under Colonel Frank, an officer, wrote one of Meade's aides, "who tried to make up for want of nerve with strong drink." Near the front Frank ran into Col. Robert McAllister's brigade. According to the latter officer, bad blood had already developed between them; their mutual dislike was on full display that morning. McAllister bristled when Frank told him he intended to pass through his brigade to attack the enemy, inferring a lack of courage in McAllister's men. McAllister told the colonel, "I had skirmishers out and that I was advancing with the line of battle and did not wish him to go ahead of me." A distinguished veteran, McAllister told Frank he was to support McAllister's left flank. Frank disagreed, arguing that his orders were to "find the enemy wherever he could find him, and whip him." When McAllister refused to allow him to pass, Frank moved around his left and soon was lost in the thickets (No. 1).

Within minutes firing exploded into the face of Frank's New Yorkers when they stumbled into the right side of Longstreet's line composed of a brigade of Georgians under Brig. Gen. Goode Bryan. The killing distance of a mere 40 yards sent men and officers tumbling to the ground while those still standing attempted to reform. Colonel Frank sent an aide back to McAllister pleading for help, but he refused to budge. Frank's orders, McAllister maintained, were to "advance with this line." When Frank pulled his men back in front of McAllister's men, the brigadier once again refused to allow them to move through their ranks. Once McAllister's own picket line became engaged, however, the stubborn general allowed Frank's men to push through to the rear. The bloodied brigade did not stop until it reached the safety of the breastworks lining the Brock Road. The fighting continued fitfully along Hancock's entire front, but the combat was heading toward a stalemate. Both sides had shot their bolt and needed rest, reordering, and a fresh supply of ammunition.[12]

At 9:00 a.m., Hancock received a message that complicated his deteriorating situation: "General Sheridan has been directed to make an attack with a division of cavalry on Longstreet's flank and rear by the Brock road." Hancock knew that two of Longstreet's divisions (Field's and Kershaw's) were in front of him, but this report implied more Rebels were moving along his left flank. Could this be Maj. Gen. George Pickett's Division? Before long gunfire was heard from the direction of Todd's Tavern—the area of the perceived threat to his left flank. Another report arrived that a body of enemy infantry was moving up the Brock Road. Only later, after the fighting ended, would Hancock learn that the gunfire was the engagement between Sheridan's and Stuart's cavalrymen (see Map Set 18), and that the column of infantry was merely "a body of several hundred convalescents who had been marched from Chancellorsville and were now following the route of the Second Corps around by Todd's Tavern."[13]

Believing he had no choice but to reinforce his left, Hancock tapped Brig. Gen. Henry Eustis's brigade, which had been dispatched north side of Plank Road to help blunt attacks there. Hancock also ordered a regiment from Carroll's brigade to reinforce his left along the Brock Road. When he realized these moves could destabilize the front line, he countermanded his orders and instead sent Colonel Leasure's brigade (Stevenson's division, IX Corps) south along the Brock Road (No. 2). Stevenson's remaining brigade under Colonel Carruth had already been pushed ahead well north of the Orange Plank Road to support Webb's brigade (No. 3).[14]

And so the second round of major fighting in the sector sputtered to a fitful halt. Longstreet had done exactly what he had been asked to do— beat back Hancock's attack, stabilize the army's right, and save Hill's Third Corps from destruction. After the war, Longstreet aide Moxley Sorrel reflected, "I have always thought that in its entire splendid history the simple act of forming line in that dense undergrowth, under heavy fire and with the Third Corps men pushing to the rear through the ranks, was perhaps its greatest performance for steadiness and inflexible courage and discipline." Historian Edward Steere agreed, observing that Longstreet's ability to halt the massive Federal onslaught was nothing short of "miraculous."[15]

Fortunately for the Confederates, Longstreet could now call upon reinforcements: Maj. Gen. Richard Anderson's Division had arrived at the Widow Tapp field (No. 4).

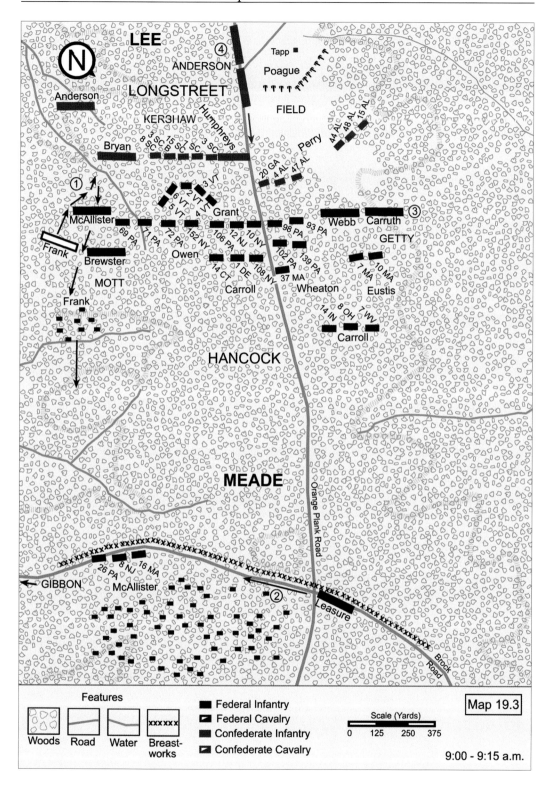

Map 19.3

9:00 - 9:15 a.m.

Features

Woods Road Water Breast-works

Federal Infantry
Federal Cavalry
Confederate Infantry
Confederate Cavalry

Scale (Yards)
0   125   250   375

Map 19.4: Hancock and Lee Realign Their Troops (9:30 - 10:30 a.m.)

With the fluid movement and heavy fighting portions of the combat at an end, at least temporarily, both sides took advantage of the breathing space to reform their ranks and reinforce their shattered lines. The Confederates had an easier time of it because fresh reinforcements in large numbers were readily available with good open space in the Widow Tapp and Chewning farms. With A. P. Hill well to the rear reforming his broken corps, General Lee wisely placed Richard Anderson's five-brigade division under Longstreet's command. The division was split into two parts. Three brigades under Brig. Gens. Abner Perrin, Edward Perry, and Nathaniel Harris remained north of the Orange Plank Road to support General Field's broken division while the remaining two brigades under Brig. Gens. William Mahone and Ambrose Wright headed south of the road to support General Kershaw's command. Two brigades of Georgians, George "Tige" Anderson's of Field's Division and William Wofford's of Kershaw's Division had not yet engaged the enemy and were still fresh. They could add their weight to any push.[16]

The broad gap between the two wings of the Confederate army continued to worry Lee. This was the area General Burnside was to have exploited, but he had not moved with sufficient vigor and purpose to reach the area in time, and when he did, a single brigade (Ramseur's) had stopped him. With Longstreet now up and the army's right stabilized, Lee finally had the luxury of sealing this critical gap. The only troops readily available belonged to A. P. Hill, whose shattered corps was shifted toward the Chewning farm. Hill's aide, Col. William Palmer, recalled after the war, "we had been there [near the Chewning house] only a short while when we were startled by the breaking down of a fence just below, and in plain view was a long line of Federal infantry clearing the fence to move forward." These troops belonged to Burnside, who was finally taking up a position between the two Confederate wings. Hill quietly instructed his aides to "Mount, walk your horses, and don't look back." This was the second time in two days that Hill had nearly been captured. Later that

morning, when Palmer encountered some Federal prisoners, one of them stopped him to ask, "Were you not at the house a short time ago?" When Palmer responded affirmatively, the man continued, "I wanted to fire on you, but my colonel said you were farmers riding from the house."[17]

The sudden appearance of Federal skirmishers worried Hill, who sent Palmer back to find Lee with the request: "if Anderson's division had arrived he [Hill] wanted a brigade of that division sent to him." Lee told Palmer, "Well, let's see General Longstreet about it." When he found Longstreet, Palmer reiterated his request. At this point none of Anderson's brigades had been engaged. "Certainly, Colonel," he agreed. "Which one will you take?" Realizing time was of the essence, Palmer replied, "The leading one," and hurried back with it.[18]

While all this was transpiring, Hill's exhausted survivors of Cadmus Wilcox's and Henry Heth's divisions were making their way toward the Chewning farm. James Lane's Brigade led Wilcox's command, halting just northwest of the farmhouse. Sam McGowan's South Carolinians were next in line and stopped on the opposite side of the house. Continuing the line to the right were Edward Thomas's and Alfred Scales's brigades. Heth's reorganized troops arrived with John Cooke's Brigade next to Scales, followed by William Kirkland's, Henry Walker's, and finally some of John Stone's men on the right.[19]

On the other side of the line, General Hancock worked to realign the troops that had been shattered during their initial early morning attack and then by Longstreet's counterattack. North of the Orange Plank Road, Sumner Carruth's men attached themselves to Alexander Webb's right. James Rice's brigade, now back in fighting trim, deployed on the left of Webb's brigade to form a solid three-brigade front. They were backed up by Henry Eustis's and Frank Wheaton's brigades. Seven Federal brigades were in position south of the Orange Plank Road, with William Brewster's and Robert McAllister's brigades of Gershom Mott's division holding the first line, and Lewis Grant's, Hobart Ward's and Alexander Hays' brigades in the second line. Joshua Owen's and Samuel Carroll's brigades comprised the third line.[20]

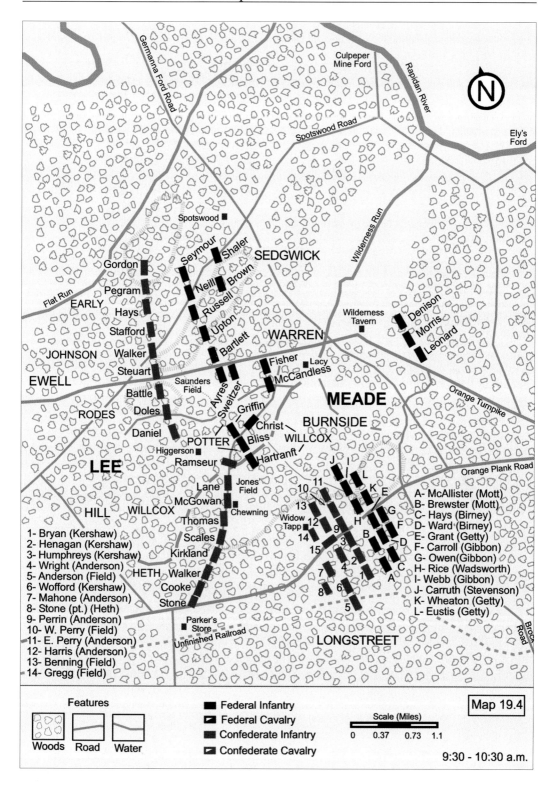

A- McAllister (Mott)
B- Brewster (Mott)
C- Hays (Birney)
D- Ward (Birney)
E- Grant (Getty)
F- Carroll (Gibbon)
G- Owen (Gibbon)
H- Rice (Wadsworth)
I- Webb (Gibbon)
J- Carruth (Stevenson)
K- Wheaton (Getty)
L- Eustis (Getty)

1- Bryan (Kershaw)
2- Henagan (Kershaw)
3- Humphreys (Kershaw)
4- Wright (Anderson)
5- Anderson (Field)
6- Wofford (Kershaw)
7- Mahone (Anderson)
8- Stone (pt.) (Heth)
9- Perrin (Anderson)
10- W. Perry (Field)
11- E. Perry (Anderson)
12- Harris (Anderson)
13- Benning (Field)
14- Gregg (Field)

Features

Woods   Road   Water

Federal Infantry
Federal Cavalry
Confederate Infantry
Confederate Cavalry

Scale (Miles)
0   0.37   0.73   1.1

Map 19.4

9:30 - 10:30 a.m.

Map Set 20: Longstreet Assaults Hancock's Left Flank

Map 20.1: Longstreet Plans an Offensive (9:00 - 10:00 a.m.)

The timely arrival of Lt. Gen. James Longstreet and his First Corps on the early morning of May 6 would never be forgotten by the men of the Army of Northern Virginia. "Old Pete" and his two fresh veteran divisions aptly demonstrated their battlefield prowess by quickly blunting the Federal onslaught on both sides of the Orange Plank Road. By doing so, they stabilized the crumbling front and in doing so, saved A. P. Hill's Third Corps and, by extension, the entire army from what looked like a severe battlefield defeat.

While the fighting still raged, the Southern leaders looked for a more promising opportunity to turn the tide of the battle than a direct frontal attack. It is unclear whether the idea emanated from Gen. Robert E. Lee, James Longstreet, or they arrived at the idea independently. The army's chief engineer, Maj. Gen. Martin L. Smith, was dispatched to reconnoiter the Federal left, a difficult task he completed by about 10:00 a.m. He informed Longstreet that heavy woods would conceal any movement along the Federal left flank and that he did not see any enemy infantry until he reached the Brock Road. Smith also reported that the unfinished bed of the Fredericksburg and Gordonsville Railroad, running roughly parallel to the Federal flank, could be used to hide the movement. In addition, a series of ridges ran northward toward the Orange Plank Road, the troughs of which would serve as lanes for the troops to reach the Federal flank. Longstreet sent Smith out again, this time with some of his own officers to "find a way for turning the extreme Union left on that road [Brock]." Smith would not return from this mission until after the flank attack finally ran out of steam.

Longstreet decided to use three fresh brigades to strike the Union left: Brig. Gen. G. T. Anderson's (Field's Division), Brig. Gen. William Wofford's (Kershaw's Division), and Brig. Gen. William Mahone's (Anderson's Division). Despite having manned the front of Field's column when it arrived near dawn that morning at the Widow Tapp field, Anderson's veteran brigade had not yet been engaged; it was shifted south of the road and remained in reserve as Kershaw's Division met and threw back Hancock's Federals. Wofford's Georgians were fresh because they had been left behind at Parker's Store to guard the wagon trains, and Mahone's Virginians were now in reserve behind Wofford. All three brigades were up and ready, so they could be moved quickly into position.[1]

In both his battle report and memoirs, General Longstreet write that he assigned his chief of staff, Lt. Col. Moxley Sorrel, to oversee the operation: "Colonel Sorrel . . . was ordered to conduct three brigades . . . by the route recommended by General Smith, have them faced to the left, and march down against Hancock's left."[2] Sorrel, who would end the war a brigadier general, would never forget what was to be the seminal opportunity of his military career. In a meeting with Longstreet, he received the following orders: "Colonel, there is a fine chance of a great attack by our right. If you will quickly get into those woods, some brigades will be found much scattered from the fight. Collect them and take charge. Form a good line, and then move, your right pushed forward and turning as much as possible to the left. Hit hard when you start, and don't start until you have everything ready. I shall be waiting for your gun fire, and be on hand with fresh troops for further advance."

Sorrel rode away from the meeting feeling that "no greater opportunity could be given to an aspiring young staff officer, and I was quickly at work. The brigades of Anderson, Mahone, and Wofford were lined up in fair order and in touch with each other. It was difficult to assemble them in that horrid Wilderness, but in an hour we were ready."[3]

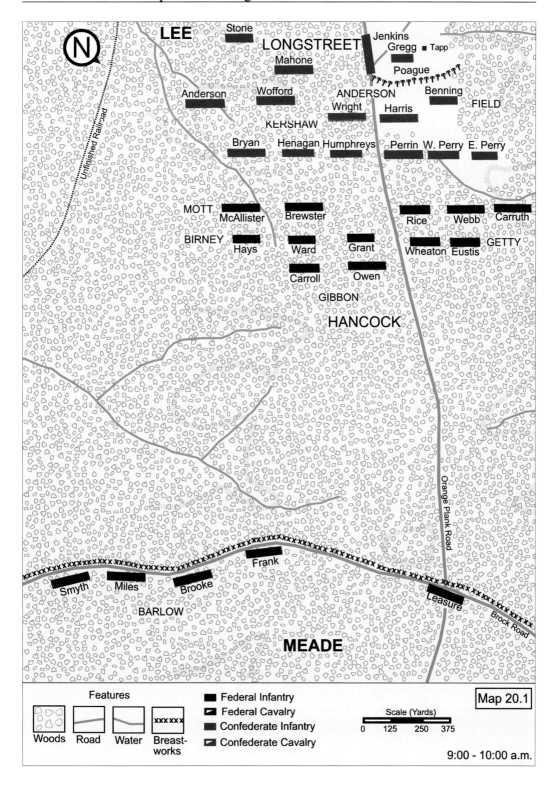

Map 20.1

9:00 - 10:00 a.m.

Map 20.2: Sorrel Gets into Position
(10:00 - 11:00 a.m.)

Longstreet's attack plan was perfect for the situations. While Sorrel attacked the Federal left flank with three fresh brigades, the remainder of Longstreet's command would press the enemy front, holding it in place to be rolled up, or helping to collapse it. The dense undergrowth, as it had since the first shot of the battle, would magnify the offensive effort.

Along the way to gather his new three-brigade command, Sorrel encountered Col. John Stone with a portion of Brig. Gen. Joseph Davis's Brigade. The unit belonged to Maj. Gen. Henry Heth's Division and although it had fought well on May 5, had collapsed on the morning of May 6 when the large-scale Federal attack swept away nearly everything facing it. Stone's men had fought north of the Orange Plank Road, but Longstreet's arrival and movements cut off the Mississippians from the rest of the brigade and division and they reformed south of the road. Their location below the road put them in position to participate in the flanking operation.[4]

Sorrel marched his column south and then along the railroad bed about one-half mile. He halted the van of Anderson's Brigade when it reached the point where the railroad bed made a sharp bend to the south and faced his entire column left (north). This put his attack column squarely on the flank and rear of the Federal left. It only took about one hour to get the brigades "lined up in fair order and in touch with each other." General Wofford made it clear that he wanted the honor of forming the right of the attack column, which would pit his Georgians against the most vulnerable part of the Federal line—its flank and rear. However, Anderson's command was in front and reached the position first, forming the right flank of the attacking line with its right aligned on a small stream. Wofford had to be content with forming on Anderson's left, with Mahone and Stone (or at least a portion of Stone's command) extending the line westward.[5]

The efficiency with which the flanking operation was organized and executed to this point impressed one historian, who observed, "Sorrel's strike force had miraculously mastered the obstructing thickets and stood ready to hit the Union flank with nearly parade-ground precision."[6] Indeed, it is difficult to envision how the operation could not have been executed with greater efficiency or precision. The left flanks of three Federal brigades were fully exposed to a long line of veteran Confederate infantry about to engulf them. It appears the unlucky recipients of the gray wave about to crash against them consisted of McAllister's brigade in the first line, Hays' brigade in the second and, farther to the right, Carroll's brigade in the third line. At least four other brigades were between these brigades and the Orange Plank Road. Most of these commands were preoccupied with the heavy Rebel reinforcements arrayed across their front. Only one Federal commander seemed concerned about the exposed nature of the left flank even though Hancock had been worried about a potential strike like the one Longstreet was about to launch. Colonel McAllister, a diligent officer, took the opportunity to reconnoiter the thickets obscuring his exposed left flank. "By crawling along from tree to tree in front I discovered a ravine," McAllister reported. Well to the front, he spotted enemy pickets and beyond them, the unfinished railroad bed filled with enemy infantry. McAllister returned to his brigade and sent an aide to inform his division commander, General Mott, about what was about to transpire.[7]

Unlike many officers with more direct combat experience, Sorrel resisted the urge to attack piecemeal before his entire column was in order. He had learned his patience by working with Longstreet, who strove to avoid dribbling his men into combat. Once he was satisfied every regiment was where it should be, Sorrel rode to the center of his line and took up a position in front of the 12th Virginia of Mahone's Brigade. The staff officer pulled off his hat and waved it over his head as he grasped his horse's reins with the other hand. "Follow me, Virginians! Let me lead you!" he yelled.[8]

Many veterans recalled Sorrel's inspiring performance. [Rank] William Smith of the 12th Virginia wrote in 1892, "The gallantry of this officer on that occasion is as vivid to me now as if it had been but yesterday. I do not remember to have seen during the whole period of the war a finer exhibition of prowess than I witnessed that day in Colonel Sorrel, in the Battle of the Wilderness."[9]

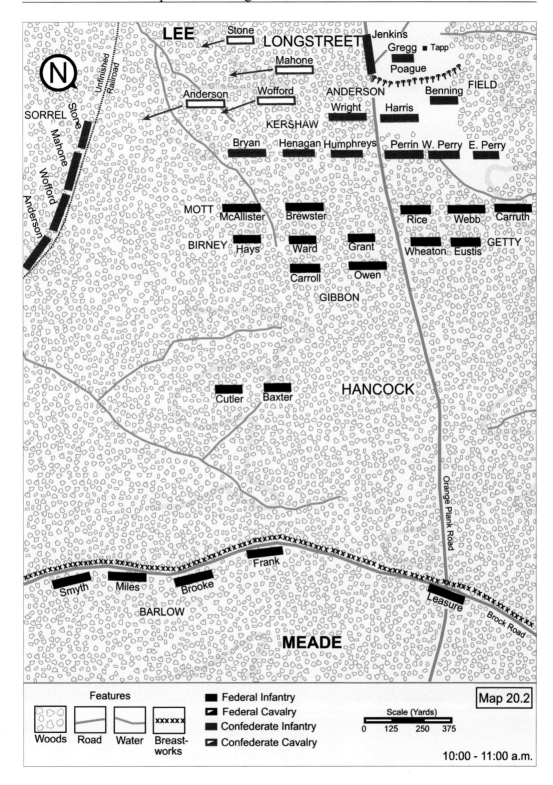

LEE

Stone

LONGSTREET

Jenkins
Gregg ■ Tapp
Poague

Mahone

Anderson   Wofford

ANDERSON
Wright   Harris   Benning   FIELD

SORREL

KERSHAW

Bryan   Henagan Humphreys   Perrin W. Perry   E. Perry

MOTT
McAllister   Brewster

Rice   Webb   Carruth
GETTY

BIRNEY
Hays   Ward   Grant   Wheaton Eustis

Carroll   Owen

GIBBON

Cutler   Baxter   HANCOCK

Orange Plank Road

Frank

Smyth   Miles   Brooke

BARLOW   Leasure   Brock Road

MEADE

Features

Woods   Road   Water   Breast-works

Map 20.2

- Federal Infantry
- Federal Cavalry
- Confederate Infantry
- Confederate Cavalry

Scale (Yards)
0   125   250   375

10:00 - 11:00 a.m.

Map 20.3: Sorrel Launches the Attack
(11:00 a.m. - noon)

The alignments of Wofford's and Stone's brigades are unclear. Anderson's Georgia brigade was likely deployed, from right to left, as follows: 11th-8th-9th-7th, and 59th, while the Virginians of Mahone's command deployed, right to left: 12th-41st-61st-16th, and 6th.

With the long gray line now ready, Sorrel launched it toward the unsuspecting Federal flank. During the advance, Mahone's men set off in a northeasterly direction and performed a gentle left-wheel to put them in line with Wofford's Georgians on their right. Once this was done, the infantrymen were close enough to make out the enemy in their front. Because the heavy fighting had died down by about 10:00 a.m., most of the Yankees in this sector were catching a well-deserved rest. A soldier in the 12th Virginia observed that the enemy was "apparently bivouacking, and little expecting any attack from that direction."[10]

The impact hit the Federal left like an unstoppable avalanche. Colonel McAllister, who knew it was coming, vainly tried to reposition his brigade by turning it 90 degrees to face the assault wave (No. 1). It was too little too late. Executing a large-scale maneuver like that in heavy brush and timber took an inordinate amount of time, and the movement was just being completed when Wofford's and Mahone's men, screaming the Rebel Yell, struck. According to McAllister, his men "held the enemy in front and delivered volley after volley into their ranks," but the long enemy line "had flanked my left" and heavy fire ripped through "my front, on my left flank, and rear." Tactically speaking, McAllister was in a no-win situation. If he had remained in place, his left flank would have been turned and crushed. His realignment, however, presented his right flank to Bryan's Georgians. While McAllister was wheeling to face Sorrel's threat from the south, Kershaw reignited his attack from the west. McAllister's brigade disintegrated. McAllister himself was nearly captured, but scores of his men were not so lucky.[11]

Because of the alignment of Sorrel's attack column, Hays' brigade, resting from its morning ordeal behind McAllister's men, was struck by Wofford (No. 2). Hit in the flank and rear, and hearing the intense gunfire in front of them, Hays' men turned to the rear and headed for the Brock Road. This was a difficult task for the sprinting Union soldiers because the thickets forced the men to keep their eyes shut, "or we would have had our eyes put out." Running blind through the brush only added to the bloody chaos.[12]

With McAllister and Hays in full rout, Sorrel's men continued advancing toward the Orange Plank Road. William Brewster's New York brigade, which did not enjoy a positive reputation as an effective fighting unit, broke when Kershaw's former brigade under Colonel Henagan renewed its attack against its front (No. 3). Behind Brewster was Hobart Ward's brigade, which was also recuperating after its initial combat with Longstreet's men. Ward's men may have held their position longer than Brewster's and thus took the full brunt of Sorrel's flank attack while its ranks were being simultaneously broken by Brewster's fleeing New Yorkers.[13]

By this time fear and in some cases outright hysteria overtook many of the Federal troops. The Confederate attackers, recalled one Union officer, seemed "like an army of ghosts rising out of the earth. . . . [S]uch an apparition will unsettle the stoutest nerves." A Southern foot soldier described the pandemonium this way: "the crackle of small arms, the bomb of the artillery, the hussah of the Yanks, the rebel yell sounding in the air." Another Confederate, writing of his younger days with pride, recalled the "woods echoing with the heavy discharge of musketry and the 'rebel yell' sounding from more than a thousand Confederate throats, the men in the finest spirits as they pressed on."[14]

Some of Ward's regiments, like the 40th New York, desperately tried to turn and face Sorrel's onslaught (No. 4). Bullets flying into them from several directions, however, convinced the veterans their situation was hopeless. The historian of the 141st Pennsylvania, also of Ward's brigade, admitted that his regiment headed toward the Brock Road "without supports, without ammunition, and with lines badly broken." Fighting on or close to the right side of Ward's brigade, Lt. Col. Charles Weygant of the 124th New York explained, "I might as well have tried to stop the flight of a cannon ball by interposing the lid of a cracker box."[15]

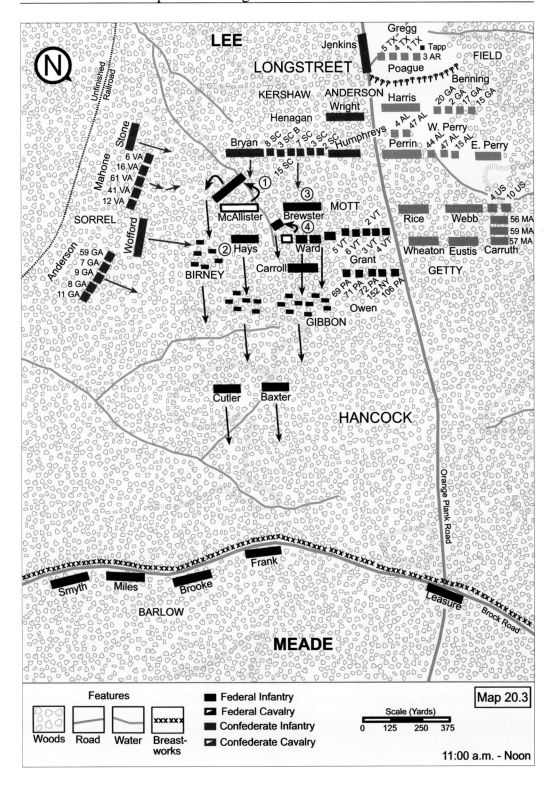

Map 20.3

11:00 a.m. - Noon

Map 20.4: Sorrel's Attack Grinds Toward the Orange Plank Road (11:00 a.m. - noon)

Within minutes the maelstrom engulfed Sam Carroll's brigade in position in the third line behind Ward's brigade. Carroll tried to swing his front around to face Sorrel's onslaught, realizing as he did so that the Rebels were also coming from the west (No. 1). According to Capt. Thomas Galwey of the 8th Ohio, the retreat began slowly: "One by one, then in twos and threes, until at last they went in such numbers as to give the appearance of a general skedaddle." The experienced men tried to remain in place. "Our veterans halloed to the faint-hearted to come back, showering bitter curses on them, but all to no purpose," admitted Galwey. Some of the Union foot soldiers were armed with Spencer repeating rifles, which only served to delay the inevitable. "There was nothing left of us now but broken little squads," wrote Galwey. "All that remained for us to do was to get back to our lines, running if possible."[16]

Despite its stunning early success, the Confederates still had to overcome a variety of obstacles. The 6th Virginia of Mahone's Brigade encountered stout resistance that forced the regiment to "double back until it had gotten to be twenty-five or thirty ranks deep," according to one officer. General Mahone appeared at this time and "in a clear shrill voice, which could be heard above the rattle of the muskets, asked, 'What regiment is this in this confusion?' Being answered that it was the Sixth Virginia, he exclaimed, 'The Sixth Virginia Regiment of my brigade—that splendidly drilled regiment—in this condition?'" Supposedly embarrassed, the men sorted out the situation and continued their advance, driving the enemy from their front.[17]

Mahone's Virginians encountered a marshy area during their approach to the Plank Road. The bog sucked at their legs and retarded their movements. When he spotted the 12th Virginia's flag-bearer struggling through the mud, Sorrel rode over and offered to carry the flag. The reply was a stern rejection of the offer, followed with the promise, "We will follow you!" Sorrel spurred his horse forward toward the enemy.[18]

The initial Rebel attack crushed five Federal brigades south of the Plank Road. Only Grant's Vermonter brigade (No. 2) and Owen's Philadelphia Brigade behind it (No. 3) remained. Grant's men had turned in a valiant performance on May 5 and did the same earlier this morning when they were shoved up to blunt Longstreet's initial eastward attack. Once Sorrel's attack was underway, Grant noted that "bullets came from the right across the Plank Road—small arms fire from Abner Perrin's advancing brigade. Grant swivelled the 4th Vermont in that direction, which fired into the Alabamians (No. 4). Although they could not see Perrin's men, the stream of bullets made it clear that a sizable force was beyond Grant's right. Humphreys's Mississippians were also approaching their front, and likely some of Henagan's South Carolinians and Virginians from Mahone command were pressing Grant's left. The colonel ordered two of his regiments to wheel in that direction (No. 5). Colonel Thomas Seaver of the 3rd Vermont tried to get the 2nd Vermont on his left to do the same, to no avail. By this time, explained Seaver, "the left of the line had broken in confusion, and in order to save my command from capture, I was obliged to retire." Grant realized further resistance was "worse than useless," and ordered his brigade to fall back to the Brock Road. "Our entire lines at this part of the army went back in disorder. All organization and control seemed to have been lost," he admitted. Private Seth Eastman of the 6th Vermont wrote that he and his comrades "were obliged to run to the right of the line as the Rebels came in on our left flank. . . . The ground was covered with the dead and wounded in indescribable confusion." Private Wilbur Fisk of the 2nd Vermont wrote, "my legs saved me. . . . We had to leave our dead and wounded . . . retreat out of that place, leaving all that we had gained in the hands of the enemy."[19]

Only Owens's Philadelphia Brigade remained as an organized unit south of the Plank Road. According to its historian, "without any apparent cause that could be seen from the position of the brigade, the troops on our left [Carroll's brigade] began to give way, and commenced falling back towards the Brock Road." The men also had to part ranks to allow Grant's Vermonters to pass. "Those pressing past . . . did not seem to be demoralized in manner, nor did they present the appearance of soldiers moving under orders, but rather of a throng of armed men who were returning dissatisfied from a muster."[20]

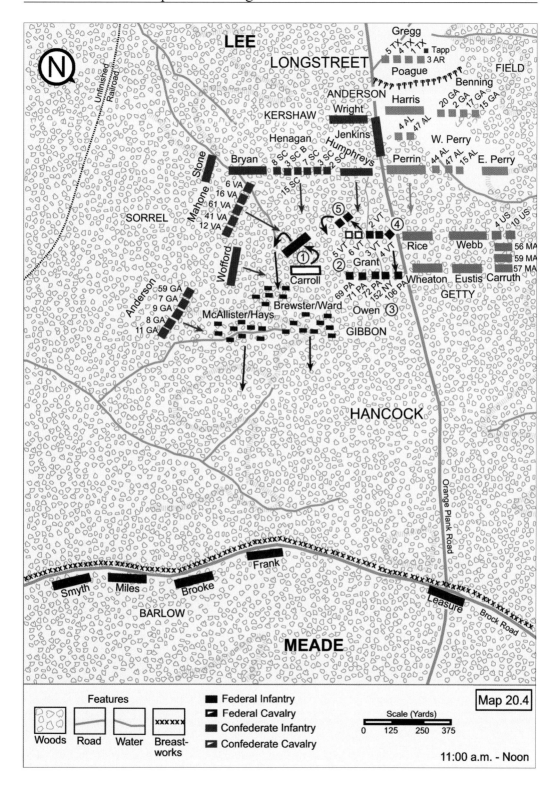

Features

Woods	Road	Water	Breast-works

■ Federal Infantry
◢ Federal Cavalry
■ Confederate Infantry
◢ Confederate Cavalry

Scale (Yards)

0   125   250   375

Map 20.4

11:00 a.m. - Noon

Map 20.5: Actions North of the Orange Plank Road (11:00 a.m. - noon)

The Rebel attack south of the Plank Road chewed up one Federal brigade after another in exactly the manner Longstreet, Sorrel, and others hoped it would. The adrenaline of success coursed through the ranks: "the men seem[ed] to have lost all sense of danger," wrote one, "although hostile bullets were doing some deadly work." Another Rebel explained that "the woods echoing with the heavy discharge of musketry and the 'rebel yell' sounding from more than a thousand Confederate throats, the men were in the finest spirits as they pressed on."[21]

North of the Plank Road, meanwhile, Brig. Gen. James Wadsworth was feeling every one of his 56 years that day. Rarely had his command been so badly manhandled as it had earlier that morning when Longstreet's First Corps veterans launched their counteroffensive. Munching on a cracker, Wadsworth confided to an aide that he was "exhausted and worn out." He worried that he was physically unfit to command his men and thought that perhaps he should turn over his division to someone else. Firing and the movement of troops south of the Orange Plank Road interrupted his introspection. He mounted his horse and within minutes discovered the entire sector was in flight. Still smarting from his defeat a few hours earlier because of Wadsworth's orders, Brig. Gen. Alexander Webb was now told by the same officer to "Go to the left and stop the retreat of those troops to our left who are flying to the Brock Road." Wadsworth then endeavored to form a new defensive line running parallel to the Orange Plank Road. He ordered the 76th New York and 56th Pennsylvania of Rice's brigade to move in that direction, and instructed an aide to find Brig. Gen. Lysander Cutler and double-quick his exhausted Iron Brigade from its resting point near the Lacy house back to the front.[22]

General Rice accompanied his regiments to their new position, where he quickly realized that Wadsworth's proposed new line along the Plank Road facing south was untenable because Confederate artillery shells were raining down amongst his men (No. 1). The undesirability of the position was compounded by the fact that Confederate infantry were moving against Rice's new right flank—Maj. Gen. Charles Field had reignited his charge against the Federal positions north of the Plank Road. According to Field, "General Longstreet informed me that some troops had been sent around to attack the enemy on his left flank, and that he wished me to attack in front at the same time. The plank road at this point was straight and level for a mile or more. Placing a couple of pieces in the road, which effectually dislodged the enemy from a breastwork which he had thrown up across it."

Field's Division was reinforced by two fresh brigades from Maj. Gen. Richard Anderson's Division. The Alabamians of Brig. Gen. Abner Perrin's command formed just to the left (north) of the Plank Road, while Brig. Gen. Edward Perry's Floridians formed some distance off Perrin's left. In between, Brig. Gen. William Perry had reformed several of his regiments that had fought Wadsworth's troops so doggedly and well earlier in the morning. Although outnumbered by the Federal brigades north of the Plank Road by a factor of two to one, these three Rebel brigades proved highly effective against the tired and skittish Federals in their front.[23]

The iron rain from above and the lead rounds zipping through their ranks proved too much for Rice's regiments and they retreated. Wadsworth believed the only hope to staunch the onslaught was a bold counterattack, but the only troops he could find were men of the 20th Massachusetts of Webb's brigade. The unit was shielded behind Rebel-built breastworks near the Plank Road. A ravine between the works and the enemy lines strengthened the position. After a contentious exchange with the 20th's commander, Col. George Macy, Wadsworth ordered it out of its protected position. Macy objected, and the general became increasingly agitated by what he considered a case of rank insubordination. Wadsworth told him that he would lead the charge. Spurring his horse, the division leader jumped the earthworks and the Bay Staters followed him (No. 2).[24]

No one seems to have spotted elements of the 8th Alabama (Perrin's Brigade) lying in wait in their front until the Alabamians opened fire. The rounds cut into Macy's unsuspecting men "from an unseen enemy only a few yards away, though invisible," recalled one of the soldiers." The officers immediately ordered the men to fall to the ground and return the fire.[25]

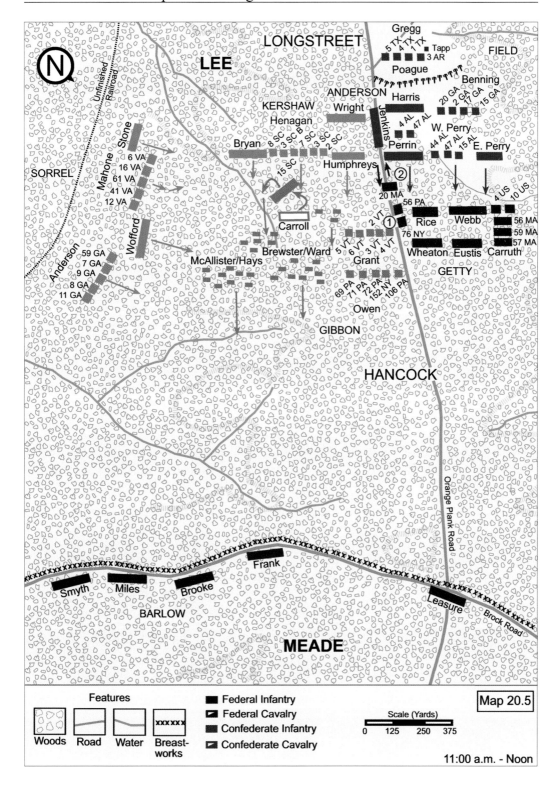

Map 20.5

11:00 a.m. - Noon

Map 20.6: The Last of the Federal Line Collapses (noon - 1:00 p.m.)

Wadsworth was riding at the front of the 20th Massachusetts along the Plank Road when the 8th Alabama fired its first volley (No. 1). The flash and surprise stunned his mount, and with Wadsworth pulling on the reins his horse headed straight for the Confederate lines. The division commander gained control of the horse before it entered the enemy's ranks and was spurring his mount back toward the Bay Staters when a round of small arms fire exploded around him. One of the bullets slammed into his head and sprayed brain matter onto an aide riding next to him, who maintained enough presence of mind to dismount and catch the general as he fell from his horse. After carefully lowering Wadsworth to the ground, the aide concluded the general had been killed instantly, hopped onto the general's horse, and galloped to safety. Wadsworth, however, was still alive. Passing Rebel soldiers dragged the fatally wounded Federal officer to the base of a tree and left him there. Southerners who recalled seeing him noted that his hat, boots, and other personal effects were already gone; someone ordered a blanket draped over the fallen general. When an infantry officer asked the aide who had accompanied Wadsworth why he had not stopped the general from riding virtually alone into such a dangerous area, he shot back, "My God…nobody could stop him!"[26]

It was about this time that General Webb returned from his failed mission to rally troops south of the Orange Plank Road. In truth, no one could have stopped the mad stampede to the rear under such circumstances. Webb found his brigade aligned parallel to the Orange Plank Road, placed there by Wadsworth as a barrier against Sorrel's advance (No. 2). Carruth's and Rice's brigades, together with handfuls of other scattered units, comprised the first line facing west above the Plank Road. They tried to advance against the Floridians and Alabamians in front of them, but were repulsed (No. 3). One Union soldier recalled that the enemy's volleys "resembled the fury of hell in intensity, and [were] deadly accurate." A soldier in the 57th Massachusetts wrote home that the firing was "so profligate that some of the boys drove into it head down and back bent, as if they were in the middle of an intense New England blizzard." The Massachusetts unit carried 548 men into this "profligate" fire and emerged with just 262.[27]

Even though Webb's position along the Plank Road left his men in danger of being hit in the front, flank, and rear, he decided to make a stand to delay the enemy advance for as long as possible. To his right and rear, however, the rest of the units north of the road (Carruth, Rice, Eustis and Wheaton) were in full retreat. General Eustis was so stunned by the rapid turn of events that he "seemed paralyzed," wrote Col. Oliver Edwards of the 37th Massachusetts. According to Edwards, Eustis asked him to take command of the brigade, which he did. Edwards immediately pulled the brigade back to the Brock Road (No. 4).[28]

With the exception of Webb's brigade, the entire Federal line was in full flight toward the Brock Road. General Field recalled that once he attacked north of the Plank Road, the "enemy was started back, but slowly, and then he broke and fled in confusion, leaving his dead and wounded thick upon the field." Small fires broke out in the woods. Some believed the flames had escaped from the campfires ignited by Union troops to make coffee, while others were certain the sparks emanated from musket discharges. The spreading fires scorched the dead and burned to death the injured, adding a dense horrid smoke to an already hellish environment.

When Sorrel's front ranks drew near the Plank Road, they met Webb's rearguard, augmented by the 56th and 57th Massachusetts of Carruth's brigade (No. 5). This improvised force was already battling a determined advance by Perrin's men from the west, and was now confronted by Sorrel's men from the south. Somehow, at least for a short time, Webb was able to maintain a stable front. A Union officer recalled that the woods along the road were "so dense that one could distinguish nothing." An aide quickly made his way to Webb with a message from the commander of the 56th Massachusetts: the enemy was edging around his flank and approaching his rear and he needed permission to withdraw. The Rebels sliding around Webb's flank were either Virginians from Mahone's Brigade or the right side of Perrin's command. Webb's response was decisive: "break like partridges through the woods for the Brock Road." The last semblance of military order among the Union troops disintegrated.[29]

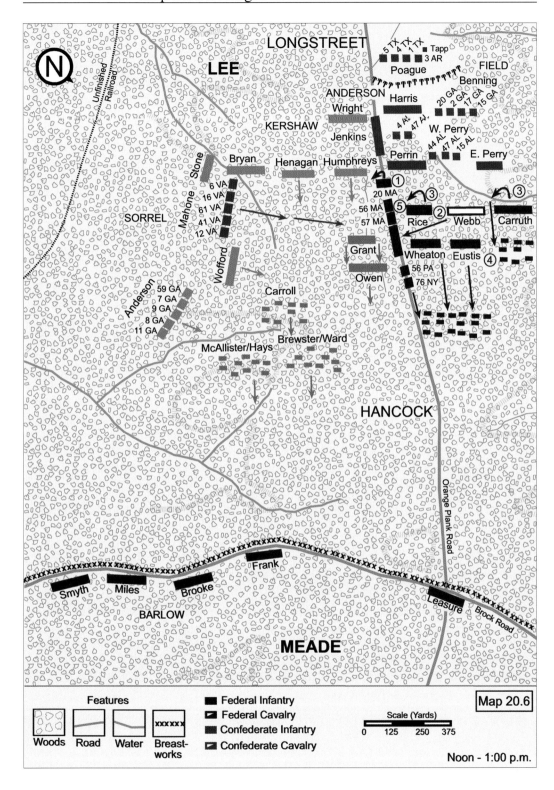

Map 20.6

Features

Woods   Road   Water   Breast-works

Federal Infantry
Federal Cavalry
Confederate Infantry
Confederate Cavalry

Scale (Yards)
0   125   250   375

Noon - 1:00 p.m.

Map 20.7: Longstreet is Wounded; The Flank Attack Ends (1:00 - 2:00 p.m.)

The men of Mahone's Brigade had never tasted such victory, but the lines were becoming ragged and disordered. Burning brush forced the 12th Virginia on the right of the line to veer right (No. 1). Thus separated, the men continued across the Plank Road while the rest of the brigade halted within 75 yards of the road. Major Richard Jones recalled that the vegetation was so thick that he did not see the Plank Road until he was within a few feet of it.[30]

Realizing that his regiment had drifted far from the rest of the brigade, Col. D. A. Weisiger ordered his 12th Virginia to turn to the left and make a wheel back toward the road. It now approached the rest of the brigade in the dense thickets. The brigade's two elements were essentially facing each other (No. 2). It was a recipe for disaster.[31]

In a career filled with successes, the morning of May 6 may have been General Longstreet's greatest. With his arrival, the situation had changed from almost certain destruction of a portion of Lee's army to decisive victory. The success put everyone in good spirits. A First Corps staffer noticed that "almost every face wore a smile, and…each officer and man felt disposed to congratulate every one he met on our success." Longstreet was especially in good spirits. General Field described an encounter with his commander: "General Longstreet rode up to me…seizing my hands, congratulated me in warm terms on the fighting of my troops and the result of the assault."[32]

Longstreet understood that victory was not complete and would not be until the vital intersection of Plank and Brock Roads was in Confederate hands. Gathering his lieutenants around him, Longstreet planned the next offensive. He was assisted by the return of Gen. Martin Smith, who had reconnoitered to Brock Road and found that the Union line there again hung in the air, inviting yet another flanking movement. Longstreet quickly ordered General Wofford to loop his brigade to the right while Gen. Micah Jenkins and his brigade spearheaded a drive up the Plank Road with the rest of

Kershaw's Division in support. Kershaw reported that his orders were to attack the "position of the enemy upon the Brock Road, before he could recover from his disaster. The order to me was to break their line and push all to the right of the road towards Fredericksburg." The attack was to be supported by two Napoleons and a 24-pounder howitzer belonging to David McIntosh's Battalion.[33]

A handsome, young officer, Micah Jenkins was a favorite among the men and officers. He had recently returned from sick leave, still not completely recovered from his lingering illness. He left all that behind when he learned that his brigade would carry a major part of the responsibility for the charge. His South Carolinians were veterans and many were proud of their new uniforms. Andrew Dunn, one of Longstreet's aides, did not like the looks of the situation, so he tried to convince his corps commander to halt and turn back, but Longstreet simply said, "That is our business" and continued down the road.[34]

As Longstreet's entourage reached Mahone's Brigade, invisible in the thickets on the south side of the Plank Road, the 12th Virginia completed its wheeling motion and reached the road. One of the Virginians recalled that, "suddenly we were startled by a sharp volley of musketry coming from a line of troops about forty or fifty yards south of the plank-road, the bullets from which volley fiercely whizzed over our heads." Someone yelled out, "Show your colors!" and the flag-bearer, the same soldier who would not relinquish his flag to Colonel Sorrel, calmly strode out onto the road surface and waved his banner.[35]

Sorrel later noted that Longstreet's party, followed by Jenkins's brigade and part of Kershaw's command, was riding in the shaded light of the dense tangle when "a shot or two went off then more, and finally a strong fusillade." Caught in between the facing lines of Mahone's Brigade, General Jenkins was shot in the head and died later that day. A staff officer and a courier were also struck and killed. Longstreet was hit in the arm, but the trajectory took it up through his throat. The impact was so forceful that, according to Sorrel, Longstreet "was actually lifted straight up and came down hard." Still in command of his senses he rode forward waving his good arm to stop the firing.[36]

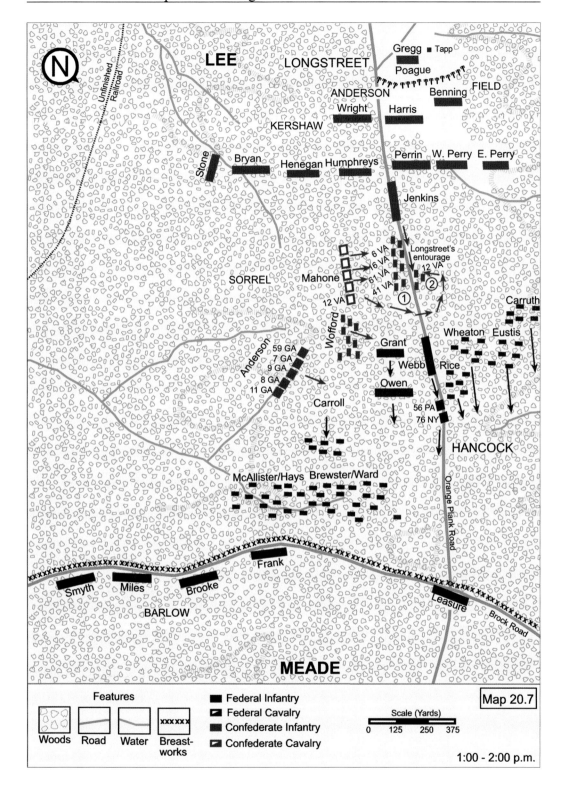

N

LEE   LONGSTREET

Gregg   ■ Tapp
Poague
ANDERSON   FIELD
Wright   Harris   Benning
KERSHAW

Bryan   Henegan Humphreys   Perrin W. Perry E. Perry

Stone

Jenkins

6 VA   Longstreet's
6 VA   entourage
SORREL   Mahone   61 VA   12 VA   Carruth
41 VA   ②
12 VA   ①

Wheaton Eustis
Anderson   59 GA   Wofford   Grant
7 GA   Webb   Rice
9 GA
8 GA   Owen
11 GA   56 PA
Carroll   76 NY

HANCOCK

McAllister/Hays Brewster/Ward

Orange Plank Road

Frank
Smyth Miles Brooke   Leasure
BARLOW   Brock Road

MEADE

Features	Federal Infantry	
	Federal Cavalry	Map 20.7
Woods Road Water Breast-works	Confederate Infantry	Scale (Yards)
	Confederate Cavalry	0 125 250 375

1:00 - 2:00 p.m.

Map 20.8: The Combatants Regroup
(1:00 - 2:00 p.m.)

Carrying the rotund general to the rear, the knot passed General Lee, with "sadness in his face." A very large man, it took three soldiers to ease General Longstreet out of his saddle and into a waiting ambulance. The bloody foam rising to his lips suggested a lung wound and together with the excessive loss of blood, the situation seemed dire. Surgeons were able to quickly stop the bleeding and Longstreet would make a full recovery.[37]

While Longstreet was receiving medical care, the last of Hancock's troops were making their way back to the defenses along Brock Road. Perhaps the best firsthand accounting of the late morning battle comes from Lt. Col. Charles Weygant, whose 124th New York of Ward's brigade was among the first to retire. He noted that his regiment was "caught up as by a whirlwind, and broken to fragments; and the terrible tempest of disaster swept on down the Union line, beating back brigade after brigade, and tearing to pieces regiment after regiment, until upwards of twenty thousand veterans were fleeing, every man for himself, through the disorganizing and already blood-stained woods, toward the Union rear." General Hancock would concede to Longstreet after the war, "You rolled me up like a wet blanket."[38]

According to military historian Robert E. L. Krick, only two brigades, Wofford's and Mahone's, sporting a total of 11 regiments did most of the damage. He noted that "the role of Stone's Mississippians is uncertain, although it must have been small." He also pointed to a contemporary newspaper article that stated, "Anderson's brigade was so far to the right and rear of the enemy that it met with little or no resistance." Therefore two Confederate brigades had defeated what amounted to a full Federal corps—over 20,000 men. Certainly, the coordinated attacks of Kershaw's and Field's divisions played a major role, as did the tangles of the Wilderness, which disrupted Federal movements and wreaked havoc on the emotions of the men.[39]

This was a time when the Union officers showed their mettle. Most encouraged their men to stay in position, and when it came time to retreat, to do so in an orderly manner. General Hancock was especially active during this time. According to Col. Lewis Grant, he "displayed almost superhuman efforts and ability in rallying the disordered troops and reforming the line to resist attack." During the Confederate onslaught, most of the officers were unsuccessful. One Vermont soldier noted that "some of the officers drew their swords and revolvers and tried their utmost to rally them…they might as well have appealed to the winds." Once at Brock Road, the men reformed their broken ranks and began the process of restoring their broken confidence. The II Corps' historian noted the disparities in how the various units returned to Brock Road: "on the right (north) of the Plank Road, where the troops came back under orders, the regiments are generally entire, though greatly depleted by losses and by straggling; but on the left of the Plank Road (south), many regiments are to be found in companies or squads." The reason is clear—Sorrel's men slammed into the Federal troops south of Plank Road, causing their units to disintegrate.[40]

Upon reaching the breastworks, the men exhibited different emotions. For Thomas Galwey of the 8th Ohio (Carroll's brigade) it was to prepare for another fight: "It was our one hope—shattered, fatigued, and out of ammunition as we were by this time—to get across the parapet and, after a short rest in the hollow ground in the rear, to re-form and be again ready for action." Wilbur Fisk of the 2nd Vermont (Grant's brigade), felt very differently: "They tried to halt us at the first line of breastworks, but I saw fresh troops coming that hadn't been in the fight at all, and I thought they might as well hold the line as me. My object was to find a safe place in the rear and, in spite of revolvers or swords, entreaties, or persuasions, I found it."[41]

While some Confederates attempted to storm the breastworks, "yelling like devils" most were content to settle down and await orders. Lee soon arrived on the scene and assessed the situation. Most of his units were in disarray and not ready to continue the offensive, he believed, so he ordered his officers to stand down and reorganize their units.[42]

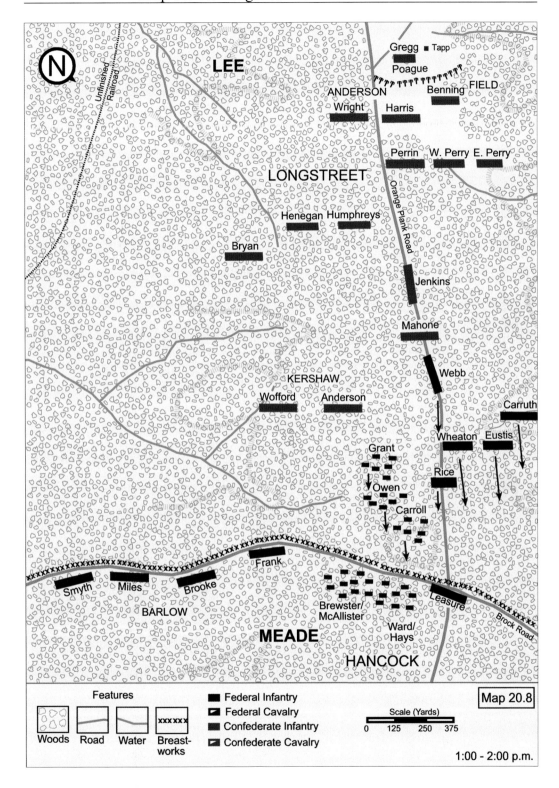

N

LEE

Gregg ■ Tapp

Poague

ANDERSON   Benning FIELD

Wright   Harris

Perrin W. Perry E. Perry

LONGSTREET

Henegan Humphreys

Bryan

Jenkins

Mahone

KERSHAW   Webb

Wofford Anderson   Carruth

Grant   Wheaton Eustis

Owen   Rice

Carroll

Frank

Smyth Miles Brooke   Leasure

BARLOW   Brewster/
McAllister

MEADE   Ward/
Hays

HANCOCK

Orange Plank Road

Unfinished Railroad

Brock Road

Features

Woods Road Water Breastworks

xxxxx

■ Federal Infantry
▱ Federal Cavalry
■ Confederate Infantry
▱ Confederate Cavalry

Map 20.8

Scale (Yards)

0   125   250   375

1:00 – 2:00 p.m.

Map Set 21: Burnside Finally Hits the Gap

Map 21.1: Burnside Arrives on Longstreet's Flank (1:00 - 1:30 p.m.)

After being temporarily blocked by Brig. Gen. Stephen Ramseur's Brigade just south of Lt. Gen. Richard Ewell's line (see Map 19.1), Maj. Gen. Ambrose Burnside pushed his three IX Corps brigades under Cols. Samuel Griffin and Zenas Bliss (Brig. Gen. Robert Potter's division), and Col. John Hartranft (Brig. Gen. Orlando Willcox's division) southward toward the Orange Plank Road. Willcox's other brigade under Col. Benjamin Christ remained behind to guard the road leading to Parker's Store. The move was in response to Lt. Gen. U. S. Grant's order of 11:45 a.m.: "Push in with all vigor so as to drive the enemy from General Hancock's front, and get in on the Orange and Fredericksburg plank road at the earliest possible moment." The message included a subtle rebuke: "Hancock has been expecting you for the last three hours, and has been making his attack and dispositions with a view of your assistance."[1]

Potter's division, in the front of the column, clawed its way through thick woods and nearly impenetrable undergrowth. Bliss' brigade led the division, followed by Griffin's brigade (No. 1). Cyrus Comstock, one of Grant's staff officers, watched with growing concern while Bliss' column approached the enemy line by the flank. He rode to Burnside and suggested, "Don't you think it would be better for Bliss to move in a line of battle?" to which the IX Corps commander replied, "If you order it, it is." Comstock shot back, "I order it," and Bliss deployed with three regiments in the first line and three in the second. According to Potter, he "reformed as quickly as possible and moved to the attack, being entirely unable to see anything from the thickness of the wood." More than terrain bothered the men. One Massachusetts soldier complained, "the heat was intense [and] the men were almost exhausted from their long march the previous day." Potter deployed both of his brigades, with Bliss in the front and Griffin behind him. Hartranft's brigade was still on the march.[2]

According to Potter, he discovered "the enemy were posted on the opposite side of a swampy ravine and were intrenched." Almost certainly he spotted the 15th and 48th Alabama regiments behind some rough works, but exactly how they arrived there is open to debate. The only troops close enough at that time were the trio of brigades north of the Orange Plank Road under Brig. Gens. Abner Perrin and Edward Perry, and Col. William Perry. According to Col. William Oates of the 15th Alabama, after General Longstreet was shot down, division leader Charles Field ordered all three brigades forward toward Brock Road to "feel for the enemy" (No. 2). Although no organized Federals were in their immediate front, no one knew where they were or how far back they had fallen. The order made Oates uncomfortable because some of his troops had ventured left (north) and encountered Burnside's infantry. When Oates reported the information to Colonel Perry, he was told "I was probably mistaken." When Oates remonstrated that he would be hit in the left flank during a move eastward toward the Brock Road, he was told to follow orders. Colonel Perry recalled the situation somewhat differently. When the initial firing fell away, he claimed to have sent an officer with a squad of men to act as videttes to the left of the brigade about noon. "Some time afterwards, information was received which strengthened my apprehensions, and caused me to send Colonel Oates in that direction with his own and the Forty eighth Alabama regiment" (No. 3). According to Perry, information from Oates convinced him "a formidable attack from that quarter was impending." Perry went on to claim he sent an aide to ask General Lee for permission to shake out his entire brigade in that direction, but the aide returned with word that he was to continue his forward movement toward the Brock Road.[3]

The small but growing firefight developing off his left posed a dilemma for the brigade commander. "At length, the indications growing more threatening toward the left, I resolved, without regard to orders, to make the movement before contemplated," he reported. It was a bold act to disobey direct orders, especially any originating from the army's commander.[4]

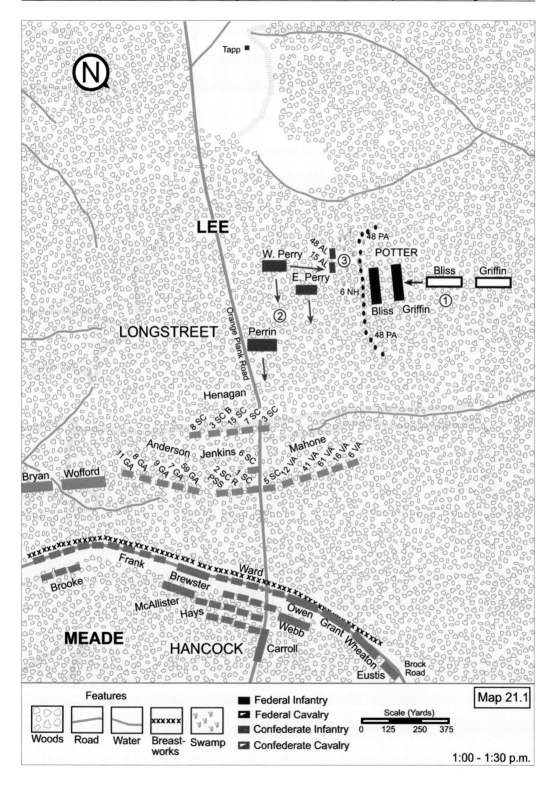

Map 21.1

Features

Woods   Road   Water   Breast-   Swamp
                        works

■ Federal Infantry
◰ Federal Cavalry
■ Confederate Infantry
◰ Confederate Cavalry

Scale (Yards)
0   125   250   375

1:00 - 1:30 p.m.

Map 21.2: Potter's Union Division Attacks the Confederate Left North of the Plank Road (1:30 - 2:30 p.m.)

After spitting out orders for the rest of his brigade to turn to the left, Colonel Perry rode forward to see how Oates' two regiments (15th and 48th Alabama) were faring. He found them facing a sizable number of Federal troops. Fortunately, the Alabamians were protected by a hastily constructed pile of logs. A Federal soldier who later stormed this barricade recalled it was constructed of "felled trees and the bodies of their dead."

Riding over to the right of the 15th Alabama, Perry observed a large gap between it and Edward Perry's Florida brigade, which was still facing eastward. As the rest of the Alabama regiments arrived, William Perry threw them into position. He sent the 4th Alabama to the right of the 15th Alabama to fill in the frontage between the two brigades (No. 1). The rest of the new arrivals (44th, 47th, and 48th Alabama) were sent to the left of the line.[5]

General Edward Perry, who had obeyed Lee's orders to maintain his eastward-moving front, realized that Colonel Perry had shift to face north and that a large body of Federal troops was deployed for battle off his left. The brigade had suffered heavily during its last major combat at Gettysburg when a Federal counterattack struck it in front and on the left. A similar situation now loomed. He quickly ordered his men to swivel to left and face the enemy (No. 2), but before they could fully comply, Burnside's troops were nearly upon them yelling the "huzzah" battle cry.[6]

While the Rebels were coming up, Potter's men methodically advanced. According to the historian of the 48th Pennsylvania (Bliss' brigade), the "movement was made through a dense wood, almost impenetrable, owing to the tangled underbrush. . . . [T]he attack [was] made where it was utterly impossible to see anything from the thickness of the woods. The enemy was posted on the opposite side of a swampy ravine behind entrenchments." Realizing that their lines did not conform to that of the enemy's, some of Bliss' regiments did "nearly a half wheel to the right" (No. 3). Now better positioned, they continued their generally southward advance.

The orders "Forward, double quick!" rang out and the line speed accelerated. "[T]he enemy poured in terrific volleys; their bullets whistled around us and thinned our ranks," recalled a Pennsylvanian, "but the advance was not checked."[7]

Exactly what transpired next is hard to discern with any confidence. Few participants left accounts of this portion of the Wilderness combat, and many of those that did, particularly on the Federal side, may have exaggerated what took place. What we do know is that the Federal troops on the left of Burnside's line overwhelmed Edward Perry's small band of Floridians (No. 4). According to Pvt. D. L. Geer of the 5th Florida, "our lines were not connected to our left, so we had it hot right here in this place. . . . Right here some of the boys were killed and most of them were taken prisoner. . . . We were cut up badly." A soldier in the 8th Florida wrote that "our brave boys fought with [their] usual daring. We were flanked and necessarily compelled to fall back, but not without disputing every inch of ground during the engagement." According to Colonel Oates, the Floridians were struck "squarely in the flank and decimated at once." Colonel Perry recalled how the Floridians on his right simply "melted away." Colonel P. D. Bowles of the 4th Alabama thought the survivors were "retreating slowly." The Florida Brigade lost about one-half of its 500 men during this brief but desperate portion of the battle.[8]

The troops that encountered and overwhelmed Perry's Floridians were positioned on Bliss' left flank. While the accounts of their attack are fairly numerous, none of them mention falling on the flank of exposed Confederate troops or infantry fighting or moving without the benefit of breastworks.

The retreat of the Floridians left Colonel Perry and his Alabama troops in a tough situation. Although they were fighting on slightly higher ground, large numbers of Federals were moving against their front and were about to engulf their right. Perry's left also hung in the air. The marshy ground in front of the Confederate position slowed the Federal advance considerably, and the rude breastworks protected the men from most of the bullets, but the situation was deteriorating rapidly. The veteran Rebels, however, remained in place, leveled their weapons, and opened fire.[9]

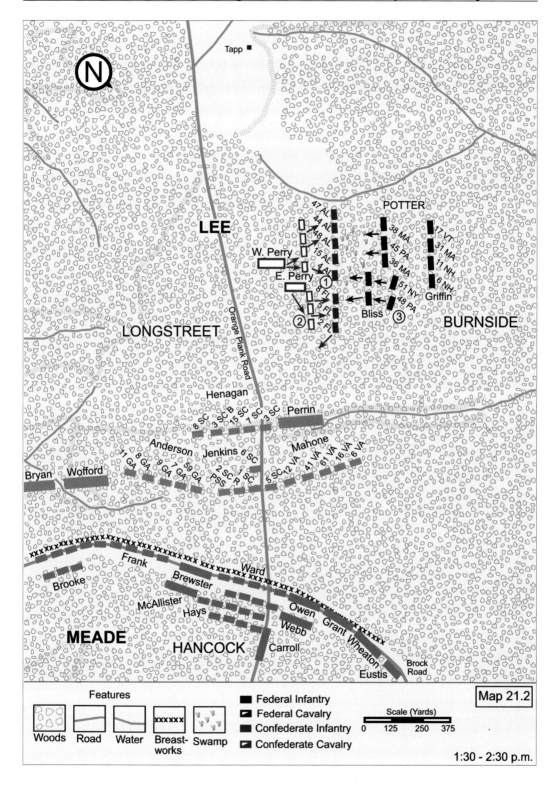

Tapp

N

LEE

POTTER

47 AL
44 AL
48 AL
15 AL
4 AL

W. Perry

E. Perry

①

②

8 FL
9 FL
5 FL
2 FL

LONGSTREET

Orange Plank Road

38 MA
45 PA
36 MA
51 NY
48 PA

Bliss ③

17 VT
31 MA
11 NH
6 NH

Griffin

BURNSIDE

Henagan

8 SC 3 SC 15 SC 7 SC 3 SC

Perrin

Anderson Jenkins 6 SC

Mahone

Bryan Wofford

11 GA 8 GA 9 GA 7 GA 59 GA

2 SC R 1 SC
PSS

5 SC 12 VA 41 VA 61 VA 16 VA 6 VA

xxxxxxxxxxxxxxxxxxxxxxx

Frank

Ward

Brooke

Brewster

xxxxxxxxxxxxx

McAllister

Hays

Owen Grant Wheaton

MEADE

HANCOCK

Webb

Carroll

xxxxxxxxx

Brock
Road

Eustis

Features

Woods Road Water Breast- Swamp
works

xxxxx

■ Federal Infantry
◪ Federal Cavalry
■ Confederate Infantry
◪ Confederate Cavalry

Scale (Yards)
0   125   250   375

Map 21.2

1:30 - 2:30 p.m.

Map 21.3: The Fighting Intensifies
(2:30 - 4:00 p.m.)

While the rest of Perry's regiments were settling into position or throwing up works, Colonel Oates launched a small but sharp counterattack with his own 15th Alabama and the 44th Alabama into the right side of Bliss' oncoming line. Although bold and audacious, the few hundred tired Alabamians were no match for the Federals. As Oates admitted after the war, "they were too numerous and the attempt failed" (No. 1).[10]

Bliss' attack produced solid results—at least initially. According to the historian of the 36th Massachusetts (in the middle of the line), "The left of our regiment first struck the rebel line, and received the severest fire, but pressed on through it, and the Thirty-sixth and Forty-fifth broke the line, went over the breastworks with a rush, and drove out the enemy [Perry's Flordians] in our front. The attack had been most determined and successful, and the regiment had complete possession of the rebel works in its front. Thus far all had gone well," continued the writer. "The Fifty-first New York, however, had broken in the attack and failed to carry the line with which it was confronted, and, in a brief time, though to us it seemed an age, the enemy rallied, moved upon swept round toward our rear [see below as the 48th Pennsylvania had also broken], and we were subjected to a fearful fire of musketry at short range" (No. 2). The 48th Pennsylvania had a similar experience: "Sharp firing at very close range ensued, followed by a savage charge, which brought the boys into the enemy's rifle pits in some places. Being unable to maintain the advantage gained, the troops fell back. Twice the charge was renewed—considerable ground was gained, but the enemy retained possession of their lines," recorded the 48th's historian. These troops may have been up against the lead elements of Benning's Brigade (see Map 21.4).[11]

The situation was grim on the Rebel side of the works. Colonel Perry knew he was in a precarious situation and could not hold much longer without support, and his ammunition was running low. An aide returned with news that reinforcements were on the way, but would they arrive in time? Fresh gunfire erupted on the left of his line, where the 47th Alabama was hit in front and rear (see next paragraph). Perry refused part of his line to face the attack (No. 3). It was the right move, but even that could not save his line, he wrote, for "they [the enemy] were too near at hand and their momentum was too great."[12]

Burnside knew he was hours behind schedule, that Hancock and Wadsworth had collapsed A. P. Hill's front, and the Federal attack had collapsed under the weight of a fresh enemy assault. The IX Corps commander's style was not to interfere with the decision-making of his division commanders, but on the afternoon of May 6 he made an exception. Burnside spurred his horse next to General Potter, who was watching Bliss' brigade attack, and yelled through the din, "Let Griffin attack!" Nodding his assent, Potter notified Col. Simon Griffin, whose brigade was in line behind Bliss, to move forward (No. 4). To add more weight to the attack, Burnside also threw in Brig. Gen. John Hartranft's brigade (Willcox's division). According to Capt. William Bolton of the 51st Pennsylvania (Hartranft's brigade), the movement to the front was slow "on account of the woods and underbrush, which was on fire." Hartranft positioned his brigade on Potter's right where, recalled Captain Bolton, "Our brigade succeeded in finding the enemy. We formed our line. The enemy was in force in front of our left." (No. 5).[13]

Griffin's brigade relieved Bliss' worn-out foot soldiers near the Rebel works, but some of Bliss' regiments remained in place and fought beside the new arrivals. According to the historian of the 6th New Hampshire (Griffin's brigade), "the front line had given way, and our advance was just in time to meet its broken ranks as they came back in confusion, followed by the rebels and a volley of shot and shell. Our men wavered for a moment when they saw the front line thus broken . . . the boys gave a cheer and rushed on, firing as they went. The rebels were surprised by this gallant charge and tried to fall back, but we were too quick for them . . . and took their first intrenched line, and captured a goodly number of prisoners."[14]

Perry's line was collapsing and he could not stop it. "Nothing was left us but an inglorious retreat, executed in the shortest possible time and without regard to order," he admitted. "It was the first time since its organization, and, until it folded its colors forever at Appomattux, it was the last, that the brigade ever was broken on the battlefield" (No. 6).[15]

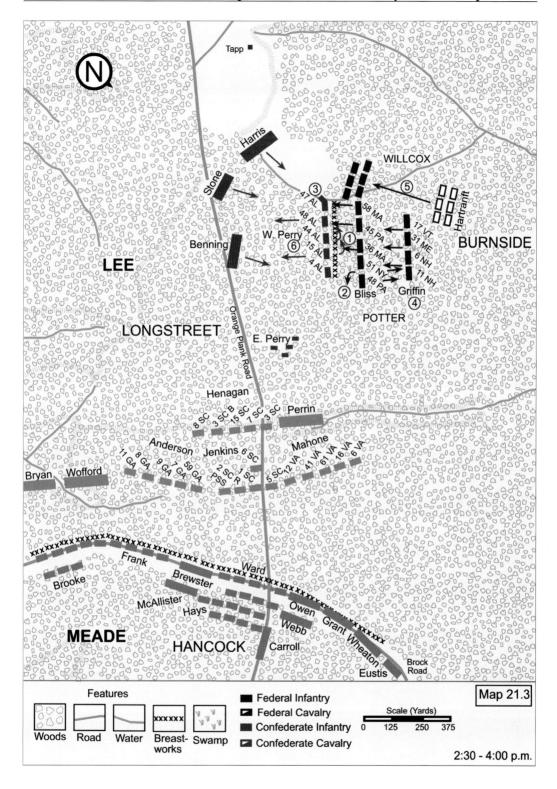

Tapp

N

Harris

Stone

WILLCOX

47 AL

③

58 MA

⑤

Hartranft

48 AL

45 PA

17 VT

BURNSIDE

44 AL

W. Perry

①

36 MA

31 ME

Benning

15 AL

⑥

51 NY

6 NH

LEE

4 AL

48 PA

11 NH

② Bliss

Griffin

④

POTTER

LONGSTREET

E. Perry

Henagan

8 SC
3 SC-B
15 SC
7 SC
3 SC Perrin

Anderson   Jenkins 6 SC   Mahone

11 GA
8 GA
9 GA
7 GA
59 GA
2 SC-R
1 SC
PSS
5 SC
12 VA
41 VA
61 VA
16 VA
6 VA

Bryan   Wofford

Orange Plank Road

xxxxxxx xxxxxxxxx   xxx xxxxxx

Frank

Ward

xxx xxxxxx

Brooke

Brewster

McAllister

Hays

Owen

Grant

Wheaton

MEADE

HANCOCK

Carroll

Webb

Brock
Road

Eustis

Features

| Woods | Road | Water | Breast-works | Swamp |

- ■ Federal Infantry
- ◪ Federal Cavalry
- ▦ Confederate Infantry
- ◪ Confederate Cavalry

Scale (Yards)

0   125   250   375

Map 21.3

2:30 - 4:00 p.m.

Map 21.4: Stalemate
(4:00 - 5:00 p.m.)

Luckily for the Rebels, Burnside's divisions were well west of Longstreet's left flank, and vegetation limited visibility and made movement difficult. Also, reinforcements were streaming into the area to end whatever Union opportunity might have existed. The arrivals came from three different divisions: Brig. Gen. Nathaniel Harris's Mississippi brigade (Anderson's Division), a portion of Col. John Stone's Brigade (Heth's Division), and Brig. Gen. Henry Benning's Brigade (Field's Division) (No. 1). These reinforcements headed toward Perry's abandoned works swarming with the bluecoats from Potter's division. On their right, Hartranft's brigade extended the line westward. One of Stone's men wrote, "an Alabama brigade [Colonel Perry's] was being heavily assaulted and was giving way. Stone saw this and moved his Brigade . . . in rear of the Alabama Brigade and ordered a charge and drove the enemy back until he occupied a position in advance of the troops on his right [Benning's]."[16]

Together with the rest of his comrades, Pvt. David Holt of the 16th Mississippi of Harris's Brigade watched as a "Yankee line of battle burst the brush. They had only a little way to run between the thick brush and our ditch, and they came at top speed shouting all the while. We greeted them with a volley from the breastworks," he wrote, "and the line seemed to melt away, some falling on the breastworks."[17]

The 11th New Hampshire, which had outpaced the rest of Griffin's brigade, spotted "a long line of gray-clad men emerging from the thick undergrowth on our left, and swinging around our flank (No. 2). The officers quickly ordered the men back to the breastworks." The historian of the 36th Massachusetts of Bliss' brigade recalled, "The regiment was loathe to give up the great advantage it had gained, and the fighting was hand to hand—terrible and bloody. The men fought gallantly; but the force upon our left was too strong, and our line was compelled to retire. Falling back slowly, with their faces toward the enemy." Colonel Perry confirmed the reinforcements "swooped down upon the enemy in the midst of their exultation and confusion, and swept them away like chaff. . . . [T]he enemy

disappeared like an apparition." When the troops forming Hartranft's left side spied Potter's troops heading for the rear, "a panic seized the left, which brought the whole line back in confusion."[18]

On the cusp of a significant victory that was now suddenly slipping through his fingers, Burnside ordered General Willcox to bring up Benjamin Christ's brigade. The sights and sounds that greeted the men were not encouraging. "As we moved to the front we passed many dead and wounded, laid out in rows along the road, the wounded attended by the surgeons and Hospital Corps," recalled an officer. Willcox rode to his right to see how his other brigade (Hartranft's) was faring. He learned some of these troops, especially the 8th Michigan, had captured part of the enemy works, "but this advantage was lost by the Second Division [Potter's] falling back before the enemy." Hartranft, continued Willcox, "held his main line until I came up with Christ's brigade, when the enemy was completely checked." The commander of the 20th Michigan of Christ's brigade, Lt. Col. Byron Cutcheon, saw it differently. "We came upon Hartranft's First Brigade badly cut up and somewhat scattered through the woods, having been repulsed and driven back." The historian of the 50th Pennsylvania, also of Christ's brigade, recalled a more dire situation than Willcox: "at one time the rebels were around us in the form of a horse shoe, then we were double quicked to a part of the field where our forces were stampeding."[19]

Willcox pushed Christ's brigade behind Hartranft's, but then moved it nearly 400 yards to the left, where it formed the left flank of the IX Corps line (No. 3). According to the 50th Pennsylvania's adjutant, "our presence had the effect of infusing new energy into the disordered and broken ranks. The enemy were driven backward until our ammunition was nearly exhausted." The fighting settled into a fitful exchange in front while the rest reorganized.[20]

With the exception of Harris's command, all of the other Confederate brigades that fought this action against Burnside had already been heavily engaged, making it impossible to ascertain their losses. In all likelihood they were substantial. On the Federal side, Potter reported that his division lost 504 men from all causes on May 6, with Bliss losing 354 and Griffin 208. In Willcox's division, Hartranft's brigade sustained the heaviest casualties with 407, and Christ the least with 119.[21]

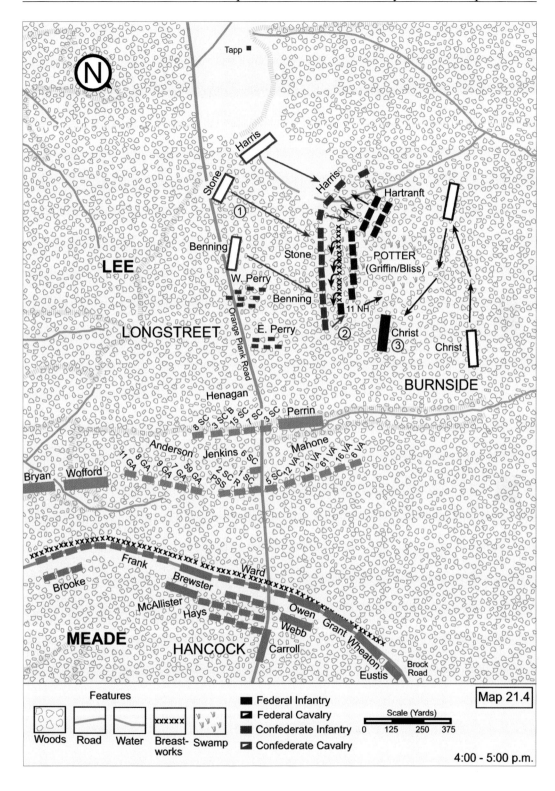

Map 21.4

4:00 - 5:00 p.m.

Map Set 22: Final Actions on the Federal Left

Map 22.1: Hancock Redeploys his Men (2:00 - 4:00 p.m.)

May 6 was a tactical roller coaster ride for both armies. The stunning initial success of Maj. Gen. Winfield Hancock's predawn assault broke apart Lt. Gen. A. P. Hill's Corps and exposed the right flank of Lt. Gen. Richard Ewell's Second Corps farther north. If Hancock could turn his men right and roll up Ewell's line, General Lee would have no choice but to retreat west (away from Richmond) to save his army.

And then Lt. Gen. James Longstreet came up. The calm veteran leadership of the First Corps leader was on full display as he fed his brigades into the battle just where they were needed, blunting the Federal assault on both sides of the Plank Road. Longstreet's arrival and success convinced Maj. Gen. George Meade to suspend offensive operations on his right against Ewell and ask V Corps commander Maj. Gen. Gouverneur Warren to send troops to reinforce Hancock. By 11:00 a.m. Warren replied that he had ordered up entrenching tools and engineers, and when the works were finished he could send about 7,700 men to Hancock's sector. This force included "two brigades of the Pennsylvania Reserves (Crawford), say about 2,200; two brigades of General Robinson, 2,000; two brigades of General Griffin, 2,000; engineer troops, 1,500." Warren's effort thinned his own front, but he assured Meade he would consult with VI Corps commander Maj. Gen. John Sedgwick to maintain a suitable defensive line.[1]

Warren was preparing to move when Lt. Col. Moxley Sorrel unleashed his devastating flanking action against Hancock's exposed left. The sudden turn of events flipped what appeared to be a decisive Federal victory into a potential major defeat. By 2:00 p.m. the head of Warren's supporting column—a brigade of Robinson's division and two regiments of heavy artillery from Col. Elisha Marshall's Provisional Brigade (IX Corps)— reached Hancock on the Brock Road. Hancock now had 18 brigades at his disposal—about one- half of Meade's force with units representing every corps in the army.[2]

With these extra troops, Hancock cobbled a strong defensive line behind the works along the Brock Road. According to Meade's aide, Lt. Col. Theodore Lyman, "General Hancock has a continuous line, but not organized enough to advance. . . . Hancock has troops enough to hold, if he can hold at all." Lyman ended with this observation: "All the enemy seems to have gone to fight Burnside. There is no enemy in Hancock's front south of Orange Plank road."[3]

In fact, Lyman was gravely mistaken. While some of Lee's troops had indeed turned to confront Burnside, most were reforming in the thickets a few hundred yards west of the Brock Road. The composition of this line General Lee put together for what he hoped would be the battle's decisive blow is unknown. It appears the line was composed of Micah Jenkins's Brigade (now under Col. John Bratton) straddling the Plank Road, with Mahone's Brigade on its left and Tige Anderson's Georgians on their right. Wofford's and then Bryan's brigades extended the front line to the right. Henagan's and Perrin's brigades were probably in the second line. Brigadier General Abner Perrin's Brigade was behind Mahone. A member of Wright's Brigade recalled that it remained in reserve during the entire battle and the same is probably true of Humphreys's. The accompanying map offers a reasonable effort to approximate their locations.[4]

How Hancock deployed his units along the vital intersection is also unclear and nearly every historian, past and present, disagree. We know Barlow's division was on the left and units from the V and VI Corps were on the right, but their alignment cannot be described with any confidence. I have utilized Gordon Rhea's interpretation. The vital intersection was defended by Birney's hardy, but now decimated division, deployed in three lines. Mott's division hunkered down on its left, followed south by Barlow's brigades, which assumed the left of the defensive line. Although General Webb never explained his exact location, Rhea nestled him within Barlow's line. Getty's brigades were just north of the intersection, along with Owen's brigade. Carruth's and Kitching's men occupied the right of the line. For a reserve, Hancock camped three brigades— Carroll's, Rice's, and Leasure's in the rear, along the Plank Road. The Federal line was further strengthened by Capt. Edwin Dow's and Capt. Frederick Edgell's batteries, a total of a dozen guns, which dropped trail at the intersection. It was a formidable defensive array.[5]

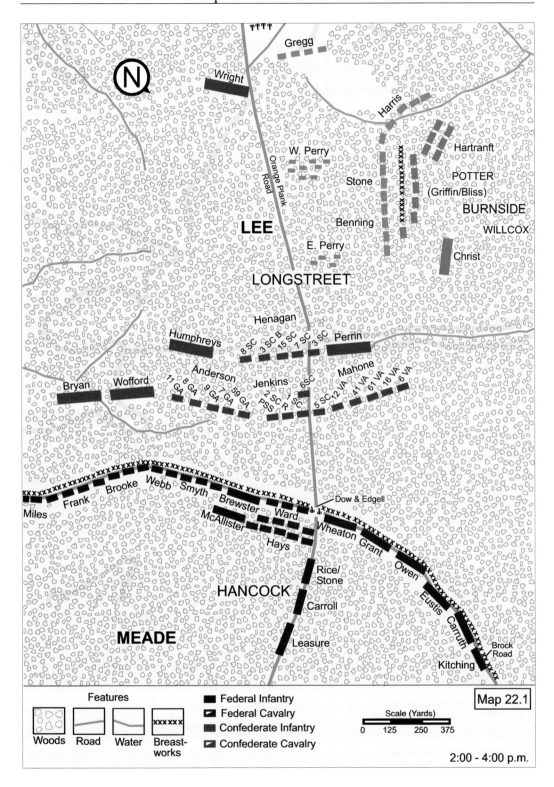

Map Set 22. Final Actions on the Federal Left

Map 22.1

Features

Woods Road Water Breast-works

Federal Infantry
Federal Cavalry
Confederate Infantry
Confederate Cavalry

Scale (Yards)
0   125   250   375

2:00 - 4:00 p.m.

Map 22.2: The Confederates Begin Attack Against the Brock Road Line (4:00 - 5:00 p.m.)

The Federals manning the breastworks along the Brock Road were about to fight yet another engagement that late afternoon of May 6. The number of Confederate brigades aligned in front of their position remains in dispute.[6]

Unsure of Lee's intentions (indeed, Meade's staffer Colonel Lyman believed the Confederates were no longer in their front), Hancock ordered Colonel Leasure's small brigade to slip from its reserve position along the Orange Plank Road and make a reconnaissance by sweeping southeast (No. 1). Leasure aligned the 21st Massachusetts on the left, the 100th Pennsylvania in the middle, and the 3rd Maryland on the right. Smoldering fires reduced visibility and increased the likelihood of friendly fire. A soldier from the 100th Pennsylvania left a vivid recollection of the harrowing experience: "the forest was quite dense and the trees burning from the explosion of shells during the previous contest. The dead and wounded of both sides lay thick along the line of march. The dust and smoke made the air almost unfit to breathe and everyone seemed to think that it was the intention to risk the loss of the brigade to find out the position of the enemy." The commander of the 3rd Maryland, Col. Joseph Sudsburg, agreed and called the sweep "one of the most disagreeable movements I have ever performed."[7]

Within minutes some of the Massachusetts men on the left stumbled into Confederates and were captured. When a Confederate line of battle materialized out of nowhere, Leasure halted his line and wheeled his men to face it (No. 2). The enemy troops melted back into the thickets, and Leasure continued his sweep (No. 3). The roughly one-half mile movement ended when the brigade reached the intersection of Brock and Plank roads (No. 4). It resumed its reserve position with the knowledge that the woods in front of Hancock's line swarmed with Rebs.[8]

Not long after Leasure's dangerous movement ended, Lee's Confederates advanced against the Brock Road. How many Rebel brigades participated in this final attack will likely never be known, but we know with certainty that George Anderson's, Micah Jenkins's and William Wofford's were among them, and the total number in position may have been as high as eight. And still the Confederate line advanced—against as many as 18 Federal brigades. Meade's aide described Lee's men as "unquenchable fellows," driven by a commander who sought decisive victory on every field. For a time it appeared as though the Confederate line would be unstoppable. One Union soldier wrote the enemy "in a line of battle on a charge, bugles sounded, seeming confident that they would carry everything before them." The approach triggered a "terrific crash of riflery all along the lines," recalled a soldier in blue. After two long days of desperate bloody fighting, most of the Federals lining these defenses realized that if they were driven from the barricades the army would likely suffer a devastating defeat. One eyewitness called the charge "impetuous and persistent . . . the most wicked assault thus far encountered—brief in duration, but terrific in power and superhuman momentum."[9]

It was a "heavy fire that made the bark fly from the saplings," observed one of the Federals. Colonel James Hagood of the 1st South Carolina (Jenkins's Brigade) recalled a similar fire and effect. He and his comrades were 200 yards from the road when Union troops opened fire, "a furious blaze of musketry [that] illuminated the dismal forest, tearing off the limbs of trees." Intense artillery fire followed. A New Yorker recalled that "the rapid fire of the foe had but slight effect on our line, behind its bullet proof cover; over the top of which we, with deliberate aim, hurled into their exposed but unwavering line an incessant and most deadly fire. Again and yet again did their shattered regiments in our front close on their colors, while fresh troops from the rear moved up and filled the gaps." Unable to close the final yards, the Confederates dropped down and opened a heavy but ineffective fire. "Our men," noted the historian of the Philadelphia Brigade, "were but little exposed." This was revenge time, and the exposed Rebels "gave [the Federal troops] and opportunity to repay the severe handling they had received in the early morning."[10]

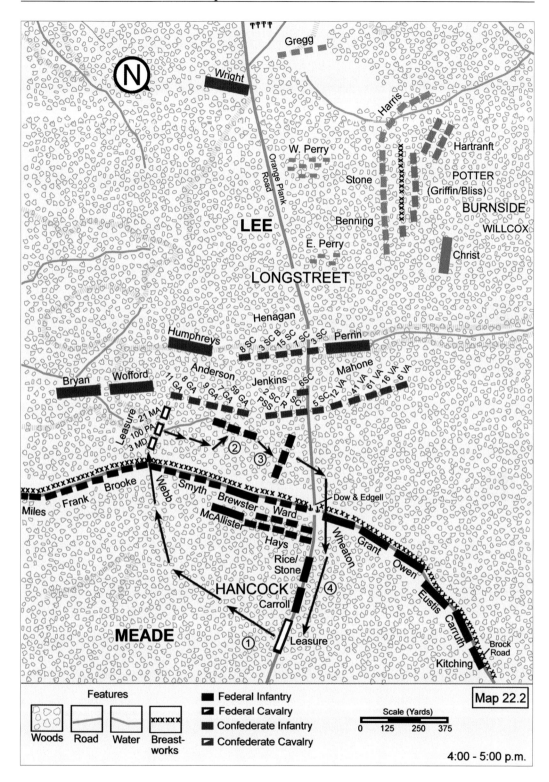

Map 22.2

Features

Woods | Road | Water | Breast-works

■ Federal Infantry
◪ Federal Cavalry
■ Confederate Infantry
◪ Confederate Cavalry

Scale (Yards)
0   125   250   375

4:00 – 5:00 p.m.

Map 22.3: The Confederates Breach the Brock Road Line (5:00 - 6:00 p.m.)

The Confederates continued attacking the Union breastworks along the Brock Road for about half an hour. Warren Cudsworth, historian of the 1st Massachusetts (McAllister's brigade, Mott's division, II Corps), left a vivid recollection of the event: "[the enemy's] first line, broken and wavering under the galling and repeated discharges of the Union infantry, was strengthened and steadied by the second, and this again by the third; both sides loading and firing in furious haste, till the rattle of at least fifty thousand muskets rose into an incessant roll and roar, and all the space between the combatants was swept by a perfect hurricane of death-dealing missiles. The enemy was losing fearfully; and the Union troops, behind their earthworks, slightly."[11]

Colonel Robert McAllister's men, who occupied a second line of breastworks south (left) of the intersection, were told by their commander "they must hold this line under all circumstances and at all hazards." To ensure compliance, McAllister and his staff rode back and forth "to prevent our men from breaking if the front line [probably Brewster's brigade] should give way." A soldier fighting in Col. Joshua Owen's brigade (Gibbon's division, II Corps) north (to the right) of the intersection recalled that the fighting was so hot that men in the rear ranks passed their muskets up to the front and after being fired, the guns were passed back to them for reloading.[12]

The historian of Hancock's II Corps, however, had a different perspective: "the attack was a real one, but was not made with great spirit; nor, it must be confessed, was the response from our side as hearty as it was wont to be. The enemy's line advanced to within about one hundred yards, and then halted and commenced firing, to which our troops replied, with noise enough, but keeping too much down behind the log intrenchements and thus discharging their muskets upward."[13]

Why only a handful of Confederate brigades stormed the Federal defenses on either side of the intersection of Brock and Plank roads remains unclear. The battle's most recent historian, Gordon Rhea, concluded that "the

Wilderness checked Lee much as it had earlier thwarted the Federals." This simple conclusion appears to be correct. Below the road, for example, Anderson's Georgians on the right of Jenkins's South Carolinians (now under John Bratton) launched their attack before Jenkins's men were ready to advance with them. Entire regiments lost their way and wandered about in the thickets—just as their Federal opponents had done over and over for two long days. The Wilderness was no place to wage a battle.[14]

Despite the chaos and heavy defensive fire, some of Lee's units managed to reach the first line of works south of the intersection and drive the Union defenders from it. According to Colonel McAllister, "the enemy's column charged the front line and the battle raged furiously.... The first line gave way and we received the shock of battle. My brigade poured volley after volley and held the enemy in check so they could not hold the first line of breastworks." Captain Edwin Dow ordered his six Napoleons to swivel to the left and open fire "with shell and case-shot, bursting them just over the first line of works, which were on fire, and shot their flag down five times." The second battery firing from the intersection under Capt. Frederick Edgell also opened fire on the same location.[15]

The breastworks "had now taken fire at more than one point, from the discharges of the musketry," confirmed the II Corps' historian. "The heat at times became intense, and the smoke, blown backward over the intrenchments, not only concealed the enemy from view, but blinded and stifled our men." Unable to maintain their positions as the breastworks caught fire, more troops vacated the works. A soldier in Col. Sam Carroll's brigade (Gibbon's division) sitting in reserve east of the intersection along the Orange Plank Road could see "through the trees their [the enemy's] little red flags waving on the parapet." The best evidence indicates that the left side of Jenkins's Brigade and a portion of Anderson's were the troops responsible for reaching the smoldering Union works.

For a short time, it appeared as though Lee's troops were going to break open Hancock's final line and take control of the vital road and intersection.[16]

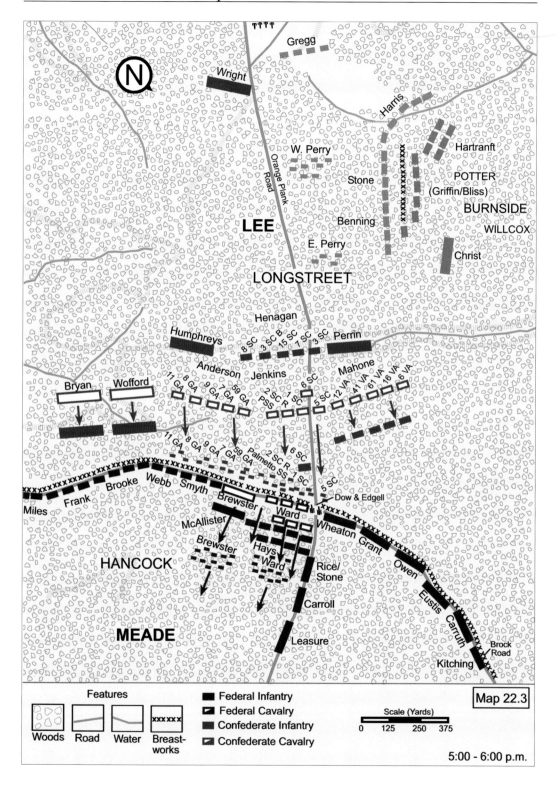

Map 22.3

5:00 – 6:00 p.m.

Features

Woods   Road   Water   Breastworks

■ Federal Infantry
◨ Federal Cavalry
■ Confederate Infantry
◨ Confederate Cavalry

Scale (Yards)

0   125   250   375

Map 22.4: Hancock Repulses the Last Confederate Attack (5:00 - 6:00 p.m.)

In addition to Brewster's men, Hobart Ward's brigade just south (left) of the intersection also broke. Ward's demeanor infuriated other Federal officers who watched the brigadier sit passively atop a caisson while his men broke. When one II Corps officer ordered him down and to rally his men, Ward claimed his horse had bolted and that he had hopped on the caisson because it was the fastest way to reach them. Soon thereafter, Ward ordered the caisson to the rear, with him still on it. Captain Dow, the battery's commander, reported that "during the action of May 6, General Ward ordered one of my caissons to the rear, thereby jeopardizing the position, owing to a scarcity of ammunition." By this time the situation was dire. According to newspaper writer Charles Page, "stragglers for the first time in this fighting streamed to the rear in large numbers, choking the roads and causing panic by their stampede and incoherent tales of frightful disaster."[17]

Lee had breached Hancock's line at its very center where the two major roads intersected. Whatever opportunity Lee had to turn the tactical success into a decisive victory, however, proved short-lived. As many as five Federal brigades behind and on either side of the breach sprang into action, and there were no Rebel infantry commands in place to drive deep and widen the opening. Colonel Leasure, whose small brigade had occupied a reserve position along the Orange Plank Road, moved his men forward to the left of the road and watched the unfolding action from several hundred yards away. He ordered both his 21st Massachusetts and 100th Pennsylvania to fix bayonets and move toward the breastworks to try to stop the troops there from vacating them (No. 1). With the enemy infantry massing along the breastworks, Leasure brought up his last regiment, the 3rd Maryland, and urged it forward by screaming at the top of his lungs, "Now, boys, show them what the Anchor and Cross Cannon mean!" Moving southeast, the regiment smashed into the Rebels at the barricade.[18]

Earlier in the action, General Hancock worried about whether Mott's division could hold its position, so he ordered Col. John Brooke

(Barlow's division), whose brigade was farther east on the Brock Road, to move west parallel to the breastworks (No. 2). "I reached General Mott's line in time to see it leave the works (which were on fire in many places) and the enemy plant their colors on them," reported Brooke, who decisively "changed front to the left, and charging drove the enemy from our front."[19]

Two brigades in General Wadsworth's division under Col. Roy Stone and Brig. Gen. James Rice had been so battered on May 5 and again on May 6 that they had been temporarily reorganized as one unit under the command of Rice and placed in reserve behind the Federal defenses. When the enemy breached the works, Hancock rode up and asked the identity of the organization, and when he got his answer, responded, "Just what I want," and ordered the units to counterattack. The assault was probably straight down the Orange Plank Road (No. 3). "Instantly the lines were formed," wrote the historian of the 150th Pennsylvania, "and, advancing swiftly, rushed upon the intrenchments, which, after a brief but bloody encounter, were freed from the clutch of the enemy."[20]

While these counterattacks hit the left and center of the breach, Colonel Carroll waited with his brigade "in the third line . . . to the right of the Plank Road." With the situation spiraling out of control, General Birney ordered Carroll to attack (No. 4). The colonel threw his brigade at the enemy just west of the intersection to "regain the breastworks, which I did in double-quick at the point of the bayonet." According to Thomas Galwey of the 8th Ohio, "Gen. Carroll . . . made us a fiery speech, and led us on the enemy. In a very short while we hustled them out of their position, taking a good many prisoners."[21]

The Confederates who had breached the Federal works held on as long as they could. According to Colonel Hagood of the 1st South Carolina, he pulled his regiment back only when "the enemy threatened to cut me off." One of the most important (and often overlooked) aspects of the defensive effort was the role played by the Union artillery (No. 5). The 12 guns of Dow's and Edgell's batteries ensured the Rebels were unable to hold or expand their gains. According to Captain Dow, his guns "checked the enemy's advance until Carroll's brigade charged the enemy with such fury as to utterly rout them."[22]

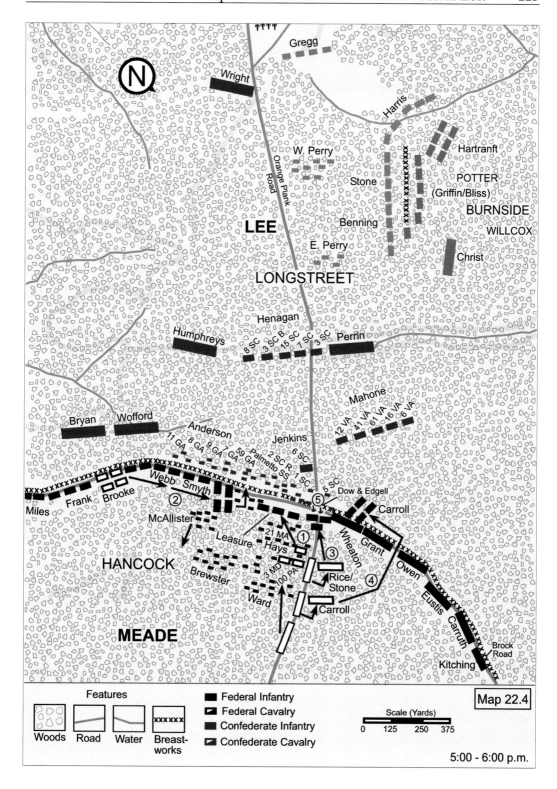

Map 22.4

5:00 - 6:00 p.m.

Features

Woods Road Water Breastworks

■ Federal Infantry
◤ Federal Cavalry
■ Confederate Infantry
◤ Confederate Cavalry

Scale (Yards)

0   125   250   375

Map Set 23: Gordon Attacks the Federal Right Flank
(6:00 a.m. - 10:30 p.m.)

Map 23.1: Gordon has a Plan
(6:00 a.m. - 8:00 a.m.)

Friend and enemy alike considered Brig. Gen. John Gordon to be one of Lee's finest general officers. He performed well on many fields, but his reputation rose significantly at Gettysburg, when his all-Georgia brigade broke apart Brig. Gen. Francis Barlow's division on Blocher's Knoll. Gordon's debut in the Wilderness on May 5 was again stellar. Launching his brigade off the Orange Turnpike into a breach in the line near Saunders' Field, Gordon threw back victorious Federal troops and helped stabilize Lt. Gen. Richard Ewell's line (see Map 5.4).[1]

Once the line was solidified, Ewell dispatched Gordon's Georgians north to occupy the left flank of his line. As his men settled into their new position before May 6 was even a few hours old, Gordon sent scouts beyond his front to ascertain what the heavy thickets in his front might be concealing. They returned about dawn with the news that the Federal line ended well to the south, and that no enemy units were in Gordon's front. The skeptical brigadier sent out another set of scouts. As Gordon wrote later, not only did the second reconnaissance verify the first report, but he was "astounded" to learn "there was not a supporting force within several miles" of the exposed flank, and that only a handful of vedettes occupied the woods in front of his Georgia boys. Gordon wrote after the war, that he "throbb[ed] with the tremendous possibilities to which such a situation invited us, provided the conditions were really as reported."[2]

Still not convinced the Federal high command would allow the army's right flank to simply hang in the air, Gordon joined some cavalrymen on yet another reconnaissance. The group encountered some light temporary breastworks, but "there was no line guarding this flank," he wrote. "As far as my eye could reach, the Union soldiers were seated on the margin of the rifle-pits, taking their breakfast. Small fires were burning over which they were boiling their coffee, while their guns leaned against the works in their immediate front." There was also an open field adjacent to the Federal flank that could be used as a staging area for an infantry attack. The plan he envisioned was straightforward. He would march a flanking force into position perpendicular to the Federal flank and drive south, rolling up the flank while the rest of Ewell's men attacked due east to pin the balance of the Federals in place. "As each of Sedgwick's brigades gave way in confusion," Gordon hoped, "the corresponding Confederate brigade, whose front was thus cleared on the general line, was to swing into column of attack on the flank, thus swelling at each step of our advance the numbers, power, and momentum of the Confederate forces as they swept down the line of works and extend another brigade's length to the unprotected Union rear."[3]

Excited by the prospects, Gordon ordered an aide, Thomas Jones, to find division commander Maj. Gen. Jubal Early and explain what he had discovered and what he proposed to do about it. Time was of the essence, he emphasized, because Maj. Gen. John Sedgwick, the Federal VI Corps commander, would surely realize his mistake soon and take steps to rectify it. Jones, however, could not find Early but he did stumble upon General Ewell. While he was in the process of briefing the Second Corps leader, the irascible Early arrived, shook his head, and speaking "rather sharply" to Jones, announced that Gordon was clearly mistaken. Major William Cowles of the 1st North Carolina Cavalry, explained Early, had reported a column of infantry on the Germanna Plank Road, which paralleled the Yankee line. This could have been Maj. Gen. Ambrose Burnside's IX Corps, which up to that time had not yet made an appearance. As Early put it in his memoirs, "the impolicy of the attempt at the time was obvious, as we had no reserves, and, if it failed, and the enemy showed any enterprise, a serious disaster would befall . . . Lee's whole army."[4]

Ewell, who according to Gordon's account appeared to be in favor of supporting the proposed attack prior to Early's arrival, informed Jones the movement could not be made at that time. Jones galloped back to deliver the disheartening news to Gordon.[5]

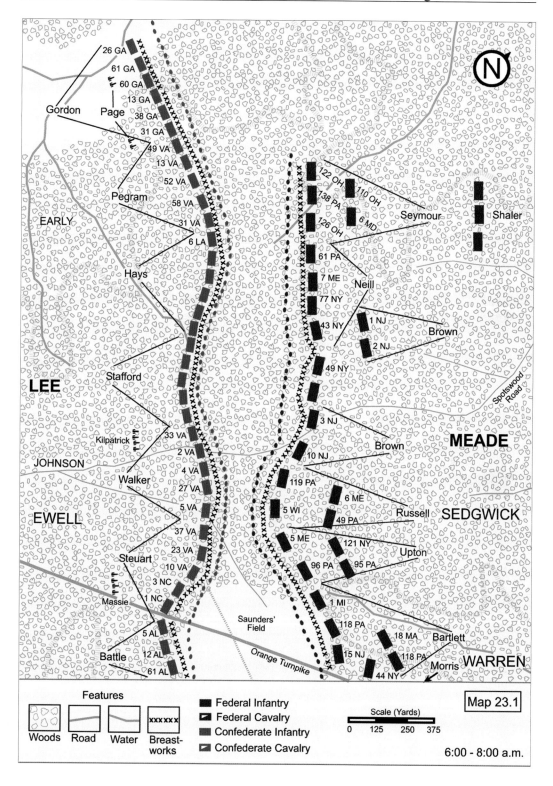

26 GA
61 GA
60 GA
13 GA
38 GA
31 GA
49 VA
13 VA
52 VA
58 VA
31 VA
6 LA

Gordon
Page
Pegram
EARLY
Hays

122 OH
110 OH
138 PA
6 MD
126 OH
61 PA
7 ME
77 NY
43 NY
49 NY
3 NJ
10 NJ
119 PA
5 WI
5 ME
96 PA
1 MI
118 PA
15 NJ
44 NY

Seymour
Shaler
Neill
1 NJ
2 NJ
Brown
Brown
MEADE
6 ME
49 PA
121 NY
95 PA
Russell
SEDGWICK
Upton
18 MA
Bartlett
118 PA
Morris
WARREN

LEE
Stafford
Kilpatrick
33 VA
2 VA
4 VA
27 VA
5 VA
37 VA
23 VA
10 VA
3 NC
1 NC
5 AL
12 AL
61 AL

JOHNSON
Walker
EWELL
Steuart
Massie
Battle

Saunders'
Field
Orange Turnpike
Spotswood Road

Features

| Woods | Road | Water | Breast-works |

Federal Infantry
Federal Cavalry
Confederate Infantry
Confederate Cavalry

Scale (Yards)
0   125   250   375

Map 23.1

6:00 - 8:00 a.m.

Map 23.2: Inaction on the Federal Right
(8:00 a.m. - 2:00 p.m.)

According to Gordon, the news enraged him. "How did Early know the location of Burnside?" he wondered. Gordon claimed to have returned with Jones between 8:00 and 9:00 a.m. on May 6 to plead his case in person. Once again Early spoke up, and as Gordon recalled the conversation, "he was so firmly fixed in his belief that Burnside's corps was where he declared it to be that he was not perceptibly affected by the repeated reports of scouts, or my statement that I myself had ridden for miles in rear of Sedgwick's right, and that neither Burnside's corps nor any other troops were there." To Gordon's chagrin, Ewell demurred a second time.[6]

History would show that Gordon was right—a great opportunity beckoned. Sedgwick's flank was "in the air," and by this time Burnside's IX Corps was not a threat to any action that far north. After passing several restless hours, by 1:00 p.m. he could no longer hold his peace and once again rode to Ewell's headquarters to plead his case. He was denied yet again.[7]

About the same time Gordon was returning from his visit to Ewell's headquarters, Brig. Gen. Robert Johnston's Brigade reached the Second Corps after a hard march from Taylorsville, Virginia, about 20 miles north of Richmond. General Lee had been requesting Johnston for weeks, but it was not until the morning of May 5 that his North Carolinians were put on the road for a long forced march. One of Johnston's men wrote after the war that "army mules fell dead in their traces under the severe strain, but without stopping for bivouac, or hardly to rest, we held out and reached the Plank Road." Once the brigade arrived, General Ewell dispatched Johnston and his men north to extend the Secon Corps' left flank beyond Gordon's command.[8]

About an hour later, on the other side of the line, General Sedgwick sent Brig. Alexander Shaler's brigade of three regiments—barely 1,000 bayonets—to report to Brig. Gen. Truman Seymour to shore the Union right flank. Stretched thin, Sedgwick had nothing else to send. Shaler passed behind Seymour's brigade to deploy on the far right flank. He put two regiments in line, and bent back the 65th New York at a right angle (facing north) to the rest of the line. Seymour's men on Shaler's left were in particularly bad shape because the earlier "very heavy" fighting had killed and wounded large numbers of men, including the "choicest and best of officers." While most of Seymour's men were safely behind breastworks, the same was not true of Shaler's three regiments, who were prevented from erecting works by especially active Rebel sharpshooters.

This end of General Sedgwick's line was further weakened when Brig. Gen. Thomas Neill's brigade (Getty's division) on Seymour's left was shifted south to cover some gaps in the line, forcing Seymour to stretch his line to compensate for the movement. The new arrivals realized they were on the army's far right—a dangerous place to be at any time and especially in the middle of the Wilderness. According to Charles Edinborough of the 67th New York, part of Shaler's brigade, the men fully expected to be flanked.[9]

Nothing about the position pleased the 37-year-old Shaler, who would later confessed, "I was in anything but a peaceful state of mind." Not only was he exposed on the far right without support, but he disliked serving under Truman Seymour. "I lost no time in informing Gen'l Seymour that I would not be held responsible for any disaster that might befall the troops at this point, calling on him for at least 4,000 to 5,000 more men to properly defend that point." Seymour tried to calm Shaler by assuring him that he would request additional reinforcements for the right. Meanwhile, Seymour sent his own 6th Maryland, which formed on the right of the 122nd New York. Several of Seymour's own regimental commanders expressed concerns about the exposed nature of their commands, but Seymour could do little except order them to remain alert and make sure their men were safe, well-fed, and ready for anything that should come their way.[10]

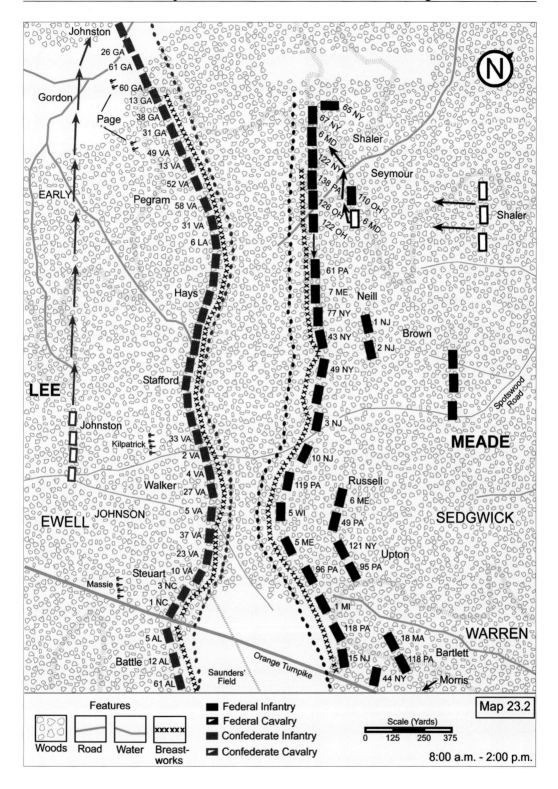

Johnston

26 GA
61 GA
60 GA
Page
13 GA
Gordon
38 GA
31 GA
49 VA
13 VA
52 VA
EARLY
Pegram
58 VA
31 VA
6 LA

65 NY
67 NY
6 MD
Shaler
122 NY
138 PA
126 OH
110 OH
6 MD
122 OH
Seymour

Shaler

Hays

61 PA
7 ME
Neill
77 NY
1 NJ
43 NY
Brown
2 NJ
49 NY

Stafford
LEE
Johnston
Kilpatrick
33 VA
2 VA
4 VA
Walker
27 VA
5 VA
EWELL
JOHNSON
37 VA
23 VA
Steuart
10 VA
Massie
3 NC
1 NC

5 AL
Battle
12 AL
Saunders'
Field
61 AL

3 NJ
MEADE
10 NJ

119 PA
Russell
6 ME
SEDGWICK
5 WI
49 PA
5 ME
121 NY
Upton
96 PA
95 PA

1 MI
118 PA
18 MA
WARREN
Bartlett
15 NJ
118 PA
Orange Turnpike
44 NY
Morris

Spotswood Road

Features

Woods Road Water Breastworks

■ Federal Infantry
◨ Federal Cavalry
■ Confederate Infantry
◨ Confederate Cavalry

Scale (Yards)
0   125   250   375

Map 23.2

8:00 a.m. - 2:00 p.m.

Map 23.3: Gordon Prepares to Launch his Attack (2:00 - 6:00 p.m.)

As the afternoon faded, the men in blue continued praying for the day to end without an attack against their weak right flank. They would not get their wish. After several requests for reinforcements, General Sedgwick finally sent some staff officers to check on his right flank. There, they did little more than metaphorically pat Shaler on the head and tell him not to worry—cavalry units were operating in the woods beyond his right and they would discover any enemy movement from that direction.[11]

Behind the Rebel line, when he saw Johnston's Tar Heels crashing their way north through the thickets toward his own brigade, Gordon mounted his horse for another ride to the Orange Turnpike and a visit with Ewell and Early. It was after 2:00 p.m. Once again, Gordon would return frustrated and unhappy. What happened next is unclear, but someone finally ordered the charge he had been advocating.[12]

The attack was to be a two-brigade flank assault with Johnston's command on the left side and Gordon's the right— about 3,500 men (No. 1). Early's remaining two brigades under Brig. Gen. John Pegram (on Gordon's right, under Col. John Hoffman) and Brig. Gen. Harry Hays (on Pegram's right) would frontally assault as the battle developed. It appears that the Virginians moved out of their breastworks in preparation for their attack; the Louisianans did not (No. 2). Unfortunately, no one briefed General Johnston on his mission and it appears that he formed behind Gordon's Brigade, not to the left of it.[13]

Moving through the thickets was difficult, especially with the fading light (No. 3). Gordon had his men moving by 5:00 p.m., first northwest and then northeast. After some amount of time, the two brigades were a few hundred yards north of, and perpendicular to, the Federal line. According to a Georgia soldier, "All orders were given in a whisper. The sharpshooters were to advance up the steep hill at . . . the double-quick; we were to advance at quick time and not to fire until we had passed over these brave fellows, who were to fall flat after the first volley."[14]

Gordon's men moved forward with grim determination (No. 4). Some of the Georgians would look back on the event and feel sorry for the unsuspecting Union troops. "Poor fellows! None of them suspected the bolt that was about to strike them." The soldiers on the receiving end did not see the approaching danger until the gray wave was within 100 yards. "We found them massed five or six lines deep, all resting, cooking and eating; with their guns stacked, their blankets spread down and some of their little tents stretched," recalled a Georgia private. Another Georgian added, "suddenly, and only a few feet away, the long line of gray-clad soldiers appeared and opened on them . . . never was lightning from the clouds more expected, and confusion reigned supreme."[15]

Before Gordon's attack began, Seymour and Shaler visited Sedgwick's headquarters. An observer recalled Seymour saying, "Well, general, we have repulsed two attacks today, but my men are pretty shaky, and I should be very fearful in case of another attack." Just then gunfire erupted to the north, and the three generals mounted and rode in the direction of the combat.[16]

Shaler's far right regiment, the 65th New York facing north, quickly crumbled (No. 5). "The enemy came up suddenly with a terrific yell and jumped over and around the shallow works in front . . . throwing this gallant regiment [the 65th New York] into a rout before the members had time to grasp their muskets from the stacks. They came pell-mell through our ranks," recalled a member of the 122nd New York (Shaler's brigade).[17] Rebel sources confirmed the sudden collapse. "We could not give them but two volleys," wrote one. "[I]t seemed like scaring up a bunch of partridges or crows . . . it was almost like shooting birds 'on the wing.'" The enemy, he added, "left stampeded and panic stricken. I am sure there were enough guns to have armed our brigade three or four times, and several car-loads of blankets, tents, clothing, etc."[18]

Gordon's initial success masked the fact that General Johnston was thrust into the attack blind. "I was entirely uninformed as to the position of the enemy and plans for the attack," claimed Johnston, "and I knew nothing of the character of the ground. It was impossible to see anything in front of the line fifty feet and I had to be guided by the noise and firing, which commenced in a few moments and soon became very warm." Most of Johnston's men drifted too far east or didn't move much at all and so played little role in this pivotal flank attack.[19]

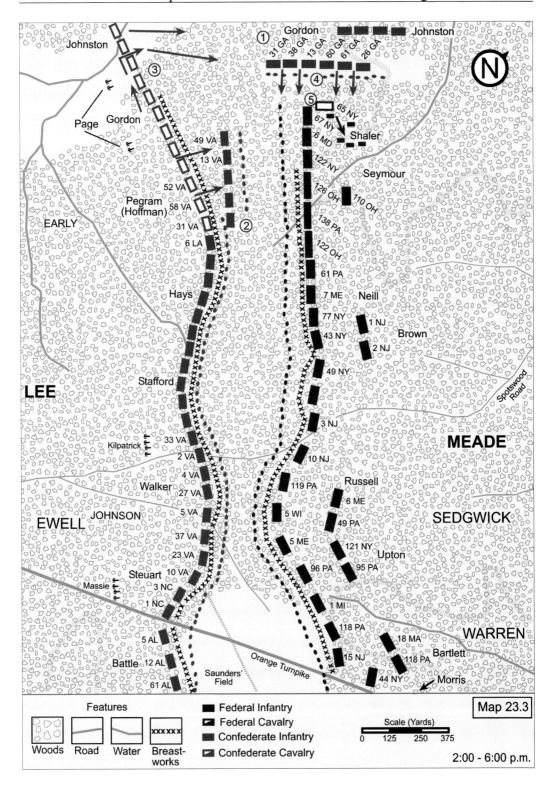

Map 23.3

Features

Woods   Road   Water   Breast-works

Federal Infantry
Federal Cavalry
Confederate Infantry
Confederate Cavalry

Scale (Yards)
0   125   250   375

2:00 - 6:00 p.m.

Map 23.4: Gordon's Attack Gains Momentum (6:00 - 8:00 p.m.)

The rout of the Federal right was only just beginning. The 67th New York of Shaler's brigade was the next command to feel the weight of Gordon's onslaught. According to Pvt. Charles Edinborough of the 67th, "we were struck square in the flank, and the first shot I fired was down the breastwork to the right." When Gordon's men swung around the regiment's rear, Edinborough and his comrades knew it was time to depart, heading south.[20]

Like a line of dominos, the fall of one triggered the collapse of another. The regiment next in line was the 6th Maryland of Seymour's brigade, fighting in the middle of Shaler's line. The Marylanders were in a tough spot. In order "to prevent capture of my whole command," wrote Col. John Horn, "I ordered my command to fall back, which was done, but they soon became mixed up with other troops and panic and confusion ensued." Some of the Federals halted on occasion to fire into the pursuing masses. A soldier in the 6th Maryland recalled that the officers would rally the men for a stand, "but a volley would kill some and wound more, and the line would give way again and fall back, and again a stand be made, but we could not stand before three advancing lines."[21]

The collapse of the 6th Maryland exposed the right and rear of the 122nd New York, Shaler's final regiment. Although attacked in flank and rear by portions of Gordon's Georgians, the men discerned that Johnston's North Carolinians deeper in their rear, "did not come on as vigorously as they yelled, and made believe that they were going to." This allowed the New Yorkers some breathing room to turn to the right and concentrate their fire against Gordon. When the Confederate artillery opened fire, the New Yorkers realized it was time to head south. A New Yorker noted, "A terrific volley, fortunately aimed a little high, poured in from the right across our flank, followed by an unearthly screeching and yelling. We caught a glimpse of a swarm of gray-coats sweeping onto us from the right rear and heard some officers cry, 'men, get back.'"[22]

With all of Shaler's men on the run, the gray cascade reached Seymour's main position. The attack had struck so quickly that many of his men were still making a mad rush for their stacked arms. Some lost the race and were swept away, while others managed a shot or two before succumbing to the maelstrom. Seymour tried unsuccessfully to rally his troops. One Federal officer described the chaotic scene: "such excitement you could form no idea of. Staff officers yelling and calling on men to rally . . . and the men throwing away their guns and running like mad men. And them Rebs a yelling as they came up on the charge with that peculiar yell they have."[23]

The 126th Ohio held the right end of Seymour's main line. Its commander, Col. William Ball, confirmed that "the regiments on my right gave way one after another." When his own regiment "was ordered to retreat," he continued, "there was not a man in the intrenchements on my right or left." When Col. Warren Keifer of the 110th Ohio realized he was under attack in his reserve position behind the 126th, he tried to pivot his men to meet the charge, but "so rapid was the enemy's advance upon the flank and rear, that time was not given to change front to meet him." Colonel Ball agreed with Keifer's observation: "So quick were the movements of the enemy that when I first discovered them in our rear, they were in rear of the center of my regiment, scattering the second line with all speed."[24]

Like Shaler's regiments, Seymour's men had no choice but to head south with all haste. Keifer's Ohioans fell back in as chaotic a state as the rest, but the regimental commander could only admit that "some confusion occurred in the retreat." The leader of the 136th Pennsylvania, Col. Matthew McClennan, blamed some of the rout on Shaler's brigade, which was "hurled upon us in confusion by an overwhelming enemy, and soon the panic spread, resulting in a disorderly and hasty retreat." Colonel Ball of the 126th Ohio agreed the net effect was a rout: "The retreat was necessarily disorderly, there being barely time to escape." Officers tried to rally their men without success. Even General Sedgwick rode into the blue masses in an effort to stop the retreat. "As some demoralized soldier came by, he [Sedgwick] would swear that unless he stopped he would cut his d_d head off, and with drawn blade he would go through the motion," recalled infantryman James Brewer of the 6th Maryland.[25]

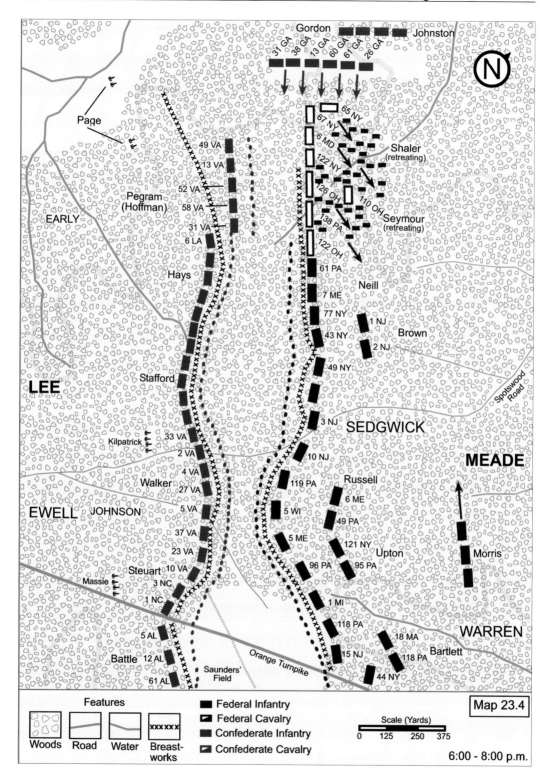

Features

Woods   Road   Water   Breastworks

▰ Federal Infantry
▱ Federal Cavalry
▰ Confederate Infantry
▰ Confederate Cavalry

Scale (Yards)
0   125   250   375

Map 23.4

6:00 - 8:00 p.m.

Map 23.5: Gordon's Attack
Loses Steam (8:00 - 9:00 p.m.)

Riding behind his brigade, Gordon observed a spectacle few commanders witness: every unit on the Federal right was in retreat. As he wrote years later, "there was nothing for the brave Federals to do but to fly. There was no time given them to file out from their works and form a new line of resistance." They attempted to do so "again and again," he added, "but in every instance the swiftly moving Confederates were upon them, pouring a consuming fire into their half-formed ranks and shivering one command after another in quick succession."[26]

By this time Gordon's men had reached the right of General Neill's brigade. "Shoot them, bayonet them, stop them any way you can!" screamed Col. George Smith of the 61st Pennsylvania. The orders were useless, and Smith and much of his regiment were swept to the rear (No. 1). Sedgwick, however, pivoted some of Neill's men to face the attack, but they were being assailed on two fronts: Gordon's men from the northwest and Pegram's (Hoffman's) Virginians from the south (see below). The 7th Maine was caught in the middle (No. 2). When some Confederates called for the unit's surrender, its commander Maj. James Jones yelled, "All others may go back, but the 7th Maine never!" When General Shaler, now without a hat or a command, encountered the 61st Pennsylvania on a wagon track, he pleaded, "For God's sake, men, make a stand on this road; if you think anything of the Army of the Potomac, make a stand on this road!" He was quickly overwhelmed by enemy soldiers and hustled off to the rear (No. 3). General Seymour, riding ahead to ascertain the location of the enemy was also nabbed and sent to the rear.[27]

By this time the natural friction inherent in an attack began breaking down the Rebel wave, which allowed the Union line to begin coalescing between the wagon track and Spotswood Road. As noted earlier, Johnston led his brigade of North Carolinians into the fight with little understanding of the terrain, the enemy, or his role. The heavy firing ahead and to his right, coupled with limited visibility, seems to have both unnerved him and scattered his men. As he later wrote, when he found Federals in front

(apparently a reforming Federal regiment), Johnston became fearful of being cut off and ordered his men to fall back (No. 4). That decision cleaved away one-half of Gordon's flanking column.[28]

Back south along Ewell's main Rebel line, meanwhile, Maj. John Daniel, General Early's aide, was busy trying to get Pegram's and Hays' brigades into action. Colonel Hoffman had already moved the Virginians out of their defenses to prepare for their part in the fight, but they were still reforming their ranks when the Georgians attacked. As Gordon's drive faltered, Pegram's men were ordered forward. Like Johnston's men, however, the Virginians quickly became confused within the smoky darkening gloom of the Wilderness. Some opened fire into the right side of Gordon's line comprised of the 31st and 38th Georgia regiments (No. 5). This caused the two regiments to grind to a halt and some of the Georgians bolted to the rear, forcing General Gordon to spend several precious minutes trying to stop the friendly fire, realign his troops, and continue forward.[29]

Major Daniel personally directed the 31st and 58th Virginia of Pegram's Brigade toward Neill's brigade. There were not many of them as they approached the Union works. Henry Wingfield of the 58th Virginia noted in his diary that "owing to the thick branches and undergrowth in the woods…our line was in considerable disorder and only some twenty men were with the flag as it was fired on." When the Union soldiers spotted the Virginians approaching through the thickets, Neill's men held their fire until the very last moment. According to surgeon George Stevens of the 77th New York, "they advanced slowly . . . until within a few feet of the Union line, when with wild yells they leaped forward, some even mounting the breastworks. But a sheet of flame instantly flashed along the whole line of our works; the astonished rebels wavered for a moment and then beat a hasty retreat" (No. 6).[30]

It does not appear that Hays' Louisianans attacked the Federal works. According to a staff officer, "though our skirmish line was hotly engaged, our Brigade took no part in this action."[31]

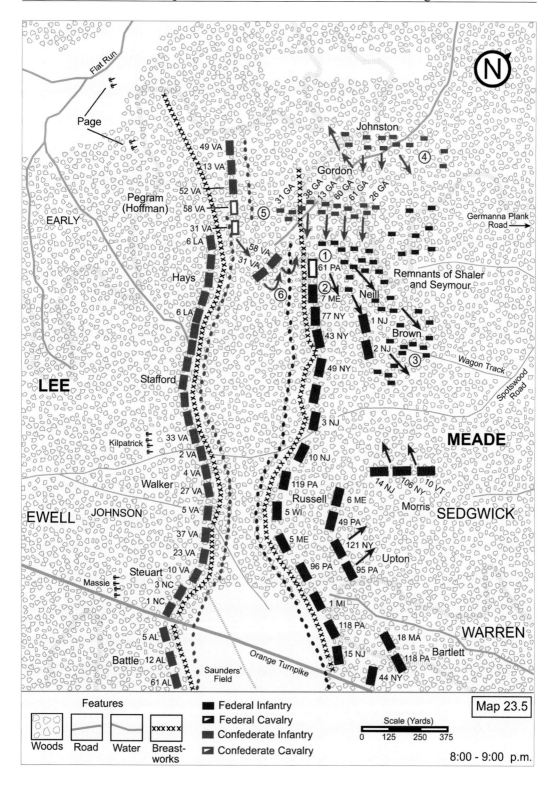

Map 23.5

Scale (Yards)
0   125   250   375

8:00 - 9:00 p.m.

Features

Woods   Road   Water   Breast-works

Federal Infantry
Federal Cavalry
Confederate Infantry
Confederate Cavalry

Map 23.6: Gordon's Attack Grinds to a Halt (9:00 - 10:30 p.m.)

Gordon's ragged lines and large clots of exhausted men pressed ahead, driving Neill's, Seymour's, and Shaler's brigades south and east. A solid line of fresh soldiers appeared in front of Gordon's men (No. 1) consisting of the 10th Vermont, 14th New Jersey, and 106th New York of Brig. Gen. William Morris's brigade (Brig. Gen. Ricketts's division). Morris was rushed north when the attack began, and arrived in time to form off Brig. Gen. David Russell's right flank —the next brigade holding Sedgwick's line below Neill's collapsed brigade. The Green Mountain boys were deploying when their leader ordered them to "join him in giving three cheers, which were given as only soldiers can give them." They were joined by some remnants of Neill's, Seymour's, and Shaler's brigades. Two more regiments, the 95th Pennsylvania and 121st New York from Colonel Upton's brigade (Brig. Gen. Horatio Wright's division), which had been on the far left of the line, had also been rushed north and formed behind Morris's men (No. 2).[32]

What happened next can only be surmised. With his attack losing momentum, Gordon turned his horse southwest to find expected support from Pegram's Brigade. He encountered the 13th, 49th, and 52nd Virginia regiments. "He [General Gordon] came to us with hat off and the tears streaming down his face and begged us to go with him and capture the Yankee breastworks," Capt. Robert Daniel Funkhouser of the 49th Virginia on Pegram's left recorded in his diary. The Virginians fought to keep some semblance of a line as they struggled through calf-deep marsh laced with vines and briers. Conflicting orders made matters worse. The first was to "dress and close to the right," and after a time, "dress and close to the left." The Virginians reached the Federal works scattered and with little regimental cohesion. Funkhouser wrote the troops struggled "through a perfect jungle standing in water which we had to wade through in pitch darkness over entirely strange ground." Even though it was now dark, the Federals knew the fighting was not yet over. According to one New Yorker, a "tired and hungry body of troops who, with bayonets fixed, lay as quiet as death awaiting the onslaught of the enemy."[33]

The snapping of twigs and twisting of brush signaled the oncoming Rebel attack. "Every man was aroused and alert," recalled a Union soldier. "Then the men heard the order, spurts of reddish-orange "fire" erupted along the Federal line. Many of Pegram's men did not realize how close they came to the Federal positions (No. 3). "We thought we saw men lying on the ground to our front, and supposing them to be our skirmishers, we marched up to them when they raised up and put their guns almost against our heads and fired." Another soldier noted the Union troops "poured a shower of balls at us." Pegram's men now headed back to their original positions.[34]

Gordon's flanking attack had run its course, and with it, the major infantry fighting in the Wilderness came to an end. Few actions in the Civil War were as decisive as this flank attack. Gordon's men (with but little support from other units) captured about half a mile of breastworks, killed or wounded 400 Federals and took another 600 prisoner, including Generals Shaler and Seymour. Gordon's losses totaled about 50, some of which were the result of friendly fire. He would subsequently be given command of Jubal Early's Division when A. P. Hill was ill. Coming to grips with the fumbled chance to decisively roll up Sedgwick's line was something Gordon was never able to do. After the war he wrote, "the greatest opportunity ever presented to Lee's army was permitted to pass."[35]

Colonel William Ball of the 122nd Ohio of Seymour's brigade revealed his frustration in his report when he wrote, "The turning of our right was the result of gross negligence on the part of some general officer, I know not whom." In a gross understatement, General Shaler confided in his diary that "the density of the woods prevented us from discovering their preparation movements & therefore the attack was something of a surprise." The Army of the Potomac's chief of staff, Andrew Humphreys, put the blame on the advance pickets when he wrote, "there must have been some neglect in the vedettes or skirmish line in keeping a lookout on that ground." Someone deployed the Federal skirmishers too close to the main line of defense. Scattered shots had been fired throughout the afternoon in that sector, so when a handful of shots were discharged during the opening moments of Gordon's attack, no one took special notice.[36]

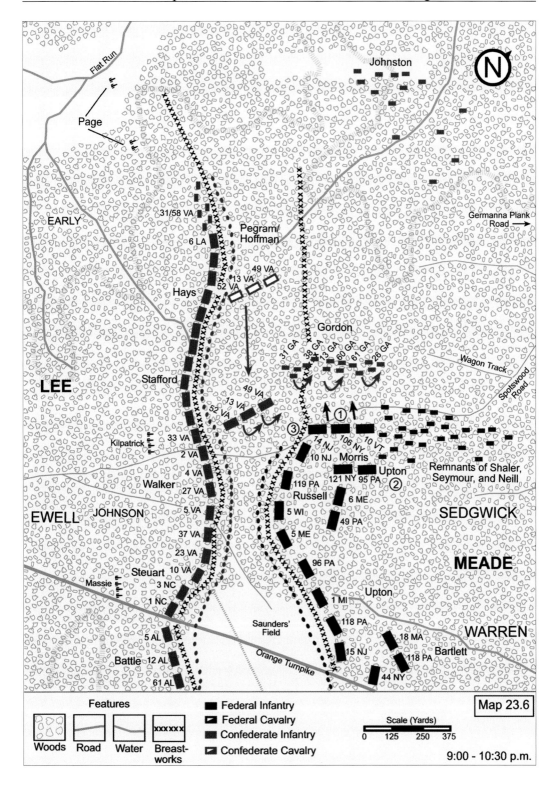

Flat Run

Page

Johnston

N

31/58 VA

EARLY

6 LA

Germanna Plank Road →

Pegram/
Hoffman

49 VA

13 VA
52 VA

Hays

Gordon

31 GA 38 GA 13 GA 60 GA 61 GA 26 GA

Wagon Track

LEE

Stafford

49 VA

13 VA

52 VA

①

Spotswood Road

Kilpatrick

33 VA

2 VA

③

14 NJ 106 NY 10 VT

10 NJ Morris

Remnants of Shaler,
Seymour, and Neill

4 VA

Walker

27 VA

119 PA

121 NY 95 PA Upton ②

Russell

6 ME

EWELL   JOHNSON

5 VA

37 VA

5 WI

5 ME

49 PA

SEDGWICK

23 VA

10 VA

96 PA

Steuart

3 NC

1 MI   Upton

MEADE

Massie

1 NC

118 PA

WARREN

5 AL

Saunders'
Field

18 MA

Bartlett

Battle 12 AL

15 NJ

118 PA

Orange Turnpike

61 AL

44 NY

Features

Woods Road Water Breastworks

Federal Infantry
Federal Cavalry
Confederate Infantry
Confederate Cavalry

Scale (Yards)
0   125   250   375

Map 23.6

9:00 - 10:30 p.m.

Map Set 24: The Battle Ends
(May 6 - 7, 1864)

Map 24.1: Federal
Opportunities Gained and Lost
(May 6, 10:00 p.m. - May 7, 11:00 a.m.)

The fighting along the far right flank of the Union army ended after 10:00 p.m. Skirmishers up and down the lines exchanged fitful small arms fire, but the major combat was finally over. The relative silence was replaced by the shrieks and pleas of the wounded. General Grant's aide Lt. Col. Horace Porter penned a vivid account: "forest fires raged; ammunition trains exploded; the dead were roasted in the conflagration; the wounded, roused by its hot breath, dragged themselves along, with their torn and mangled limbs, in the mad energy of despair, to escape the ravages of the flames; and every bush seemed hung with shreds of blood-stained clothing."[1]

Federal losses were horrendous. According to the official returns, the Army of the Potomac lost 17,666, broken down as follows: 2,246 killed, 12,037 wounded, and 3,383 captured. Historian Gordon Rhea estimates that the army lost about 17 percent of its effective strength in the two-day battle. Each of the three infantry corps (II, V, and VI) reported more than 5,000 casualties, with the independent IX Corps reporting fewer than 1,700. The army's cavalry corps entered the fighting with 12,424 effectives and reported 710 losses, with 97 killed, 416 wounded, and 197 captured/missing. For the infantry divisions, those fighting on the left on May 5 and 6 sustained the greatest losses: Brigadier General Getty's four-brigade division (VI Corps) lost 2,994 men, followed by Maj. Gen. David Birney's two-brigade division (II Corps), with 2,242. Among the brigades Alexander Hays' brigade (Birney's division, II Corps) and Lewis Grant's brigade each lost over 1,300 men (or nearly as many as the entire IX Corps). Losses among the army's officers were particularly high: 209 killed, wounded, and captured. Losses among the army's general officers were severe with James Wadsworth and Alexander Hays killed or mortally wounded, George Getty, Henry Baxter, and Roy Stone, wounded, and Generals Shaler and Seymour captured.[2]

Grant, who believed that Lee's reputation was overblown, came to respect his opposite after just two days of combat. Grant was heard to remark that "Joe Johnston would have retreated after two days of such punishment." But not Lee, whose army was wounded, but still full of fight.[3]

There was plenty of blame to go around for the failure of the superior Army of the Potomac to decimate and possibly destroy Lee's army. Starting at the top, Grant's major responsibility was to give general orders to Meade about the movements of the army and to coordinate its activities with the IX Corps, which remained in an independent capacity. Grant performed poorly in both arenas. The army's Provost Marshal, Brig. Gen. Marsena Patrick wrote in his diary that "I do not see that Grant does anything but sit quietly about, whittle, smoke."[4]

Perhaps Grant's biggest disappointment was Meade. He knew Meade had a reputation of being slow and methodical, and was not aggressive. It was obvious to Grant he would need to take a more assertive role in this theater. He was also not overly enthusiastic about the performance of the corps commanders. Both Warren and Sedgwick were too cautious and at times, too stubborn. Hancock, commonly perceived to be Meade's best corps leader, was reduced to hand-wringing on the afternoon of May 6 as the destruction of his entire wing seemed possible. However, he continued to hold Meade's confidence, who wrote, "Bully Hancock is the only one of my corps commanders who will always go right in when I order him."[5]

The Federal army's high iniitial morale was now lagging. According to General Webb, the soldiers "felt deep mortification" by not besting Lee's men. "From personal contact with the regiments who did the hardest fighting, I declare that the individual men had no longer the confidence in their commanders, which had been their best and strongest trait during the past year."[6]

Grant's first fight with Lee did not go particularly well. Despite tremendous disparities in the size and equipment of his army, Grant allowed the battle to be fought on Lee's terms. The tangles of the Wilderness negated all of Grant's considerable advantages. According to a recent historian, "the outnumbered Confederates had pummeled both exposed Union flanks, and Grant could count himself lucky that Lee had not taken advantage of the gaping hole that Burnside's tardiness had created in the center of the Union lines."[7]

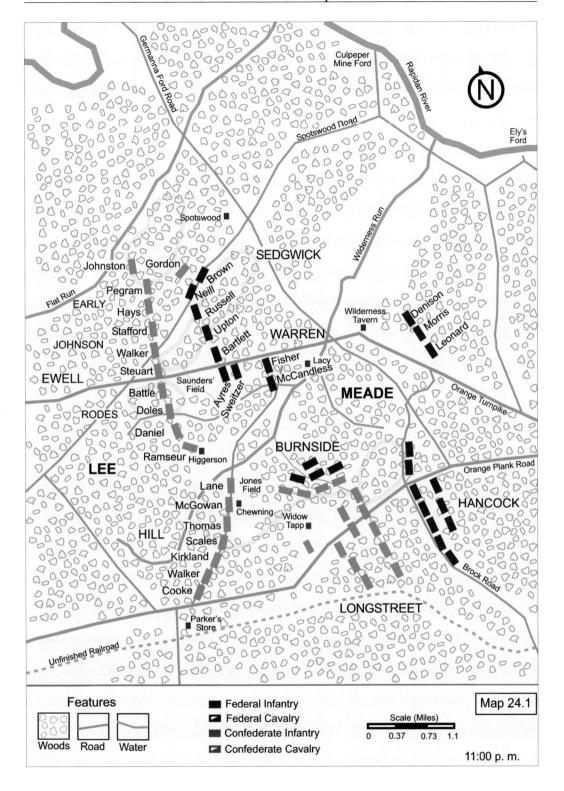

Map 24.1

11:00 p. m.

Map 24.2: Confederate Opportunities Gained and Lost (May 5-6)

A recently published exhaustive study of Lee's losses concluded that the Army of Northern Virginia's casualties at the Wilderness amounted to 11,033. With the army estimated to number 66,140, the drain in manpower was almost 17 percent, about the same as the Federal's. The breakdown of the army's losses is: 1,477 killed, 7,633 wounded, and 1,923 captured or missing. Hill's Third Corps sustained the most casualties (4,730), followed by Longstreet's First Corps (3,059) and Ewell's Second Corps (2,692). The army's cavalry corps entered the fighting with 9,320 effectives and reported 516 losses, with 59 killed, 437 wounded, and 20 captured/missing. For the infantry divisions, Harry Heth's Division sustained the most casualties at 2,292, followed by Charles Field's Division (1,918). Four brigades: Gordon's, Kirkland's, Lane's, and McGowan's each lost more than 2,000 men. Losses among the army's officers were probably high, but are not easily quantifiable. Lee lost some irreplaceable general officers in the Wilderness thickets, including those killed or mortally wounded: Brigadier Generals John Jones, Leroy Stafford, and Micah Jenkins; and wounded: James Longstreet, Henry Benning, and John Pegram.[8]

Outnumbered and out-equipped, Lee entered the campaign with many questions on his mind. What role would Grant play with the Army of the Potomac? He knew from almost a year's experience that Meade was slow and methodical, but all reports showed Grant to be the opposite. Then there were questions about Lee's own army. While the numbers had grown to be close to what he commanded at Gettysburg, the men had spent a long hard winter without adequate food or clothing. Would Longstreet reach the army in time? How effectively would Ewell and Hill lead their men after many setbacks during the summer and fall campaigns? Lee was becoming increasingly worried about his own health. Would he be able to handle the rigors of a new campaign? Most of these questions would be answered by the end of the first week in May.

Longstreet did arrive, just in time, and his experience and the fighting abilities of his troops changed the day. Less clear was the performance of the three other principals: Lee, Hill and Ewell. Some historians believe that the Wilderness could have been as great a victory for Lee as that of Chancellorsville, a year before. The difference was the absence of both Stonewall Jackson and Lee's characteristic aggressiveness. As indicated earlier, a recent historian believed Lee put his troops in motion a day too late and when he did, he issued contradictory orders to his lieutenants, Ewell and Hill. Lee "vacillated between two courses of action: on one hand he wanted to seize the initiative and hit Grant's flank while the Federals were bogged down in the Wilderness, but on the other he did not want his scattered troops to be lured into a major engagement." Gordon Rhea went a bit further in his indictment of Lee. He took issue with the commonly held belief that Lee had "trapped Grant in the Wilderness." "He was merely the fortunate beneficiary of sloppy Federal planning and reconnaissance." He went on to write that "his failure to take affirmative steps to impede Grant's progress or to accelerate his own army's response exposed the Confederates to peril." Rhea bluntly noted that "Lee made several decisions during the battle which put his army and his cause in serious jeopardy." Perhaps Lee's most serious shortcoming during the battle was his inability to coordinate the two wings of his army, and as a result they fought as independent entities.[9]

Lee's lieutenants performed surprisingly well, despite their poor showings at Gettysburg. The always dependable Longstreet delivered his First Corps at the most timely moment, despite navigating difficult logistical issues. Ewell, who had shown so much timidity at Gettysburg, mounted a good defensive effort on May 5 and 6, keeping two Federal Corps at bay, although some questions continue to exist about his ability to effectively coordinate his large command. The ever aggressive A. P. Hill also performed well in a defensive mode on May 5. He has been criticized for not adequately preparing his men for Hancock's hammer blows on the early morning of May 6. However, historian Peter Carmichael convincingly argues that the culprit was not Hill, but Lee, who stubbornly insisted that Longstreet's legions would arrive on time.[10]

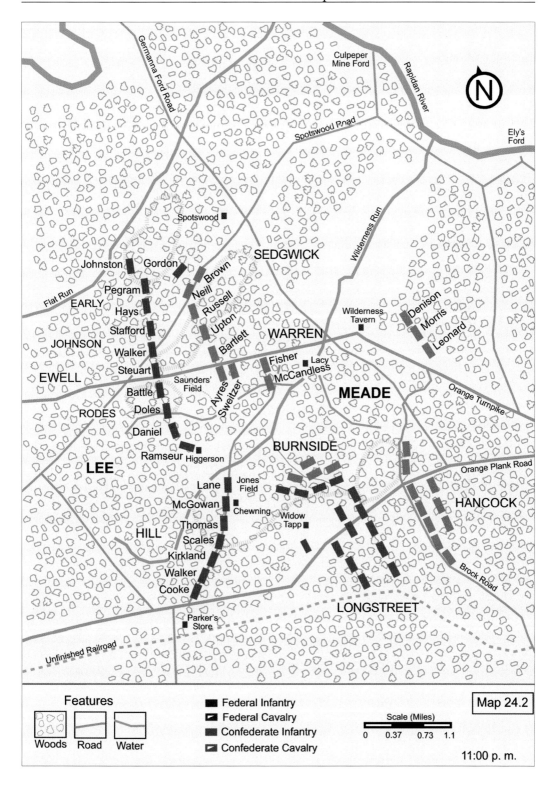

Features

Woods   Road   Water

■ Federal Infantry
◪ Federal Cavalry
■ Confederate Infantry
◪ Confederate Cavalry

Scale (Miles)

0   0.37   0.73   1.1

Map 24.2

11:00 p. m.

Map 24.3: The Campaign Continues
(May 7, 1864)

Both leaders realized that nothing could be gained from remaining in the Wilderness. Federal aide Lt. Morris Schaff accurately summed up the situation: "two days of deadly encounter; every man who could bear a musket had been put in; and now on the defensive behind breastworks; the cavalry drawn back; the trains seeking safety beyond the Rapidan; thousands and thousands of killed and wounded…the air pervaded with a lurking feeling of being face to face with disaster."[11]

The armies remained in position on May 7 as the leaders planned their next moves. Most active were the medical corps, carrying men to safety and doing what they could to save lives and patch up those who could possibly fight another day.

With the lull in the fighting, both Lee and Grant were tasked with determining their future course of action. Grant sent the following communication to General Halleck at 7:00 a.m. on May 7: "At present we can claim no victory over the enemy, neither have they gained a single advantage. The enemy pushed out of his fortification to prevent their position being turned, and have been sooner or later driven back in very instance. Up to this hour the enemy have not shown themselves in force within a mile of our lines."[12]

Sitting with Horace Porter, studying a map, Grant revealed that there was nothing to be gained from continued fighting in the Wilderness. According to Porter, Grant decided that "if he [Lee] falls back and entrenches, my notion is to move promptly toward the left. This will, in all probability, compel him to try and throw himself between us and Richmond, and in such a movement I hope to be able to attack him in a more open country, and outside of his breastworks."[13]

Considering the possibilities, Grant pointed to Spotsylvania Court House. By moving the army to that location, Grant would slide between Lee and Richmond, forcing Lee to rapidly parry the move, leaving his breastworks and driving him out into the open. The army would move in two columns within supporting distance of each other. The VI Corps, followed by the IX Corps, would head east to Chancellorsville, then work south toward Spotsylvania via narrow country roads. Once this column began its trek, the V Corps would step onto Brock Road and head south toward Spotsylvania, moving behind the II Corps. Once the path was clear, the latter corps would take up the march. Stealth was of the utmost importance, Meade was told. The movement would begin after dark. This was a graphic indication that Grant had now assumed a much more active role in directing the activities of the Army of the Potomac.[14]

Lee eagerly reviewed the steady stream of reports assembling in his tent. The enemy was inactive on the morning of May 7 and showed no signs of resuming an offensive action. What was Grant planning? Reviewing the evidence and trying to predict Grant's thinking, Lee decided that a rapid march toward Spotsylvania Court House, while a gamble, would be his best move. Major General Richard Anderson, now in command of the First Corps, was told to prepare his men for a rapid night march. Time was of the essence, as Lee knew he had to beat his adversary to this critical junction point. With the growing smoke from the fires in the Wilderness, Anderson took the initiative and modified his orders—instead of moving out at 3:00 a.m. on May 8, he decided to hit the road at 11:00 a.m. on May 7. The movement of both armies toward Spotsylvania would ensure continued bloody combat through the month of May.[15]

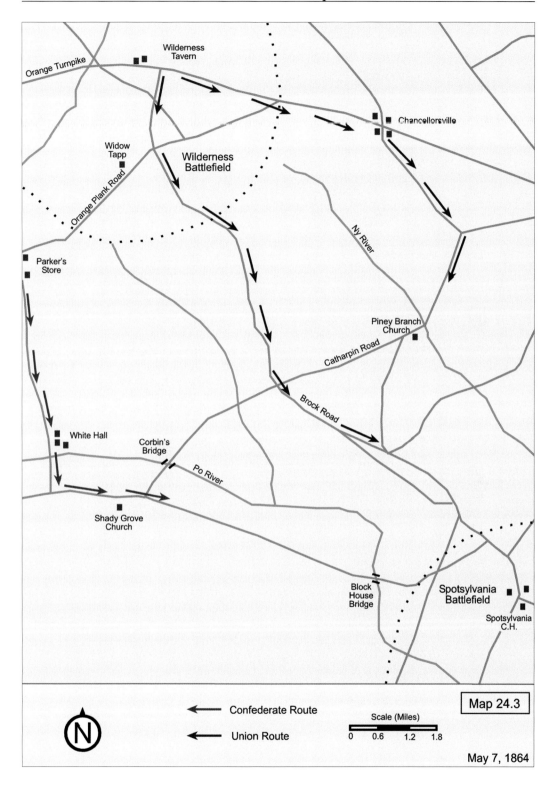

Map 24.3

May 7, 1864

Confederate Route

Union Route

Scale (Miles)

0   0.6   1.2   1.8

Appendix

Orders of Battle

ARMY OF THE POTOMAC
Maj. Gen. George G. Meade

Second Corps
Maj. Gen. Winfield Hancock

First Division
Brig. Gen. Francis C. Barlow

First Brigade
Col. Nelson A. Miles

26th Michigan, Maj. Lemuel Saviers
61st New York, Lt. Col. K. Oscar Broady
81st Pennsylvania, Col. H. Boyd McKeen
140th Pennsylvania, Col. John Fraser
183rd Pennsylvania, Col. George P. McLean

Second Brigade
Col. Thomas A. Smyth

28th Massachusetts, Lt. Col. George W. Cartwright
63rd New York, Maj. Thomas Touhy
69th New York, Capt. Richard Moroney
88th New York, Capt. Denis F. Burke
116th Pennsylvania, Lt. Col. Richard C. Dale

Third Brigade
Col. Paul Frank

39th New York, Col. Augustus Funk
52nd New York, Maj. Henry M. Karples
57th New York, Lt. Col. Alford B. Chapman
111th New York, Capt. Aaron P. Seeley
125th New York, Lt. Col. Aaron B. Myer
126th New York, Capt. Winfield Scott

Fourth Brigade
Col. John R. Brooke

2nd Delaware, Col. William P. Baily
64th New York, Maj. Leman W. Bradley
66th New York, Lt. Col. John S. Haremell
53rd Pennsylvania, Lt. Col. Richards McMichael
145th Pennsylvania, Col. Hiram L. Brown
148th Pennsylvania, Col. James A. Beaver

Second Division
Brig. Gen. John Gibbon

Provost Guard
2nd Company Minnesota Sharpshooters,
Capt. Mahlon Black

First Brigade
Brig. Gen. Alexander S. Webb

19th Maine, Col. Selden Connor
1st Company Andrew (Massachusetts) Sharpshooters,
Lt. Samuel G. Gilbreth
15th Massachusetts, Maj. I. Harris Hooper
19th Massachusetts, Maj. Edmund Rice
20th Massachusetts, Maj. Henry L. Abbott
7th Michigan, Maj. Sylvanus W. Curtis
42nd New York, Maj. Patrick J. Downing
59th New York, Capt. William McFadden
82nd New York (2nd Militia), Col. Henry W. Hudson

Second Brigade
Brig. Gen. Joshua T. Owen

152nd New York, Lt. Col. George W. Thompson
69th Pennsylvania, Maj. William Davis
71st Pennsylvania, Lt. Col. Charles Kochersperger
72nd Pennsylvania, Col. De Witt C. Baxter
106th Pennsylvania, Capt. Robert H. Ford

Third Brigade
Col. Samuel S. Carroll

14th Connecticut, Col. Theodore G. Ellis
1st Delaware, Lt. Col. Daniel Woodall
14th Indiana, Col. John Coons
12th New Jersey, Lt. Col. Thomas H. Davis
10th New York Battalion, Capt. George M. Dewey
108th New York, Col. Charles J. Powers
4th Ohio, Lt. Col. Leonard W. Carpenter
8th Ohio, Lt. Col. Franklin Sawyer
7th West Virginia, Lt. Col. Jonathan H. Lockwood

Third Division
Maj. Gen. David B. Birney

First Brigade
Brig. Gen. J. H. Hobart Ward

20th Indiana, Col. William C. L. Taylor
3rd Maine, Col. Moses B. Lakeman

40th New York, Col. Thomas W. Egan
86th New York, Lt. Col. Jacob H. Lansing
124th New York, Col. Francis M. Cummins
99th Pennsylvania, Lt. Col. Edwin R. Biles
110th Pennsylvania, Lt. Col. Isaac Rogers
141st Pennsylvania, Lt. Col. Guy H. Watkins
2nd U.S. Sharpshooters, Lt. Col. Homer R. Stoughton

Second Brigade
Brig. Gen. Alexander Hays

4th Maine, Col. Elijah Walker
17th Maine, Col. George W. West
3rd Michigan, Col. Byron R. Pierce
5th Michigan, Lt. Col. John Pulford
93rd New York, Maj. Samuel McConihe
57th Pennsylvania, Col. Peter Sides
63rd Pennsylvania, Lt. Col. John A. Danks
105th Pennsylvania, Col. Calvin A. Craig
1st U.S. Sharpshooters, Maj. Charles P. Mattocks

Fourth Division
Brig. Gen. Gershom Mott

First Brigade
Col. Robert McAllister

1st Massachusetts, Col. Napoleon B. McLaughlen
16th Massachusetts, Lt. Col. Waldo Merriam
5th New Jersey, Col. William J. Sewell
6th New Jersey, Lt. Col. Stephen R. Gilkyson
7th New Jersey, Maj. Frederick Cooper
8th New Jersey, Col. John Ramsey
11th New Jersey, Lt. Col. John Schoonover
26th Pennsylvania, Maj. Samuel G. Moffett
115th Pennsylvania, Maj. William A. Reilly

Second Brigade
Col. William R. Brewster

11th Massachusetts, Col. William Blaisdell
70th New York, Capt. William H. Hugo
71st New York, Lt. Col. Thomas Rafferty
72nd New York, Lt. Col. John Leonard
73rd New York, Lt. Col. Michael W. Burns
74th New York, Col. Thomas Holt
120th New York, Capt. Abram L. Lockwood
84th Pennsylvania, Lt. Col. Milton Opp

Artillery Brigade
Col. John C. Tidball

Maine Light, 6th Battery (F), Capt. Edwin B. Dow
Massachusetts Light, 10th Battery,
Capt. J. Henry Sleeper
New Hampshire Light, 1st Battery,
Capt. Frederick M. Edgell
1st New York Light, Battery G, Capt. Nelson Ames
4th New York Heavy, 3rd Battalion,
Lt. Col. Thomas Allcock
1st Pennsylvania Light, Battery F,
Capt. R. Bruce Ricketts
1st Rhode Island Light, Battery A,
Capt. William A. Arnold
1st Rhode Island Light, Battery B,
Capt. T. Frederick Brown
4th U.S., Battery K, Lt. John W. Roder
5th U.S., Batteries C and I, Lt. James Gilliss

Fifth Corps
Maj. Gen. Gouverneur K. Warren

Provost Guard
12th New York Battalion, Maj. Henry W. Rider

First Division
Brig. Gen. Charles Griffin

First Brigade
Brig. Gen. Romeyn B. Ayres

140th New York, Col. George Ryan
146th New York, Col. David T. Jenkins
91st Pennsylvania, Lt. Col. Joseph H. Sinex
155th Pennsylvania, Lt. Col. Alfred L. Pearson
2nd U.S., Companies B, C, F, H, I, and K,
Capt. James W. Long
11th U.S., Companies B, C, D, E, F, and G, First
Battalion, Capt. Francis M. Cooley
12th U.S., Companies A, B, C, D, and G, 1st Battalion,
Maj. Luther B. Bruen
12th U.S., Companies A, C, D, F, and H,
2nd Battalion, Maj. Luther B. Bruen
14th U.S., 1st Battalion, Capt. Edward McK. Hudson
17th U.S., Companies A, C, D, G, and H, 1st Battalion,
Capt. James F. Grimes
17th U.S., Companies A, B, and C, 2nd Battalion,
Capt. James F. Grimes

Second Brigade
Col. Jacob B. Sweitzer

9th Massachusetts, Col. Patrick R. Guiney

22nd Massachusetts, Col. William S. Tilton
32nd Massachusetts, Col. George L. Prescott
4th Michigan, Lt. Col. George W. Lurebard
62nd Pennsylvania, Lt. Col. James C. Hull

Third Brigade
Brig. Gen. Joseph J. Bartlett

20th Maine, Maj. Ellis Spear
18th Massachusetts, Col. Joseph Hayes
1st Michigan, Lt. Col. William A. Throop
16th Michigan, Maj. Robert T. Elliott
44th New York, Lt. Col. Freeman Conner
83rd Pennsylvania, Col. Orpheus S. Woodward
118th Pennsylvania, Col. James Gwyn

Second Division
Brig. Gen. John C. Robinson

First Brigade
Col. Samuel H. Leonard

16th Maine, Col. Charles W. Tilden
13th Massachusetts, Capt. Charles H. Hovey
89th Massachusetts, Col. Phineas S. Davis
104th New York, Col. Gilbert G. Prey

Second Brigade
Brig. Gen. Henry Baxter

12th Massachusetts, Col. James L. Bates
83rd New York (9th Militia), Col. Joseph A. Moesch
97th New York, Col. Charles Wheelock
11th Pennsylvania, Col. Richard Coulter
88th Pennsylvania, Capt. George B. Rhoads
90th Pennsylvania, Col. Peter Lyle

Third Brigade
Col. Andrew W. Denison

1st Maryland, Maj. Benjamin H. Schley
4th Maryland, Col. Richard N. Bowerman
7th Maryland, Col. Charles E. Phelps
8th Maryland, Lt. Col. John G. Johannes

Third Division
Brig. Gen. Samuel W. Crawford

First Brigade
Col. William McCandless

1st Pennsylvania Reserves, Col. William C. Talley
2nd Pennsylvania Reserves,
Lt. Col. Patrick McDonough
6th Pennsylvania Reserves, Col. Wellington H. Ent
7th Pennsylvania Reserves, Maj. LeGrand B. Speece
11th Pennsylvania Reserves, Col. Samuel M. Jackson
13th Pennsylvania Reserves (1st Rifles),
Maj. William R. Hartshorne

Third Brigade
Col. Joseph W. Fisher

5th Pennsylvania Reserves, Lt. Col, George Dare
8th Pennsylvania Reserves, Col. Silas M. Baily
10th Pennsylvania Reserves, Lt. Col. Ira Ayer, Jr
12th Pennsylvania Reserves, Lt. Col. Richard Gustin

Fourth Division
Brig. Gen. James S. Wadsworth

First Brigade
Brig. Gen. Lysander Cutler

7th Indiana, Col. Ira G. Grover
19th Indiana, Col. Samuel J. Williams
24th Michigan, Col. Henry A. Morrow
1st New York Battalion Sharpshooters,
Capt. Volney J. Shipman
2nd Wisconsin, Lt. Col. John Mansfield
6th Wisconsin, Col. Edward S. Bragg
7th Wisconsin, Col. William W. Robinson

Second Brigade
Brig. Gen. James C. Rice

76th New York, Lt. Col. John E. Cook
84th New York (14th Militia), Col. Edward B. Fowler
95th New York, Col. Edward Pye
147th New York, Col. Francis C. Miller
56th Pennsylvania, Col. J.William Holmann

Third Brigade
Col. Roy Stone
Lt. Col. John Irvin

121st Pennsylvania, Capt. Samuel T. Lloyd
142nd Pennsylvania, Maj. Horatio N. Warren
143rd Pennsylvania, Col. Edmund L. Dana
149th Pennsylvania, Lt. Col. John Irvin
150th Pennsylvania, Capt. George W. Jones

Artillery Brigade
Col. Charles S. Wainwright
Massachusetts Light, Battery C,
Capt. Augustus P. Martin
Massachusetts Light, Battery E,
Capt. Charles A. Phillips
1st New York Light, Battery D,
Capt. George B. Winslow
1st New York Light, Batteries E and L,
Lt. George Breck
1st New York Light, Battery H, Capt. Charles E. Mink
4th New York Heavy., 2nd Battalion,
Maj. William Arthur
1st Pennsylvania Light, Battery B,
Capt. James H. Cooper
4th U.S., Battery B, Lt. James Stewart
5th U.S., Battery D, Lt. Benjamin F. Rittenhouse

Sixth Corps
Maj. Gen. John Sedgwick

Escort
8th Pennsylvania Cavalry, Company A,
Capt. Charles E. Fellows

First Division
Brig. Gen. Horatio G. Wright

First Brigade
Col. Henry W. Brown

1st New Jersey, Lt. Col. William Henry, Jr.
2nd New Jersey, Lt. Col. Charles Wiebecke
3rd New Jersey, Capt. Samuel T. DuBois
4th New Jersey, Lt. Col. Charles Ewing
10th New Jersey, Col. Henry O. Ryerson
15th New Jersey, Col. William H. Penrose

Second Brigade
Col. Emory Upton

5th Maine, Col. Clark S. Edwards
121st New York, Lt. Col. Egbert Olcott
95th Pennsylvania, Lt. Col. Edward Carroll
96th Pennsylvania, Lt. Col. William H. Lessig

Third Brigade
Brig. Gen. David A. Russell

6th Maine, Maj. George Fuller
49th Pennsylvania, Col. Thomas Hulings

119th Pennsylvania, Maj. Henry P. Truefitt, Jr.
5th Wisconsin, Lt. Col. Theodore B. Catlin

Fourth Brigade
Brig. Gen. Alexander Shaler

65th New York, Col. Joseph E. Hamblin
67th New York, Col. Nelson Cross
122nd New York, Lt. Col. Augustus W. Dwight

Second Division
Brig. Gen. George W. Getty.

First Brigade
Brig. Gen. Frank Wheaton

62nd New York, Col. David J. Nevin
93rd Pennsylvania, Lt. Col. John S. Long
98th Pennsylvania, Col. John F. Ballier
102nd Pennsylvania, Col. John W. Patterson
139th Pennsylvania, Lt. Col. William H. Moody

Second Brigade
Col. Lewis A. Grant

2nd Vermont, Col. Newton Stone
3rd Vermont, Col. Thomas O. Seaver
4th Vermont, Col. George P. Foster
5th Vermont, Lt. Col. John R. Lewis
6th Vermont, Col. Elisha L. Barney

Third Brigade
Brig. Gen. Thomas H. Neill

7th Maine, Col. Edwin C. Mason
43rd New York, Lt. Col. John Wilson
49th New York, Col. Daniel D. Bidwell
77th New York, Maj. Nathan S. Babcock
61st Pennsylvania, Col. George F. Smith

Fourth Brigade
Brig. Gen. Henry L. Eustis

7th Massachusetts, Col. Thomas D. Johns
10th Massachusetts, Lt. Col. Joseph B. Parsons
37th Massachusetts, Col. Oliver Edwards
2nd Rhode Island, Lt. Col. Samuel B. M. Read

Third Division
Brig. Gen. James B. Ricketts

First Brigade
Brig. Gen. William H. Morris

14th New Jersey, Lt. Col. Caldwell K. Hall
106th New York, Lt. Col. Charles Townsend
151st New York, Lt. Col. Thomas M. Fay
87th Pennsylvania, Col. John W. Schall
10th Vermont, Lt. Col. William W. Henry

Second Brigade
Brig. Gen. Truman Seymour

6th Maryland, Col. John W. Horn
110th Ohio, Col. J. Warren Keifer
122nd Ohio, Col. William H. Ball
126th Ohio, Col. Benjamin F. Smith
67th Pennsylvania (detachment),
Capt. George W. Guss
138th Pennsylvania, Col. Matthew R, McClennan

Artillery Brigade
Col. Charles H. Tompkins

Maine Light, 4th Battery (D), Lt. Melville C. Kimball
Massachusetts Light, 1st Battery (A),
Capt. William H. McCartney
New York Light, 1st Battery, Capt. Andrew Cowan
New York Light, 3rd Battery, Capt. William A. Harn
4th New York Heavy, 1st Battalion,
Maj. Thomas D. Sears
1st Rhode Island Light. Battery C,
Capt. Richard Waterman
1st Rhode Island Light, Battery E,
Capt. William B. Rhodes
1st Rhode Island Light, Battery G,
Capt. George W. Adams
5th U.S., Battery M, Capt. James McKnight

Ninth Corps
Maj. Gen. Ambrose E. Burnside

Provost Guard
8th U.S. Infantry, Capt. Milton Cogswell

First Division
Brig. Gen. Thomas G. Stevenson

First Brigade
Col. Sumner Carruth

35th Massachusetts, Maj. Nathaniel Wales
56th Massachusetts, Col. Charles E. Griswold
57th Massachusetts, Col. William F. Bartlett
59th Massachusetts, Col. J. Parker Gould
4th U.S., Capt. Charles H. Brightly
10th U.S., Maj. Samuel B. Hayman

Second Brigade
Col. Daniel Leasure

3rd Maryland, Col. Joseph M, Sudsburg
21st Massachusetts, Lt. Col. George P. Hawkes
100th Pennsylvania, Lt. Col. Matthew M. Dawson

Artillery

Maine Light, 2nd Battery (B), Capt. Albert F. Thomas
Massachusetts Light, 14th Battery,
Capt. Joseph W. B. Wright

Second Division
Brig. Gen. Robert B. Potter

First Brigade
Col. Zenas R. Bliss

36th Massachusetts, Maj. William F. Draper
58th Massachusetts, Lt. Col. John C. Whiton
51st New York, Col. Charles W. LeGendre
45th Pennsylvania, Col. John I. Curtin
48th Pennsylvania, Lt. Col. Henry Pleasants
7th Rhode Island, Capt. Theodore Winn

Second Brigade
Col. Simon G. Griffin

31st Maine, Lt. Col. Thomas Hight
82nd Maine, Maj. Arthur Deering
6th New Hampshire, Lt. Col. Henry H. Pearson
9th New Hampshire, Lt. Col. John W. Babbitt
11th New Hampshire, Col. Walter Harriman
17th Vermont, Lt. Col. Charles Cummings

Artillery

Massachusetts Light, 11th Battery,
Capt. Edward J. Jones
New York Light, 19th Battery,
Capt. Edward W. Rogers

Third Division
Brig. Gen. Orlando B. Willcox

First Brigade
Col. John F. Hartranft

2nd Michigan, Col. William Humphrey
8th Michigan, Col. Frank Graves
17th Michigan, Col. Constant Luce
27th Michigan, Maj. Samuel Moody
109th New York, Col. Benjamin F. Tracy
51st Pennsylvania, Lt. Col Edwin Schall

Second Brigade
Col. Benjamin C. Christ

1st Michigan Sharpshooters, Col. Charles V. De Land
20th Michigan, Lt. Col. Byron M. Cutcheon
70th New York, Col. David Morrison
60th Ohio, Lt. Col. James N. McElroy
50th Pennsylvania, Lt. Col. Edward Overton, Jr.

Artillery

Maine Light, 7th Battery (G),
Capt. Adelbert B. Twitchell
New York Light. 34th Battery, Capt. Jacob Roemer

Fourth Division
Brig Gen. Edward Ferrero

First Brigade
Col. Joshua K. Sigfried

27th U. S. Colored Troops, Lt. Col. Charles J. Wright
30th U.S. Colored Troops, Col. Delavan Bates
39th U.S. Colored Troops. Col. Ozora P. Stearns
43rd U.S. Colored Troops, Lt. Col. H. Seymour Hall

Second Brigade
Col. Henry G. Thomas
30th Connecticut (colored), detachment,
Capt Charles Robinson
19th U.S. Colored Troops, Lt. Col. Joseph G. Perkins
23rd U.S. Colored Troops,
Lt. Col Cleaveland J. Campbell

Artillery

Pennsylvania Light, Battery D, Capt. George W. Durell
Vermont Light, 3rd Battery, Capt. Romeo H. Start

Cavalry

3rd New Jersey, Col. Andrew J. Morrison
22nd New York, Col. Samuel J. Crooks
2nd Ohio, Lt. Col. George A. Purington
13th Pennsylvania, Maj, Michael Kerwin

Reserve Artillery
Capt. John Edwards, Jr.

New York Light, 27th Battery, Capt. John B. Eaton
1st Rhode Island Light, Battery D,
Capt. William W. Buckley
1st Rhode Island Light, Battery H,
Capt. Crawford Allen, Jr.
2nd U.S., Battery E, Lt. James S. Dudley
3rd U.S.. Battery G, Lt. Edmund Pendleton
3rd U.S., Batteries L and M, Lt. Erskine Gittings

Provisional Brigade
Col. Elisha G. Marshall

24th New York Cavalry (dismounted),
Col. William C. Raulston
14th New York Heavy Artillery,
Lt. Col. Clarence H. Corning
2nd Pennsylvania Provisional Heavy Artillery,
Col. Thomas Wilhelm

Cavalry Corp
Maj Gen. Philip H. Sheridan

Escort
6th U.S., Capt. Ira W. Claflin

First Division
Brig. Gen. Alfred T. A. Torbert

First Brigade
Brig. Gen. George A. Custer

1st Michigan, Lt. Col. Peter Stagg
5th Michigan, Col. Russell A. Alger
6th Michigan, Maj. James H. Kidd
7th Michigan, Maj. Henry W. Granger

Second Brigade
Col. Thomas C. Devin

4th New York, Lt. Col. William R. Parnell

6th New York, Lt. Col. William H. Crocker
9th New York, Col. William Sackett
17th Pennsylvania, Lt. Col. James Q. Anderson

Reserve Brigade
Brig. Gen. Wesley Merritt

19th New York (1st Dragoons), Col. Alfred Gibbs
6th Pennsylvania, Maj. James Starr
1st U.S., Capt. Nelson B. Sweitzer
2nd U.S., Capt. Theophilus F. Rodenbough
5th U.S., Capt. Abraham K. Arnold

Second Division
Brig. Gen. David McM. Gregg

First Brigade
Brig. Gen. Henry E. Davies, Jr.

1st Massachusetts, Maj. Lucius M. Sargent
1st New Jersey, Lt. Col. John W. Kester
6th Ohio, Col. William Stedman
1st Pennsylvania, Col. John P. Taylor

Second Brigade
Col. J. Irvin Gregg

1st Maine, Col. Charles H. Smith
10th New York, Maj. M. Henry Avery
2nd Pennsylvania, Lt. Col. Joseph P. Brinton
4th Pennsylvania, Lt. Col. George H. Covode
8th Pennsylvania, Lt. Col. Samuel Wilson
16th Pennsylvania, Lt. Col. John K. Robison

Third Division
Brig. Gen. James H. Wilson

Escort
8th Illinois (detachment), Lt. William W. Long

First Brigade
Col. Timothy M. Bryan, Jr.
Col. John B. McIntosh

1st Connecticut, Maj. Erastus Blakeslee
2nd New York, Col. Otto Harhaus
5th New York, Lt. Col. John Hammond
18th Pennsylvania, Lt. Col. William P. Brinton

Second Brigade
Col. George H. Chapman

3rd Indiana, Maj. William Patton
8th New York, Lt. Col. William H. Benjamin
1st Vermont, Lt. Col. Addison W. Preston

Artillery
Brig. Gen. Henry J. Hunt

Artillery Reserve
Col. Henry S. Burton

First Brigade
Col. J. Howard Kitching

6th New York Heavy, Lt. Col. Edmund R. Travis
15th New York Heavy, Col. Louis Schirmer

Second Brigade
Maj. John A. Tompkins

Maine Light, 5th Battery (E),
Capt. Greenleaf T. Stevens
1st New Jersey Light, Battery A,
Capt. William Hexamer
1st New Jersey Light, Battery B, Capt. A. Judson Clark
New York Light, 5th Battery, Capt. Elijah D. Taft
New York Light, 12th Battery,
Capt. George F. McKnight
1st New York Light, Battery B, Capt. Albert S. Sheldon

Third Brigade
Maj. Robert H. Fitzhugh

Massachusetts Light, 9th Battery, Capt. John Bigelow
New York Light, 15th Battery, Capt. Patrick Hart
1st New York Light, Battery C, Lt. William H. Phillip
New York Light, 11th Battery, Capt. John E. Burton
1st Ohio Light, Battery H, Lt. William A. Ewing
5th U.S., Battery E, Lt. John R. Brinckle

Horse Artillery

First Brigade
Capt. James M. Robertson

New York Light, 6th Battery, Capt. Joseph W. Martin
2nd U.S., Batteries B and L, Lt. Edward Heaton
2nd U.S., Battery D, Lt. Edward B. Williston
2nd U.S., Battery M,
Lt. Alexander C. M. Pennington, Jr.
4th U.S., Battery A, Lt. Rufus King, Jr.
4th U.S., Batteries C and E, Lt. Charles L. Fitzhugh

Second Brigade
Capt. Dunbar R. Ransom

1st U.S., Batteries E and G, Lt. Frank S. French
1st U.S., Batteries H and I, Capt. Alanson M. Randol
1st U.S., Battery K, Lt. John Egan
2nd U.S., Battery A, Lt. Robert Clarke
2nd U.S., Battery G., Lt. William N. Dennison
3rd U.S., Batteries C, F, and K, Lt. James R. Kelly

*   *   *

ARMY OF NORTHERN VIRGINIA
General Robert E. Lee

First Corps
Lt. Gen. James Longstreet

Kershaw's Division
Brig. Gen. Joseph B. Kershaw

Kershaw's Brigade
Col. John Henagan

2nd South Carolina, Lt. Col. Franklin Gaillard,
Maj. William Wallace
3rd South Carolina, Col. James D. Nance,
Lt. Col. William D. Rutherford
7th South Carolina, Capt. Elijah J. Groggans,
8th South Carolina, Lt. Col. Eli T. Stackhouse
15th South Carolina, Col. John B. Davis
3rd South Carolina Battalion, Capt. B. M. Whitener

Wofford's Brigade
Brig. Gen. William T. Wofford

16th Georgia, Col. B. Edward Stiles
18th Georgia
24th Georgia, Col. Christopher C. Sanders
Cobb's (Georgia) Legion, Lt. Col. Luther J. Glenn,
Lt. Col. William D. Conyers
Phillips (Georgia) Legion, Lt. Col. Joseph Hamilton,
Maj. John S. Norris
3rd Georgia Battalion Sharpshooters,
Lt. Col. Nathan L. Hutchins, Jr.

Humphreys' Brigade
Brig. Gen. Benjamin G. Humphreys

13th Mississippi, Maj. George L. Donald

17th Mississippi, Capt. Jesse C. Cochran
18th Mississippi, Maj. George B. Gerald,
Capt. William H. Lewis
21st Mississippi, Col. D. N. Moody

Bryan's Brigade
Brig. Gen. Goode Bryan

10th Georgia, Col. Willis C. Holt
50th Georgia, Col. Peter McGlashan,
Maj. John M. Spence
51st Georgia, Col. Edward Ball
53rd Georgia, Col. James P. Simms

Field's Division
Maj. Gen. Charles W. Field

Jenkins' Brigade
Brig. Gen. Micah Jenkins

1st South Carolina, Col. James R. Hagood
2nd South Carolina (Rifles), Col. Robert E. Bowen,
Lt. Col. David L. Donald
5th South Carolina, Col. A. Coward,
Maj. Thomas C. Beckham
6th South Carolina, Col. John Bratton,
Lt. Col. John M. Steedman
Palmetto (South Carolina) Sharpshooters,
Col. Joseph Walker

Law's Brigade
Col. William F. Perry

4th Alabama, Col. Pinckney D. Bowles
15th Alabama, Col. Alexander A. Lowther,
Maj. William C. Oates
44th Alabama, Col. William F. Perry,
Lt. Col. John A. Jones
47th Alabama, Col. Michael J. Bulger
48th Alabama, Lt. Col. William M. Hardwick,
Maj. John W. Wigginton

Anderson's Brigade
Brig. Gen. George T. Anderson

7th Georgia, Col. John R. Towers
8th Georgia, Col. Edward F. Hoge
9th Georgia, Maj. William M. Jones
11th Georgia, Lt. Col. William Luffman
59th Georgia, Lt. Col. Bolivar H. Gee

Gregg's Brigade
Brig. Gen. John Gregg

3rd Arkansas, Col. Van H. Manning,
Capt. Frank Thach
1st Texas, Lt. Col. Frederick S. Bass,
Maj. Richard J. Harding
4th Texas, Col. John P. Bane
5th Texas, Lt. Col. King Bryan, Capt. Tacitus T. Clay

Benning's Brigade
Brig. Gen. Henry L. Benning,
Col. Dudley Mc. DuBose

2nd Georgia,
15th Georgia, Col. Dudley M. Du Bose,
Maj. Peter J. Shannon
17th Georgia, Col. Wesley C. Hodges,
Maj. William A. Barden
20th Georgia, Lt. Col. Eli M. Seago

Artillery
Brig. Gen. E. Porter Alexander

Huger's Battalion, Lt. Col. Frank Huger

Brooks Arillery (South Carolina),
Capt. William W. Fickling
Madison Light Artillery (Louisiana),
Capt. George V. Moody, Lt. Dent Burroughs
Parker Light Artillery (Virginia),
Capt. William W. Parker
Bedford Artillery (Virginia), Capt. J. Donnell
Co. C. 12th Virginia Artillery (Virginia),
Capt. Osmond B. Taylor
Ashland Artillery (Virginia), Capt. James Woolfolk

Haskell's Battalion, Maj. John C. Haskell

3rd North Carolina Artillery (North Carolina),
Capt. John R. Potts, Lt. Henry G. Flanner
2nd Palmetto Light Artillery (South Carolina),
Capt. Hugh R. Garden
Nelson Light Artillery (Virginia),
Capt. James N. Lamkin
1st North Carolina Artillery (North Carolina),
Capt. James N. Lamkin
Cabell's Battalion, Col. Henry C. Cabell

Pulaski Artillery (Georgia), Lt. Morgan Callaway
Troup Artillery (Georgia), Capt. Henry H. Carlton

1st Co. Richmond Howitzers (Virginia),
Capt. Edward S. McCarthy, Lt. Robert M. Anderson
1st North Carolina Artillery (North Carolina),
Capt. Basil C. Manly

Second Corps
Lt. Gen. Richard S. Ewell

Early's Division
Maj. Gen. Jubal A. Early

Hays' Brigade
Brig. Gen. Harry T. Hays

5th Louisiana, Lt. Col. Bruce Menger
6th Louisiana, Maj. William H. Manning
7th Louisiana, Maj. J. Moore Wilson
8th Louisiana, Col. Alcibiades De Blanc
9th Louisiana, Col. William Peck

Pegram's Brigade
Brig. Gen. John Pegram, Col. John S. Hoffman

13th Virginia, Col. James B. Terrill,
Maj. Charles T. Crittenden
31st Virginia, Col. John S. Hoffman,
Maj. William P. Cooper
49th Virginia, Col. J. Catlett Gibson,
Lt. Col. Charles B. Christian
52nd Virginia, Col. James H. Skinner,
Lt. Col. Thomas Watkins
58th Virginia, Col. Francis H. Board,
Lt. Col. John G. Kasey

Gordon's Brigade
Brig. Gen. John B. Gordon

13th Georgia, Lt. Col. Samuel W. Jones
26th Georgia, Col. Edmund N. Atkinson
31st Georgia, Col. Clement A. Evans,
Lt. Col. John H. Lowe
38th Georgia, Lt. Col. Phillip E. Davant,
Maj. Thomas Bomar
60th Georgia, Lt. Col. Thomas J. Berry
61st Georgia, Col. John H. Lamar

Johnson's Division
Maj. Gen. Edward Johnson

Stonewall Brigade
Brig. Gen. James A. Walker

2nd Virginia, Lt. Col. William W. Randolph,
Capt. Charles H. Stewart
4th Virginia, Col. William Terry
5th Virginia, Col. John H. S. Funk
27th Virginia, Lt. Col. Charles L. Haynes
33rd Virginia, Lt Col. George Huston

Jones' Brigade
Brig. Gen. John M. Jones,
Col. William A. Witcher

21st Virginia, Col. William Witcher,
Lt. Col. William P. Moseley
25th Virginia, Col. John C. Higginbotham
42nd Virginia ———
44th Virginia, Col. Norvell Cobb
48th Virginia, Col. Robert H. Dungan
50th Virginia, Col. Alexander S. Vandeventer

Steuart's Brigade
Brig. Gen. George H. Steuart

1st North Carolina, Col. Hamilton A. Brown
3rd North Carolina, Col. Stephen D. Thruston
10th Virginia, Col. Edward T. H. Warren,
Lt. Col. D. H. Lee Martz
23rd Virginia, Lt. Col. John P. Fitzgerald
37th Virginia, Col. Titus V. Williams

Stafford's Brigade
Brig. Gen. Leroy A. Stafford, Col Zebulon York

1st Louisiana, Maj. Edward D. Willett
2nd Louisiana, Col. Jesse M. Williams
10th Louisiana, Lt. Col. Henry D. Monier
14th Louisiana, Col. Zebulon York
15th Louisiana, Col. Edmund Pendleton

Rodes' Division
Maj. Gen. Robert E. Rodes

Daniel's Brigade
Brig. Gen. Junius Daniel

32nd North Carolina, Col. Edmund C. Brabble
43rd North Carolina, Capt. Cary Whitaker
45th North Carolina, Col. Samuel H. Boyd
53rd North Carolina, Col. William A. Owens
2nd North Carolina Battalion, Maj. James J. Iredell

Doles' Brigade
Brig. Gen. George Doles

4th Georgia, Col. Philip Cook
12th Georgia, Col. Edward Willis
44th Georgia, Col. William H. Peebles

Ramseur's Brigade
Brig. Gen. Stephen D. Ramseur

2nd North Carolina, Col. William R. Cox
4th North Carolina, Col. Bryan Grimes
14th North Carolina, Col. R. Tyler Bennett
30th North Carolina, Col. Francis M. Parker

Battle's Brigade
Brig. Gen. Cullen A. Battle

3rd Alabama, Col. Charles Forsyth
5th Alabama, Col. Josephus M. Hall
6th Alabama, Col. James N. Lightfoot
12th Alabama, Col. Samuel B. Pickens
61st Alabama, Col. William G. Swanson

Johnston's Brigade
Brig. Gen. Robert D. Johnston

5th North Carolina, Col. Thomas M. Garrett
12th North Carolina, Col. Henry E. Coleman
20th North Carolina, Col. Thomas F. Toon
23rd North Carolina, Col. Charles C. Blacknall

Artillery
Brig. Gen. Armistead L. Long

Hardaway's Battalion
Lt. Col. Robert A. Hardaway

Powhatan (Virginia) Artillery, Capt. Willis J. Dance
1st Rockbridge Artillery (Virginia),
Capt. Archibald Graham
Salem Flying (Virginia) Artillery,
Capt. Charles B. Griffin
Co. K,1st Virginia Artillery, Captain Lorraine F. Jones
Co. D. 1st Virginia Artillery,
Capt. Benjamin H. Smith, Jr.

Braxton's Battalion
Lt. Col. Carter M. Braxton

Alleghany (Virginia) Artillery,
Capt. John C. Carpenter
Stafford Light (Virginia) Artillery,
Capt. Raleigh L Cooper

Lynchburg "Lee" (Virginia) Artillery,
Capt. William W. Hardwicke

Nelson's Battalion
Lt. Col. William Nelson

Co. A, 31st Virginia Artillery,
Capt. Thomas J. Kirkpatrick
Fluvanna Artillery(Virginia) battery,
Capt. John L. Massie
Georgia Battery, Capt. John Milledge, Jr.

Cutshaw's Battalion
Maj. Wilfred E. Cutshaw

Charlottesville (Virginia) Artillery,
Capt. James McD. Carrington
Staunton (Virginia) Artillery,
Capt. Asher W. Garber
Courtney (Virginia) Artillery, Capt. William Tanner

Page's Battalion
Maj. Richard C. M. Page

King William (Virginia) Artillery,
Capt. William P. Carter
Orange (Virginia) Artillery,
Capt. Charles W. Frey
Page's (Virginia) Artillery, Maj. Richard C. M. Page
Jeff Davis (Alabama) Artillery, Capt. William J. Reese

Third Corps
Lt. Gen. Ambrose P. Hill

Anderson's Division
Maj. Gen. Richard H. Anderson

Perrin's Brigade
Brig. Gen. Abner Perrin

8th Alabama, Lt. Col. Hilary A. Herbert,
Capt. Duke Nall, Capt. Henry C. Lea
9th Alabama,
10th Alabama, Lt. Col. James E. Shelley
11th Alabama, Col. John C. C. Sanders
14th Alabama, Lt. Col. James A. Broome

Harris' Brigade
Brig. Gen. Nathaniel H. Harris

12th Mississippi, Col. Merrie B. Harris

16th Mississippi, Col. Samuel E: Baker
19th Mississippi, Col. Thomas J. Hardin
48th Mississippi, Col. Joseph McJayne

Mahone's Brigade
Brig. Gen. William Mahone

6th Virginia, Lt. Col. Henry W. Williamson
12th Virginia, Col. David A. Weisiger
16th Virginia, Lt. Col. Richard O. Whitehead
41st Virginia, Lt. Col. Joseph P. Minetree
61st Virginia, Col. Virginius D. Groner

Wright's Brigade
Brig. Gen. Ambrose R. Wright

3rd Georgia
22nd Georgia
48th Georgia, Lt. Col. Matthew R. Hall
2nd Georgia Battalion, Maj. Charles J. Moffett

Perry's Brigade
Brig. Gen. Edward A. Perry

2nd Florida, Capt. C. Seton Fleming
5th Florida, Col. Thompson B. Lamar
8th Florida, Lt. Col. William Baya

Heth's Division
Maj. Gen. Henry Heth

Davis's Brigade
Col. John M. Stone

2nd Mississippi, Col. John M. Stone
11th Mississippi, Col. Francis M. Green
26th Mississippi, Col. Arthur Reynolds
42nd Mississippi, Col. William A. Feeney,
Lt. Col. Andrew McNelson
55th North Carolina, Capt. Walter A. Whitted

Cooke's Brigade
Brig. Gen. John R. Cooke

15th North Carolina, Col. William MacRae
27th North Carolina,
Lt. Col. William H. Yarborough
46th North Carolina, Col. William L. Saunders
48th North Carolina, Col. Samuel H. Walkup

Kirkland's Brigade
Brig. Gen. William W. Kirkland

11th North Carolina, Col. William J. Martin
26th North Carolina, Col. John R. Lane,
Lt. Col. John T. Jones
44th North Carolina, Col. Thomas C. Singletary,
Maj. Charles M. Stedman
47th North Carolina, Col. George H. Faribault
52nd North Carolina, Lt. Col. Benjamin F. Little

Walker's Brigade
Brig. Gen. Henry H. Walker

40th Virginia
47th Virginia, Col. Robert M. Mayo
55th Virginia, Col. William S. Christian
22nd Virginia Battalion, Lt. Col Edward P. Tayloe

Archer's Brigade
Brig. Gen. James J. Archer

13th Alabama, Col. Birkett D. Fry
1st Tennessee (Provisional Army),
Maj. Felix G. Buchanan
7th Tennessee, Lt. Col. Samuel G. Shepard
14th Tennessee, Col. William McComb

Wilcox's Division
Maj. Gen. Cadmus M. Wilcox

Lane's Brigade
Brig. Gen. James H. Lane

7th North Carolina, Lt. Col. William Lee Davidson,
Capt. James G. Harris
18th North Carolina, Col. John D. Barry
28th North Carolina, Lt. Col. William H. A. Speer
33rd North Carolina, Lt. Col. Robert V. Cowan
37th North Carolina, Col. William M. Barbour

Scales' Brigade
Brig. Gen. Alfred M. Scales

13th North Carolina, Col. Joseph H. Hyman
16th North Carolina, Col. William A. Stowe
22nd North Carolina, Col. Thomas S. Galloway, Jr.
34th North Carolina, Col. William L. J. Lowrance
38th North Carolina, Lt. Col. John Ashford

McGowan's Brigade
Brig. Gen. Samuel McGowan

1st South Carolina (Provisional Army),
Lt. Col. Washington P. Shooter
12th South Carolina, Col. John L. Miller
13th South Carolina, Col. Benjamin T. Brockman
14th South Carolina, Col. Joseph N. Brown
1st South Carolina (Orr's Rifles),
Lt. Col. George McD. Miller

Thomas' Brigade
Brig. Gen. Edward L. Thomas

14th Georgia, Col. Robert W. Folsom,
Maj. Washington L. Goldsmith
35th Georgia, Col. Bolling H. Holt
45th Georgia
49th Georgia, Lt. Col. John T. Jordan

Artillery
Col. R. Lindsay Walker

Poague's Battalion
Lt. Col. William T. Poague

Madison Light Artillery (Mississippi),
Capt. Thomas J. Richards
Co. A., 12th Virginia Artillery,
Capt. Addison W. Utterback
1st North Carolina Artillery,
Capt. Arthur B. Williams
Albemarle Everett (Virginia), James W. Wyatt

Pegram's Battalion
Lt. Col. William J. Pegram

Letcher Artillery (Virginia), Capt. Thomas A. Brander
Purcell Artillery (Virginia), Capt. George M. Cayce
Crenshaw Artillery (Virginia), Capt. Thomas Ellett
Fredericksburg Artillery (Virginia),
Capt. Edward A. Marye
Pee Dee Artillery (South Carolina),
Capt. William E. Zimmerman

McIntosh's Battalion
Lt. Col. David G. McIntosh

Johnson's/Clutter's (Virginia) Battery,
Capt. Valentine J. Clutter
2nd Rockbridge Artillery (Virginia),
Capt. William K. Donald
Hardaway Artillery (Alabama),
Capt. William B. Hurt
Danville (Virginia) Battery, Lt. Berryman Z. Price

11th Sumter (Georgia) Battalion
Lt. Col. Allen S. Cutts

Company A, Capt. Hugh M. Ross
Company B, George M. Patterson
Company E (C), Capt. John T. Wingfield

Richardson's Battalion
Lt. Col. Charles Richardson

Norfolk Light Artillery Blues (Virginia),
Capt. Charles R. Grandy
Donaldsonville Artillery (Louisiana),
Capt. R. Prosper Landry
Huger Artillery (Virginia), Capt. Joseph D. Moore
Lewis Artillery (Virginia), Capt. Nathan Penick

Cavalry Corps
Maj. Gen. James E. B. Stuart

Hampton's Division
Maj. Gen. Wade Hampton

Young's Brigade
Brig. Gen., Pierce M. B. Young

7th Georgia, Col. Lt. Col. Joseph L. McAllister
Cobb's (Georgia) Legion, Col. Gilbert J. Wright
Phillips (Georgia) Legion, Capt. Hugh Buchanan
20th Georgia Battalion, Lt. Col. John M. Millen
Jeff. Davis (Mississippi) Legion,
Col. J. Frederick Waring

Rosser's Brigade
Brig. Gen. Thomas L. Rosser

7th Virginia, Col. Richard H. Dulany
11th Virginia, Col. Oliver R. Funsten
12th Virginia, Lt. Col. Thomas B. Massie
35th Virginia Battalion, Lt. Col. Elijah White

Butler's Brigade
Brig. Gen. Matthew C. Butler
1st South Carolina, Col. John L. Black
2nd South Carolina, Col. Thomas J. Lipscomb
4th South Carolina, Col. B. Huger Rutledge
5th South Carolina, Col. John Dunovant
6th South Carolina, Col. Hugh K. Aiken

Fitzhugh Lee's Division
Maj. Gen. Fitzhugh Lee

Lomax's Brigade
Brig. Gen. Lundsford L. Lomax

5th Virginia, Col. Henry C. Pate
6th Virginia, Col. John S. Green
15th Virginia, Col. Charles R. Collins

Wickham's Brigade
Brig. Gen. Williams C. Wickham

1st Virginia, Lt. Col. William A. Morgan
2nd Virginia, Col. Thomas T. Munford
3rd Virginia, Col. Thomas H. Owen
4th Virginia, Col. William H. F. Payne

William H. F. Lee's Division
Maj. Gen. William H. F. Lee

Chambliss's Brigade
Brig. Gen. John R. Chambliss, Jr.

9th Virginia, Col. Richard L. T. Beale
10th Virginia, Col. J. Lucius Davis
13th Virginia, Col. Jefferson C. Phillips

Gordon's Brigade
Brig. Gen. James B. Gordon

1st North Carolina, Col. William H. Cheek
2nd North Carolina, Col. Clinton M. Andrews
3rd North Carolina, Col. John A. Baker
4th North Carolina, Col. Dennis D. Ferebee
5th North Carolina, Col. Stephen B. Evans

Horse Artillery
Maj. R. Preston Chew

Breathed's Battalion
Maj. James Breathed

Washington Artillery (South Carolina),
Capt. James F. Hart
1st Stuart Horse Artillery (Virginia),
Capt. Philip Preston Johnston
McGregor's Battery (Virginia),
Capt. William M. McGregor
Lynchburg Beauregards Artillery (Virginia),
Capt. John J. Shoemaker
Ashby Artillery (Virginia), Capt. James W. Thomson

Endnotes

Map Set 1: Preparing for a New Kind of War

1. *United States War Department, The War of the Rebellion: A Compilation of the Official Records of the Union and Confederate Armies*, 128 vols. (Washington: U. S. Government Printing Office, 1880-1901), Series 1, vol. 33, 1,114, 1,285. Hereafter cited as *OR*. All references are to Series 1 unless otherwise noted. Clifford Dowdey and Louis H. Manarin, *The Wartime Papers of R. E. Lee* (New York: Bramhall House, 1961), 672; Joseph T. Glatthaar, *General Lee's Army: From Victory to Collapse* (New York: Free Press, 2008), 355; Francis G. Ruffin to Maj. A. M. Allen, March 9, 1864, Francis Ruffin Letterbook, Francis G. Ruffin Papers, Virginia Historical Society.

2. W. R. Montgomery to Aunt Frank, January 19, 1864. William R. Montgomery Papers, Fredericksburg National Military Park (hereafter, FNMP); Glatthaar, *General Lee's Army: From Victory to Collapse*, 355.

3. George Washington Hall Diary, March 27-29, 1864 entries, George Washington Hall Papers, Library of Congress; James Stanton to Brig. Gen. James Gordon, April 28, 1864, James B. Gordon Papers, North Carolina Division of Archives and History.

4. Glatthaar, *General Lee's Army: From Victory to Collapse*, 357-58.

5. Gary W. Gallagher, *Lee and His Generals in War and Memory* (Baton Rouge, LA: Louisiana State University Press: 1998), 80; Dowdey and Manarin, *The Wartime Papers of R. E. Lee*, 589-90.

6. Andrew A. Humphreys, *The Virginia Campaign, 1864 and 1865* (New York: Da Capo Press, 1995), 2.

7. John J. Hennessy, "I Dread the Spring: The Army of the Potomac Prepares for the Overland Campaign," in Gary W. Gallagher, ed., *The Wilderness Campaign* (Chapel Hill, NC: University of North Carolina Press, 1997), 66; George R. Agassiz, ed., *Meade's Headquarters, 1863-1865; Letters of Colonel Theodore Lyman from the Wilderness to Appomattox* (Boston: The Atlantic Monthly Press, 1922), 58-59, 61. A surgeon who prepared for the attack later wrote, "all along the heights could be seen battery upon battery . . . ready to belch their iron . . . into the stiffened freezing flesh of the best blood of America. As I looked out . . . my heart died within me." Meade was under intense pressure from Washington to end 1863 with a victory. James M. Grenier, Janet L. Coryell, and James R. Smither, eds., *A Surgeon's Civil War: The Letters and Diary of Daniel M. Holt, MD.* (Kent, OH: Kent State University Press, 1994), 160. The attack was planned by Maj. Gen. Gouverneur Warren. However, Warren called off the attack at the last minute when he discovered the strength of the Confederate right flank and the unacceptable losses that would be sustained had he gone forward with the plan. This experience may have influenced his behavior during the earlier stages of the Wilderness on May 5, 1864.

8. Bradley M.Gottfried, *Kearny's Own: The History of the First New Jersey Brigade in the Civil War* (New Brunswick, NJ: Rutgers University Press, 2005), 141-42; Hennessy, "I Dread the Spring," 70, 80.

9. Gottfried, *Kearny's Own*, 152.

10. Humphreys, *The Virginia Campaign, 1864 and 1865*, 1; Hennessy, "I Dread the Spring," 80-81.

11. Hennessy, "I Dread the Spring," 82-93. What to do with Burnside posed a dilemma for Grant, for Burnside led the Army of the Potomac during the failed Fredericksburg campaign in December 1862. Burnside's seniority over Meade added to the problem. Protocol demanded Burnside be put in charge of the army (over Meade), but Grant knew the men would never support that and he was not in favor of it. The only viable solution was to keep Burnside and his IX Corps separate from the Army of the Potomac, reporting not to Meade but directly to Grant. This solution, as will be discussed later, created its own set of problems. Gordon C. Rhea, *The Battle of the Wilderness, May 5-6* (Baton Rouge, LA: Louisiana State University Press, 1994), 48.

12. Humphreys, *The Virginia Campaign, 1864 and 1865*, 3; Charles S. Wainwright, *A Diary of Battle: The Personal Journals of Colonel Charles S. Wainwright, 1861-1865*, Allan Nevins, ed. (New York: Harcourt, Brace, and World, 1962), 335. Meade made the recommendation to the War Department on March 4, 1864.

13. *OR* 33, 725; Hennessy, "I Dread the Spring," 84. Sykes went west to command the Department of Kansas for the remainder of the war. He served with the Regular Army in a variety of posts until his death in 1880. Ezra J. Warner, *Generals in Blue: Lives of the Union Commanders* (Baton Rouge, LA: Louisiana State University Press, 1964), 493.

14. Robert Garth Scott, *Into the Wilderness with the Army of the Potomac* (Bloomington, IN: Indiana University Press, 1988), 5; Humphreys, *The Virginia Campaign, 1864 and 1865*, 5.

15. Horace Porter, *Campaigning with Grant* (Bloomington, IN: Indiana University Press, 1961), 46-47.

16. Ulysses S. Grant, *The Personal Memoirs of U. S. Grant*, 2 vols. (New York: Charles L. Webster & Company, 1886), vol. 2, 116-17; George Meade, *The Life and Letters of George Gordon Meade, Major General, United States Army*, 2 vols. (New York: New York, Charles Scribner's Sons, 1913), vol. 2, 154; Rhea, *The Battle of the Wilderness*, 43-44; Hennessy, "I Dread the Spring," 93.

17. Wainwright, *A Diary of Battle*, 338.

18. *OR* 33, 1036; Alfred C. Young, *Lee's Army During the Overland Campaign: A Numerical Study* (Baton Rouge, LA: Louisiana State University Press, 2013), 2, 7-8.

19. Rhea, *The Battle of the Wilderness*, 30.

20. *OR* 36, pt. 1, 12; Rhea, *The Battle of the Wilderness*, 46; Brooks D. Simpson, "Great Expectations: Ulysses S. Grant, The Northern Press, and the Opening of the Wilderness Campaign," in Gary W. Gallagher, ed., *The Wilderness Campaign* (Chapel Hill, NC: University of North Carolina Press, 1997), 6-7.

21. Grant, *Personal Memoirs*, vol. 2, 133; Gordon C. Rhea, "Union Cavalry in the Wilderness: The Education of Philip H. Sheridan and James H. Wilson." in Gary W. Gallagher, ed., *The Wilderness Campaign*, 107-8. In his meeting with Lincoln and Halleck, Grant stated that little had been accomplished by the cavalry, and he believed it had the potential to well under a more "thorough" leader. Halleck asked, "How would Sheridan do?" to which Grant replied, "The very man I want."

22. *Glatthaar, General Lee's Army: From Victory to Collapse*, 363; Dowdey and Manarin, *The Wartime Papers of R. E. Lee*, 688. These detached brigades included Brig. Gen. Robert Hoke's and Brig. Gen. Richard Johnston's.

23. Heros von Borcke, *Memoirs of the Confederate War for Independence* (Philadelphia: Lippincott, 1867), 22-23.

24. Randolph H. McKim, *A Soldier's Recollections* (New York: Longmans, Green, 1910), 134.

25. Gallagher, *Lee and His Generals in War and Memory*, 80-83. A. P. Hill's prolonged periods of sickness were long thought to be psychological, brought about by stressful situations. James I. Robertson, however, in *General A. P. Hill: The Story of a Confederate Warrior* (New York: Random House, 1987), 11, offered evidence that Hill's recurring bouts of illness were the result of the advanced stages of venereal disease.

26. Dowdey and Manarin, *The Wartime Papers of R. E. Lee*, 684-85; Gallagher, *Lee and His Generals in War and Memory*, 78-80.

27. Rhea, *The Battle of the Wilderness*, 22.

28. Edward Porter Alexander, *Military Memoirs of a Confederate: A Critical Narrative* (New York: C. Scribner's Sons, 1907), 497; Rhea, *The Battle of the Wilderness*, 22.

Map Set 2: The Armies Approach the Wilderness

1. Grant, *Personal Memoirs*, vol. 2, 118.

2. *OR* 33, 828.

3. Humphreys, *The Virginia Campaign, 1864 and 1865*, 9-12.

4. Rhea, *The Battle of the Wilderness*, 52; Humphreys, *The Virginia Campaign, 1864 and 1865*, 11.

5. Grant, *Personal Memoirs*, vol. 2, 135, 137.

6. *OR* 36, pt. 2, 331-34; Humphreys, *The Virginia Campaign, 1864 and 1865*, 421-23. The canvas bridges were removed on the evening of May 4, once the three infantry corps had crossed; the wooden bridges were left for the wagons and the IX Corps to use. Scott. *Into the Wilderness with the Army of the Potomac*, 23-24.

7. *OR* 36, pt. 2, 355.

8. *OR* 36, pt. 2, 337.

9. C. F. Atkinson, *Grant's Campaigns of 1864 and 1865: The Wilderness and Cold Harbor* (London: H. Rees, Ltd., 1908), 103; Humphreys, *The Virginia Campaign, 1864 and 1865*, 11-13; Rhea, *The Battle of the Wilderness*, 54-58.

10. Francis Walker, *History of the Second Army Corps in the Army of the Potomac* (New York: Charles Scribner's Sons, 1887), 408; *OR* 36, pt. 1, 350.

11. *OR* 36, pt. 2, 361-62; Thomas W. Hyde, *Following the Greek Cross; or, Memories of the Sixth Army Corps* (Boston: Houghton, Mifflin and Company, 1894), 182.

12. Rhea, *The Battle of the Wilderness*, 64-65; *OR* 36, pt. 1, 306.

13. Agassiz, *Meade's Headquarters*, 87; Morris Schaff, *The Battle of the Wilderness* (Houghton Mifflin Company, 1910), 85; Alanson A. Haines, *History of the Fifteenth Regiment New Jersey Volunteers* (New York: Jenkins & Thomas, Printers, 1883), 140-41.

14. Charles A. Page, *Letters of a War Correspondent* (Boston, L. C. Page and Company, 1899), 48; Ulysses S. Grant, "Preparing for the Campaigns of 1864," in Robert U. Johnson and Clarence C. Buel, eds., *Battles and Leaders of the Civil War* (New York: The Century Company, 1887), vol. 4, 97. Articles in this series are hereafter noted by author, title, and series.

15. The "horse collar" was composed of half of a pup tent (another soldier carried the other half) rolled tightly and covered with a gum blanket on the outside and tied with twine on both ends. Inside was extra clothing along with rations, etc. Carried over the shoulder, it resembled a horse collar. Scott, *Into the Wilderness with the Army of the Potomac*, 17.

16. Frank Wilkeson, *Recollections of a Private Soldier in the Army of the Potomac* (New York: G.P. Putnam's Sons, 1887), 43.

17. Porter, *Campaigning with Grant*, 44; OR 36, pt. 2, 371-72.

18. Rhea, *The Battle of the Wilderness*, 71; OR 36, pt. 2, 380.

19. OR 36, pt. 1, 318; 36, pt. 2, 378; Rhea, *The Battle of the Wilderness*, 74-75.

20. Edwin B. Houghton, *The Campaigns of the Seventeenth Maine* (Portland, ME: Portland, Short & Loring, 1866), 164-65; Charles H. Weygant, *History of the One Hundred and Twenty-Fourth Regiment, N.Y.S.V.* (Newburgh, NY: Journal Printing House, 1877), 271-72.

21. B. L. Wynn, "Lee Watched Grant at Locust Grove," *Confederate Veteran*, XXI (1913), 68. The lookouts on Clark's Mountain had seen ominous clouds of dust across the river on the afternoon of May 3. While probably only cavalry moving closer to the river, it was a telltale sign that Grant's spring offensive was about to begin. Scott, *Into the Wilderness with the Army of the Potomac*, 25.

22. James Longstreet, *From Manassas to Appomattox: Memoirs of the Civil War in America* (Indiana University Press, 1960), 556-57; OR 36, pt. 1, 1054; Rhea, *The Battle of the Wilderness*, 82-85.

23. William Dame, *From the Rapidan to Richmond and the Spottsylvania Campaign* (Baltimore: Green-Lucas Company, 1920), 71-72; Rhea, *The Battle of the Wilderness*, 87.

24. Rhea, *The Battle of the Wilderness*, 85-86; OR 36, pt. 1, 1,036-38, 1,070; Jubal A. Early, *Lieutenant-General Jubal A. Early, C.S.A.: Autobiographical Sketch and Narrative of the War Between the States* (Philadelphia: J. B. Lippincott Company, 1912), 344-45; Longstreet, *From Manassas to Appomattox*, 557. George Pickett's Division (Longstreet's Corps) was still at Petersburg, and Robert Johnston's Brigade (Rodes' Division) was at Hanover Junction. The latter was on the march but would not arrive until May 6. Scott, *Into the Wilderness with the Army of the Potomac*, 27.

25. OR 36, pt. 2, 948.

26. Walker, *History of the Second Army Corps*, 409; Scott, *Into the Wilderness with the Army of the Potomac*, 21.

Map Set 3: May 5: Initial Contact

1. Scott, *Into the Wilderness with the Army of the Potomac*, 31; Earl J. Hess, *Trench Warfare Under Grant and Lee: Field Fortifications in the Overland Campaign* (Chapel Hill, NC: University of North Carolina Press, 2007), 20; www.nps.gov/frsp/photos multimedia/tavern.htm.

2. William Swan, "The Battle of the Wilderness," in *Papers of the Military Historical Society of Massachusetts* (Boston: The Military Historical Society of Massachusetts, 1905), vol. 4, 117-63; OR 36, pt. 1, 580; Gordon C. Rhea, "Union Cavalry in the Wilderness: The Education of Philip H. Sheridan and James H. Wilson," in Gary W. Gallagher, ed., *The Wilderness Campaign*, 116; Tom Huntington, *Searching for George Gordon Meade: The Forgotten Victor of Gettysburg* (Mechanicsburg, PA: Stackpole Books, 2013), 253.

3. Armistead L. Long, *Memoirs of Robert E. Lee: His Military and Personal History* (New York: J. M. Stoddardt & Company, 1886), 327.

4. OR 36, pt. 2, 371, 375, 389; Rhea, *The Battle of the Wilderness*, 91-92; Rhea, "Union Cavalry in the Wilderness," 117.

5. OR 36, pt. 1, 1070, 1,090.

6. Robert Stiles, *Four Years Under Marse Robert* (New York: Neale, 1910), 245.

7. OR 36, pt. 1, 1070; Campbell Brown, *Campbell Brown's Civil War: With Ewell and the Army of Northern Virginia* (Baton Rouge, LA: Louisiana State University Press, 2001), 247. General Ewell claimed in his report that it was about 8:00 a.m. when he sent Brown to find General Lee. Brown, however, recorded on July 1, 1864, that Ewell had dispatched him at about 6:00 a.m., which is probably more accurate because Brown was a meticulous and reliable observer writing less than two months after the event. OR 36, pt. 1, 1,070.

8. John H. Worsham, *One of Jackson's Foot Cavalry: His Experience and What He Saw During the War 1861-1865* (New York: Neale Publishing Company, 1912), 200.

9. Humphreys, *The Virginia Campaign, 1864 and 1865*, 423-24.

10. Scott, *Into the Wilderness with the Army of the Potomac*, 32.

11. OR 36, pt. 2, 371; Scott, *Into the Wilderness with the Army of the Potomac*, 32-33.

12. McHenry Howard, *Recollections of a Maryland Confederate Soldier and Staff Officer Under Johnston, Jackson and Lee* (Baltimore, MD: Williams &

Wilkins Company, 1914), 270-71; Henry W. Thomas, *History of the Doles-Cook Brigade, Army of Northern Virginia, C.S.A.* (Atlanta: The Franklin Printing and Publishing Company, 1903), 76; Rhea, *The Battle of the Wilderness*, 126-27; Gregg S. Clemmer, *Old Alleghany: The Life and Wars of General Ed Johnson* (Hearthside Publishing Company, 2004), 535. John M. Jones' Brigade led the division during the march, accompanied by Milledge's Battery. Kirkpatrick's and Massie's batteries of Nelson's Battalion also accompanied Ed Johnson's Division. Cadmus M. Wilcox, "Lee and Grant in the Wilderness," *Annals of the War Written by Leading Participants North and South, Alexander K. McClure, ed.* (Philadelphia: The Times Publishing Company, 1879), 489; Edward Steere, *The Wilderness Campaign* (Harrisburg, PA: The Stackpole Publishing Company, 1960), 138. Steere's monograph is one of the finest written on the battle, and a model battle study of its day and in many respects remains so. George Steuart was shy one regiment (the 37th Virginia), which was left behind to picket the Rapidan River. It missed the opening fight with Griffin's division, but arrived in time to participate in the fight with Horatio Wright's division. Thomas M. Rankin, *37th Virginia Infantry* (Lynchburg, VA: H. E. Howard, Inc., 1987), 79.

13. Rhea, *The Battle of the Wilderness*, 95-98; Swan, "The Battle of the Wilderness," 127.

14. *OR* 36, pt. 1, 580; *OR* 36, pt. 2, 413.

15. *OR* 36, pt. 2, 413, 416.

16. Long, *Memoirs of Robert E. Lee*, 327; Charles S. Venable, "General Lee in the Wilderness Campaign," in *Battles and Leaders of the Civil War*, vol. 4, 240-41.

17. Venable, "General Lee in the Wilderness Campaign," 240-41; William L. Royall, *Some Reminiscences* (New York: The Neale Publishing Company, 1909), 28.

18. Brown, *Campbell Brown's Civil War*, 247; *OR* 36, pt. 1, 124. A young soldier wrote to his local newspaper, "It was the first time that our boys had enjoyed the advantage of fortifications, and they did everlastingly pile up the Yankees every time they charged our works." *Macon Daily Telegraph*, May 26, 1864.

19. Joseph Hayes Journal, May 5, 1864, Joshua Chamberlain Collection, Library of Congress; *OR* 36, pt. 1, 575, 589; Rhea, *The Battle of the Wilderness*, 101-2.

20. *OR* 36, pt. 2, 876, 885-86; Louis N. Boudrye, *Historic Records of the Fifth New York Cavalry, First Ira Harris Guard* (Albany, NY: J. Munsell, 1865), 122; George W. Toms, "The 5th N. Y. Cav. At the Wilderness," *National Tribune*, July 8, 1886; William B. Cary, "The Wilderness Fight," *National Tribune*, February 1, 1912. Rhea, "Union Cavalry in the Wilderness," 117-18; Walter Clark, *Histories of the Several Regiments and Battalions from North Carolina in the Great War 1861-'65*, 5 vols. (Wilmington, NC: Broadfoot Publishing Company, 1996), vol. 3, 94. Hereafter, *N.C. Regiments*; Louis H. Manarin, *North Carolina Troops, 1861-1865: A Roster*, 15 vols. (Raleigh, NC: State Department of Archives and History, 1966), vol. 3, 461; I. J. Lichtenberg, "The Wilderness: How the 5th N.Y. Cav. Had a hand in Opening the Fight," *National Tribune*, September 30, 1886. Cary's men probably encountered the 47th North Carolina.

21. William N. McDonald, *A History of the Laurel Brigade, Originally the Ashby Cavalry of the Army of Northern Virginia* (Baltimore: The Johns Hopkins University Press, 2002), 225.

22. Humphreys, *The Virginia Campaign, 1864 and 1865*, 23-24; *OR* 36, pt. 1, 189; *OR* 36, pt. 2, 404, 406; Steere, *The Wilderness Campaign*, 104.

23. *OR* 36, pt. 2, 416-18; Scott, *Into the Wilderness with the Army of the Potomac*, 37; Rhea, *The Battle of the Wilderness*, 104-5. Crawford's orders were: "The movement toward Parker's Store is suspended. You will halt, face toward Mine Run, and connect with General Wadsworth on your right." *OR* 36, pt. 2, 417.

24. John J. Pullen, *The Twentieth Maine: A Volunteer Regiment in the Civil War* (Philadelphia: J. B. Lippincott Company, 1957), 182; Hess, *Trench Warfare Under Grant and Lee*, 22.

25. Schaff, *The Battle of the Wilderness*, 129-30; Rhea, *The Battle of the Wilderness*, 104-5.

26. *OR* 36, pt. 2, 403.

27. Steere, *The Wilderness Campaign*, 104, 107-8.

28. D. H. Robbins, "Thrice Distinguished: Who Opened the Fight in the Wilderness," *National Tribune*, May 13, 1909; Clark, *N.C. Regiments*, vol. 3, 27; Steere, *The Wilderness Campaign*, 114-15. The deployment of Kirkland's regiments is unclear. According to one study, they were deployed from left to right as follows: 11th North Carolina-47th North Carolina-44th North Carolina-26th North Carolina-52nd North Carolina. John Michael Priest, *Nowhere to Run: The Wilderness, May 4th and 5th, 1864* (Shippensburg, PA: White Mane Publishing Company, 1995), 41.

29. *OR* 36, pt. 1, 886; pt. 2, 885; Robbins, "Thrice Distinquished,"; Josiah R. Sypher, *History of the Pennsylvania Reserve Corps: A Complete Record of the Organization, and of the Different Companies, Regiments, and Brigades Containing Descriptions of Expeditions* (Lancaster, PA: Elias Barr & Co.), 1865), 510;

Howard Thomson and William Rauch, *History of the "Bucktails," Kane Rifle Regiment of the Pennsylvania Reserve Corps* (Philadelphia: Electric Printing Company, 1906), 292.

30. Rhea, "Union Cavalry in the Wilderness," 119.

31. OR 36, pt. 1, 896-97; Dennis E. Frye, *12th Virginia Cavalry* (Lynchburg, VA: H. E. Howard, Inc., 1988), 64.

32. James H. Wilson, *Under the Old Flag: Recollections of Military Operations in the War for the Union, The Spanish War, and the Boxer Rebellion*, 2 vols. (New York: Appleton and Company, 1912), vol. 1, 381; McDonald, *A History of the Laurel Brigade*, 225-26.

33. OR 36, pt. 1, 877, 897, 903; Steere, *The Wilderness Campaign*, 89, 92; Rhea, *The Battle of the Wilderness*, 113.

34. OR 36, pt. 2, 418; Sypher, *History of the Pennsylvania Reserve Corps*, 510; Samuel P. Bates, *History of the Pennsylvania Volunteers: Prepared in Compliance with Acts of the Legislature*, 5 vols. (Harrisburg, PA: B. Singerly, State Printer, 1869), vol. 1, 553; Steere, *The Wilderness Campaign*, 149. Crawford's regimental deployments, as described by Sypher, did not respect the brigade organization as the two lines were composed of regiments from both brigades.

35. Rhea, *The Battle of the Wilderness*, 139-40.

36. OR 36, pt. 2, 423-24; Steere, *The Wilderness Campaign*, 120-22.

37. Porter, *Campaigning with Grant*, 50; Rhea, *The Battle of the Wilderness*, 132-34.

38. OR 36, pt. 1, 676; OR 36, pt. 2, 407, 420; Agassiz, *Meade's Headquarters*, 91; Steere, *The Wilderness Campaign*, 89. Getty once bragged, "If I was ordered to march my division across the Atlantic Ocean, I'd do it. At least, I would march them up to their necks in the sea, and then withdraw and report that it was impractical to carry out the order." Hazard Stevens, "The Sixth Corps in the Wilderness," in *Papers of the Military Historical Society of Massachusetts*, 14 vols. (Boston: Military Historical Society of Massachusetts (1881-1918), vol. 4, 180.

39. Stevens, "The Sixth Corps in the Wilderness," vol. 4, 189-90.

40. OR 36, pt. 1, 676. General Ewell apparently observed Getty's division crossing the turnpike behind Warren's men as it moved south and reported the movement to General Lee. Steere, *The Wilderness Campaign*, 144.

41. Theodore Gerrish, *Army Life: A Private's Reminiscences of the Civil War* (Portland, ME: Hoyt, Fogg, and Donham, 1882), 159; Mary Genevie

Green Brainard, *Campaigns of the One Hundred and Forty-Sixth Regiment, New York State Volunteers* (New York: G. P. Putnam's Sons, 1915), 187.

42. Rhea, *The Battle of the Wilderness*, 125, 127.

Map Set 4: The Fight for Saunders Field

1. OR 36, pt. 1, 676; Stevens, "The Sixth Corps in the Wilderness," vol. 4, 189-90; Rhea, *The Battle of the Wilderness*, 135-36.

2. Rhea, *The Battle of the Wilderness*, 137-41; Washington Roebling Report, Gouverneur Warren Collection, New York State Archives.

3. Steere, *The Wilderness Campaign*, 132-33; Rhea, *The Battle of the Wilderness*, 138-41.

4. Swan, "The Battle of the Wilderness," 129-30.

5. Monroe Cockrell, ed. *Gunner with Stonewall: Reminiscences of William Thomas Poague, Lieutenant, Captain, and Lieutenant Colonel of Artillery, Army of Northern Virginia, C.S.A.* (Jackson, TN: McCowat-Mercer Press, 1857), 87-88. The Union army experienced similar difficulties posting artillery pieces.

6. Charles Seiser, ed., "August Seiser's Civil War Diary," in Rochester Historical Society Publication, XXII, 189; Schaff, *The Battle of the Wilderness*, 151-52.

7. Swan, "The Battle of the Wilderness," 130; Orrin Cook Memoirs, FNMP; *Rochester Democrat and American*, May 20, 1864.

8. OR 36, pt. 2, 41920; Swan, "The Battle of the Wilderness," 130; Steere, *The Wilderness Campaign*, 133-35.

9. Rhea, *The Battle of the Wilderness*, 143.

10. OR 36, pt. 1, 227, 555, 559, 567, 575, 580, 589; Charles Haynes Diary, May 5, 1864, FNMP; Steere, *The Wilderness Campaign*, 153; Amos M. Judson, *History of the Eighty-Third Regiment of Pennsylvania Volunteers* (Alexandria, VA: Stonewall House, 1985), 94; Brainard, *Campaigns of the One Hundred and Forty-Sixth Regiment, New York State Volunteers,* 187; Brian A. Bennett, *Sons of Old Monroe: A Regimental History of Patrick O'Rorke's 140th New York Volunteer Infantry* (Dayton, OH: The Press of Morningside Bookshop, 1999), 394.

11. OR 36, pt. 1, 1,070; Hess, *Trench Warfare Under Grant and Lee*, 23; Porter Farley, "Reminiscences of the 140th New York Volunteer Infantry," in Rochester Historical Society Publication, XXII (1944), 239; Eugene Arus Nash, *A History of the Forty-Fourth Regiment, New York Volunteer Infantry* (Chicago: R. R. Donnelley & Sons, Company, 1911), 184; Timothy J. Reese, *Sykes' Regular Infantry Division, 1861-1864: A History*

of Regular United States Infantry Operations in the Civil War's Eastern Theater (Jefferson, NC: McFarland Press, 1990), 301. Thomas Wood of the 3rd North Carolina recalled that although there were "not more than two picks to a regiment," they improvised with hollowed-out canteens and bayonets. Thomas Wood Memoir, FNMP.

12. Holman S. Melcher, *"An Experience in the Battle of the Wilderness," in War Papers Read Before the Commandery of the State of Maine, Military order of the Loyal Legion of the United States* (Portland, ME: The Thurston Print, 1898), vol. 1, 77; Pullen, *The Twentieth Maine*, 185; Farley, "Reminiscences of the 140th New York Volunteer Infantry," 22.

13. Richard L. Armstrong, *25th Virginia Infantry* (H. E. Howard, Inc., 1990), 75; John D. Chapla, *18th Virginia Infantry* (Lynchburg, VA: H. E. Howard, Inc., 1989), 70; *OR 36*, pt. 1, 580. The 25th Virginia's losses totalled six dead, two wounded, and 86 prisoners. Armstrong, 25th Virginia Infantry, 75. The alignment of Jones' Brigade, like so many in the Wilderness, is subject to interpretation or ample guesswork, but it appears as though the 21st Virginia held the left and the 50th Virginia held the right. Chapla, the 48thVirginia's historian, argues the 48th regiment was in place second from the right, while Frank O'Reilly, *Battle of the Wilderness Map Set* (Fort Washington, PA: Eastern National, 2003), Map 1, places it on the far right of Jones' front. I have chosen to follow Chapla's conclusion, but I have used the Wilderness map set to position the remaining regiments.

14. Melcher, "An Experience in the Battle of the Wilderness," vol. 1, 77.

15. Farley, "Reminiscences of the 140th New York Volunteer Infantry," 23; Rhea, *The Battle of the Wilderness*, 145, 147; William H. Powell, *The Fifth Army Corps* (New York: G. P. Putnam's Sons, 1896), 608-9; Bennett, *Sons of Old Monroe*, 392, 395; James Colledge, "The Wilderness: The Place Where the First Battle of the Campaign was Fought," *National Tribune*, April 30, 1891. The historian of the V Corps described Ayres' charge across Saunders Field: "unimpeded by under- growth . . . rushed impetuously across the opening, undaunted by a fire that thinned its ranks, and never slackened its speed until the wood were gained, where they expected to close with the bayonet." Powell, *The Fifth Army Corps*, 608. Sergeant Charles Bowen of the 12th U.S. Regulars noted in his diary that his brigade was "sent into battle through a perfect thicket of stunted pines, we got mixed up together." Charles Thomas Bowen Letters, September 20, 1861-April 19, 1865, FNMP.

16. S. D. Thurston, "Report of the Conduct of General George H. Steuart's Brigade from the 5th to the 12th of May, 1864, inclusive," *Southern Historical Society Papers*, vol. 14 (1886), 148; Bennett, *Sons of Old Monroe*, 393. According to Thomas Wood of the 3rd North Carolina, Steuart's Brigade was not on the edge of Saunders Field at this time. Wood was standing near General Steuart when Steuart gave the command, "Forward guide center." Wood recalled, "our front was a wilderness of small old-field pine trees, with branches near the ground, that were much lower than the men's heads. We received a heavy volley before we saw the enemy, and before a volley was returned." Kneeling down, they could see the legs of the enemy. "It was a killing fire," he recalled. Wood Memoir.

17. August Selser Diary, FNMP; Bennett, *Sons of Old Monroe*, 396.

18. Howard, *Recollections of a Maryland Confederate Soldier*, 271; Greg Mertz, personal communication. The fact that Captain Howard raised the issue to division commander Johnson (who failed to notice that his men were not properly aligned to return an effective fire), and then did not communicate the same issue to his immediate superior, General Steuart (who likewise seems not to have noticed the improper alignment) raises a larger issue about command competency. Another staff officer in this corps, a Prussian captain named Oscar Hinrichs, maintained one of the most detailed and opinionated accounts of the war only recently published as *Stonewall's Prussian Mapmaker: The Journals of Captain Oscar Hinrichs, edited and annotated by Richard Brady Williams* (Chapel Hill, NC: University of North Carolina Press, 2014). The Prussian, who worked closely with both Johnson and Steuart, did not hold either man in high esteem. During the fall campaigns of 1863, Hinrichs observed that Steuart "had a very poor [status and reputation]" within the army. He did not handle his brigade well at Gettysburg, and went on to lose complete control of his brigade almost immediately at Payne's Farm on November 27, 1863, during the Mine Run Campaign. Ed Johnson recklessly attacked and immediately lost control of his entire division at Payne's Farm the moment it stepped off. When he was captured on May 12, 1864, in the Mule Shoe at Spotsylvania, Hinrichs told his journal, "the Yankees may keep [him]." Williams, *Stonewall's Prussian Mapmaker*, xii, 95.

19. *OR 36*, pt. 1, 640; *Rochester Democrat and American*, July 23, 1864.

20. Brainard, *Campaigns of the One Hundred and Forty-Sixth Regiment, New York State Volunteers*, 190-91; Raymond W. Smith, ed. *Out of the*

Wilderness: The Civil War Memoir of Cpl. Norton C. Shepard, 146th New York Volunteer Infantry (Hamilton, NY: Edmonston Publishing, Inc., 1998), 5.

21. William Snakenberg, "Memoirs of W. P. Snakenberg," 31-32, FNMP; Reese, *Sykes' Regular Infantry Division*, 306.; George Markle Diary, Gettysburg National Military Park. According to Sergeant Bowen of the 12th U.S. Infantry, "a strong force came in front & thus we were exposed to a terrific cross fire which mowed down men by the scores. No troops could stand this and our left broke & ran. This of course made bad worse & the entire line broke." Bowen Letters.

22. Jones' Brigade was the largest in Johnson's Division, fielding almost 1,900 men. Young, *Lee's Army During the Overland Campaign*, 81; Capt. J. W. Williams, "Company D at the Battle of the Wilderness: Pen Sketches of the 'Greensboro Guards,' Co. D of the Fifth Alabama, C.S.A.", *Greensboro Record*, July 2, 1903.

23. Joseph Hayes Journal; John W. Daniel, "My Account, May 5," John W. Daniel Collection, University of Virginia; John R. King, *My Experience in the Confederate Army and in Northern Prisons* (Clarksburg, WV: Stonewall Jackson Chapter of the United Daughters of the Confederacy, 1917), 182; Civil War Letters of Abram Schultz Miller written to his wife, Julia Virginia Miller, 1861-1864, The Handley Library, Winchester, VA; Melissa Delcour, "The Country Loses a Noble Soldier: The Battles of Brigadier General John Marshall Jones," *Civil War Regiments*, vol. 6, no. 4 (1999), 139, offers a detailed investigation into Jones' service in the Wilderness and his death. Some believe Jones was killed when he refused to surrender to some enlisted men. Priest, *Nowhere to Run*, 70. Captain McHenry Howard heard that Jones, "apparently disdaining to fly, was killed while sitting on his horse gazing at the approaching enemy." Howard, *Recollections of a Maryland Confederate Soldier*, 273. To his wife on May 20, 1864, North Carolina staff officer Benjamin Justice observed, "Gen. Jones's Brigade . . . behaved badly in the face of the foe, & Gen. Jones sacrificed his life in the vain effort to rally his men, & rather than survive his disgrace of his command, preferred death." Benjamin Justice Letters, FNMP.

24. OR 36, pt. 1, 1,070; Cullen Andrews Battle, *Third Alabama! The Civil War Memoir of Brigadier General Cullen Andrews Battle, CSA* (Tuscaloosa, AL: The University of Alabama Press, 2000), 105-6; James W. Roberts, "The Wilderness and Spottsylvania, May 4-12, 1864: Narrative of a Private Soldier," *The Quarterly Periodical of the Florida Historical Society*, vol. 8 (October, 1932), 60; J. B. Stamp, "Ten Months Experience in Northern Prisons," *Alabama Historical Quarterly*, vol. 18 (Winter, 1956), 486. Captain J. W. Williams of the 5th Alabama recalled long after the war, "We went forward in a perfect line, and when we reached a point where we could see the Virginia brigade, they were still holding their position. We moved up into Jones' troops, halted, and were ordered to lie down. . . . When I raised by head, and cast my eyes down the line all were gone . . . [and] the Yankees were coming, wild with excitement." Williams, "Company D at the Battle of the Wilderness." Staff officer Benjamin Justice, who had also criticized Jones' men, complained to his wife, "Battle's Brigade (Ala.) have established a disgraceful reputation for running at every encounter with the foe." Justice to wife, May 20, 1864.

25. John J. Hennessy, ed., *Fighting with the Eighteenth Massachusetts: The Civil War Memoir of Thomas H. Mann* (Baton Rouge, LA: LSU Press, 2000), 235-36; Judson, *History of the Eighty-Third Regiment of Pennsylvania Volunteers*, 94; Stamp, "Ten Months Experience in Northern Prisons," 486.

26. Bennett, *Sons of Old Monroe*, 397; Farley, "Reminiscences of the 140th New York Volunteer Infantry," 240.

27. Rhea, *The Battle of the Wilderness*, 150; D. P. Marshall, *History of Company K, 155th Pennsylvania Volunteer Zouaves* (n.p: 1888), 155-56. 191; OR 36, pt. 1, 555, 557.

28. Farley, "Reminiscences of the 140th New York Volunteer Infantry," 28-29; Norman Leader, "The Bloodied Guns of Winslow's Battery," *Virginia Country's Civil War Quarterly*, vol. 6, 16.

29. Joseph Hayes Journal; Judson, *History of the Eighty-Third Regiment of Pennsylvania Volunteers*, 94; Roberts, "The Wilderness and Spottsylvania, May 4-12, 1864," 60; (Philadelphia: J. L. Smith, Map Publisher, 1905), 400; OR 36, pt. 1, 573, 575.

30. Roberts, "The Wilderness and Spottsylvania, May 4-12, 1864," 60; Gerrish, *Army Life*, 163-64, 168-69; Melcher, "An Experience in the Battle of the Wilderness," vol. 1, 79-82. The men were surprised to see the appearance of General Bartlett. One veteran recalled that he was always "distinctly dressed. In the thickest of a fight his men could not mistake him, and the enemy could not complain that they had not in him a shining mark whenever there was an opportunity to make a selection." Survivors' Association, *History of the 118th Pennsylvania Volunteers*, 401.

31. Worsham, *One of Jackson's Foot Cavalry*, 201; Judson, *History of the Eighty-Third Regiment of Pennsylvania Volunteers*, 94.

32. Howard, *Recollections of a Maryland Confederate Soldier*, 272. Carroll Waldron of the 146th New York recorded in his diary that troops were "passing in our rear from right to left. As I supposed our troops but suddenly it dawned upon me that they were rebels and I raised my gun to fire at them, but my Captain who lay at my elbow put my gun down and said don't fire." Waldron was soon captured by the surging Confederates. Carroll Scott Waldron, "The War Memoir of Carroll Scott Waldron," FNMP.

33. Clark, *N.C. Regiments*, vol. I, 150-51, 200-201.

34. Abner R. Small, *The Road to Richmond* (Berkeley, CA: University of California Press, 1957), 132.

35. Daniel G. Macnamara, *The History of the Ninth Regiment Massachusetts Volunteer Infantry* (New York: Fordham University Press, 2000), 372-73. V Corps artillery brigade commander, Col. Charles Wainwright, noted in his report, "The guns were fought to the last, and lost as honorably as guns could be lost." OR 36, pt. 1, 640.

36. Bennett, *Sons of Old Monroe*, 409, 411; Melcher, "An Experience in the Battle of the Wilderness," vol. 1, 79-82.

Map Set 5: Wadsworth's Division Enters the Fight (May 5)

1. Rufus Dawes, *Service with the Sixth Wisconsin Volunteers* (Madison, WI: The State Historical Society of Wisconsin, 1962), 259; Craig L. Dunn, *Iron Men, Iron Will: The Nineteenth Indiana Regiment of the Iron Brigade* (Indianapolis, IN: Guild Press, 1995), 240; Henry B. Harshaw and Richard Lester, "Operations of the 'Iron Brigade' in the Spring Campaign of 1864," Oshkosh Public Museum. An alternate explanation of the deployment is with the first line composed, from left to right, of the 24th Michigan, 19th Indiana, 2nd Wisconsin, and 7th Wisconsin, and a second line with the 6th Wisconsin on the right and 7th Indiana on the left. Lance J. Herdegen, *The Iron Brigade in Civil War and Memory: The Black Hats from Bull Run to Appomattox and Thereafter* (El Dorado Hills, CA: Savas Beatie, LLC, 2012), 480; Orson B. Curtis, *History of the Twenty-Fourth Michigan of the Iron Brigade* (Detroit, MI: Winn & Hammond, 1891), 231. This interpretation was apparently first presented by Orson Curtis in his 24th Michigan book. A careful analysis using two primary sources (Dawes, and Harshaw and Lester) suggests otherwise.

2. Richard E. Matthews, *The 149th Pennsylvania Volunteer Infantry Unit in the Civil War* (Jefferson, NC: McFarland Press, 1994), 134-35; Peter Tomasak, ed., *Avery Harris Civil War Journal* (Luzerne, PA: Luzerne National Bank, 2000), 113; Rhea, *The Battle of the Wilderness*, 162. The brigade's battle report does not indicate regimental deployment. However, Avery Harris's journal and the modern history of the 149th Pennsylvania suggest the brigade was in two lines. This departs from O'Reilly's Map 1 in *Battle of the Wilderness Map Set*.

3. O'Reilly, *Battle of the Wilderness Map Set*, Map 1.

4. Survivors' Association, *History of the 121st Regiment, Pennsylvania Volunteers: "An Account from the Ranks,"* (n.p., n.p.: 1905), 76.

5. Tomasak, *Avery Harris Civil War Journal*, 115; Rhea, *The Battle of the Wilderness*, 157-58.

6. Matthews, *The 149th Pennsylvania*, 135.

7. Schaff, *The Battle of the Wilderness, 152; Curtis, History of the Twenty-Fourth Michigan*, 231; Matthews, *The 149th Pennsylvania*, 135.

8. OR 36, pt. 1, 617; Dunn, *Iron Men, Iron Will*, 241-42; Dawes, *Service with the Sixth Wisconsin Volunteers*, 260. Buckles survived his wound and was awarded the Medal of Honor for his gallantry.

9. Curtis, *History of the Twenty-Fourth Michigan*, 231; Rhea, *The Battle of the Wilderness*, 157. General Doles was killed at Cold Harbor in June 1864 and so never filed a battle report for the Wilderness.

10. Harshaw and Lester, "Operations of the 'Iron Brigade'"; Herdegen, *The Iron Brigade*, 482.

11. *History of the 121st Pennsylvania*, 77.

12. OR 36, pt. 1, 623.

13. Thomas, *History of the Doles-Cook Brigade*, 14; Matthews, *The 149th Pennsylvania*, 137.

14. Thomas, *History of the Doles-Cook Brigade*, 76; Curtis, *History of the Twenty-Fourth Michigan*, 231. The six-map series of the battle prepared by the National Park Service shows the 44th Georgia on the left flank of Doles' Brigade. However, the regimental accounts in Thomas's history (76, 477) clearly show the 4th Georgia as I have it.

15. Thomas, *History of the Doles-Cook Brigade*, 76; Henry Davenport to father, May 7, 1864, Sarah Pfeiffer Collection, Atlanta History Center.

16. *History of the 121st Pennsylvania*, 77; Tomasak, 115.

17. *History of the 121st Pennsylvania*, 77; Matthews, *The 149th Pennsylvania*, 137; David Neely Diary, May 5, 1864 entry, FNMP; Rhea, *The Battle of the Wilderness*, 163; OR 36, pt. 1, 610. Samuel Foust of the 149th Pennsylvania recorded in his diary, "Our

division made a grand charge on the Rebs and had to retreat perfectly panic stricken." Andersonville National Historic Site. The commander of the regiment, Col. John Irvin, succinctly noted in his report, "formed in line along bottom of gully, delivered a very heavy volley; fell back to Wilderness Run." Pennsylvania Historical Society.

18. Clark, *N.C. Regiments*, vol. 4, 44; *OR* 36, pt. 1, 623. Captain George Hugunin of the 147th New York (Rice's brigade) claimed that Daniel's Brigade had no skirmish line, "but 3 or 4 lines of battle." He also noted an unusual movement of the North Carolina troops: "when the first line fired they lay down—the next marched over them, fired & laid down & and so on when the first had loaded & ready again. Of course it knocked our line out." George Hugunin Memoir, FNMP.

19. John W. Daniel, "My Account, May 5," Rhea, *The Battle of the Wilderness*, 159-60; G. W. Nichols, *A Soldier's Story of his Regiment* (Kennesaw, GA: Continental Book Company, 1961), 141. A foot soldier in Gordon's 26th Georgia claimed he observed stress pass between General Gordon and his division commander, Jubal Early. "General Gordon, advance your line," ordered Early. Gordon responded, "As soon as I can form it, I will." Before Gordon had completed his task, Early returned and ordered him, "Forward." Gordon calmly responded, "I cannot General, until I form my line." When ready, Gordon finally ordered the advance. *Savannah Morning News*, July 20, 1864.

20. Steere, *The Wilderness Campaign*, 168-70; Rhea, *The Battle of the Wilderness*, 160; O'Reilly, *Battle of the Wilderness Map Set*, Map 1. Further proof of Gordon's orientation comes from the history of Doles' Brigade and the events described by Rufus Dawes, a Union officer in the 6th Wisconsin. Thomas, *History of the Doles-Cook Brigade, 76; Dawes, Service with the Sixth Wisconsin Volunteers*, 260.

21. Pharris DeLoach Johnson, ed., *Under the Southern Cross: Soldier Life with Gordon Bradwell and the Army of Northern Virginia* (Macon, GA: Mercer University Press, 1999), 151-52; Isaac G. Bradwell, "Battle of the Wilderness," *Confederate Veteran*, vol. 16 (1908), 448; *Savannah Morning News*, July 20, 1864.

22. Dawes, *Service with the Sixth Wisconsin Volunteers*, 260.

23. Herdegen, *The Iron Brigade*, 482; Dunn, *Iron Men, Iron Will*, 242; Civil War Diary of Capt. George Britton, University of Wisconsin, (Eau

Claire Research Center), Eau Claire, Wisconsin; *Civil War Diary of Capt. Alexander B. Pattison, Co. A, 7th Regiment of Indiana Infantry Volunteers*, FNMP.

24. *OR* 36, pt. 1, 623, 1077; Alton J. Murray, *South Georgia Rebels: The True Experiences of the 26th Regiment Georgia Volunteer Infantry, Lawton-Gordon-Evans Brigade* (St. Mary's, GA: Murray, 1976), 149. According to Thomas Devereux of the 43rd North Carolina, Daniel's Brigade "killed a large number [of enemy troops] and took a large number of prisoners." Thomas Devereux to his mother, May 6, 1864, Thomas Devereux Papers, North Carolina Division of Archives and History, Raleigh, North Carolina. Some historians argue Gordon moved his entire brigade south to Higgerson's Field. However, Gordon clearly reported (*OR* 36, pt. 1, 1,077) that he divided his brigade into three parts just south of Saunders Field. While he does not specifically mention the fight between three of his regiments and McCandless' men in Higgerson's Field, the movement patterns of the Georgia regiments support this view.

25. Dawes, *Service with the Sixth Wisconsin Volunteers*, 261.

26. Wayne Mahood, *General Wadsworth: The Life and Times of Brevet Major General James S. Wadsworth* (New York: Da Capo, 2003), 231; L. Allison Wilmer, et al., *History and Roster of Maryland Volunteers* (Baltimore, MD: Press of Guggenheimer, Weil & Co., 1898), 265.

27. Daniel H. Mowen, "Reminiscences of the Civil War by a Veteran in the Union Army," FNMP; Swan, "The Battle of the Wilderness," 131; *OR* 36, pt. 1, 623; Dawes, *Service with the Sixth Wisconsin Volunteers*, 261.

28. Wilmer, *History and Roster of Maryland Volunteers*, 265; *OR* 36, pt. 1, 601, 604; Charles Phelps Diary, May 5 entry, Charles E. Phelps Collection, Maryland Historical Society, Baltimore, MD. According to Daniel Mowen of the 7th Maryland, it was a fighting retreat. "The men reloaded while marching by the rear rank, then halting, facing front and firing at short intervals." Mowen, "Reminiscences of the Civil War."

29. Rhea, *The Battle of the Wilderness*, 164-65; Augustus Buell, *The Cannoneer: Recollections of Service in the Army of the Potomac* (Washington: *The National Tribune* Company, 1890), 159-61. While Buell provided a colorful account of the action, he was not with his unit at the battle and relied upon others for this information. Greg Mertz, park ranger, personal communication. A member of the 31st Georgia wrote to his local newspaper that the regiment's advance "for nearly two miles was eminently successful, driving the Yankees before

them, killing and wounding large numbers." Gregory C. White, *A History of the 31st Georgia Volunteer Infantry* (Baltimore, MD: Butternut and Blue, 1997), 114. Doles' Brigade lost 271 and Daniel's fewer than 100. Young, *Lee's Army During the Overland Campaign*, 282, 284.

30. Joseph Gibbs, *Three Years in the Bloody Eleventh: The Campaigns of a Pennsylvania Reserves Regiment* (University Park, PA: Pennsylvania State University Press, 2002), 257-58; Evan Morrison Woodward, *Our Campaigns: The Second Regiment Pennsylvania Reserve Volunteers* (Shippensburg, PA: Burd Street Press, 1995), 246; Sypher, *History of the Pennsylvania Reserve Corps*, 511; Bates, *History of the Pennsylvania Volunteers*, vol. 1, 729.

31. Bates, *History of the Pennsylvania Volunteers*, vol. 1, 729-30; Sypher, *History of the Pennsylvania Reserve Corps*, 511-12; F. L. Hudgins, "With the 38th Georgia Regiment," *Confederate Veteran*, vol. 26 (1918), 163; Nichols, *A Soldier's Story of his Regiment*, 143-44.

32. Gibbs, *Three Years in the Bloody Eleventh*, 259; Bates, *History of the Pennsylvania Volunteers*, vol. 1, 588, 854.

33. Dunn, *Iron Men, Iron Will*, 243; Robert Monteith, "Battle of the Wilderness, and Death of General Wadsworth," Wisconsin *MOLLUS* (Milwaukee, WI: Burdick, Armitage & Allen, 1891), 411; Hugunin Memoir.

34. Swan, "The Battle of the Wilderness," 131; Mahood, *General Wadsworth*, 232; Tomasak, *Avery Harris Civil War Journal*, 116; Schaff, *The Battle of the Wilderness*, 159; Dawes, *Service with the Sixth Wisconsin Volunteers*, 261.

35. Schaff, *The Battle of the Wilderness*, 166-67; Steere, *The Wilderness Campaign*, 182-83; David W. Lowe, *Meade's Army: The Private Notebooks of Lt. Col. Theodore Lyman* (Kent, OH: Kent State University Press, 2007), 134.

36. Wilkeson, *Recollections of a Private Soldier in the Army of the Potomac*, 66-67; Rhea, *The Battle of the Wilderness*, 170-71.

37. Brainard, *Campaigns of the One Hundred and Forty-Sixth Regiment, New York State Volunteers*, 91.

38. OR 36, pt. 1, 540; Gouverneur Warren to Charles Porter, November 21, 1875, Warren Collection, New York State Archives; Rhea, *The Battle of the Wilderness*, 173.

39. Rhea, *The Battle of the Wilderness*, 173-74.

Map Set 6: Wright's Division Engages the Confederate Left

1. OR 36, pt. 1, 665; Rhea, *The Battle of the Wilderness*, 176.

2. OR 36, pt. 1, 659-60; Steere, *The Wilderness Campaign*, 244; Gottfried, *Kearny's Own*, 164-65.

3. Rhea, *The Battle of the Wilderness*, 178; OR 36, pt. 1, 665; Lewis Luckenbill Diary, May 5, 1864 entry, FNMP.

4. Clemmer, *Old Alleghany*, 542; Rhea, *The Battle of the Wilderness*, 179-80. There is considerable confusion about the positions of Walker's and Stafford's brigades at this time. It is clear the two brigades exchanged positions during the afternoon, but there is debate as to when this took place. Both Rhea and Steere posit the exchange occurred early in the afternoon, but strong evidence suggests the shift occurred after the fight between Johnson's and Wright's divisions. The latter view is backed up by firsthand accounts from members of Stafford's Brigade, and members of Brown's First New Jersey brigade recalled fighting Stafford's Louisianans. The only way to reconcile these accounts is for Stafford's Brigade to be deployed on Steuart's left and on Walker's right. This conclusion has also been accepted by Frank O'Reilly (*Battle of the Wilderness Map Set*, Map 2).

5. George T. Stevens, *Three Years in the Sixth Corps: A Concise Narrative of Events in the Army of the Potomac, from 1861 to the Close of the Rebellion, April 1865* (Albany, NY: S. R. Gray, 1866), 305; OR 36, pt. 1, 665; Frederick David Bidwell, *History of the Forty-Ninth New York Volunteers* (Albany, NY: J. B. Lyon Company, Printers, 1916), 43; William Holmes Morse Diary, May 5, 1864 entry, FNMP.

6. OR 36, pt. 1, 660.

7. George W. Bicknell, *History of the Fifth Regiment Maine Volunteers* (Portland, ME: Hall L. Davis, 1871), 303-4; OR 36, pt. 1, 665; Clark S. Edwards, "War Reminiscences of the Bethel Company," FNMP.

8. Gottfried, *Kearny's Own*, 164-65; John Judd Diary, May 5, 1864 entry, Kansas State Historical Society; Edwin Halsey Diary, May 5, 1864 entry, U.S. Army Military History Institute, Carlisle, PA; Edwin Halsey to sister, May 19, 1864, FNMP; Joseph G. Bilby, "A Jersey Journey: Being the Perambulations of the 10th New Jersey Infantry, Late Olden's Legion," *Military Images*, vol. 16, No. 5 (March-April 1995), 11. The precise alignment of the brigade's second line remains unclear.

9. Bates, *History of the Pennsylvania Volunteers*, vol. 1, 1,241; Robert S. Westbrook, *History of the 49th Pennsylvania Volunteers* (Altoona, PA: n.p., 1898), 187.

10. Bidwell, *History of the Forty-Ninth New York Volunteers*, 43-44. Edward H. Fuller, *Battles of the Seventy-Seventh New York State Foot Volunteers* (n.p., n.p., 1901), 16; Letter to Editor of The Saratogian,

June 9, 1864. The order of Neill's regimental alignment remains in question.

11. *OR 36*, pt. 1, 665-66.

12. Rhea, *The Battle of the Wilderness*, 180.

13. Rev. James B. Sheeran, *Confederate Chaplain: A War Journal* (Milwaukee, WI: The Bruce Publishing Company, 1960), 87. James McCown, a new recruit to the 5th Virginia, expressed his dread prior to the fight: "After forming in line there is an awful silence. . . . He that a short while ago jested is now grave. Many are seen during this quiet to take out their Bibles and read and silently ask God to spare and shield them in the hour of battle. How awful is this inaction, silence. . . ." James McCown Diary, May 5, 1864 entry, Handley Library, Winchester, VA.

14. Issac O. Best, *History of the 121st New York State Infantry* (Chicago: J. H. Smith, 1921), 118-19.

15. *OR 36*, pt. 1, 665; Bicknell, *History of the Fifth Regiment Maine Volunteers*, 304; Salvatore G. Cilella, Jr., *Upton's Regulars: The 121st New York Infantry in the Civil War* (Lawrence, KS: Kansas University Press, 2009), 287. The 96th Pennsylvania of Upton's brigade faced bullets fired by men from Johnson's Division, as well as friendly fire from some of the troops from Leonard's brigade in their rear. Henry Kaiser Diary, May 5, 1864 entry, FNMP.

16. Halsey Diary, May 5, 1864; *OR 36*, pt. 1, 666; Lewis Van Blarcom Speech, FNMP. While most authors and cartographers place the 15th New Jersey toward the center of Wright's line, the regiment's commander, Col. Charles Penrose clearly states in his report that Sedgwick moved the regiment to the left. Charles Penrose, "Official Report of the Movement of the Fifteenth Reg. N.J. During Grant's Wilderness Campaign," U.S. Army Military History Institute, Carlisle, Pennsylvania

17. Bicknell, *History of the Fifth Regiment Maine Volunteers*, 304. Terrence Murphy, *10th Virginia Infantry* (Lynchburg, VA: H. E. Howard, 1989), 93. The quote about the casualties comes from the recollections of Pvt. James Huffman. He recalled that Sedgwick's men charged across the field several times, but it is clear his memory was faulty.

18. Haines, *History of the Fifteenth Regiment New Jersey Volunteers*, 145.

19. Haines, *History of the Fifteenth Regiment New Jersey Volunteers*, 145.

20. Charles R. Paul, "Campaign of 1864," Murray S. Smith Collection, U.S. Army Military History Institute, 1-2; Gottfried, *Kearny's Own*, 165.

21. Bates, *History of the Pennsylvania Volunteers*, vol. 1, 1241.

22. James I. Robertson, Jr. *The Stonewall Brigade* (Baton Rouge, LA: LSU Press, 1963), 219; J. S. Dozle, "Reminiscences of the Wilderness," Hotchkiss Papers, Library of Congress; Lowell Reidenbaugh, *27th Virginia Infantry* (Lynchburg, Va.: H.E. Howard, 1982), 95.

23. William G. Bean, *The Liberty Hall Volunteers: Stonewall's College Boys* (Charlottesville, Va.: University of Virginia Press, 1964), 186; McCown Diary, May 5, 1864 entry; Gottfried, *Kearny's Own*, 166.

24. Thomas S. Doyle Memoirs, Library of Congress; Dennis E. Frye, *2nd Virginia Infantry* (Lynchburg, Va.: H.E. Howard, 1984), 86-87.

25. Reidenbaugh, *27th Virginia Infantry*, 95; Lowell Reidenbaugh, *33rd Virginia Infantry* (Lynchburg, Va.: H.E. Howard, 1987), 81-82; Doyle Memoirs.

26. Westbrook, *History of the 49th Pennsylvania Volunteers*, 187.

27. Terry L. Jones, *Lee's Tigers: The Louisiana Infantry in the Army of Northern Virginia* (Baton Rouge, LA: LSU Press, 1987), 196; Henry E. Handerson, *Yankee in Gray: The Civil War Memoirs of Henry E. Handerson with a Selection of His Wartime Letters* (Cleveland, OH: Press of Western Reserve University, 1962), 70.

28. Jones, *Lee's Tigers*, 196; Handerson, *Yankee in Gray*, 70.

29. Terry L. Jones, "Leroy Augustus Stafford," in William C. Davis, ed., *The Confederate General* 6 vols. (Harrisburg, PA: National Historical Society, 1991), vol. 5, 194-95; Westbrook, *History of the 49th Pennsylvania Volunteers*, 187; G. M. G. Stafford, *General Leroy August Stafford: His Forebears and Descendants* (New Orleans, LA: Pelican Publishing Company, 1943), 44-45, 50-51; Rhea, *The Battle of the Wilderness*, 181; Terry L. Jones, *The Civil War Memoirs of Captain William J. Seymour: Reminiscences of a Louisiana Tiger* (Baton Rouge, LA: Louisiana State University Press, 1991), 109; Jones, *Lee's Tigers*, 196-97. Stafford was a wealthy plantation owner prior to the war. He fought with distinction at the head of the 9th Louisiana from Jackson's 1862 Valley Campaign into the Wilderness. When promoted to the rank of brigadier general and given command of the second Louisiana brigade, the men were initially unhappy with the selection. However, with time, they came to respect and appreciate him. Jones, "Leroy Augustus Stafford," 194-95.

30. Jones, *Lee's Tigers*, 197; *OR 36*, pt. 1, 1028. It is of interest to note that Lee's communication also

reported the death of Gen. John M. Jones, but no tribute was provided for him.

31. Larry Maier, *Rough & Regular: A History of Philadelphia's 119th Regiment of Pennsylvania Volunteer Infantry* (Shippensburg, PA: Burd Street Press, 1997), 158; Haines, *History of the Fifteenth Regiment New Jersey Volunteers*, 145-46.

32. Bidwell, *History of the Forty-Ninth New York Volunteers*, 44.

33. Jones, *Civil War Memoirs of Captain William J. Seymour*, 109.

34. James P. Gannon, *Irish Rebels, Confederate Tigers: A History of the 6th Louisiana Volunteers, 1861-1865* (Mason City, IA: Savas Publishing Company, 1998), 226-27; Jones, *Lee's Tigers*, 198; Jones, *Civil War Memoirs of Captain William J. Seymour*, 109.

35. Bidwell, *History of the Forty-Ninth New York Volunteers*, 44; A. T. Brewer, *History of the Sixty-First Regiment Pennsylvania Volunteers* (Philadelphia: Art Engraving & Printing Co., 1911), 82.

36. Jones, *Civil War Memoirs of Captain William J. Seymour*, 109-10; Gannon, *Irish Rebels, Confederate Tigers*, 227-28; W. S. Dunlop, *Lee's Sharpshooters or the Forefront of Battle: A Story of Southern Valor That Never Has Been Told* (Dayton, OH: Morningside, 1988), 390. There are many references to the 25th Virginia of Jones' Brigade in this sector. The assertion began in the report of Col. Oliver Edwards of the 37th Massachusetts (Eustis's brigade). Morris Schaff repeated this in *The Battle of the Wilderness*, 165. Many secondary authors followed suit, though with little critical analysis. One author wrote, "Richard Ewell, at Colonel John C. Higginbotham's insistence, detached the badly mauled 25th Virginia to accompany the Louisianans. The colonel proudly led his fifty men and the regimental colors up the trail behind Hays' brigade." Priest, *Nowhere to Run*, 118-19. Priest cited the regimental history of the 25th Virginia as his source (Armstrong, *25th Virginia Infantry*, 75), but he is in error, for Armstrong explicitly indicated the small regiment remained near the turnpike and reformed there. Historian Terry Jones repeated the error and mistakenly wrote that the 25th Virginia was part of Walker's Brigade and was "the only regiment that actually joined in the attack." Jones, *Lee's Tigers*, 197. It must also be remembered the 25th Virginia was on the skirmish line in Saunders Field and lost heavily during the early fighting (see Map 4.3). It was not in any shape to participate in an attack on the opposite side of Ewell's line. Unfortunately, the six-part battlefield map follows Steere's and Priest's convention and places the regiment on

Harry Hays' left flank. The only units in this position were from John Pegram's Virginia brigade.

37. Stevens, *Three Years in the Sixth Corps*, 306; Jones, *Lee's Tigers*, 198; Gannon, *Irish Rebels, Confederate Tigers*, 228.

38. James Bumgardner, "Pegram's Brigade, Early's Division: Ewell's Corps in the Battle of the Wilderness," *Richmond Daily Times*, October 8, 1905; Richard B. Kleese, *49th Virginia Infantry* (Lynchburg, VA: H. E. Howard, Inc., 2002), 43-44; Rankin, *37th Virginia Infantry*, 79

39. The specific location of Brown's regiments is impossible to ascertain. This map, therefore, relies heavily upon the second map of the six-map series produced by the Fredericksburg and Spotsylvania National Military Park.

40. Stevens, *Three Years in the Sixth Corps*, 306-7.

41. Hyde, *Following the Greek Cross*, 185. According to an officer in Pegram's Brigade, "The timber and undergrowth in front was so dense, that the attacking force could not have been seen until it appeared within twenty or thirty yards of the Confederate line." Bumgardner, "Pegram's Brigade, Early's Division: Ewell's Corps in the Battle of the Wilderness."

42. Rhea, *The Battle of the Wilderness*, 184.

Map Set 7: The Renewed Attack Against the Confederate Left

1. Steere, *The Wilderness Campaign*, 131-32; OR 36, pt. 2, 404; Hyde, *Following the Greek Cross*, 183-84.

2. *OR* 36, pt. 2, 414.

3. Steere, *The Wilderness Campaign*, 252; *OR* 36, pt. 1, 722, 728; Rhea, *The Battle of the Wilderness*, 245.

4. *OR* 36, pt. 2, 414.

5. Steere, *The Wilderness Campaign*, 253.

6. *OR* 36, pt. 1, 728; Rhea, *The Battle of the Wilderness*, 243.

7. Warner, *Generals in Blue*, 432-33; *OR* 36, pt. 1, 728, 730, 736; Francis Cordrey Diary, May 5 entry, FNMP; Osceola Lewis, *History of the One Hundred and Thirty Eighth Pennsylvania Volunteer Infantry* (Norristown, PA: Wills, Iredell, and Jenkins, 1866), 82; George B. Imler Diary, May 5, 1864 entry, Richmond National Military Park.

8. *OR* 36, pt. 1, 731; Thomas E. Pope, *The Weary Boys: Colonel J. Warren Keifer & the 110th Ohio Volunteer Infantry* (Kent, OH: Kent State University Press, 2002), 58.

9. *OR* 36, pt. 1, 728; Francis Cordrey, "In the Wilderness: What a Private Saw and Felt in that Horrible Place," *National Tribune*, June 21, 1894.

10. Robert J. Driver, *52nd Virginia Infantry* (Lynchburg, VA: H. E. Howard, Inc., 1986), 49-50; Samuel E. Buck, *With the Old Confeds* (Baltimore, MD: H. E. Houck & Co., 1925), 104; Walbrook D. Swank, *Stonewall Jackson's Foot Cavalry* (Shippensburg, PA: Burd Street Press, 2001), 34; Bumgardner, "Pegram's Brigade, Early's Division: Ewell's Corps in the Battle of the Wilderness."

11. *OR 36*, pt. 1, 731. Keifer recalled that the attack began about 7:00 p.m. Steere, *The Wilderness Campaign*, 254.

12. Driver, *52nd Virginia Infantry*, 50; Robert J. Driver, *58th Virginia Infantry* (Lynchburg, VA: H. E. Howard, Inc., 1990), 58. OR 36, pt. 1, 731; Joseph Warren Keifer, *Slavery and Four Years of War: A Political History of Slavery in the United States Together With a Narrative of the Campaigns and Battles of the Civil War in Which the Author Took Part: 1861-1865*, 2 vols. (New York: G. P. Putnam Sons, 1900), vol. 2, 83-86; Henry Wyatt Wingfield Diary, May 5, 1864 entry, FNMP.

13. *OR 36*, pt. 1, 72; Jones, *Civil War Memoirs of Captain William J. Seymour*, 111; J. Warren Keifer to Wife, May 10, 1864, Library of Congress. Colonel Horn noted in his report, "I had no support upon my left, the regiment on my left having fallen back as soon as checked by the enemy." This would have been the 110th Ohio—Colonel Keifer's regiment. The disparity in losses would appear to support this observation. OR 36, pt. 1, 736. John Pegram survived his wound and returned to his command on August 7, 1864. He married on January 19, 1865, and died in battle at Hatcher's Run exactly three weeks later. Walter S. Griggs, "John Pegram," *The Confederate General*, vol. 5, 7.

14. Driver, *52nd Virginia Infantry*, 50.

15. Steere, *The Wilderness Campaign*, 255-56; Brewer, *History of the Sixty-First Regiment Pennsylvania Volunteers*, 82.

16. Steere, *The Wilderness Campaign*, 256; Rhea, *The Battle of the Wilderness*, 249; Alfred S. Roe, *The Thirty-Ninth Regiment Massachusetts Volunteers, 1862-1865* (Worchester, MA: Regimental Veteran Association, 1914), 167; G. N. Galloway, "Annuals of the War," *Philadelphia Weekly Times*, January 8, 1881.

17. Buck, *With the Old Confeds*, 104-5. Captain Charles Taylor of the 2nd New Jersey (Brown's brigade) recorded in his journal: "remained under arms all night but little sleep"—a sentiment expressed by many other soldiers in the field. Charles Melville Taylor Diary, May 5 entry, FNMP.

Map Set 8: The Orange Plank Road: Getty and Heth Fight for the Crossroads

1. Alexander Boteler Diary, May 5, 1864, in Brooks Collection, Library of Congress; Royall, Some Reminiscences, 28; Venable, "General Lee in the Wilderness Campaign," 241; Sylvester F. Hildebrand, "Fifty Years Ago First Troops to Leave Apollo," Apollo (PA) *Sentinel* (April 21, 1911); Anonymous account, Harold C. George Papers, Library of Congress. The identity of these Federal troops is unknown, but they appeared suddenly while Lee and A. P. Hill sat conversing under a tree. Alexander Boteler, one of Jeb Stuart's aides, was stirred from his slumber by the sounds of urgent voices and saw "all the generals in full flight from the field followed by their respective aides and couriers."

2. Wilcox, "Lee and Grant in the Wilderness," 492.

3. James L. Morrison, ed., *The Memoirs of Henry Heth* (Westport, CT: Greenwood Press, 1974), 182-83; Wilcox, "Lee and Grant in the Wilderness," 492. Wilcox encountered General Gordon near the Chewning farm (see Map 10.1).

4. Janet Hewitt, ed., *Supplement to the Official Records of the Civil War*, 100 vols. (Wilmington, NC: Broadfoot, 1999), pt. 1, vol. 6, 703-4. Hereafter *OR Supplement*; OR 36, pt. 2, 410; Billy Ellis, *Tithes of Blood: A Confederate Soldier's Story* (Murfreesboro, TN: Southern Heritage Press, 1997), 146; Steere, *The Wilderness Campaign*, 200-201. Brigadier General Joseph Davis, who normally commanded the brigade, was in Richmond at this time, which left Colonel Stone in command. Only the disposition of Cooke's Brigade and a portion of Stone's are known. Steven H. Stubbs, *Duty-Honor-Valor: The Story of the Eleventh Mississippi Infantry Regiment* (Philadelphia, MS: Dancing Rabbit Press, 2000), 515-16. Henry "Mud" Walker's Brigade was the result of the consolidation of Col. John Brockenbrough's Virginia brigade and Brig. Gen. James J. Archer's Brigade. Both units had suffered heavily at Gettysburg, where the latter officer was captured; Brockenbrough was simply inept and his brigade a model of inefficiency and neglect. Walker, therefore, boasted eight regiments, all of whom were undersized. F. Ray Sibley, Jr., *The Confederate Order of Battle: The Army of Northern Virginia* (Shippensburg, PA: White Mane Publishing Co., 1996), 292.

Like so many aspects of the Wilderness Campaign, the precise location of Heth's defensive stand (i.e., A. P. Hill's front on May 5) athwart the Orange Plank Road, remains something of a mystery. Most authors discuss the location in only general terms, implying it was just into the thickets east of the Widow Tapp field. Indeed, this is where nearly maps drawn to date place Heth's line. Considered another way, these maps (which are also wildly inconsistent in their placement), have led readers to conclude that Heth's main line was anywhere from one- half a mile to as far as a full mile west of the Brock Road. A careful study of available firsthand sources, however, has led me to conclude this was not the case.

The issue was first raised by my publisher and editor, Theodore P. Savas, during discussions about the various sources on this part of the May 5 battlefield. Theodore P. Savas, personal communication. Major General Henry Heth's own report, *OR Supplement*, pt. 1, vol. 6, 703, details that his May 5 advance (Cooke's brigade) "continued to drive the enemy, until it reached a point where the Brock Road crossed the plank road." Heth goes on to discuss the arrival of his other brigades and their placement in a growing line, but does not mention falling back any distance at all. After a long afternoon and evening of heavy fighting, Heth reported, "About dark my division fell back about 500 yards and night put an end to the operations." That position would be much closer to where virtually every other historian and cartography place the main May 5 battle. Throughout the fighting on May 5, Heth's men launched a number of small counter-thrusts that threatened or came within sight of the Brock Road. This would have been impossible if Heth's main line was one-half mile or more west of the road.

Federal sources also imply Heth's position was much closer to the Brock Road then generally believed. For example, Col. Thomas Seaver of the 3rd Vermont reported that his men moved off the Brock Road, and passing through "the skirmish line for about 200 yards, we met the enemy." On Seaver's right, Lt. Col. Stephen Pingree of the 4th Vermont reported that his regiment moved forward "50 to 75 rods [one rod = 5.5 yards, so 275-412 yards] . . . and advancing some 25 yards beyond . . . concealed foe at a distance of less than 75 yards." In other words, the farthest distance in Pingree's estimate was only .29 miles. *OR 36*, pt. 1, 711. Other sources in the Vermont Brigade mention descending into a swale, roughly the left end of the brigade line, and getting hit by Heth's men as they ascend the next ridge. That swale today is roughly 400 yards from the intersection. Generals Getty and

Wheaton also position Heth's line much closer to the intersection. Federal sources also mention minie balls fired by Heth's men zipping around them on the Brock Road during the fighting that afternoon.

As a result of these and other sources, I have concluded Heth's skirmish line was established perpendicular to the Orange Plank Road about 300 yards from the Brock Road intersection, with Heth's main line about 100-150 yards behind that. In other words, Heth's main line of battle utilized most of May 5 was only 400-450 yards west of the Brock Road intersection. Today, a housing development occupies most of this area, which obliterated any evidence of Heth's line there. The smaller works much farther back by the Widow Tapp Farm marked by the National Park Service as Heth's main line, believe historians Chris Mackowski and Kris White (both of whom have worked at the park and know the terrain well) are simply works thrown up later that night by troops in the rear, or Heth's men when they fell back before being overrun the next morning. Chris Mackowski and Kristopher D. White, personal communication.

5. Agassiz, *Meade's Headquarters*, 134; Steere, *The Wilderness Campaign*, 199, 201; *OR 36*, pt. 1, 677; George B. Godfrey, "The Wilderness," *National Tribune*, January 22, 1891; Richard A. Sauers and Peter Tomasak, *Ricketts' Battery: A History of Battery F, 1st Pennsylvania Light Artillery* (n.p.: Luzerne National Bank, 2001), 157.

6. Stevens, "The Sixth Corps in the Wilderness," 192; D. A. Jones to Father, May 20, 1864, FNMP. Colonel Thomas Seaver of the 3rd Vermont noted that the brush restricted visibility to fewer than 40 yards. *OR 36*, pt. 1, 709.

7. *OR 36*, pt. 1, 697; Dunlop, *Lee's Sharpshooters*, 368-69; Dunbar Rowland, *Military History of Mississippi, 1803-1888: Taken from the Official and Statistical Register of the State of Mississippi, 1908* (Spartansburg, S.C.: Reprint Co., 1978), 49; Ellis, *Tithes of Blood*, 143; *OR Supplement*, pt. 1, vol. 6, 703. The left side of Grant's skirmish line did not receive orders to advance. Colonel Thomas Seaver of the 3rd Vermont reported, "the skirmishers not advancing, I passed them." *OR 36*, pt. 1, 709.

8. *OR Supplement*, pt. 1, vol. 6, 703-4.

9. *OR 36*, pt. 1, 681-82; 696-97; Howard Coffin, *The Battered Stars: One State's Civil War Ordeal During Grant's Overland Campaign* (Woodstock, VT: Countryman Press, 2002), 105-7. Edward Holton of the 6th Vermont wrote home after the battle, "We soon found out to our sorrow that we were close to the Rebs, as at the first fire we lost a large

number of our men, but we rallied." Edward Holton to Katie, May 10, 1864, FNMP. Luther Harris of the 4th Vermont recalled that "when the enemy succeeded in checking the rout, and the battle took on lines and order, then the advancing party flung itself on the ground and began a fierce fire of musketry, working their way forward on their faces until, so far as distance was concerned, stones could have been used as missels." Luther Harris Memoir, FNMP.

10. *OR* 36, pt. 1, 697; George C. Benedict, *Vermont in the Civil War*, 2 vols. (Burlington, VT: The Free Press Association, 1886), vol. 1, 424-25.

11. *OR* 36, pt. 1, 682.; Berea Willsey Diary entry, May 5, 1864, FNMP; Harold C. George Papers, Library of Congress; Albert M. Haywood to brother, May 9, 1864, FNMP.

12. Ellis, *Tithes of Blood*, 144.

13. Steere, *The Wilderness Campaign*, 206-7; *OR* 36, pt. 1, 711; Emil and Ruth Rosenblatt, eds. *Hard Marching Every Day—The Civil War Letters of Private Wilbur Fisk* (Lawrence, KS: University of Kansas Press, 1992), 215; Charles B. Brockway, "Across the Rapidan." *Philadelphia Weekly Times*, January 7, 1882; Sauers and Tomasak, *Ricketts' Battery*, 158; Peter S. Chase, *Reunion Greeting Together with a Historic Sketch* (Brattleboro, VT: Phoenix Job Printing Office, 1891), 50-51; Benjamin F. Hurlburd letter to Reverend, June 26, 1864, FNMP; Bradley M. Gottfried, "To Fail Twice: Brockenbrough's Brigade at Gettysburg," *Gettysburg Magazine*, Issue 23 (July, 2000), 66-75.

14. *OR* 36, pt. 1, 681-82, 691; George H. Uhler, "Camps and Campaigns of the 93d Regiment Pennsylvania Volunteers," 18-19, FNMP.

15. Robert Hunt Rhodes, ed., *All For The Union: The Civil War Diary and Letters of Elisha Hunt Rhodes* (New York: Orion Books, 1958), 144; Joseph K. Newell, *Ours: Annals of the Tenth Regiment, Massachusetts Volunteers, in the Rebellion* (Springfield, MA: C. A. Nichols & Co., 1875), 258.

16. James Bowen, *History of the Thirty-Seventh Regiment Massachusetts Volunteers, in the Civil War of 1861-1865* (Holyoke, MA: C. W. Bryan & Company, 1884), 275-76.

17. *OR* 36, pt. 1, 677.

18. Coffin, *The Battered Stars*, 109-10; Brockway, "Across the Rapidan"; Sauers and Tomasak, *Ricketts' Battery*, 158-59.

19. *OR* 36, pt. 1, 677; Sauers and Tomasak, *Ricketts' Battery*, 159.

20. Dunlop, *Lee's Sharpshooters*, 370-71; *OR* 36, pt. 1, 677.

21. *OR* 36, pt. 1, 691, 698.; Harris *Memoir*, FNMP.

Map Set 9: Getty is Reinforced on the Orange Plank Road

1. Walker, *History of the Second Army Corps*, 411-12; *OR* 36, pt. 1, 318; *OR* 36, pt. 2, 406; Rhea, *The Battle of the Wilderness*, 188.

2. *OR* 36, pt. 1, 318; *OR* 36, pt. 2, 407-10; Rhea, *The Battle of the Wilderness*, 188-90.

3. Charles C. Perkis Memoir, *Civil War Times Illustrated* Collection, USMHI; Rhea, *The Battle of the Wilderness*, 94-95.

4. Walker, *History of the Second Army Corps*, 412-13; Ruth L. Silliker, *The Rebel Yell & the Yankee Hurrah: The Civil War Journal of a Maine Volunteer* (Camden, ME: Down East Books, 1985), 143.

5. *OR* 36, pt. 2, 410; Rhea, *The Battle of the Wilderness*, 190-91; Walker, *History of the Second Army Corps*, 414; Steere, *The Wilderness Campaign*, 199-200. Hancock's report implies that he sent reinforcements on his own volition. *OR* 36, pt. 1, 320.

6. Steere, *The Wilderness Campaign*, 207-8; *OR* 36, pt. 1, 697.

7. *OR* 36, pt. 1, 697; Frederick Clark Floyd, *History of the Fortieth (Mozart) New York Volunteers, which was composed of Four Companies from New York, Four Companies from Massachusetts, and Two Companies from Pennsylvania* (Boston: F. H. Gilson Company, 1909), 216; Homer D. Musselman, *47th Virginia Infantry* (Lynchburg, VA: New Papyrus Publishing, 2010), 74-75; Richard O'Sullivan, *55th Virginia Infantry* (Lynchburg, VA: H. E. Howard, Inc., 1989), 127.

8. The 26th Mississippi (Davis's/Stone's Brigade) was shifted to the left to form behind the 27th North Carolina around this time, presumably because of only light pressure against Heth's left flank. Stubbs, *Duty-Honor-Valor*, 518.

9. Thomas D. Marbaker, *History of the Eleventh New Jersey Volunteers: Its Organization to Appomattox to Which is Added Experiences of Prison Life and Sketches of Individual Members* (Trenton, NJ: MacCrellish & Quigley, Book and Job Printers, 1898), 162; Warren Cudworth, *History of the First Regiment Massachusetts Infantry from the 25th of May, 1861, to the 25th of May, 1864; Including Brief References to the Operations of the Army of the Potomac* (Boston: Walker, Fuller & Co., 1886), 459; Cornelius Van Santvoord, *The One Hundred and Twentieth New York State Volunteers: A Narrative for the Union* (Rondout, NY: Kingston and Freeman, 1894), 113.

10. *OR* 36, pt. 1, 487, 492, 496, 498; Charles B. Darling, *Historical Sketch of the First Regiment Infantry, Massachusetts Volunteer Militia* (Boston: n.p., 1890), 459.

11. *OR* 36, pt. 1, 487, 492, 498; Cudworth, *History of the First Regiment Massachusetts Infantry*, 489; Steere, *The Wilderness Campaign*, 212-13.

12. *OR* 36, pt. 1, 483; Steere, *The Wilderness Campaign*, 210-11; O'Reilly, *Battle of the Wilderness Map Set*, Map 3.

13. Cudworth, *History of the First Regiment Massachusetts Infantry*, 459.

14. *OR* 36, pt. 1, 488, 492.

15. *OR* 36, pt. 1, 488, 492, 499.

16. James I. Robertson, Jr., ed., *The Civil War Letters of General Robert McAllister* (New Brunswick, NJ: Rutgers University Press, 1965), 415-16.

17. Silliker, *The Rebel Yell & the Yankee Hurrah*, 143; George W. Verrill, "The Seventeenth Maine at Gettysburg and in the Wilderness," Maine *MOLLUS* (Portland, ME: The Thurston Print, 1898), vol. 1, 273.

18. C. A. Stevens, *Berdan's Sharpshooters in the Army of the Potomac, 1861-1865* (St. Paul, MN: The Price-McGill Company, 1892), 401; *OR* 36, pt. 1, 485; William B. Kent to brother, May 4, 1894, FNMP; William H. Green, "From the Wilderness to Spotsylvania," Maine *MOLLUS* (Portland, ME: Lefavor-Tower Company, 1902), vol. 2, 92. The actual route of Hays' march is in dispute. While some postulated Hays came up behind Wheaton's brigade, one credible historian believed Carroll's brigade later occupied that space, and argued that Hays' men moved farther to the right, to support Eustis's troops. Steere, *The Wilderness Campaign*, 210-11.

19. Steere, *The Wilderness Campaign*, 215; Stephen Chase Memoir, U.S. Army Military History Institute.

20. Kent to brother, May 4, 1894; William B. Jordan, Jr., *Red Diamond Regiment: The 17th Maine Infantry, 1862-1865* (Shippensburg, PA: White Mane Publishing Company, 1996), 133. The loss of Mattocks was cheered by the men. As Pvt. John Halsey confessed, "I can't think of any officer I'd sooner part with, for he was very pompous and had yards and yards of superfluous red tape about him." Silliker, *The Rebel Yell & the Yankee Hurrah*, 144.

21. David H. King, *Personal Recollections of the War: A Record of Service with the Ninety-Third New York Volunteer Infantry, 1861-1865* (Milwaukee, WI: Swain and Tate Company, 1895), 91; Frank Rood to mother and father, May 6, 1864,

Navarro College (Pearce Civil War Collections), Corsicana, Texas.

22. Samuel Dunham, "Death of Gen. Hays: Where and How he Fell at the Battle of the Wilderness," *National Tribune*, November 12, 1885; Jack D. Welsh, *Medical Histories of Union Generals* (Kent, OH: Kent State University Press, 1996), 164; Gilbert Adams Hays, *Under the Red Patch: Story of the Sixty-Third Regiment Pennsylvania Volunteers, 1861-1865* (Pittsburgh, PA: Sixty-third Pennsylvania Volunteers Regimental Association, 1908), 232; Walker, *History of the Second Army Corps*, 416. Some troops claimed Hays was drinking whisky from his canteen at the front. When the strap became tangled, Hays shifted to continue drinking, but the act moved his head directly into the path of a Rebel bullet. Rhea, *The Battle of the Wilderness*, 203-4.

23. Daniel G. Crotty, *Four years Campaigning in the Army of the Potomac* (Grand Rapids, MI: Dygert Bros. & Co., 1874), 126; Steere, *The Wilderness Campaign*, 211-12.

24. Bates, *History of the Pennsylvania Volunteers*, vol. 2, 252; Robert S. Robertson to parents, May 7, 1864, FNMP; *OR* 36, pt. 1, 483.

25. Three of Ward's regiments (20th Indiana, 40th New York, and 141st Pennsylvania) had earlier pushed their way forward to help support Grant's Vermonters, but their actions thereafter remain unclear. Regimental histories for the latter two regiments suggest they held their positions well to the front through the late afternoon, but specifics are difficult to come by. Floyd, *History of the Fortieth (Mozart) New York Volunteers*, 216; David Craft, *History of the One Hundred Forty-First Regiment, Pennsylvania Volunteers, 1862-1865* (Towanda, PA: Reporter-Journal Printing Co., 1885), 177-78. The official report filed for the 40th New York notes only that the regiment relieved the troops in front of it [Grant's brigade] and "fought in line of battle until dark." *OR* 36, pt. 1, 473.

26. Civil War Diary of William Owen, May 5, 1864 entry, FNMP. The historian of the 99th Pennsylvania claimed his regiment was on the "extreme left of the division." Bates, *History of the Pennsylvania Volunteers*, vol. 3, 510. The same was true of the 110th Pennsylvania. Bates, *History of the Pennsylvania Volunteers*, vol. 3, 983. Both were holding the far left, with one regiment in the first line and the other behind it in the second.

27. Weygant, *History of the One Hundred and Twenty-Four Regiment*, 287.

28. Amos G. Bean diary, May 5, 1864 entry, FNMP.

29. Lowe, *Meade's Army*, 134-35; Agassiz, *Meade's Headquarters*, 91-92.

30. *OR* 36, pt. 1, 430.

31. Rhea, *The Battle of the Wilderness*, 208. Kirkland's fifth regiment, the 52nd North Carolina, was guarding the wagon train and so was not with the brigade during the fighting. Clark, *N.C. Regiments*, vol. 3, 244-45.

32. Earl J. Hess, *Lee's Tar Heels: The Pettigrew-Kirkland-MacRae Brigade* (Chapel Hill, NC: University of North Carolina Press, 2002), 210-12. The 47th North Carolina offers a good example of the shifting of units. The 47th, which was first sent to the left of the line, was later recalled to form just to the right of the Orange Plank Road.

Map Set 10: Wilcox's Division and the Rest of Hancock's II Corps Enter the Fight

1. Wilcox, "Lee and Grant in the Wilderness," 492; *OR Supplement*, pt. 1, vol. 6, 713-15; J. F. J. Caldwell, *The History of a Brigade of South Carolinians known as "Gregg's" and Subsequently as McGowan's Brigade* (Philadelphia: King and Baird Printers, 1866), 127-28.

2. Steere, *The Wilderness Campaign*, 219-21.

3. *OR* 36, pt. 1, 615; *OR* 36, pt. 2, 414-15; Roebling Report, Warren Collection, New York State Archives; Rhea, *The Battle of the Wilderness*, 208, 230-31.

4. Wilcox, "Lee and Grant in the Wilderness," 492; Rhea, *The Battle of the Wilderness*, 231-32.

5. Clark, *N.C. Regiments*, vol. I, 594, vol. 3, 74.

6. William P. Saville, *History of the First Regiment, Delaware Volunteers: From the Commencement of the "Three Months' Service" to the Final Muster Out at the Close of the Rebellion* (Wilmington, DE: The Historical Society of Delaware, 1884), 106; Henry Roback, *The Veteran Volunteers of Herkemer and Oswego Counties in the War of the Rebellion* (Utica, NY: L. C. Childs, 1888), 67-68; Bradley M. Gottfried, *Stopping Pickett: The History of the Philadelphia Brigade* (Shippensburg, PA: White Mane Publishing Company, 1999), 197. Theodore Castor of the 3rd Michigan (Hays' brigade) noted in his memoir that the enemy were "laying on the ground and waiting for us and when we got close enough they fired into us and made our boys drop like snow flakes." Theodore Castor Memoir, FNMP.

7. *OR* 36, pt. 1, 682, 697. Although Grant suggested that II Corps replacements were up before he vacated his position, this may not have been the case. See Map 10.3. Wheaton, on Grant's right, never commented on whether his brigade was reinforced or on the matter of falling back during the early evening hours.

8. Caldwell, *The History of a Brigade of South Carolinians*, 128; Steere, *The Wilderness Campaign*, 227-28.

9. Caldwell, *The History of a Brigade of South Carolinians*, 128 29.

10. Clark, *N.C. Regiments*, vol. 3, 27, 75, 118.

11. Steere, *The Wilderness Campaign, 224. The evidence of a "vigorous attack" by Carroll is less clear than Steere postulates. William Landon, "The Fourteenth Indiana Regiment, Letters to the Vincennes Western Sun. Indiana Magazine of History*, vol. 34, no. 1 (September 1934), 90; *OR* 36, pt. 1, 429-30.

12. *OR Supplement*, pt. 1, vol. 6, 704, 715, 775. Since Heth's men had been launching frequent small-scale attacks throughout the afternoon, his recommendation to Wilcox almost certainly meant a more general, large-scale assault to break the enemy line completely and win the day there. Heth, of course, had no way of knowing the full scope of the Federal juggernaut confronting him.

13. Caldwell, *The History of a Brigade of South Carolinians*, 128-29; Dunlop, *Lee's Sharpshooters*, 398.

14. Rhea, *The Battle of the Wilderness*, 226; Stevens, "The Sixth Corps in the Wilderness," 192-93.

15. Caldwell, *The History of a Brigade of South Carolinians*, 129.

16. Charles H. Banes, *History of the Philadelphia Brigade: Sixty-Ninth, Seventy-First, Seventy-Second, and One Hundred and Sixth Pennsylvania Volunteers* (Philadelphia: J. B. Lippincott & Co., 1876), 227-28; Joseph R. C. Ward, *History of the One Hundred and Sixth Regiment, Pennsylvania Volunteers, 2d brigade, 2d division, 2d corps. 1861-1865* (Philadelphia: Grant, Faires, & Rodgers, 1883), 239; Roback, *The Veteran Volunteers of Herkemer and Oswego Counties*, 67-68; Gottfried, *Stopping Pickett*, 1997.

17. Caldwell, *The History of a Brigade of South Carolinians*, 129-31; Sauers and Tomasak, *Ricketts' Battery*, 159. The men from Wheaton's and Getty's brigades also claimed the honor of recapturing the guns. ."As an eye witness," wrote a VI Corps staff officer long after the battle, "I know that the brave Vermonters and men of [Wheaton's] brigade . . . surged forward at the crisis without orders and drove the enemy from the guns, and that the presence of the Second Corps made no difference in the result. I know, too, that Hancock in the evening claimed that his troops recaptured the guns, and that Getty was indignant thereat, and earnestly protested that his division retook them unaided." Stevens, "The Sixth Corps in the Wilderness," 193.

18. George A. Bowen Diary, May 5, 1864 entry, FNMP; *OR Supplement*, pt. 1, vol. 6, 776.

19. Caldwell, *The History of a Brigade of South Carolinians*, 129-30; Dunlop, *Lee's Sharpshooters*, 398.

20. Clark, *N.C. Regiments*, vol. 1, 675, vol. 2, 588.

21. Clark, *N.C. Regiments*, vol. 3, 27-28.

22. Clark, *N.C. Regiments*, vol. 3, 305; George Pearsall to Sarah Pearsall, May 7, 1864, North Carolina Division of Archives and History; T. P. Williams, *The Mississippi Brigade of Brig. Gen. Joseph R. Davis: A Geographic Account of its Campaigns and a Biographical Account of its Personalities, 1861-1865* (Dayton, OH: Morningside Press, 1999), 135-36.

23. Williams, *The Mississippi Brigade of Brig. Gen. Joseph R. Davis*, 134-38; Clark, *N.C. Regiments*, vol. 3, 305; Dunlop, *Lee's Sharpshooters*, 373.

24. *OR Supplement*, pt. 1, vol. 6, 715; W. F. Smith, "Longstreet to the Rescue of Thomas' Brigade," *Atlanta Journal*, September 21, 1901.

25. *OR* 36, pt. 1, 370; Steere, *The Wilderness Campaign*, 226; Scott, *Into the Wilderness with the Army of the Potomac*, 90; George S. Young Diary, May 5, 1864 entry, FNMP.

26. Steere, *The Wilderness Campaign*, 232-33.

27. *OR* 36, pt. 2, 411.

28. Richard F. Welch, *The Boy General: The Life and Careers of Francis Channing Barlow* (Kent, OH: Kent State University Press, 2003), 99-100.

29. St. Clair A. Mulholland, *The Story of the 116th Pennsylvania Regiment Volunteers in the War of the Rebellion: The Record of a Gallant Command* (Philadelphia: F. McManus, Jr., and Co., 1903), 186.

30. *OR* 36, pt. 1, 407.

31. *OR Supplement*, pt. 1, vol. 6, 731; Allen Paul Speer, *Voices from Cemetery Hill: The Civil War Diary, Reports, and Letters of Colonel William Henry Asbury Speer* (1861-1864) (Johnson City, TN: The Overmountain Press, 1997), 127-28; Michael C. Hardy, *The Thirty-Seventh North Carolina Troops: Tar Heels in the Army of Northern Virginia* (Jefferson, NC: McFarland and Company, 2013), 181; W. Keith Alexander, "Fought them Like Tigers: Colonel Clark Moulton Avery and the 33rd North Carolina Infantry, May 5-6, 1864," in *Civil War Regiments*, vol. 6, No. 4 (1999), 62-63. During the initial stages of the advance, the men believed McGowan's South Carolinians were in front of them and the ineffectual fire sprayed in their direction was from "friendly" sources. Alexander, "Fought them Like Tigers," 62.

32. *OR Supplement*, pt. 1, vol. 6, 731, 753.

33. *OR Supplement*, pt. 1, vol. 6, 731-32, 766.

34. Lane Robert Laird Stewart, *History of the One Hundred and Fortieth Regiment, Pennsylvania Volunteers* (Philadelphia: Franklin Bindery, 1912), 180; OR 36, pt. 1, 407; Joseph S. Wicklein Memoir, FNMP.

35. Susan Williams Benson, ed., *Berry Benson's Civil War Book: Memoirs of a Confederate Scout and Sharpshooter* (Athens, GA: University of Georgia Press, 1992), 62-63; *OR Supplement*, pt. 1, vol. 6, 731-32, 754.

36. *OR Supplement*, pt. 1, vol. 6, 759-60.

37. Randy Bishop, *The Tennessee Brigade: A History of the Volunteers of the Army of Northern Virginia* (Bloomington, IN: AuthorHouse, 2005), 273; Rhea, *The Battle of the Wilderness*, 237-38; OR 36, pt. 1, 615; Steere, *The Wilderness Campaign*, 241-42.

Map Set 11: Afternoon Cavalry Actions

1. Rhea, *The Battle of the Wilderness*, 253.

2. A. D. Slade, *A. T. A. Torbert: Southern Gentleman in Union Blue* (Dayton, OH: Morningside Press, 1992), 95; OR 36, pt. 1, 803.

3. *OR* 36, pt. 1, 788; OR 36, pt. 2, 427, 429; Rhea, "Union Cavalry in the Wilderness," 123.

4. W. A. Rodgers, "the 18th Pa. Cav. Had Lively Work in the Mine Run Fight," *National Tribune*, May 27, 1897; Rhea, *The Battle of the Wilderness*, 256-57; Connecticut Adjutant-General, *Annual Report of the Adjutant-General of the State of Connecticut for the Year Ending March 31, 1865* (New Haven, CT: Carrington, Hotchkiss, 1865), 411; Connecticut Adjutant-General, *Record of Service of Connecticut Men in the Army and Navy of the United States During the War of the Rebellion* (Hartford, CT: Case, Lockwood and Brainard, 1889), 57; McDonald, *A History of the Laurel Brigade*, 226-27.

5. Henry R. Pyne, *Ride to War: The History of the First New Jersey Cavalry* (New Brunswick, NJ: Rutgers University Press, 1961), 186; OR 36, pt. 1, 860.

6. Rhea, *The Battle of the Wilderness*, 258; Rhea, "Union Cavalry in the Wilderness," 123. Gregg's defensive-offensive line is unclear. Gordon Rhea, in his *The Battle of the Wilderness*, 258, notes that the line consisted of the 1st Massachusetts Cavalry, 1st New Jersey Cavalry, and 10th New York Cavalry. However in his essay "Union Cavalry in the Wilderness," 123, Rhea wrote the Jerseymen were joined by the "1st Massachusetts Cavalry, the 6th Ohio, and perhaps the 10th New York."

7. *OR* 36, pt. 1, 860; Pyne, *Ride to War*, 224-25; McDonald, *A History of the Laurel Brigade*, 228-34.

8. William P. Lloyd, *History of the First Regiment Pennsylvania Reserve Cavalry, From its Organization,*

August, 1861, to September, 1864, with a List of Names of All Officers and Enlisted Men Who Have Ever Belonged to the Regiment (Philadelphia: King and Baird, 1864), 90-91; Luther W. Hopkins, *From Bull Run to Appomattox: A Boy's View* (Baltimore, MD: Fleet-McGinley, 1914), 145-48; Rhea, "Union Cavalry in the Wilderness," 124.

9. McDonald, *A History of the Laurel Brigade*, 233; OR 36, pt. 1, 853; Rhea, "Union Cavalry in the Wilderness," 124-25.

Map Set 12: The May 5 Fighting Ends, and the Armies Prepare for May 6

1. Clark, *N.C. Regiments*, vol. 3, 75.
2. Stevens, "The Sixth Corps in the Wilderness," 192-93; Caldwell, *The History of a Brigade of South Carolinians*, 131.
3. William Y. W. Ripley, *Vermont Riflemen in the War for the Union: A History of Company F, First United States Sharpshooters* (Rutland, VT: Tuttle & Co., 1883), 146.
4. Francis Rew Letters, FNMP; Robert Pratt Diary, May 5, 1864 entry, FNMP.
5. Schaff, *The Battle of the Wilderness*, 214; Survivors' Association, *History of the 118th Pennsylvania Volunteers*, 403; Porter, *Campaigning with Grant*, 53.
6. Stubbs, *Duty-Honor-Valor*, 517-18; W. G. Nelms, "Unfinished Report on the Campaign of 1864," in *The Lamar Rifles: A History of Company G, Eleventh Mississippi Regiment, C.S.A., With the Official Roll, Giving Each Man's Record From Time of Enlistment to Twenty-Ninth of March, Eighteen Hundred and Sixty-Five* (Roanoke, VA: Stone Printing Co., 1902), 60; OR Supplement, pt. 1, vol. 6, 704.
7. According to historian Peter Carmichael, "Ewell orchestrated a magnificent defense. He seemed to anticipate each Federal thrust, adeptly shifting his troops north of the turnpike to repel the final Union attacks of the day." He also noted that Ewell fought more than double the number of his own troops without the support of Lee, who spent the day with A. P. Hill on the Orange Plank Road front. Peter S. Carmichael, "Escaping the Shadow of Gettysburg: Richard S. Ewell and Ambrose Hill at the Wilderness," in Gary Gallagher, ed., *The Wilderness Campaign* (Chapel Hill, NC: University of North Carolina Press, 1997), 148-50. First Corps artilleryman E. Porter Alexander wrote that Ewell "whipped everything that attacked him but he even sallied out on some rash ones & captured two guns & quite a lot of prisoners." Alexander also praised

A. P. Hill, claiming that "few troops in the Army of Northern Virginia exhibited more resolve and determination." Gary W. Gallagher, ed., *Fighting for the Confederacy: The Personal Recollections of General Edward Porter Alexander* (Chapel Hill, NC: University of North Carolina Press, 1989), 353. Hill's biographer labeled May 5 as Hill's "most brilliant as a corps commander." Robertson, *General A. P. Hill*, 260.

8. Steere, *The Wilderness Campaign*, 284.
9. Porter, *Campaigning with Grant*, 53-54. Hancock made his headquarters that night on the Orange Plank Road about 100 yards from the vital crossroads with the Brock Road. Warren's headquarters remained in the spacious Lacy house, and Sedgwick camped on Spotswood Road near the road to Germanna Ford. Rhea, *The Battle of the Wilderness*, 263.
10. Rhea, *The Battle of the Wilderness*, 264.
11. Porter, *Campaigning with Grant*, 54.
12. OR 36, pt. 2, 406.
13. OR 36, pt. 2, 404-5; Rhea, *The Battle of the Wilderness*, 266-67. Because his was an independent command, General Burnside did not participate in the evening conference with Meade. Instead, he established headquarters near the Lacy house. William Marvel, *Burnside* (Chapel Hill, NC: The University of North Carolina Press, 1991), 353. Part of Meade's communicat- ion to Grant read: "After conversing with my corps commanders, I am led to believe that it will be difficult, owing to the dense thicket in which their commands are located, the fatigued condition of the men rendering it difficult to rouse them early enough, and the necessity of some daylight, to properly put in reinforce- ments." He suggested the attack begin at 6:00 a.m. Grant was probably disappointed, but Meade's reasoning was sound. He reluctantly granted a delay until 5:00 a.m. His aide relayed the response to Meade: "if delayed until 6 o'clock the enemy will take the initiative, which he [Grant] desires specially to avoid." Meade and his commanders thought it was a fair compromise. OR 36, pt. 2, 404-5. Burnside's biographer, William Marvel, took issue with the assertion that his subject was a slow marcher, and believed the argument was the result of pettiness amongst several officers, but the perception took hold and spread throughout the army. Marvel, *Burnside*, 352.
14. Rhea, *The Battle of the Wilderness*, 272-78; Jones' Brigade suffered the heaviest losses (597) of any in Ewell's Corps. About half of the casualties (292), were men who had been captured or were

missing. Young, *Lee's Army During the Overland Campaign*, 270.

15. Wilcox, "Lee and Grant in the Wilderness," 494; Morrison, *The Memoirs of Henry Heth*, 184; Dunlop, *Lee's Sharpshooters*, 32; Carmichael, "Escaping the Shadow of Gettysburg," 151-52; Robert K. Krick, "'Lee to the Rear,' the Texans Cried," in *The Wilderness Campaign*, Gary W. Gallagher, ed. (Chapel Hill, NC: University of North Carolina Press, 1997), 163. Although Heth claimed to have made three trips to his corps commander, historian Peter Carmichael, "Escaping the Shadow of Gettysburg," 151-52, thinks the evidence shows that Heth may well have exaggerated his interactions with A. P. Hill. Regardless of the number or nature of the interactions, the real culprit, argues Carmichael, was General Lee, who believed Longstreet would soon be up and did nothing to stabilize the front. Historian Robert K. Krick, "'Lee to the Rear,' the Texans Cried," 163, argued there was "ample blame to spread around."

16. Royall, *Some Reminiscences*, 30-31; Wilcox, "Lee and Grant in the Wilderness," 494; Morrison, ed. *The Memoirs of Henry Heth*, 184; Carmichael, "Escaping the Shadow of Gettysburg," 153. Heth also made the trek to Lee's tent, but could not find him.

17. Steere, *The Wilderness Campaign*, 303-9.

18. Rhea, *The Battle of the Wilderness*, 273. Although positioning Longstreet deep in his rear has been criticized by some, there were several reasons for Lee's decision. He was unsure whether Meade intended to turn his right or left flank, and he had to be prepared for either contingency. In addition, he had to shield his supply line with the Shenandoah Valley until he knew his left was not threatened. In addition, leaving Longstreet at Gordonsville gave Lee deeper strategic maneuvering options.

19. D. Augustus Dickert, *History of Kershaw's Brigade with Complete Roll of Companies, Biographical Sketches, Incidents, Anecdotes, Etc.* (Morningside Press, 1976), 344-45; Longstreet, *From Manassas to Appomattox*, 559; Rhea, *The Battle of the Wilderness*, 280.

20. Catlett to John Daniel, January 7, 1907, Daniel Collection, University of Virginia. Taliaferro was the third messenger from Lee. With each courier, the message became more impatient. Worrying about Taliaferro's safety, Longstreet told him "the Yankees are on this road and you better be careful." Rhea, *The Battle of the Wilderness*, 278.

21. Zach C. Waters and James C. Edmonds, *A Small but Spartan Band: The Florida Brigade in Lee's Army of Northern Virginia* (Tuscaloosa, AL: The University of Alabama Press, 2010), 99.

22. Cockrell, *Gunner with Stonewall*, 88.

Map Set 13: Fighting Begins on the Union Right (May 6)

1. Schaff, *The Battle of the Wilderness*, 227-29; Porter, *Campaigning with Grant*, 56.

2. OR 36, pt. 1, 1040, 1071; Isaac G. Bradwell, "The Second Day's Battle of the Wilderness," *Confederate Veteran*, vol. 28 (1920), 20; Rhea, *The Battle of the Wilderness*, 318.

3. Brewer, *History of the Sixty-First Regiment Pennsylvania Volunteers*, 83.

4. Bidwell, *History of the Forty-Ninth New York Volunteers*, 44; Brewer, *History of the Sixty-First Regiment Pennsylvania Volunteers*, 83; Rhea, *The Battle of the Wilderness*, 318-19. Albert Reid soberly recorded in his diary that "a man falls now almost every moment." May 6, 1864 entry, FNMP.

5. OR 36, pt. 1, 1071; Donald C. Pfanz, *Richard S. Ewell: A Soldier's Life* (Chapel Hill, NC: University of North Carolina Press, 1998), 370; Brewer, *History of the Sixty-First Regiment Pennsylvania Volunteers*, 83-84; Bidwell, *History of the Forty-Ninth New York Volunteers*, 44, also in Neill's brigade, did not confirm that the New Yorkers joined in the counterattack.

6. Keifer, *Slavery and Four Years of War*, vol. 2, 85-86; Samuel Burwell Memoir, FNMP; OR 36, pt. 1, 732. According to the historian of the 138th Pennsylvania, during "the movement we were to 'swing our right.' But instead of encountering a feeble picket line we found strong columns opposing us. The 'swinging' movement exposed the Brigade to both a front and flank fire, the severity of which checked its further advance." Lewis, *History of the One Hundred and Thirty Eighth Pennsylvania Volunteer Infantry*, 82.

7. OR 36, pt. 1, 540. As noted earlier, James Wadsworth's division on Warren's left was ordered to march south and attack the left flank of A. P. Hill's Third Corps.

8. Marvel, *Burnside*, 352-53; Rhea, *The Battle of the Wilderness*, 324-25; OR 36, pt. 1, 906, 927, 934; Charles Wood Diary, May 6, 1864 entry, U.S. Army Military History Institute, Carlisle, PA.

9. Lowe, *Meade's Army*, 136; Roebling Report, Warren Papers, New York State Archives; Rhea, *The Battle of the Wilderness*, 325. See Map Set 1, note 12, for why Burnside's command operated independent of the Army of the Potomac.

10. Byron M. Cutcheon, "Autobiography," Byron M. Cutcheon Papers, Bentley Historical Library, University of Michigan; Rhea, *The Battle of the Wilderness*, 325.

11. Schaff, *The Battle of the Wilderness*, 231-32.

12. Lowe, *Meade's Army*, 136.

13. Nash, *A History of the Forty-Fourth Regiment, New York Volunteer Infantry*, 185-86; Judson, *History of the Eighty-Third Regiment of Pennsylvania Volunteers*, 195.

14. OR 36, pt. 1, 540; OR 36, pt. 2, 449.

15. OR 36, pt. 1, 540; OR 36, pt. 2, 449, 450.

16. Steere, *The Wilderness Campaign*, 320-21.

17. Nash, *A History of the Forty-Fourth Regiment, New York Volunteer Infantry*, 185.

18. OR 36, pt. 2, 450, 457.

19. OR 36, pt. 1, 906; Rhea, *The Battle of the Wilderness*, 326.

20. OR 36, pt. 1, 906; *Thirty-Sixth Massachusetts Committee of the Regiment, History of the Thirty-Sixth Regiment Massachusetts Volunteers* (Boston: Press of Rockwell and Churchill, 1884), 150; Rhea, *The Battle of the Wilderness*, 326.

Map Set 14: Hancock Strikes A. P. Hill's Third Corps

1. Steere, *The Wilderness Campaign*, 310.

2. The Confederate positions at this time are unclear. Edward Thomas's Brigade's location is a good example. Gordon Rhea, a modern history of a regiment in Thomas's Brigade, and the historian of McGowan's Brigade, all postulated that Thomas's command formed on McGowan's right. Rhea, *The Battle of the Wilderness*, 284; John J. Fox, *Red Clay to Richmond: Trail of the 35th Georgia Infantry Regiment, C.S.A.* (Winchester, VA: Angle Valley Press, 2004), 249-50; Caldwell, *The History of a Brigade of South Carolinians*, 179. Steere, however, places it to the right of Scales. Steere, *The Wilderness Campaign*, 311. O'Reilly's *Battle of the Wilderness Map Set*, Map 3, places Thomas in its original position on the left of the line. I have placed Edward Thomas' Brigade on the right of McGowan's. It appears Lane's Brigade deployed in a "fish hook" orientation with the 18th, 37th, and part of the 33rd North Carolina regiments facing northeast and the 23rd, 28th, 7th, and part of the 33rd North Carolina regiments facing northwest. Hardy, The *Thirty-Seventh North Carolina Troops*, 181.

3. It is unlikely there will ever be unanimous agreement about where each Confederate brigade began the day when Hancock attacked about dawn. Steere, in his seminal work *The Wilderness Campaign*, 311, wrote: "Evidence concerning the positions taken by Kirkland and Walker . . . is so vague a nature as to prohibit a definite statement." Once Wilcox's Division arrived late on the afternoon of May 5, Heth pulled Kirkland back. Its movements thereafter are in dispute. O'Reilly's Battle of the Wilderness Map Set, Map 3 shows the brigade in the same position, but the brigade history and a regimental history suggest it occupied the front line, with Stone's Brigade somewhere to its left. See also Musselman, *47th Virginia Infantry*, 41; Robert E. Krick, *40th Virginia Infantry* (Lynchburg, VA: H. E. Howard, Inc., 1985), 41. Rhea, The Battle of the Wilderness, 284; Hess, Lee's Tar Heels, 213-14.

4. Clark, *N.C. Regiments*, vol. I, 676, 744, vol.2, 446. Wilcox, "Lee and Grant in the Wilderness," 495. .Even with instructions from A. P. Hill to let their men sleep, the disastrously exposed nature of their fronts almost required Generals Wilcox and Heth to instruct their brigadiers to dig in to some degree and/or rearrange the fronts to prepare to receive a possible—and even likely—enemy attack. It is highly doubtful either officer would have suffered any negative consequences for taking such action, and their accounts of that night and excuses for failing to act were all written with hindsight as to what transpired thereafter—and with an eye on protecting their own reputations. In my opinion, neither Heth nor Wilcox comes off well here.

5. Clark, *N. C. Regiments*, vol. 1, 676; Thomas Alfred Martin, "Autobiography," FNMP.

6. OR 36, pt. 1, 321, 430; Walker, *History of the Second Army Corps*, 420.

7. Robert Stoddart Robertson, *Personal Recollections of the War: A Record of Service with the Ninety-Third New York Vol. Infantry, and the First Brigade, First Division, Second Corps, Army of the Potomac* (Milwaukee, WI: Swain & Tate Co., Printers and Publishers, 1895), 93; Roback, *The Veteran Volunteers of Herkemer and Oswego Counties*, 68.

8. Van Santvoord, *The One Hundred and Twentieth New York State Volunteers*, 114; OR 36, pt. 1, 320-21, 430; Scott, *Into the Wilderness with the Army of the Potomac*, 111-12. The deposition of Federal regiments is from O'Reilly's six-part map series published by the Fredericksburg National Military Park. The position of certain units is unclear. For example, Map 3 places Brewster's brigade in the front line, but all other published works place it in the second line. I have followed the more popular convention and left Brewster in the second line. However, I have followed this map set with regard to the general position of the second line. Both Rhea and Steere place Eustis's and part of

Wheaton's brigades in the first line, but recessed from Birney's division. It is doubtful Hancock would not have deployed a solid front line on both sides of the Plank Road.

9. OR 36, pt. 1, 596, 615; Dawes, *Service with the Sixth Wisconsin Volunteers*, 261-62; Rhea, *The Battle of the Wilderness*, 283; Monteith, "Battle of the Wilderness," 412-13. The resupply almost did not take place when the men carrying the 20,000 rounds of ammunition nearly blundered into Confederate lines.

10. John A. Foster reminiscences, Foster and Foster Papers, Perkins Special Collections Library, Duke University.

11. Hays, *Under the Red Patch*, 234; Van Santvoord, *The One Hundred and Twentieth New York State Volunteers*, 114-15.

12. Thomas Chamberlin, *History of the One Hundred and Fiftieth Regiment, Pennsylvania Volunteers, Second Regiment, Bucktail Brigade* (Philadelphia: F. McManus, Jr. & Co., Printers, 1905), 215.

13. Steere, *The Wilderness Campaign*, 295.

14. Wilcox, "Lee and Grant in the Wilderness," 495-96.

15. OR 36, pt. 1, 488.

16. *N.C. Regiments*, vol. I, 675; Martin, "Autobiography."

17. Verrill, "The Seventeenth Maine at Gettysburg and in the Wilderness," 277. Daniel Crotty of the 3rd Michigan told a different story. "They pour a volley into our ranks . . . both sides stand and take a fearful fire, and the whole line seems to be one vast sheet of flame in the early morn. The number that fall on both sides is fearful, for we are fighting at very close range. We charge on their lines with great odds, but they stand their ground like a solid wall of masonry. The roar of musketry, the dying groans of the wounded, the hellish yells of the rebels, and the shouts and cheers of the Union men, mingle together, all making a noise and confusion that is hard to describe." Crotty indicated that they finally drove the enemy about a mile, though that is certainly an exaggeration. Crotty, *Four years Campaigning in the Army of the Potomac*, 127.

18. Fox, *Red Clay to Richmond*, 252-53; George H. Mills, *History of the 16th North Carolina Regiment* (Hamilton, NY: Edmonston Pub., 1897), 47; Smith, "Longstreet to the Rescue of Thomas' Brigade." According to a Georgian, "we [had] nearly exhausted our ammunition when our right flank was nearly all captured and killed and we were ordered to fall back." George W. Hall Diary, May 6, 1864.

19. Jordan, *Red Diamond Regiment*, 136-37; N.C. Regiments, vol. 2, 665; James H. Lane Report, Lane Collection, Auburn University; *OR Supplement*, pt. 1, vol. 6, 733-34. Perhaps embarrassed by the disaster, General Lane wrote after the battle, "brave men are sometimes forced to turn their back to the foe." Lane was not about to blame his men or himself, however, adding, "if a mistake was made either on the night of the 5th or morning of the 6th, the fault was elsewhere than with my command." *OR Supplement*, pt. 1, vol. 6, 733.

20. *OR Supplement*, pt. 1, vol. 6, 775.

21. *OR Supplement*, pt. 1, vol. 6, 777; Caldwell, *The History of a Brigade of South Carolinians*, 132-33.

22. Hess, *Lee's Tar Heels*, 213-15; *N.C. Regiments*, vol. I, 595. Poague's artillery battalion attempted to stem the tide, but many of the shells flew over the Iron Brigade. The commander of the 19th Indiana, Col. Samuel Williams, instructed his men to ignore the harmless shells. Williams was struck and killed shortly thereafter. Alan D. Gaff, *On Many a Bloody Field: Four Years in the Iron Brigade* (Bloomington, IN: Indiana University Press, 1996), 344.

23. Rhea, *The Battle of the Wilderness*, 288-89; Samuel Finley Harper to father, May 6, 1864, North Carolina Division of Archives and History.

24. Dunlop, *Lee's Sharpshooters*, 376-78; Rhea, *The Battle of the Wilderness*, 289; Clark, *N.C. Regiments*, vol. 3, 305.

25. Clark, *N.C. Regiments*, vol. I, 744, vol. 2, 446.

26. Clark, *N.C. Regiments*, vol. 2, 446, vol. 3, 118; OR 36, pt. 1, 623; A. P. Smith, *History of the Seventy-Sixth Regiment New York Volunteers* (Courtland, NY: Truair, Smith and Miles, Printers, 1867), 291.

27. Cockrell, *Gunner with Stonewall*, 89.

28. Charles D. Page, *History of the Fourteenth Regiment, Connecticut Vol. Infantry* (Meriden, CT: The Horton Printing Co., 1906), 242.

29. Lowe, *Meade's Army*, 136-37.

30. Walker, *History of the Second Army Corps*, 422.

31. Cockrell, *Gunner with Stonewall*, 89; Clark, *N.C. Regiments*, vol. 2, 446, vol. 3, 118; OR 36, pt. 1, 623; Jennings Cropper Wise, *The Long Arm of Lee: The History of the Artillery of the Army of Northern Virginia* (New York: Oxford University Press, 1959), 767; Smith, *History of the Seventy-Sixth Regiment New York Volunteers*, 291. There is some confusion about the position and action of Williams's Battery of Poague's Battalion. Accounts from members of Cooke's Brigade, repeated by Steere, *The Wilderness Campaign*, 332-33, suggest the battery fought alongside the North Carolinians. Major Poague never mentioned detaching Williams's Battery or attempting to push a battery

through heavy woods to assume such a dangerous position. Either way, Poague's Battalion was in a position to enfilade part of the Union advance. Members of Rice's brigade recalled the destructive fire of a Confederate battery. Steere seemed to believe there were two separate batteries involved here. Cockrell, *Gunner with Stonewall*, 89.

Map Set 15: Longstreet Reaches the Battlefield

1. Walker, *History of the Second Army Corps*, 422; George A. Hussey and William Todd, *History of the Ninth Regiment N.Y.S.M. (Eighty-Third N.Y. Volunteers), 1845-1888* (New York: n.p., 1889), 325.

2. Dawes, *Service with the Sixth Wisconsin Volunteers*, 262; OR 36, pt. 1, 611, 677; Walker, *History of the Second Army Corps*, 422-23.

3. Alexander, *Military Memoirs of a Confederate: A Critical Narrative*, 503.

4. Caldwell, *The History of a Brigade of South Carolinians*, 133.

5. Cockrell, *Gunner with Stonewall*, 89-90.

6. Douglas Southall Freeman, *Robert E. Lee*, 4 vols. (New York: Charles Scribner's Sons, 1936), vol. 3, 286-87; Wilcox, "Lee and Grant in the Wilderness," 496.

7. Wise, *The Long Arm of Lee*, 767; Cockrell, *Gunner with Stonewall*, 89-90; Harper, "Reminiscences."

8. Gregg's men arrived in second position behind Brig. Gen. George "Tige" Anderson's Georgia brigade, which was ordered to shift right (south) of the Orange Plank Road, which put Gregg's men in front on the left. According to General Field, Longstreet initially ordered him to "form line of battle on the right of and perpendicular to the road, and check the enemy's advance." Field ordered Anderson's Brigade accordingly, but as it moved off, Field received another order to "form in the quickest order I could and charge with any front I could make." As a result, General Field threw Gregg's Texans forward. C. W. Field, "Campaign of 1864 and 1865: Narrative of Major-General C. W. Field," *Southern Historical Society Papers*, vol. 14 (1886), 543.

9. Charles Venable, "The Campaign from the Wilderness to Petersburg," *Southern Historical Society Papers*, vol. 14 (1873), 525-26; A. C. Jones, "Lee in the Wilderness," *Philadelphia Weekly Times*, May 8, 1880; Freeman, *Robert E. Lee*, vol. 3, 286-87. The rapid pace of their long march

exhausted Longstreet's men. Most reached the field at dawn after only five hours of rest and their haversacks empty. Krick, "'Lee to the Rear,' the Texans Cried," 164-65.

10. Venable, "The Campaign from the Wilderness to Petersburg," 525. After the war, a Rebel cannoneer wrote rather poetically in describing Longstreet's entrance into the fight: "like a fine lady at a party, Longstreet was often late in his arrival at the ball. But he always made a sensation and that of delight, when he got in, with the grand old First Corps sweeping behind him as his train." Dame, *From the Rapidan to Richmond and the Spotsylvania Campaign*, 85. Historian Robert K. Krick painstakingly researched the many versions of the "Lee to the rear" incident and discovered at least 38 accounts of the event from men who were on the field that morning. Krick, "'Lee to the Rear,' the Texans Cried," 181.

11. OR 36, pt. 1, 596, 611. The historian of the 76th New York indicated that his brigade (Rice's) formed at right angles to the Orange Plank Road. Smith, *History of the Seventy-Sixth Regiment New York Volunteers*, 291.

12. Field, "Campaign of 1864 and 1865," 543; Jeffrey D. Stocker, *From Huntsville to Appomattox: R. T. Coles' History of the 4th Regiment, Alabama Volunteer Infantry, C.S.A., Army of Northern Virginia* (University of Tennessee Press, 1996), 160. Some have questioned how expeditiously General Longstreet made the march from Gordonsville to the battlefield. However, according to Robert K. Krick, who is not known as a Longstreet acolyte, Old Pete's "pace was as vigorous as ought to have been expected and in fact far prompter and more rapid than Longstreet's metabolism usually preferred." One soldier recalled, "we walked fast and double quick as much as we could," and another described the hurried pace a "turkey trot." Krick, "'Lee to the Rear,' the Texans Cried," 164-65; James B. Rawls, "Veteran's Sketch of Life from Battle of Chickamauga to Arrival Home," *United Daughters of the Confederacy Magazine* 52 (June 1989), 17; "Kershaw's Brigade," *Carolina Spartan* (Spartansburg, S.C.), May 26, 1864.

13. Joe Kershaw was leading Maj. Gen. Lafayette McLaws's Division. Field, "Campaign of 1864 and 1865," 543; Wilcox, "Lee and Grant in the Wilderness," 496; OR 36, pt. 1, 1061; Steere, *The Wilderness Campaign*, 341; William F. Perry, "Reminiscences of the Campaign of 1864 in Virginia," *Southern Historical Society Papers*, VII (1879), 51.

14. Longstreet, *From Manassas to Appomattox*, 560-61.

15. Royall, *Some Reminiscences*, 32.

16. OR 36, pt. 1, 321; Silliker, *The Rebel Yell & the Yankee Hurrah*, 145.

Map Set 16: Longstreet Counterattacks North of the Orange Plank Road

1. Jones, "Leroy Augustus Stafford," in Davis, ed., *The Confederate General*, vol. 3, 38; Stewart Sifakis, *Who Was Who in the Civil War* (Facts on File, 1988), 265.

2. O'Reilly, *Battle of the Wilderness Map Set*, Map 3; B. A. Aycock, "The Lone Star Guards," *Confederate Veteran*, vol. XXXI (March, 1923), 101; Dickert, *History of Kershaw's Brigade*, 345.

3. O. T. Hanks, *History of Captain B. F. Benton's Company, Hood's Texas Brigade, 1861-1865* (Austin, TX: Morrison Books, 1984), 28-29; Calvin L. Collier, *They'll Do To Tie To!: 3rd Ark. Infantry Regiment—C.S.A.* (Democrat Printing and Litho. Company, 1995), 175-76; E. M. Law, "From the Wilderness to Cold Harbor," in *Battles and Leaders of the Civil War* (New York: The Century Company, 1887), vol. 4, 125; Phil K. Faulk, "Battle of the Wilderness," *Philadelphia Weekly Times*, October 25, 1884.

4. R. C. "Texans Always Move Them," *The Land We Love*, vol. V, 485. Houghton, *The Campaigns of the Seventeenth Maine*, 169; OR 36, pt. 1, 617.

5. B. L. Aycock, "A Sketch: The Lone Star Guards," FNMP; Hanks, *History of Captain B. F. Benton's Company*, 29; J. B. Polley, *Hood's Texas Brigade: Its Marches, Its Battles, Its Achievements* (Dayton, OH: Morningside Bookshop, 1976), 232.

6. Polley, *Hood's Texas Brigade*, 232.

7. Polley, *Hood's Texas Brigade*, 232-33; Field, "Campaign of 1864 and 1865," 544: Perry, "Reminiscences of the Campaign of 1864 in Virginia," 51.

8. George McRae, "With Benning's Brigade in the Wilderness," *Atlanta Journal*, August 17, 1901; J. H. Gresham, "Benning's Brigade in the Wilderness Again," *Atlanta Journal*, September 7, 1901; Augusta (GA) *Chronicle and Sentinel*, June 1, 1864; Joseph Fuller Diary, May 6, 1864 entry, FNMP.

9. *Wilderness Map Study*, Map No. 3; McRae, "With Benning's Brigade in the Wilderness"; Augusta (GA) *Chronicle and Sentinel*, June 1, 1864; Gresham, "Benning's Brigade in the Wilderness Again"; Perry, "Reminiscences of the Campaign of 1864 in Virginia," 51.

10. Perry, "Reminiscences of the Campaign of 1864 in Virginia," 52; Augusta (GA) *Chronicle and Sentinel*, June 1, 1864; McRae, "With Benning's Brigade in the Wilderness." To Phil Faulk of the 11th Pennsylvania (Baxter's brigade), "it seemed as if more than one-half of our line had gone down like stubble before the tongue of fire. A solid sheet of death, red hot as a flame from hell, darted upon our ranks." Faulk, "Battle of the Wilderness."

11. Gresham, "Benning's Brigade in the Wilderness Again"; John Rozier, ed., *The Granite Farm Letters: The Civil War Coorespondence of Edgeworth and Sallie Bird* (Athens, GA: University of Georgia Press, 1988), 164.

12. Augusta (GA) *Chronicle and Sentinel*, June 1, 1864.

13. The Wilderness Campaign is one of the most confusing battles of the entire Civil War, and this is especially so in the Orange Plank Road sector. The confusion stems from both the heavy vegetation, which made it difficult for anyone to determine where they were or who they were fighting (or who was fighting alongside them), and the constant nature of steady combat combined with heavy losses during the ensuing weeks, which left little time for the filing of reports and many officers dead, injured, captured, or mustered out. For example, Edward Steere, the first historian to tackle the battle in a serious book-length modern fashion, did not attempt to discern which Federal commands battled Gregg's and Benning's brigades. He also concluded that Perry's (Law's) Brigade struck Wadsworth's division. Gordon Rhea followed Steere's convention. Rhea, however, broke with Steere when he concluded Perry's men struck Baxter's brigade (Robinson's division, Warren's V Corps) and then Eustis's and Wheaton's brigades (Getty's division, Sedgwick's VI Corps). More recently, author John Priest argued that Gregg's Texans were turned back by Webb's brigade (Gibbon's division, Hancock's II Corps), but this seems unlikely, and that Carroll's brigade (Gibbon's division, Hancock's II Corps) battled first Benning and then Perry. The historian of Perry's (Law's) Brigade also believed his men fought Carroll's brigade, but went on to add Ward's brigade (Birney's division, Hancock's II Corps) to the mix. The historian of the II Corps, Frances Walker, skirted the issue entirely by referring to commands at the divisional level, and when he mentioned brigades, he did so in vague terms. The plain fact is that in many cases, we will never know with conclusive proof which units engaged in direct combat that morning. Steere, *The Wilderness Campaign*, 344-54; Rhea, *The Battle of the*

Wilderness, 301-7; John Michael Priest, *Victory Without Triumph: The Wilderness, May 6th & 7th, 1864* (Shippensburg, PA: White Mane Publishing Company, 1996), 49-59; J. Gary Laine and Morris M. Penny, *Law's Alabama Brigade in the War Between the Union and the Confederacy* (Shippensburg, PA: White Mane Publishing Co., Inc., 1966), 240-47; Walker, *History of the Second Army Corps*, 423-28.

14. *OR 36*, pt. 1, 287; Mahood, *General Wadsworth*, 240. Evander Law was not in charge of his brigade and was under arrest in the rear because he had run afoul of Longstreet during the East Tennessee Campaign. He would not rejoin his brigade until the battle of Cold Harbor in June, where he was severely wounded. Colonel Kitching's two regiments comprised the 1st Brigade, attached to the Artillery Reserve division under Col. Henry S. Burton, all part of Brig. Gen. Henry Hunt's artillery command.

15. Laine and Penny, *Law's Alabama Brigade in the War Between the Union and the Confederacy*, 217-24; P. D. Bowles, "Battle of the Wilderness: The 4th Alabama in the Slaughter Pen, May 6, 1864," *Philadelphia Weekly Times*, October 4, 1884; Stocker, *From Huntsville to Appomattox*, 160; William C. Oates, *The War Between the Union and the Confederacy and its Lost Opportunities with a History of the 15th Alabama Regiment and the Forty-Eight Battles in Which it was Engaged* (Dayton, OH: Morningside Bookshop, 1985), 344.

16. Bowles, "Battle of the Wilderness"; Stocker, *From Huntsville to Appomattox*, 161; Young, *Lee's Army During the Overland Campaign*, 54.

17. Bowles, "Battle of the Wilderness."

18. Perry, "Reminiscences of the Campaign of 1864 in Virginia," 52-53.

19. OR 36, pt. 1, 596, 619; Mahood, *General Wadsworth*, 241; Welsh, *Medical Histories of Union Generals*, 23.

20. Perry, "Reminiscences of the Campaign of 1864 in Virginia," 53-54; Steere, *The Wilderness Campaign*, 296; William A. Jordan, *Some Events and Incidents During the Civil War* (Montgomery, AL: The Paragon Press, 1909), 74-76.

21. Perry, "Reminiscences of the Campaign of 1864 in Virginia," 54.

22. William H. Locke, *The Story of the Regiment* (Philadelphia: J. B. Lippincott, 1868), 326-27.

23. Mahood, *General Wadsworth*, 244; OR 36, pt. 1, 682.

24. Bowen, *History of the Thirty-Seventh Regiment Massachusetts*, 279-80.

25. Bowen, *History of the Thirty-Seventh Regiment Massachusetts*, 279-80; James L. Bowen, "In the Wilderness," *Philadelphia Weekly Times*, June 27, 1885; Mahood, *General Wadsworth*, 244; Henry G. Pearson, *James S. Wadsworth of Geneseo: Brevet Major General, U.S.V.* (New York: Charles Scribner's Sons, 1913), 283.

26. Bowles, "Battle of the Wilderness"; Bowen, *History of the Thirty-Seventh Regiment Massachusetts*, 279-80; Bowen, "In the Wilderness"; Uhler, "Camps and Campaigns of the 93d Regiment Pennsylvania Volunteers."

27. Bowles, "Battle of the Wilderness"; OR 36, pt. 1, 446-47.

28. Bowles, "Battle of the Wilderness"; Perry, "Reminiscences of the Campaign of 1864 in Virginia," 56-57; Stocker, *From Huntsville to Appomattox*, 161-62; Franklin Sawyer, *A Military History of the 8th Regiment Ohio Vol. Inf'y: It's Battles, Marches and Army Movements* (Cleveland, OH: Fairbanks & Co. Printers, 1881), 162-63.

29. Sawyer, *A Military History of the 8th Regiment Ohio Vol.*, 162.

30. Thomas Francis Galway, *The Valiant Hours* (Harrisburg, PA: The Stackpole Company, 1961), 199; Laine and Penny, *Law's Alabama Brigade in the War Between the Union and the Confederacy*, 241.

31. Galway, *The Valiant Hours*, 199; Sawyer, *A Military History of the 8th Regiment Ohio Vol.*, 163.

32. Sawyer, *A Military History of the 8th Regiment Ohio Vol.*, 163; Charles Myerhoff, "In the Wilderness: The Charge of Carroll's Celebrated Brigade," *National Tribune*, October 23, 1890.

33. Perry, "Reminiscences of the Campaign of 1864 in Virginia," 54; Oates, *The War Between the Union and the Confederacy*, 347.

34. OR 36, pt. 1, 437; Mahood, *General Wadsworth*, 241-42.

35. OR 36, pt. 1, 596, 619; Mahood, *General Wadsworth*, 241.

36. OR 36, pt. 1, 437-38; Seldon Connor, "In the Wilderness," Maine *MOLLUS* (Portland, ME: Lefavor-Tower Company, 1915), vol. 4, 218-19; Richard F. Miller, *Harvard's Civil War: A History of the Twentieth Massachusetts Volunteer Infantry* (Hanover, NH: University Press of New England, 2005), 337; Rhea, *The Battle of the Wilderness*, 336-37; George A. Bruce, *The Twentieth Regiment of Massachusetts Volunteer Infantry 1861-1865* (Boston: Houghton, Mifflin, and Co., 1906), 353. Webb later wrote that he took with him the 15th Massachusetts, 19th Maine, 7th Michigan, and 42nd and 82nd New York, but he was probably mistaken about the 19th Maine. Its commander, Col. Selden Connor, specifically reported that he

and his regiment remained on the left side of the Orange Plank Road and was attached to Brig. Gen. Joshua Owen's brigade of Gibbon's division. Webb likely meant the 20th Massachusetts, and simply made a mistake.

37. Miller, *Harvard's Civil War*, 337; Martha D. Perry, ed., *Letters from a Surgeon of the Civil War* (Boston: Little, Brown, and Co., 1906), 166-70; *OR* 36, pt. 1, 437.

38. *OR* 36, pt. 1, 437.

Map Set 17: Longstreet Counterattacks South of the Orange Plank Road

1. *OR* 36, pt. 1, 1061; *OR Supplement*, pt. 1, vol. 6, 662-63; Steere, *The Wilderness Campaign*, 341; Dickert, *History of Kershaw's Brigade*, 346. According to Andrew Werts of the 3rd South Carolina, "We quickened our step [to the battlefield] formed a line of battle as best we could in the face of the retreating army bolting through our ranks." Andrew Werts Memoir, FNMP. This stampede of fugitives cut the 3rd South Carolina into two wings and threw it into chaos, which reduced its effectiveness. Enemy soldiers apparently got between the wings, forcing the unit to fall back to be reorganized before moving forward again. Simeon Pratt to Baxter, May 16, 1864, James Drayton Nance Papers, South Carolina Library, Columbia, SC.

2. Dickert, *History of Kershaw's Brigade*, 347; Mac Wyckoff, *A History of the 3rd South Carolina Infantry: 1861-1865* (Fredericksburg, VA: Sergeant Kirkland's Museum and Historical Society, Inc., 1995), 171; Thomas Belue Diary, May 6, 1864 entry, Archive Department, Winthrop College, Rock Hill, SC.

3. Ripley, *Vermont Riflemen*, 148-51; Rhea, *The Battle of the Wilderness*, 310.

4. Craft, *History of the One Hundred Forty-First Regiment, Pennsylvania Volunteers*, 181.

5. Dickert, *History of Kershaw's Brigade*, 347.

6. *OR Supplement*, pt. 1, vol. 6, 659.

7. W. Garth Johnson, "Barksdale-Humphreys Mississippi Brigade," *Confederate Veteran*, vol. I (1893), 207.

8. Johnson, "Barksdale-Humphreys Mississippi Brigade," 207. According to Brig. Gen. Goode Bryan, "the discipline of the command was sorely tried, for while forming line of battle in a dense thicket under a severe fire of the enemy the line was constantly broken through by men hurrying to the rear." *OR*, 36, pt. 1, 1063.

9. Dickert, *History of Kershaw's Brigade*, 347.

10. Ibid; Johnson, "Barksdale-Humphreys Mississippi Brigade," 207.

11. *OR* 36, pt. 1, 446, 488-89; Rhea, *The Battle of the Wilderness*, 310; John E. Kittle Diary, May 6, 1864 entry, FNMP.

12. Lowe, *Meade's Army*, 136-37.

13. *OR* 36, pt. 1, 446-47; Rhea, *The Battle of the Wilderness*, 310-11.

14. Rosenblatt, *Hard Marching Every Day*, 216. Benjamin Hulburd wrote home about the advance toward the enemy on May 6: "And what a sight! Such heaps of dead. Such numbers slain. Foe mixed with foe promiscuously." Benjamin Hulburd to Reverend, June 26, 1864, FNMP.

15. Lewis A. Grant, "In the Wilderness," *National Tribune*, January 28, 1897.

16. *OR* 36, pt. 1, 699; Grant, "In the Wilderness."

17. *OR* 36, pt. 1, 1063; James W. Freeman Diary, May 6, 1864 entry, FNMP; Van Santvoord, *The One Hundred and Twentieth New York State Volunteers*, 114-15.

18. Charles W. Cowtan, *Services of the Tenth New York Volunteers in the War of the Rebellion* (New York: C. H. Ludwig, 1882), 249-50.

19. Cowtan, *Services of the Tenth New York*, 250.

20. Page, *History of the Fourteenth Regiment, Connecticut Vol. Infantry*, 238.

21. Grant, "In the Wilderness."

22. *OR* 36, pt. 1, 699; Grant, "In the Wilderness."

23. *OR* 36, pt. 1, 1063.

24. Rosenblatt, *Hard Marching Every Day*, 216; Grant, "In the Wilderness"; Hulburd to Reverend, June 26, 1864.

25. Coffin, *The Battered Stars*, 134; Grant, "In the Wilderness."

26. Coffin, *The Battered Stars*, 134-35; Richard Crandall Diary, May 6, 1864 entry, Vermont Historical Society; John L. Richards to Mother and Almira, May 30, 1864, FNMP.

Map Set 18: Cavalry Action Along the Brock Road

1. *OR* 36, pt. 1, 321. Some Confederate officers speculated there were as many as two Confederate divisions moving on Hancock's left flank: George Pickett's Division (which was not with the Army of Northern Virginia), and Richard Anderson's Division (which was marching along Orange Plank Road behind Longstreet's men to rejoin A. P. Hill's Division). Humphreys, *The Virginia Campaign, 1864 and 1865*, 41; Rhea, "Union Cavalry in the Wilderness," 126-27.

2. *OR* 36, pt. 1, 877-78; *OR* 36, pt. 2, 468-69; J. H. Kidd, *Personal Recollections of a Cavalryman with Custer's Michigan Cavalry Brigade in the Civil War*

(Ionia, MI: Sentinel Printing Company, 1908), 264-65.

3. OR 36, pt. 1, 816; Steere, *The Wilderness Campaign*, 377, 379. Custer's deployment is unclear. I have used Steere's convention, but Robert Scott believed the 6th Michigan was behind the 1st Michigan. Scott, *Into the Wilderness with the Army of the Potomac*, 139.

4. OR 36, pt. 1, 816.

5. Frank M. Myers, *The Comanches: A History of White's Battalion, Virginia Cavalry, Laurel Brig., Hampton Div., A.N.V. C.S.A* (Marietta, GA: Continental Book Co., 1956), 63-65; McDonald, A *History of the Laurel Brigade*, 234.

6. Myers, *The Comanches*, 265; Edward G. Longacre, *Lee's Cavalrymen: A History of the Mounted Forces of the Army of Northern Virginia* (Mechanicsburg, PA: Stackpole Books, 2002), 279.

7. Kidd, *Personal Recollections of a Cavalryman*, 266-67.

8. Rhea, "Union Cavalry in the Wilderness," 127; Kidd, *Personal Recollections of a Cavalryman*, 267; OR 36, pt. 1, 816.

9. McDonald, A *History of the Laurel Brigade*, 234-35; Kidd, *Personal Recollections of a Cavalryman*, 268. Two of Custer's regiments were specially trained to use sabers, while the other two were carbine specialists. (Kristopher White, former park ranger, personal communication).

10. OR 36, pt. 1, 816; Kidd, *Personal Recollections of a Cavalryman*, 268.

11. OR 36, pt. 1, 816.

12. OR 36, pt. 1, 816, 833; Edward G. Longacre, *Lincoln's Cavalrymen: A History of the Mounted Forces of the Army of the Potomac 1861-1865* (Mechanicsburg, PA: Stackpole Books, 2000), 260.

13. Robert J. Trout, *Galloping Thunder: The Stuart Horse Artillery Battalion* (Mechanicsburg, PA: Stackpole Books, 2002), 462; William Chew's Report, Leigh Collection, U.S. Army Military History Institute; John J. Shoemaker, *Shoemaker's Battery: Stuart Horse Artillery, Pelham's Battalion, Army of Northern Virginia* (Gaithersburg, MD: Butternut Press, n.d.), 70-71.

14. McDonald, A *History of the Laurel Brigade*, 234; Trout, *Galloping Thunder*, 462-63. McDonald, A *History of the Laurel Brigade*, 236; Chew Report; Shoemaker, *Shoemaker's Battery*, 70-71.

15. OR 36, pt. 1, 853.

16. OR 36, pt. 1, 816, 833.

17. OR *Supplement*, pt. 1, vol. 6, 619; McDonald, A *History of the Laurel Brigade*, 236; Jeffry D. Wert, *Cavalryman of the Lost Cause: A Biography of J.E.B. Stuart* (New York: Simon & Schuster, 2008), 341; Patrick A. Bowmaster, ed.,

"A Confederate Cavalryman at War: The Diary of Sergeant Jasper Hawse of the 14th Regiment Virginia Militia, the 17th Virginia Cavalry Battalion, and the 11th Virginia Cavalry," Independent Study Project, Virginia Tech University, December, 1994; Frank M. Myers Letter, May 16, 1864, Frank Myers Correspondence, Civil War Times Collection, U.S. Army Military History Institute.

Map Set 19: Federal Command Confusion

1. Porter, *Campaigning with Grant*, 54; OR 36, pt. 2, 337; Steere, *The Wilderness Campaign*, 322.

2. OR 36, pt. 1, 906, 927; *Committee of the Regiment, Thirty-Sixth Regiment Massachusetts Volunteers*, 150; Rhea, *The Battle of the Wilderness*, 326-27. It appears Bliss' contribution was the 48th Pennsylvania, which marched along Griffin's left flank.

3. OR 36, pt. 1, 906; Rhea, *The Battle of the Wilderness*, 328. According to General Burnside, the men were exposed to a "brisk artillery and infantry fire of the enemy." OR 36, pt. 1, 906.

4. OR 36, pt. 1, 927, 1081.

5. Clark, *N.C. Regiments*, vol. I, 721; OR 36, pt. 1, 934; William H. Randall, "Reminiscences," William H. Randall Papers, Bentley Historical Library, University of Michigan. According to Charles Wood of the 11th New Hampshire, "Went up to their works; found them too strong and moved by the left flank to the 3d Division and formed with them." Charles Wood Diary, May 6, 1864 entry. Civil War Misc. Collection, U.S. Army Military History Institute.

6. OR 36, pt. 1, 928; Rhea, *The Battle of the Wilderness*, 329; Roebling Report, Warren Collection, New York State Archives. Historian Edward Steere was sharply critical of the IX Corps commander when he observed, "Burnside was neither quick nor tough. Here his dilatory movements in the Wilderness are on a par with his sluggish action at Antietam." Steere, *The Wilderness Campaign*, 325.

7. Rhea, *The Battle of the Wilderness*, 332. Hancock and the rest of the Union high command could not account for Longstreet's third division under Maj. Gen. George Pickett, which at this time was operating closer to Richmond and was not with the Army of Northern Virginia.

8. OR 36, pt. 1, 325.

9. According to Hancock's report, OR 36, pt. 1, 321, "Frank's brigade . . . was sent to feel the enemy's right. . . . I do not know why my order to attack with Barlow's division was not more fully carried out. . . . [H]ad my left advanced as directed by me in several orders, I believe the overthrow of the enemy would have been assured." Gibbon's

report is silent on the issue of a 7:00 a.m. order. The division commander was incensed after the war when he learned what Hancock had written in his report. "I never received the order referred to nor ever heard of the charge connected with it until years after that report was written," claimed Gibbon in his memoirs. John Gibbon, *Personal Recollections of the Civil War* (Dayton, OH: Morningside Bookshop, 1988), 389-91. Division commander Barlow corroborated Gibbon by writing that he was ordered only to send in Frank's brigade. OR 36, pt. 1, 389. Historian Edward Steere concluded otherwise and believed Gibbon willfully disobeyed Hancock's orders, but provides no supporting evidence. Steere, *The Wilderness Campaign*, 362. Gordon Rhea describes the situation but does not provide his own perspective. Rhea, *The Battle of the Wilderness*, 332-34.

10. OR 36, pt. 1, 917; Joseph F. Carter, "Leasure's Brigade: Another Account of the Fight at the Salient Angle," *National Tribune*, September 25, 1890.

11. OR 36, pt. 1, 437-38. Webb noted in his report that when his men reformed, the units were intermingled with Carruth's brigade so that "no regiment in the line had on its flanks regiments of its own corps." OR 36, pt. 1, 438.

12. OR 36, pt. 1, 488-89; Martin W. Husk, *The 111th New York Volunteer Infantry: A Civil War History* (Jefferson, NC: McFarland Press, 2009), 117-19; Diary of John Nelson Brown, May 6, 1864 entry, FNMP. Colonel Frank, wrote staff officer Morris Schaff, was a "whiskey-pickled, lately- arrived, blusterous German." Schaff, *The Battle of the Wilderness*, 260. If true, his description might help explain McAllister's obvious exasperation with the man.

13. OR 36, pt. 2, 442; OR 36 pt. 1, 322.

14. Rhea, *The Battle of the Wilderness*, 340; OR 36, pt. 1, 322; OR 36, pt. 2, 443.

15. Moxley Sorrell, Bell Irvin Wiley, ed., *Recollections of a Confederate Staff Officer* (Jackson, TN: McCowat-Mercer Press, 1958), 230; Steere, *The Wilderness Campaign*, 387.

16. C. Irvine Walker, *The Life of Lieutenant General Richard Heron Anderson of the Confederate States Army* (Charleston, SC: Art Publishing Company, 1917), 159. Longstreet recalled that Richard Anderson's Division arrived at 8:00 a.m. and was put under his command. Longstreet, From Manassas to Appomattox, 561. The prior activities of Tige Anderson's Brigade are unclear. Both General Field, in his postwar recollections, and a recent history of one of Anderson's regiments, claim the brigade actually led Field's

Division to the battlefield. The unit was ordered to the right of the Orange Plank Road, and the rest of the division was thrust to the left of the road. This meant the Georgians under Tige Anderson would have had to cut through Kershaw's Division to get to their assigned position, which seems unlikely. It is more probable the brigade was in the rear of the column and made the movement to the right after Kershaw's units had cleared the road. Field, "Campaign of 1864 and 1865," 543; Warren Wilkinson and Steven E. Woodworth, *A Scythe of Fire: The Civil War Story of the Eighth Georgia Infantry Regiment* (New York: William Morrow, 2002), 285-86.

17. Royall, *Some Reminiscences*, 33.

18. Royall, *Some Reminiscences*, 33-34. The leading brigade was apparently Nathaniel Harris's Mississippi outfit. It arrived too late to participate in the brief fight with Colonel Leasure's brigade of Stevenson's division (IX Corps). See Map Set 21 for more details.

19. O'Reilly, *Battle of the Wilderness Map Set*, Map 4.

20. Rhea, *The Battle of the Wilderness*, 352.

Map Set 20: Longstreet Assaults Hancock's Left Flank

1. Longstreet, *From Manassas to Appomattox*, 562; Steere, *The Wilderness Campaign*, 392.

2. OR 36, pt. 1, 1055, 1090; Longstreet, *From Manassas to Appomattox*, 562; Edward P. Alexander, "Grant's Conduct in the Wilderness Campaign," Annual Report of the American Historical Association for the Year 1908 , 2 vols. (Washington, Government Printing Office, 1909), vol. 1, 226; Bradley M. Gottfried, "Mahone's Brigade: Insubordination or Miscommunication?", *Gettysburg Magazine*, no. 18 (January, 1998), 67-76. There is some dispute as to who was in command of the attack column. Despite Longstreet's contemporary and postwar claim that it was Moxley Sorrel, General Mahone claimed otherwise. In his official report, Mahone wrote, "as the senior brigadier, I was directed by Lieutenant-General Longstreet, charged with the immediate direction of this movement." The weight of the evidence and common sense favors Longstreet's version of events that he entrusted his capable staff officer to this important task. Artillerist E. Porter Alexander, a trustworthy witness and never one to shy away from an honest opinion, considered Sorrel a capable and "particularly gallant officer." The Mahone of early May 1864, on the other hand, was still largely

unknown within the army and not considered a particularly capable officer ready for higher command. His nearly invisible performance at Gettysburg, the Army of Northern Virginia's last major pitched battle, left some openly questioning his ability to lead large numbers of troops in battle. After reviewing the evidence, historian Robert E. L. Krick concluded that Sorrel did indeed direct the flank attack, but admitted the record is muddled on the issue. Robert E. L. Krick, "Like a Duck on a June Bug," in Gary Gallagher, ed., *The Wilderness Campaign* (Chapel Hill, NC: University of North Carolina Press, 1997), 242-43. Krick, "Like a Duck on a June Bug," 242-43.

3. Sorrel, *Recollections of a Confederate Staff Officer*, 231-32. Sorrel is a trustworthy eyewitness whose memoirs are considered among the finest published. His description of Longstreet's orders that "some brigades will be found much scattered from the fight" does not mean they had seen combat, but that the nature of the fighting had left them in various locations as circumstances dictated.

4. Henry Heth Report, Eleanor S. Brockenbrough Library, Museum of the Confederacy; Williams, *The Mississippi Brigade of Brig. Gen. Joseph R. Davis*, 147-48. The role of Stone's (Davis's) Brigade in the attack is still debated. Sorrel, who specifically lists gathering up and attacking with Anderson, Mahone, and Wofford, does not mention Stone's (Davis's) participation. Sorrel, *Recollections of a Confederate Staff Officer*, 231-32. It is possible Sorrel merely overlooked Stone's men during the confusion of the charge. General Heth suggests Stone's men did play a role, but his account is vague on that issue. See Henry Heth's Report. Gordon Rhea suggested the worn-out brigade was in reserve and did not participate in the assault. Rhea, *The Battle of the Wilderness*, 357. Robert E. L. Krick, however, in Krick, "Like a Duck on a June Bug," 245, and a history of the 11th Mississippi (one of the brigade's regiments), Stubbs, *Duty-Honor-Valor*, 527, clearly place the brigade on the left side of the attacking column. O'Reilly, *Battle of the Wilderness Map Set*, Map 4, takes a middle road, positing that only the 55th North Carolina and 26th Mississippi (two regiments in the brigade) were involved in the flank attack, while the remainder of the brigade formed much farther north along the road leading to the Chewning farm. I believe the evidence suggests some portion of the brigade was involved in the flank

attack, and if so, this might explain why Moxley Sorrel overlooked the brigade's participation.

5. Krick, "Like a Duck on a June Bug," 243-44; A. J. McWhirter, "General Wofford's Brigade in the Wilderness, May 6th," *Atlanta Journal*, September 21, 1901; Sorrel, *Recollections of a Confederate Staff Officer*, 232; Wilkinson and Woodworth, *A Scythe of Fire*, 286.

6. Richard M. Coffman, *To Honor These Men: A History of Phillips Georgia Legion Infantry Battalion* (Macon, GA: Mercer University Press, 2007), 204-5; Krick, "Like a Duck on a June Bug," 244.

7. O'Reilly, *Battle of the Wilderness* Map Set, Map 4. In piecing together the information about troop depositions, Gordon Rhea believed that Frank's brigade was still in the sector, probably "posted below and somewhat behind McAllister." However, a more recently published unit history of the 111th New York concluded these men had stampeded to the rear and halted only when they reached the defenses lining the Brock Road. Rhea, *The Battle of the Wilderness*, 358n; Husk, *The 111th New York Volunteer Infantry*, 119; OR 36, pt. 1, 489.

8. O'Reilly, *Battle of the Wilderness Map Set*, Map 4; Krick, "Like a Duck on a June Bug," 245.

9. George S. Bernard, *War Talks of Confederate Veterans* (Petersburg, VA: Fenn & Owen, Publishers, 1892), 88, 90, 95; John R. Turner, "The Battle of the Wilderness: The Part Taken by Mahone's Brigade," *Southern Historical Society Papers*, vol. 20, 81-82.

10. Bernard, *War Talks of Confederate Veterans*, 88.

11. McWhirter, "General Wofford's Brigade in the Wilderness," Krick, "Like a Duck on a June Bug," 246; OR 36, pt. 1, 489-90; Rhea, *The Battle of the Wilderness*, 359.

12. Samuel B. Wing, *The Soldier's Story: A Personal Narrative* (Phillips, ME: Phonographic Steam Book and Job Print, 1898), 65.

13. Van Santvoord, *The One Hundred and Twentieth New York State Volunteers*, 114-15.

14. Mason Whiting Tyler, *Recollections of the Civil War* (New York: G. P. Putnam's Sons, 1912), 154; W. M. Abernathy, "Our Mess: The Southern Army Gallantry and Privations, 1861-1865," W. M. Abernathy Collection, Mississippi Department of Archives and History, Jackson, Mississippi; Turner, "The Battle of the Wilderness," *Southern Historical Society Papers*, vol. 20, 75.

15. OR 36, pt. 1, 473-74; Craft, *History of the One Hundred Forty-First Regiment, Pennsylvania Volunteers*, 181; Weygant, *History of the One Hundred and Twenty-Fourth Regiment*, 293. Hancock almost lost one of his division commanders when a cannon ball arced down the Orange Plank Road and

exploded under General Birney's horse. Both rider and horse somehow emerged unhurt, but the animal was temporarily unmanageable. Weygant, *History of the One Hundred and Twenty-Fourth Regiment*, 293-94.

16. Galway, *The Valiant Hours*, 199. Galway noted that the rough and thick vegetation caused "our clothes to be literally torn to shreds."

17. Turner, "The Battle of the Wilderness," *Southern Historical Society Papers*, vol. XX, 86.

18. Turner, "The Battle of the Wilderness," *Southern Historical Society Papers*, vol. XX, 70.

19. Carol Reardon, "The Other Grant: Lewis A. Grant and the Vermont Brigade in the Battle of the Wilderness," in Gary W. Gallagher, ed., *The Wilderness Campaign* (Chapel Hill, NC: University of North Carolina Press, 1997), 233; *OR 36*, pt. 1, 699, 710; Coffin, *The Battered Stars*, 136; Rosenblatt, *Hard Marching Every Day*, 216.

20. Banes, *History of the Philadelphia Brigade*, 231-33. A soldier in the 52nd New York of Owen's brigade recalled that his brigade's retreat was orderly and offered some resistance: "We commenced falling back; not in any rush, however, but firing as we went from behind logs and trees, the enemy following cautiously after us." J. J. Walley, "In the Wilderness: Another Account of the Fight at the Angle," *National Tribune*, December 18, 1890.

21. Turner, "The Battle of the Wilderness," *Southern Historical Society Papers*, vol. 20, 73-74.

22. Monteith, "Battle of the Wilderness," 414-15; Smith, *History of the Seventy-Sixth Regiment New York Volunteers*, 291-92; Rhea, *The Battle of the Wilderness*, 362-63. Writing many years after the battle, Webb claimed that Wadsworth gave "me the most astonishing and bewildering order— which was to leave the twelve regiments under my command at his (Wadsworth's) disposal, and go to the left and find four regiments, and stop the retreat of those troops of the left of our line who were flying to the Brock Road. Alexander S. Webb, "Through the Wilderness," in *Battles and Leaders of the Civil War*, vol. 4, 159-60.

23. Field, "Campaign of 1864 and 1865," 544; Perry, "Reminiscences of the Campaign of 1864 in Virginia," 57; *OR 36*, pt. 1, 624; *Waters and Edmonds, A Small but Spartan Band*, 103.

24. Smith, *History of the Seventy-Sixth Regiment New York Volunteers*, 291-92; William Mali to Edward Robins, October 26, 1888; Gustave Magnitzky to Edward Robins, September 21, 1888, *MOLLUS* Collection, Houghton Library, Harvard University; Rhea, *The Battle of the Wilderness*, 364; Robert Garth Scott, ed., *Fallen Leaves: The Civil War Letters of Major Henry Livermore Abbott* (Kent, OH: Kent State University Press, 1991), 251-52; Bruce, *The Twentieth Regiment of Massachusetts*, 353; Miller, *Harvard's Civil War*, 338. Colonel Macy of the 20th Massachusetts had orders from General Webb to "hold the position we were then in at any cost." A few hours later, Wadsworth came "galloping up in a very wild and exciting manner" and snapped at Macy, "What are you doing there, who commands here?" The division leader was surprised to find a large body of troops manning the works while the rest of the line was falling to pieces. When Colonel Macy identified the regiment and explained he had been placed there by General Webb, Wadsworth, in an "excited" manner corrected the young man: "I command these troops and order you to go forward," he yelled. "Very well, sir," Macy declared, "but we are the 2nd Corps." William Mail did not hear this exchange, but it was obviously not pleasant, for Wadsworth was yelling and waving his arms. Wadsworth decided to lead the charge himself; he always believed no effective leader should ask more than what he could or would do himself. William Mail to Edward Robins, October 26, 1888, FNMP; Miller, *Harvard's Civil War*, 338; Mahood, *General Wadsworth*, 247-48. The location of the attack launched by the 20th Massachusetts is up for debate. The histories of the regiment put the attack south of the Orange Plank Road, but others believe it straddled the road. The latter argument makes sense because the regiment was hit by fire from the 8th Alabama in position north of the road, and this is also the location of Wadsworth's mortal wounding.

25. Miller, *Harvard's Civil War*, 338; Humphreys, *The Virginia Campaign, 1864 and 1865*, 55 (note 1); Rhea, *The Battle of the Wilderness*, 365. The entire regiment did not make the charge. The German recruits "were so terrified that they lay like logs and no amount of rough handling, even with bayonets, had any effect upon them whatsoever," noted surgeon John Perry. A young soldier in the 8th Alabama (Perrin's Brigade) recalled. "As the Yankees advanced our men poured volley after volley into their lines before their hitherto victorious progress could be stayed. Finally they faltered and began to give way; then the yell and charge," as the Alabamians counterattacked. Miller, *Harvard's Civil War*, 338-39; S. W. Vance, "Heroes of the Eighth Alabama Infantry," *Confederate Veteran*, vol. 7 (November, 1899), 492-93.

26. Dawes, *Service with the Sixth Wisconsin Volunteers*, 262; Herdegen, *The Iron Brigade*, 491-92; Gilbert E. Govan and James W. Livingood, eds., *The Haskell Memoirs: The Personal Narrative of a*

Confederate Officer (New York: G. P. Putnam's Sons, 1960), 64-65. Many Rebels claimed to have killed Wadsworth. See Mahood, *General Wadsworth*, 248-50. However, a burst of rounds from the 8th Alabama seems the most logical conclusion. The round that killed him entered near the top of his forehead, and the general lingered two days before expiring on May 8, 1864. Welsh, *Medical Histories of Union Generals*, 355. Major General Andrew A. Humphreys, the army's chief of staff, wrote to Wadsworth's son to explain that, during these "two days of desperate fighting . . . he [Wadsworth] was conspicuous beyond all others for his gallantry, prompter than all others in leading his troops again and again into action. In all these combats he literally led his men, who inspired by his heroic bearing continually renewed the combat, which but for him they would have yielded." A lieutenant colonel in Alexander Hays' brigade agreed, writing that Wadsworth's "presence on the field under the hottest fire inspirited and encouraged the men, and they will ever cherish with pride the memory of the chivalric bravery exhibited by [Wadsworth] in this battle." OR 36, pt. 1, 234; Andrew Humphreys to Mary Craig Wadsworth, September 3, 1864, Wadsworth Family Papers, Library of Congress. Wadsworth was evacuated to a Confederate hospital at Parker's Store, where a farmer named Patrick McCracken arrived to see him. McCracken was a local Irish immigrant farmer who had a run-in with Wadsworth in 1862, while Wadsworth was military governor of the District of Columbia. McCracken was accused of being a Confederate spy and hauled up before Wadsworth, who threw out the charge and sent the Irishman back home to Spotsylvania County. When he learned Wadsworth had been wounded, McCracken arrived with a pail of fresh milk and a desire to tend to the stricken officer. When he died, the farmer carried the corpse home to his land and buried him. When his body was given back to the Union army, Wadsworth's widow was told of McCracken's kindness and thanked him by sending him an undisclosed amount of money, which must have been substantial because McCracken opened a general store shortly thereafter. Former National Park ranger Kristopher White, personal communication.

27. OR 36, pt. 1, 438; Wilkeson, *Recollections of a Private Soldier in the Army of the Potomac*, 71-72; Warren Wilkinson, ed., *Mother May You Never See the Sights I have Seen: The Fifty-Seventh Massachusetts Veteran Volunteers in the Last Year of the Civil War* (New York: Harper and Row, 1990), 73-76; Christopher L. Kolakowski, "A Rough Place and a Hard Fight: Thomas Stevenson's Division on the Brock and Plank Roads," May 6, 1864, in *Civil War Regiments*, vol. 6, no. 4, 34-35. Webb indicated in his postwar account that the 19th Maine and "another regiment" were aligned along the road. However, his after-battle report indicated his entire brigade was in position. Webb, "Through the Wilderness," 161; OR 36, pt. 1, 438.

28. Smith, *History of the Nineteenth Regiment of Maine*, 137-43; OR 36, pt. 1, 438; Webb, "Through the Wilderness," 161.

29. Field, "Campaign of 1864 and 1865," 545; OR 36, pt. 1, 438; John Day Smith, *History of the Nineteenth Regiment of Maine Volunteer Infantry 1862-1865* (Minneapolis, MN: The Great Western Printing Company, 1909), 160-61; Waters and Edmonds, *A Small but Spartan Band*, 104; Ronald G. Griffin, *The 11th Alabama Volunteer Regiment in the Civil War* (Jefferson, NC: McFarland & Company, 2008), 177-78; Rhea, *The Battle of the Wilderness*, 365-66; Krick, "Like a Duck on a June Bug," 251; Francis W. Palfrey, ed., *Memoir of William Francis Bartlett* (Boston: Houghton, Osgood and Company, 1878). 99-101; Stephen Minot Weld, *Dairy and Letters of Stephen Minot Weld* (n.p.: The Riverside Press, 1912), 286.

30. Z. Boylstron Adams, "In the Wilderness," in *Civil War Papers Read Before the Commandery of the State of Massachusetts*. Three volumes (Boston, MA: The Commandery, 1900), vol. 2, 378; Bernard, *War Talks with War Veterans*, 312.

31. Turner, "The Battle of the Wilderness," *Southern Historical Society Papers*, vol. 20, 70.

32. Field, "Campaign of 1864 and 1865," 545.

33. Longstreet, *From Manassas to Appomattox*, 563; OR 36, pt. 1, 1062; Sorrel, *Recollections of a Confederate Staff Officer*, 243; David Gregg McIntosh, "A Ride on Horseback in the Summer of 1910," in David Gregg McIntosh Papers, Southern Historical Collection, University of North Carolina.

34. Govan and Livingood, *The Haskell Memoirs*, 65; Turner, "The Battle of the Wilderness," *Southern Historical Society Papers*, vol. 20, 95.

35. Turner, "The Battle of the Wilderness," *Southern Historical Society Papers*, vol. 20, 74.

36. Sorrel, *Recollections of a Confederate Staff Officer*, 233-34; Krick, "Like a Duck on a June Bug," 257; Stiles, *Four Years Under Marse Robert*, 247. Jenkins had ridden in an ambulance to the battlefield on May 5. He was struck in the forehead during the friendly fire fusillade. One side of his body was paralyzed and he died within five hours of being

wounded. Jack D. Welsh, *Medical Histories of Confederate Generals* (Kent, OH: Kent State University Press, 1995), 115. Some, including a physician, believed the bullet that struck Longstreet entered his throat and traveled down to his shoulder. Given that Longstreet was on horseback and the soldiers firing were on the ground, it seems logistical the bullet initially entered his shoulder area and traveled up to his neck. Welsh, *Medical Histories of Confederate Generals*, 143.

37. Stiles, *Four Years Under Marse Robert*, 247; Welsh, *Medical Histories of Confederate Generals*, 143; William B. Styple, *Writing & Fighting the Confederate War: The Letters of Peter Wellington Alexander Confederate War Correspondent* (Kearny, NJ: Belle Grove Publishing Company, 2002), 212-13. The situation was eerily similar to Stonewall Jackson's mortal wounding. Also the result of friendly fire, Jackson's mortal wounding occurred a year and four days earlier, along the same road and under low-light conditions, although three miles distant. Krick, "Like a Duck on a June Bug," 257.

38. Weygant, *History of the One Hundred and Twenty-Fourth Regiment*, 293; Longstreet, *From Manassas to Appomattox*, 568.

39. Krick "Like a Duck on a June Bug," 247-48; "Wofford's Georgia Brigade," *Atlanta Southern Confederacy*, June 15, 1864.

40. Walker, *History of the Second Army Corps*, 429-30; Rosenblatt, *Hard Marching Every Day*, 217; Grant, "In the Wilderness." J. J. Walley of Owen's brigade recalled that when the men reached the defenses along Brock Road, their officers yelled, "Boys, we are going to stop; every man fall in here." He noted that his brigade was three lines deep behind these breastworks. Walley, "In the Wilderness: Another Account of the Fight at the Angle."

41. Galway, *The Valiant Hours*, 199-200; Rosenblatt, *Hard Marching Every Day*, 217.

42. Krick "Like a Duck on a June Bug," 255; Steere, *The Wilderness Campaign*, 406-9; Field, "Campaign of 1864 and 1865," 545.

Map Set 21: Burnside Finally Hits the Gap

1. OR 36, pt. 2, 460-61; ibid., pt. 1, 942. Burnside claimed his slow progress was related to the "obstacles in the way of General Potter's movement were much more formidable than was at first supposed; a dense and almost impenetrable undergrowth caused considerable confusion, irregularity, and delay." The 11:45

a.m. order was probably framed in response to an earlier message drafted at 10:00 a.m. by Grant's aide, Cyrus Comstock (who was with Burnside at the time), and received at army headquarters at 10:50 a.m.: "Burnside has gained 1½ miles to the left to connect with Wadsworth [this was not true], and now moves at once toward Hancock's firing, with Potter's division deployed, supported by a brigade. I should think Hancock's firing a mile away." OR 36, pt. 1, 906.

2. OR 36, pt. 1, 928 934, 943; Committee of the Regiment, *Thirty-Sixth Regiment Massachusetts Volunteers*, 152; Byron M. Cutcheon, *The Story of the Twentieth Michigan Infantry, July 15, 1862 to May 30, 1865: Embracing Official Documents on File . . .* (Lansing, MI: Robert Smith Printing Co., 1904), 105. Colonel John Hartranft reported that he formed in support of Bliss' brigade, facing southwest, which is at odds with General Willcox's divisional report. According to Lt. Col. Byron Cutcheon of the 20th Michigan (Col. Benjamin Christ's brigade, Willcox's division), when Christ's brigade arrived it was initially placed behind Hartranft's and then moved 350 yards to the left, where it formed the left flank of the IX Corps. This supports Willcox's report and I have used this disposition on the accompanying maps. OR 36, pt. 1, 942, 948, 976.

3. OR 36, pt. 1, 928; Oates, *The War Between the Union and the Confederacy*, 349. The actions of Abner Perrin's Alabama brigade during this period of the battle are unclear. Some authors (Rhea, The Battle of the Wilderness, 400), posit that Perrin's command also turned to face to the left (north) to confront Burnside's advance, but firsthand accounts and the history of the 11th Alabama suggest the brigade continued eastward toward the Brock Road. Vance, "Heroes of the Eighth Alabama Infantry,"492-93; Griffin, *The 11th Alabama Volunteer Regiment in the Civil War*, 177-78.

4. Perry, "Reminiscences of the Campaign of 1864 in Virginia," 60-61.

5. Committee of the Regiment, *Thirty-Sixth Regiment Massachusetts Volunteers*, 153; Perry, "Reminiscences of the Campaign of 1864 in Virginia," 61.

6. Waters and Edmonds, *A Small but Spartan Band*, 107; Lyman Jackman and Amos Hadley, *History of the Sixth New Hampshire Regiment in the War for the Union* (Concord, NH: Republican Press Association, 1891), 220.

7. Committee of the Regiment, *Thirty-Sixth Regiment Massachusetts Volunteers*, 152-53; Oliver Christian Bosbyshell, (Philadelphia: Avil Printing Company, 1895), 148.

8. Oates, *The War Between the Union and the Confederacy*, 350; Perry, "Reminiscences of the Campaign of 1864 in Virginia," 61; Bowles, "Battle of the Wilderness"; D. L. Geer, "Memories of the War," *Florida Index*, January 26, 1906; "From Virginia," Gainesville Cotton States, June 4, 1864; Waters and Edmonds, *A Small but Spartan Band*, 106-7. One of the wounded was Gen. Edward Perry. A minie ball struck him in the foot and, bleeding profusely, the officer needed help to dismount. The wound became infected, and although he did not lose his limb, he was unable to return to active duty and served in the reserves in Alabama. Welsh, *Medical Histories of Confederate Generals*, 169.

9. Bob Mariani, "Private Henry Murdock's Red Badge of Courage," *North South Trader*, vol. 8 (no. 1), November- December, 1980, 39; Oates, *The War Between the Union and the Confederacy*, 350.

10. Oates, *The War Between the Union and the Confederacy*, 350.

11. Committee of the Regiment, *Thirty-Sixth Regiment Massachusetts Volunteers*, 153-54; Bosbyshell, *The 48th in the War*, 148; Frederick E. Cushman, *History of the 58th Regt. Massachusetts Vols. From the 15th day of September, 1863, to the Close of the Rebellion* (Washington, DC: Gibson Brothers, Printers, 1865), 6.

12. Perry, "Reminiscences of the Campaign of 1864 in Virginia," 61.

13. Jackman and Hadley, *History of the Sixth New Hampshire Regiment*, 220; Marvel, *Burnside*, 357; Richard A. Sauers, ed., *The Civil War Journal of Colonel Bolton, 51st Pennsylvania, April 20, 1861-August 2, 1865* (Conshohocken, PA: Combined Publishing, 2000), 198; *OR 36*, pt. 1, 948. Colonel Hartranft was mistaken about the time of this attack when he stated it occurred at 10:00 a.m. Rhea, *The Battle of the Wilderness*, 387.

14. Jackman and Hadley, *History of the Sixth New Hampshire Regiment*, 221; Dewitt Morrill Diary, May 6, 1864 entry, FNMP.

15. Perry, "Reminiscences of the Campaign of 1864 in Virginia," 61-62.

16. Nelms, "Unfinished Report on the Campaign of 1864," 61-62; Williams, *The Mississippi Brigade of Brig. Gen. Joseph R. Davis*, 148-50; Austin C. Dobbins, *Grandfather's Journal: Company B, Sixteenth Mississippi Infantry Volunteers, Harris' Brigade, Mahone's Division, Hill's Corps, A.N.V.* (Dayton, OH: Morningside Books, 1988), 191. According to General Harris's report, "we encountered the enemy, moving in columns by the flank, to the rear of the brigades of Davis [Stone], [Edward] Perry, and Law [William Perry], with the evident intention of cutting off and capturing them, as those brigades were isolated, both flanks exposed and, owing to the density of the woods, unaware of the approach of the enemy from this direction . . . forming a junction with the brigades of Davis, Perry and Law, desperate and repeated efforts were made by the enemy to dislodge us, but they were repulsed with heavy loss, and this position was maintained until after dark." *OR Supplement*, vol. 6, 696.

17. Thomas D. Cockrell and Michael B. Ballard, eds., *A Mississippi Rebel in the Army of Northern Virginia: The Civil War Memoirs of Private David Holt* (Baton Rouge, LA: Louisiana State University Press, 1995), 242-43.

18. Leander W. Cogswell, *A History of the Eleventh New Hampshire Regiment Volunteer Infantry in the Rebellion War, 1861-1865* (Concord, NH: Republican Press Association, 1891), 348; Perry, "Reminiscences of the Campaign of 1864 in Virginia," 62; *OR 36*, pt. 1, 948; Committee of the Regiment, *Thirty-Sixth Regiment Massachusetts Volunteers*, 154. A soldier in Hartranft's 17th Michigan wrote, "Made the last charge on the enemy just before dusk & lost heavily by it . . . harder fighting I never saw before & never wish to see again." Coco Collection, U.S. Army Military History Institute, Carlisle, PA.

19. *OR 36*, pt. 1, 942-43; Cutcheon, *The Story of the Twentieth Michigan Infantry*, 107; Lewis Crater, *History of the Fiftieth Regiment, Penna. Vet. Vols., 1861-65* (Reading, PA: Coleman Printer House, 1884), 51; A. M. Gambone, *Major-General John Frederick Hartranft: Citizen Soldier and Pennsylvania Statesman* (Baltimore, Butternut and Blue Press, 1995), 96. Christ received orders between 2:00 and 3:00 p.m. to rejoin the rest of the division. Rather than be thrown into confusion by trying to march through the woods like the three brigades preceding him, Willcox brought Christ's men back to the Lacy house and took a more direct route. *OR 36*, pt. 1, 941.

20. Cutcheon, *The Story of the Twentieth Michigan Infantry*, 107; Crater, *History of the Fiftieth Regiment*, 51; Frederick Lehman to Parents, May 15, 1864, Lehman Family Papers, Bentley Historical Library, University of Michigan, Ann Arbor, MI; John Irwin Diary, May 6, 1864 entry, FNMP.

21. *OR 36*, pt. 1, 132. Some of Christ's losses were sustained during the encounter with General Ramseur's Brigade earlier in the day.

*Map Set 22: Final Actions
on the Federal Left*

1. *OR* 36, pt. 2, 452; Steere, *The Wilderness Campaign*, 416.

2. Steere, *The Wilderness Campaign*, 418; *OR* 36, pt. 2, 452-53.

3. *OR* 36, pt. 2, 444.

4. James R. Hagood, "Memoirs of the First South Carolina Regiment of Volunteer Infantry in the Confederate War," South Carolina Library, University of South Carolina, 145; James J. Baldwin, *The Struck Eagle: A Biography of Brigadier General Micah Jenkins* (Shippensburg, PA: Burd Street Press, 1996), 284; Wilkinson and Woodworth, *A Scythe of Fire*, 287; Coffman, *To Honor These Men*, 206; Charles H. Andrews, "Diary of the 3rd Georgia Infantry Regiment, 1861-1865, copy owned by author. Southern newspaper correspondent Peter Alexander wrote that the attack line moved in the form of a "letter V, with the sharp point towards the enemy . . . [Anderson's Brigade] formed the apex of the line." Styple, *Writing & Fighting the Confederate War*, 213. Rhea interpreted this passage to mean that Anderson was on Jenkins's left. This seems unlikely, given the brigade's position well south of the Orange Plank Road. Mahone's Brigade would be much more likely to have assumed this position.

5. The actual alignment of the three reserve brigades is unclear. While some (Rhea, *The Battle of the Wilderness*, 390-92; O'Reilly, *Battle of the Wilderness Map Set*, Map 5) place Carroll closer to the barricades than Rice, first-person accounts, unit histories, and subsequent attack routes suggest the alignment was Rice-Carroll-Leasure. *OR* 36, pt. 1, 324, 447; William Gilfillan Gavin, *Infantryman Pettit: The Civil War Letters of Corporal Frederick Pettit* (Shippensburg, PA: White Mane Publishing Company, 1990), 145; Kolakowski, "A Rough Place and a Hard Fight," 38-41; John Black to William Hofmann, October 23, 1872, Winfield Scott Hancock Papers, Perkins Special Collections Library, Duke University, Durham, North Carolina.

6. Steere, *The Wilderness Campaign*, 422-23. Steere postulated that as many as a dozen brigades (four each from Heth's, Field's, and Kershaw's divisions) advanced into action. This analysis is suspect as Heth's brigades were at the Chewning farm guarding the space between A. P. Hill's and Richard Ewell's Corps. Several other brigades were also facing Burnside's thrust from the north Therefore, it appears General Lee had seven brigades aligned against Hancock's Brock Road line, and with Wright's and Humphreys's reserve units, the number could have swelled to

nine—a small number against the 18 brigades the Union fielded in this sector.

7. William Gilfillan Gavin, *Campaigning with the Roundheads: The History of the One Hundredth Pennsylvania Volunteer Infantry Regiment in the American Civil War, 1861-1865* (Dayton: Morningside Press, 1989), 387; Kolakowski, "A Rough Place and a Hard Fight," 37; Charles F. Walcott, *History of the Twenty-First Regiment Massachusetts Volunteers in the War for the Preservation of the Union, 1861-1865* (Boston: Houghton, Mifflin and Company, 1882), 316; Carter, "Leasure's Brigade: Another Account of the Fight at the Salient Angle."

8. Kolakowski, "A Rough Place and a Hard Fight," 37-38. According to one account, the expedition may have ended when Colonel Leasure encountered General Mott, who screamed, "Colonel, for God's sake, get your men out of here!" Gavin, *Campaigning with the Roundheads*, 387-89.

9. Agassiz, *Meade's Headquarters*, 97; Smith, *History of the Nineteenth Regiment of Maine*, 138; Cudworth, *History of the First Regiment Massachusetts Infantry*, 462-63; Weygant, *History of the One Hundred and Twenty-Fourth Regiment*, 296; Page, *Letters of a War Correspondent*, 55. While Longstreet's Corps and Anderson's Division were engaged with Hancock's II and Burnside's IX corps, Heth's and Wilcox's divisions were resting in the rear. According to James Conner of Stone's Brigade, the men were ordered to build 18-inch high earthworks they could lie behind. James Conner Memoir, FNMP.

10. Coffman, *To Honor These Men*, 205; John Daniel McDonell, "Recollections of the War," FNMP; Weygant, *History of the One Hundred and Twenty-Fourth Regiment*, 296; Banes, *History of the Philadelphia Brigade*, 233; Hagood, "Memoirs," 146.

11. Cudworth, *History of the First Regiment Massachusetts Infantry*, 463.

12. *OR* 36, pt. 1, 489-90; Walley, "In the Wilderness: Another Account of the Fight at the Angle."

13. Walker, *History of the Second Army Corps*, 432. The initial attack stunned the defenders, who were mostly exhausted and in some cases still unorganized. "The first few minutes we were staggered," admitted a reporter. Page, *Letters of a War Correspondent*, 55.

14. Rhea, *The Battle of the Wilderness*, 393-94; Natalie J. Bond and Osmun L. Coward, eds., *The South Carolinians: Colonel Asbury Coward's Memoirs* (New York: Vantage Press, 1968), 136.

15. The unit in the front line in front of McAllister was almost certainly Brewster's brigade

(Mott's division). *OR 36*, pt. 1, 489-90, 514, 519; Joseph F. Carter, "In the Wilderness: The Controversy Between Carroll's and Leasure's Brigades." *National Tribune*, January 1, 1891. According to a soldier in the 17th Indiana of Carroll's brigade, "the men in charge of those brass guns were, I think, the bravest I ever saw." John O. Donald, "The Wilderness: To What Battery Did the Two Guns Belong?" *National Tribune*, April 9, 1891.

16. Walker, *History of the Second Army Corps*, 432; Rhea, *The Battle of the Wilderness*, 394; Joseph F. Carter, "In the Wilderness: The Troops at the Crossroads Saved by the Wall of Fire." *National Tribune*, April 7, 1892; Josiah Murphey Diary, May 6, 1864 entry, Boston Public Library, Boston, MA; Galway, *The Valiant Hours*, 201.

17. *OR 36*, pt. 1, 514; Page, *Letters of a War Correspondent*, 55; Nelson E. Miller, "What the 20th Ind. did at the Junction of the Brock and Plank Roads," *National Tribune*, January 21, 1892. A few days later on May 12, division leader David Birney found General Ward (who was wounded in the head) drunk. General Hancock removed Ward from command and charged him with "misbehavior and intoxication in the presence of the enemy during the battle of the Wilderness" and had him arrested. Despite the charges, Ward was honorably mustered out of the Army of the Potomac on July 18, 1864. Many of Ward's associates were shocked by the news as he had always been singled out by his superiors for bravery and ability. Ward's troops had fought through the hell of the Wilderness for both days and the stress may have caused Ward to finally break. Warner, *Generals in Blue*, 538; Rhea, *The Battle of the Wilderness*, 394.

18. Joseph M. Sudsburg, "In the Wilderness: The Colonel of the 3rd Md. Takes a Hand in the Controversy," *National Tribune*, January 15, 1891; Gavin, *Campaigning with the Roundheads*, 394-96; Ira B. Goodrich, "Helped Save the Day: A Massachusetts Comrade's Testimony for Leasure's Brigade, *National Tribune*, April 30, 1891; Carter, "Leasure's Brigade: Another Account of the Fight at the Salient Angle."

19. *OR 36*, pt. 1, 408. Brooke probably went in on Colonel Leasure's left.

20. Chamberlin, *History of the One Hundred and Fiftieth Regiment, Pennsylvania Volunteers*, 212-13.

21. *OR 36*, pt. 1, 324, 447; Galway, *The Valiant Hours*, 201; Cowtan, *Services of the Tenth New York*, 255-56; O. G. Daniels, "At the Crossroads: The Charge Made by Carroll's Brigade," *National Tribune*, December 4, 1890. Although wounded in the arm during the earlier part of the day,

Carroll resolutely refused to relinquish command. For reasons that remain unclear, General Hancock officially recognized only Carroll's and Brooke's attacks in his report; the assaults conducted by units in the V Corps and IX Corps were ignored, possibly because Hancock believed their recognition would come from their own corps commanders.

22. *OR 36*, pt. 1, 514, 1069; Daniel Handy to wife, May 8, 1864, FNMP.

Map Set 23: Ewell Attacks the Federal Right

1. Preeminent Southern scholar Douglas Freeman described General Gordon as possessing "a certain freshness, a boldness, a freedom, an originality in sound military design." Douglas Southall Freeman, *Lee's Lieutenants: A Study in Command*. 3 vols. (New York: Charles Scribner's Sons, 1944), vol. 3, xxxiv.

2. John B. Gordon, *Reminiscences of the Civil War* (New York: Charles Scribner's Sons, 1903), 243-44; *OR 36*, pt. 1, 1,077. Gordon's memoir is one of the best by a Confederate general, but it is also laced with self-aggrandizement and no little exaggeration and self-promotion, and so needs to be read and relied upon, as do all memoirs, with some level of healthy skepticism.

3. Gordon, *Reminiscences*, 244-47.

4. Gordon, *Reminiscences*, 255; Thomas Jones to John Daniel, July 3, 1904 and December 29, 1904, Daniel Collection, University of Virginia; Early, *Autobiographical Sketch and Narrative*, 348. Gordon and Early had clashed the day before when the latter ordered an attack before Gordon's Brigade was ready for action. See Map Set 5.4, note 19.

5. Jones to Daniel, December 29, 1904; Early, *Autobiographical Sketch and Narrative*, 348.

6. Gordon, *Reminiscences*, 255.

7. Barry Popchock, "Lost Opportunity in the Wilderness," *Columbiad*, vol. 3, no. 2 (Summer, 1999), 24; Rhea, *The Battle of the Wilderness*, 409-10.

8. Clark, *N.C. Regiments*, vol. 1, 288, vol. 2, 241; Rhea, *The Battle of the Wilderness*, 410.

9. *OR 36*, pt. 1, 514, 728-29; Stevens, *Three Years in the Sixth Corps*, 310-11; Charles Edin- borough, "The Sixth Corps at the Wilderness," *National Tribune*, January 7, 1885; George R. Lincoln, "The First Long Island Regiment," *The Brooklyn Union*, May 13, 1864; Z. T. Griffen, "The Wilderness: The Disaster to Shaler's and Seymour's Brigades," *National Tribune*, March 11, 1886; James H. Brewer, "The Wilderness: The Turning of the Right Wing of the Army," *National Tribune*, June 14, 1888; Samuel C. Kerr, "In the Wilderness: Turning the

Right Flank on May 6, 1864," *National Tribune*, July 11, 1889; Z. T. Griffen, "The Wilderness: The Turning of the Right Flank, May 6, 1864," *National Tribune*, August 15, 1889.

10. Alexander Shaler *Diary*, May 6, 1864 entry, New York Historical Society, Albany, New York; Brewer, "The Wilderness: The Turning of the Right Wing of the Army"; *OR 36*, pt. 1, 736-37. Colonel Matthew McClennan of the 138th Pennsylvania showed his displeasure in his official report of the battle when he noted that when the attack began that evening, "the troops were cooking supper (by order of the brigade commander)." *OR 36*, pt. 1, 751.

11. Edinborough, "The Sixth Corps at the Wilderness"; Popchock, "Lost Opportunity in the Wilderness," 26.

12. Who actually unleashed the charge against Sedgwick's right flank is disputed. Gordon claimed General Lee settled the vexing issue by instructing Ewell to attack General Meade's right flank to divert troops away from the Brock Road defenses. Gordon, *Reminiscences*, 258. Ewell never mentioned receiving specific orders, only that he was finally able to conduct a personal reconnaissance of his left flank just before sunset. *OR 36*, pt. 1, 1,070-71. General Early also claimed credit for advocating for the attack. Early, *Autobiographical Sketch and Narrative*, 348-49. Gordon Rhea found many portions of Gordon's memories of this event to be "troubling," because they ran counter to Lee's leadership style, that the timing was inconsistent, and that Gordon penned his memoirs in the early years of the Twentieth Century. Rhea believed Lee may have discussed the possibility of an attack with Ewell even before the attack on Hancock's troops, and that Ewell may have brought up Gordon's idea, which Lee then approved. Rhea, *The Battle of the Wilderness*, 415-16. Either way, Ewell ordered Early to assemble troops to assault and turn the enemy's right flank. Freeman, *Lee's Lieutenants*, vol. 3, 370-71; Popchock, "Lost Opportunity in the Wilderness," 26.

13. *OR 36*, pt. 1, 1071; Popchock, "Lost Opportunity in the Wilderness," 26; Rhea, *The Battle of the Wilderness*, 423; Robert Johnston Report, Daniel Collection, University of Virginia. Hoffman led John Pegram's Brigade.

14. Johnson, *Under the Southern Cross*, 157; Bradwell, "Second Day's Battle of the Wilderness," 20; *Savannah Morning News*, July 20, 1864.

15. Nichols, *A Soldier's Story of His Regiment*, 148; Bradwell, "Second Day's Battle of the Wilderness," 20.

16. Charles Whittier, "Reminiscences," Boston Public Library; Rhea, *The Battle of the Wilderness*, 419.

17. Zeno T. Griffen, "In the Wilderness: The Turning of the Right Flank, May 6, 1864;" *OR 36*, pt. 1, 737.

18. Edinborough, "The Sixth Corps at the Wilderness"; Nichols, *A Soldier's Story of His Regiment*, 148.

19. Robert Johnston Report, Daniel Collection, University of Virginia; Rhea, *The Battle of the Wilderness*, 422. According to Capt. Benjamin Collins of the 12th North Carolina, "The Brig. without resting was almost immediately formed on our extreme left and moving forward struck the right of Grant's army in flank." His memoir suggests the brigade played an instrumental role in the flank attack, but its actual impact is subject to debate. Benjamin M. Collins, "Reminiscence of the Overland Campaign," Southern Historical Collection, University of North Carolina, Chapel Hill, NC. In a letter after the war, General Johnston deflected any assertion that his men were overly heroic: "It was just a day of plain hard fighting," he wrote. Johnston was upset with his division commander, Jubal Early: "I suppose Gen Early thought because we came off the field in good order that we hadn't any severe struggle during the day and therefore he ordered me to cover the retreat of the army." Robert Johnston to John Daniel, June 30, 1905. J. W. Daniel Papers, Duke University, Durham, NC. Thomas Jones, an aide to General Gordon, wrote after the war, "I am not sure, for I was not with it, that Robt. D. Johnston's brigade got under fire that evening. . . . I feel quite sure that some of his command was halted or thrown into confusion that evening." Thomas Jones to John Daniel June 30, 1904, J. W. Daniel Papers, Duke University, Durham, NC.

20. Edinborough, "The Sixth Corps at the Wilderness."

21. *OR 36*, pt. 1, 737; Brewster, "The Wilderness"; "Letter from the 126th Ohio," *Steubenville Weekly Herald*, May 17, 1864.

22. Griffen, "In the Wilderness The Disaster to Shaler's and Seymour's Brigades;" "Letter from the 126 Ohio," *Steubenville Weekly Herald*, May 17, 1864; Hyland C. Kirk, *Heavy Guns and Light: History of the 4th New York Heavy Artillery* (New York: Dillingham, 1890), 160. According to General Ewell, some of Harry Hays' Brigade was "partly moved out of his works to connect with Gordon."

OR 36, pt. 1, 1,071; It is unclear whether a junction ever came about.

23. Jack to Samuel Bradbury, May 19, 1864, Samuel Bradbury Papers, Duke University; Kirk, *Heavy Guns and Light*, 160.

24. OR 36, pt. 1, 732, 745. Thomas S. Berry, "In the Wilderness," *National Tribune*, October 3, 1889. Charles E. Garlinger, "Another Account," *National Tribune*, October 17, 1889. The 6th Maryland was part of Seymour's brigade and was farther right, but in between two of Shaler's regiments, making the 126th Ohio the right unit of the bulk of Seymour's brigade line.

25. OR 36, pt. 1, 732, 752; Brewer, "The Wilderness: The Turning of the Right Wing of the Army." According to James Brewer of the 6th Maryland, Sedgwick stood on a log, "and one instant begging the men for God's sake to rally, and the next moment, as some demoralized solider came by, he would swear that unless he stopped he would cut his d__d head off, and with his drawn blade he would go through the motion."

26. Gordon, *Reminiscences*, 249.

27. Popchock, "Lost Opportunity in the Wilderness," 31; A. L. Syphers, "In the Wilderness: Was the Right Flank Turned May 6?", *National Tribune*, June 13, 1889; Rhea, *The Battle of the Wilderness*, 420. C. E. Stevens's recollection demonstrates the desperate nature of the fight: "Our left [77th New York] clung to the breastworks . . . our right was at right angles to the works, forming the base for a new line." C. E. Stevens, "Not a Fighting Regiment," *National Tribune*, October 8, 1908.

28. Johnston Report. According to Johnston, "if proper information had been given me, I could have accomplished a great deal more and believe that the results of the action would have been… nd more disastrous to the enemy." Johnston's brigade alignment is not known. However, it appears the 23rd North Carolina was on its right flank, for it was sent forward to support Gordon's flank when additional support was requested prior to the Tar Heels falling back.

29. OR 36, pt. 1, 1,078; John M. Ashcraft, 31st Virginia Infantry (Lynchburg, VA: H. E. Howard, 1988), 65; Jones to Daniel, July 3, 1904.

30. Popchock, "Lost Opportunity in the Wilderness," 31; Stevens, *Three Years in the Sixth Corps*, 318; Wingfield Diary, May 6, 1864 entry, FNMP; Driver, *58th Virginia Infantry*, 59. Henry Wingfield also recorded in his diary, "Our brigade was attached to his [Gordon's] but owing to the fact that our Genl. Pegram had been wounded on the previous day we failed to connect but came up afterwards. Just as we were about making the junction desired we were ambuscaded by the Yankees."

31. Jones, *Civil War Memoirs of Captain William J. Seymour*, 114-15. The brigade's modern historian noted, "Hays was supposed to join the attack once the Federal flank was dislodged . . . the Tigers' participation was limited to heavy skirmishing." Jones, *Lee's Tigers*, 199.

32. OR 36, pt. 1, 666, 723; J. Payne, "The Wilderness: The Turning of the Right Flank, May 6, 1864," *National Tribune*, July 18, 1889.

33. Driver, *52nd Virginia Infantry*, 52-53; Kleese, *49th Virginia Infantry*, 46-47; Laura Virginia Hale and Stanley S. Phillips, *History of the Forty-Ninth Virginia, C.S.A., "Extra Billy Smith's Boys:" Based on the Unpublished Memoirs of Captain Robert Daniel Funkhouser, Company D, 49th Virginia Infantry, C.S.A.* (n.p., n.p., 1981), 109; Kirk, *Heavy Guns and Light*, 166-67. According to an officer in the 52nd Virginia, his unit moved forward in the black thickets and took fire from the rear and front: "There was not support. . . . The line after moving a short distance toward the Federal works fell back. The men knew nothing of Gordon's progress and success on their left; they evidently felt that a charge by them against the Federal works was hopeless. A few officers urged the line forward until it dissolved." Bumgardner, "Pegram's Brigade, Early's Division: Ewell's Corps in the Battle of the Wilderness." While it is conceivable that only one attack was made by the brigade, Daniel's account (see Map 23.5) clearly states he only moved two regiments forward.

34. Kirk, *Heavy Guns and Light*, 166-67; Hale and Phillips, *History of the Forty-Ninth Virginia*, 109. Pegram's Brigade lost 168 men during this charge. Young, *Lee's Army During the Overland Campaign*, 278.

35. OR 36, pt. 1, 737, 1078; Gordon, *Reminiscences*, 103-4; Popchock, "Lost Opportunity in the Wilderness," 34; Freeman, *Lee's Lieutenants*, vol. 3, 391; According to Colonel Horn of the 6th Maryland, "General Shaler did all that [a] man could do to rally his troops, being captured by the enemy while so engaged." OR 36, pt. 1, 737. Gordon rode Shaler's horse "Abe," which he renamed "General Shaler" for the rest of the war before selling him at Appomattox to finance his trip home to Georgia. Popchock, "Lost Opportunity in the Wilderness," 37. Gordon's Brigade entered the battle with almost 2,300 men and lost a combined 319 from all sources on May 5 and 6. Most of these occurred during the May 5 afternoon fighting south of the Orange Turnpike.

Young, *Lee's Army During the Overland Campaign*, 94, 276.

36. *OR* 36, pt. 1, 745-46; Shaler *Diary*, May 6, 1864 entry; Humphreys, *The Virginia Campaign, 1864 and 1865*, 50.

Map Set 24: The Battle Ends
(May 6 - 7, 1864)

1. Porter, *Campaigning with Grant*, 72-73.

2. *OR* 33, pt. 1, 1036; *OR* 36, pt. 1, 119-37, 285, 853, 875; Powell, *The Fifth Army Corps*, 629-31; Walker, *History of the Second Army Corps*, 435-40; Rhea, *The Battle of the Wilderness*, 436.

3. Agassiz, *Meade's Headquarters*, 102.

4. David S. Sparks, ed., *Inside Lincoln's Army: The Diary of Marsena Rudolph Patrick, Provost Marshal General, Army of the Potomac* (New York: Thomas Yoseloff, 1964), 369.

5. Rhea, *The Battle of the Wilderness*, 432-33; Lyman Journal, May 6, 1864, Lyman Papers, Massachusetts Historical Society.

6. Webb, "Through the Wilderness," 163.

7. Stephen R. Taaffe, *Commanding the Army of the Potomac* (Lawrence, KS: Kansas University Press, 2006), 156.

8. Young, *Lee's Army During the Overland Campaign*, 21, 232, 24546; Freeman, *Lee's Lieutenants*, vol. 3, 372.

9. Carmichael, "Escaping the Shadow of Gettysburg," 146; Rhea, *The Battle of the Wilderness*, 442-43.

10. Rhea, *The Battle of the Wilderness*, 444-45; Carmichael, "Escaping the Shadow of Gettysburg," 152-53.

11. Schaff, *The Battle of the Wilderness*, 326.

12. *OR* 36, pt. 2, 480.

13. Porter, *Campaigning with Grant*, 65-66.

14. *OR* 36, pt. 1, 1041; *OR* 36, pt. 2, 968, 971; Freeman, *Lee's Lieutenants*, vol. 3, 375-80.

15. *OR* 36, pt. 2, 481.

Bibliography

Archival Sources

Andersonville National Historic Site
  Samuel Foust Diary

Atlanta History Center
  Sarah Pfeiffer Collection

Auburn University
  James H. Lane Collection

Boston Public Library, Boston, Massachusetts
  Josiah Murphey Diary
  Charles Whittier, "Reminiscences."

Duke University (Perkins Special Collections Library), Durham, North Carolina
  Samuel Bradbury Papers
  J. W. Daniel Papers
  Foster and Foster Papers
  Winfield Scott Hancock Papers

Fredericksburg National Military Park, Fredericksburg, Virginia
  Albert M. Haywood Letters
  Albert Reid Diary
  Amos G. Bean diary
  Andrew Werts Memoir
  Aycock, B. L. "A Sketch: The Lone Star Guards."
  Benjamin F. Hurlburd Letters
  Benjamin Justice Letters
  Carroll Scott Waldron, "The War Memoir of Carroll Scott Waldron"
  Charles Haynes Diary
  Charles Melville Taylor Diary
  Charles Thomas Bowen Letters
  D. A. Jones Letters
  Daniel Handy Letters
  Daniel H. Mowen, "Reminiscences of the Civil War by a Veteran in the Union Army."
  David Neely Diary
  Dewitt Morrill Diary
  Edward Holton Letters
  Francis Cordrey Diary
  Francis Rew Letters
  George A. Bowen Diary
  George S. Young Diary
  George Hugunin Memoir
  George H. Uhlen, "Camps and Campaigns of the 93d Regiment Pennsylvania Volunteers."
  Henry Kaiser Diary

Henry Wyatt Wingfield Diary
James Conner Memoir
James W. Freeman Diary
John E. Kittle Diary
John Nelson Brown Diary
John Irwin Diary
John Daniel McDonell, "Recollections of the War"
John L. Richards Letters
Joseph S. Wicklein Memoir
Lewis Luckenbill Diary
Lewis Van Blarcom Speech
Luther Harris Memoir
Orrin Cook Memoirs
Porter Farley, "The 140th New York . . . Wilderness, May 5, 1984."
Robert Pratt diary
Robert S. Robertson Letters
William Snakenberg, "Memoirs of W. P. Snakenberg."
Samuel Burwell Memoir
Theodore Castor Memoir
Thomas Wood Memoir
Thomas Alfred Martin, "Autobiography."
W. R. Montgomery Letters
William B. Kent Letters
William Mail Letters
William Holmes Morse Diary
William Owen Diary

Gettysburg National Military Park
George Markle Diary

Handley Library, Winchester, Virginia
James McCown Diary

Harvard University (Houghton Library), Boston, Massachusetts
Mollus Collection

Kansas State Historical Society, Topeka, Kansas
John Judd Diary

Library of Congress, Washington, D.C.
Brooks Collection
Thomas S. Doyle Memoirs
Harold C. George Papers
J. Warren Keifer Papers
George Washington Hall Diary
Hotchkiss Papers
Joseph Hayes Journal (Joshua Chamberlain Collection)
Wadsworth Family Papers

Massachusetts Historical Society, Boston, Massachusetts
Lyman Papers

Mississippi Department of Archives and History, Jackson, Mississippi
W. M. Abernathy Collection

Museum of the Confederacy (Eleanor S. Brockenbrough Library), Richmond, Virginia
Henry Heth Report

Navarro College (Pearce Civil War Collections), Corsicana, Texas
Clark S. Edwards Papers
Frank Rood Letters

New York Historical Society, Albany, New York
Alexander Shaler Diary

New York State Archives, Albany, New York
Washington Roebling Report (Gouverneur Warren Collection)
Gouverneur Warren Collection

North Carolina Division of Archives and History, Raleigh, North Carolina
Thomas Devereux Papers
Samuel Finley Harper Letters
James B. Gordon Papers
George Pearsall Letters

Oshkosh Public Museum
Henry B. Harshaw and Richard Lester, "Operations of the 'Iron Brigade' in the Spring Campaign of 1864."

Pennsylvania Historical Society
Col. John Irvin Report

Richmond National Military Park
George B. Imler Diary

South Carolina Library, Columbia, South Carolina
James Drayton Nance Papers

Tennessee State Library and Archives, Nashville, Tennessee
Brown-Ewell Papers

University of Michigan (Bentley Historical Library), Ann Arbor, Michigan
Byron M. Cutcheon Papers
Lehman Family Papers
William H. Randall Papers

University of North Carolina (Southern Historical Collection), Chapel Hill, North Carolina
Benjamin M. Collins, "Reminiscence of the Overland Campaign."
Joseph Fuller Diary
David Gregg McIntosh Papers

University of South Carolina (South Caroliniana Library), Columbia, South Carolina
James R. Hagood, "Memoirs of the First South Carolina Regiment of Volunteer Infantry in the Confederate War."

University of Virginia, Charlottesville, Virginia
John W. Daniel Collection

University of Wisconsin, (Eau Claire Research Center), Eau Claire, Wisconsin
Civil War Diary of Capt. George Britton

U.S. Army Military History Institute, Carlisle, Pennsylvania
Stephen Chase Memoir
Coco Collection
Edwin Halsey Diary
Edwin Halsey Letters
Leigh Collection
Frank Myers Correspondence
Charles Penrose, "Official Report of the Movement of the Fifteenth Reg. N.J. During Grant's Wilderness Campaign."
Charles C. Perkins Memoir
Murray S. Smith Collection
Charles Wood Diary

Vermont Historical Society, Burlington, Vermont
Richard Crandall Diary

Virginia Historical Society, Richmond, Virginia
Francis G. Ruffin Papers

Virginia Tech University, Blacksburg, Virginia
Bowmaster, Patrick A., ed. "A Confederate Cavalryman at War: The Diary of Sergeant Jasper Hawse of the 14th Regiment Virginia Militia, the 17th Virginia Cavalry Battalion, and the 11th Virginia Cavalry." Independent Study Project (December 1994).

Winthrop College (Archive Department), Rock Hill, SC.
Thomas Belue Diary

Newspapers

Augusta (GA) Chronicle and Sentinel, June 1, 1864
Gainesville Cotton States, June 4, 1864
Macon Daily Telegraph, May 26, 1864
Rochester Democrat and American, July 23, 1864
The Saratogian, June 9, 1864
Savannah Morning News, July 20, 1864

Official Documents

Hewitt, Janet, ed. *Supplement to the Official Records of the Civil War*, 100 Voumes. Wilmington, NC: Broadfoot Publishing Co., 1999).

United States War Department, *The War of the Rebellion: A Compilation of the Official Records of the Union and Confederate Armies*, 128 volumes (Washington: U. S. Government Printing Office, 1880-1901.

Books

Agassiz, George R. ed., *Meade's Headquarters, 1863-1865: Letters of Colonel Theodore Lyman from the Wilderness to Appomattox*. Boston: The Atlantic Monthly Press, 1922.

Alexander, Edward Porter. *Military Memoirs of a Confederate: A Critical Narrative*. New York: C. Scribner's Sons, 1907.

Armstrong, Richard L. *25th Virginia Infantry*. H. E. Howard, Inc., 1990.

Ashcraft, John M. *31st Virginia Infantry*. Lynchburg, VA: H. E. Howard, 1988.

Atkinson, C. F. *Grant's Campaigns of 1864 and 1865: The Wilderness and Cold Harbor*. London: H. Rees, Ltd., 1908.

Baldwin, James J. *The Struck Eagle: A Biography of Brigadier General Micah Jenkins*. Shippensburg, PA: Burd Street Press, 1996.

Banes, Charles H. *History of the Philadelphia Brigade: Sixty-Ninth, Seventy-First, Seventy-Second, and One Hundred and Sixth Pennsylvania Volunteers*. Philadelphia: J. B. Lippincott & Co., 1876.

Bates, Samuel P. *History of the Pennsylvania Volunteers: Prepared in Compliance with Acts of the Legislature*. Harrisburg, PA: B. Singerly, State Printer, 1869. Five Volumes.

Battle, Cullen Andrews. *Third Alabama! The Civil War Memoir of Brigadier General Cullen Andrews Battle, CSA*. Tuscaloosa, AL: The University of Alabama Press, 2000.

Bean, William G. *The Liberty Hall Volunteers: Stonewall's College Boys*. Charlottesville, Va.: University of Virginia Press, 1964.

George C. *Vermont in the Civil War*. Two volumes. Burlington, VT: The Free Press Association, 1886.

Bennett, Brian A. *Sons of Old Monroe: A Regimental History of Patrick O'Rorke's 140th New York Volunteer Infantry*. Dayton, OH: The Press of Morningside Bookshop, 1999.

Benson, Susan Williams, ed. *Berry Benson's Civil War Book: Memoirs of a Confederate Scout and Sharpshooter*. Athens, GA: University of Georgia Press, 1992.

Bernard, George S. *War Talks of Confederate Veterans*. Petersburg, VA: Fenn & Owen, Publishers, 1892.

Best, Issac O. *History of the 121st New York State Infantry*. Chicago: J. H. Smith, 1921.

Bidwell, Frederick David. *History of the Forty-Ninth New York Volunteers*. Albany, NY: J. B. Lyon Company, Printers, 1916.

Bicknell, George W. *History of the Fifth Regiment Maine Volunteers*. Portland, ME: Hall L. Davis, 1871.

Bishop, Randy. *The Tennessee Brigade: A History of the Volunteers of the Army of Northern Virginia*. Bloomington, IN: AuthorHouse, 2005.

Bond, Natalie J. and Osmun L. Coward, eds., *The South Carolinians: Colonel Asbury Coward's Memoirs*. New York: Vantage Press, 1968.

Bosbyshell, Oliver Christian. *The 48th in the War: Being a Narrative of the Campaigns of the 48th Regiment Pennsylvania Volunteers During the War of the Rebellion*. Philadelphia: Avil Printing Company, 1895.

Boudrye, Louis N. *Historic Records of the Fifth New York Cavalry, First Ira Harris Guard*. Albany, NY: J. Munsell, 1865.

Bowen, James. History of the Thirty-Seventh Regiment Massachusetts Volunteers, in the Civil War of 1861-1865. Holyoke, MA: C. W. Bryan & Company, 1884.

Brainard, Mary Genevie Green. *Campaigns of the One Hundred and Forty-Sixth Regiment, New York State Volunteers*. New York: G. P. Putnam's Sons, 1915.

Brewer, A. T. *History of the Sixty-First Regiment Pennsylvania Volunteers*. Philadelphia: Art Engraving & Printing Co., 1911.

Brown, Campbell. *Campbell Brown's Civil War: With Ewell and the Army of Northern Virginia.* Baton Rouge, LA: Louisiana State University Press, 2001.

Bruce, George A. *The Twentieth Regiment of Massachusetts Volunteer Infantry 1861-1865.* Boston: Houghton, Mifflin, and Co., 1906.

Buck, Samuel E. *With the Old Confeds.* Baltimore, MD: H. E. Houck & Co., 1925.

Buell, Augustus. *The Cannoneer: Recollections of Service in the Army of the Potomac.* Washington: The National Tribune Company, 1890.

Caldwell, F. J. *The History of a Brigade of South Carolinians known as "Gregg's" and Subsequently as McGowan's Brigade.* Philadelphia: King and Baird Printers, 1866.

Chapla, John D. *48th Virginia Infantry.* Lynchburg, VA: H. E. Howard, Inc., 1989.

Cilella, Salvatore G. Jr., *Upton's Regulars: The 121st New York Infantry in the Civil War.* Lawrence, KS: Kansas University Press, 2009.

Chamberlin, Thomas. *History of the One Hundred and Fiftieth Regiment, Pennsylvania Volunteers, Second Regiment, Bucktail Brigade.* Philadelphia: F. McManus, Jr. & Co., Printers, 1905.

Chase, Peter S. *Reunion Greeting Together with a Historic Sketch.* Brattleboro, VT: Phoenix Job Printing Office, 1891.

Clark, Walter. *Histories of the Several Regiments and Battalions from North Carolina in the Great War 1861-'65.* Five volumes. Wilmington, NC: Broadfoot Publishing Company, 1996.

Clemmer, Gregg S. *Old Alleghany: The Life and Wars of General Ed Johnson.* Hearthside Publishing Company; 2004.

Cockrell, Monroe ed. *Gunner with Stonewall: Reminiscences of William Thomas Poague, Lieutenant, Captain, and Lieutenant Colonel of Artillery, Army of Northern Virginia, C.S.A.* Jackson, TN: McCowat-Mercer Press, 1857.

Cockrell, Thomas D. and Michael B. Ballard, eds., *A Mississippi Rebel in the Army of Northern Virginia: The Civil War Memoirs of Private David Holt.* Baton Rouge, LA: Louisiana State University Press, 1995.

Coffin, Howard. *The Battered Stars: One State's Civil War Ordeal During Grant's Overland Campaign.* Woodstock, VT: Countryman Press, 2002.

Coffman, Richard M. *To Honor These Men: A History of Phillips Georgia Legion Infantry Battalion.* Macon, GA: Mercer University Press, 2007.

Cogswell, Leander W. *A History of the Eleventh New Hampshire Regiment Volunteer Infantry in the Rebellion War, 1861-1865.* Concord, NH: Republican Press Association, 1891.

Collier, Calvin L. *They'll Do To Tie To!: 3rd Ark Infantry Regiment—C.S.A.* Democrat Printing and Litho. Company, 1995.

Connecticut Adjutant-General. *Annual Report of the Adjutant-General of the State of Connecticut for the Year Ending March 31, 1865.* New Haven, CT: Carrington, Hotchkiss, 1865.

_____. *Record of Service of Connecticut Men in the Army and Navy of the United States During the War of the Rebellion.* Hartford, CT: Case, Lockwood and Brainard, 1889.

Cowtan, Charles W. *Services of the Tenth New York Volunteers in the War of the Rebellion.* New York: C. H. Ludwig, 1882.

Craft, David. *History of the One Hundred and Forty-First Pennsylvania Volunteers, 1862-1865.* Towanda, PA: Reporter-Journal Printing Co., 1885.

Crater, Lewis. *History of the Fiftieth Regiment, Penna. Vet. Vols., 1861-65.* Reading, PA: Coleman Printer House, 1884.

Crotty, Daniel G. *Four years Campaigning in the Army of the Potomac.* Grand Rapids, MI: Dygert Bros. & Co., 1874.

Cudworth, Warren. *History of the First Regiment Massachusetts Infantry from the 25th of May, 1861, to the 25th of May, 1864; Including Brief References to the Operations of the Army of the Potomac.* Boston: Walker, Fuller & Co., 1886.

Curtis, Orson B. *History of the Twenty-Fourth Michigan of the Iron Brigade.* Detroit, MI: Winn & Hammond, 1891.

Cushman, Frederick E. *History of the 58th Regt. Massachusetts Vols. From the 15th day of September, 1863, to the Close of the Rebellion.* Washington, DC: Gibson Brothers, Printers, 1865.

Cutcheon, Bryon M. *The Story of the Twentieth Michigan Infantry, July 15, 1862 to May 30, 1865: Embracing Official Documents on File. . .* Lansing, MI: Robert Smith Printing Co., 1904.

Dame, William *From the Rapidan to Richmond and the Spottsylvania Campaign.* Baltimore: Green-Lucas company, 1920.

Darling, Charles B. *Historical Sketch of the First Regiment Infantry, Massachusetts Volunteer Militia.* Boston: n.p., 1890.

Dawes, Rufus *Service with the Sixth Wisconsin Volunteers.* Madison, WI: The State Historical Society of Wisconsin, 1962.

Dickert, D. Augustus. *History of Kershaw's Brigade with Complete Roll of Companies, Biographical Sketches, Incidents, Anecdotes, Etc.* Moningside Press, 1976.

Dobbins, Austin C. *Grandfather's Journal: Company B, Sixteenth Mississippi Infantry Volunteers, Harris' Brigade, Mahone's Division, Hill's Corps, A.N.V.* Dayton, OH: Morningside Books, 1988.

Dowdey, Clifford and Louis H. Manarin, *The Wartime Papers of R. E. Lee.* New York: Bramhall House, 1961.

Driver, Robert J. *52nd Virginia Infantry.* Lynchburg, VA: H. E. Howard, Inc., 1986.

____. *58th Virginia Infantry.* Lynchburg, VA: H. E. Howard, Inc., 1990.

Dunlop, W. S. *Lee's Sharpshooters or the Forefront of Battle: A Story of Southern Valor That Never Has Been Told.* Dayton, OH: Morningside, 1988.

Dunn, Craig L. *Iron Men, Iron Will: The Nineteenth Indiana Regiment of the Iron Brigade* Indianapolis, IN: Guild Press, 1995.

Early, Jubal A. *Lieutenant-General Jubal A. Early, C.S.A.: Autobiographical Sketch and Narrative of the War Between the States.* Philadelphia: J. B. Lippincott Company, 1912.

Ellis, Billy. *Tithes of Blood: A Confederate Soldier's Story.* Murfreesboro, TN: Southern Heritage Press, 1997.

Floyd, Frederick Clark. *History of the Fortieth (Mozart) New York Volunteers, which was composed of Four Companies from New York, Four Companies from Massachusetts, and Two Companies from Pennsylvania.* Boston: F. H. Gilson Company, 1909.

Fox, John J. *Red Clay to Richmond: Trail of the 35th Georgia Infantry Regiment, C.S.A.* Winchester, VA: Angle Valley Press, 2004.

Freeman, Douglas Southall. *Robert E. Lee.* Four volumes. New York: Charles Scribner's Sons, 1936.

____. *Lee's Lieutenants: A Study in Command.* Three volumes. New York: Charles Scribner's Sons, 1944.

Frye, Dennis E. *2nd Virginia Infantry.* Lynchburg, Va.: H.E. Howard, 1984.

____. *12th Virginia Cavalry.* Lynchburg, VA: H. E. Howard, Inc., 1988.

Fuller, *Edward H. Battles of the Seventy-Seventh New York State Foot Volunteers.* n.p.: n.p., 1901.

Gaff, Alan D. *On Many a Bloody Field: Four Years in the Iron Brigade.* Bloomington, IN: Indiana University Press, 1996.

Galway, Thomas Francis. *The Gallant Hours.* Harrisburg, PA: The Stackpole Company, 1961.

Gallagher, Gary W., ed. *Fighting for the Confederacy: The Personal Recollections of General Edward Porter Alexander.* Chapel Hill, NC: University of North Carolina Press, 1989.

____. *The Wilderness Campaign.* Chapel Hill, NC: University of North Carolina Press, 1997.

____. Lee and His Generals in War and Memory. Baton Rouge, LA: Louisiana State University Press: 1998.

Gambone, A. M. *Major-General John Frederick Hartranft: Citizen Soldier and Pennsylvania Statesman.* Baltimore, Butternut and Blue Press, 1995.

Gannon, James P. *Irish Rebels, Confederate Tigers: A History of the 6th Louisiana Volunteers, 1861-1865.* Mason City, IA: Savas Publishing Company, 1998.

Gavin, William Gilfillan, *Campaigning with the Roundheads: The History of the One Hundredth Pennsylvania Volunteer Infantry Regiment in the American Civil War, 1861-1865.* Dayton: Morningside Press, 1989.

_____. *Infantryman Pettit: The Civil War Letters of Corporal Frederick Pettit*. Shippensburg, PA: White Mane Publishing Company, 1990.

Gerrish, Theodore. *Army Life: A Private's Reminiscences of the Civil War*. Portland, ME: Hoyt, Fogg, and Donham, 1882.

Gibbon, John. *Personal Recollections of the Civil War*. Dayton, OH: Morningside Bookshop, 1988.

Gibbs, Joseph. *Three Years in the Bloody Eleventh: The Campaigns of a Pennsylvania Reserves Regiment*. University Park, PA: Pennsylvania State University Press, 2002.

Glatthaar, Joseph T. *General Lee's Army: From Victory to Collapse*. New York: Free Press, 2008.

Gordon, John B. *Reminiscences of the Civil War*. New York: Charles Scribner's Sons, 1903.

Gottfried, Bradley M. *Stopping Pickett: The History of the Philadelphia Brigade*. Shippensburg, PA: White Mane Publishing Company, 1999.

_____. *Kearny's Own: The History of the First New Jersey Brigade in the Civil War*. New Brunswick, NJ: Rutgers University Press, 2005.

Govan, Gibert E. and James W. Livingood, eds., *The Haskell Memoirs: The Personal Narrative of a Confederate Officer*. New York: G. P. Putnam's Sons, 1960.

Grant, Ulysses S. *The Personal Memoirs of U. S. Grant*. Two volumes. New York: Charles L. Webster & Company, 1886.

Grenier, James M., Janet L. Coryell, and James R. Smither, eds. *A Surgeon's Civil War: The Letters and Diary of Daniel M. Holt, MD*. Kent, OH: Kent State University Press, 1994.

Griffin, Ronald G. *The 11th Alabama Volunteer Regiment in the Civil War*. Jefferson, NC: McFarland & Company, 2008.

Haines, Alanson A. *A History of the Fifteenth Regiment New Jersey Volunteers*. New York: Jenkins & Thomas, Printers, 1883.

Hale Laura Virginia and Stanley S. Phillips. *History of the Forty-Ninth Virginia, C.S.A., "Extra Billy Smith's Boys:" Based on the Unpublished Memoirs of Captain Robert Daniel Funkhouser, Company D, 49th Virginia Infantry, C.S.A*. n.p., n.p., 1981.

Handerson, Henry E. *Yankee in Gray: The Civil War Memoirs of Henry E. Handerson with a Selection of His Wartime Letters*. Cleveland, OH: Press of Western Reserve University, 1962.

Hanks, O. T. *History of Captain B. F. Benton's Company, Hood's Texas Brigade, 1861-1865*. Austin, TX: Morrison Books, 1984.

Hardy, Michael C. *The Thirty-Seventh North Carolina Troops: Tar Heels in the Army of Northern Virginia*. Jefferson, NC: McFarland and Company, 2013.

Hays, Gilbert Adams. *Under the Red Patch: Story of the Sixty-Third Regiment Pennsylvania Volunteers, 1861-1865*. Pittsburgh, PA: Sixty-third Pennsylvania Volunteers Regimental Association, 1908.

Hennessy, John J., ed. *Fighting with the Eighteenth Massachusetts: The Civil War Memoir of Thomas H. Mann*. Baton Rouge, LA: LSU Press, 2000.

Herdegen, Lance J. *The Iron Brigade in Civil War and Memory: The Black Hats from Bull Run to Appomattox and Thereafter*. El Dorado Hills, CA: Savas Beatie, LLC, 2012.

Hess, Earl J. *Lee's Tar Heels: The Pettigrew-Kirkland-MacRae Brigade*. Chapel Hill, NC: University of North Carolina Press, 2002.

_____. *Trench Warfare Under Grant and Lee: Field Fortifications in the Overland Campaign*. Chapel Hill, NC: University of North Carolina Press, 2007.

Hopkins, Luther W. *From Bull Run to Appomattox: A Boy's View*. Baltimore, MD: Fleet-McGinley, 1914.

Houghton, Edwin B. *The Campaigns of the Seventeenth Maine*. Portland, ME: Portland, Short & Loring, 1866.

Howard, McKinley. *Recollections of a Maryland Confederate Soldier and Staff Officer under Johnston, Jackson and Lee*. Baltimore, MD: Williams & Wilkins Company, 1914.

Humphreys, Andrew A. *The Virginia Campaign, 1864 and 1865*. New York: Da Capo Press, 1995.

Huntington, Tom. *Searching for George Gordon Meade: The Forgotten Victor of Gettysburg*. Mechanicsburg, PA: Stackpole Books, 2013.

Husk, Martin W. *The 111th New York Volunteer Infantry: A Civil War History*. Jefferson, NC: McFarland Press, 2009.

Hussey, George A. and William Todd, *History of the Ninth Regiment N.Y.S.M. Eighty-Third N.Y. Volunteers), 1845-1888*. New York: n.p., 1889.

Hyde, Thomas W. *Following the Greek Cross; or, Memories of the Sixth Army or, Memories of the Sixth Army Corps*. Boston: Houghton, Mifflin and Company, 1894.

Jackman, Lyman and Amos Hadley, *History of the Sixth New Hampshire Regiment in the War for the Union*. Concord, NH: Republican Press Association, 1891.

Johnson, Pharris DeLoach ed., *Under the Southern Cross: Soldier Life with Gordon Bradwell and the Army of Northern Virginia*. Macon, GA: Mercer University Press, 1999.

Jones, Terry L. *Lee's Tigers*. Baton Rouge, LA: LSU Press, 1987.

_____. *The Civil War Memoirs of Captain William J. Seymour: Reminiscences of a Louisiana Tiger*. Baton Rouge, LA: Louisiana State University Press, 1991.

Jordan, William B. *Red Diamond Regiment: The 17th Maine Infantry, 1862-1865*. Shippensburg, PA: White Mane Publishing Company, 1996.

Jordan, William C. *Some Events and Incidents During the Civil War*. Montgomery, AL: The Paragon Press, 1909.

Judson, Amos M. *History of the Eighty-Third Regiment of Pennsylvania Volunteers*. Alexandria, VA: Stonewall House, 1985.

Keifer, Joseph Warren. *Slavery and Four Years of War: A Political History of Slavery in the United States Together With a Narrative of the Campaigns and Battles of the Civil War In Which the Author Took Part: 1861-1865*. New York: G. P. Putnam Sons, 1900.

Kidd, J. H. *Personal Recollections of a Cavalryman with Custer's Michigan Cavalry Brigade in the Civil War*. Ionia, MI: Sentinel Printing Company, 1908.

King, David H. *Personal Recollections of the War: A Record of Service with the Ninety-Third New York Volunteer Infantry, 1861-1865*. Milwaukee, WI: Swain and Tate Company, 1895.

King, John R. *My Experience in the Confederate Army and in Northern Prisons*. Clarksburg, WV: Stonewall Jackson Chapter of the United Daughters of the Confederacy, 1917.

Kirk, Hyland C. *Heavy Guns and Light: History of the 4th New York Heavy Artillery* (New York: Dillingham, 1890.

Kleese, Richard B. *49th Virginia Infantry*. Lynchburg, VA: H. E. Howard, Inc., 2002.

Krick, Robert E. *40th Virginia Infantry*. Lynchburg, VA: H. E. Howard, Inc., 1985.

Laine, J. Gary and Morris M. Penny, *Law's Alabama Brigade in the War Between the Union and the Confederacy*. Shippensburg, PA: White Mane Publishing Co., Inc., 1966.

Lewis, Osceola. *History of the One Hundred and Thirty Eighth Pennsylvania Volunteer Infantry*. Norristown, PA: Wills, Iredell, and Jenkins, 1866.

Lloyd, William P. *History of the First Regiment Pennsylvania Reserve Cavalry, From its Organization, August, 1861, to September, 1864, with a List of Names of All Officers and Enlisted Men Who Have Ever Belonged to the Regiment*. Philadelphia: King and Baird, 1864.

Locke, William H. *The Story of the Regiment*. Philadelphia: J. B. Lippincott, 1868.

Long, Armistead L. *Memoirs of Robert E. Lee: His Military and Personal History*. New York: J. M. Stoddardt & Company, 1886.

Longacre, Edward G. *Lincoln's Cavalrymen: A History of the Mounted Forces of the Army of the Potomac 1861-1865*. Mechanicsburg, PA: Stackpole Books, 2000.

_____. *Lee's Cavalrymen: A History of the Mounted Forces of the Army of Northern Virginia*. Mechanicsburg, PA: Stackpole Books, 2002.

Longstreet, James. *From Manassas to Appomattox*. Indiana University Press, 1960.

Lowe, David W. *Meade's Army: The Private Notebooks of Lt. Col. Theodore Lyman*. Kent, OH: Kent State University Press, 2007.

McDonald, William N. *A History of the Laurel Brigade, Originally the Ashby Cavalry of the Army of Northern Virginia*. Baltimore: The Johns Hopkins University Press, 2002.

Macnamara, Daniel G. *The History of the Ninth Regiment Massachusetts Volunteer Infantry*. New York: Fordham University Press, 2000.

Mahood, Wayne. *General Wadsworth: The Life and Times of Brevet Major General James S. Wadsworth*. New York: Da Capo, 2003.

Maier, Larry *Rough & Regular: A History of Philadelphia's 119th Regiment of Pennsylvania Volunteer Infantry*. Shippensburg, PA: Burd Street Press, 1997.

Manarin, Louis H. *North Carolina Troops, 1861-1865: A Roster*. Fifteen Volumes. Raleigh, NC: State Department of Archives and History, 1966.

Marbaker, Thomas D. *History of the Eleventh New Jersey Volunteers: Its Organization to Appomattox to which is added Experiences of Prison Life and Sketches of Individual Members*. Trenton, NJ: MacCrellish & Quigley, Book and Job Printers, 1898.

Marshall, D. P. *History of Company K, 155th Pennsylvania Volunteer Zouaves*. n.p: n.p., 1888.

Marvel, William. *Burnside*. Chapel Hill, NC: The University of North Carolina Press, 1991.

Matthews, Richard E. *The 149th Pennsylvania Volunteer Infantry Unit in the Civil War*. Jefferson, NC: McFarland Press, 1994.

Meade, George *The Life and Letters of George Gordon Meade, Major General, United States Army*. New York: New York, Charles Scribner's Sons, 1913.

Miller, Richard F. *Harvard's Civil War: A History of the Twentieth Massachusetts Volunteer Infantry*. Hanover, NH: University Press of New England, 2005.

Mills, George H. *History of the 16th North Carolina Regiment*. Hamilton, NY: Edmonston Pub., 1897.

Morrison, James L., ed. *The Memoirs of Henry Heth*. Westport, CT: Greenwood Press, 1974.

Mulholland, St. Clair A. *The Story of the 116th Pennsylvania Regiment Volunteers in the War of the Rebellion: The Record of a Gallant Command*. Philadelphia: F. McManus, Jr., and Co., 1903.

Murphy, Terrence *10th Virginia Infantry*. Lynchburg, VA: H. E. Howard, 1989.

Murray, Alton J. *South Georgia Rebels: The True Experiences of the 26th Regiment Georgia Volunteer Infantry, Lawton-Gordon-Evans Brigade*. St. Mary's, GA: Murray, 1976.

Musselman, Homer D. *47th Virginia Infantry*. Lynchburg, VA: New Papyrus Publishing, 2010.

Myers, Frank M. *The Comanches: A History of White's Battalion, Virginia Cavalry, Laurel Brig., Hampton Div., A.N.V. C.S.A*. Marietta, GA: Continental Book Co., 1956.

Nash, Eugene Arus. *A History of the Forth-Fourth Regiment, New York Volunteer Infantry*. Chicago: R. R. Donnelley & Sons, Company, 1911.

Newell, Joseph K. *Ours: Annals of the Tenth Regiment, Massachusetts Volunteers, in the Rebellion*. Springfield, MA: C. A. Nichols & Co., 1875.

Nichols, G. W. *A Soldier's Story of his Regiment*. Kennesaw, GA: Continental Book Company, 1961.

Oates, William C. *The War Between the Union and the Confederacy and its Lost Opportunities with a History of the 15th Alabama Regiment and the Forty-Eight Battles in Which it was Engaged*. Dayton, OH: Morningside Bookshop, 1985.

O'Sullivan, Richard. *55th Virginia Infantry*. Lynchburg, VA: H. E. Howard, Inc., 1989.

Page, Charles A. *Letters of a War Correspondent*. Boston, L. C. Page and Company, 1899.

Page, Charles D. History of the Fourteenth Regiment, Connecticut Vol. Infantry. Meriden, CT: The Horton Printing Co., 1906.

Palfrey, Francis W., ed, *Memoir of William Francis Bartlett*. Boston: Houghton, Osgood and Company, 1878.

Pearson, Henry G. *James S. Wadsworth of Geneseo: Brevet Major General, U.S.V*. New York: Charles Scribner's Sons, 1913.

Perry, Martha D., ed. *Letters from a Surgeon of the Civil War*. Boston: Little, Brown, and Co., 1906.

Pfanz, Donald C. *Richard S. Ewell: A Soldier's Life*. Chapel Hill, NC: University of North Carolina Press, 1998.

Polley, J. B. *Hood's Texas Brigade: Its Marches, Its Battles, Its Achievements*. Dayton, OH: Morningside Bookshop, 1976.

Pope, Thomas E. *The Weary Boys: Colonel J. Warren Keifer & the 110th Ohio Volunteer Infantry*. Kent, OH: Kent State University Press, 2002.

Porter, Horace. *Campaigning with Grant*. Bloomington, IN: Indiana University Press, 1961.

Powell, William H. *The Fith Army Corps*. New York: G. P. Putnam's Sons, 1896.

Priest, John Michael. *Nowhere to Run: The Wilderness, May 4th and 5th, 1864*. Shippensburg, PA: White Mane Publishing Company, 1995.

_____. *Victory Without Triumph: The Wilderness, May 6th and 7th, 1864*. Shippensburg, PA: White Mane Publishing Company, 1996.

Pullen, John J. *The Twentieth Maine*. Philadelphia: J. B. Lippincott Company, 1957.

Pyne, Henry R. *Ride to War: The History of the First New Jersey Cavalry*. New Brunswick, NJ: Rutgers University Press, 1961.

Rankin, Thomas M. *37th Virginia Infantry*. Lynchburg, VA: H. E. Howard, Inc., 1987.

Reese, Timothy J. *Sykes' Regular Infantry Division, 1861-1864: A History of Regular United States Infantry Operations in the Civil War's Eastern Theater*. Jefferson, NC: McFarland Press, 1990.

Reidenbaugh, Lowell. *27th Virginia Infantry*. Lynchburg, Va.: H.E. Howard, 1982.

_____. *33rd Virginia Infantry*. Lynchburg, Va.: H.E. Howard, 1987

Rhea, Gordon C. *The Battle of the Wilderness, May 5-6*. Baton Rouge, LA: Louisiana State University Press, 1994.

Rhodes, Robert Hunt, ed. *All For The Union—The Civil War Diary and Letters of Elisha Hunt Rhodes*. New York, Orion Books, 1958.

Ripley, William Y. W. *Vermont Riflemen in the War for the Union: A History of Company F, First United States Sharpshooters*. Rutland, VT: Tuttle & Co., 1883.

Roback, Henry. *The Veteran Volunteers of Herkemer and Oswego Counties in the War of the Rebellion*. Utica, NY: L. C. Childs, 1888.

Robertson, James I. *The Stonewall Brigade*. Baton Rouge, LA: LSU Press, 1963.

_____. Robertson, Jr., ed. *The Civil War Letters of General Robert McAllister*. New Brunswick, NJ: Rutgers University Press, 1965.

_____. *General A. P. Hill: The Story of a Confederate Warrior. New York: Random House, 1987*.

Robertson, Robert Stoddart. Personal Recollections of the War: A Record of Service with the Ninety-Third New York Vol. Infantry, and the First Brigade, First Division, Second Corps, Army of the Potomac. Milwaukee, WI: Swain & Tate Col, Printers and Publishers, 1895.

Roe, Alfred S. *The Thirty-Ninth Regiment Massachusetts Volunteers, 1862-1865*. Worcester, MA: Regimental Veteran Association, 1914.

Rosenblatt, Emil and Ruth, eds. *Hard Marching Every Day—The Civil War Letters of Private Wilbur Fisk*. Lawrence, KS: University of Kansas Press, 1992.

Rowland, Dunbar. *Military History of Mississippi, 1803-1888: Taken from the Official and Statistical Register of the State of Mississippi, 1908*. Spartansburg, S.C.: Reprint Co., 1978.

Royall, William L. *Some Reminiscences*. New York: The Neale Publishing Company, 1909.

Rozier, John., ed., The Granite Farm Letters: The Civil War Coorespondence of Edgeworth and Sallie Bird. Athens, GA: University of Georgia Press, 1988.

Sauers, Richard A., ed. *The Civil War Journal of Colonel Bolton, 51st Pennsylvania, April 20, 1861-August 2, 1865*. Conshohocken, PA: Combined Publishing, 2000.

Sauers, Richard A. and Peter Tomasak, *Ricketts' Battery: A History of Battery F, 1st Pennsylvania Light Artillery*. n.p.: Luzerne National Bank, 2001.

Saville, William P. *History of the First Regiment, Delaware Volunteers: From the Commencement of the "Three Months' Service" to the Final Muster Out at the Close of the Rebellion*. Wilmington, DE: The Historical Society of Delaware, 1884.

Sawyer, Franklin. *A Military History of the 8th Regiment Ohio Vol. Inf'y: It's Battles, Marches and Army Movements*. Cleveland, OH: Fairbanks & Co. Printers, 1881.

Schaff, Morris *Battle of the Wilderness*. Houghton Mifflin Company, 1910.

Scott, Robert Garth. *Into the Wilderness with the Army of the Potomac.* Bloomington, IN: Indiana University Press, 1988.

_____. *Fallen Leaves: The Civil War Letters of Major Henry Livermore Abbott.* Kent, OH: Kent State University Press, 1991.

Sheeran, Rev. *James B. Confederate Chaplain: A War Journal.* Milwaukee, WI: The Bruce Publishing Company, 1960.

Sibley, F. Ray. *The Confederate Order of Battle: The Army of Northern Virginia.* Shippensburg, PA: White Mane Publishing Co., 1996.

Sifakis, Stewart. *Who Was Who in the Civil War.* Facts on File, 1988.

Silliker, Ruth L. *The Rebel Yell & the Yankee Hurrah: The Civil War Journal of a Maine Volunteer.* Camden, ME: Down East Books, 1985.

Shoemaker, John J. *Shoemaker's Battery: Stuart Horse Artillery, Pelham's Battalion, Army of Northern Virginia.* Gaithersburg, MD: Butternut Press, n.d.

Slade, A. D. *A. T. A. Torbert: Southern Gentleman in Union Blue.* Dayton, OH: Morningside Press, 1992.

Small, Abner R. *The Road to Richmond.* Berkley, CA: University of California Press, 1957.

Smith, A. P. *History of the Seventy-Sixth Regiment New York Volunteers.* Courtland, NY: Truair, Smith and Miles, Printers, 1867.

Smith, John Day. *History of the Nineteenth Regiment of Maine Volunteer Infantry 1862-1865* (Minneapolis, MN: The Great Western Printing Company, 1909.

Smith, Raymond W. ed. *Out of the Wilderness: The Civil War Memoir of Cpl. Norton C. Shepard, 146th New York Volunteer Infantry.* Hamilton, NY: Edmonston Publishing, Inc., 1998.

Sparks, David S., ed. *Inside Lincoln's Army: The Diary of Marsena Rudolph Patrick, Provost Marshal General, Army of the Potomac.* New York: Thomas Yoseloff, 1964.

Speer, Allen Paul. *Voices from Cemetery Hill: The Civil War Diary, Reports, and Letters of Colonel William Henry Asbury Speer. 1861-1864.* Johnson City, TN: The Overmountain Press, 1997.

Stafford, G. M. G. *General Leroy August Stafford: His Forebears and Descendants.* New Orleans, LA: Pelican Publishing Company, 1943.

Steere, Edward. *The Wilderness Campaign.* Harrisburg, PA: The Stackpole Publishing Company, 1960.

Stevens, C. A. *Berdan's Sharpshooters in the Army of the Potomac, 1861-1865.* St. Paul, MN: The Price-McGill Company, 1892.

Stevens, George T. *Three Years in the Sixth Corps: A Concise Narrative of Events in the Army of the Potomac, from 1861 to the Close of the Rebellion, April 1865.* Albany, NY: S. R. Gray, 1866.

Stewart, Lane Robert Laird. *History of the One Hundred and Fortieth Regiment, Pennsylvania Volunteers.* Philadelphia: Franklin Bindery, 1912.

Stiles, Robert. *Four Years Under Marse Robert.* New York: Neale, 1910.

Stocker, Jeffrey D. *From Huntsville to Appomattox: R. T. Coles' History of the 4th Regiment, Alabama Volunteer Infantry, C.S.A., Army of Northern Virginia.* University of Tennessee Press, 1996.

Stubbs, Steven H. *Duty-Honor-Valor: The Story of the Eleventh Mississippi Infantry Regiment.* Philadelphia, MS: Dancing Rabbit Press, 2000.

Survivors' Association. *History of the 118th Pennsylvania Volunteers—Corn Exchange Regiment: from their first engagement at Antietam to Appomattox . . .* Philadelphia: J. L. Smith, 1905.

Survivors' Association, *History of the 121st Regiment, Pennsylvania Volunteers: "An Account from the Ranks."* n.p., n.p.: 1905.

Swank, Walbrook D. *Stonewall Jackson's Foot Cavalry.* Shippensburg, PA: Burd Street Press, 2001.

Styple, William B. *Writing & Fighting the Confederate War: The Letters of Peter Wellington Alexander Confederate War Correspondent.* Kearny, NJ: Belle Grove Publishing Company, 2002.

Sypher, Josiah R. *History of the Pennsylvania Reserve Corps: A Complete Record of the Organization and of the Different Companies, Regiments and Brigades Containing Descriptions of Expeditions.* Lancaster, PA: E. Barr, 1865.

Taaffe, Stephen R. *Commanding the Army of the Potomac.* Lawrence, KS: Kansas University Press, 2006.

Thirty-Sixth Massachusetts Committee of the Regiment, *History of the Thirty-Sixth Regiment Massachusetts Volunteers.* Boston: Press of Rockwell and Churchill, 1884.

Thomas, Henry W. *History of the Doles- Cook Brigade, Army of Northern Virginia, C.S.A.* Atlanta: The Franklin Printing and Publishing Company, 1903.

Thomson, O. R. Howard and William Rauch, *History of the "Bucktails", Kane Rifle Regiment of the Pennsylvania Reserve Corps.* Philadelphia: Electric Printing Company, 1906.

Tomasak, Peter ed. *Avery Harris Civil War Journal.* Luzerne, PA: Luzerne National Bank, 2000.

Trout, Robert J. *Galloping Thunder: The Stuart Horse Artillery Battalion.* Mechanicsburg, PA: Stackpole Books, 2002.

Tyler, Mason Whiting. *Recollections of the Civil War.* New York: G. P. Putnam's Sons, 1912.

Van Santvoord, Cornelius. *The One Hundred and Twentieth New York State Volunteers: A Narrative for the Union.* Rondout, NY: Kingston and Freeman, 1894.

von Borcke, *Heros. Memoirs of the Confederate War for Independence.* Philadelphia: Lippincott, 1867.

Wainwright, Charles S. *A Diary of Battle: The Personal Journals of Colonel Charles S. Wainwright, 1861-1865,* Allan Nevins, ed. New York: Harcourt, Brace, and World, 1962.

Walcott, Charles F. *History of the Twenty-First Regiment Massachusetts Volunteers in the War for the Preservation of the Union, 1861-1865.* Boston: Houghton, Mifflin and Company, 1882.

Walker, C. Irvine. *The Life of Lieutenant General Richard Heron Anderson of the Confederate States Army.* Charleston, SC: Art Publishing Company, 1917.

Walker, Francis. *History of the Second Army Corps in the Army of the Potomac.* New York: Charles Scribner's Sons, 1887.

Ward, Joseph R. C. *History of the One Hundred and Sixth Regiment, Pennsylvania Volunteers, 2d brigade, 2d division, 2d corps. 1861-1865.* Philadelphia: Grant, Faires, & Rodgers, 1883.

Warner, Ezra J. *Generals in Blue: Lives of the Union Commanders.* Baton Rouge, LA: Louisiana State University Press, 1964.

Waters Zach C. and James C. Edmonds, *A Small but Spartan Band: The Florida Brigade in Lee's Army of Northern Virginia.* Tuscaloosa, AL: The University of Alabama Press, 2010.

Welch, Richard F. *The Boy General: The Life and Careers of Francis Channing Barlow.* Kent, OH: Kent State University Press, 2003.

Weld, Stephen Minot. *Dairy and Letters of Stephen Minot Weld.* n.p.: The Riverside Press, 1912.

Welsh, Jack D. Medical Histories of Confederate Generals. Kent, OH: Kent State University Press, 1995.

_____. *Medical Histories of Union Generals.* Kent, OH: Kent State University Press, 1996.

Wert, Jeffry D. *Cavalryman of the Lost Cause: A Biography of J.E.B. Stuart.* New York: Simon & Schuster, 2008.

Westbrook, *Robert S. History of the 49th Pennsylvania Volunteers.* Altoona, PA: np, 1898.

Weygant, Charles H. *History of the One Hundred and Twenty-Fourth Regiment, N.Y.S.V.* Newburgh, NY: Journal Printing House, 1877.

White, Gregory C. *A History of the 31st Georgia Volunteer Infantry.* Baltimore, MD: Butternut and Blue, 1997.

Wiley, Bell Irvin, ed. Recollections of a Confederate Staff Officer. Jackson, TN: McCowat-Mercer Press, 1958.

Wilkeson, Frank. *Recollections of a Private Soldier in the Army of the Potomac.* New York: G.P. Putnam's Sons, 1887.

Wilkinson, Warren, ed. *Mother May You Never See the Sights I have Seen: The Fifty–Seventh Massachusetts Veteran Volunteers in the Last Year of the Civil War.* New York: Harper and Row, 1990.

Wilkinson, Warren and Steven E. Woodworth, *A Scythe of Fire: The Civil War Story of the Eight Georgia infantry Regiment.* New York: William Morrow, 2002.

Williams, Richard Brady, *Stonewall's Prussian Mapmaker: The Journals of Captain Oscar Hinrichs.* University of North Carolina Press: Chapel Hill, NC, 2014.

Williams, T. P. *The Mississippi Brigade of Brig. Gen. Joseph R. Davis: A Geographic Account of its Campaigns and a Biographical Account of its Personalities, 1861-1865.* Dayton, OH: Morningside Press, 1999.

Wilmer, L. Allison, et al., *History and Roster of Maryland Volunteers*. Baltimore, MD: Press of Guggenheimer, Weil & Co., 1898.

Wilson, James H. *Under the Old Flag: Recollections of Military Operations in the War for the Union, The Spanish War, and the Boxer Rebellion*. 2 vols. New York: Appleton and Company, 1912.

Wing, Samuel B. *The Soldier's Story: A Personal Narrative*. Phillips, ME: Phonographic Steam Book and Job Print, 1898.

Wise, Jennings Cropper. *The Long Arm of Lee: The History of the Artillery of the Army of Northern Virginia*. New York: Oxford University Press, 1959.

Woodward, Evan Morrison. *Our Campaigns: The Second Regiment Pennsylvania Reserve Volunteers*. Shippensburg, PA: Burd Street Press, 1995.

Worsham, John H. *One of Jackson's Foot Cavalry: His Experience and What He Saw During the War 1861-1865*. New York: Neale Publishing Company, 1912.

Wyckoff, Mac. *A History of the 3rd South Carolina Infantry: 1861-1865*. Fredericksburg, VA: Sergeant Kirkland's Museum and Historical Society, Inc., 1995.

Young, Alfred C. *Lee's Army During the Overland Campaign: A Numerical Study*. Baton Rouge, LA: Louisiana State University Press, 2013.

Articles and Essays

Adams, Z. Boylstron. "In the Wilderness." in *Civil War Papers Read Before the Commandery of the State of Massachusetts*. Three volumes. Boston, MA: The Commandery, 1900), vol. 2, 373-402.

Alexander, Edward P. "Grant's Conduct in the Wilderness Campaign." *Annual Report of the American Historical Association for the Year 1908*. 2 vols. Washington, Government Printing Office, 1909.

Alexander, W. Keith "Fought them Like Tigers: Colonel Clark Moulton Avery and the 33rd North Carolina Infantry, May 5-6, 1864." in *Civil War Regiments*, Vol. Six, No. 4 (1999), 47-76.

Aycock, B. A. "The Lone Star Guards." *Confederate Veteran*, vol. XXXI (March, 1923), 101-103.

Bumgardner, James. "Pegram's Brigade, Early's Division: Ewell's Corps in the Battle of the Wilderness." *Richmond Daily Times*, October 8, 1905.

Berry, Thomas S. "In the Wilderness." The *National Tribune*, October 3, 1889.

Bilby, Joseph G. "A Jersey Journey: Being the Perambulations of the 10th New Jersey Infantry, Late Olden's Legion." *Military Images*, vol. XVI, No. 5 (March-April 1995), 5-11.

Bowen, James L. "In the Wilderness." *Philadelphia Weekly Times*, June 27, 1885.

Bowles, P. D. "Battle of the Wilderness: The 4th Alabama in the Slaughter Pen, May 6, 1864." *Philadelphia Weekly Times*, October 4, 1884.

Bradwell, Isaac G. "Battle of the Wilderness." *Confederate Veteran*, vol. XVI (1908), 447-448.

____. "The Second Day's Battle of the Wilderness." *Confederate Veteran*, XXVIII (1920), 20-22.

Brewer, James H. "The Wilderness The Turning of the Right Wing of the Army." *National Tribune*, June 14, 1888.

Brockway, Charles B. "Across the Rapidan." Philadelphia Weekly Times, January 7, 1882.

C., R. "Texans Always Move Them." *The Land We Love*, vol. V, 485.

Carmichael, Peter S. "Escaping the Shadow of Gettysburg: Richard S. Ewell and Ambrose Hill at the Wilderness." In Gary Gallagher, ed. *The Wilderness Campaign*. Chapel Hill, NC: University of North Carolina Press, 1997, 136-159.

Carter, Joseph F. "Leasure's Brigade: Another Account of the Fight at the Salient Angle." *National Tribune*, September 25, 1890.

____. "In the Wilderness: The Controversy Between Carroll's and Leasure's Brigades." *National Tribune*, January 1, 1891.

____. "In the Wilderness: The Troops at the Crossroads Saved by the Wall of Fire." The *National Tribune*, April 7, 1892.

Cary, William B. "The Wilderness Fight." The *National Tribune*, February 1, 1912.

Colledge, James. "The Wilderness: The Place Where the First Battle of the Campaign was Fought." *National Tribune*, April 30, 1891.

Connor, Seldon. "In the Wilderness." *Maine MOLLUS*, vol. 4, Portland, ME: Lefavor-Tower Company, 1915, 200-229.

Cordrey, Francis. "In the Wilderness: What a Private Saw and Felt in that Horrible Place." *National Tribune*, June 21, 1894.

Daniels, O. G. "At the Crossroads: The Charge Made by Carroll's Brigade." *National Tribune*, December 4, 1890.

Delcour, Melissa "The Country Loses a Noble Soldier: The Battles of Brigadier General John Marshall Jones." *Civil War Regiments*, vol. 6, no. 4 (1999), 120-147.

Donald, John O. "The Wilderness: To What Battery Did the Two Guns Belong?" *National Tribune*, April 9, 1891.

Dunham, Samuel. "Death of Gen. Hays: Where and How he Fell at the Battle of the Wilderness." *National Tribune*, November 12, 1885.

Edinborough, Charles. "The Sixth Corps at the Wilderness." *National Tribune*, January 7, 1885.

Farley, Porter. "Reminiscences of the 140th New York Volunteer Infantry." *Rochester Historical Society Publication*, XXII (1944), 199-263.

Faulk, Phil K. "Battle of the Wilderness." *Philadelphia Weekly Times*, October 25, 1884.

Field, C. W. "Campaign of 1864 and 1865: Narrative of Major-General C. W. Field." *Southern Historical Society Papers*, vol. XIV (1886), 543-547.

Garlinger, Charles E. "Another Account." *The National Tribune*, October 17, 1889.

Godfrey, George B. "The Wilderness." *National Tribune*, January 22, 1891.

Goodrich, Ira B. "Helped Save the Day: A Massachusetts Comrade's Testimony for Leasure's Brigade." *The National Tribune*, April 30, 1891.

Gottfried, Bradley M. "Mahone's Brigade: Insubordination or Miscommunication?" *Gettysburg Magazine*, No. 18 (January, 1998), 67-76.

____. "To Fail Twice: Brockenbrough's Brigade at Gettysburg." *Gettysburg Magazine*, Issue 23 (July, 2000), 66- 75.

Grant, Lewis A. "In the Wilderness." *National Tribune*, January 28, 1897.

Grant, Ulysses S. "Preparing for the Campaigns of 1864." in *Battles and Leaders of the Civil War*, vol. 4, 97-117.

Geer, D. L. "Memories of the War." *Florida Index*, January 26, 1906.

Green, William H. "From the Wilderness to Spotsylvania." in *MOLLUS- Maine*, vol. II. Portland, ME: Lefavor-Tower Company, 1902, 91-104.

Griffen, Z. T. "The Wilderness: The Disaster to Shaler's and Seymour's Brigades." *National Tribune*, March 11, 1886.

____. Griffen, Z. T. "The Wilderness: The Turning of the Right Flank, May 6, 1864." National Tribune, August 15, 1889.

Hennessy, John J. "I Dread the Spring: The Army of the Potomac Prepares for the Overland Campaign." in *The Wilderness Campaign*, Gary W. Gallagher, ed. Chapel Hill, NC: University of North Carolina Press, 1997, 66-105.

Hildebrand, Sylvester F. "Fifty Years Ago First Troops to Leave Apollo." *Apollo (PA) Sentinel* (April 21, 1911.

Hudgins, F. L. "With the 38th Georgia Regiment." *Confederate Veteran*, vol. XXVI (1918), 161-163.

Jones, A. C. "Lee in the Wilderness." *Philadelphia Weekly Times*, May 8, 1880.

Jones, Terry L. "Leroy Augustus Stafford," in William C. Davis, ed., *The Confederate General*. Harrisburg, PA: National Historical Society, 1991, vol. 5, 194-95.

Johnson, W. Garth. "Barksdale-Humphreys Mississippi Brigade." *Confederate Veteran*, vol. I (1893), 206-207.

Kerr, Samuel C. "In the Wilderness: Turning the Right Flank on May 6, 1864." *National Tribune*, July 11, 1889.

"Kershaw's Brigade," *Carolina Spartan* (Spartansburg, S.C.), May 26, 1864.

Kolakowski, Christopher L. "A Rough Place and a Hard Fight: Thomas Stevenson's Division on the Brock and Plank Roads, May 6, 1864." in *Civil War Regiments*, Vol. 6, no. 4, 25-46.

Krick, Robert K. "'Lee to the Rear,' the Texans Cried." in Gary Gallagher, ed., *The Wilderness Campaign*. Chapel Hill, NC: University of North Carolina Press, 1997, 164-65.

———. "Like a Duck on a June Bug," in Gary Gallagher, ed., *The Wilderness Campaign*. Chapel Hill, NC: University of North Carolina Press, 1997, 236-264.

Landon, William. "The Fourteenth Indiana Regiment, Letters to the Vincennes Western Sun." in *Indiana Magazine of History*. Vol. 34, No. 1 (September 1934), 90.

Law, E. M. "From the Wilderness to Cold Harbor," *Battles and Leaders of the Civil War*, vol. IV, 125.

Leader, Norman. "The Bloodied Guns of Winslow's Battery." *Virginia Country's Civil War Quarterly*, vol. 6, 15-20.

"Letter from the 126th Ohio." *Steubenville Weekly Herald*, May 17, 1864.

Lichtenberg, I. J. "The Wilderness: How the 5th N.Y. Cav. Had a hand in Opening the Fight." *National Tribune*, September 30, 1886.

Lincoln, George R. "The First Long Island Regiment." *The Brooklyn Union*, May 13, 1864.

McWhirter, A. J. "General Wofford's Brigade in the Wilderness, May 6th. *Atlanta Journal*, September 21, 1901.

Mariani, Bob. "Private Henry Murdock's Red Badge of Courage," *North South Trader*, vol. VIII (no. 1), November-December, 1980, 39.

Nelson E. Miller, "What the 20th Ind. did at the Junction of the Brock and Plank Roads." The *National Tribune*, January 21, 1892.

Melcher, Holman S. "An Experience in the Battle of the Wilderness." in *War Papers Read Before the Commandery of the State of Maine, Military order of the Loyal Legion of the United States*. Portland, ME: The Thurston Print, 1898. vol. 1, 73-84.

Monteith, Robert. "Battle of the Wilderness, and Death of General Wadsworth. *Wisconsin MOLLUS*. Milwaukee, WI: Burdick, Armitage & Allen, 1891. 410-415.

Myerhoff, Charles. "In the Wilderness: The Charge of Carroll's Celebrated Brigade." *National Tribune*, October 23, 1890.

Nelms, W. G. "Unfinished Report on the Campaign of 1864," in *The Lamar Rifles: A History of Company G, Eleventh Mississippi Regiment, C.S.A., With the Official Roll, Giving Each Man's Record From Time of Enlistment to Twenty-Ninth of March, Eighteen Hundred and Sixty-Five*. Roanoke, VA: Stone Printing Col, 1902, 60.

Payne, J. "The Wilderness: The Turning of the Right Flank, May 6, 1864." *National Tribune*, July 18, 1889.

Perry, William F. "Reminiscences of the Campaign of 1864 in Virginia," *Southern Historical Society Papers*, VII (1879), 49-63.

Popchock, Barry. "Lost Opportunity in the Wilderness." in Columbiad, vol. 3, no. 2 (Summer, 1999), 21-37.

Reardon, Carol. "The Other Grant: Lewis A. Grant and the Vermont Brigade in the Battle of the Wilderness." in Gary W. Gallagher, ed., *The Wilderness Campaign*. Chapel Hill, NC: University of North Carolina Press, 1997, 201-235.

Rhea, Gordon C. "Union Cavalry in the Wilderness: The Education of Philip H. Sheridan and James H. Wilson." in Gary W. Gallagher, ed., *The Wilderness Campaign*. Chapel Hill, NC: University of North Carolina Press, 1997), 106-135.

Rawls, James B. "Veteran's Sketch of Life from Battle of Chickamauga to Arrival Home." *United Daughters of the Confederacy Magazine* 52 (June 1989), 15-18.

Robbins, D. H. "Thrice Distinguished: Who Opened the Fight in the Wilderness." *National Tribune*, May 13, 1909.

Roberts, James W. "The Wilderness and Spottsylvania, May 4-12, 1864: Narrative of a Private Soldier," *The Quarterly Periodical of the Florida Historical Society*, Vol. 8 (October, 1932), 60.

Rodgers, W. A. "The 18th Pa. Cav. Had Lively Work in the Mine Run Fight." *National Tribune*, May 27, 1897.

Seiser, Charles, ed. "August Seiser's Civil War Diary," in *Rochester Historical Society Publication*, XXII, 189.

Simpson, Brooks D. "Great Expectations: Ulysses S. Grant, The Northern Press, and the Opening of the Wilderness Campaign." In Gary W. Gallagher, ed., *The Wilderness Campaign*. Chapel Hill, NC: University of North Carolina Press, 1997, 1-35.

Smith, W. F. "Longstreet to the Rescue of Thomas' Brigade." *Atlanta Journal*, September 21, 1901.

Stamp, J. B. "Ten Months Experience in Northern Prisons." *Alabama Historical Quarterly*, vol. 18 (Winter, 1956), 486-498.

Stevens, C. E. "Not a Fighting Regiment." *The National Tribune*, October 8, 1908.

Stevens, Hazard. "The Sixth Corps in the Wilderness." in *Papers of the Military Historical Society of Massachusetts, 14 vol. Boston: Military historical Society of Massachusetts*, (1881-1918), Mass. Vol. IV, 176-203.

Sudsburg, Joseph M. "In the Wilderness: The Colonel of the 3rd Md. Takes a Hand in the Controversy." *National Tribune*, January 15, 1891.

Swan, William. "The Battle of the Wilderness." In *Papers of the Military Historical Society of Massachusetts*. Boston: The Military Historical Society of Massachusetts, 1905. Vol. 4, 117-163.

Syphers, A. L. "In the Wilderness: Was the Right Flank Turned May 6?" *National Tribune*, June 13, 1889.

Thurston, S. D. "Report of the Conduct of General George H. Steuart's Brigade from the 5th to the 12th of May, 1864, inclusive." *Southern Historical Society Papers*, vol. XIV (1886), 146-151.

Toms, George W. "The 5th N. Y. Cav. At the Wilderness." *The National Tribune*, July 8, 1886.

Turner, John R. "The Battle of the Wilderness: The Part Taken by Mahone's Brigade." *Southern Historical Society Papers*, vol. XX, 81-2.

Vance, S. W. "Heroes of the Eighth Alabama Infantry," *Confederate Veteran* vol. VII (November, 1899), 492-93.

Venable, Charles S. "The Campaign from the Wilderness to Petersburg," *Southern Historical Society Papers*, XIV (1873), 522-27.

____. "General Lee in the Wilderness Campaign," in *Battles and Leaders of the Civil War*. New York: The Century Company, 1887, vol. 4, 240-46.

Verrill, George W. "The Seventeenth Maine at Gettysburg and in the Wilderness." in *MOLLUS-Maine*, (Portland, ME: :The Thurston Print, 1898), vol. 1 259-282.

Walley, J. J. "In the Wilderness: Another Account of the Fight at the Angle." *National Tribune*, December 18, 1890.

Webb, Alexander S. "Through the Wilderness," in *Battles and Leaders of the Civil War*. New York: The Century Company, 1887, vol. 4, 152- 169.

Wilcox, Cadmus M. "Grant and Lee in the Wilderness," *Annals of the War Written by Leading Participants North and South*, Alexander K. McClure, ed. Philadelphia: The Times Publishing Company, 1879, 485-501.

Williams, Capt. J. W. "Company D at the Battle of the Wilderness: Pen Sketches of the 'Greensboro Guards,' Co. D of the Fifth Alabama, C.S.A." *Greensboro Record*, July 2, 1903.

Wofford's Georgia Brigade." *Atlanta Southern Confederacy*, June 15, 1864.

Wynn, B. L "Lee Watched Grant at Locust Grove." *Confederate Veteran*, XXI (1913), 68.

Index

28); *26th*, 260 (Map Set 3, note 23), 108, 148; *27th*, 271 (Map Set 9, note 8); *28th*, 122; *33rd*, 120, 277 (Map Set 14, note 2); *34th*, 116; *37th*, 120, 277 (Map Set 14, note 2), 146; *38th*, 120, 146; *43rd*, 265 (Map Set 5, note 24), *44th*, 108, 260 (Map Set 3, note 23), 148; *45th*, 58, 116; *46th*, 128; *47th,* 260 (Map Set 3, note 20, 23), 273 (Map Set 9, note 32), 108; *48th*, 150; *52nd*, 261 (Map Set 3, note 31), 273 (Map Set 9, note 31); *53rd*, 56; *55th*, 118, 285 (Map Set 20, note 4); *93rd*, 144; *120th*, 144; *121st*, 236; *152nd*, 144

North Anna River, 10, 20

Oates, William, 164, 168, 210, 212, 214

Ohio Units: *Infantry: 8th*, 112, 116, 166, 168, 200, 208, 224; *110th*, 86, 88, 269 (Map Set 7, note 13), 136, 232; *122th*, 86, 236; *126th*, 86, 232, 293 (Map Set 23, note 24)

Olustee, battle of, 86

Orange and Alexandria Railroad, 4, 12

Orange Court House, 2, 12, 28, 98

Owen's (Joshua) brigade, actions on May 5, 108, 112, 114, 116, 120; May 6, 144, 282 (Map Set 16, note 36), 174, 176, 178, 192, 200, 218, 220, 222

Page, Charles, 178, 224

Palmer, William, 142, 192

Parker's Store, 22, 26, 28, 30, 32, 260 (Map Set 3, note 23), 38; May 5, 98, 134, 138, 142; May 6, 186, 194, 286 (Map Set 20, note 25), 210

Parker's Store Road, 26, 34, 36

Patrick, Marsena, 238

Patton, William, 16

Payne's Farm, Battle of, 262 (Map Set 4, note 18)

Pearson, Henry, 186

Pegram, John, 88, 269 (Map Set 7, note 13), 293 (Map Set 23, note 30), 240

Pegram's (John) Brigade, 80, 82, 268 (Map Set 6, note 41), 86, 88, 230, 292 (Map Set 23, note 13), 293 (Map Set 23, note 30), 234, 236

Pegram's (William) Battalion, 186

Pennsylvania Units: *Artillery: Rickett's,* 90, 94, 96, 116; *Cavalry: 1st,* 126; *17th*, 184; *18th,* 124; *Infantry: 1st Reserves,* 36; *2nd Reserves,* 36, 64; *5th Reserves,* 36; *6th Reserves,* 36; *7th Reserves,* 36, 64;

8th Reserves, 36; *10th Reserves,* 36; *11th Reserves,* 36, 64; *12th Reserves,* 36; *13th Reserves,* 34, 36; *11th*, 158, 280 (Map Set 16, note 10), 164; *26th*, 102; *48th*, 140, 186, 212, 214; *49th*, 72, 76, 78; *50th*, 216; *56th*, 56, 150, 202; *57th*, 102, 106, 234; *61st*, 88, 136, 234; *62nd,* 42; *63rd*, 102, 106, 144; *83rd,* 30, 42, 44, 48, 50; *90th*, 88; *91st*, 42, 46; *93rd,* 94; *95th*, 72, 74, 236; *96th*, 72, 267 (Map Set 6, note 15); *98th*, 94; *99th*, 272 (Map Set 9, note 26); *100th*, 220, 224; *105th*, 102; *110th*, 272 (Map Set 9, note 26); *115th*, 102, 104; *116th*, 120; *118th*, 42, 44; *119th*, 72, 76, 78; *121st*, 54, 56, 58; *136th*, 232; *138th*, 86, 276 (Map Set 13, note 6), 292(Map Set 23, note 10); *139th*, 94; *141st*, 100, 272 (Map Set 9, note 25) , 172, 198; *142nd*, 54; *143rd*, 54, 66; *149th*, 58, 265 (Map Set 5, note 17) , 164; *150th*, 54, 224; *155th*, 42, 46

Penrose, Charles, 267 (Map Set 6, note 16)

Perrin's (Abner), Brigade, 192, 200, 202, 204, 210, 218

Perry, Edward, 212, 289 (Map Set 21, note 8)

Perry's (Edward) Brigade, 192, 202, 210, 212, 214, 289 (Map Set 21, note 16)

Perry, John, 170, 286 (Map Set 20, note 25)

Perry, William, 156, 160, 162, 164, 210, 212, 214, 216

Perry's (William) Brigade, initial actions on May 6, 156, 162, 280 (Map Set 16, note 13), 164, 166, 170, 176, 202; fight with IX Corps, 212, 214, 216, 289 (Map Set 21, note 16)

Pickett's (George) Division, 282 (Map Set 18, note 1), 190, 283 (Map Set 19, note 7)

Pickett's Charge, 4, 102

Pingree, Stephen, 270 (Map Set 8, note 4)

Pleasonton, Alfred, 8

Po River, 180

Poague, William, 40, 150, 154, 278 (Map Set 14, note 31)

Poague's (William) Battalion, 40, 90, 112, 134, 278 (Map Set 14, note 22, 31), 150, 152, 154, 158, 172

Polley, J. B., 158

Porter, Horace, 22, 128, 238, 242

Potter, Robert, 186, 210, 214

Potter's (Robert) Division, 130, 140, 186, 210, 288 (Map Set 21, note 1), 212, 216

Raleigh, NC, 2

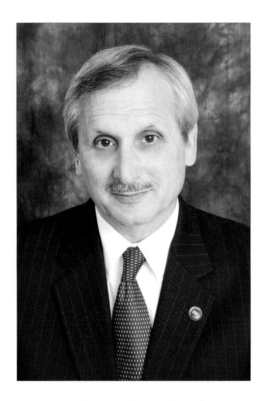

About the Author

Bradley M. Gottfried holds a Ph.D. in Zoology from Miami University. He has worked in higher education for more than three decades as a faculty member and administrator and is currently the President of the College of Southern Maryland.

An avid Civil War historian, Dr. Gottfried is the author of ten books, including *The Battle of Gettysburg: A Guided Tour* (1998); *Stopping Pickett: The History of the Philadelphia Brigade* (1999); *Brigades of Gettysburg* (2002); *Roads to Gettysburg* (2002); *Kearny's Own: The History of the First New Jersey Brigade* (2005), *The Maps of Gettysburg* (2007), *The Artillery of Gettysburg* (2008), *The Maps of First Bull Run* (2009), *The Maps of Antietam* (2011), and *The Maps of the Bristoe Station and Mine Run Campaigns* (2013). Brad has finished work on his next book, *The Maps of Fredericksburg,* and is working on both *The Maps of Spotsylvania,* and (with co-editor Theodore P. Savas) completing *The Gettysburg Campaign Encyclopedia.*